# Art Museums of America

## A Guide to Collections in the United States and Canada

# BY LILA SHERMAN

William Morrow and Company, Inc.
New York   1980

*To*
*Burton, David, and Roger.*

Library of Congress Cataloging in Publication Data

Sherman, Lila.
  Art museums of America.

  Includes index.
  1. Art museums—United States—Guide-books.
2. Art museums—Canada—Guide-books. I. Title.
N510.S45     708′.13     79-20022
ISBN 0-688-03570-1

Printed in the United States of America.

First Edition
1 2 3 4 5 6 7 8 9 10

# PREFACE

This book attempts to celebrate, in a practical way, the great surge toward the arts that has taken place in the United States. Americans are, in fact, discovering America, and particularly the expanding resources of their museums.

From the beginning, I decided to limit the focus of the book to the fine arts museums. I would include only those museums that conformed (with a few exceptions) to a specific definition: nonprofit galleries or museums with permanent collections maintained for the purpose of the exhibition, not sale, of artwork, with particular emphasis on paintings, prints, and sculpture as opposed to historical displays (artifacts), decorative arts, crafts, or other special interests.

I have not attempted to evaluate, only to elucidate. In talking about the collections, if I have used a value word, generally speaking it was not descriptive of my own judgment, but rather a statement of fact based on the current acknowledged evaluation of a famous collection: that the Metropolitan Museum is a great institution is not my judgment; it is a fact of the institution. Beyond attempting to describe the force and focus and often the history of the collections (lesser interests of a museum or minor collections are often omitted), I have tried to give a feeling of place—the particular quality of each location; to ferret out the facts of the buildings —when, by whom, and in what style they were built, altered, or replaced; to indicate the activities and facilities that would be most interesting to visitors, as opposed to local residents whose memberships entitle them to other benefits and graces; to be specific about parking, on-premises restaurants, admission policies, and open hours (eating and drinking facilities often change with the seasons; admission charges, with the economy); and to include directions when they were supplied to me by the museums themselves.

As the work progressed, I found that there are many art centers that take over the functions of a regional or community museum (with permanent collections and temporary exhibitions) in addition to their admirable roles as cultural and educational centers. Many of them are included here. Of course, I have missed some, as I have missed some museums and galleries, and I hope to adjust that deficiency in a future edition. Meanwhile, the response to my importunings of hundreds of museums and galleries across this land was wonderful and awesome.

Indeed, and as I hope perusers of this book will clearly see, the great art of this country and of other cultures is here on this continent for us to study and enjoy.

From the information gathered for the book, I have prepared an appendix which I believe is unique, and which could prove a useful tool for travelers, art students, and professionals. Should a reader care to know where in this country the good collections of, say, Renaissance art are located, he or she can find that information in this listing. The major museums, the great sprawling institutions with collections that span the ages of history and range the continents, are listed under the category "General." Other museums are listed under the categories (schools of art, countries, centuries) in which they have particularly strong collections. The listing of a museum under one category does not imply that it lacks resources in other areas, but only that it has declared itself strong in that particular area.

Fifty state art councils aided me in my research, and I thank them. I am also grateful to all the museum directors and their staffs who provided me with information, assistance, and encouraging words such as "Send us a copy!" or "A great idea!" or "We need it!"

There were two reference sources that were invaluable in this project: the American Association of Museums' *Official Museum Directory* (National Register Publishing Co., Inc., 1976) and the *American Art Directory* (R. R. Bowker Co., 1976).

—L. S.

# CONTENTS

## CANADA

**8**              CONTENTS

# ALABAMA

**BIRMINGHAM: Birmingham Museum of Art.** 2000 Eighth Ave. N., 35203 ☐ Founded in 1950, the Birmingham Museum of Art came to its present home, the Oscar Wells Memorial Building, in 1959. The starkly modern structure, finished in green marble and travertine, is located at the north edge of Woodrow Wilson Park in downtown Birmingham. In its almost 30 years of existence its holdings have increased by leaps and bounds; indeed, two new wings have been added since 1966 to accommodate the growing collection. It all began with a Samuel H. Kress collection of Italian Renaissance and Northern European works. Through the years acquisitions included the Frances Oliver collection of porcelain and silver, and the Beeson collection, one of the world's great stores of old Wedgwood. More of the Old Masters were added, as well as American paintings of the 19th century, German late Gothic sculpture, Dutch and Flemish 17th-century paintings, and English 18th-century works; pre-Columbian art including an excellent group of Inca gold and Indian tribal arts; art of the American West including 12 Remington bronzes; the Rives collection of archaeological artifacts from the ancient Near East. Modern art is represented by local and regional as well as nationally prominent artists, ranging from Impressionist to contemporary. The museum plans about 6 to 10 special exhibitions a year, usually complementing the permanent collection, sometimes displaying the works of contemporary artists. Tours are led by trained docents on request. A reference library of about 1,500 volumes is available to the public. The museum shop sells cards, jewelry, toys, and reproductions. The Museum Art Educational Council sponsors classes in painting, pottery, weaving, and batik. There is a monthly lecture series and special lectures in connection with exhibitions. Recent catalogs include *Kress Collection, Greek and Austrian Festival of Arts, Hans Grohs, The Tiepolos: Painters to Princes and Prelates, Rubens and Humanism.* Free parking behind the museum. Mon.–Sat. 10–5; Thurs. 10–9; Sun. & holidays 2–6; closed Christmas & New Year's Day. Free. (22nd St. exits of I-20 & I-59.)

**GADSDEN: Gadsden Museum of Fine Arts.** 856 Chestnut St., 35901 ☐ Near the center of this industrial city, which is surrounded by farming countryside and the foothills of Lookout Mountain, is the Gadsden Museum of Fine Arts. In a renovated old home, the museum's small, general collection of paintings, sculpture, and prints includes such artists as Sargent, José Guevara, and Al Carraway. The first 3 months of each year are taken by jury shows of local interest; exhibits change every month thereafter, each featuring a different artist who is often present at the opening. A program of events for the year is published in July. Tours can be arranged upon request. Mon.–Sat. 10–4 (winter), 10–5 (summer); Sun. 2–5; receptions on first Sun. of every month 3–5. Free. (One block from the main street [Broad], between 8th & 9th Sts.)

**HUNTSVILLE:   Huntsville Museum of Art.** 700 Monroe St., S.W., 35801 ☐ The English settled here in 1805; the first constitutional convention of the State of Alabama met here in 1819; the Space Age, in the form of the George C. Marshall Space Flight Center, arrived here in 1960; and a civic center to accommodate a growing population was built here in 1975. The 5-unit Von Braun Civic Center, on 8 acres in downtown Huntsville, houses a sports arena, concert and exhibit halls, a playhouse, and the Huntsville Museum of Art, in which American graphic arts predominate. There is also a collection of Japanese and Chinese objects in porcelain, jade, bronze, and ivory. Major exhibits are changed 2 to 3 times a year; small complementary exhibits are changed monthly. Cameras are not permitted. The museum sponsors lectures and concerts, children's programs, tours, in-school lectures for city and county fifth and sixth grades. Docents are available by appointment to lead tours. The museum library is open by special permission. A sales gallery offers jewelry, books, prints, stationery, handcrafted and seasonal items. Parking facilities are located nearby. Tues.–Sat. 10–5; Thurs. 7–9; Sun. 1–5. Free.

**MOBILE: Fine Arts Museum of the South.** Museum Drive, Langan Park, 36608 ☐ About 10 miles from downtown Mobile, at the edge of a lake in Langan Park and surrounded by gardens, a golf course, a baseball field, and a children's theater, is the Fine Arts Museum of the South. The informality of its environment pervades the museum itself: "Come in bare feet or bathing suits if you like," they say, "but come and enjoy what's here." Built in 1964, it was expanded in 1976 with the addition of a $1-million wing that triples the exhibition space of the original structure. A 2-story-high sculpture in silver and gold, entitled "Youth," was designed by Richard Lippold to commemorate the new wing. In this open space, surrounded by a mezzanine, is displayed the museum's collection of contemporary paintings. Close by in another gallery, traditional decorative arts are displayed. African art, sports art, folk arts, and contemporary crafts occupy other areas of the new addition. Touring exhibits appear here regularly. Cameras are allowed by permission only. Education programs for adults and children are available, as well as lecture series and concerts. Tours by special request to the education department. Parking facilities. Tues.–Sat. 10–5; Sun. 12–5. Free. (From I-65, turn west on Springhill Ave.)

**MONTGOMERY: Montgomery Museum of Fine Arts.** 440 South McDonough St., 36104 ☐ The Confederacy's first capital, the city of Montgomery still bears the grace and distinction of its past. The museum, a 2-story brick structure completed in 1959, is located near the downtown area, surrounded by businesses and some older residences. American art predominates among some 450 works that include portraits by 19th-century American primitives, a large collection of paintings by the 19th-century American Frederick W. Freer, works by "the Eight," and paintings, prints, and drawings by many well-known American artists of the 20th century. Southern artists are represented in a large collection of works on paper. Old Master prints, a small group of French Impressionist paintings, and a diverse selection of decorative arts broaden the range of the museum. Four to 5 shows run concurrently; there is a complete change every 4 to 8 weeks. Typically, some exhibitions are organized by the museum staff, and some are loaned from other institutions. Cameras by permission only. Lectures are scheduled to coordinate with exhibitions; films are shown regularly on Thursday evenings; and there is a Sunday afternoon concert series. The education department offers guided tours on advance request to school groups, clubs, civic organizations; it schedules films for children, programs for senior citizens, and lectures. Museum publications include exhibition catalogs (sold in the shop), a quarterly calendar of events for members, and an annual report. The shop also sells stationery, jewelry, crafts, and books. Parking at side of building. Tues.–Sat 10–5; Thurs. 10–10, Sun. 1–6. Free. (About ½ mile off I-85. Exit at Union or Court St.; continue to South McDonough St.; take McDonough [one way] to ½ block past High St. intersection; museum is on the left.)

**TUSCALOOSA: University of Alabama Art Gallery.** Mailing address: Box F, University, AL 35486 ☐ The University of Alabama was established early in the 19th century, when Tuscaloosa was the capital of Alabama and cotton was king. Except for 4 buildings that still stand, the university was burned to the ground by Union troops. Garland Hall, in which the Art Gallery is located, was built 20 years later (1886) in the old Quadrangle, a beautiful and historic area on the old campus. A remodeled space in the hall became the Art Gallery in 1967; there, the university's small collection of predominantly modern paintings, drawings, and prints is displayed. Also on view are examples of Chinese ceramics, primitive artwork, and photography. The gallery plans 9 or 10 loan exhibitions per year and 4 or 5 shows of faculty and student works. Daily 8–5; Sun. 2–5; closed university holidays. Free.

# ALASKA

**ANCHORAGE:** **Anchorage Historical and Fine Arts Museum.** 121 West Seventh Ave., 99501 ☐ The Anchorage Historical and Fine Arts Museum occupies an entire block in Anchorage, Alaska's largest city, set high on a bluff overlooking Cook Inlet and near the wild and beautiful Kenai Peninsula. The modern, brick-faced structure, its exterior softened by a cast concrete cornice frieze designed by Alex Combs, was built to celebrate the Alaska Purchase Centennial in 1967 and opened to the public in 1968. The initial collections housed there, after removal from the Loussac Library and the City Hall Annex, belonged to the Cook Inlet Historical Society; these objects, dating from the Russian period (1741–1867) to the present, are still on permanent loan from the society. In a decade, the subject areas of the museum broadened to cover not only the history but the anthropology and art of Alaska from prehistory to the present. Currently, the principal collections consist of native artifacts representing the four major aboriginal cultures of Alaska (Eskimo, Aleut, Athapaskan, and Tlingit-Haida), and of 19th- and 20th-century Alaskan paintings. The paintings include works by late-19th-century artists who traveled up the coast and others who settled in Alaska in the early 1900s, among them "Muir Glacier" by Thomas Hill, "The Trapper" by Sydney Laurence, and "Resurrection Bay" by Rockwell Kent. Loan exhibits change monthly, and there is a new one-person show of a contemporary Alaskan artist every month. Three statewide juried exhibitions are mounted annually: the All Alaska Juried Art Exhibition in February; the Festival of Native Arts in June; and a craft show, Earth, Fire, and Fibre, in November. Cameras are permitted with occasional exceptions.

Lectures, films, craft demonstrations, and panel discussions are presented on a regular basis by the museum in addition to a Sunday concert series, organized by the University of Alaska in Anchorage, and Tuesday evening nature programs, sponsored by the Sierra Club. Intensive tour programs are offered to both children and adults; guided tours for classes and other groups can be arranged by appointment, but during the summer months there are regularly scheduled tours. A noncirculating library of about 1,000 volumes is open to the public. A shop sells contemporary native art, museum and other related publications, reproductions, slides, and postcards. The museum publishes exhibition catalogs, a newsletter, and occasional papers. Some of its publications are: *Sydney Laurence, an Alaskan Impressionist* and *Eustace Ziegler* by R.L. Shalkop, and *Russian*

*Orthodox Art in Alaska* by R.L. and Antoinette Shalkop. Parking space on museum grounds. Winter, Tues.–Sat. 9–5, Sun. 1–5; summer (Memorial Day to Labor Day), Mon., Wed., Fri., Sat. 9–5, Tues. & Thurs. 9–9, Sun. 1–5. Free. (As for directions, "If you have driven as far as Anchorage," they say in Anchorage, "you will have no trouble finding us.")

# ARIZONA

**PHOENIX: Phoenix Art Museum.** 1625 North Central Ave., 85004 ☐ The largest city in Arizona is the home of the Phoenix Art Museum, which, about a mile from the heart of the city, shares a cultural complex with the main branch of the city library and the Phoenix Little Theater. It began in 1925 with the formation of the Phoenix Fine Arts Association, an alliance of art-conscious women who had been active in state fair art displays. A small collection was amassed and housed in an old building until 1959 when, with both private and public funds, the present gallery was constructed. In 1965 space was tripled by the opening of a new wing. The museum is especially proud of its Western and Mexican art. It also has impressive displays of Renaissance, Baroque, 18th-century, 19th-century English and French, and contemporary art. Sixteen Thorne miniature rooms, a costume institute, and a fine collection of Chinese porcelains broaden still further the range of exhibits. Some notable holdings are Rufino Tamayo's "Two Figures in Red," which hangs along with "Lush Spring," a painting by Helen Frankenthaler, who was one of his students; Thomas Moran's "Grand Canyon"; Carlo Dolci's "Salome With the Head of John the Baptist"; and Labille Guiard's "Madame Adelaide."

The museum has a regular schedule of wide-ranging exhibits that change about every 6 weeks. Group tours are available, as well as tours for the deaf. A branch museum, Sun City–Phoenix Art Museum, opened in 1976 in a retirement community near the outskirts of Phoenix. The reference library of some 2,500 volumes is open to the public Tues.–Fri. 10–4:30. The museum sponsors a series of art classes, a 3-year educational program for docents, and in the spring and fall, a lecture series. Free public concerts are held Oct.–May. Publications include a monthly membership calendar and catalogs of major exhibitions. A shop carries jewelry, art books, reproductions, postcards, and craft items. Free parking on museum grounds. Tues.–Sat. 10–5; Wed. 10–9; Sun. 1–5. Free. (At corner of McDowell & Central Aves.)

**SCOTTSDALE: Scottsdale Center for the Arts.** 7383 Scottsdale Mall, 85251 ☐ Surrounded by the restaurants, boutiques, and galleries of a bustling new 12-acre civic plaza, the 3-year-old Scottsdale Center for the Arts adds to the charm and excitement of this resort/suburb of Phoenix. Exhibits change here monthly, and works of art are displayed in nearby city buildings and permanent outdoor locations. Louise Nevelson's steel sculpture "Windows to the West" is among the center's holdings. Docents are available; tours can be arranged on request. Cameras are permitted. There is a museum shop, a parking garage, a 175-seat cinema, and an 800-seat theater. Art classes, workshops, and demonstrations are held; lectures and concerts are scheduled regularly. Daily 10–5. Free. (2 blocks east of Scottsdale Rd. on 2nd St.; 2 blocks south of Indian School Rd. on Civic Center Plaza.)

**TEMPE: University Art Collections.** Arizona State University, 85281 ☐ The University Art Collections are housed in the Matthews Center (1935) on the campus of Arizona State University, the state's oldest institution of higher learning. The nucleus of this collection, several American paintings, was given to the university by Oliver B. James in 1950 and was displayed in the library. Having expanded into a notable collection of American art, one of the most definitive west of the Mississippi, it was moved from the library. In addition to paintings, American acquisitions over the years range from all manner of Americana, crafts, 19th-century crockery, and contemporary ceramics to graphics and 19th- and 20th-century sculpture. Some of the artists represented are Gilbert Stuart, Ryder, Remington, Benjamin West, Peto, Winslow Homer, Henri, Glackens, Prendergast, Luks, Bellows, Marin, Phillip C. Curtis, Fritz Scholder, and John James Audubon. Rembrandt and Dürer are among the Old Masters in the collection of European prints; European paintings and sculpture from the 16th century to the present enlarge the scope of the museum. Exhibits in the 2 permanent galleries—American Art and European Art—change monthly. Tours for groups are available with advance notice. Cameras are permitted only under specific conditions. Although there is no regular schedule, the Collections sponsors speakers, poetry readings, and workshops. Brochures and booklets are available in the shop, which also sells jewelry, cards, and reproductions. Mon.–Fri. 10–5; Sun. 1–5; closed state and legal holidays. Free. (The most direct street approaches to the museum are Mill Ave. or University Ave. Matthews Center is on the main mall of the campus. Visitor parking on campus.)

**TUCSON: Tucson Museum of Art.** 235 West Alameda, 85701 ☐ The Tucson Museum of Art celebrated its 50th birthday in 1974, only 2 years before the city of Tucson celebrated its 200th. The city's history, influenced by Spanish, Mexican, and Indian settlers, is reflected not only in the holdings of this markedly western museum, but also in its modern exterior, an open ramp system fashioned out of concrete that leads underground and is surrounded by traditional territorial houses and Mexican adobes built in the 19th century. In 1962, the Tucson Fine Arts Association (the founding group) changed its name to the Tucson Art Center and settled in the historic Judge Samuel Kingan home until 1975 when, again changing its name, the Tucson Museum of Art moved into its present home adjacent to El Presidio Park and near the downtown governmental complex. In 20,000 feet of exhibit space, with the latest in museum security, environment, and support facilities, the museum, the first phase of a larger building program, is especially strong in pre-Columbian, Spanish Colonial, Mexican, Southern contemporary, and 19th- and 20th-century American art, as well as Western Americana. Exhibits here change every 5 or 6 weeks, making 10 or 15 special shows yearly. On the same block, designated a historic district, is La Casa Cordova, the state's first and only Mexican museum, a restored adobe that displays Mexican furnishings and artifacts. Also in the historic district is the Knox Corbett House, which houses the museum school, a fully staffed and multifaceted facility; the Romero House, with the school studios; the Edward Nye Fish House (1868), with the Tucson Museum of Art research library; and the Hiram Sanford Stevens House, which is under study for restoration. The library of some 6,000 volumes and 16,000 slides is open to the public. Throughout the year the museum presents film series, art history lectures, art technique demonstrations, and various music and dance programs open to the public free of charge. In addition, the museum sponsors scholarships for the art school, artist-in-residence, public-school outreach, and museum guided-tour programs for the handicapped, a business and community lecture and speakers' bureau, and joint public programs with other museums and cultural agencies.

Guided tours in English and Spanish (exhibition labels and catalogs are also in 2 languages) are offered from 10 to 5 by appointment; docent tours Fridays at 1:30. Cameras by permission only. Publications include monthly calendars for members, exhibition catalogs, and other special catalogs. A sales shop features crafts by Tucson artists, cards, magazines, catalogs, and an art rental and sales gallery. Parking within a one-block radius. Tues.–Sat. 10–5; Sun. 1–5; closed holidays. Free. (Take Congress St. exit off I-10, turn left onto Granada, then right onto Alameda.)

**University of Arizona Museum of Art.** Olive and Speedway, 85721 ☐ The beautifully landscaped campus of the University of Arizona occupies almost 300 acres of this resort city that boasts near perfect weather. There are 2 museums here; the Arizona State Museum, displaying the archaeology and ethnology of Arizona, and the university's Museum of Art. A Samuel H. Kress collection of Renaissance works (including a 26-panel retablo from the cathedral of Ciudad Rodrigo, Spain) enriches this pre-dominantly contemporary museum. The Gallagher Memorial collection consists of over 170 contemporary paintings and sculptures from many countries; the C. Leonard Pfeiffer collection of exclusively American paintings; and the Samuel Latta Kingan collection of 19th-century American paintings. Pollock, Stamos, and de Kooning works hang here, as do paintings by Miró and Léger. Works by Moore, Archipenko, and Maillol are among a growing sculpture group. Special exhibitions and retrospectives are scheduled regularly. The museum has an outreach program that brings the public schools in closer proximity to the arts; a docent program supplies trained guides for school tours and other groups. Catalogs of the permanent collections and all special exhibits are sold at the museum's book shop. The library (500 volumes) is available for research. Mon.–Sat. 10–5; Sun. 2–5. Free.

**YUMA:    Yuma Art Center.** 281 Gila St. Mailing address: P.O. Box 1471, Yuma 85364 ☐ The Yuma Art Center is housed in a Spanish Colonial Revival structure built in 1926 by the Southern Pacific Railroad and restored almost 50 years later in time for American bicentennial celebrations. The center's collection focuses on contemporary Arizona artists, and exhibitions change monthly. Bilingual tours can be arranged by appointment. Cameras are permitted. In addition to lectures, given in cooperation with Arizona Western College, and concert series, the center sponsors a wide range of artist-in-residence programs in the visual and performing arts. A shop offers work, both fine arts and crafts, of Yuma artists. Tues.–Sun. 10–5; closed national holidays. Free. (From the east, exit from I-8 at Giss Pkwy. and take second right onto Gila St. From the west, exit at 4th Ave. and turn left onto 1st St.; go west 6 blocks and then turn right.)

# ARKANSAS

**HARRISON:** · **Bryant Art Museum.** Route 1, 72601 ☐ The amassing of a private collection is very often linked to the beginnings of a museum. And so it was with the Bryant Art Museum, located in the midst of the Ozarks, 7 miles south of Harrison and 2 miles north of Dogpatch, U.S.A., at the intersection of 2 small state highways. Tom Bryant, Sr., had acquired a sizable collection of 17th-, 18th-, 19th-, and 20th-century European and American works of art, which he had on display in his home in suburban Chicago. In 1961, 2 years after purchasing a schoolhouse, vintage 1931, near his vacation cottage in Arkansas, he began renovations of the building with an eye toward moving the collection there and making it available to the public. By 1963, the Bryant Art Museum was a reality. The main gallery was once the gymnasium and auditorium; a chapel now occupies what was a storage place for cordwood. Religious paintings, mythological paintings, English landscapes, and pastoral scenes are among over 60 works hung in the 2 main galleries; the artists include George Morland, George Inness, Bernard DeHoog, Edouard Cortez, Gustave Jean Jacquet, Benjamin Constant, and John Constable. "The Thundercloud" by Inness is a particular delight in this diverse collection, and a 1550 unattributed religious painting in the style of Raphael, the most unusual. During June, July, and August, the museum opens exhibit space for one-person shows by local artists. Cameras are permitted. Two smaller galleries offer contemporary paintings, antiques, pottery, china, glass, and ceramics for sale as well as the usual books, prints, and postcards. Weekdays 9–5; Sun. 1–5. Admission: $1 for adults; 50¢ for students. (Take Rt. 7, south of Harrison, to Rt. 206; direction signs will help you from there.)

**JONESBORO:   Arkansas State University Art Gallery.** Fine Arts Center. Mailing address: Box 846, State University 72467 ☐ This gallery, on the 800-acre campus of the university, was founded as a part of the Division of Art in 1967, when the Fine Arts Center, a modern brick and concrete building, was completed. The collection, consisting primarily of 20th-century works, was brought together from corridors and offices throughout the university. Exhibits (catalogs are published) now change monthly; lectures are scheduled through the year. Parking nearby. Mon.–Thurs. 8–5; Fri. 8–12 noon; Sun. 1–5. (Caraway Rd. and Aggie Rd. will get you there.)

**LITTLE ROCK:   Arkansas Arts Center.** MacArthur Park. Mailing address: P.O. Box 2137, Little Rock 72203 ☐ The Arkansas Arts Center presents a contemporary facade of glass, brick, and copper among the historic sites in MacArthur Park, about ½ mile from downtown Little Rock, in the Quapaw Quarter of the city. Dedicated to all the arts, it provides the "City of Roses" with 5 exhibition galleries in which up to 35 shows per year are mounted. About 15 are organized by the center itself—some competitive, some educational, and some featuring regional artists or private collections. The permanent collection has some 2,000 objects including paintings, prints, photographs, sculptures, textiles, and decorative arts. There is also an unusual collection of American jazz—some 4,000 records from the 1930s and 1940s. Emphasis in acquisitions, however, is in the area of prints and drawings. Some of the artists represented are Odilon Redon, Diego Rivera, George Inness, Charles Bird King, John Henry Byrd, James Peale, Andrew Wyeth, Richard Diebenkorn, Georgia

O'Keeffe, Willem de Kooning, Arthur Dove, Mark Tobey, Francesco Bassano, John Hesselius, Thomas Moran, Samuel F. B. Morse, Giacomo Palma, Francesco-Giuseppe Casanova, Gilbert Stuart, and Alexander Hewig Wyant. Specifically, Peale's "George Washington," Bassano's "Adoration of the Shepherds," and Redon's "Andromeda" are points of interest. Cameras can be used by permission only. This collection was started in 1927 by the Fine Arts Club of Arkansas in the Pulaski County Court House. In 1937, it was moved to the Museum of Fine Arts, which opened in MacArthur Park. The present structure opened in 1963 and was expanded in 1975. Before 1963, about 30 percent of the collection was stored. At present, an antebellum house is under renovation, soon to be utilized for the decorative arts.

Activities of the center are myriad. The School of Visual Arts, Theatre and Dance offers classes in crafts and the arts to students of all ages. Lectures, workshops, and demonstrations are conducted throughout the year. A regular series of Artists-in-Action demonstration/lectures is offered on Sundays at 2 p.m. from September through May. Docent tours are available for each exhibit, and special tours can be arranged in advance. School aids, workshops, classes for teachers, a Neighborhood Arts Program, and a State Services Department that sponsors, among other things, an Artmobile and traveling artists, are all facets of the center's involvement with its own community and the larger state community. A research library of over 6,000 volumes is open to the public. A shop sells books, jewelry, crafts, gifts, cards, African art, and handmade toys. The Vineyard Restaurant serves lunch Mon.–Fri. 11:30–1:30. Parking area accommodates 900 cars; special area for the handicapped. Publications include members' bulletin, annual catalog, film and class schedules, and sundry brochures. Mon.–Sat 10–5; Sun. & holidays 12 noon–5. Free, but donations may be made at the gallery entrance. (In the park at the corner of Commerce & 9th Sts. Take the 9th St. exit from I-30; the park is 3 blocks west of the highway.)

**PINE BLUFF:   Southeast Arkansas Arts and Science Center.** Civic Center, 71601 □ One of the oldest cities in Arkansas, founded as a trading post in 1819, Pine Bluff is the home of the Southeast Arkansas Arts and Science Center, a modern structure designed by Arkansas native son Edward Durell Stone. Holdings of the center include 19th-century European paintings and 20th-century American paintings and prints. A Little Firehouse Studio is used for the center's visual arts program. Among its special activities the center sponsors a museum school, lectures, concerts, and other educational programs. Guided tours available. Publications include a semimonthly calendar of events and exhibit catalogs. Mon.–Fri. 9–5. Free.

# CALIFORNIA

**BERKELEY: University Art Museum, Berkeley.** 2626 Bancroft Way, 74720 ☐ The largest university museum in the world, the University Art Museum opened in 1970 after almost a decade of planning and building. In 1963, a survey of the campus recommended the addition of an art museum, and in the same year, Hans Hofmann donated 45 of his paintings and a quarter-million dollars to the university. These two events led to what is now the spectacular cantilevered concrete and glass museum at Berkeley. The young architects chosen by national competition designed a striking building with exposed concrete walls. Inside, the 31,050 square feet of exhibition space divided into eleven galleries are bathed in natural light that filters through skylights and floor-to-ceiling windows. The temperature and humidity in each gallery are controlled individually; electronic and ultrasonic devices detect smoke, fire, and motion throughout. Although the collection is eclectic and most periods of Asian as well as Western art are represented, the largest number of artworks come from 20th-century America and Europe. This modern collection is represented by Rothko, de Kooning, Bearden, Reinhardt, Still, Frankenthaler, Gottlieb, Mitchell, Wiley, Clarke, Francis, and William Allan among the Americans; European painters such as Francis Bacon, Miró, Léger, and Magritte; and sculptors Maillol, Calder, Smith, Pomodoro, Paolozzi, Lye, Voulkos, and Cornell. The 19th-century works include paintings by Cézanne, Rosso, Carpeaux, Blakelock, Bierstadt, and Ensor. Broadening the range of the collection further are 16th-century masterworks by Rubens, Carracciolo, and Savoldo. Because of a generous gift from Hans Hofmann, the museum holds the largest collection anywhere of his paintings; they are displayed in the Hans Hofmann Gallery. (The museum also houses Hofmann's archives.) Japanese paintings and woodblock prints on extended loan are exhibited in the Oriental Gallery, and an impressive collection of ancient and primitive art from the university's Lowie Museum of Anthropology occupies another section of this diverse facility. Cameras with shielded flash (no tripods or plug-ins) are generally permitted.

Approximately 20 exhibitions, some traveling, some on extended loan, and some from the permanent collection, are mounted annually, accompanied by informative, scholarly catalogs. The Pacific Film Archive is one of the very few that combines archive facilities and regular film showings.

Some 3,000 prints stored here, including an important group of Japanese films, are available for study in special screening rooms, and about 800 of them are screened for the public each year in the museum's 200-seat theater. The museum also sponsors lecture series, video screenings, concerts, and dance performances. The bookstore is a potpourri of gift items, art books, catalogs, posters, cards, calendars, jewelry, and craft materials. The Swallow Restaurant (Tues.–Sun. 11:30–7:30) offers a continental menu with wine. Parking lots nearby. Wed.–Sun. 11–5. Free. (On Bancroft Way just below College Ave. From US 80 take Ashby Ave. exit, drive east on Ashby toward the hills; turn left on Telegraph Ave.; right on Durant Ave.; left on College; left again on Bancroft.)

**CLAREMONT: Galleries of the Claremont Colleges.** Mailing address: Lang Art Gallery, Scripps College, 91711. Montgomery Art Gallery, Pomona College, 91711 ☐ Lang Art Gallery, and Montgomery Art Gallery, with shared resources and staff, together form the Galleries of Claremont Colleges, 6 institutions of higher learning in the Pomona-Walnut Valley of the Los Angeles Basin. The **Lang Art Gallery** was built facing an expansive green on the Scripps College campus in 1926, in the modified California Spanish architectural style of many Southern California structures. The collections housed here are predominantly American—paintings, drawings, and prints; the Young collection of American painting (1880–1930) includes such distinguished works as "Four Fishwives" by Winslow Homer and "Smiling Sara" by Mary Cassatt. The paintings of Henry McFee form another collection. Other notable assemblages are the Johnson collection of Japanese woodblock prints; the Dorothy Adler Routh collection of cloisonné; a group of modern Southern California ceramics; an Oriental costume collection; the Nagel collection of ancient and medieval sculpture, painting, and decorative art; the Bruce collection of ancient Cypriot pottery; and the Claremont University Center collection of American Indian pottery (including pre-Columbian), basketry, and beadwork. Exhibitions change monthly; a Ceramics Annual, the oldest of this kind of event in the country, is mounted in the spring; the Young collection of American painting is exhibited in the fall. The museum is host to a lecture series sponsored by the Scripps Fine Arts Foundation, which also supplies docents for group tours and scholarships to Scripps College students. Sept.–May, daily 1–5; Wed. eve. 7–9. Free. (On the corner of Columbia and 9th Sts. Exit from San Bernardino Freeway at Claremont-Indian Hill Blvd.; go north to 10th St., east on 10th to Columbia, then south on Columbia. Or take Foothill Blvd. [US 66] to Dartmouth Ave.; go south to 10th St., east on 10th to Columbia, then south on Columbia.)

The **Montgomery Art Gallery,** a modern concrete-slab construction built in 1958 and extensively renovated and expanded in 1976, faces a large green and a sculpture garden on the Pomona College campus. Here, a print collection encompasses a wide variety of graphic art from the United States and Europe and includes major holdings of prints by Goya. A collection of Renaissance and medieval paintings from the Kress Foundation, photographic works by well-known contemporary American artists, and a small group of American and European paintings comprise the balance of the museum's holdings. A lecture series and scholarships are sponsored by the Rembrandt Club, the museum's support group, as is an artist lecture series for which the College Art Department also takes partial responsibility. Tours are conducted by docents and staff. The Galleries publish exhibition catalogs and miscellaneous books and brochures. Sept.–May, daily 1–5, Wed. eve. 7–9. Free. (On the northeast corner of Bonita & College Ave. Take San Bernardino Freeway to Claremont-Indian Hill Blvd. Go north to Bonita Ave., then east to College Ave. Or take Foothill Blvd. [US 66] to College Ave., go south to Bonita Ave.)

**DOWNEY:   Downey Museum of Art.** 10419 S. Rives Ave., 90241 ☐ The Downey Museum of Art was founded in 1952 to house the work of Southern California artists, some of whom are Billy Al Bengston, Shirley Pettibone, Jim Bolin, and Lukman Glasgow. Four galleries display the paintings, sculpture, graphics, and photographs of these and other contemporary artists. Exhibits rotate approximately every 6 weeks. Cameras are not permitted. This active small museum supports a school and a docent program and sponsors lectures, concerts, and guided tours. Catalogs accompany each exhibit. A research file is kept on the permanent collection and the rotating exhibits. Parking nearby. Wed.–Sun. 1–5. Free. (Leave the Santa Ana Freeway at Paramount Blvd. Turn right onto Paramount and go to Florence Ave.; make a right turn onto Florence, then a left onto Rives.)

**FRESNO:   Fresno Art Center.** 3033 East Yale Ave., 93703 ☐ The art center here has an interesting crop of American contemporary paintings and prints, mixed with some choice Oriental items, and Mexican and pre-Columbian paintings. An 18th-century Swedish panel painting by Johannes Nilsson brings a profusion of Sweden's folk scenes across 2 continents to the art enthusiasts of Fresno. The center supplies its community with an art center's services: lectures, classes, concerts, dance recitals, tours, and the like. In fact, its service extends throughout the San Joaquin Valley by means of a traveling exhibit of Mexican art which it sends to Mexican communities. Paintings, postcards, and books are for sale. Daily 10–4:30; Tues., Wed., Thurs. 7:30–9:30. Free. (In Radio Park, northeast of Fresno.)

**LAGUNA BEACH:  Laguna Beach Museum of Art.** 307 Cliff Drive, 92651 ☐ This museum began with the artists who came to this beautiful and hospitable environment to paint. An art colony grew up, and from its ranks, in 1918, the art association, to establish a gallery for promoting, exhibiting, and selling the members' work. The gallery became a reality and grew through the years until in 1972 the Laguna Beach Art Association, in its enlarged quarters, became the Laguna Beach Museum of Art. In their own milieu, the artists who founded the organization are memorialized in a collection of their own works—among them are Benjamin C. Brown, Norman Chamberlain, R. Clarkson Coleman, Arthur Hill Gilbert, Edgar Payne, William Wendt, and Karl Yens. The museum, in brief, shows the work of early and contemporary California artists (1900–1940, 1960–1970). The temporary exhibition schedule provides about 12 new shows each year including invitationals, retrospectives, student shows, and a juried exhibition. Special arrangements must be made for the use of cameras. The museum educational council sponsors lecture series on art history and tours to other museums. Catalogs accompany special exhibits. A limited library with biographical material on the early artists of the area is open to the public upon written request. A bookstore sells crafts, jewelry, Japanese woodblock prints, cards, and ceramics. There is a restaurant next door. Parking at city meters only. Daily 11:30–4:30; closed Tues. Free. (At the corner of North Coast Highway & Cliff Drive.)

**LA JOLLA:  La Jolla Museum of Contemporary Art.** 700 Prospect St., 92037 ☐ San Diego's popular resort community, La Jolla, combines the pleasures of a beautiful coastline and fine beaches with a lush landscape and an urban center with its attendant cultural facilities, among them the La Jolla Museum of Contemporary Art. In 1937 a group of local artists used the former home of Ellen Browning Scripps to display their work; this showplace was the forerunner of what became the present museum in 1970. The 1913 mission-style building, located within easy walking distance of La Jolla's business center, houses a notable collection of contemporary art—the only museum in Southern California to specialize in this period. Among the many artists represented are Richard Diebenkorn, Marsden Hartley, Joan Miró, Robert Motherwell, Nathan Oliveira, Claes Oldenburg, Arshile Gorky, Roy Lichtenstein, and Jim Dine. New exhibits are mounted every 6 weeks. Cameras can be used by permission only. The museum library is open to the public. Art classes for young people are offered in fall and spring. Concerts sponsored by local nonprofit organizations are held in the museum auditorium. The docent program offers guided tours to groups and Senior Days, in which lectures and films are shown to those over 45. Five or 6 exhibition catalogs are published annually and a newsletter monthly. A museum shop sells catalogs, art books, jewelry, and postcards. Street parking limited. Tues–Fri. 10–5; Wed. 7–10; Sat. & Sun. 12:30–5; closed Jan. 1. Free. (Leave I-5 [north] at La Jolla Village Dr.; driving south, leave it at Ardath Rd. Take either road to Torrey Pines Rd., turn right onto Prospect.)

**LONG BEACH: Long Beach Museum of Art.** 2300 East Ocean Blvd., 90803 ☐ The city of Long Beach opened a Municipal Art Center in 1951. Six years later the city designated its art center as the Long Beach Museum of Art. Made with California brick, cedar shingle, and redwood beams, the museum and its sculpture garden are located on a bluff overlooking the ocean. Housed here is a potpourri of paintings, sculpture, prints, and drawings predominantly by American and especially West Coast artists—and one of the most complete video art archives on the western seaboard. The museum always maintains an exhibit of video art by contemporary artists. Other exhibits change monthly. A chamber music series, a lecture series, gallery talks, and a summer film symposium are offered by the museum. In addition, it is developing an art outreach program in the schools and libraries of the city. The library (1,200 volumes) is open to the public by appointment. The Carriage House Bookshop has books (including rare volumes, first editions, and out-of-print art selections), master prints, cards, crafts, and folk art, and also runs a coffee, tea, and pastry concession with seating in a garden setting looking out onto the sculpture garden and the ocean beyond. Parking on the street only. Wed.–Sun. 12–5. Free.

**LOS ANGELES: Los Angeles County Museum of Art.** 5905 Wilshire Blvd., 90036 ☐ A broad central plaza and a sculpture garden form an impressive approach to the three elevated modern pavilions that make up the Los Angeles County Museum of Art. One of them, the Ahmanson Gallery, houses the permanent collections. All changing exhibits take place in the central Frances and Armand Hammer Wing; here also, on an upper level in Lytton Halls, is the museum's contemporary art collection. In the Leo S. Bing Center to the east are the Bing Theater and other museum facilities. Gathered by some famous collectors—Hearst, the Heeramanecks, Hammer—the museum's holdings range from prehistory through the 20th century, with special strengths in Indian, Nepalese, Tibetan, and Islamic art, Postimpressionist paintings, and 19th- and 20th-century sculpture. Recent acquisitions include a Cubist sculpture by Picasso; major works by Guido Reni, Hals, de la Tour, and Winslow Homer; a 16th-century Italian polychromed wood sculpture; and nearly 2,000 Near Eastern and Central Asian objects dating from the last thousand years before Christ. Paintings by Rembrandt, Rubens, and El Greco hang here; later Europeans include Cézanne and Degas. Cropsey, Copley, Stuart, Bingham, Inness, Hassam, and Eakins are among the Americans. Works by Rodin and others fill the sculpture garden. Four major exhibits and about 17 smaller ones are installed each year. Hand-held cameras with flashcubes are permitted.

Lectures, films, theater programs, concerts, a formal educational program for children, a docent program, and guided tours are offered here. The Textile and Costumes Research Center and the Conservation Center are foremost in the West. Publications include catalogs, an annual report, and descriptive bulletins. The library (53,000 volumes) can be used by students and scholars. A large variety of items are for sale in the museum shop. The Plaza Cafe provides indoor and outdoor eating. Parking in lot off Carson Avenue one block east of museum. Tues.–Fri. 10–5; Sat. & Sun. 10–6; 2nd Tues. of month 12–9. Admission $1 for adults; 50¢ for sr. citizens, students, children 5–17; under 5 free; free 2nd Tues. of month.

**Municipal Art Gallery.** Barnsdall Park, 4804 Hollywood Blvd., 90027 ☐ The Municipal Art Gallery makes its home in Hollywood. Originally, it was located in a building designed by Frank Lloyd Wright in 1954 to house his 60 Years of Living Architecture exhibition; since 1971 it has been in an adjoining structure that bears a stylistic relationship to Wright's. Although there is no permanent collection, visitors find changing exhibitions that focus on contemporary local talent, with occasional historical presentations. A yearly Christmas show is dedicated to the interests of young audiences; a biannual juried show alternates with a biannual newcomer's invitational. Art classes, internships, concerts, lectures, and a variety of other special educational programs involving dialogue between professionals and laymen of all ages are offered. Tours are scheduled daily. Books, jewelry, art journals, cards, toys, and folk art are sold in the gallery shop. Tues.–Sun. 12–5. Free; voluntary contributions welcome. (One block west of the intersection of Hollywood Blvd. and Vermont Ave; accessible via Hollywood and Santa Monica Freeways.)

**University Galleries, University of Southern California.** University Park, 90007 ☐ Elizabeth Holmes Fisher, over a period of many years, gave 72 paintings to the University of Southern California, and in 1939 she donated the funds to build the Fisher Gallery. Other donations were received subsequently, among them the Armand Hammer collection. Today, the University Galleries own 400-some paintings. A major portion are Dutch and Flemish works from the 16th and 17th centuries; there are 9 paintings from the Barbizon school and 11 from the Hudson River school. A few Oriental porcelains, 139 Chinese bronze mirrors, prints from the 18th and 19th centuries, and a fine collection of Georgian silver round out this excellent amalgam of gifts and acquisitions. Outstanding are two Rubens works from the Hammer collection: "Venus Wounded by a Thorn" and "The Nativity." Exhibitions—architectural, photographic, graphic, student—change monthly. No flashes are allowed; a permission-to-photograph form must be signed. The gallery is used primarily as a teaching aid in university courses. From time to time exhibiting artists lecture. Catalogs are published with most shows. The School of Architecture and Fine Arts, of which the galleries are part, has a research library open to the public. A cafeteria in the Commons, several snack shops, and a sit-down restaurant are on campus. Parking limited; fee of $1 charged in campus lots. Mon.–Fri. 12–5; occasionally Sun. for special exhibitions. Free. (Reached from Harbor Freeway (north- or southbound), Exposition exit. From Santa Monica Freeway (east- or westbound) take Hoover-Vermont exit. Go to Exposition Blvd. between Hoover & Figueroa Sts.)

**Frederick S. Wight Art Gallery of University of California at Los Angeles.** 405 Hilgard Ave., 90024 ☐ All around the Frederick S. Wight Art Gallery of UCLA, in recognition of the felicity of living with works of art, are placed great works of art. The idea for this sculpture garden, full of the creative outpourings of the 19th and 20th centuries, was former chancellor of the university Franklin D. Murphy's, and the garden bears his name. Works by Arp, Calder, Lachaise, Lipchitz, Moore, Rodin, and Noguchi, among many others, are set for easy viewing and comfort: one can sit around them or on them, or lean against them, on grass, under trees, or on terraces. Inside is a collection of 15th- to 19th-century Italian, Spanish, Dutch, Flemish, and English paintings; an African, an Oceanic, and a pre-Columbian collection; and a smaller group of 19th- and 20th-century paintings. The Grunwald Center for the Graphic Arts makes its home here, filling an entire section of the building, with prints ranging back to the 15th century and including German Expressionist works, French Impressionists, Japanese woodblock prints, a complete set of Tamarind lithography workshop impressions, all of Renoir's prints (only one is missing), and an exceptional collection of Matisse's, Rouault's, and Picasso's. Changing exhibitions are scheduled regularly. This university museum sponsors lectures by visiting scholars or faculty members, seminars, gallery talks, and tours. Catalogs are published with special exhibitions. The art library contains 45,000 volumes; there is a collection of 158,000 slides. Tues.–Fri. 11–5; Sat. & Sun. 1–5; closed Aug. Grunwald Center for the Graphic Arts, Mon.–Fri. 9–12, 1–5. Free.

**MALIBU:  J. Paul Getty Museum.** 17985 Pacific Coast Highway, 90265 ☐ Overlooking the Pacific Ocean at Malibu is a 1st-century Roman villa, created in the image of the Villa Dei Papiri by J. Paul Getty to provide a classical environment for his collection of Greek and Roman art. The original villa was located near Pompeii and was buried by lava from Vesuvius in 79 A.D. Excavations made during the 18th century revealed the floor plan that was re-created by Getty in 1974 with the help of a professor of art history who specialized in ancient architecture. Three separate collections, begun in the 1930s, make up the holdings of this splendid edifice, which replaced Getty's own home, a short distance away, as their showplace. The Greek and Roman antiquities collection, occupying the ground floor that encircles an inner peristyle garden, contains sculpture and mosaics, the Landsowne "Herakles," Mazarin "Venus," and Elgin "Throne," 4th-century Attic gravemarkers, and both Greek and Roman portraits. Western European paintings and the French decorative arts collection are on the upper floor. Western art from the 13th to the 20th centuries, with strong emphasis on Renaissance and Baroque, is on view, enhanced by the presence of works by Raphael, Rembrandt, Rubens, de la Tour, Van Dyck, Gainsborough, and Boucher. The decorative arts collection, some of which is installed in period rooms, ranges from the late 17th century to about 1800. Furniture, carpets, tapestries, clocks, and chandeliers from the salons of French nobility and indeed from the royal household evoke the life of 18th-century France.

Activities of the museum include concerts (held on the third Thursday of each month, Sept.–June, at 1:30), lectures (Thursdays at 8:30), special education programs for visiting school children, and orientation lectures by docents every 15 minutes (audio cassette tours and guidebooks are also available). The 15,000-volume library is open by appointment to scholars, as is an archive with over 150,000 photographs of artworks. Three conservation laboratories, not open to the public, service each of the collections. The bookstore offers guidebooks, catalogs, and other museum publications, as well as reproductions and gift items. A Garden Tea Room is open 10:30–2:30 for lunch, 2:30–4:30 for snacks. Proof of parking serves as the means of admission to the museum; therefore advance parking reservations are advisable for guaranteed admission. Visitors who arrive without a reservation are admitted only if parking is available; they may not park outside the museum grounds and walk in. Reservations for a specific date (morning or afternoon arrival) may be obtained by writing to the reservations office or by telephoning (213-454-6541). Visitors arriving by taxi, bicycle, or public bus (ask the bus driver for a museum pass) are admitted without a reservation and must walk up a steep hill to the museum. Mon.–Fri. 10–5 (June–Sept.); Tues.–Sat. 10–5 (Oct.–May). Free. (One mile north of Sunset Blvd.; reached from Santa Monica Freeway [west].)

**MONTEREY: Monterey Peninsula Museum of Art.** 559 Pacific St., 93940 ☐ On a peninsula dedicated to year-round amusement (several golf courses border the Pacific and attract tourists from all over the world) and in a city rich in the history of California, the Monterey Peninsula Museum of Art, appropriately, is dedicated to the folk art of the world and to artwork of the California region. Two sculptures by Sir Jacob Epstein, a portrait painted by Samuel F. B. Morse (inventor of the telegraph), and "Gathering Storm" by George Inness enhance the museum's collections, which also include a notable assemblage of works by American photographers. Two exhibitions, mounted in 2 galleries, change every month; emphasis ranges from painting to sculpture, graphic arts, photography, textile arts, group shows, and one-person shows. Cameras are permitted. The museum offers 3 full-semester classes; a Museum on Wheels, a program in which a folk art collection is taken to the schools in 3 rural counties and staff instructors give classes in crafts; and a scholarship and intern program for art students at the local college. Docent tours for groups and the use of the library on weekdays can be arranged by appointment; the library is open to the public on Saturday afternoons. Publications include a monthly bulletin, *Courier; Yesterday's Artists on the Monterey Peninsula* by Helen Spangenberg; and other brochures and catalogs. The museum shop offers jewelry, books, cards, folk art, posters, and museum replicas for sale. Parking on the street or in public parking lots within a block of the museum. Tues.–Fri. 10–4; Sat. & Sun. 1–4. Free.

**NEWHALL: William S. Hart County Park.** 24151 North Newhall Ave., 91321 ☐ William S. Hart was the epitome of the 1920s Western film hero—strong and silent, gentle but deadly. In 1925 Hart retired as the silver screen's premier cowboy, wrote several books, and spent his declining years, until 1946 when he died, on his Horseshoe Ranch near Newhall. Here he collected works of art and artifacts relating to the American West that had nourished him since childhood. Displayed on the walls of his retirement home is an excellent collection of paintings by Russell, De Yong, and Remington. Period furnishings, sculptures, ivory and wood carvings, and an interesting collection of Western and Indian artifacts are the other attractions of this historic house. Cameras are not permitted. The museum offers guided tours every day. On Saturday evenings in August and September, William S. Hart silent films are shown free of charge. Parking on the grounds where wide open spaces invite wandering and picnicking (grounds open every day, 10 to dusk). A descriptive brochure is available. Tues.–Sun. 10–5; closed Thanksgiving, Christmas, and Jan. 1. Free; donations accepted. (Take SR 14 to San Fernando Rd. and go west to Newhall Ave.)

**NEWPORT BEACH: Newport Harbor Art Museum.** 850 San Clemente Dr., 92660 ☐ In 1977, after 16 years of existence and only 7 years of collecting, the Newport Harbor Art Museum opened the doors of its spanking new building. Located in Newport Center, one of the largest retailing and commercial developments in Southern California, it is accessible to the series of expensive coastal residential towns that make up the city of Newport Beach. The harbor it overlooks has long been a haven for many of the yachts that ply the Pacific coastal waters. The collections housed here are devoted to modern art, and most specifically to American artists at work within the last 30 years. Although small, the permanent collection includes a notable roster of painters: Josef Albers, Robert Irwin, Gene Davis, Ludwig Sander, Kenzo Okada, Julian Stanczak, and Paul Wonner. New acquisitions include paintings by John McLaughlin and John Paul Jones. The museum has a regular schedule of special exhibits; some typical shows have been Robert Rauschenberg in Black and White; Edward Hopper; a Reginald Marsh retrospective; paintings by Walter Darby Bannard; Mary Cassatt paintings; 10 Major Works by Mark Rothko. Catalogs are published for most of these special exhibitions. Cameras may be used with permission only; no tripods or flash.

The museum sponsors lecture and film series, concerts, regular art classes and lecture courses, and also offers guided tours that are available to groups by prearrangement. One or 2 docent tours are conducted daily. A small library is available by special permission. The museum book shop stocks books, jewelry, prints, cards, and other gift items. A new restaurant in the outdoor sculpture garden provides wine and beer with its menu. Parking on the museum grounds. Donation. (From the San Diego Freeway, take Jamboree Rd. south to Santa Barbara; left on Santa Barbara; left on San Clemente Dr. The museum is on the left. From the Coast Hwy. [SR 1], go east on Jamboree Rd. to Santa Barbara; right on Santa Barbara; left on San Clemente.)

**NORTHRIDGE:   Fine Arts Gallery, California State University, Northridge.** 18111 Nordhoff St., 91330 ☐ The only major exhibition space in the San Fernando Valley, the Fine Arts Gallery brings art to a population of some 2 million. The university's collection is stored in the library and drawn upon for 6 exhibitions per year. It includes contemporary American works, especially from Southern California (Hans Burkhardt, a Southern Californian, has donated 40 of his paintings), drawings and prints by Mark Tobey and Arshile Gorky, African artifacts, and sculptures. A strong docent program serves the visiting public—the gallery has about 30,000 visitors per academic year; guided tours are conducted by both docents and graduate art historians. Tues.-Fri. 10-4; Sun. 1-4; closed in summer. Free. (Take Nordhoff St. [west] exit from San Diego Freeway.)

**OAKLAND:   Mills College Art Gallery.** 94613 ☐ Mills College, with a present enrollment of about 1,000 women, was founded in 1852, its gallery, in 1927. Some 5,000 feet of display area houses an outstanding collection of over 3,000 prints and drawings from Europe and America. Paintings, sculpture, textiles, Indian artifacts, and ceramics are also features of the permanent collection. Exhibits change monthly; the smaller Antonio Prieto Gallery, also on the campus, is devoted to crafts and ceramics. Wed.–Sun. 12–4; closed during college vacations. Free. (Take MacArthur Freeway [580] to the MacArthur Blvd. exit; turn right at front gate.)

**Oakland Museum.** 1000 Oak St., 94607 ☐ The Oakland Museum (opened in 1969) is an amalgam of the old Oakland Art Museum (founded 1916), the Snow Museum of Natural History (founded 1922), and the Oakland Public Museum (founded 1910). These elements now constitute the art, natural science, and history departments of the new museum. Designed by the architectural firm of Kevin Roche and John Dinkeloo Associates, the Oakland Museum quickly gained recognition as a landmark urban museum. On the shore of Lake Merritt, gardens, pools, courts, and lawns are interspersed among the levels of a 3-tiered structure, the roof of one tier serving as the garden for another. The collections gathered under these several roofs and in several sculpture courts describe the arts of California, and its natural sciences and history. Defining California arts are paintings by early artist-explorers, Gold Rush paintings, Victorian landscapes, and sculptures by such as Peter Vouldos and Arthur Putnam. Bierstadt's Western landscapes share the walls with contemporaries such as Diebenkorn and Clyfford Still. A variety of changing exhibits are held frequently in a central Great Hall. There is a gallery for one-person or group shows for contemporary Californians and an Art Observatory and Gallery that display the study collections, a multimedia program, photographs, and prints. The Oakland Museum Association supports an educational and cultural program including lectures, films, concerts, and guided tours; provides docents; and coordinates volunteer activities. It provides and services a museum store and an art rental and sales gallery. Several catalogs are published yearly. The library (1,500 volumes) is available for use on the premises. A restaurant overlooks one of the many gardens. Tues.–Thurs., Sat. 10–5; Fri. 10–10; Sun. 10–6. Admission 25¢ per gallery.

**PACIFIC PALISADES: Will Rogers State Historic Park.** 14253 Sunset Blvd., 90272 ☐ Western art—paintings by Charles M. Russell and Edward Borein, for example—hangs on the walls of Will Rogers's home. On 186 acres of ranch country, the house still contains the furniture he used and his cowboy mementos; on the ranch are corrals, stables, and riding trails. Park open 7–7 in summer; 7–6 in winter. Museum open daily 10–5. Admission $1.50 per car.

**PALO ALTO:   Stanford University Museum of Art.** Stanford University, 94305 ☐ Like many of the cultural institutions of California and the American West, Stanford University and its museum came about through the beneficence of a man enriched by the 1869 completion of the transcontinental railroad. Leland and Jane Lathrop Stanford founded the university in 1885 in memory of their only child, Leland, Jr., who died of typhoid fever in Florence at the age of fifteen. In 1891 the museum was dedicated. A neoclassic structure designed after a Greek museum that Leland, Jr., had admired, it was one of the first major public buildings to be constructed of steel-reinforced concrete. The additions that were completed in 1905 made it the largest private museum in the world at the time; the distinction was short-lived, however, when much of the structure and its contents were destroyed by the earthquake of 1906. Housed in this university museum is a collection that includes Oriental, pre-Columbian, African, North American Indian, and Melanesian art; Western art from the Renaissance to the present; and ancient art from Greece, Rome, and Egypt. Outstanding are the 18th- and 19th-century French and English prints and drawings; paintings from the Ming Dynasty; bronzes from the Chou Dynasty; and a large collection of sculpture by Rodin. Permission to use a camera must be granted by the curator.

In addition to 2 temporary exhibits, each running for about 2 months, the museum runs the Thomas Welton Stanford Art Gallery on the campus, with changing exhibits and portions of the permanent collection. The art department of the university sponsors a series of Wednesday evening lectures during the school year, and the Committee for Art, the museum's support organization, sponsors a lecture series throughout the year called "Art Plus." Educational services include presentations for schoolrooms and other facilities, and docent tours. In the gallery bookshop, located in the T. W. Stanford Art Gallery, books, including a host of museum publications, posters, cards, catalogs, and jewelry are sold. Parking facilities limited. Tues.–Fri. 10–4:45 Sat. & Sun. 1–4:45; closed Christmas, Jan. 1, July 4. Free. (Take I-101 University Ave. [west] exit. University becomes Palm Dr. Turn right off Palm Dr. to Museum Way and go to the end.)

**PASADENA:   Norton Simon Museum.** 411 Colorado Blvd., 91105 ☐ Among the magnificent old estates of Pasadena is a modern museum, modern in both structure and artistic emphasis. The Norton Simon Museum was founded in 1924 as the Pasadena Art Museum. After several decades passed during which the museum focused on the exhibition of contemporary art, its name was changed to the Pasadena Museum of Modern Art. When financial problems brought about a reorganization under the aegis of Norton Simon, the museum's name was again changed, a stunningly modern H-shaped complex was built, and long-term loans from the Norton Simon Foundation and Norton Simon Inc. Foundation were hung. The nucleus of the permanent collection is the splendid assemblage of German Expressionist paintings given to the museum by Galka Scheyer, American agent of the "Blue Four"—Paul Klee, Alexei von Jawlensky, Lyonel Feininger, and Wassily Kandinsky. These painters, all of whom came from a loosely knit Munich group that formed around 1911 and called itself Der Blaue Reiter, were linked together by Scheyer when she brought their work to the United States. The Norton Simon Museum is one of the principal repositories of works by Klee and Jawlensky. Broadening the range of its modern collection are paintings by Archipenko, Diebenkorn, Duchamp, de Kooning, Francis, Miró, Nolde, Picasso, and Schwitters. Works by Degas, Maillol, and Rubens are among the European holdings; bronzes from the Chola Dynasty (850–1267) are among those from southern Asia. The library is open by appointment only, and tours are limited. A catalog of the Scheyer collection can be obtained at the bookshop, as well as art books, prints, cards, posters, and slides. Thurs.–Sun. 12–6. Adults $1.50, children free; students, senior citizens 50¢. (At the corner of Orange Grove and Colorado Blvd., near the intersection of freeways 134 and 210.)

**RIVERSIDE: Riverside Art Center.** 3425 Seventh St., 92501 ☐ The Riverside Art Center's beginnings, like those of many art centers across the country, can be traced to a founding group of artists and community leaders dedicated to the concept that the visual arts are necessary to a growing community. It has a small permanent collection—many art centers do not—that is "loosely woven together [by] sentimental, educational, and esthetic values." For the most part, the collection consists of contemporary American art. Among the graphics, however, are lithographs by Picasso, Chagall, Wunderlich, and Appel. Exhibits change every 4 to 6 weeks, but the permanent collection is always on view. Studio art instruction is available to members year round; lectures are given by exhibiting artists and others regularly. A monthly newsletter to members and a magazine about art and artists are published. The center offers member artists' work for sale or rent. Tues.–Sat. 10–5; Sun. 12–5. Free. (At the corner of Seventh & Lime. From Hwy. 91 [north], exit at 7th St.; from 91 [south], exit at University Ave.)

**SACRAMENTO: E. B. Crocker Art Gallery.** 216 O St., 95814 ☐ Less than 20 years after gold was discovered in the American River near Sacramento and the Gold Rush of 1849 began, the E. B. Crocker Art Gallery was aborning. In 1869, when Judge Edwin Crocker retired as counsel to the Central Pacific, the railroad that his brother had been instrumental in completing, he began to direct his energies to his family and home, and to the construction of a large entertainment center and art gallery adjacent to his home for his four eligible daughters. Built in the style of a 16th-century Italian villa, the gallery was completed in 1872. Two years in advance of that event, Crocker took his family to Europe to search for and buy the works of art that would ultimately fill up this masterpiece of architecture that Seth Babson had been commissioned to design. They spent most of their time in Germany, restricted in their movement by the vagaries of the Franco-Prussian War, and most particularly in Dresden; they purchased some 700 paintings and over 1,000 master drawings. In 1872 the collection was brought to San Francisco, framed, and exhibited, and the next year was moved to Sacramento for installation in its permanent home. The judge died a few years later, leaving the care of the collection to his widow, who by 1885 had deeded both gallery and contents to the city of Sacramento. Eventually the Crocker home was also given over to the city and was remodeled to be used as a gallery annex. The R. A. Herold Memorial wing was added to the gallery to accommodate the now expanding collection. Today, the permanent collection continues the diversity that the original 700 paintings, although preponderantly German and more or less impulsively acquired, began. Works range from Italian Renaissance to 20th-century French; Dutch and Flemish still lifes, landscapes, and tavern scenes; Baroque mythology; Old Masters; early German portraits; and select decorative art pieces. The 19th-century German genre and landscape paintings constitute one of the largest collections of this sort outside Germany. And the drawings, stored for many years and rediscovered in the 1930s, are major treasures of the museum; they include works by Dürer, Rubens, Van Dyck, Rembrandt, Boucher, Fragonard, David, and Ingres. Later acquisitions added to this diversity: a collection of Korean ceramics, gathered by a Crocker daughter, is unique; a group of Chinese porcelain and ceramics dating from the 7th through the 19th century is being expanded; Japanese art is represented by sculpture, prints, and armor. The judge's interest in California painters resulted in a collection of 19th-century American artists, among them Charles C. Nahl, William Keith, and Thomas Hill. Nahl's "Sunday Morning in the Mines" is on permanent view. Modern American works have been added to the collection in recent years.

Special activities of the museum include lectures, films, and free Sunday afternoon concerts. A Children's Art Experience is held the last Saturday of every month. Docent tours are held Tues.-Fri. 10 & 11 a.m.; Wed.-Fri. 12:30; Sat. 2. Facilities include a library (by special permission only), and a gallery bookstore which offers catalogs, art books, and gift items for sale. Tues. 2–10; Wed.–Sun. 10–5; closed Thanksgiving, Christmas, & Jan. 1. Free. (Near Old Sacramento and the Capitol Mall.)

**SALINAS: Hartnell College Gallery.** 156 Homestead Ave., 93901 ☐ Salinas, where John Steinbeck was born, is the home of Hartnell College. The 2,500-square-foot gallery here is located near the downtown area of this mainly agricultural community. It houses a small but interesting collection of 1930s works by San Francisco Bay area WPA artists. Exhibits are changed monthly. Mon.–Fri. 10–4; Fri. 6–9.

**SAN DIEGO: Fine Arts Gallery of San Diego.** Balboa Park. Mailing address: Box 2107, 92112 ☐ The Fine Arts Gallery of San Diego is an ornate Spanish plateresque structure built in 1926 in Balboa Park, a thousand acres of recreation, culture, botanical gardens, and zoo in the center of San Diego. The collections housed here range from Italian Renaissance paintings to Spanish Baroque; 19th- and 20th-century European and American; Asian art including works from India, China, Japan, Korea, Persia, and Southeast Asia; and an impressive selection of American, European, and Oriental prints. A sculpture garden displays contemporary works. About 25 special exhibits are mounted each year; generally, they last from 4 to 8 weeks. Cameras can be used for noncommercial purposes with existing light only. A large research library is open to members only. The gallery's educational program is extensive; in addition to classes for children and adults, it sponsors lectures, gallery talks, and film series. Docent tours are offered and a 45-minute recorded "Director's Tour" is available for a $1 rental fee. The gallery store sells books (many of them museum publications), jewelry, prints, postcards; there is also an art sales and rental gallery. Parking directly in front of the gallery. Tues–Sun. 10–5. Free. (SR 163 goes through Balboa Park; Laurel St. takes you to the front of the gallery. From I-5 traveling south, take the Sassafras exit; turn left on Laurel. Use the El Prado parking area.)

**Timken Art Gallery.** Balboa Park, 92112 ☐ The Timken Art Gallery, a small, rectilinear structure built in 1965, is also part of the enchanting Balboa Park. Severely simple and elegant, with a bronze, glass, and travertine exterior, the gallery, one building among the many museums, theaters, restaurants, and sports facilities, overlooks the spacious plaza that was once part of the Panama-California International Exposition. A short walk away is its most famous neighbor, the San Diego Zoo. The collection housed in this gem of a museum was assembled by two unmarried sisters, Anne and Amy Putnam. By 1950, the Putnam Foundation was formed to provide for the future expansion of this already important group of paintings. In 1958, the Timken Foundation of Canton, Ohio (Amelia C. Bridges, a member of the Timken family, had founded and supported the Fine Arts Society of San Diego until her death and succession by the Putnam sisters) offered to pay a substantial part of the cost of a new gallery to house these paintings. Before this, and after the formation of the foundation, purchases made by the sisters were placed on loan at the Metropolitan Museum of Art in New York and the National Gallery in Washington. The gallery has 6 rooms; in one is a collection of Russian icons; another contains a group of American paintings; the remaining 4 rooms contain the Putnam sisters' collection of Old Masters from Dutch-Flemish, French, Spanish, and Italian schools of painting, including Rembrandt, Rubens, Fragonard, Petrus Christus, Bruegel, Boucher, Veronese, Corot, and David. A Remington and an Eastman Johnson are among the American paintings. A rare series of 16th-century French tapestries hangs in the main rotunda. The collection is on display continuously and without change; with only the few exceptions of paintings on loan, the exhibits are permanent. Tours can be arranged on Wednesdays and Thursdays. Three pamphlets, each covering a segment of the collection, are available free of charge. Parking nearby. Tues.–Sat. 10–4:20; Sun. 1:30–4:20; closed major holidays and Sept. Free.

**SAN FRANCISCO: Asian Art Museum of San Francisco, The Avery Brundage Collection.** Golden Gate Park, 94118 ☐ The Asian Art Museum was built between 1960 and 1966 to house the Avery Brundage Collection of Oriental Art, which was given to the city of San Francisco and remained in the basement of the M. H. de Young Memorial Museum until 1966. Valued at some $30 million, it consists of nearly 10,000 objects—sculptures, lacquers, paintings, bronzes, ceramics, jades, and decorative objects—"illustrating major periods and stylistic developments of the arts of Asia from Iran to Japan and from Mongolia to Indonesia." Departments include China, Korea, Japan, Indonesia, the Philippines, the Himalayan countries, and Southeast Asia. A policy of rotation (80 percent of the holdings are in storage) results in continually changing exhibits. In addition, the museum hosts 3 traveling exhibits a year. A branch museum in Japan Center, on Geary Boulevard, also displays portions of the collection on a rotating basis; these exhibits change 3 or 4 times a year. Cameras are not permitted.

The museum offers an intern program for advanced graduate students in Asian art and culture and a 2-semester course on the arts of China for students, docents, and the general public through the San Francisco State University Extension Service. The Conservation Department accepts interns from graduate programs in conservation. Lectures, study groups, and loan exhibitions are sponsored by the Society of Asian Art for participation by its members. Educational materials and gallery aids are designed for circulation, and workshops are held for teachers. The museum collaborates with and supports other institutions identified with Asian art and culture. Docent tours are conducted every day; special group or school tours are also available in English or European or Asian languages. The library of over 12,000 volumes is open to the public Mon.-Fri. 1:30-4:45. A museum shop, shared with the adjoining M. H. de Young Memorial Museum, offers the museum's impressive selection of books on Oriental art, jewelry, prints, and postcards. Daily, 10-5. Free on 1st day of each month; other days adults, 75¢; youths 25¢; children and seniors, free.

**The Fine Arts Museums of San Francisco, M. H. de Young Memorial Museum.** Golden Gate Park, 94118 ☐ By dint of the boldness and energy of M. H. de Young (owner of the San Francisco *Chronicle)* and his cadre of art-enthusiastic San Franciscans, a museum was fashioned out of the debris of the 1894 California Midwinter International Exposition. At the closing of the fair in 1895, the Arts Building and the Royal Pavilion were left standing; de Young and his group set about filling them with the objects that had been on display in various government exhibits. Thus, the M. H. de Young Museum was established in one of the most beautiful parks in the world. Impressive among the de Young purchases at the time were the primitive art objects from the South Seas and Africa; they now have their own galleries. Subsequent acquisitions enriched the museum with objects from all periods of art in the Western World, beginning with ancient Egypt. The Roscoe and Margaret Oakes collection focuses on Dutch, Flemish, and British art of the 17th, 18th, and 19th centuries. Works by Hals, Van Dyck, Gainsborough, Reynolds, Constable, and Goya share space with Rembrandt's "The Rabbi," "Tribute Money" by Rubens, "St. Francis" and "St. John the Baptist" by El Greco, "The Courtship" by Eakins, and Bouts's "Virgin and Child." The outstanding American section includes not only Eakins's work, but also Frederick Church's, Harnett's, Copley's, and Stuart's. And the Flemish tapestries, hung just beyond the entrance to the museum, are spectacular in size and in workmanship. Special exhibits change frequently. Cameras, but not flashes or tripods, are permitted.

An art school offers classes in drawing, painting, design, printmaking, photography, filmmaking, textiles, metal arts, sculpture, and ceramics. Lectures are given frequently on both the permanent collection and temporary exhibitions. Other educational activities include an outreach program, an art apprentice program that trains volunteers, and, in 1978, an International Symposium on Early Irish Art and Culture. Tours are led by docents every day. Numerous catalogs on the permanent and traveling exhibitions are available in the museum shop together with other books, magazines, jewelry, reproductions, and slides. Café de Young is a cafeteria; wine is available. Parking nearby. Daily 10-5. Admission 75¢ for adults; 25¢ for young people; free for children under 12, senior citizens, and recognized educational groups.

**The Fine Arts Museums of San Francisco, California Palace of the Legion of Honor.** Lincoln Park, 94121 ☐ The California Palace of the Legion of Honor and the M. H. de Young Memorial Museum merged in 1972 as a department of the city and county of San Francisco. The Palace of the Legion of Honor was a gift to the city by Mr. and Mrs. Adolph B. Spreckles, whose idea it was to duplicate the original Palace of the Legion of Honor in Paris and to dedicate its American twin structure to the memory of Californians who died in World War I. It opened in 1924 on a stretch of land in Lincoln Park, a headland above the Pacific that looks out to the Golden Gate, the bay, and the mountains. Unique as a replica in America of a neoclassical-style palace, the museum is also unique in its concentration on the creative arts of France. An extensive Rodin sculpture collection (which Rodin himself helped to select) is said to be one of the finest in the country, as is the medieval and Renaissance tapestry collection. French paintings, sculpture, decorative arts, and period rooms include works from the 16th to the 20th century, with special emphasis given the 18th and 19th. The largest graphics collection in the western United States is housed here as well, a resource of the Achenbach Foundation for the Graphic Arts—approximately 100,000 European, American, and Asian prints ranging from the 15th century to the present. The grandeur of this museum is exemplified in some of its masterpieces: Rodin's "The Thinker," for example, and his "The Burghers of Calais" and "St. John the Baptist"; a tapestry from the series "The Apocalypse," made around 1380; an 18th-century Parisian room; La Tour's "Old Man" and "Old Woman"; Monet's "Water Lilies"; and Cézanne's "Rocks in the Park of the Château Noir." There are continually changing special exhibitions. Cameras without flashes or tripods are permitted.

Lectures, concerts, and a drama festival are held regularly. In 1976 an International Tapestry Symposium was one of the museum's educational efforts. Docent tours for schools and other special groups are offered. Catalogs published here include *Rodin Sculpture: A Critical Catalog of the Spreckles Collection* and *French Drawings: A Critical Catalog;* they are for sale in the book shop, where visitors can also buy prints and postcards. The Café Chanticleer is a cafeteria; wine is available. Parking on grounds. Daily 10–5. Admission 75¢ for adults; 25¢ for youths; free for children under 12, senior citizens, and recognized educational groups.

**San Francisco Museum of Modern Art.** Van Ness Ave. at McAllister St., 94102 ☐ Another exposition figured in the early life of yet another San Francisco museum. The San Francisco Museum of Art was founded in 1916 by the city's Art Association, and from then until 1926 it was housed in the Palace of Fine Arts of the Panama-Pacific International Exposition. Incorporated as a nonprofit institution independent of the Art Association in 1921, the museum became a private institution dedicated to the art of the 20th century in 1935. In that year it opened new facilities at the San Francisco Civic Center, and not until 1976 did it change its name to San Francisco Museum of Modern Art. Today it occupies 2 floors of the War Memorial Veterans' Building. Here, the 20th century presides; a few antecedents from the late 1800s only serve to strengthen the review of modern art displayed in paintings, sculpture, drawings, prints, photographs, and a few decorative objects. An extraordinary group by Matisse includes "Jeune Fille aux Yeux Verts" and "Le Serfe" (a 1903 bronze); there are 28 paintings by Clyfford Still, as well as works by Gorky ("Enigmatic Combat"), Pollock ("Guardians of the Secret"), Rauschenberg ("Collection"), and Jasper Johns ("Lands End"). An active program of temporary exhibits brings new shows every 6 to 8 weeks. The use of cameras (permanent collection only) requires written permission from the director.

The Education Department offers classes in drawing, painting, ceramics, photography, dance, mime, animated film, and history of art, plus classes for children in art and movement. Lectures and forums relating to current exhibitions or topics relevant to modern art are frequent. In addition, the museum sponsors poetry readings, dance, jazz, avant garde, and chamber music programs. The museum offers training for individuals with art backgrounds through its docent program. Docents then conduct gallery tours for adults and children and lecture to schools and community groups. Tours are offered 3 days a week. Catalogs and brochures are published for almost all exhibitions organized by the museum; a catalog of the permanent collection was published in 1970. The Louise Sloss Ackerman Fine Arts Library, a research and reference library, is open to the public 3 afternoons a week (Mon.-Wed. 1-5). The museum book shop sells books, magazines, cards, prints, jewelry, posters, and gifts. The museum cafe is self-service, including wine. Three parking lots within a 3-block radius, but street parking is most common; parking is a problem. Tues.-Fri. 10-10; Sat. & Sun. 10-5. Admission $1-$1.50 to temporary exhibits; free to permanent collection galleries.

**SAN JOSE: Rosicrucian Egyptian Museum.** Rosicrucian Park, 95191 □ Founded in 1929 by Dr. H. Spencer Lewis to house his private collection of antiquities, the Rosicrucian Egyptian Museum now contains the largest collection of ancient Egyptian works in the western United States. The museum, a replica of an Egyptian temple surrounded by lawns and fountains, moved to its present site in Rosicrucian Park in 1966. Assyrian and Babylonian artifacts (small clay figures, carved seals, cuneiform tablets, deity figures) may also be seen, but the preponderance of the exhibits are Egyptian, ranging from ancient times to the Coptic Christians and the

Roman period. The art gallery, changing exhibits every month, features the work of artists from Northern California. Tours are available on a regular schedule, and larger group tours can be prearranged. Cameras without flash bulbs are permitted. The museum shop has a wide selection of Egyptian-style jewelry, postcards, posters, books, and other souvenirs. Tues.–Fri. 9–5; Sat, Sun., Mon. 12–5. Free. (SR 17 to The Alameda; turn right on Naglee.)

**San Jose Museum of Art.** 110 S. Market St., 95113 ☐ The San Jose Museum of Art was founded in 1968 in an old (1892) building with a long history as a post office and then a library. It houses a permanent collection of paintings chiefly by contemporary Californians, or depicting California scenes. Many changing exhibitions feature local, regional, national, and traveling shows. Classes are held for adults and children; lectures, gallery talks, and tours are also offered. A docent program is conducted in conjunction with California State University. A traveling instructional museum, "Let's Look at Art," is part of the museum's outreach program. A sales and rental gallery and a gift shop offer a variety of items and exhibition catalogs. Tues.–Sat. 10–4:30; Sun., holidays 12–4. Free.

**SAN MARINO: Huntington Library, Art Gallery and Botanical Gardens.** 1151 Oxford Rd., 91108 ☐ Twelve miles northeast of Los Angeles and hard by Pasadena is San Marino, home of the Huntington Library, Art Gallery and Botanical Gardens, a triple miracle in this quiet residential community. Built in 1909 in the tradition of 19th-century British manors, what is now the art gallery was the home of railroad executive Henry E. Huntington, who built a second building, the great columned library, in 1919. The two buildings are surrounded by 207 acres of gardens, the third wonder of this awesome institution. Huntington and his wife, the widow of his uncle Collis P. Huntington, whose fortune came from the building of railroads, lived among the exquisite rarities they collected with the help of the incomparable Sir Joshua Duveen. The gallery, with pleasing effect, retains the domestic setting of that home. Huntington particularly admired the art that emanated from Britain in the 18th and 19th centuries, and the combination of his limitless resources and Duveen's impeccable taste resulted in one of the finest collections of this period outside England. "Pinkie," a portrait of Sarah Moulton-Barrett by Sir Thomas Lawrence, Gainsborough's "Blue Boy," Sir Joshua Reynolds's "Mrs. Siddons as the Tragic Muse," and Constable's "View on the Stour" are some of the masterpieces here. Mrs. Huntington, Arabella, loved the decorative arts of 18th-century France—the furniture, tapestries, porcelain, and sculpture—and the painters of the Renaissance. Out of this predilection grew one of the richest collections of these periods in the United States, the major portion of which is displayed in the library building.

The library specializes in British and American history and literature. A half million books are housed here, some 350,000 of which are rare. Among the treasures are a Gutenberg Bible, the Ellesmere manuscript of Chaucer's *Canterbury Tales,* manuscripts of Benjamin Franklin's *Autobiography* and Thoreau's *Walden,* a unique collection of early editions of Shakespeare, and a first edition of Audubon's double-elephant folio of *Birds of America.* The library is primarily a research facility for qualified scholars; permission to use it must be granted by the Reader Service or, in the case of the Art Reference Library, the Curator of the Art Collection. Cameras are permitted in both library and gallery, but flash equipment and tripods are not.

Gardens arranged by horticultural or botanical interest have some 9,000 plants from all over the world. A Shakespeare garden displays the flora used in Elizabethan gardens; a rose garden contains the largest collection of tea roses in the United States; the camellia collection comprises 6 acres of the largest variety in the world. Other displays can be seen in a palm, a Japanese, and a desert garden, where is assembled the largest outdoor collection of desert plants extant.

The Huntington's activities include changing exhibits devoted to British drawings and British and Continental prints on the second floor of the gallery; docent classes for schoolchildren in each area of specialization; 15-minute talks and dramatic, musical or dance programs at least once a month; educational training programs for docents; lectures for support groups; scholarly conferences and seminars; and fellowships for post-Ph.D. scholarly research. The Huntington Library publishing program is one of the oldest in Southern California. Three or four scholarly books are published each year as well as *The Huntington Quarterly; The Calendar,* a bi-monthly newsletter; and an annual report. The bookstore offers materials related to the Huntington. A series of self-guide tour pamphlets for the gallery, the library, and some of the gardens are available for 10¢; taped tours of the gallery can be rented for 50¢; docent tours of the grounds take place at 1 p.m. on weekdays. Free parking on the grounds. Tues–Sun. 1–4:30; closed major holidays and October. Free. (From Pasadena Freeway [SR 11] continue on Arroyo Pkwy. to California Blvd. and turn right onto Allen Ave.; turn left onto Orlando Rd. and right onto Oxford. From San Bernardino Freeway [I-10], exit onto San Gabriel Blvd. [north]. Turn left onto Huntington Dr., right onto San Marino Ave., and left onto Stratford. Stratford runs into Oxford. From Foothill Freeway [I-210], exit onto Rosemead Blvd. [south]; turn right onto California Blvd. and then left onto Allen Ave. Follow directions as from Pasadena Freeway. From Ventura Freeway [SR 134], going toward Pasadena, exit on Orange Grove Blvd. [south]. Turn left onto California, then follow directions as from Pasadena Freeway.)

**SANTA BARBARA: Santa Barbara Museum of Art.** 1130 State St., 93101 ☐ A Spanish Colonial building erected in 1914 to house the Central Post Office was remodeled in 1939 to house the Santa Barbara Museum of Art. This event was sparked by a letter to the Santa Barbara *News Press* from artist Colin Campbell Cooper in which he suggested that the city should have a museum, and that the old post office was the perfect place. Ultimately, the post office building was bought from the U.S. Government by the County of Santa Barbara and leased to the museum corporation. It opened in 1941 with a fine collection of Oriental musical instruments, Greek and Roman antiquities, Old Master paintings (Zurbarán's "A Franciscan Monk"), English paintings (a portrait of Gainsborough by William Hoare), drawings by European artists from the Renaissance to the 18th century, drawings and prints from the 19th and 20th centuries (Marin, Miró, Matisse), American art predominantly from the West Coast (Copley's "General Joshua Winslow" and an unknown painter's "The Buffalo Hunter"), and the Alice Schott antique doll collection. Permission is needed for the use of cameras. The museum offers lectures and films, and supports an art education outreach program by its docent council. A slide library, a Contemporary Graphics Center, and an art rental gallery are valuable resources. Docents guide tours Tues.–Sun. at 12:30 and by appointment. A museum shop sells catalogs and cards. Parking in a city parking lot, which allows 90 minutes free. Tues.–Sat. 11–5; Sun. 12–5. Free. (SR 101 passes through Santa Barbara. Coming from the north, take the Carrillo St. off ramp; go left on Carrillo, left on Chapala, and right on Anapamu. Coming from the south, go right on the State St. exit, proceed on State to Anapamu.)

**University of California, Santa Barbara Art Museum.** 93106 ☐ The university museum, opened in 1960, overlooks a lagoon on the campus. Its exhibits are notable, especially the Morgenroth collection of over 400 Renaissance medals and plaques; the Story collection of European Master prints, ranging from the 15th to the 18th centuries; the Sedgwick collection of European Master paintings from the 15th through the 17th century; and a group of architectural drawings by Southern California architects. Changing exhibits, including faculty and student shows, accompany the display of the permanent works throughout the year. An agreement form must be signed in order to photograph the exhibits. A small library that is part of the Morgenroth collection is open to the public. Catalogs are sold at the museum desk. Parking and restaurant facilities on campus or in the nearby community. Tues.–Sat. 10–4; Sun & holidays 1–5. Free. (From US 101 south, the Ward Memorial/UCSB exit leads directly to the main entrance of the campus. From 101 north take the Storke Rd. exit toward the ocean to El Colegio, which leads to the west entrance.)

**SANTA CLARA: de Saisset Art Gallery and Museum.** University of Santa Clara, 95053 ☐ In the Spanish Colonial motif of the Jesuit University of Santa Clara, of which it is a part, the de Saisset Art Gallery and Museum stands as a memorial to Ernest de Saisset. It was built in 1955, adjacent to the Mission Santa Clara de Asis, with funds left by his sister, Isabelle de Saisset, to house the paintings done by her brother. In addition to these paintings, the museum's holdings represent many eras and diverse styles, among them, 17th-century Dutch-Flemish; 19th-century American (including Chase, Moran, Keith, Tryon); 19th-century English (Millais, Turner); and 17th-century Spanish. It is the West Coast repository of a collection of New Deal Art consisting of photographs, paintings, drawings, and sculpture. In its Oriental collection, ranging from the 7th century to the present, is a pair of clay horsemen (618 A.D.) from the T'ang Dynasty and Imperial Temple jars from the Ch'ing Dynasty (1662–1722). Graphics include lithographs, engravings, and etchings by such masters as Engelbrecht, Huret, Dürer, Hogarth, Van Leyden, Bartolozzi, Stenhardt; 10th-century Japanese woodblock prints; and works by Picasso, Vlaminck, Rouault, Chagall, Scholder, and Fried. In a gallery known as the Mission Room is an extensive collection dealing with the Costanoan Indians, the early mission fathers, and the history of the university. The African collection has artifacts from various tribes. There are also distinguished collections of tapestries, porcelain, 19th- and 20th-century sculpture, photography, and video art. Cameras are not permitted, except by special permission.

The museum sponsors concert series featuring violinists and a guitar society, and lectures in the form of a humanities forum. Tours of the gallery, available on Wednesday mornings, include the university observatory and mission. Publications are limited to catalogs of special exhibits. A museum shop offers books, handcrafted jewelry, postcards and cards, and antique items all under $25. Parking facilities in front of the museum. Tues.–Fri. 10–5; Sat. & Sun. 1–5; closed June–Sept. & major holidays. Free. (On the University of Santa Clara campus; first building on the right upon entering the main gates to the university. From SR 17, take the Alameda off ramp going west and follow it to the main entrance to the university. It will be on your left. From US 101, take the de la Cruz Blvd. exit and follow the signs to Santa Clara and the university. The entrance will be on your right.)

**Triton Museum of Art.** 1505 Warburton Ave., 95050 ☐ The Triton Museum comprises four buildings that blend the elements of Oriental and Spanish architecture; it is located on 7 landscaped acres. Founded in San Jose in 1965 by Mr. and Mrs. W. Robert Morgan, it was moved to its present site opposite the Santa Clara Civic Center in 1967. The permanent collection of this quadripavilion and expanding complex is devoted to American painting; California artists are featured, especially a large group of paintings by Theodore Wores. A developing collection of American ceramic and glass began in 1974 with the bequest of the Vivien Woodward Elmer majolica collection. One to 3 exhibitions are mounted simultaneously and change every 4 to 6 weeks. The 1866 Jamison-Brown house was moved to the museum grounds in 1970 and has since served as a meeting place and to house part of the permanent collection. Art classes, lectures, concerts, workshops, and tours are scheduled throughout the year. Docents conduct group tours and also lecture in the schoolrooms of Santa Clara. Exhibition announcements, a newsletter, and occasional exhibit catalogs are published. Books, postcards, and prints are offered at a small sales desk. Parking facilities of the Civic Center also serve museum visitors. Tues.–Fri. 12–4; Sat. & Sun. 12–5. Free. (Take SR 17 to The Alameda; going northwest, turn right onto Monroe St., then left onto Warburton. Or take US 101 to San Tomas Expwy.; go south; turn left onto Scott, then left onto Warburton. Or take I-280 to Winchester Blvd.; follow it north as it turns into Lincoln; Lincoln ends at the museum on Warburton.)

**STOCKTON: Pioneer Museum and Haggin Galleries.** 1201 North Pershing Ave., 95203 ☐ The Pioneer Museum and Haggin Galleries, one of the cultural centers of Stockton, was founded in 1928 to preserve historical objects relating to the city, the San Joaquin Valley, and the state of California. Soon after, Eila Haggin McKee became interested in the museum as a showcase for some 180 paintings left to her by her father. The modified neoclassic structure was built in Victoria Park, one of Stockton's largest, on land donated by the city in 1930; in 1973 it was expanded the third time. The gallery houses 19th-century French Academy and Salon paintings and 19th-century American landscape paintings. The French collection includes "Nymphs Bathing" by Adolphe William Bouguereau, "Gathering for the Hunt" by Rosa Bonheur, "The Artist and His Model" by Jean Léon Gérôme, and works by Vibert, Laurencin, de la Peña, Gauguin, Harpignies, Monchablon, Richet, Renoir, and Worms. "Sunset in Yosemite Valley" by Albert Bierstadt and "Stagecoach" by Edward Lamson Henry hang with works by Bradford, Cropsey, Coulter, Deakin, Hart, Childe Hassam, George Inness, David Johnson, William Keith, Leyendecker, and Maxfield Parrish. Exhibitions are scheduled every 6 to 8 weeks throughout the year. Cameras can be used by permission only; no flashbulbs. The museum sponsors occasional lectures during the year, classes during the summer only. A docent council prepares educational programs. Guided tours are given on Saturdays; advance notice is required for special group tours. A bimonthly calendar of events is published. The library is open by special permission only. Although there are no eating facilities in the museum, there are picnic and barbecue facilities in the park, as well as tennis courts, playgrounds, ponds, and a swimming pool. Tues.–Sun. 1:30–5; park open 6 a.m.–11 p.m. Free. (Take I-5 to Pershing-Oak St. exit.)

# COLORADO

**COLORADO SPRINGS: Colorado Springs Fine Arts Center.** 30 West Dale St., 80903 □ This famous resort town at the base of Pikes Peak, with plains extending eastward and mountains westward, and with Manitou Springs and Pike National Forest within easy reach, has, as an added icing on its cake, an impressive and active Fine Arts Center. The 1936 Art Deco building, with intimations of southwestern Pueblo architecture, is near downtown Colorado Springs. Overlooking Monument Valley Park, with a spectacular view of Pikes Peak, it was one of the first "multi-purpose institutions of its kind, housing both museum and performing arts facilities," as well as an excellent (15,000-volume) library. It has 2 separate collections, one of southwestern Spanish Colonial and American Indian art (a gift of Alice Bemis Taylor known as the Taylor Museum collection) and one of 19th- and 20th-century American art with emphasis on the Southwest (the fine arts collection). Five galleries are utilized for both touring exhibits and exhibits mounted from the permanent fine arts collection; 2 other galleries are used for changing exhibits of the Taylor Museum collection, considered to be one of the finest of its kind in the world. Among the museum's American paintings are Sargent's "Lady in White," Kuhn's "Trio," and Dove's "Fog Horns." Other painters represented are Bierstadt, Callahan, Lawson, and Sage. Special exhibits change regularly at intervals of about 4 to 8 weeks and are planned to provide the greatest variety possible. Cameras may be used with permission from the information desk.

In addition to the museum, the center, with a 450-seat auditorium and a 150-seat music room, supports a performing arts program and an educational program including art courses, docent tours, lectures, and films. The Bemis Art School for Children, known across the country, is a highlight of the center's educational efforts. The library, which specializes in books on art and anthropology, is open to the public. Many publications, including monthly membership journals and exhibition catalogs, emanate from the center. A museum shop sells books, jewelry, cards, southwestern Spanish and Indian crafts, and museum replicas; a Collector's Gallery sells and rents contemporary art works. Parking facilities close by. Tues. & Thurs. 10–9; Wed., Fri., Sat. 10–5; Sun. 1:30–5; closed Thanksgiving, Christmas, Jan. 1. Free. (Take I-25 to Uintah St. [exit 62]. Go east to Cascade Ave., south to Dale St., west to the center. Or take Nevada Ave. [US 85] and go west on Dale.)

**DENVER: Denver Art Museum.** 100 West 14th Ave. Pkwy., 80204 ☐ Denver's Art Museum is the largest arts resource between Kansas City and Los Angeles. The spectacular modern edifice—twin towers connected by a central core, faced with faceted glass tiles that reflect the shifting lights of the city—opened in 1971 at the south end of the Civic Center in downtown Denver. Seven levels of galleries, stacked vertically in pairs and equipped with the most modern temperature controls and security mechanisms, contain the diverse collection of this interesting museum that has served an 8-state region from its beginnings in 1893 as The Artists' Club. Changing exhibits are installed on the main floor. Above, in ascending order, are the other major collections: African, Oceanic, and Northwest Coast Indian works; an outstanding North American Indian collection gathered from almost every tribe known; art from the Americas, displayed in environmental settings, including New World Art (pre-Columbian works, Spanish Colonial paintings, the finest collection of Spanish Peruvian religious art in the country, and Southwestern santos), and paintings from 18th- and 19th-century North American artists; European art—paintings, drawings, and sculpture by Van Dyck, Tintoretto, Rubens, Veronese, Monet, Pissarro, Renoir, Matisse, Utrillo, Picasso, Modigliani, Degas, Chagall, and Toulouse-Lautrec—represented by the Samuel H. Kress collection of Renaissance art, the Simon Guggenheim Memorial Collection, and the European collection of Edward and Tullah Hanley, as well as 3 period rooms in French Gothic, English Tudor, and Spanish Baroque; Oriental art—porcelains, bronzes, scrolls, and stone figures from China, Japan, India, and other Far Eastern countries—highlighted by a 13th-century South Indian bronze of the Hindu god Shiva and a 10th-century Chinese wood sculpture of Kuan-yin, goddess of mercy; and textiles and costumes, located at the top of the stack of galleries. Exhibitions change regularly; many are borrowed from the world's leading museums.

A variety of art education and service programs are offered by the museum, including a wide range of lectures, seminars, workshops, and symposia, performing arts events, and films. Guided tours are made available to some 75,000 visitors annually (1976 attendance reached almost 528,000). Statewide programs include tours, distribution of film strips, slide and tape cassettes, brochures, loans, and college and school programs. An extensive library (40,000 volumes) of American Indian and native arts is among the museum's assets. A shop offers jewelry, museum replicas, books, postcards, posters, and catalogs. A cafeteria with a shaded patio is open Tues.–Sat. 11–3; Sun. 1–3; Wed. until 8 p.m.; wine and cocktails are available. Tues.–Sat. 9–5; Sun. 1–5; Wed. eve. 6–9; closed major holidays. Free. (The Civic Center is bounded by West Colfax Ave., West 14th Ave., Broadway, & Cherokee St.)

# CONNECTICUT

**BRIDGEPORT: Housatonic Museum of Art.** 510 Barnum Ave., 06608 ☐ The Housatonic Community College is the proud possessor of one of the surprising collections in Connecticut. Scattered through this 5-story school facility, in classrooms, offices, library, and bookstore (a 2nd-floor gallery has changing exhibits) are over 1,000 works—drawings, paintings, prints, and sculpture—the preponderance of which come from 19th- and 20th-century Europe and America. Works by Mary Cassatt, Cézanne, Daumier, Dubuffet, Dürer, Renoir, Rodin are scattered through the galaxy of 20th-century stars such as Arp, Avery, Baskin, Calder, Chagall, de Kooning, Dine, Levine, Lichtenstein, Miró, Motherwell, Oldenburg, Rauschenberg, Rivers, Shahn, Shinn, Stamos, Stella, and Larry Zox. Eight monthly exhibitions are mounted in the gallery from September through May; generally they are drawn from outside sources. Occasional lectures are held and catalogs that relate to the special exhibits are sponsored by the museum. Tours can be arranged in advance. Other functions of this museum are carried out through the facilities of the college—art classes, library, cafeteria. Parking lot across the street. Mon.–Thurs. 8 a.m.–9 p.m.; Fri. 8–4. Free. (From exit 28 on I-95, take East Main St. north to Barnum Ave.)

**COS COB: Bush-Holley House.** 39 Strickland Rd., 06807 ☐ Elmer Livingston MacRae attracted many of the artists and writers of his time to his home in Cos Cob, near Greenwich. They stayed together, and together they plotted the coup of 1913, the Armory Show in New York. Today the house is the headquarters of the Greenwich Historical Society. The furniture, fireplaces, and paintings are as they were, and on the grounds stand a barn and gallery, and the John Rogers Museum with some of the genre sculptures that made Rogers's reputation. Tues.–Fri. 10–12, 2–4; Sat., Sun. 2–4. Admission $1 for adults, 25¢ for children. (Off US 1.)

**FARMINGTON:   Hill-Stead Museum.** 06032 ☐ Alfred Atmore Pope, having amassed a fortune in Cleveland as head of the Cleveland Malleable Iron Company, chose a 150-acre tract of unspoiled Connecticut land for his retirement home. In 1900 he commissioned Stanford White, then at the height of his career, to design it. Pope's daughter Theodate (later Mrs. John Wallace Riddle), an aspiring young architect, took an active part in the project, and together they produced a graceful neo-Colonial house that could function not only as a home, but also as a showcase for Pope's sizable art collection. Hill-Stead served its dual purpose well for almost half a century until Mrs. Riddle bequeathed the house and its contents to be maintained as a museum in memory of her parents. The walls of this gracious house, with all its original furnishings, are hung with a beautiful selection of French Impressionist paintings—works by Degas, Monet, Manet, Cassatt, Carrière. Indeed, each room is a small gallery. In the drawing room hangs Manet's "The Guitar Player" and "Absinthe Drinker," Degas's "The Tub," and Monet's "View of the Bay and the Maritime Alps at Antibes." Whistler's "Symphony in Violet and Blue" and Degas's "Jockeys" can be seen in the dining room. The morning room contains Monet's "Boats Leaving the Harbor." Upstairs are Carrière's "Maternity," Cassatt's "Mother and Two Children," and etchings and engravings by Dürer and Piranesi. Throughout are the decorative arts, furniture, rugs, silver, and porcelains of a well-appointed, tasteful collector's home. The house can be viewed only with a museum guide, and the library can be used by special permission. A museum shop offers postcards, slides, and booklets prepared by the museum for sale. Parking on the museum grounds. Wed., Thurs., Sat., Sun. 2–5; closed Thanksgiving, Christmas. Admission $1 for adults, 50¢ for children under 12. (Exit 39 of I-84 at Farmington. Entrances to the museum are on Farmington Ave. & Mountain Rd.)

**GREENWICH:   Bruce Museum.** Steamboat Rd., 06830 ☐ The Bruce Museum was established in 1908 by Robert M. Bruce as a natural history, historical, and art museum. The art here is from 17th-century Italy, 19th-century Western Europe, and 20th-century America, and there are porcelain and ivory objects from the Orient. Temporary exhibits are mounted regularly. The museum sponsors lectures, films, and concerts. A docent program provides guides for tours. The library (1,000 volumes) has books on both art and science. Mon.–Fri. 10–5; Sun. 2–5. Free.

**HARTFORD:   Connecticut Historical Society.** 1 Elizabeth St., 06105 ☐ The Connecticut Historical Society, founded in 1825 as a research library and record museum on Connecticut, moved its holdings in 1950 from the Wadsworth Atheneum, where they had been housed since 1844, to the Curtis Veeder home on 8 acres of land in the suburbs of Hartford. Although primarily a historical museum, with excellent collections of 17th- and 18th-century Connecticut-made furniture, the society also has a collection of some 600 portraits dating from the 17th century to the present. It includes works by Johnston, Durand, Trumbull, Earle, Moulthrop, Jennys, and Samuel F. B. Morse. The society also owns a sizable collection of lithographs by the Kellogg Brothers firm and engravings by Abel Buell and Amos Doolittle, two of Connecticut's earliest engravers. Exhibitions change regularly, and "live" storage makes it possible for visitors, by appointment, to view items of particular interest that are not on display. The society's library of 70,000 volumes, 1½ million manuscripts, bound newspapers, maps, prints, and photographs is open to the public (Mon–Sat. 9:30–5:30); especially notable is the collection on New England genealogy. Publications are released annually on subjects relating to Connecticut; a quarterly bulletin, an annual report, and catalogs of the collection are also available. The society holds lecture series during the fall and winter and provides guided tours for large groups by prearrangement. Mon.–Sat 1–5; closed holidays. Free. (At the junction of Asylum Ave. and Elizabeth St. From I-84 [west] exit at Asylum St. and go west; from I-84 [east] exit at Sigourney St., go north, then west on Asylum.)

**Wadsworth Atheneum.** 600 Main St., 06103 ☐ The Wadsworth Atheneum, located in the center of the "Insurance Capital of the World," is one of the oldest public art museums in the United States. In the summer of 1841, Daniel Wadsworth, together with several other Hartford citizens, raised $20,000 for the creation of an art gallery. Wadsworth contributed his family homestead at 600 Main Street for the museum's home, and a year later the Wadsworth Atheneum was granted a charter by the state. Since 1844, when the original Gothic Revival building was completed, the museum has grown in every direction: In 1910 the Morgan Memorial (housing J. P. Morgan, Sr.'s collection and memorializing his father Junius) was built in the style of the Renaissance; also in 1910, the Tudor-style Colt Memorial was added; 1932 saw the addition of the modern Avery Memorial; and 1965, the James Lippincott Goodwin Building, still more modern. Surprisingly, the 5 cleverly interconnected buildings form a pleasing whole. The collection housed here is massive; it consists of over 30,000 objects and is valued at almost $100 million. Its strength is in classical bronzes, Baroque paintings, 18th-century porcelain, American furniture, English and American silver, 19th-century French and American paintings, and 20th-century art. Caravaggio's "The Ecstasy of St. Francis" is one of the very few by that 16th-century master in this country. There are also gems by Poussin, Goya, El Greco, Rubens, Rembrandt, Delacroix, and Toulouse-Lautrec, to mention only a few. Exhibitions change regularly in only some of the galleries. Cameras are permitted, but flashes must be shielded.

The museum screens foreign films and American revivals in its impressive Avery Theater. It also offers occasional concerts and lectures in conjunction with exhibitions. The Lions Gallery of the Senses is an educational facility for both the visually impaired and the sighted, emphasizing sensory exploration of art works. The MATRIX Gallery of contemporary art sponsors lectures by artists whose work is displayed there. Educational programs for schools and demonstrations on artistic processes are scheduled throughout the year. Publications include a myriad of books and catalogs. Guided tours are available on Saturdays and Sundays, and mini-lectures at noon on some weekdays. Special group tours can be arranged through the Education Office. The library is open to the public by appointment. EAT Restaurant is open Tues.–Fri. 11:30–2; beer and wine are available with lunch; snack bar open during same hours. Parking facilities within easy walking distance. Admission $1 for adults, 50¢ ages 12–18. (From I-91 or I-84, coming from either direction, take the exit marked Downtown Hartford, Capitol Area, or Capitol Ave.; go to Prospect St., then to Main.)

**MIDDLETOWN: Davison Art Center.** Wesleyan University, 301 High St., 06457 ☐ A collection of prints and drawings, presented to Wesleyan University by George and Harriet Davison between 1938 and 1953, is housed in the pre-Civil War Alsop House, renamed in honor of the Davisons. Several thousand prints and drawings describe the history of printmaking from the 15th century on. Works by Dürer, Cranach, Rembrandt, and Piranesi, among others, can be seen here. The Millet collection is said to be among the most complete anywhere of this artist. From the 19th and 20th centuries, American and English printmakers predominate; and from the Orient, Japanese prints. Temporary exhibitions are scheduled regularly. Lectures, films, concerts, recitals, and gallery talks are a few of the center's other scheduled activities. The library (16,000 volumes) is open for use under university regulations. Mon.–Sat. 10–4; Sun. & holidays 2–5; closed weekends June–Aug. Free.

**NEW BRITAIN: New Britain Museum of American Art.** 56 Lexington St., 06052 ☐ Several parks are scattered through what is somewhat unromantically called the "Hardware City." The New Britain Museum of American Art is located in a turn-of-the-century home adjacent to one of them. The house was left by its owner to be used as a free public art museum in 1937. The fine collection of American art on display here began in 1903 with a bequest by John Butler Talcott. From 1903 to 1937 it was housed in the New Britain Public Library. By 1977, the museum had been enlarged thrice—in 1950, in 1964 with the addition of 3 galleries, and again in 1977. The entire spectrum of American art can be seen here, some 3,000 items from the Colonial period up to the present. Early and striking primitive portraits contrast with later works by Gilbert Stuart and Thomas Sully. Landscapes from the Hudson River school are highlighted by Frederick Church's "Haying Near New Haven," and from the Barbizon school, by several George Inness works. The Ashcan school is represented by Henri, Luks, Glackens, Shinn, and Sloan, and their colleagues in the protesting "Eight," Prendergast, Lawson, and Davies. There are genre paintings by Edward Lamson Henry, William Mount, and Eastman Johnson, and trompe l'oeil paintings by William Harnett and John Peto. Thomas Hart Benton's murals "The Arts in America" occupy their own gallery; displayed elsewhere are several Wyeths, Copleys, Whistlers, and Sargents. Another fine collection spans 100 years of American illustration. Exhibitions change from October through June approximately every 6 weeks. Cameras are permitted. Series of lectures, films, field trips, and docent tours (either multilingual or especially oriented for the blind and deaf) are arranged by the museum. Publications include catalogs of the collections and several monographs on American artists. The research library of books on American art is available for use on the premises. A museum shop sells catalogs, prints, postcards, Christmas cards, and gift items. Parking on the street. Tues.–Sun. 1–5; special arrangements for group morning visits. Free. (Take exit 35 off I-84. Lexington St. is off West Main St.)

**NEW HAVEN:   Yale University Art Gallery.** Chapel St. at York. Mailing address: 2006 Yale Station, 06520 ☐ Yale's art collection began in 1718 with a gift of a portrait of George I from Elihu Yale. The Collegiate School of Saybrook, Connecticut, subsequently took his name, and in 1745 the Yale College Charter made it permanent. In 1831 John Trumbull, the "patriot-artist," then old and financially insecure after an active and successful career, donated his unsold paintings and miniatures, a substantial collection, to Yale in exchange for which he received an annuity. Trumbull himself designed the neoclassical building that was to house his paintings, and in 1832 the Trumbull Gallery, the first college art museum in America, opened on what was then the New Haven Green. Trumbull and his wife are buried under the part of the gallery housing his works. In 1866 the collections were moved to a new School of Fine Arts building, Street Hall, on the corner of Chapel and High Streets. The next move was made in 1928, when Harvard-educated Edward S. Harkness contributed the funds for a new Art Gallery, a Tuscan Romanesque building modeled after a palace in Viterbo, Italy, by Egerton Swartout, and connected to

Street Hall by a bridge across High Street. The present building, one of architect Louis I. Kahn's first major works, and the first modern building at Yale, incorporates parts of the old Art Gallery for its American collections and sculpture gallery. The Trumbull paintings of the Revolutionary period were only the beginnings of a now major museum with works of all countries and all major periods. The James Jackson Jarves collection of early Italian paintings was acquired in 1871, the first assemblage of its kind in America. Subsequently, the museum acquired the Rebecca Darlington Stoddard collection of over 600 Greek and Roman vases; the Dura-Europos collection of antiquities from the university's excavations in the Syrian desert; the Griggs collection of Italian painting and medieval art; the Moore collections of textiles and of Near and Far Eastern art; the Linton collection of African sculpture; the Olsen collection of pre-Columbian art; the Garvan and related collections of American painting and decorative arts; the Société Anonyme collection of 20th-century art (formed by Katherine Dreier and Marcel Duchamp); and the Rabinowitz and the Stephen Clark collections of master paintings. In addition, the museum houses a notable group of old master prints and drawings and contemporary photographs. Among the best known works on view are van Gogh's "Night Cafe," John Trumbull's "The Declaration of Independence," Joseph Stella's "Brooklyn Bridge," and Antonio Pollaiuolo's "Hercules and Deianira." Special exhibitions are scheduled regularly every month. Permission is required for use of cameras; no flashbulbs are allowed.

The museum has a full schedule of events and services. Gallery talks are held 3 times a week from mid-September to mid-May; "à la carte" lectures are given on Wednesdays from October through April—members of the faculty, curators, or invited scholars lecture briefly on a single work of art while visitors dine al fresco on lunches they have been invited to bring; on Sundays from October to April the museum offers a series of films, lectures, and concerts. Group tours can be arranged by appointment; tours for public educational institutions are free; charge for all private groups. Filmstrips, slides of the collection, and reproduction sets are available for loan. The many exhibition catalogs, books relating to the gallery collections, a monthly calendar of events, a bulletin, cards, and gifts are available at the Sales and Information Desk. Metered parking on the street, parking lots nearby. Tues.–Sat. 10–5; Thurs. 6–9 (mid-Sept.–mid-May); Sun. 2–5; closed Thanksgiving, Christmas, Jan. 1, July 4. Free. (Leave I-91 at Downtown New Haven exit. At the end of the ramp, turn right onto York St. and go to Chapel.)

**Yale Center for British Art.** 1080 Chapel St. Mailing address: Box 2120 Yale Station, 06520 ☐ The Yale Center for British Art is still another treasure of one of the country's great universities. It was completed in 1975, a year after its architect, Louis I. Kahn, died, and was dedicated in 1977. The building, its contents, and funds for its maintenance and operation were the gift of Paul Mellon, who graduated from Yale University with the class of 1929. In this spectacular modern structure—pale wood paneling lines two interior wells—is housed the most important collection of British art outside England. Ranging from the late 16th to mid-19th century, it consists of 1,800 paintings, 7,000 drawings, 5,000 prints, 20,000 rare books, and sculpture. Among the paintings are William Turner's "Dort" (Dordrecht), Constable's "Hadleigh Castle," Hogarth's "Beggars' Opera," Sir Anthony Van Dyck's "Mountjoy Blount, Earl of Newport," and George Stubbs's "A Lion Attacking a Horse." A semi-permanent installation of paintings traces the development of British art; 2 major special exhibitions are mounted each year; and every 3 months a new prints and drawings exhibit is on display. Cameras are permitted, tripods and flashbulbs only by special arrangement.

The research library, containing 10,000 volumes on British art, is open to the public. Prints, drawings, and rare books also may be consulted by visitors in a specially equipped study room; a photography archive contains 60,000 photographs depicting British art. The public education department of the museum, staffed with a gallery lecturer and volunteer aides, arranges lectures, films, symposia, and concerts in the 200-seat auditorium, as well as gallery talks and group visits. Publications include *Yale Center for British Art* by Jules David Prown; *Selected Paintings, Drawings and Books,* Preface by Edmund Pillsbury; *The Pursuit of Happiness* by J. H. Plumb; and *English Landscape 1630-1850,* Introduction and Entries by Christopher White. These books and others on British art, postcards, slides of the collection, and catalogs are sold in the museum shop. Commercial parking lot behind the building. Tues.-Sat. 10-5; Sun. 2-5; closed Thanksgiving, Christmas, July 4, Jan. 1. Free. (Leave I-91 at Downtown New Haven exit. At end of ramp, turn right onto York Street and go 2 blocks. The parking lot entrance is before the second light.)

**NEW LONDON:** **Lyman Allyn Museum.** 100 Mohegan Ave., 06320 ☐ A whaling captain's daughter, Harriet U. Allyn, bequeathed the money for a museum in this seafaring town in memory of her father, captain of one of the vessels in the great whaling fleet that sailed from New London in the first half of the 19th century. The Lyman Allyn Museum was founded in 1926; the neoclassical building, designed by Charles A. Platt, opened to the public in 1932 with the grand total of 13 objets d'art in its permanent collection. Today, after almost 50 years of purchases and acquisitions, extensive renovations, and several expansions, the museum houses over 12,000 objects from civilizations that flourished within a time range of some 5,000 years. Since 1950, it has been under the management of Connecticut College and administered by the president of the college. Although the diversity and range of the collection is broad, the museum is strong in Old Master drawings, American decorative arts, and paintings by Connecticut artists. Probably the best known works here are by 2 American painters, Thomas Cole ("Mount Etna from Taormina, Sicily") and Andrew N. Wyeth ("Crows"). Also on permanent display are Egyptian, Greek, and Roman antiquities, medieval and Renaissance art, Oriental objects, primitive art, American and European paintings, furniture, silver, and decorative arts. Dollhouses and furniture, dolls and toys add to the variety. Exhibits are scheduled once a month all year long. An 1829 Federal stone house, the Deshon-Allyn house on the museum grounds, is furnished with late Federal and Empire furniture and has been designated a Registered National Landmark.

The museum offers art classes for both adults and children; sponsors lectures and lecture series, concerts, movies, and tours; has an active school program featuring guided tours led by trained docents; and provides guides for visitors and groups on request. Publications include a *Handbook* of the museum and books on regional painting and decorative arts. The library (about 10,000 volumes) is open to researchers in art history; books may not be removed. A museum shop sells cards, silver, jewelry, and antiques, acquired from the United States and abroad. Parking near the museum. Tues.-Sat. 1-5; Sun. 2-5; closed Thanksgiving, Christmas, and Jan. 1. Free. (Take Briggs St. exit from I-95. Follow signs to museum entrance on south side of Connecticut College campus and opposite the U.S. Coast Guard Academy.)

**NORWICH:   Slater Memorial Museum and Converse Art Gallery.** The Norwich Free Academy, 108 Crescent St., 06360 □ A Romanesque structure with a tower rising 130 feet above the campus of the Norwich Free Academy is the home of the Slater Memorial Museum, dedicated in 1886. Adjacent to it stands the Converse Art Gallery, built some 20 years later. Together they form a museum with rich resources in Oriental art, American decorative and fine arts, art from Africa and the South Sea islands, Greek sculpture casts, American Indian artifacts, marine items, textiles, and guns. Rotating exhibits are mounted monthly. The museum sponsors demonstrations, craft programs, special activities for children; guided tours are available by appointment. Publications include a pamphlet about the museum and exhibition catalogs. Parking nearby. Sept–May: Mon.-Fri. 9-4, Sat. & Sun. 1-4; June–Aug.: Tues.-Sun. 1-4; closed holidays. Free. (Take exit 81E off Conn. Tpke.)

**OLD LYME:   Lyme Historical Society, Florence Griswold House.** 96 Lyme St., 06371 □ This sleepy village on the Connecticut River, with its tree-lined streets and picturesque surroundings, attracted a group of American artists at the turn of the century and for about 2 decades after. Their vision of the world resisted the 20th-century pull toward the urban realism of the Ashcan School and the abstractions introduced in the 1913 Armory Show. Some that came cleaved to the French Barbizon school—a world of romance and muted colors that proclaimed the dignity of man in nature on canvases that, without a "finished" look, seemed to capture the essence of that relationship. Others, under the influence of Childe Hassam and Walter Griffin, were intrigued by the joyous colors of the French Impressionists and experimented in their techniques. This early art colony was established and nurtured by Florence Griswold, whose house served as living quarters for her flock of young artists. The house, an 1817 Georgian structure designed by Samuel Belcher, who also designed the Old Lyme Congregational Church, still bears the jubilant remains of the group that worked there—landscapes adorn the walls and door panels, and caricature sketches, the mantel. The paintings displayed derive from those 2 decades of creative productivity; Barbizon art is represented by such painters as Ranger, Howe, Cohen, and Dessar; and Impressionism by Hassam, Metcalf, Griffin, and many others. Local decorative arts and historic artifacts, toys, china add to the interest of this graceful museum. In addition, the Goodman Presentation Case, a collection of small paintings by Lyme Art Association members, is on view. Three to 4 new exhibits are mounted annually; the museum opens its summer season with a new show every June. Cameras are permitted. Activities sponsored by the museum include an annual lecture series, guided tours by trained docents, films, and field trips. The museum archives—documents relating to the town's history—are open to the public (Mon.-Fri. 10-5), as is a book shop, where the museum's publication *Miss Florence and the Artists of Old Lyme* by Arthur Heming can be purchased. Summer, Tues.-Sat. 10-5, Sun. 1-5; winter, closed Mon. & Tues. Free. (block from I-95 exit 70.)

**RIDGEFIELD: Aldrich Museum of Contemporary Art.** 258 Main St., 06877 ☐ In a white clapboard and shuttered post-revolutionary house, built in 1783 by two ex-lieutenants on a wide, tree-lined street, surrounded by a gracious lawn and other 18th- and 19th-century houses, is the Aldrich Museum of Contemporary Art. The building was known as "Old Hundred" after 100 years' use as a grocery and hardware store; in 1883 a descendant of one of the builders made it her home. From 1929 to 1964 it was in use as a church, and in 1964, after some interior renovation, selections from the collection of couturier Larry Aldrich went on display in the new museum. Visual surprises begin just beyond the paneled front door where the feeling of history disappears and the present bursts forth through the bold statements of the contemporary paintings hung here. The museum's cleanly modern, dramatically lighted galleries, utilizing the economy of line and the polished wood floors of a typical New England interior, display the most innovative of contemporary sculpture and paintings by both established artists and those whose work is not yet well known. Continuing the contrasts, the spacious stretch of lawn in the rear forms a sculpture garden, but there are no classical forms here; nonobjective sculptures of all dimensions and materials dot the landscape, modern contours at rest on the sod of old New England. Open year-round, the museum mounts 4 major exhibitions a year (one a season), each lasting approximately 3 months. Most well known is the annual Contemporary Reflections exhibit, a springtime display of the painting and sculpture of artists without major New York City gallery affiliations. Other exhibits are built around particular themes or feature works from other famous private collections. Among the artists represented in the Aldrich collection are sculptors Grosvenor, Morris, Forrest Myers, Padovano, Pomodoro, Anthony Caro, and Paolozzi; works by Louise Nevelson, Picasso, Stella, Al Held, Carl Andre, Robert Indiana, and others grace the indoor galleries. Cameras are permitted.

Art history seminars, concerts, lectures, art film programs, panel discussions, travel programs, a public service docent training program, special educational projects with colleges and universities, pilot projects for schools, and continuing education programs, are all part of the museum's philosophy of involvement. Regular gallery tours are offered on Saturday afternoons; group tours are available by appointment for a fee. Publications include an illustrated catalog of each major exhibit and a quarterly newsletter for members. A terrace with tables and chairs overlooks the sculpture garden. Parking adjacent to the garden. Sat., Sun., Wed. 1–5; sculpture garden open daily. Admission $1 for adults, 50¢ for students and children; sculpture garden is free. (When you get near Ridgefield, take Rt. 35 [it becomes Main St. in Ridgefield] through the business center. The museum is just beyond, on the left.)

**STORRS:   William Benton Museum of Art.** University of Connecticut, 06268 ☐ The William Benton Museum of Art, situated in the center of the main campus of the University of Connecticut, opened during the presidency of Homer Babbidge. Under his direction in 1966, it became the new resident of "The Beanery," a 1920s Gothic building that had served as a dining hall for faculty and students. The 200-item collection that opened the new museum in 1966 has grown to nearly 2,000 objects. Among them, American art from 1900 to 1920 and German graphics of the late 19th and early 20th century are central. The time range of the collection is broad, beginning in the pre-Columbian 15th century and including the contemporary world. George Bellows and Ernest Lawson paintings, a Mary Cassatt pastel, 2 oils by Benjamin West, and an excellent portrait by Jan de

Bray are among the significant works on display. At least 5 large exhibits and 10 small gallery exhibits are mounted each academic year; however, any work of art in the collection can be viewed in storage by prearrangement. In addition, a print room is open, also only by appointment. Cameras are permitted with restrictions. Lectures and concerts related to the special exhibits are scheduled, as well as films, gallery talks, and demonstrations. Tours can be arranged by appointment. Much care and attention is given the many publications that emanate regularly from the museum; an annual bulletin includes essays by staff members or outside authorities on several works from the permanent collection. A museum shop sells catalogs, books, jewelry, artifacts, cards, and other gift items. Parking information for visitors from University Information Booth near Police Department at north end of the campus on Rt. 195; campus shuttle buses travel from general parking area to points near the museum. Mon.–Sat. 10–4:30, Sun. 1–5. Free.

**WATERBURY: Mattatuck Museum.** 119 West Main St., 06702 ☐ An industrial city, the hub of a cluster of affluent villages in western Connecticut, Waterbury is proud of its long history as the "brass center of the world." The Mattatuck Museum here, located on the town Green, began in 1877 as a historical society, to collect and interpret the history of the region of Mattatuck. The acquisition of paintings proceeded more or less aimlessly until the 1950s, when the museum developed a policy to concentrate on acquiring a comprehensive collection of Connecticut artists. Pertinent to this decision was a major bequest by the estate of Kay Sage containing her works, those of her husband Yves Tanguy, and of Alexander Calder. The Connecticut Artist Collection now includes works by John Turnbull, Ammi Phillips, Field, Church, Earl, Wier, Kensett, Shattuck, Vickery, Gorky, Gabo, Albers, and Avery. Frequent exhibits feature works of contemporary Connecticut artists. The school-related sevices sponsored by the museum are extensive and include classes in fine arts, local history, and art appreciation, plus gallery activities and after-school programs. Lectures and concerts are scheduled regularly. Special tours are available by appointment. The museum publishes a *Pictorial History of Waterbury, Connecticut,* assorted pamphlets, and a catalog of the Connecticut Artist Collection. The library is open by appointment only. The museum shop sells books relating to Waterbury History. Parking in a municipal garage across the Green. Tues.–Sat. 12–5; Sun. 2–5 (except July & Aug.). Free (small fee for group tours). (Exit 21 off I-84. Go north on Meadow St. to West Main St.; then east to the Green.)

# DELAWARE

**REHOBOTH BEACH: Rehoboth Art League, Inc.** Henlopen Acres. Mailing address: P.O. Box 84, 19971 ☐ The small winter population of this seashore resort community has sustained an active art league since 1938. In fact, since then there have been several expansions in the form of another restoration in 1949, an addition in 1964, and a new building for classes in 1970. The small permanent collection of paintings, on display from Oct. 1 to Mar. 31, is almost exclusively the work of artist members. The league has a regular schedule of special exhibits beginning in the spring and continuing through Sept. Cameras are not permitted. Children's art classes are offered during the summer in painting, drawing, printmaking, ceramics, and music. Concerts are sometimes held. A brochure of the year's exhibits is published annually. A small sales desk offers books, jewelry, postcards. Limited parking on grounds. May–Sept, 10–5. Free. (Enter town over canal bridge on Rehoboth Ave.; turn right on Columbia Ave. to 2nd St., left on 2nd into Dodds Lane, opposite Henlopen Acres Yacht Basin.)

**WILMINGTON: Delaware Art Museum.** 2301 Kentmere Parkway, 19806 ☐ The Delaware Art Museum is located near the center of Wilmington, Delaware's largest city. It is a sturdy building, recently renovated and air-conditioned, designed in 1938 in the Georgian Colonial style frequently seen in this city. The museum began in 1912 when a group of citizens organized the Wilmington Society of the Fine Arts to preserve the work of Wilmington illustrator and teacher Howard Pyle. Today one of its strengths is its holdings of works by American illustrators—over 500 of Pyle's works are enhanced by a large collection of paintings and drawings by his students. Another interesting group consists of about 500 posters by turn-of-the-century artists, mainly American. Also on permanent exhibit is the Bancroft collection of English Pre-Raphaelite paintings, one of the best in the country, which includes works by Ford Madox Brown, Dante Gabriel Rossetti ("Found"), Sir Edward Burne-Jones ("The Prioress' Tale"), Sir John Millais ("The Waterfall"), Frederick Shield, and Frederick Sandys; and the works of 19- and 20-century American painters such as N. C. Wyeth, Frank Schoonover, Winslow Homer ("Milking Time"), Thomas Eakins, Edward Hopper ("Summertime"), John Sloan, Robert Indiana, and a group of 14 paintings by Andrew Wyeth ("Tenant Farmer" is one). The museum mounts special exhibitions, on loan or from the permanent collection, at approximately 6-week intervals. There is also an annual juried exhibit of paintings, prints, sculpture, and photographs, and one of crafts. A 20,000-volume reference library mounts separate exhibits of book illustrators and designers in the Library Gallery; illustrations of Dickens, wood engravings by Winslow Homer, and illustrations by Charles Dana Gibson, for example, have been shown. A Downtown Gallery in the Bank of Delaware (901 Market Street) designs special exhibits to stimulate interest in art in those who live in, work in, and visit the center city. The H. Fletcher Brown Wing has special craft exhibits from the permanent collection and from the classes and workshops conducted by the museum. An annual crafts fair is held on the grounds of the musuem, usually in June. Cameras can be used in the galleries with prior permission from the curatorial department; no tripods or flashes are permitted.

The museum offers classes in art, crafts, and photography for children and adults, and short-term intensive workshops in various mediums for adults. Lectures, gallery talks, concerts, and films are held at irregular intervals. "ArtReach" is a program of visual education in the schools and community. Guided tours are available on the third Tues. of each month or by appointment. The many books and catalogs published here are available at the museum store, which also sells jewelry, crafts, posters, reproductions, and slides. A sales and rental gallery carries contemporary graphics and drawings on consignment from galleries in Washington, New York, and Philadelphia. The library is open to the public Mon.–Fri. 10–4:30. Parking facilities nearby. Mon.–Sat. 10–5; Sun. 1–5. Admission $1 for adults, 50¢ for students, free for children and senior citizens. (From I-95, take the Delaware Ave. [Rt. 52] exit 7. Proceed north on Delaware Ave. to Bancroft Pkwy. Turn right to Kentmere Pkwy.; turn left onto Kentmere. By public transportation, take the Delaware Ave. bus #10 from downtown Wilmington to Woodlawn Ave. Walk north on Woodlawn about 4 blocks.)

**Henry Francis du Pont Winterthur Museum.** 19735 ☐ The Henry Francis du Pont Winterthur Museum, one of the great houses in the land, with probably the greatest assemblage of American decorative arts in the world, is an outstanding work of art itself. The original house was built in 1839 by Evalina Gabrielle du Pont and James Antoine Bidermann, great-aunt and great-uncle of the late Henry Francis du Pont and named after Bidermann's birthplace in Switzerland. Henry's grandfather acquired the estate from the Bidermanns' son, and in 1927 Henry Francis du Pont inherited the property. He brought his family there and began to install woodwork and paneling that came from rooms in old houses along the eastern seaboard. He furnished these relocated rooms the way they might have looked during various periods of the country's history with the antiques he acquired. This project lasted until 1951, when he and his family moved to other quarters and the house was opened to the public as a museum. By this time, Winterthur had been expanded several times and included 100 period rooms, a visual record of the American domestic scene from 1640 to 1850. After du Pont's death in 1969, the entire property, including 60 acres of gardens on the 900-acre tract of rolling Delaware countryside and the du Pont's home from 1950 to 1969, was deeded to the museum.

Everything in this remarkable museum is native American, or was imported and used by Americans in their homes. Furniture, ceramics, glass, metals, textiles, needlework, paintings, prints, folk art, Shaker rooms, all can be viewed in what has grown to over 200 room settings. Outstanding is the Philadelphia Chippendale furniture; a 9-shell, block-front high chest made by Goddard and Townsend of Newport; Chinese export porcelain; fractur painting; early New England silver; and 6 matched silver tankards made and signed by Paul Revere. Paintings by Benjamin West, John Singleton Copley, Gilbert Stuart, and John Trumbull, among others, grace the walls of these reproduced homes, as they would have in bygone days. Cameras are not permitted here. Thirty miles to the south are 2 historic houses owned and administered by Winterthur. Both the Corbit-Sharp House and the Wilson-Warner House are magnificent 18th-century restorations in the historic area of Odessa, Delaware.

The museum sponsors 2 graduate degree programs jointly with the University of Delaware, one in early American culture, and one in the conservation of artistic and historic objects. A 3-week intensive summer institute for professionals in the field is also offered. Lecture series are scheduled, as well as school tours for elementary, high school, and college groups. All tours are guided by staff members. There are different tours each season for which no appointment is needed; they are given daily except Mon. and generally include the South Wing ("14 period rooms showing the chronological development of architectural and furniture styles from 1684–1840"), the gardens, and in the fall, the H. F. du Pont House. The charge ($2–$5.50) changes with the seasons. For a complete tour, during which half of the musuem is shown in the morning and the other half in the afternoon, an appointment is necessary and can be made through the reservations office (302-656-8591). These tours are offered daily except Sun., Mon., Thanksgiving, Dec. 24, Christmas, Jan. 1, and July 4. The charge is $6 per person. There are also special subject tours from 10 to 2 in which visitors select specific sections of the collections to visit ($5 per person). The museum shop offers the many books and publications published by Winterthur, as well as gift items, slides, postcards, and spring and fall plants for sale. A cafeteria is open 8–4. (Winterthur is located on Rt. 52 [exit 7 off I-95], 6 miles north of Wilmington and 6 miles south of US 1.)

# DISTRICT OF COLUMBIA

**WASHINGTON, D.C.: Corcoran Gallery of Art.** 17th and New York Ave., N.W., 20006 □ William Wilson Corcoran made a large enough fortune in banking to enable him to assume, in 1848, almost the entire cost of the Mexican War by buying nearly all of the $16 million worth of government bonds issued to finance the war. Indeed, the transaction enriched him further when he took the bonds to London and sold $5 million worth at the subsequently higher market value. Thus encumbered with such a great deal of money, he began to concentrate solely on the good uses of it—in philanthropies to educational and religious institutions, and in art. He began the Corcoran Gallery of Art in 1859; James Renwick had designed the building and Corcoran had been collecting enough American works to fill it. But construction was interrupted by the Civil War; Corcoran, partial to the Confederacy, left the country, and it was not until 1872 that he was able to launch his gallery and resume the purchase of American art objects. He died in 1888, after which his collection was moved to its present home. (The original building was taken over by a curatorial department of the National Collection of Fine Arts and is now called the Renwick Gallery.) The Corcoran collection starts with pre-Revolutionary portraits and follows the course of American creativity up to the very active present. The work of Copley ("Jacob Fowle"), Stuart, and Rembrandt Peale ("Washington Before Yorktown") is displayed here; Bierstadt's "The Last of the Buffalo" epitomizes the group of artists, all here, who cataloged America's thrust westward, and the paintings of Cole, Durand, Church, and Kensett bespeak the Hudson River school. A crowd pleaser is "The Old House of Representatives" by Samuel F. B. Morse, which identifies 86 of the occupants of that august chamber. Moving later into the 19th century and the beginning of the 20th, the museum shows works of Homer ("A Light on the Sea"), Eakins ("The Pathetic Song"), and Sargent ("Madame Pailleron"); Bellows's "Forty-two Kids" shows the appeal of New York's waterfront in the era of the Ashcan school; Mary Cassatt and Marsden Hartley, of Impressionism and abstraction. Sculptors Powers, Remington, Saint-Gaudens, and Daniel Chester French are well represented. Along about 1928, a gift came to the Corcoran which veered from the gallery's stated determination to concentrate only on American art. William A. Clark, United States senator from Montana, bequeathed his collection of paintings and drawings by Dutch, Flemish, English, and French artists (Rembrandt's "A Musician," Degas's "Ballet School,"

**59**

works of Corot, Rubens, Renoir, Pissarro, Gainsborough, Reynolds); tapestries; an 18th-century French salon; laces; rugs; and other items distinctly non-American. This beautiful gift has been given its own wing. Another diversion from the American art scene are the many bronzes by French sculptor Antoine-Louis Barye, bought by Corcoran. Otherwise, in the Corcoran Gallery, American art predominates. A schedule of exhibitions features contemporary American artists, Washington area artists, and historical shows of American art.

The Corcoran School of Art is housed in its own wing and offers undergraduate and graduate-level courses. Formally organized educational programs are also available to children and adults. The gallery offers lectures, films, concerts, gallery talks, and free guided tours. The library (4,500 volumes) is available for inter-library loan and is open to the public by special request. A calendar of events, catalogs, reproductions, and handbooks of the collections are published and sold. Tues.–Sun. 11–5. Admission $1 for adults, 50¢ for students, military E-4 and below; free for senior citizens, children, clergy.

**Dimock Gallery.** George Washington University, Lower Lisner Auditorium, 730 21st St., N.W., 20052 ☐ George Washington University is located in the heart of the capital, and the Dimock Gallery in the heart of the university, the Lisner Auditorium. It is dedicated, as is the university, to fulfill the hopes of George Washington to increase opportunities for higher education in literature, science, and art. The art deco building that houses this gallery opened in 1946 to display the university's holdings of 19th- and 20th-century American art, Joseph Pennell etchings and lithographs, the W. Lloyd Wright collection of Washingtoniana, and a fine collection of American portraiture, including many images of George Washington by such painters as Rembrandt Peale and Gilbert Stuart. The best known of these, Gilbert Stuart's Monro-Lenox portrait, was purchased by the university at auction in 1949. A teaching facility of the university, the gallery schedules 8 to 10 changing exhibits per year. Lectures, films, slide shows, and classes are held in conjunction with the temporary exhibits. Catalogs or pamphlets are prepared for many of the exhibits. Public parking at several locations near the gallery. Mon.–Fri. 10–5; closed major holidays. Free.

**Diplomatic Reception Rooms.** Department of State, 2201 C St., N.W., 20520 ☐ The Fine Arts Committee of the State Department has, through gifts and loans from businesses, foundations, and private owners, furnished the Diplomatic Reception Rooms. These rooms are used by the President, Vice President, Secretary of State and other cabinet members and by the Chief Justice to receive and entertain distinguished visitors from all over the world. Since 1961, when the State Department moved into its new building in the area of Washington known as Foggy Bottom, a voluntary program, the Americana Project, has striven to fill these rooms with paintings and examples of antique American furniture and decorative arts, consistent with the times of the men whose names they bear: John Quincy Adams, Thomas Jefferson, Benjamin Franklin, James Monroe, James Madison, Martin Van Buren, and Henry Clay. The more than 125,000 visitors who pass through them annually see part of America's artistic heritage—an outstanding collection of American 18th- and 19th-century paintings and decorative objects arranged in beautifully designed period rooms. The Thomas Jefferson State Reception Room was recently renovated to reflect Jefferson's taste for the classic style of Andrea Palladio that was popular in late 18th-century America. American Chippendale furnishings are enhanced by portraits by Henry Inman and Robert Edge Pine. In the John Quincy Adams State Drawing Room is the English Sheraton tambour writing desk on which the 1783 Treaty of Peace was signed between England and the United States, and Benjamin West's unfinished painting, "Signing of the Preliminary Treaty of Peace, Paris, 1782" hangs above it. On the walls of this most beautiful of reception rooms are portraits by Charles Willson Peale, Charles Robert Leslie of London, Rembrandt Peale, and Gilbert Stuart. In the gallery entrance are 19th-century landscapes by Thomas Hill, Granville Perkins, A. T. Bricher, and A. Weidenbach; and in the James Monroe Reception Room, where the furniture comes from the period when Monroe was president, are portraits by Edward Savage. The rooms continue to be added to; funds for maintaining the collection and for adding to it are still being sought by the Fine Arts Committee. Tours, by reservation only, are conducted Mon.–Fri. at 9:30, 10:30, and 3:30. Call the tour office or write to Tours at the Department of State. Parking is difficult.

**Dumbarton Oaks Research Library and Collection.** 1703 32nd St., N.W., 20007 ☐ It was at Dumbarton Oaks in 1940 that the conference leading to the founding of the United Nations took place. A Georgian-style mansion, built in 1801, it was owned by Mr. and Mrs. Robert Woods Bliss, who filled it with the treasures of the Byzantine Empire, from the 4th to the 15th century. In 1940, the Blisses gave their house and its gardens, their extraordinary collection, their library, and funds to maintain all three to Harvard University as a research center in Byzantine and medieval humanities. Byzantine mosaics, textiles, bronzes, sculpture, ivories, metalwork, and jewelry tell the story of the empire and of an astute and discerning collector. After 1940 Bliss changed his tack, and sailed into the waters of pre-Columbian art. By the time of his death in 1962 he had amassed a sizable collection in this area and had given it, as well, to Harvard, to be housed in Dumbarton Oaks. A Philip Johnson addition to the mansion—8 circular glass galleries—shields these striking treasures from the outdoors and at the same time makes them part of it; the limestone and wood used to carve out the religious symbols and ornaments of the early Americas seems to be in place here. Pottery, textiles, and gold work dating from 800 B.C. to the 16th century are all on display. There is also a small collection of European and American paintings in the original house and a Garden Library, which has a fine collection of rare books, prints, and drawings on landscape architecture and gardening. Guided tours for students and professional groups are conducted, and lectures and seminars on 3 fields of research—Byzantine and pre-Columbian art and landscape architecture—are held. The 3 libraries (86,000 volumes on Byzantine subjects, 6,000 volumes on pre-Columbian subjects, 9,000 volumes on gardening) are all available for inter-library loan and are open to accredited scholars by special permission. Handbooks of the collections are published and are available. Tues.–Sun. 2–4:45. Free.

**Freer Gallery of Art.** 12th Street & Jefferson Dr., S.W., 20560 ☐ The Freer Gallery of Art houses one of the world's great collections of Oriental art. In 1906, Charles Lang Freer, whose fortune was made in the manufacture of cars and railroads, and who was instrumental in forming the American Can and Foundry Company, presented his collections and funds to build the Freer Gallery to the Smithsonian Institution. Ground on the Mall was broken in 1916; the building, designed by Charles A. Platt of New York in the style of a Florentine Renaissance palace, opened in 1923, 4 years after the death of its benefactor. Some 12,000 objects that had been in Freer's home in Detroit became available to the public: the magnificent Oriental collection and a large number of works by James McNeill Whistler (a friend of Freer) and some of his contemporaries. The ancient Orient is represented by bronze, jade, sculpture, painting, lacquer, pottery, porcelain, manuscripts, metal, and glass; the works come from China, Japan, Korea, Tibet, India, Indochina, Iran, Iraq, Syria, Asia Minor, Byzantium, plus Egypt. Cameras are permitted, but flashes must be covered.

The museum's library of about 40,000 volumes, pamphlets, and periodicals (many in Chinese and Japanese) is open to the public Mon.–Fri. 10–4:30. Books, papers, booklets, and journals relative to the collection are published from time to time: *Ars Orientalis,* a scholarly journal on the arts of Asia, appears irregularly but invariably (the series reached Volume X in 1975), as do *Oriental Studies* and *Occasional Papers.* A 45-minute film on *The Art of Hyōgushi* is available for sale or rent. Books, jewelry, prints, postcards, stationery items, and needlepoint kits are sold in the museum's shop. Conducted tours are offered daily at 2; guided tours for groups can be arranged in advance. Parking nearby. Daily 10–5:30; closed Christmas. Free.

**Hirshhorn Museum and Sculpture Garden.** Smithsonian Institution, Independence Ave. at 8th St., S.W., 20560 ☐ The man who amassed this fabulous, often controversial, collection came to the United States in 1905 at the age of 6, the twelfth of thirteen fatherless, immigrant children. He began selling newspapers at the age of 12, set himself up in business as a broker at the age of 17, and was soon on his way to fulfilling the rags-to-riches American dream. It was the idea of mining uranium in Canada that catapulted this already successful man into a vast fortune. The Hirshhorn Museum and Sculpture Garden came about as a result of this fortune. Joseph H. Hirshhorn made a gift to the nation in 1966 and 1972 of some 6,000 works of art, collected over a span of 40 years. The museum was created by an Act of Congress on November 7, 1966, authorizing the site on the Mall, and naming the Smithsonian Institution as its administrator. In 1967 a design by Gordon Bunshaft of Skidmore, Owings & Merrill of New York was approved by the National Capital Planning Commission; construction began in 1970. The 4-story circular, reinforced-concrete structure, raised above a plaza on 4 huge piers and rising to a height of 82 feet around an open inner court, opened in the fall of 1974. Among the cluster of Smithsonian buildings along the Mall and set against a backdrop of stolid government architecture, the Hirshhorn Museum proclaims its modernity, as each of its neighbors proclaims its own era. Within its confines, and in the adjacent 1.3-acre sunken sculpture garden with its rectangular reflecting pool, is one of the nation's largest and most comprehensive collections of modern art, cataloging the changing styles of paintings and sculpture from the late 19th century to the present. The collection is especially strong in European and American sculpture of the late 19th and 20th centuries, American painting from 1880 to the present, and the last 3 decades of European painting. Among the works of art on view (some for the first time) are Henry Moore's "King and Queen," the only cast in the Western Hemisphere; Rodin's "The Burghers of Calais"; Brancusi's "Sleeping Muse," his only representation of this theme; Eakins's second "Portrait of Mrs. Eakins" (the first and earlier portrait hangs in the Metropolitan Museum in New York); Mondrian's "Composition in Blue and Yellow"; Rothko's "Red, Blue, and Orange"; Maillol's "Nymph"; Calder's "Two Disks"; Giacometti's "Dog"; and Matisse's "Backs I–IV," his most ambitious sculpture. The museum mounts 4 to 6 special exhibitions a year. In addition, it presents special loan exhibitions, group exhibitions, and one-person exhibitions by an international representation of artists. Cameras are permitted; no flashbulbs.

Special activities scheduled by the museum take place in its 280-seat auditorium, including a series of films on art and films by young filmmakers, a lecture series, and concerts. The museum has a reference library, open to the public by special permission only. Some fellowships are available through the Smithsonian Institution. Catalogs are published with each new exhibition; 2 catalogs cover the entire collection: *An Introduction to the Hirshhorn Museum and Sculpture Garden* and the more detailed and larger *Selected Paintings and Sculpture from the Hirshhorn Museum and Sculpture Garden.* All are available in the museum shop along with postcards, slides, posters, jewelry, and sundry gift items. An outdoor cafe is open during the warm weather (usually mid-April–Oct. 1). Parking garage in the National Air and Space Museum, a half-block from the museum. Daily 10–5:30; Apr. 1–Labor Day 10–9; closed Christmas. Free.

**Museum of African Art.** Frederick Douglass Institute, 316–318 A St., N.E., 20002 ☐ A Victorian row house on Capitol Hill, nestled in the shadow of the Supreme Court, is the home of the Museum of African Art. It was the home of Frederick Douglass, a former slave who became an advisor to President Lincoln, and the museum is an affiliate of the cultural institute that bears his name. Since 1964, when the museum was founded to help promote and render familiar to Americans the great artistic heritage of Africa, which until then had not been widely appreciated, the walls and gallery space here have been devoted exclusively to African art and culture. The collection, one of the largest and most diverse of its kind in the United States, consists of some 6,500 works—traditional carvings, musical instruments, and textiles. Although the art of the entire continent is represented, the exhibits show particular strength in works from Nigeria, Ghana, Liberia, the Ivory Coast, and Zaire. They change regularly, and often consist of private collections on loan. Permission is needed for use of cameras.

The museum's educational programs range from elementary school to college-level accredited courses. Traditional African music, dance concerts, African films, and lectures on African art are scheduled regularly, and workshops in African crafts are held during the summer months. The library of 6,000 volumes and periodicals on African culture and history is open to the public only on request. Some 150,000 slides and motion pictures, which make up the Eliot Elisofon Photographic Archives, are available for study. Publications of the musuem include exhibition catalogs and audiovisual materials; they are available at the front desk. The museum shop offers traditional African sculpture, textiles, clothing, jewelry, instruments, and crafts for sale. Walk-in gallery tours are conducted weekdays at 2; group tours, by appointment. Most tour group leaders are African and speak their native tongue as well as English, French, and Spanish. Mon.–Fri. 11–5; weekends & holidays 12–5. Free; contributions recommended.

**National Collection of Fine Arts.** 8th & G Sts., N.W. 20560 ☐ The National Collection of Fine Arts is our national museum of American art.

It began with the founding of the Smithsonian Institution in 1846 when provision was made for a national fine arts collection. This first assemblage of artworks, which in fact, predated the formation of the Institution, was enlarged during the late 1800s and soon after the turn of the century was designated as the National Gallery of Art. More expansion, several major gifts, and transfers to the collection of art objects held by various government agencies took place during the early 1900s. By 1937, the collection became officially known as the National Collection of Fine Arts. In 1968, 10 years after the Old U.S. Patent Office, a century-old neoclassical building, was turned over to the Smithsonian and had undergone extensive renovations, the National Collection of Fine Arts opened to the public in its own home there (it had been installed first in the original Smithsonian building and later in the National Museum of Natural History). Some 21,000 works are now housed there, a visual demonstration of America's developing artistic consciousness. The collection contains American art from the 18th century to the present and includes American miniatures, late 19th- and early 20th-century painting and sculpture, including the Impressionists, Federal Art Project works; George Catlin paintings (466 in all); and sculpture by Hiram Powers. Some of the more outstanding works are Gilbert Stuart's "John Adams" (1826); Benjamin West's "Self Portrait" (1819); Alvan Fisher's "Niagara Falls with Rainbow" (1820); Thomas Moran's "Grand Canyon of the Yellowstone" (1893-1901); Alexander Calder's "Nenuphar" (1968); and Franz Kline's "Merce C" (1961). There are 86 works by Thomas Moran, 63 by Romaine Brooks, 1,000 by William H. Johnson, 18 by Albert Ryder, and 9 by Winslow Homer (in addition to 25 by him on long-term loan).

The **Renwick Gallery** (17th St. & Pennsylvania Ave., N.W.) is a curatorial department of the National Collection—a "national showcase for American creativity in design, crafts, and the decorative arts." The 2 collections combined mount approximately 25 special exhibits annually.

The library, with some 30,000 volumes, is one of the major centers for research in American art (open 10-5 weekdays to graduate students and qualified scholars). Several other facilities of this museum are distinctive: a major archive of photographs and slides; a computerized inventory of American paintings executed before 1914 (at present there are more than 180,000 listings); and an Explore Gallery for young people. Educational programs include internships for graduate students at District of Columbia universities; a "Discover Graphics" program for high school students; junior internships, also for high school students; a spring festival for children with films, demonstrations, performances, and tours; and pre- and post-doctoral fellowships. Publications—a catalog, an illustrated checklist, or a book—are issued in conjunction with all special exhibits. In addition, the collection publishes a monthly newsletter, brochures, and a gallery guide, all of which are available at the museum shops at both the NCFA and the Renwick Gallery, together with prints, postcards, and slides. Walk-in tours are conducted by trained docents at noon on weekdays and 2 on Sundays. Group tours can be arranged through the museum. A cafeteria serves light meals, including wine and beer. Public parking nearby; or take the Metro to Gallery Place station. Open 10–5:30; closed Christmas. Free.

**National Gallery of Art.** 6th St. & Constitution Ave., N.W., 20565 ☐ The youngest of the major art museums in the United States, the National Gallery of Art nevertheless bears the weighty responsibility of officialdom. It was established by an Act of Congress in 1937, with the Chief Justice of the United States as chairman of its board and the Secretaries of State and Treasury as members. Andrew Mellon, Secretary of the Treasury under Presidents Harding, Coolidge, and Hoover, gave his private collection of paintings and sculpture to the government to form the nucleus of what was to be the national collection and then donated funds for the construction of a building to house it. John Russell Pope was commissioned to design the edifice, to rise in the shadow of the Capitol. It is one of the largest marble structures in the world, classic in design with a colonnaded portico and a central rotunda. The sculpture halls to the east and west of the rotunda lead to inner garden courts and more than 80 galleries. Soon after its opening in 1941 the gallery was filled with masterpieces given to their government by some of the famous collectors of the country. Mellon's gift of paintings, 21 of which he had acquired from the Hermitage in Leningrad, was generous—his collection represented the creative arts from the 13th century to the 19th, including Raphael's "Alba Madonna," van Eyck's "Annunciation," Botticelli's "Adoration of the Magi," several paintings by Rembrandt, and several by Vermeer, Gilbert Stuart's famous portrait of George Washington, and Edward Savage's "The Washington Family." Mellon contributions to the gallery did not cease with Andrew's; his daughter Ailsa Mellon Bruce provided funds for some of the gallery's most important purchases: the only Leonardo da Vinci ("Ginevra de' Benci") outside Europe, Rubens's "Daniel in the Lions' Den," van der Weyden's tiny but brilliant "Saint George and the Dragon," and many American paintings. The gifts that followed Mellon's were equally impressive: Samuel H. Kress's contribution of Italian art began before the gallery opened and has been continued by the Kress Foundation through the years. Among the masterpieces on display as a result of Kress generosity is the great tondo by Fra Angelico and Fra Filippo Lippi entitled "The Adoration of the Magi," El Greco's "Laocoön," and extraordinary paintings by Giorgione, Titian, Memling, Poussin, Watteau, Fragonard, and Ingres, among others. Joseph A. Widener gave a collection of 14 Rembrandts, 8 Van Dycks, 2 Vermeers, Italian, Spanish, English, and French paintings, and French sculpture. The Chester Dale collection brought the insouciance of the French Impressionsts to the gallery: paintings by most of the French masters from the 19th and early 20th centuries including Manet, Cézanne, Renoir, Monet, Degas, and one American, George Bellows. In 1972 the W. Averell Harriman Foundation enriched the gallery's French collection still further by adding works by such as Picasso, Cézanne, and Gauguin. Walt Kuhn's "The White Clown" was another Harriman gift. Lessing J. Rosenwald was the donor responsible for the gallery's wealth in the graphic arts—more than 30,000 prints and drawings span 9 centuries and most countries and cultures. The Index of American Design describes the craftsmanship of Americans in some 17,000 watercolor illustrations and 22,000 photographs.

Since the summer of 1978, the National Gallery of Art has expanded into a new building—the East Building—on the Mall, a development made possible by still more Mellon generosity; the building is a gift to the nation from Paul Mellon, his sister Ailsa Mellon Bruce, and the Andrew Mellon Foundation. I. M. Pei and Partners designed this modern classic of a building that makes no concessions to the stolid, unyielding look of the nation's capital. Flanking the original building on its east side, the new wing is a huge and angular sculpture in its own right and it matches the original building in both color and structural material (it is faced with the same pink Tennessee marble). But where the Pope building's comfortable symmetry and familiar classical shapes blend with the restrained governmental architecture and monuments of Washington, the East Building soars in the triangulated shapes and angles of a new and dramatic architectural statement. Two unequal triangular towers (the trapezoidal site bisected diagonally created these shapes), the larger housing the museum, the smaller, the new Center for Advanced Study in the Visual Arts, are joined by another triangle, an 80-foot-high skylighted court, overhung by glass and steel tetrahedrons that repeat the angles of the building itself. In this connecting core, on several levels that open onto it, moves the traffic of the museum, across bridges and through galleries. Contemporary art has its home here, encountered first in Calder's giant mobile that hangs from the geometric sky of this breathtaking great hall. Calder was invited to create this work for this building; Henry Moore, Joan Miró, Robert Motherwell, and Anthony Caro were others invited to contribute to the permanent installations. The inaugural exhibitions included modern art from Europe, particularly the school of Paris; Abstract Expressionists of the New York school (Motherwell's "Spanish Elegy," de Kooning's 6 "Women," Gorky's "The Plow and the Song," Pollock's "poured" paintings, Rothko, David Smith, and Barnett Newman's "Stations of the Cross" paintings); Picasso and Cubism; Matisse—Cutouts (another gift from Paul

Mellon); a European Painting and Sculpture group that includes work by Balla, Boccioni, Severini, Giacometti, Max Beckmann, and Miró (an early work that belonged to Ernest Hemingway). Reaching into the past are exhibits of Piranesi; of master drawings and watercolors; and of small French paintings (more Mellon beneficence, this one from Ailsa).

Lectures are given regularly by guest speakers and members of the staff; the A. W. Mellon Lectures in the Fine Arts are a series delivered in the spring of every year. Tours are available through the week; special tours can be arranged in advance. Electronic guide lectures are also available. Films are shown (free) in the auditorium; concerts are held (free) in the East Garden Court, Sun. evenings Sept.–June. The Office of Extension Services supplies lecture texts, color slides, and films for educational purposes. The publications office sells reproductions, slides, films, catalogs, and other publications. The library has 65,500 volumes pertaining to the fine arts and related fields. Four fellowship programs are operative, each of different duration. Weekdays 10–5; Sun. 12–9. Apr. 1–Labor Day, weekdays 10–9; Sun. 12–9. Free.

**National Portrait Gallery.** F St. at 8th, N.W., 20560 □ The National Portrait Gallery was established in 1962 by an Act of Congress to collect, exhibit, and study portraits of "men and women who have made significant contributions to the history, development, and culture of the people of the United States, and of the artists who created such portraits." At first, the gallery was housed in the Arts and Industries Building in the Smithsonian's complex on the Mall. In 1968 the collection was moved to the Greek Revival building that was erected between 1836 and 1867 to house the U.S. Patent Office and the Department of the Interior. The gallery occupies the original wing that was completed in 1840 from a design by William P. Elliot and Ithiel Town, modified by Robert Milles, who supervised the construction. The extension added between 1849 and 1867 was supervised by Thomas U. Walter and Edward C. Clark. A fire in 1877 occasioned the restoration of the third floor in a Victorian Renaissance style; and finally, the entire building was renovated between 1965 and 1967. The gallery's collection consists of portraits of famous Americans from the late 18th century to the present—all the presidents and other eminent Americans—exhibited in chronological sequence. The gallery has 2 major loan exhibitions per year dealing with various aspects of American history and portraiture as well as approximately 10 small exhibits of a similar nature. Photographing is allowed only with curatorial permission.

Special classes are offered to area schoolchildren through the art education department. Occasionally, the gallery sponsors lectures and concerts. A Speakers' Bureau supplies presentations by staff members for interest groups in the D.C. vicinity; arrangements can be made through the education office. Docents are available upon request 10–3 Mon.–Fri. and 11–3 on weekends. All major loan exhibitions are accompanied by full-scale catalogs. In addition, the gallery publishes an illustrated checklist of its permanent collection and other books related to its holdings. The Catalog of American Portraits, a national inventory of important American portraits, including information about the sitter and artist, as well as a photograph of each portrait, is open by application to qualified researchers. The library (16,000 volumes) is available for inter-library loan; it too is open by application to qualified researchers. A gallery shop features books, reproductions, biographies, and portraits related to American history. The cafeteria-style restaurant, open daily and from May to Oct., is supplemented by a kiosk in the adjacent courtyard; beer and wine are available. Several public parking lots within a block radius. Daily 10–5:30; closed Christmas. Free.

**The Phillips Collection.** 1600–1612 21st St., N.W., 20009 ☐ Just off Massachusetts Avenue, in the neighborhood of embassies, is the home of the Phillips Collection. It was founded in 1918 by Duncan Phillips as a memorial to his father and brother, who died during the flu epidemic that engulfed the world that year. Subtitled "A Museum of Modern Art and Its Sources," it opened in 1921 with the stated purpose of showing contemporary works in the context of and as influenced by works from the past. At that time, housed in the Phillips home, an 1897 brownstone near Dupont Circle, it was the first museum of modern art in the United States. By 1930, the collection displaced the family; they moved to other quarters and left the entire house to serve as their museum. Thirty years later, still more room was needed, and a new wing was added. The more than 2,000 works now housed there reflect the personal taste of Duncan Phillips and his wife Marjorie, both of whom were artists themselves. They believed that modernity was a phenomenon, even in the 15th century, of the evolution of art; that the initiators of all ages were the modernists of their time, stimulating the movement of art. This philosophy produced a variegated collection that includes what the Phillipses considered to be the best of the old and the new, but emphasizing 19th- and 20th-century European and American paintings. Fine examples of the masters of 20th-century painting can be seen in units of Braque, Bonnard, Kokoschka, Rouault, Marin, Dove, O'Keeffe, Hartley, Knaths, Gatch, and Avery; 19th-century units include Daumier, Corot, Delacroix, and Monticelli. Probably the best-known painting in the collection is Renoir's "Luncheon of the Boating Party." The Ryder paintings are impressive, and the units of Bonnard and Braque are famous. Six Cézannes include a beautiful self-portrait; Matisse works include his "Studio, Quai St. Michel" and the later "Egyptian Curtain." "Miss Van Buren" by Eakins is an example of great American portraiture. Daumier's "Uprising," one of his masterpieces, can be viewed with John Sloan's "Wake of the Ferry," the best-known work in the collection of "the Eight." Visitors particularly admire the unit of Paul Klee paintings, and the collection of works by John Marin is one of the largest anywhere. Van Gogh, Degas, and Monet are well represented, as is Delacroix, with his world-famous "Paganini." Loan exhibitions of contemporary American or European artists are scheduled throughout the year. Hand-held cameras without flashbulbs or tripods are permitted.

The museum sponsors occasional lectures and a regular series of weekly concerts from September through May. Docent tours for groups can be arranged in advance. Books and catalogs relating to the collection are published by the museum; a sales desk and a small shop offer these and postcards, notepaper, color reproductions, photographs, and slides. Parking in lots and garages within a block of the museum. Tues.–Sat. 10–5; Sun. 2–7; closed Thanksgiving, Christmas, Jan. 1, July 4, Labor Day. Free.

**Renwick Gallery.** See National Collection of Fine Arts.

**Smith-Mason Gallery-Museum.** 1207 Rhode Island Ave., N.W., 20005 ☐ General John Alexander Logan (1826–1886) astride a fiery horse looks out over Logan Circle. Here, founded only a dozen years ago, is the Smith-Mason Gallery-Museum, a 4-story Victorian building across from the park that surrounds the monument to the general. The collection housed here—paintings, sculpture, and graphics by living artists from the United States and the Caribbean islands—is on permanent display. In addition, there are regularly scheduled special exhibits. Cameras are not permitted. Volunteers conduct guided tours of the museum. A sales desk offers small gift items. Park on the street in front of the gallery. Tues.–Fri. 12–4; Sat. 10–5; Sun. 2–5. Free.

# FLORIDA

**CLEARWATER: Florida Gulf Coast Art Center.** 22 Ponce de Leon Blvd., Belleair, 33516 ☐ The Florida Gulf Coast Art Center adds to the list of tourist attractions that have made this resort city, overlooking the Gulf of Mexico, grow. It was founded by Georgine Shillard Smith in 1947 and houses her collection of paintings. The permanent collection also contains a Buddhist shrine, a George Innis Singer group, and an assemblage of early American and contemporary artists. Exhibits change monthly. Cameras are permitted. Classes in art and sculpture are given in 10-week sessions throughout the year. The center also sponsors lectures, concerts, and scholarship programs for students in the county. The library is open to members only or by special permission. Tours are available by appointment. A members' sales gallery offers works of artist members. Parking on the grounds. Tues.–Sat. 10–4; Sun. 3–5. Free. (Go west on Rt. 686 [Bay Dr.] to Indian Rocks Rd., right on Indian Rocks to Rosery, left on Rosery, and right on Ponce de Leon Blvd.)

**CORAL GABLES: Lowe Art Museum.** University of Miami, 1301 Miller Dr., 33146 □ The Lowe Art Museum, an arm of the University of Miami, is a major cultural facility in the community. It houses works of premium caliber and interest: a Samuel H. Kress collection of Renaissance, Baroque, and Rococo paintings and sculpture; the Virgil Barker (historian and author; the museum's first director) collection of American art spanning the entire spectrum of styles and periods in the country; the Alfred Barton collection of American Indian art and artifacts; an Oriental collection; European art; ancient art; a pre-Columbian collection; graphics; and sculpture. A regular schedule of changing exhibitions is maintained throughout the year. The museum's activities include lectures, films, gallery talks, concerts, dance programs, and an extensive children's educational program. Its library of some 5,000 volumes is available to the public. Catalogs are published with special exhibitions. Docent tours are conducted upon request. Mon.–Fri. 12–5; Sat. 10–5; Sun. 2–5; closed Christmas, Jan. 1. Free.

**Metropolitan Museum and Art Centers, Inc.** 1212 Anastasia Ave., 33134 □ With the panache that could only have occurred in the 1920s, entrepreneur George Merrick set about to create an "American Riviera." Parks and parkways, landscaping and homes were planned; buildings were to conform to the Mediterranean-Spanish style of architecture. The Metropolitan Museum and Art Centers has its central facility in one of the buildings (now a Registered National Historical Landmark) that was created as a result of Merrick's dream. The collection housed here is eclectic, but has particular strengths in contemporary Latin American paintings, the sculpture of Jacques Lipchitz, and historic costumes. Also notable are the Marks collection of European painting since 1945 and the contemporary American paintings. Other collections cover the areas of Oriental, African, and pre-Columbian art, graphics, and archaeology. Many special exhibits are mounted each year in the main building and the 2 branches, one in North Miami (12340 N.E. Eighth Ave.) and one in Miami Beach (2100 Washington Ave.). Cameras are permitted, but not flash equipment.

The art school of the museum enrolls 5,000 to 6,000 part-time students; some 100 courses are offered in 6-week sessions. A children's 2-week summer camp has a large enrollment. Lecture, concert, and film series are scheduled regularly, interspersed with special seminars and demonstrations. A small general art library is open to members only. Guided tours Tues.-Thurs. 11-1 and by appointment for large groups; Spanish-speaking guides and a recorded tour are also available. A museum newsletter is published bimonthly; catalogs accompany special exhibitions. A museum shop sells books, prints, postcards, ceramics, and gift items. A restaurant and bar are located in the building. Parking on the grounds and nearby. Tues., Wed. 10-10; Thurs., Fri. 10-6; Sat., Sun. 1-6. Free. (Take US 1 to Lejune Rd., then to Anastasia Ave. Or take Bird Rd. to Alhambra Circle, then to Anastasia.)

**DAYTONA BEACH: Museum of Arts and Sciences.** 1040 Museum Blvd., 32014 ☐ Fulgencio Batista, former president of Cuba, left 42 Cuban paintings, 21 photo panels, pottery, a sugar mill, and a large library of leatherbound books in Daytona Beach before he left for Spain. A modern building was erected for the museum in 1971, and the collection now resides in the splendid state-owned Tuscawilla Park near the center of the city. Exhibits here change regularly through the winter months, but the permanent Cuban collection is on display during the summer. The museum sponsors art and science classes, museum trips, lectures, and concerts. A planetarium and a nature trail signal the science orientation of the education program. The library of general reference works is available to members only. Publications include a bimonthly newsletter and catalogs. The sales desk has mainly children's items. Parking on the grounds. Tues.-Fri. 9-5; Sat. 12-5; Sun. 1-5. Admission 50¢ per person, $1 per family. (From I-95 go east on 92 to Barnett Bank [Seneca]; go south for 3 blocks to Museum Blvd.)

**FORT LAUDERDALE: Fort Lauderdale Museum of Art.** Address at press time: 426 East Las Olas Blvd., 33301 ☐ The new Fort Lauderdale Museum of Art, scheduled for opening in 1981, occupies a 16-acre site between the ocean and the intracoastal waterway in the 2900 block of N.E. 9th Street; it is a paradigm of modern facilities in both appearance (a low-lying travertine marble structure) and function (incorporating space for educational and community as well as exhibition activities). The collection is a significant assemblage of pre-Columbian Indian artifacts from North, Central, and South America; 19th- and 20th-century West African tribal sculpture, basketry, and textiles; Abstract Expressionist paintings of the 1950s; and a representation of contemporary Florida artists. African war masks, ancestor figures, and carved reliefs come from such tribes as Bakuba, Ibo, and Wum. Pre-Columbian works include a rare classic Mayan feather receptacle, a Mississippi Southern Cult stone mask, and a Mexican classic period maskette (Olmec style). James Brooks, James Rosenquist, Le Corbusier, Anuszkiewicz, and Dennis Miller Bunker are among the artists represented.

Temporary and traveling exhibits are scheduled regularly; tours can be arranged in advance. The museum sponsors a wide range of educational programs for adults and children including art classes, demonstrations, lectures, and extensive docent activities. Publications include exhibition catalogs, quarterly bulletins, and a monthly calendar. A non-circulating library is available to members only. A museum shop sells jewelry replicas and other museum-quality items. Parking nearby. Tues.–Sat. 10–4:30; Sun. 12–5; closed holidays. Free. (For new museum, take Sunrise Blvd. east and turn south on Birch Rd.)

**GAINESVILLE: University Gallery.** University of Florida, 32611 ☐ Set amid the rolling hills of northern Florida, the University Gallery, founded in 1965 as part of the College of Architecture and Fine Arts, is prominent on the University of Florida campus. The contemporary building, designed by a Jacksonville architectural firm, houses fine collections of African, Indian, and Latin American art. A new exhibit is mounted bi-monthly. Special permission is needed for cameras. The gallery sponsors lectures and concerts, and the support organization supplies docents for public-school programs. Numerous catalogs are published for the special exhibitions; the majority deal with African, Indian, and Latin American art. Parking available. Mon.–Fri. 9–5; Sun. 1–5. Free. (On US 441, several blocks past University Ave., the town's main east-west thoroughfare.)

**JACKSONVILLE: Cummer Gallery of Art.** 829 Riverside Ave., 32204 ☐ The Cummer Gallery of Art was founded in 1958, as directed by the will of Mrs. Ninah May Holden Cummer, who bequeathed the bulk of her estate and her art collection to form a museum foundation for the people of Jacksonville. A neoclassical building, looking out over formal gardens in the rear and the broad expanse of the St. Johns River beyond, was erected on the site of her former home. The gallery opened in 1961 with a display of the entire collection of some 65 objects and paintings, including the rare 14th-century Agnolo Gaddi "Madonna and Child," European and American paintings of the 19th century, prints, and decorative objects. Today, the Cummer Gallery houses an outstanding selection of paintings through the 20th century, tapestries, furniture, sculpture, graphics, decorative arts, and the great Wark collection of early Meissen porcelain, the finest of its kind in the country and matched only by the Royal Collections in Dresden and the Schneider collection in Munich. Some of the most notable paintings are "The White Rowboat: St. John's River" and "Waiting for a Bite" by Winslow Homer; "Marine Off Big Rock" by John Kensett; Rubens's "Entombment of Christ"; "Mrs. Nicholas Douty" by Thomas Eakins; "Maria Walpole, Countess of Waldegrave" by Sir Joshua Reynolds; and "Adam and Eve" by Philippe Van Dyck. The Tudor Room, formerly the Cummer drawing room, was dismantled and installed in the gallery as a stunning example of 16th-century English decor. Special exhibitions are scheduled every 6 to 8 weeks. Cameras are permitted; no flashes or tripods.

Activities of the gallery include an art history course and a docent-in-training program. A concert series, lectures, film programs, school outreach programs, and trips to other museums both in the United States and abroad are also sponsored. The library is open to members, students with a request from a professor, and the general public by application. Publications include a *Handbook of the Permanent Collection* and monographs on subjects relating to the collection. The museum shop sells books, jewelry, prints, postcards, original art objects, and antique porcelains. Parking across the street. Tues.–Fri. 10–4; Sat. 12–5; Sun. 2–5. Free. (Near the intersection of Riverside Ave. & Post St. From I-95 south take Park St. exit; turn left on Park, left on Post, left on Riverside. From I-95 north & I-10, take Stockton exit; turn left on Stockton, left on Post, left on Riverside.)

**Jacksonville Art Museum.** 4160 Boulevard Center Dr., 32207 ☐ Another of Jacksonville's repositories of art is the Jacksonville Art Museum, chartered in 1948 after about 10 years as an art club. Its present home, located in an office park several miles from the center of the city, was completed in 1966, and its expansion in 1973. The collection housed here, with the stated goal of serving the community as an educational facility, is dedicated to the display of contemporary art, but it also includes pre-Columbian and African art and one of the nation's fine collections of Oriental porcelains and ceramics from Neolithic to 18th-century works. Special changing exhibits last from several weeks to months. The use of cameras is permitted occasionally.

As many as 19 art classes are held throughout the year, as are lectures and concerts. The education department offers workshops, seminars, and other events. The museum is host to a Visual Arts Center, operated by the Duval County school system, which provides teachers across the country with resource materials—reproductions, slides, and prints—for classroom use. Publications include a monthly calendar and information guide for members, frequent exhibition catalogs, and a complete catalog of the Koger Collection of Oriental porcelains and ceramics. Regularly scheduled docent tours are available for groups. A museum shop offers reproductions, books, jewelry, cards, gifts, and children's items for sale. There are picnic grounds facing a creek and a heavily wooded area. Parking available. Tues. Wed. Fri. 10–4; Thurs. 10–10; Sat. & Sun. 1–5; closed legal holidays & Aug. Free. (In the Koger Executive Center south of the city, between Beach & Atlantic Blvds. Heading north on I-95, take Beaches exit; heading south, take Emerson exit.)

**KEY WEST: Martello Gallery and Museum.** South Roosevelt Blvd., 33040 ☐ The Martello Gallery and Museum is housed in a martello tower (a circular masonry fortress) built in 1861 to protect Fort Taylor, on the promontory of Key West, from enemy landings. The fort was never completed; improved weaponry—rifled cannon with exploding shells—made this ancient Mediterranean-style citadel defense obsolete. Today the structure's vaulted rooms, built as storage vaults for ammunition, provisions, and water, serve as galleries for the museum's collection of paintings and an exhibition of artifacts from old Key West. Memorabilia from the residences in Key West of Ernest Hemingway, Tennessee Williams, and other literary lights are also exhibited. In addition, the museum displays some of the unique wildlife that flourishes in the Keys. There are monthly exhibits in the 9 art galleries during the 6-month winter season. Cameras are permitted. A shop offers gift items for sale. Parking on the grounds. Daily 9:30–5. Admission $1.50 for adults, 25¢ for children 7–16, military free. (From US 1 to Key West, take A1A onto South Roosevelt Blvd. If you get to the airport, you've gone too far.)

**LAKELAND: Polk Public Museum.** 800 East Palmetto St., 33801 ☐ In the central highlands of Florida, the Polk Public Museum is a repository of the arts, the sciences, and history. It began in 1966 as a children's museum housed in a small church building and was moved to its present home in 1970. The small permanent collection includes contemporary regional paintings and sculpture, some pre-Columbian objects, early American and Floridian artifacts, fossils, and rocks and gemstones. Exhibits change regularly. Cameras can be used only with special permission. Classes in art, history, and science are held 3 times a year. The museum also sponsors occasional lectures, concerts, and films as well as tours to other museums, local, in other states, and abroad. The children's program includes "suitcase museums" that are sent to the schools, and in the summer, classes and field trips. The library, with some 300 volumes of art, pottery, china, and flowers is open to the public daily. A museum shop sells original artwork, books, jewelry, museum replicas, and handcrafts. Tours of the museum can be arranged by appointment. Parking available. Mon.–Fri. 10–5; Sat. 10–4; Sun. 1–4. Free. (Go to downtown Lakeland by way of Lake Morton Dr. to Palmetto. The museum is just behind the Lakeland Public Library.)

**MIAMI: Miami Art Center, Inc.** 7867 North Kendall Dr., 33156 ☐ A Latin American gallery at the Miami Art Center displays the Martinez-Canas collection of Latin American paintings. Some Far Eastern, African, pre-Columbian, and African art, some European and American paintings and decorative arts, and a group of antique toys occupy a permanent collection gallery. Costumes are displayed in another separate gallery. The center has an active schedule of changing exhibitions. It sponsors seminars for businesspeople interested in the arts, lectures, gallery talks, and 100 tours per year; classes and workshops for adults and children; and a program for graduate students from the University of Miami and Florida International University. Catalogs accompany temporary exhibits. Crafts and books are sold. Mon.–Thurs. 10–9:30; Sat. & Sun. 1–6. Donations accepted; admission $1 for special exhibitions and lectures.

**Vizcaya, Dade County Art Museum.** 3251 South Miami Ave., 33129 □ Looking out on Biscayne Bay and protected by a great stone breakwater that could be a huge, moored barge festively adorned with statuary, is the museum known as Vizcaya. This extraordinary limestone and tile-roofed building was finished in 1916 to serve as the home of James Deering, one of the founders of International Harvester Company. Designed by Paul Chalfin, looking for all the world like an Italian Renaissance palace with some 10 acres of formal gardens and 20 of natural hammock jungle, the interior holds no disappointments. European decorative arts and interior architectural elements (doorways, wall panels, ceilings from European palaces) from the 16th to the 19th centuries, classical and medieval pieces, Italian and French furnishings are felicitously arranged around airy loggias and a central court. Works by Lachaise, Calder, Thevenez, and Chandler are scattered among objects from the Renaissance, Baroque, and neoclassical periods in Europe—tapestries, rugs, pottery and porcelains, ivories, musical instruments, and sculptures.

Guided tours are conducted every day except Christmas, beginning every 15 minutes, from 9:30 to 3:30 (Spanish and French tours are available by appointment). There is an active school program both in the museum and in the schools. A descriptive booklet, *Vizcaya Museums and Gardens,* is available at a small gift shop, as are slides, postcards, jewelry, pottery, and reproductions. Light meals and snacks are sold at the cafe. Parking on museum grounds. Daily 9:30–5:30; closed Christmas. Admission $3.50 plus tax for adults, $1 plus tax for children. (One block from the intersection of US 1 [Dixie Hwy.] & South Miami Ave., near the turnoff to the Rickenbacker Causeway. Or from I-95, take the 25th Rd. exit. Watch the direction signs.)

**MIAMI BEACH:   Bass Museum of Art.** 2100 Collins Ave., 33139 □ Belying its reputation for mindless indulgence—this city is, after all, well known as "Broadway with Palms"—Miami Beach hosts the noteworthy Bass Museum of Art. Housed in what was formerly the public library, which was built of native coral rock in 1934, it was renovated in 1963 to accommodate the John and Johanna Bass collection of paintings, sculpture, vestments, and tapestries. It is in the heart of this pleasure city, near the new public library, in a park that is always open, and abutting Collins Avenue, the main artery that services the sweep of pleasure domes along the 8-mile-long beach. Rembrandt, Rubens, and Botticelli reside here, along with the French Impressionists, medieval sculptures, modern paintings, and church vestments and tapestries—in all, some 500 objects of art. The collection is on display permanently; the use of cameras is permitted under controlled conditions. The public library's excellent art collection is available to visitors of the museum. Guided tours for groups can be arranged in advance. A shop offers prints, postcards, and a catalog of the collection for sale. Tues.–Sat. 10–5. Free.

**ORLANDO: Loch Haven Art Center.** 2416 North Mills Ave., 32803 ☐ Loch Haven Park, about 5 miles from the center of Orlando, is the site of museums, a planetarium, 2 lakes, and the Loch Haven Art Center. The center was founded in 1926 but moved to its present location in 1969. The pre-Columbian collection is held to be one of the most representative in the Southeast, spanning more than 3,000 years of art history and ranging over all of Latin America. Among the contemporary American graphics are works by Calder, Johns, Motherwell, Nesbitt, and Trova. Painting, sculpture, and graphics of the 20th century include works by O'Keeffe, Lichtenstein, and Sheeler. Exhibits rotate every 4 to 6 weeks. Cameras are usually permitted. Classes for children and adults, lectures, films, workshops, and concerts fill the schedule of events. An Art Enrichment Program exposes over 15,000 schoolchildren to the art world by means of a lecture, an exhibition tour, and an audiovisual presentation. Tours are conducted during all exhibitions. Catalogs and periodicals are published in conjunction with exhibitions. The library (1,000 volumes) is open to the public with special permission. The art center shop sells original jewelry, pottery, reproductions, art books, cards, prints, and gift items. Parking on the grounds. Tues.–Sat. 1–5; Sun. 2–5. Free. (Exit from I-4 at Princeton; Loch Haven Park signs mark exit. The center is also accessible from Mills Ave. [Hwy. 17-92; it is at the corner of Princeton] or Rollins St.)

**ORMOND BEACH: Tomoka State Park Museum.** Tomoka State Park. Mailing address: P.O. Box 695, 32074 ☐ The repository of the paintings and sculpture of Fred Dana Marsh (1872–1961) is his memorial, built in 1967 by the state of Florida in the beautiful woodland of Tomoka State Park. In addition to the Marsh collection, the museum has exhibits on Florida geology, wildlife, Indian artifacts, and history. Cameras are permitted. Guided tours are conducted when requested. Parking on the grounds, which are open from 8 until sundown every day. Wed.–Sun. 9–5. Admission 25¢. (Go to North Beach St. in Ormond Beach.)

**PALM BEACH: Henry Morrison Flagler Museum.** Whitehall Way. Mailing address: Box 969, 33480 ☐ "Whitehall" is the restored mansion of Henry Morrison Flagler, one of the founders of the Standard Oil Company and singlehandedly the developer of the entire east coast of Florida from Jacksonville to Key West—the railroad he built covered that route—and the founder of St. Augustine, Daytona, Palm Beach, and Miami as resort cities along the railroad route. Today an American palace, the home he built for his second bride, can be seen as it was when it was inhabited by its owners. The furniture, porcelains, paintings, silver, glass, dolls, lace, costumes, indeed, the architecture itself, reflect the taste and style of the late 19th and early 20th centuries. Mr. Flagler's private railroad car, "Rambler," built in 1886, has been restored and is also on exhibit on the museum grounds. All the displays are permanent. The museum sponsors occasional lectures, and schoolchildren are accommodated with tours by specially trained volunteers. Guided tours for other groups are also available daily, on the hour. The archives are open to researchers upon request. Postcards, booklets, and slides are sold at the reception desk. Parking on the premises. Tues.–Sun. 10–5; closed Christmas. Admission $1.50 for adults, 50¢ for children. (Whitehall Way is just off Cocoanut Row.)

**Society of the Four Arts.** Four Arts Plaza, 33480 ☐ Towering old palms, like Greek columns, adorn the entrance to the Four Arts Gallery, which looks out over Palm Beach's Lake Worth. The Four Arts Society, of which the gallery is an integral part, was incorporated in 1936 to encourage an appreciation of the arts by presenting exhibitions, lectures, concerts, and films, and by maintaining a fine library and garden. From its first commercial-building home, it moved in 1938 to a newly constructed, Spanish-style structure that served to house the library, exhibition galleries, and an auditorium for lectures and concerts. Today that building is devoted to the Four Arts Library, and the auditorium and galleries are located in another Spanish-style building across the plaza. The permanent collection, consisting primarily of 19th- and 20th-century American and European paintings and sculpture, is small but includes works by such notable artists as John Marin, Maurice Prendergast, John Singer Sargent, A. B. Davies, Jean Arp, Ernest Trova. Here also can be seen Rodin's "The Age of Bronze," and Isamu Noguchi's 25-foot stainless steel sculpture-fountain "Intetra." Four exhibitions, usually on loan from large museums or private collectors, are held each year between December 1 and April 15. Cameras are permitted; special permission is needed for flash equipment. The gallery sponsors a series of lectures and concerts from January through March, as well as films and educational programs for children. The library of some 27,000 volumes, strong in art references, is open to the public. Catalogs (published for each exhibition) and postcards are for sale at the reception desk.

Parking is available on the grounds. Dec.–mid-Apr., Mon.–Sat. 10–5; Sun. 2–5. Library open Mon.–Sat. 10–5; closed Sat. May–Nov. Free. (From Florida Tpke. & I-95, take exit 40; go east on Okeechobee Blvd.; cross Lake Worth on Royal Park Bridge to Royal Palm Way.)

**PENSACOLA: Museum of the Americas.** 105 West Gonzalez St., 32501
☐ The collections of the Museum of the Americas are on view by appointment or in loan exhibitions elsewhere. Two collections gathered by Earle W. Newton relating to Anglo-American and Hispanic studies are in storage in Pensacola pending the completion of buildings in St. Augustine, Florida and Brookfield, Vermont. Included in the works to be shown are about 200 English paintings dating from 1580 to 1820; American paintings related to the English school (1680–1820); English mezzotints (1650–1800); a complete collection of Hogarth paintings and engravings; Spanish furniture; Latin American folk art; and pre-Columbian artifacts, especially from Peru and Mexico. The museum also has a sizable library open for research by special permission only.

**ST. PETERSBURG: Museum of Fine Arts.** 255 Beach Dr. North, 33701
☐ The Museum of Fine Arts is located in Straub Waterfront Park, the cultural and boating hub of the city, overlooking Tampa Bay. It opened in 1965 in its neo-Palladian home with diverse collections that represent a wide range of time and place. The sculpture from India is particularly fine among the pieces from the Far East. A collection of American and European works—paintings, sculpture, graphic and decorative arts—includes paintings by 20th-century Georgia O'Keeffe ("Poppy") and Ben Shahn ("Antennas"); 19th-century Frederick Church ("Falls Near Tequendama"), Thomas Moran ("Florida Landscape"), and Jasper Cropsey ("Fountain of the Sibyl"); a 17th-century Dutch painting by Abraham Bloemaert ("Christ with the Woman at the Well"); and a painting from the circle of Perugino ("Adoration of the Christ Child"). Two period rooms, one Jacobean and one Georgian, a collection of contemporary American photographs, and a group of pre-Columbian pottery and gold broaden the scope of this small but well-run and attractive museum. Exhibits change monthly. Limited use of cameras is permitted.

The museum sponsors lectures, concerts, and films, programs for children, and seminars. The library, which includes a picture file and slides, is open to the public during regular museum hours. *Mosaic,* a bimonthly newsletter, and *Pharos,* a scholarly quarterly devoted to research on the museum's collections, are available at the museum shop, which also sells books, jewelry, prints, and postcards, as well as museum reproductions in sculpture and the decorative arts. Parking close by. Tues.–Sat. 10–5; Sun.

1-5; closed Christmas, Jan. 1. Pay what you wish, but you must pay something. (Take I-275 to 5th Ave. North; go east to Beach Dr. North, then south 2 blocks to the museum.)

**SARASOTA: John and Mable Ringling Museum of Art.** 5401 Bay Shore Rd. Mailing address: P.O. Box 1838, 33578 ☐ When Sarasota became the winter quarters of Ringling Bros. and Barnum & Bailey early in the century, John, youngest of the five brothers, began to build his home there and became involved with interests apart from the circus. One of these, a real estate venture, took him to Italy for the purpose of buying sculpture—which he did in great quantity. But instead of serving as statuary for a commercial enterprise, the pieces he bought (among them a bronze casting of Michelangelo's "David") formed the nucleus of the museum that was to bear his name. The museum building, designed by John H. Phillips after an Italian Renaissance palace, with north and south galleries enclosing a formal terraced sculpture garden, was completed in 1930. At John's death in 1936, the museum closed, a legal imbroglio ensued, and it was not until ten years later, the estate settled and the gift of the museum acceptable to the state, that it reopened. The works under this palatial roof make up one of the most extensive collections of the Italian Baroque school in the United States; one of the largest collections of Rubens paintings and cartoons for tapestries in the United States; a major collection of Cypriot works; and a representative collection of European decorative arts from the medieval period through the 18th century. Contemporary art, particularly by Florida artists, is shown in separate galleries. The catalog of paintings is impressive: Rubens's "Portrait of the Archduke Ferdinand," "Portrait Head of a Young Monk," and "Thetis Plunging Achilles into the River Styx," to name only a few; Rembrandt's "Portrait of a Lady" and "The Deposition"; Van Dyck's "St. John the Evangelist" and "St. Andrew the Apostle"; Hals's "Portrait of Pieter Jacobs Olycan"; Bassano's allegories of Fire and Water, "Adoration of the Shepherds," and "Christ in the Garden of Olives." Canalettos, Piero di Cosimos, Poussins, Veroneses, Velázquezes, El Grecos, and Gainsborough's huge "Portrait of General Philip Honywood" can be seen through the sprawling galleries that skirt the central gardens over which "David" holds kingly court. The museum's curator of contemporary art mounts changing exhibits throughout the year. The Museum of the Circus, with circus memorabilia gathered from around the world, and the Ringling Residence, filled with the opulence of the twenties, also brought together from all over the world, are other points of interest on this huge estate. And in the Museum of Art is the Asolo Theater, an 18th-century Venetian theater taken from a palace in Asolo, Italy, in which one of the better drama companies in the country performs. Cameras are permitted, but flashbulbs and tripods are not.

A state facility, the museums sponsor a myriad of educational and special activities, beginning with the hosting of high school students whose bimonthly visits are part of their school art program. Art lecture series and lectures on the various exhibits take place regularly. Concerts are held in the Asolo Theater. A Museum Careers Program (an internship program for University of South Florida Students); a State Services Program providing consultation and curatorial services, museum education, slide sets, an Art Caravan, and circulating exhibitions to communities statewide; and circulating exhibitions are among other services of the Ringling Museums. The Art Reference Library is open to the public weekdays 9–4. Publications include catalogs of each of the museums and a *Ringling Museums Souvenir Book.* Docents conduct tours in each museum twice daily, 4 times daily during the winter holiday season. A gift shop sells books, jewelry, prints, postcards, and reproductions. A small restaurant on the grounds near the Museum of the Circus offers light meals. Parking across the road in front of the museum. Mon.–Fri. 9–10; Sat. 9–5; Sun. 11–6. Admission $3.25 (combination ticket for all museums); children under 12 free with adults; Museum of Art free on Sat. (One block west of US 41 [Tamiami Trail], just south of Sarasota-Bradenton Airport; also 3 miles north of downtown area.)

**TALLAHASSEE:  LeMoyne Art Foundation, Inc.** 125 North Gadsden, 32301 ☐ The LeMoyne gallery opened in Florida's capital city in 1964, and moved to its present home, a clapboard house built in 1854, some time later. The mid-19th-century neoclassical building houses a concentration of 20th-century works. Exhibits change monthly; they include traveling shows, one- or two-artist shows, and retrospectives. Cameras are permitted. Classes are offered 4 times a year. The gallery also sponsors lectures, films, and television and radio programs. Docents are available by appointment to educational groups. A small research library is open by special permission only. Works of art are sold here, and a museum shop carries crafts, jewelry, batik, and prints (originals are available as well as reproductions). Park on the street or in nearby garages. Tues.–Sat. 10–5; Sun. 2–5. Free. (From Monroe St. turn east on Park and go 2 blocks to Gadsden.)

**TAMPA:  University Galleries.** College of Fine Arts, University of South Florida, 33620 ☐ The planned cultural complex at the University of South Florida will include a separate gallery building to house the permanent collection, now installed in galleries in 3 campus buildings (the Fine Arts Building, the Teaching Auditorium, and the Student Services Building). It will bring together the graphics of contemporary artists such as Rauschenberg, Rosenquist, Dine, Calder, and Anuszkiewicz; photographers Caponigro, Hine, Minor White, and Velsmann; paintings; sculpture; ceramics; a pre-Columbian collection from Mexico and Costa Rica; folk art from Guatemala; and some West African masks and sculpture. Exhibitions now change monthly. Cameras can be used only with permission from the exhibitions coordinator or security officer. All the educational activities usually connected to a museum are here carried out by the university art department. The main university library houses all art reference books and is open to the public daily. Catalogs are prepared for major exhibits. Parking on campus; temporary parking permits obtainable at the visitor center, main university entrance. Teaching Gallery and Small Gallery in the Fine Arts Building open Mon.–Fri. 8–5; Theater Gallery in the USF Teaching Auditorium lobby, Mon.–Fri. 8–5, and evenings and weekends during theater events; Fine Arts Gallery in Student Services Building Mon.–Fri. 9–1, 2–5, Sat. 10–1, 2–4. Free. (Take I-75 north or south to Fowler Ave. exit; go east to main university entrance. Or take US 301 north or south to Fowler Ave. exit and go west to main entrance.)

**WEST PALM BEACH:   Norton Gallery and School of Art.** 1451 South Olive Ave., 33401 ☐ The Norton Gallery and School of Art is a low-lying, clean-lined, symmetrical white building that looks out over Lake Worth. The expansive green that stretches out from the entrance and the profusion of palms that adorn the area give credence to the role of West Palm Beach as a resort. The gallery is one of the resort attractions; indeed, it lays claim to being "one of the most important small museums in the United States." The Elizabeth Calhoun and Ralph Hubbard Norton private collection opened this museum in 1941. Through the years it has expanded to include a notable assemblage of late 19th- and early-20th-century French paintings and sculpture; American works from 1900 to 1950; and a Chinese collection of some 200 objects that fall into 5 major areas: archaic bronzes, archaic jades, Buddhist sculpture, later jade carvings, and ceramics. The French group includes works by Gauguin, Cézanne, Renoir, Monet, Pissarro, Matisse, Brancusi, Maillol, Picasso, and Braque; in the American group are works by painters such as Bellows, O'Keeffe, Hopper, Marin, Sheeler, Davis, Dove, Demuth, Shahn, and Pollock. Gauguin's "The Agony in the Garden" hangs here, as well as Braque's "Still Life on Red Tablecloth," Stuart Davis's "New York Mural," and Cézanne's "The Artist's Son"—all superior examples of the oeuvres of these artists. An interior open garden, patterned after the Brookgreen Gardens in South Carolina, displays outstanding works of sculpture. Temporary exhibits are scheduled throughout the year, some planned and executed by the museum from the permanent collection and some loan or traveling exhibits. Cameras, but not flashbulbs or tripods, are permitted.

The Norton School of Art offers instruction in painting, drawing, composition, sculpture, ceramics, and art appreciation, as well as classes for children. The children's program also includes daily docent tours, concerts, and a puppet theater. The gallery sponsors lectures, an international film classic series, a concert series, and art tours in the United States and abroad. The library, containing a comprehensive collection of art biographies, art reference materials, and major periodicals, is open to the public for research. Docent tours are conducted on Sundays at 2, year round, and daily during the winter months. A museum shop offers gift and paper items, jewelry, reproductions, and catalogs for special exhibits. Parking facilities adjoin the museum. Tues.–Fri. 10–5; Sat. & Sun. 1–5. Free. (Take Flagler Dr. to Lakeview and turn south on US 1 [Dixie Hwy.]. Or from I-95 go east on Okeechobee Blvd. to US 1 south.)

**WINTER PARK:** **Cornell Fine Arts Center.** Rollins College, 32789 ☐ In 1977 the George D. and Harriet W. Cornell Fine Arts Center made its debut on the campus of Rollins College on the shore of Lake Virginia. The permanent collection housed in this Spanish-American-style, rambling structure consists of 19th- and 20th-century American paintings, European paintings from the Renaissance through the 19th century, bronzes, sculptures, and prints. The prize of the center, however, is the Smith Watch Key Collection, comprising over 1,200 keys and recognized as the most complete of its kind in the world. Exhibits based on the permanent collection are mounted in one gallery, while others are reserved for student and faculty art, local artists and collections, and traveling exhibits. One or more galleries are changed regularly. Cameras are not permitted. Courses in art, ceramics, and weaving are offered by the college Creative Arts program in the center. Docents are present for tours on request. Parking space adjacent to the center. Tues.–Fri. 10–5; Sat. & Sun. 1–5. Free. (Leave I-4 at Fairbanks exit; go east to Park Ave. and Fairbanks in Winter Park; go right on South Park, left on Holt Ave. Proceed east through the campus to the center, which is on the lakefront.)

**Morse Gallery of Art.** 133 East Welbourne Ave., 32789 ☐ The Morse Gallery of Art began its existence on the Rollins College campus in 1942 and remained there until it was moved to its present home amid the Old World ambience of downtown Winter Park. Here are housed the familiar artworks of Louis Comfort Tiffany: the stained glass, pottery, iridescent glass, metalware, enamelware, oils, watercolors, and furniture. Indeed, in this gallery are assembled more Tiffany stained-glass windows than anywhere else in the world. Also on exhibit are paintings and pottery by other 19th-century Americans and some European glass of the same period.

Docents are available, as is a gallery sales desk offering books, postcards, and slides. Parking space nearby. Tues.-Sat. 11-5; Sun. 2-5. Small entrance fee. (From I-4, take Fairbanks Ave. exit; go north on Park Ave. to the first street beyond the second traffic light and turn right.)

# GEORGIA

**ALBANY:   Banks Haley Gallery.** 813 North Slappey Blvd., 31701 ☐ Thirty miles from the birthplace of Jimmy Carter, in the "pecan center of the world," is the Banks Haley Gallery, owned and operated by the Southwest Georgia Art Association. Opened in 1969, the building consists of 3 circular units, situated in a small city park not far from the center of town. The permanent collection is small, but the gallery's exhibits, which it secures from larger museums and outlying colleges and universities, change monthly. Functioning as an art center, it offers a large number and variety of classes, lectures, chamber music and jazz concerts, films, and discussion groups. The Albany Arts Festival, a juried exhibition, and the Georgia Art Bus are among the springtime activities; an arts festival for the handicapped is held periodically; and an exhibit of high school art is mounted, also in the spring. Scholarships are offered for all classes. Guided tours are conducted for special groups. Brochures and/or program notices accompany the special exhibits. A museum shop sells original prints, drawings, paintings, pottery, jewelry, handcrafted items, and museum replicas. Parking on street around the park. Daily 2-5; closed Thanksgiving, Christmas, Jan. 1, July 4. Free. (North Slappey Boulevard is accessible from US 19 & US 82.)

**ATHENS:   Georgia Museum of Art.** University of Georgia, Jackson St., 30602 ☐ The Georgia Museum of Art, on the main campus of the University of Georgia, came about through the efforts and enthusiasms of one man, Alfred H. Holbrook. An estates lawyer, his interest in art germinated in his law practice and burst into full flower when, at the age of 70, he retired from the law and moved his "century of American art" (100 paintings executed between 1840 and 1940) to the university. In 1945 these paintings, the Eva Underhill Holbrook Memorial Collection, were formally presented to the University of Georgia. They established the Georgia Museum of Art, which opened in the old library, refitted as a museum, in 1948 with Holbrook as the appointed director. Holbrook augmented the original collection, the number of galleries was increased over the years, and by the time of his death at age 99½ in 1974, his gifts totaled some 800 paintings, drawings, and sculptures. Additional university purchases and gifts of other donors brought the museum's acquisitions to more than 3,500 works of art; today the total has reached over 4,000 objects. American art from 1850 to the present predominates in the painting collection; emphasis in the print collection is on both American and European works, the earliest dating from circa 1490. Temporary exhibitions change about every 5 weeks. Cameras are not permitted. The museum sponsors lectures and concerts and, as a university facility, an education program for undergraduate and graduate students. The large (50,000 volumes) reference library serves students and researchers associated with the university. A quarterly bulletin, a monthly newsletter, and exhibition catalogs are published here. Parking nearby. Mon.–Fri. 8–5; Sat. 9–12; Sun. 2–5; closed legal and academic holidays. Free.

**ATLANTA: High Museum of Art.** 1280 Peachtree St., N.E., 30309 ☐ In 1926 Mrs. Joseph M. High gave her home on Peachtree Street to the Atlanta Art Association to house a museum and art school. Thirty years later the High Museum expanded into a 2-story building adjacent to the house with galleries, offices, and a 400-seat auditorium. Then, in 1962, the museum joined with the Atlanta College of Art, the Atlanta Symphony, and a resident theater company to form the Atlanta Arts Alliance. Thus allied, the groups raised money for the present building, the Atlanta Memorial Art Center, the focal point of which is the museum. And central to the museum is a Kress collection consisting of works from the 14th to the 18th century—particularly Italian Renaissance and northern European. A Bellini ("Madonna and Child") is included here, and a Tiepolo. A small but outstanding collection of 18th- and 19th-century American paintings includes a Copley and a Charles Willson Peale, a Doughty and a Blakelock. American art from 1850 on is also represented in graphics, photography, early furniture, and some modern paintings. African objects, English and American silver and glass, and an outstanding display of 18th-century European ceramics are also among the holdings of this interesting museum. Special exhibits are mounted for one- to two-month periods; some are organized locally, others are on loan. Cameras may be used with special permission of the registrar.

The museum holds series of "Adventures in Looking" classes for school-age children. Lectures and films are important aspects of museum activities; seminars and workshops are offered on special subjects. Slide shows are taken into the community by Speakers' Bureau volunteers. Some exhibitions are organized as teaching aids; volunteer teachers give tours and lead workshops for schoolchildren. Demonstrations, poetry readings, and musical programs are scheduled in conjunction with exhibitions. Guided tours are led by docents on Mon.–Fri. 10:30–1; special groups, by appointment 7 days a week; bilingual tours can be arranged. The museum publishes a calendar each month and catalogs for special exhibitions. The library (5,000 volumes) is available to members and students of the Atlanta College of Art. Books, jewelry, decorative items, and paper goods are sold at the museum shop. Parking garage in the center. Mon.–Sat. 10–5; Sun. 1–5; closed Christmas, New Year's Day, Memorial Day, and Labor Day. Free. (Take 14th St. exit off I-85 & 75 [the downtown connector]. Go east 3 blocks on 14th St. and turn north onto Peachtree St. The center is between 15th and 16th Sts. on Peachtree. Or the #10 MARTA bus stops directly in front of the building.)

**AUGUSTA: Gertrude Herbert Memorial Institute.** 506 Telfair St., 30901 ☐ The Gertrude Herbert Memorial Institute of Art is the long name of a small 3-story frame house built in 1818 by Nicholas Ware. It was known as Ware's Folly, and in 1937 it became known as the Gertrude Herbert Memorial Institute. Its handsome exterior sets the scene for a collection of some European Renaissance and modern paintings, sculpture, and graphics. Exhibitions change monthly, and include circulating, one-person, and group shows. Films, lectures, and some classes are given here, and there is a small art library. Tues.–Fri. 10–12, 2–5; Sat. 3–5. Free.

**COLUMBUS: Columbus Museum of Arts and Crafts, Inc.** 1251 Wynnton Rd., 31906 ☐ At the western border of Georgia, across the Chattahoochee River from Alabama and just below the series of waterfalls that supply it with power, the city of Columbus grew modern while retaining much of the original 1828 city plan. History is perceptible on the streets, in the houses, in the opera house, and in the Columbus Museum of Arts and Crafts, which is the repository of the Creek Indian culture that flourished here in the early 1800s. Also gathered here are some early European paintings (English, Flemish, Dutch, Italian), American paintings, sculpture, and graphics (both early and contemporary), some Oriental ivory, a gun collection, and a doll collection. There is a needlework gallery, a selection of costumes, and some African sculpture. Exhibits change regularly. Tours, lectures and gallery talks, classes and workshops are offered. The library (375 volumes) covers art and Indian history. Tues.–Sat. 10–5; Sun. 2–5. Free.

**MOUNT BERRY: Martha Berry Museum and Art Gallery.** Berry College. Mailing address: P.O. Box 189, 30149 ☐ Located near Rome, Georgia, on the beautiful Berry family estate, the Marth Berry Museum and Art Gallery opened in 1972 to perpetuate the memory of Martha Berry and to house the collections assembled through the years by the abutting Berry College and Berry Academy, which she founded in 1902. The

30,000-acre campus provides a magnificently bucolic setting for this Greek Revival edifice. In addition to Martha Berry memorabilia, the museum's holdings are representative of many periods and places. The 18th-century French collection is the strongest; there are Italian, French, English, and American paintings from the 15th to the 20th centuries; and there is also European furniture. Notable items: a George Romney painting and one by Thomas Sully; 2 miniatures by Jean-Baptiste-Siméon Chardin, both entitled "Mother with Two Children"; sea scenes by Frederick Judd Waugh; "Old Lyme Church in the Snow" by Guy C. Wiggins; a Giotto; and a Sebastiano Ricci. A schedule of exhibits includes an annual quilt festival and special seasonal shows. The museum functions as a laboratory for the art, industrial arts, and home economics departments of Berry College. Lectures, musicales, and poetry readings are regular events. Guided lecture tours are offered to special groups on request. A sales desk has books, postcards, stationery, and gift items for sale. Parking adjoining the building. Tues.–Sat. 10–5; Sun. 1–5. Free; voluntary contributions are welcome. (The museum and art gallery are across the Martha Berry Hwy. from the Berry College campus at Mount Berry, adjoining Rome.)

**SAVANNAH: Telfair Academy of Arts and Sciences.** 121 Barnard St., Telfair Square, P.O. Box 10081, 31402 ☐ William Jay, the brilliant young English architect who introduced Regency architecture to America, designed the home of Alexander Telfair. An amalgam of Greek and Roman elements, with an impressive front portico, it was built in 1818 and occupied by the Telfair family until 1875. With the death of the last member of the family, the mansion was bequeathed to the Georgia Historical Society as a museum. After some renovation, the formal opening to the public of this extraordinary mansion took place in 1886, attended by Jefferson Davis. The rest of the bequest could now be seen: paintings purchased in Italy, family portraits, silver, porcelain, and furniture. The museum's first director, Carl Brandt, had already begun to expand the family collection with objects—casts of Elgin marbles and classical sculpture, and mural decorations—that today are more interesting as a reflection of late 19th-century taste than as artworks. But he also acquired works by Europeans working in Munich and Düsseldorf, and by the English narrative painters. It was Gary Melchers, an American expatriate painter, who brought 20th-century art to the museum. His purchases in Europe included many paintings by his French and German contemporaries. American Ashcan realists and Impressionists were also added to the museum's holdings by Melcher and his successors. As a result, the museum now has an interesting assemblage of "the Eight"; Twachtman, Metcalf, Hassam are among the Impressionists; and Melchers, Stewart, and MacEwen among the expatriates. One of Bellows's finest works, "Snow-

Capped River," was acquired in 1911. Early American portraits from many Savannah homes found their way to the museum by gift or purchase. Another collection of interest is the large group of drawings and pastels by Kahlil Gibran. The Waring print collection contains etchings, engravings, woodcuts, and lithographs dating back some 400 years and includes works by Hogarth, Piranesi, Goya, and Holbein. Close behind the Telfair house, and owned and administered by the academy, is the Owens Thomas House, another William Jay masterpiece, in which are displayed decorative arts in period settings dating from the Federal era. Both buildings have been designated National Historic Landmarks.

The museum sponsors lectures, films, gallery talks, seminars, concerts, jazz festivals, and a chamber music series. Guided tours for groups are also offered. The Telfair family library is available for use upon request. A newsletter and catalogs are published. Tues.–Sat. 10–4:30; Sun. 2–5; closed major holidays. Admission $1.

# HAWAII

**HONOLULU: Contemporary Arts Center of Hawaii.** 605 Kapiolani Blvd., 96813 ☐ Here, near the ocean and with a view of nearby mountains, close to the University of Hawaii, the Iolani Palace, and the state capitol in downtown Honolulu, is Hawaii's Contemporary Arts Center. Unexpectedly, it is one of the occupants of a bustling building owned by the *Honolulu Advertiser,* a major daily newspaper. The center's collection—about 500 works executed in Hawaii by Hawaiians (or non-natives who live or work in Hawaii) since the beginning of the century—is installed throughout the building. And in the center gallery there is a new exhibit every month, usually featuring local artists. Occasionally exhibits travel here from mainland United States or from Japan. Guided tours of the entire building, including the gallery area, are conducted by appointment. Catalogs accompany some of the exhibits. A sales desk offers exhibition work for sale. The news building cafeteria is open to the public. Parking area adjacent to the building. Mon.–Fri. 8–5; Sat. 8–12. Free. (Corner of Kapiolani Blvd. & South St. in the downtown access area.)

**Honolulu Academy of Arts.** 900 South Beretania St., 96814 ☐ The meeting of East and West in Honolulu is no mere state of mind. It is pragmatic fact—in the streets where Buddhist temples abut Christian churches and old Chinese markets compete with modern shopping centers; in the faces of the people whose ancestry has combined cultures and races; and in the art that is gathered in its museum, the only general museum in the central Pacific. The Honolulu Academy of Arts was founded in 1927 by Mrs. Charles Montague Cooke, who was descended from New England missionaries. Within the 25 galleries that are grouped around the most inviting and beautiful courtyards to be found almost anywhere is art from both Asia and the Western Hemisphere. Among the Asian fine arts are Chinese and Japanese paintings and sculpture from early history to the present. (The *Alice Cooke Spalding House* at 2411 Makiki Heights Drive is the academy's repository for Asian decorative arts. It houses an important group of Korean ceramics.) The West is represented by ancient Mediterranean and medieval Christian art; and European and American art including a Kress collection of Italian Renaissance paintings; later paintings by artists such as Monet ("Water Lilies") and other Impressionists; Whistler, Sargent, and Eakins of the Americans; and moderns Frankenthaler, Rauschenberg, and David Smith, to name a few. The temporary exhibition schedule packs more than 35 shows into each busy year; a wide variety of themes representing the cultural diversity in Honolulu utilizes objects from the museum or on loan.

Lectures, films, gallery talks, concerts, and dance recitals fill the schedule of special events. The academy's educational program includes creative art classes for children; a studio program and Graphic Arts Center that offers professional courses in drawing and printmaking and a resident artist program that brings master printmakers to the academy to conduct the workshops; an extension program that brings art to the neighboring islands; and guided tours of the museum itself. Catalogs of special exhibitions, art books, pamphlets, and the *Honolulu Academy of Arts Journal* (biennial) are published here. Many of these are available at the book shop, which also handles reproductions, slides, cards, and antique ceramics. The library (24,000 volumes) is open for scholarly research; a restaurant is open for less scholarly pursuits. Academy: Tues.–Sat. 10–4:30; Sun 2–5. Free. Spalding House: Tues.–Sun. 1–4:30. No charge Tues.; Wed.–Sun. $1 for adults, 75¢ for senior citizens, 25¢ for students, children free.

**Tennent Art Foundation.** 203 Prospect St., 96813 ☐ The Tennent Art Foundation gallery, built in 1954 to house the paintings of Hawaii's artist Madge Tennent, is located in a Hawaiian garden near the center of downtown Honolulu. Her works, about 50 paintings and drawings, depict the Hawaiian people, particularly women. They alone are on exhibit here. Cameras are permitted. Lectures and occasional concerts are held in the gallery. Tours are conducted by appointment. Madge Tennent's collection of books is available for use in the gallery. A newsletter, *Prospectus,* is published. Notecards and color reproductions are for sale at the sales desk.

Parking nearby. Tues.–Sat. 10–12; Sun. 2–4. Free. (Go to the top of Ward Ave. and bear left on Prospect St.)

**LIHUE, KAUAI:  Kauai Museum.** 4428 Rice St. Mailing address: P.O. Box 248, 96776 ☐ In the center of Lihue, the seat of government of Kauai, the Kauai Museum is dedicated to telling the story of the island, its history, and the ethnic origins of its people. Two buildings, one designed by architect Hart Wood in the early 1900s and one built in 1960, house the collections. In the William Hyde Rice Building is a permanent exhibit, The Story of Kauai, which tells the history of the island from its geological formation through the 19th century. In the Albert Spencer Wilcox Building is a permanent exhibit on the Hawaiian Calabash, and changing exhibits on ethnic heritage, and changing art exhibits. The museum owns several paintings of Kauai by artists of the 19th and 20th centuries. Slide lectures and movies are scheduled occasionally. The library, specializing in Kauai, is open for research by special permission. Three publications have been produced by the museum and are available at the museum shop, which also offers other books, baskets and tapa from the South Pacific, and Hawaiian design jewelry for sale. Parking in the nearby shopping center. Mon.–Fri. 9:30–4:30; Sat. 9–1. Admission fee $2 for adults; children free.

# IDAHO

**BOISE:  Boise Gallery of Art.** Julia Davis Park. Mailing address: Box 1505, 83701 ☐ The Boise Gallery of Art is located in Julia Davis Park along with a zoo, a rose garden, an amusement park, and a State Historical Museum. Run by the Boise Art Association, the gallery opened in 1936 with Oriental art, American and European paintings, sculpture, graphics, and works by Idaho artists. Temporary exhibits of graphics, photography, crafts, and architecture are scheduled regularly; there is one annual exhibition of works by Idaho artists. The gallery offers classes, tours, lectures, concerts, films, and an arts festival. A bulletin, an annual report, and a catalog of the annual Idaho artists are published. The library (1,000 volumes) is open for reference work by permission. Books and magazines are on sale, as well as some work by Northwest artists. Tues., Thurs., Fri. 10–5; Wed. 10–9; Sat., Sun. 12–5. Free.

# ILLINOIS

**CHAMPAIGN: Krannert Art Museum.** University of Illinois, 500 Peabody Dr., 61820 ☐ In the twin cities of Champaign and Urbana, the University of Illinois has over 35,000 students who utilize more than 160 buildings. One of these, the Krannert Art Museum, is a major museum in the state. It was designed by a student of Mies van der Rohe, Ambrose Richardson, with a simple marble-faced exterior and an elegant reflecting pool, and was built (in 1961) to house a collection that was scattered throughout the campus. Now, mustered here in wood-paneled galleries, is an assemblage of objects and paintings that, covering many periods and styles, reflects a general history of art: 2 collections of Oriental art; the Meyers collection of early American furniture and art; the Lorado Taft collection of sculpture; the Trees collections of paintings; WPA paintings, sculptures, and prints; the Olsen collection of pre-Columbian art; the Moore collection of classical and 18th- and 19th-century European and American decorative arts; contemporary drawings and prints, paintings, and sculpture; and the Krannert collection of Old Masters. A biennial exhibition of American painting and sculpture mounted here has resulted in the museum's acquisition, through purchase, of a stunning selection of American art. In the same way, as host to the American Craftsmen exhibit, the museum has enlarged its collection of contemporary crafted objects. Other exhibitions, a faculty show, and occasional one-man shows, are scheduled regularly throughout the year; traveling exhibits that are slated for large museums are shown here, sometimes as premiere openings. Cameras can be used for educational purposes only, and only with written permission. The museum's Lorado Taft Lectureship Fund supports lecture series; gallery talks, demonstrations, children's programs, and graduate museum training courses are also supported by the museum. A semiannual *Bulletin* is published as well as exhibition catalogs. Parking close by. Mon.–Sat. 9–5; Sun. 2–5; closed national holidays. Free.

**CHICAGO: Art Institute of Chicago.** Michigan Ave. at Adams St., 60603 ☐ The Art Institute of Chicago looks out over Lake Michigan from Chicago's downtown Grant Park. In 1882 it held its first exhibition under that name—it began as the Chicago Academy of Fine Arts, formed by a group of Chicago businessmen—in a property on Michigan Avenue and Van Buren Street. Some 10 years later it was the inheritor of the Italian

Renaissance-style building which it still occupies; the building had been constructed for the World's Congress of Religions during the World's Columbian Exposition of 1893, after which it was to be turned over to the Art Institute as a permanent home. New modern facilities connected to the original building were completed in 1977. A glimpse of the beauty and diversity of this collection can be seen at the base of an impressive stairwell: El Greco's incomparable "Assumption of the Virgin" and the 14th-century Spanish Ayala Altar share this space. The museum's holdings go on from there to unfold the progress of art from the classical world to the present. One of the world's finest collections of Impressionists and Postimpressionists can be seen here. Also superlative are the Japanese prints and Chinese sculptures and bronzes dating from the pre-Han through the early Ch'ing dynasties; the unique Thorne Rooms, authentic reproductions in miniature of European and American rooms offering a study of interior design from the 13th century to the present; a print and drawings collection that spans 5 centuries from the 15th to the present. A photography collection, begun in 1949, shares the space of the Department of Prints and Drawings. Turkish and Greek island embroideries, Indian sculpture and miniatures, English pottery, English and American furniture and silver, textiles, and primitive art are other facets of this gem of a museum. Some of the most well-known works are the T'ang Dynasty (618–906 A.D.) Horse; Louise Nevelson's "America Dawn"; Grant Wood's "American Gothic"; Mary Cassatt's "The Bath"; Rembrandt's "Young Girl at an Open Half-Door"; Gustave Caillebotte's "Paris, A Rainy Day"; Renoir's "On the Terrace"; Cézanne's "Basket of Apples"; Seurat's "Sunday Afternoon on the Island of La Grande Jatte"; and Picasso's "Daniel-Henry Kahnweiler." In addition to the permanent hangings, the institute has many temporary exhibitions, some organized by the institute itself, others traveling exhibits mounted by outside institutions. A permit must be obtained for cameras.

A mainstay of Chicago's cultural life, the institute initiates and supports many programs and activities. Its School of Art is an undergraduate and graduate college; fellowships and scholarships are offered to qualified students. Classes for children and young artists are available in the Young Artists Studio. Many lectures are scheduled regularly during the year by the Department of Museum Education, which also offers gallery talks by prearrangement to hundreds of groups each year. The Junior Museum of the Art Institute has a number of educational programs for schoolchildren and their families. A triannual brochure listing all exhibitions and a variety of catalogs are published. The facilities include a large reference library that is open to members, visiting scholars, and graduate students who present a professor's letter indicating the reason for their request. In addition, and attached to the institute, is the Goodman Theater Center (a resident theater company), a children's theater company, a Studio Theater, and a Film Center. The museum store sells a variety of items—books, cards and stationery, jewelry, artworks, woven fabrics, decorative pieces, posters, slides, scarves, reproductions, and many and varied gift items. For the hungry, there is a cafeteria and a more formal dining room and, during the summer, an outdoor garden restaurant. Several parking facilities in Grant Park near the institute. Mon.–Wed., Fri. 10:30–4:30; Thurs. 10:30–8; Sat. 10–5; Sun. & holidays 12–5. Admission fee is discretionary; Thurs. free.

**Chicago Center for Contemporary Photography.** 600 South Michigan Ave., 60605 ☐ The Chicago Center for Contemporary Photography writes: "Chicago has a great variety of cultural and educational institutions which merit the art tourist's attention." This Columbia College program merits that attention. Occupying the ground floor, lower level, and mezzanine of the college's main building, in the heart of the city, the center collects and displays photographic works by living artists. The display is not permanent; a revolving schedule (exhibits change every 6 weeks) brings the center's 500 prints to light though the year. Some of the photographers represented are Michael Bishop, Aaron Siskind, Harry Callahan, Robert Heinecken, Keith Smith, Barbara Morgan, Roger Mertin, Linda Connor, Arnold Newman, Emmet Gowin, Garry Winogrand, Lee Friedlander. Cameras are permitted. The center coordinates the Contemporary Trends Lecture Series; provides gallery speakers for interested groups; publishes exhibition catalogs and a series of announcement posters; and holds slide presentations. Photographs on exhibit can be purchased at the reception desk. Public parking available, but not free. Mon.–Sat. 10–5. Free. (At corner of Harrison St.)

**Martin D'Arcy Gallery of Art.** Loyola University, 6525 North Sheridan Rd., 60626 ☐ The Martin D'Arcy Gallery is the museum of Loyola University, one of the largest Catholic universities in the nation. It was begun in 1969 by its present director, Rev. Donald F. Rowe, S.J., with a single work of art, and has been expanded slowly to its present total of 140 carefully chosen objects. Its location in the university library—it has its own refurbished area—gives it the serene and contemplative atmosphere that was conceived by its director: a place where "an individual work of art can assert itself on the minds and emotions of a viewer." The gallery is unique in Chicago, and perhaps in the country. Students and visitors linger quietly, relax on the comfortable sofas and chairs, read, listen to soft classical and Renaissance music that is piped in, enjoy the fresh flower arrangements and the view of Lake Michigan, and literally experience the works, both religious and secular, on view. These fine objects were all executed in Western Europe between 1100 and 1700 A.D., "when attention to detail and a direct appeal to an intimate personal experience were paramount." Objects from medieval and Renaissance Europe in ivory, gold, silver, enamel, and bronze are gathered here, as well as textiles, manuscripts, paintings, and sculpture. Among them the Flemish oak sculpture, dated around 1520, "Lamentation Over the Body of Christ," is notable. Other treasures are a 16th-century jewel box from Nuremberg, believed to have belonged to Queen Christina of Sweden; another possession of Christina's, a sculptural composition, "The Flagellation," said to have been given her by Pope Alexander VII in 1655; a beaten silver censer made in Genoa in about 1630; "The Annunciation," a Limoges enamel on copper, made about 1515; rare stained glass from Canterbury Cathedral, made about 1220; "A Birdcatcher," cast bronze Flemish or German 17th-century genre figure; an engraved rock crystal beaker, made in late-16th-century Germany. The museum's purpose is to. show the permanent collection; special exhibits are rare. There have been only two major exhibits, the works taken from the gallery's collection and private Chicago collections; "Enamels, the XII to the XVI Century," and "The Art of Jewelry, 1450 to 1650." Scholarly catalogs accompanied both exhibits, and are still available.

Cameras are permitted here, and tours are available on request. The library of about 15,000 volumes is open to students and others who obtain special permission. Parking on the campus. Open whenever school is in session (call if in doubt) Mon.–Fri. 12–4; Tues. & Thurs. 6:30–9:30; Sun. 1–4. Free. (The campus is 5 miles north of downtown Chicago. Take Lake Shore Drive; it turns into Sheridan Rd.)

**Museum of Contemporary Art.** 237 East Ontario St., 60611 ☐ In 1967 a group of art-involved Chicagoans founded this first museum in the Midwest devoted to contemporary art. That same year the museum set up house in the turn-of-the-century building that was to be its home in the center of the city. In short order, the building was transformed by architect and founding member Daniel Brenner into a contemporary structure, the starkly square exterior embellished only by a 50-foot frieze by Swiss sculptor Zoltan Kemeny. Ten years later, to celebrate its birthday, the museum expanded into an adjacent brownstone. From the beginning, with its first young director Jan Van Der Marck, the museum sought to explore the "untried, unproved, the problematical, and the controversial" in art. Thus, every area of contemporary art is displayed here: painting, sculpture, graphics, photography, architecture, and crafts, as well as the less traditional earth and body works, conceptual art, and video and performance art. The 20th-century painting, sculpture, graphics, and photography include works by Albers, Christo, Matta, Olitski, Samaras, Walker Evans, Cornell, and Paschke; the Robert B. Mayer Memorial Loan includes works by Dubuffet, John Chamberlain, Nevelson, Pearlstein, Rosenquist, Segal, Warhol, Wesselman, and Westermann. Twelve special exhibitions are mounted annually. These range from the well-known masters (Calder, Lindner, Pollock, Kline, Braque, Rockwell) to the less-known vanguard artists (Dan Flavin, Robert Irwin, Frida Kahlo) to the well-known contemporaries (Oldenburg, Warhol, Rosenquist, Lichtenstein, Rauschenberg). Group theme shows (contemporary crafts, African fabrics, new British painting and sculpture, for example) are also mounted. Cameras without flash are permitted in the galleries.

MCA has active Affiliate Branches, volunteer groups throughout the city and suburbs which explore contemporary art with regularly scheduled programs of meetings with artists, tours of private collections, architectural tours, trips to other museums, and craft demonstrations. The museum proper sponsors its own lecture series, concert series, poetry readings, film screenings, and dance and theater performances; also children's events such as puppet and mime shows, dance concerts, and plays. Guided tours are offered by prearrangement (Spanish and French tours available by appointment); Saturday Gallery Walks to nearby galleries are led by staff assistants (also on Tues. and Thurs.); videotapes provide discussions of current exhibits. A bimonthly calendar and exhibition catalogs are published. The museum has a reference library (1,000 volumes, artists' files, magazines, and catalogs) open to scholars by appointment. The museum shop offers a varied inventory for sale: catalogs, art books, calendars, cards, and posters, jewelry, crafts, gifts, and clothing accessories. Public and meter parking nearby. Mon.–Sat. 10–5; Thurs. 10–8; Sun. 12–5. Admission $1 for adults; 50¢ for children under 16 and senior citizens. (2 blocks west of Lake Shore Drive, or 1½ blocks east of 600 North Michigan Ave.)

**Lorado Taft Midway Studios.** 6016 Ingleside Ave., 60637 ☐ Lorado Taft's studio, once a simple brick barn, is now part of the University of Chicago's Department of Art. Taft started there in 1906 (the building was of 1890 vintage) and spent the next 30 years there teaching sculpture students of the Chicago Art Institute and working with his associates. The studio has since become a National Historic Landmark housing his works—maquettes and portrait busts for which he was famous. Since it is affiliated with the university, the studio has exhibits of student painting, sculpture, graphics, and ceramics. Tours and lectures are scheduled. Mon.–Fri. 9–5; Sat., Sun. 12–5. Free.

**University of Chicago, Oriental Institute Museum.** 1155 East 58th St., 60637 ☐ The art and archaeology of the ancient Near East—Egypt, Assyria, Babylonia, Syria, Palestine, Anatolia, Nubia, and Iran—is covered, better perhaps than anywhere else in the world, by this distinguished institution. It was founded in 1919 by an Egyptologist. Later, expeditions were sent to other countries. Today, the museum's treasures from this part of the world (from 5000 B.C. to A.D. 1100) reveal a history of creativity, fine craftsmanship, and aesthetic sophistication—in bronze, ivory, stone, and many other mediums. Temporary exhibits are installed to complement the permanent collection. The museum sponsors lectures and films related to its field of study. The educational program here is available to undergraduate and graduate students of the University of Chicago. A docent council provides guides for tours of the collections. A *Guide to Near East Collections of the Oriental Institute Museum* and occasional pamphlets are published and sold here; also sold are books, reproductions, prints, cards and slides. Tues.–Sat. 10–4; Sun. 12–4. Free.

**FREEPORT: Freeport Art Museum.** Highland Area Arts Council, 511 South liberty, 61032 ☐ The Highland Area Arts Council operates the Freeport Art Museum, in which is assembled the eclectic collection of a late-born art enthusiast. William T. Rawleigh's success in selling medicinal remedies, herbs, spices, cooking items, and beauty products sent him all over the world in search of more raw materials for his products. In addition to finding these materials he found the excitement of the art world. His purchases were shipped back home to form the nucleus of the Rawleigh Museum, incorporated in 1920, and today called the Freeport Art Museum. Italian paintings and sculpture dating from the early 1900s, American Indian art, Art Nouveau pottery, *pietre dure,* Far Eastern textiles, and primitive and Oriental art are on display here. Of particular note is an immense Ch'ing Dynasty lacquer screen. Traveling exhibitions change every month; special exhibits regularly feature local and regional artists. Cameras are permitted. The museum and arts council sponsorships include an artist-in-residence program, films and chamber music concerts, poetry readings and theatrical programs, a school for the arts, and tours of the museum for students and adults. A monthly newsletter is published, and catalogs accompany special exhibits (the museum has its own small press). Parking nearby. Wed.–Sun. 10–5. Free; entrance charge of $1 to special exhibits, 25¢ for children. (US 20 to Carroll St., Carroll to Iroquois, Iroquois to South Liberty.)

**MT. VERNON: Mitchell Art Museum.** Richview Rd. Mailing address: P.O. Box 923, 62864 ☐ The Mitchell Art Museum, established in 1973, has a Main Gallery and a Hall Gallery in which are displayed its permanent collection of late-19th- and early-20th-century paintings and sculpture, some small carvings and bronzes, jade, and cut glass. Many exhibits have been mounted here since its opening. The museum sponsors lectures, tours, classes, concerts, a docent program, a school loan service, and competitive art shows. A newsletter is published quarterly. The library (275 volumes) has materials on artists represented in the collection. The gift shop offers postcards, books, slides, and prints for sale. Tues.–Sun. 1–5. Free.

**QUINCY: Quincy Art Center.** 1515 Jersey St., 62301 ☐ Joseph Lyman Silsbee, who is distinguished mainly by his close connection with Frank Lloyd Wright, designed the building that houses the Quincy Art Center in 1888. In 1923 the center moved in with a collection of paintings, sculpture, graphics, and crafts by contemporary Americans and Europeans. It sponsors an annual competition of area artists, tours, lectures, films, gallery talks, concerts, and classes. A scholarship program offers assistance for art classes to underprivileged children. The library (250 volumes) is available for use on request. A brochure and a calendar of events are published. Tues.–Sun. 2–5. Free.

**ROCKFORD: Burpee Art Museum.** Rockford Art Association, 737 North Main St., 61103 ☐ The Burpee Art Museum is located in the heart of Rockford, producer of screw products and fasteners, and one of the largest machine-tool producers in the world. Almost in defiance of its industrial surroundings, the museum looks like an Italian villa on a spacious site serenely looking out over the Rock River that splits this large city in two. Its history suggests the beginnings of many small museums and art centers across the country—an art association was formed in the early 1900s, a benefactor (in this case Mr. and Mrs. Harry Burpee) purchased a house to be used for a museum in the 1930s, the art association became a coresident in the museum building, and the city was thus provided with an art center. The collection housed here is predominantly North American; the paintings are from the late 1800s and early 1900s. Among them are "View near Byron, Rock River, Illinois" by George Robertson; "The Boat Yard" by Paul Puzinas; and "Portrait of Mrs. Mathilda Hitchcock Knowlton" by George P. A. Healy. A standing female nude, "Knowledge," by Lorado Taft, is among the museum's sculptures. Exhibitions are scheduled throughout the year. Cameras are permitted. Art classes for children and classes for adults in various crafts as well as lectures and slide presentations are offered by the museum. A school program, "Show Me a Picture," sends art education into the public schools. A Greenwich Village Fair is held on the museum grounds every fall. The library is open to the public. Guided tours are conducted only by prearrangement. A newsletter, brochures, and exhibition catalogs are published regularly. Tues.–Fri. 12–5; Sat. & Sun. 1–5. Free. (On a one-way section of North Main St. [SR 2], about 1 minute north of Business 20.)

**SPRINGFIELD: Springfield Art Association.** 700 North Fourth St., 62702 ☐ Edwards Place, a historic museum to which the Art Gallery of the Springfield Art Association was added, was built in 1833, 4 years before Springfield was named and became a town, and 4 years before Abraham Lincoln moved there to make it his home for the 24 years before he left for Washington. The gallery was added in 1955, an adaptation of the Victorian house it abuts. The gallery's permanent collection consists of 40 pieces of African art, Japanese and Chinese ceramics and bronzes, prints, contemporary crafts, jade, Persian rugs and textiles, and a large collection of Victorian furniture. Some of the paintings displayed here are by George Healy, George Grosz, Maurice de Vlaminck, A. Y. Jackson, among others. Exhibitions are scheduled every 6 to 7 weeks. Cameras are permitted. The gallery's activities include a museum school, lectures on special exhibits, film series, concerts, artist demonstrations, and book reviews. An outreach program sends docents into public and private elementary schools with original art and reproductions to conduct discussions. Exhibition tours are given on request; tours through Edwards Place are conducted daily, 2–4. The library facility is open to members, students of the school of art, and others by special permission. A sales and rental gallery offers original prints, pottery, jewelry, paintings, and textiles. Parking can be found nearby. Tues.–Sun. 2–4, or by special request. Free.

# INDIANA

**ANDERSON: Alford House—Anderson Fine Arts Center.** 226 West Historial 8th St., 46016 ☐ The Anderson Fine Arts Center was given a gift of a group of contemporary Hoosier artists' paintings. The 3 galleries here show these and other American and European paintings. Half the temporary exhibits are devoted to area artists and the other half to traveling or one-person shows. A 5-state competitive exhibit takes place in November. The activities here are typical of a community fine arts center: lectures, classes, films, concerts, tours. Paintings are loaned to local schools. There is a sales and rental gallery and a shop that sells crafted items, gifts, cards, and books. Catalogs accompany some exhibits. Tues. 10–5, 7–9; Wed., Sat. 10–5; Sun. 2–5. Free.

**BLOOMINGTON: Indiana University Art Museum.** 47401 ☐ Construction of the new Indiana University Art Museum began in the spring of 1978 on land adjacent to the Fine Arts Building, which had been its home. I. M. Pei's impressive triangular design triples the gallery space of the museum to accommodate an expanding collection and the Fine Arts Library. Three permanent exhibit galleries and a special exhibit gallery, conservation laboratories, a print study room, and meeting rooms for faculty and students are included in the interior plans. Classical art is one of the strong points of this museum; recently a large Cycladic idol, a Black Figure amphora by the Amasis Painter and a Red Figure cup by the Brygos Painter, two Roman marble busts, and an Etruscan bronze mirror have been acquired. The collection of primitive art is among the finest in the United States; purchases and loans from the Raymond and Laura Wielgus collection include a seated Teotihuacan figure and a sacred flute figure from New Guinea; other recent acquisitions are a Benin head and a Tchokwe chief's chair. Western art is represented by J. M. W. Turner (a seascape), Claude Monet, E. L. Kirchner, Emil Nolde, Alexei Jawlensky, Fernand Léger, Yves Tanguy, Picasso, Stuart Davis, Jackson Pollock, and Morris Louis; modern sculpture, by Auguste Rodin, Joseph Cornell, Jean Arp, Alexander Archipenko, Jacques Lipchitz, Marino Marini, and George Segal. There are drawings by Egon Schiele, Franz Marc, Juan Gris, Raoul Dufy, and Arthur G. Dove. Among the graphics are a trial proof set of Goya's "Caprichos," an impression of Picasso's etching the "Minotauromachia" and 47 plates of his "Suite Vollard," an important collection of Max Beckmann graphics, Dürer engravings, and Rembrandt etchings. The museum has an active exhibition schedule throughout the year designed to accommodate a wide range of interests: traveling shows, exhibits from the permanent collection, and loan exhibits. Cameras are not permitted. Lectures and lecture series are held; a docent program has been initiated recently, as has an outreach program into surrounding counties. Guided tours are available (Tues.–Fri. 9–5). The library is open to the public. A shop sells books, jewelry, prints, postcards, and the many publications produced by the museum. Tues.–Sat. 9–5. Free. (At the center of the campus, near 7th St. & Jordan.)

**EVANSVILLE:  Evansville Museum of Arts and Science.** 411 S.E. Riverside Dr., 47713 ☐ The Evansville Museum of Arts and Science looks out over the Ohio River onto the rich farmlands of Kentucky to the south. The contemporary building, several solid, asymmetrical masses with a central marble facade, was begun in 1956 and opened to the public in 1959. (The museum had previously been, for 30 years, in what was once a stagecoach inn.) Some of the works on view were purchased in 1904 from the foreign exhibits at the Louisiana Purchase Exposition in St. Louis by the town's Federation of Women's Clubs, whose efforts to start a museum then were aborted by the destruction of the mansion bought for the purpose. The works were later dispersed among the city schools. The art collection has grown to include Old Masters; French Impressionists; American landscapes and contemporary paintings, prints, and sculpture; 18th- and 19th-century English portraits; a Gothic period room; and a reproduction of a 19th-century street scene. The museum has 500 American paintings, 900 American and European graphics, and 100 European paintings. The sculpture collection ranges from before the Christian era to contemporary. Also assembled here are groups of American Indian arts and crafts; black African, Egyptian, Oceanic, and Oriental art; arms and armor; and Victorian decorative arts. Among the notable accessions are Georges Rouault's "Three Clowns," a "Self Portrait" and "Mary Magdalene" by Titian, "Girl With Fruit" by Fernand Léger, Murillo's "Madonna and Child," "Old North Carolina" by William M. Harnett, "Pamet River Road" by Edward Hopper, a Renoir pastel "Portrait of a Boy," a sculpture by Louise Nevelson, a marble Roman torso made in about the 1st century B.C., and a Sung period Kuan Yin stone head. The exhibits in 2 galleries change monthly, except in July and August. Purchases from 2 annual competitive juried shows—the Mid-States Art Exhibition and the Mid-States Crafts Exhibition—have contributed to the enlarging contemporary collection. Cameras are permitted.

The museum has an active schedule of classes in art, astronomy, antiques, and sciences. It sponsors occasional lectures, films, musicales, and an annual artist-in-residence program. Various clubs—stamp, camera, coin, astronomy—are offshoots of the educational program. The library is open to the public Tues.–Fri. 10–5. Publications include exhibition catalogs, a monthly bulletin, *Architectural Heritage of Evansville,* and a walking tour guide of the neighboring 19th-century historic preservation district. Guided tours are available by prearrangement. A shop offers books, toys, reproductions, some original arts and crafts, and other small items for sale. Parking on the grounds. Tues.–Sat. 10–5; Sun. 12–5. Free. (US 41 to Southlane Dr. [Rt. 41-A]. The museum is located where Southlane becomes S.E. Riverside.)

**FORT WAYNE: Fort Wayne Museum of Art.** 1202 West Wayne St., 46804 ☐ A Victorian mansion on a sleepy, tree-lined residential street at the west end of downtown Fort Wayne has been the home of the 80-year-old Fort Wayne Museum of Art since 1950. The museum has over 1,000 objects ranging from ancient to modern times. Its aim is to specialize in national and regional art. Today its collection consists of paintings, sculpture, graphics, prints, photographs, African art, Japanese woodcuts, WPA textiles, Indiana artists, and antiquities. Exhibits are changed every 6 to 8 weeks in the main building and the new young people's wing. Cameras can be used with special permission. The art school associated with the Fort Wayne Museum of Art is part of the Indiana-Purdue Fort Wayne campus. The museum itself sponsors lectures, films, special exhibits, and workshops. Docents are on hand to conduct school tours daily and evening tours for adults. A museum shop offers books, jewelry, postcards, and crafts for sale; an art sales and rental gallery is also active. Tues.–Sun. 1–5; Sat. 10–5; closed major holidays. Free. (At West Wayne & College Sts.)

**GOSHEN: Goshen College Art Gallery.** Harold and Wilma Good Library, Goshen College, 1700 S. Main St., 46526 ☐ Goshen College, a Mennonite liberal arts college in the heart of fertile Goshen County, has a one-room art gallery in the Good Library, which was built in 1968. The small permanent collection consists primarily of contemporary works by regionally known artists. Exhibits change monthly; there are occasional ethnic and folk art shows; student exhibits take place in March and April. Cameras are permitted. *Mennonite Artists Contemporary 1975,* an illustrated catalog published by the college, contains biographies of about 50 Mennonite artists. Mon.–Sat. 8–5; Tues. until 10; Sun. 1–5; no exhibits in August. Free. (1½ miles south of town on SR 15.)

**INDIANAPOLIS: Indianapolis Museum of Art.** 1200 West 38th St., 46208 ☐ The Indianapolis Art Association, the forebear of the Museum of Art, was incorporated in 1883, about 75 years after George Pogue and his family settled in the Delaware Indian territory at the confluence of the White River and Fall Creek, the wilderness site of what was to become the seat of government of Indiana. In 1895 a bequest was made by John Herron to build a museum and school at 16th and Pennsylvania Streets; they were completed in 1906, and both museum and school remained in that location until 1966, when the J. K. Lilly estate, Oldfields, some 50 acres landscaped by the sons of Frederic Law Olmstead, was accepted as a gift from the children of J. K. Lilly, Jr. as a site for a new museum. The Lilly residence, built in the style of an 18th-century French château, was opened that year as the Lilly Pavilion of Decorative Arts. By 1970, the Krannert Pavilion of the new Indianapolis Museum of Art was opened, an impressive, clean-lined, 3-story structure designed by Mies van der Rohe-trained Ambrose Richardson, with soaring columns at the entrance. Richardson was the same architect who had conceived the Krannert Museum at the University of Illinois ten years earlier. The museum expanded at a rapid pace: In 1972, the Clowes Pavilion, a gift of the Clowes Fund, was inaugurated to house the medieval, Renaissance, Spanish, and Baroque collection of Dr. G. H. Clowes, who had been research director for Eli Lilly and Company; in 1973, the Showalter Pavilion with a 730-seat theater; and in 1974, two branch museums—the **Downtown Gallery** in the American Fletcher National Bank and the **Indianapolis Museum of Art at Columbus.** Today the Krannert and Clowes Pavilions house collections of paintings, sculpture, and decorative arts from both Western and non-

Western traditions that span the history of art. The museum attempts to remain general; it has departments of Oriental art, African, Oceanic, American Indian decorative arts, prints, and Western painting and sculpture. However, certain collections are exceptional: the Chinese art, for example—porcelains, bronzes, paintings, and jades—to which Eli Lilly was particularly drawn, is one of the finest Oriental collections in the country; the J. M. W. Turner watercolors; the 17th-century Dutch and Flemish paintings; the late-19th-century French paintings; the 18th-century English portraits; the Indiana paintings; the European porcelains; and an unusual textile study center. The museum has 4 special exhibition galleries that provide about 20 rotating exhibits annually, complementing the permanent collection. The limited use of cameras is permitted; sketching and copying is permitted only with dry materials such as pencil, chalk, charcoal, and crayon.

Among the many activities of this most beautifully situated museum is the National Endowment for the Arts-sponsored State Traveling Exhibition Program (STEP) by which towns and cities all over the state share the collections of IMA. Specially prepared exhibits are made available by IMA to all qualified museums, educational facilities, community centers, and other institutions with the necessary display space. The museum's two active branches function as part of an expanding outreach program—one in downtown Indianapolis as a facility easily available to people in that area; and one in Columbus, Indiana, 45 miles south of Indianapolis, that holds 6 exhibitions yearly on a broad spectrum of themes. A panoply of art classes, lectures, concerts, films, and film seminars are held by the museum for members and the public, and for various affiliated organizations. An NEA-sponsored pilot adult education program confers academic credit for a Learning Museum Program. Docents lead regularly scheduled tours (2 p.m. daily), as well as tours for groups, the handicapped, and gifted children, and extension tours in the schools. The noncirculating reference library of some 18,000 volumes is open to the public; a film library rents films; and the color slide collection numbers about 50,000. The museum shop offers a large variety of items for sale, and books and catalogs published by the museum; the rental gallery has a fine selection of original works. A luncheonette and more formal Garden-on-the-Green Restaurant (wine sold here), where parties can be catered upon special request, are on the premises. Other facilities include the 7-tier outdoor concert terrace used during the summer; the "touch gallery," Artery; a Video Gallery where past programs can be reviewed; IMA Art World, a Sunday morning television program. Each pavilion has its own parking area. Tues.–Sun: Krannert/Clowes/greenhouses 11–5; Lilly 1–4; Garden-on-the-Green Restaurant 11–2; IMA Columbus Mon.–Fri. 10–4:30, Sat. 10–2:30, Sun. 12–4; Downtown Gallery Mon.–Fri. 9–5. Free. (Entire complex—139 acres open to the public during museum hours—is 15 minutes from the center of Indianapolis. By car, start at the central intersection of Indianapolis—Washington and Meridian Sts. Go 38 blocks north on Meridian from Washington to 38th St.; then go 12 blocks west from Meridian. Or take a city bus that leaves from the center of the city every half hour.)

**MUNCIE: Ball State University Art Gallery.** 2000 University Ave., 47306 ☐ Muncie, Indiana, sociologists Robert and Helen Lynd's typical small Midwestern city—"Middletown"—was aided in the course of its growth by 5 members of the Ball family. The Ball brothers made their famous jars, supported other industries, and contributed to educational and cultural endeavors here. Ball State University was one of those contributions. In 1936 a modified Gothic building, the Arts Building, was completed on the campus, and the university's art collection was installed there. Among the works are Italian Renaissance paintings and furniture; 19th-century American paintings; 20th-century paintings, prints, and drawings; and a Ball-Kraft collection of Roman glass. Changing exhibits feature the museum's own collection and frequent loan exhibitions. Cameras without flashes are permitted. The museum sponsors occasional lectures, and the music department presents concerts in the sculpture court. Guided tours are offered by appointment. Postcards and catalogs— *Ancient Glass Collections* and *Nineteenth Century American Paintings*—are for sale at the gallery desk. Two parking garages are within walking distance. Sept.–June: Mon.–Fri. 9–4:30, 7–9; Sat. & Sun. 1:30–4:30. July–Aug.: Mon.–Fri. 9–4:30; Sat. & Sun. 1:30–4:30; closed university holidays. Free. (Campus is 1 mile northwest of downtown. The Arts Building is 2 buildings west of the intersection of North McKinley Ave. & Riverside Ave.)

**NASHVILLE: T. C. Steele State Memorial.** R.R. #1, 47448 ☐ Theodore Clement Steele, Indiana painter who worked between 1870 and 1926, organized the well-known Brown County Art Colony, which still flourishes today. Between Belmont and Nashville, close by the Brown County State Park and sprawling Lake Monroe, are 211 acres of trees, ravines, streams, and hills that once surrounded Steele's home. Here is the 1907 barn-type studio that houses about 150 of his paintings. Open year round, daily 9–5. Admission 50¢ for adults, free for children under 12. (The entrance is 8 miles west of Nashville on Rt. 46 to Belmont.)

**RICHMOND: Art Association of Richmond.** McGuire Hall, Whitewater Blvd., 47374 ☐ The Art Association of Richmond, Indiana, founded in 1897, has a collection of paintings, sculpture, prints, and decorative arts. There are about 15 exhibits scheduled each year. The association carries on the activities of an active art center; it offers lectures, workshops, films, gallery talks, concerts, dance and drama evenings, and classes. Art is loaned to industries and schools. The library (1,200 volumes) is available for public use. Labor Day–June, Mon.–Fri. 9–4; Sun. & holidays 2–5. Free.

**SOUTH BEND:   Art Gallery, University of Notre Dame.** O'Shaughnessy Hall. Mailing address: Notre Dame, IN 46556 □ A potpourri of over 4,000 items from ancient to modern paintings, sculpture, prints, drawings, ceramics, tapestries, and photographs is gathered in Notre Dame's art gallery. Established in 1917 (the university's original art collection had been decimated in a fire in the 1850s) and moved to a new building (O'Shaughnessy Hall) in 1952, the gallery serves both the university and the community. An F. J. Fisher collection provides visitors with a glimpse of 16th-century Italian and 18th-century French and English painting; a Kress study collection contributes Italian paintings dating from the trecento to the 18th century, as well as Spanish and Dutch works; a gift from G. David Thompson introduces the contemporary world of art; and a memorial collection in the name of Dr. Tom Dooley adds primitive art to the gallery's diversity. There are many bright spots here: works by Van Dyck, Tintoretto, Veronese, a Lely portrait of Mary II of England, and from among the Americans, Thomas Eakins's "The Reverend Philip R. McDevitt." The Thompson collection of contemporaries includes work by Moholy-Nagy, Noguchi, Stamos, and Karel Appel. Special exhibits drawn from the permanent collection are complemented by loan exhibitions that come to the gallery from other museums or private collections. Lectures, guided tours, gallery talks, concerts, poetry readings, and art seminars are all activities that the gallery sponsors through the year. The library (7,600 volumes) is available for research. Catalogs and monographs are published and sold here, along with postcards of items in the collection. Mon.–Fri. 10–4:45; Sat. & Sun. 1–5. Free.

**TERRE HAUTE:   Sheldon Swope Art Gallery.** 25 South Seventh St., 47807 □ The Sheldon Swope Art Gallery, established by a bequest from Sheldon Swope in 1942, enriches downtown Terre Haute with an infusion of 19th- and 20th-century painting and sculpture. Contemporary artists are prominent here (Warhol and di Suvero among them), as are not-so-contemporary but 20th-century painters Wood, Hopper, Benton, Burchfield, and Soyer, and 19th-century Bierstadt and Inness. Scattered among these are holdings of primitive and Far Eastern artwork and some ancient and Renaissance art. Exhibitions are changed monthly; there is a special Wabash Valley Annual exhibition every March. Gallery talks for school and other groups are offered, and special tours are arranged for students from the colleges and universities in the area. Occasional films and concerts are also held here. The gallery publishes a monthly calendar, a newsletter, and catalogs of the permanent collection. A library (3,000 volumes) is available for general research. Books, postcards, replicas are for sale. Sept. 4–July 31, Tues.–Fri. 10–5; Sat. 12–5; Sun. 2–5. Free.

**VALPARAISO: University Art Galleries and Collections.** Valparaiso University, 46383 ☐ Valparaiso University owns about 700 artworks that are put on display on a rotating basis principally in the Moellering Library. There is no museum building. American landscapes from mid-19th century to the present predominate among the paintings, which also include "Rust Red Hill" by Georgia O'Keeffe and works by Eastman Johnson, Frederick Edwin Church, William Glackens, John Sloan, Childe Hassam, John Marin, Charles Burchfield, and others. Monthly loan exhibits are shown during the school year, selections from the permanent collection Nov.–Mar. Moellering Library open Mon.–Fri. 9–9; Sat. 9–5; Sun. 1–10. Free. (Take US 30 to SR 2 [north] to campus entrance, in southeast section of town.)

# IOWA

**CEDAR FALLS: University of Northern Iowa Gallery of Art.** 27th Street and Hudson Rd., 50613 ☐ Farmlands surround the University of Northern Iowa, which now has a spanking new art gallery. The collection, formerly in various university buildings, has been brought together under one roof, which it shares with the department of art. Emphasizing 20th-century art from Europe and America, it includes artists such as Albers, Arp, Baskin, Bonnard, Braque, Calder, Cassatt, Cézanne, Chagall, Dali, Daumier, Degas, Derain, Feininger, Goya, Grosz, Kollwitz, Lasansky, Léger, Matisse, Moore, Picasso, Renoir, Severini, Signac, Tobey, Villon, and Wood. Temporary exhibitions change every 5 to 7 weeks, with a hiatus in July and August. Permission is needed for cameras. Lectures and concerts are sponsored by the museum, which also goes out into community schools and organizations with its docent program. Guided tours are available by appointment. A luncheon counter/restaurant is located in Maucker Student Union, close to the gallery. Parking nearby. Tues.–Sat. 10–3, Wed. 10–9; Sun. 1–5.

**CEDAR RAPIDS: Cedar Rapids Art Center.** 324 Third Street S.E., 52301 ☐ Grant Wood grew up in Cedar Rapids, about 20 miles away from

Anamosa, where he was born. In 1973, the Cedar Rapids Art Center, in memoriam, opened a special gallery to exhibit his works. The balance of the permanent collection here includes other regional painters, works by Marvin Cone, prints, decorative arts, and crafts. Temporary exhibits are scheduled through the year. Classes, films, lectures, and concerts are held regularly. Newsletters and catalogs for selected exhibits are prepared. The library (1,200 volumes) can be used on the premises. A gift shop offers works of art, jewelry, and crafted items. Tues.–Wed., Fri., Sat. 10–5; Thurs. 10–8:30. Free.

**DAVENPORT: Davenport Municipal Art Gallery.** 1737 Twelfth St., 52804 ☐ The Davenport Municipal Art Gallery was established in 1925 just about 90 years after the city was founded by Col. George Davenport and Antoine LeClaire. It is part of a municipal art center, 2 segments of which are completed. This gallery has several distinctions: It was among the first municipal galleries in Iowa; it has an excellent Spanish Colonial collection, said to be one of the best outside Mexico; its Haitian collection is notable; and it houses an unequaled gathering of Iowa-born Grant Wood paintings and memorabilia in a special Grant Wood Gallery. There are other interesting features here and some surprises: Rembrandt prints and Japanese prints; a Remington "Bronco Buster"; and "Portrait of Sarah K. Siddons" by Lawrence. Exhibits change monthly, and include an annual Mid-Mississippi Valley Competition and 2 annual out-of-doors Beaux Arts Fairs. Activities in this city facility are myriad: studio classes for adults and children in painting, drawing, pottery, and graphics; lectures; films; demonstrations; and concerts. A docent program and an Art Force Gallery for Children educate 2 more segments of the art audience. A sales-rental gallery and a gallery shop (selling ceramics, glass, metal, and weavings) are available to visitors. The library (5,000 volumes) is open for use on the premises. The journal *Preview* is published quarterly, and catalogs are published to accompany exhibits. Tues.–Sat. 10–4:30; Sun. 1–4:30. Free.

**DES MOINES: Des Moines Art Center.** Greenwood Park, 50312 ☐ The Des Moines Art Center was designed by Eliel Saarinen, one of the great architects of this century. Its strong geometric shapes in rhythm with the contour of the sloping parkland it occupies, the new museum was widely acclaimed as a major architectural achievement when it opened to the public in 1948, fifteen years after James Edmundson, a Des Moines businessman, made a bequest to finance its construction. In 1968 the building was expanded by the addition of a 250-seat auditorium and a large sculpture gallery designed by I. M. Pei, another master architect. The sculpture court seems to emerge from the edge of the large reflecting pool, which the building encloses. Two hundred years of artistic achievement are displayed here; American and European paintings and sculpture, highlighted by an impressive contemporary collection, are bathed in the natural and artificial light that illuminates unadorned, airy interior spaces. Acquisitions are continually enlarging the pre-Columbian, African, and Oceanic arts collections as well as the Western painting and sculpture from mid-18th century to the present. The roster of artists represented in this relatively new assemblage is imposing: Rodin ("Pierre de Wiessant," one of the "Burghers of Calais"), Arp, Brancusi, Giacometti, David Smith, Barlach, Bordelle, Calder, Oldenburg, Cornell, Jasper Johns, Wiley, Rauschenberg, Morris Louis, John Singer Sargent ("The Pailleron Children"), Stanton, MacDonald-Wright, Hopper ("Automat"), Rothko, Stella, Bellows, Henri ("Ballet Girl in White"), Monet ("Cliffs at Entretat"), and others. Constantly changing shows are either drawn from the permanent collection or are traveling exhibits, or exhibits organized by the museum itself, sometimes as loan shows prepared for travel to other institutions across the country. The use of cameras is permitted for the permanent collection only, without tripods or flashes; a release slip must be signed.

The education department conducts both adults' and children's classes for two 16-week semesters and a 6-week summer session. Instruction in ceramics, drawing, jewelry making, painting, photography, and weaving are included in an ever widening range of programs for people in the community; scholarships are available to school children for studio classes. Artist-in-residence and ceramicist-in-residence programs add to the center's educational resources, as does the strong docent training program, which makes guided tours available (Tues.–Fri.; appointments necessary for groups at least 2 weeks in advance of the visit). The center also sponsors lectures, films, and musical and dance programs regularly. A bimonthly bulletin is published for members, and catalogs accompany exhibits that originate in the museum. The research library of more than 5,000 volumes is open to the public Tues.–Sat. 11–5. Postcards, catalogs, and notepapers are available at the reception desk. The museum shop offers books, paintings, sculpture, jewelry, and pottery for sale. Parking nearby. Tues.–Sat. 11–5; Sun. 12–5; holidays 1–5. Free. (Exit from I-235 at 42nd St.; go to Grand Ave. at Polk Blvd. in Greenwood Park.)

**FORT DODGE:   Blanden Art Gallery.** 920 3rd Ave. South, 50501 ☐ It is said by the people in Fort Dodge that the Blanden Art Gallery was the first art museum built in Iowa. It was dedicated in 1931 in memory of Elizabeth Mills Blanden, wife of Mayor George Blanden of Fort Dodge. A neo-Italian Renaissance structure of gold-colored brick, one of many old historic homes in the area, it houses a remarkable collection of early-20th-century paintings by European and American artists—Chagall, Miró, Beckmann, Hofmann, Soyer, Glackens, Rouault, Tamayo; several Henry Moore sculptures, a Calder mobile, and a Marini sculpture; an interesting selection of Japanese woodcuts and Oriental decorative arts; and contemporary graphics and posters. Some outstanding works are "The Cry of the Gazelle at Daybreak" by Miró; "Festival of Flowers, Nice" by Beckmann; "The Fantastic Horsecart" by Chagall; "The Dance" by Tamayo; Marini's "Cavalier"; a watercolor ("Central Park") and an oil ("Edge of the Woods") by Prendergast; and "Nirvana" by Hans Hofmann. Changing monthly exhibits feature regional art; the museum utilizes exhibitions mounted by the Iowa Arts Council and the Smithsonian Institution. Cameras are permitted. The educational activities include 6-week workshop sessions; film and lecture series; and, through the Community College, jewelry, silversmith, and painting classes. Tours are available only with 2-week advance notice. A newsletter is published bimonthly. The library is open to the public. A sales and rental shop offers jewelry, pottery, porcelain, prints, paintings, cards, and macramé weaving supplies. Parking behind the building or on the street. Tues.–Sun. 1–5; closed holidays. Free. (US 20 [5th Ave. S.] into Fort Dodge to 12th St.; go north on 12th for 2 blocks and turn west onto 3rd Ave. S. Go 1½ blocks on 3rd.)

**IOWA CITY:   University of Iowa Museum of Art.** Riverside Dr., 52242 ☐ In 1934, when few institutions were engaged in the teaching of fine arts, the University of Iowa hired one of Iowa's native sons, Grant Wood, "painter of the soil," to teach the graphic and plastic arts. But it was not until 1969 that the university opened an art museum. Housed here in this modern facility is the Owen and Leone Elliott collection, which contains a mixture of early-20th-century paintings from Europe—Picasso, Utrillo, Soutine, and Vlaminck, for example; Old Master prints; English 18th-century silver; and Chinese jade. The university collection expands the 20th-century holdings to Americans—Pollock, Hartley, Stuart Davis, and many others, and adds pre-Columbian and African art and a fine group of lithographs from the Tamarind Workshop. About 20 exhibitions a year are drawn from the permanent collection; some are exhibits on loan. The importance of graphics in the tradition of this gallery is emphasized by the Print and Drawing Study Club. Guided tours, lectures, gallery talks, films, and concerts are sponsored by the gallery. Catalogs are published occasionally. Mon.–Fri. 10:30–5; Sat. 10–5; Sun. 1–5. Free.

**MARSHALLTOWN:   Fisher Community Center.** 50158 ☐ Marshalltown's residents (30,000 and increasing) owe their Community Center to Bill Fisher, an industrialist who built it in 1958 to house his collection of Impressionist paintings. Surrounding it is a parklike environment, enhanced by a pond, some well-placed sculpture, and a fountain. The Fisher collection is a joyful aggregation of color and light—Bonnard, Vuillard, Matisse ("Portrait de Madame Matisse dans la Grace"), Sisley, Cassatt, Monet, Pissarro, Degas ("Dancers on Stage"), and more. The center's changing exhibitions feature contemporary work, often of local origin. Cameras are permitted; no flashbulbs. Classes, lectures, concerts, and film series are offered here, and recorded tours are available. A museum shop is located on Main Street. Parking is plentiful. Free. (From US 30 to Marshalltown, take Center St. [SR 14] to Anson St.)

**MASON CITY:   Charles H. MacNider Museum.** 303 Second St., S.E., 50401 ☐ The Charles H. MacNider Museum makes its home in a Tudor mansion built in 1920; it opened as a public arts center in 1966. A small permanent collection assembled here has 20th-century American art and Iowa art as its focus. It includes works by Arthur Dove, Thomas Hart Benton, Alfred Maurer, William Baziotes, Sam Francis, Jack Levine, Ben Shahn, Morris Graves, Peter Hurd, Nathan Oliveira, and others. Exhibits change monthly, and in the fall the museum sponsors an annual state-wide Iowa Crafts Exhibition. Cameras are usually permitted. An active art center, the museum schedules art classes for children and adults. Films, music events, and speakers are also frequently programmed. Group tours are conducted on the second Sunday of each new exhibit; other tours are given upon request. A newsletter is published every month, and small catalogs accompany many of the exhibits. A library (500 volumes) is open to the public. The sales/rental gallery features original work by over 60 Midwestern artists. Tues., Thurs. 10–9; Wed., Fri. 10–5; Sun. 2–5; closed national holidays. Free. (Accessible from US 18 or 65, or I-35.)

**SIOUX CITY:   Sioux City Art Center.** 513 Nebraska St., 51101 ☐ The Sioux City Art Center is one of many cultural and recreational facilities in what Siouxians regard as the "mecca" of the Great Plains. A turn-of-the-century building in the downtown area houses a permanent collection of some 400 objects of local and regional significance. Three galleries have monthly changing exhibits and an annual 4-state competitive show. Cameras are permitted. The center offers classes for adults and children, sponsors lecture-workshop series with nationally known artists, and hosts chamber music concerts. Tours are available on request. The library is open to members only. A sales and rental gallery offers original paintings for sale to the public, for rent to members. Tues.–Sat. 10–5; Sun. 1–5; closed holidays & Aug. Free.

# KANSAS

**ELLSWORTH:   Rogers House Museum Gallery.** Snake Row, 67439 ☐
Between low rolling hills and flatlands to the west is Ellsworth, home of
Charles B. Rogers, who in 1968 founded a museum to exhibit his art
collection. The 1869 building that became the showplace of this collection
was used as a hotel until its conversion—cowboys and cattlemen driving
herds from Texas to Ellsworth for shipment east stayed here in this 2-story
structure on what was once the main street facing the railroad tracks.
Exhibits vary, but the American West predominates, in both historical and
modern representations. There is a gallery of flower paintings and a
display of "Christmas 'Round the World"—paintings showing the stories,
customs, and legends of Christmas in many countries. The use of cameras
is not encouraged. A gallery shop offers cards, small craft items, original
prints, watercolors, and oils, and some books for sale; *The Great West
Illustrated* and *Country Neighbors,* both by Charles B. Rogers, can be
purchased. Mon.–Sat. 10–5; Sun. 1–5; closed Christmas. Admission 50¢
for adults, 25¢ for children. (At the edge of town on the corner of Rt. 14 &
South Main St.)

**EMPORIA:   University Art Gallery, Emporia State University.** 1200
Commercial St., 66801 ☐ Emporia was made famous by the *Emporia
Gazette,* edited by Pulitzer Prize-winning native son William Allen White.
Today the city of some 23,000 population boasts a diversified economy
with fine educational opportunities enhanced by the presence of Emporia
State University. The art gallery here, created to enrich the cultural
opportunities of some 6,000 students, has changing exhibits every month.
The permanent collection is seldom on view. Exhibitions are also mounted
in several other locations on the campus. Cameras are permitted. The art
department offers a complete range of courses in the arts. Visiting artists
give lectures and demonstrations periodically. Gallery calendars are
available on request. Weekdays 9–5. Free. (The gallery is in the
Humanities Building on the Market St. side of the campus.)

**HAYS:   Visual Arts Center, Fort Hays State University.** North Campus
Dr., 67601 ☐ The Visual Arts Center at Fort Hays State University has
been an entity since 1953. It grew extensively through the succeeding
years, and in 1978 ground was broken for a new facility. The permanent

collection here consists of the Vyvyan Blackford collection of paintings; regionalist prints of the 1930s; contemporary European and American prints; an International Graphic Society collection; and a National Small Paintings, Prints, and Drawings collection. Both regional and national exhibitions change monthly; a juried National Exhibition of Small Paintings and Drawings is held each spring. Cameras are permitted. Guest artists are invited to give lectures, workshops, and concerts. Parking nearby. Mon.–Fri. 8–5. Free.

**LAWRENCE: Helen Foresman Spencer Museum of Art.** University of Kansas, 66045 ☐ In January 1978 the Museum of Art of the University of Kansas changed its name and moved into a new building. Shining white Indiana limestone renders this neoclassical building especially dramatic on the beautiful 900-acre, tree-lined campus. The original museum was dedicated in Spooner Hall, an old Romanesque building, in 1928, ten years after an eclectic collection of some 9,000 objects had been given to the university by Sallie Casey Thayer, a Kansas City art collector who had gathered paintings and decorative art objects from all over the world. A half-century later, a gift by Helen Foresman Spencer resulted in the new building and the new name. The collection here is a comprehensive one, particularly noteworthy in the areas of medieval art; 17th- and 18th-century art, especially German and Austrian; American painting; graphics; and photography. The museum houses a Samuel H. Kress study collection of Italian Renaissance paintings, Old Master prints and paintings from the Max Kade Foundation, and the Gene Swenson collection emphasizing contemporary art. There are also strong representations of American needlework (quilts and samplers), American glass, Oriental decorative arts, Korean ceramics, and Japanese woodblock prints. The galleries in the new museum suggest the breadth of its holdings: There is an Oriental gallery, a Renaissance, medieval, and ancient, a 17th-, 18th-, 19th-, and 20th-century gallery, and one each for Americana, for tribal arts, and for changing exhibitions. A Venetian presepio (crèche) complete with original architecture is one of the most popular attractions. Masterworks in the collections include sculptures by Tilman Riemenschneider, Giovanni Bologna, and Don Judd; paintings by Guercino, Sebastiano Ricci, Winslow Homer, Dante Gabriel Rossetti, and James Rosenquist; graphics by Mantegna, Dürer, Rembrandt, and Johns. Six traveling exhibits drawn from the permanent collection are scheduled annually, to be shown first in the Kress Foundation gallery; and 6 special exhibits a year are on display in the Raymond White gallery for graphics. A Traveling Art Museum sends special exhibits to libraries, colleges, banks, and other locations all over the state. Cameras are permitted, but not flashes.

The museum schedules lectures and concerts in the auditorium, which seats 260, and the courtyard (concerts are held here 2 Sundays a month at 2:30). Educational programs include the training of docents who work both in the galleries and outside the museum in innovative outreach programs for the public schools. Guided tours are available to groups who apply in advance; a self-guide tour brochure is also available. The publications department is responsible for the frequent exhibition catalogs; the *Register of the Museum of Art,* a scholarly publication sent to Friends of the museum; *Sally Casey Thayer and Her Collection,* a biography of the founder and the story of the collection; *A Handbook of the Collections,* illustrating more than 350 objects in the collection; and a bimonthly *Calendar.* These are sold at a shop, which also stocks postcards, other books, and gift items. At current writing, the art library is housed in the Watson Library on campus, but plans to move it to the lower level of the new building are under consideration. Food is available (with beer) at the Student Union across the street from the museum. Parking lot adjacent to the building. Tues.–Sat. 10–4; Sun. 1:30–4. Free. (From the turnpikes, drive on 6th or 9th St. to Mississippi St.; go south on Mississippi to 1301. The museum is on the edge of the campus.)

**LINDSBORG: Birger Sandzen Memorial Gallery.** 401 North First St., 67456 ☐ Birger Sandzen came from Sweden to Lindsborg, Kansas, to teach at Bethany College for two years, and remained for the rest of his life. Teacher, lecturer, artist-in-residence, a believer in "outreach" before the concept became common, his many oils, watercolors, and prints appeared in exhibits around the country in the twenties and are now housed in this Memorial Gallery at Bethany. Built in 1957 through the efforts of Sandzen's son-in-law Charles P. Greenough III, the simple modern building opens onto a courtyard in which a fountain, "The Little Triton," by compatriot Carl Milles predominates. In addition to the works of Sandzen, paintings by Raymer and Kansas native Henry Varnum Poor, a Hartley, a Nordfeldt, a Curry, and some others are displayed here. Exhibits, mostly on loan, are changed monthly Sept.–May. The gallery hosts an occasional concert or recital. Guided tours are available. *The Graphic Work of Birger Sandzen,* two reproductions of paintings by Sandzen, stationery, and postcards are offered at a sales desk. Park in the rear of the church across the street or on the street. Wed.–Sun. 1–5. Admission 50¢ for adults, 25¢ for children. (Take Old Highway 81 from I-135; go to Olsson & First Sts.)

**TOPEKA: Topeka Public Library, Gallery of Fine Arts.** 1515 West 10th St., 66604 ☐ Since 1902 the Topeka Public Library has been the repository of the Edward Wilder collection of art glass, pottery, and statuary. Since

1953 the library has been at its present site in the center of town, and in 1976 a complete renovation secured the new gallery. In addition to the Wilder collection, there are watercolors of historical local scenes by Pauline Shirer; drawings by Kansas WPA artist Rolland Ayres; a miscellaneous group of paintings and graphics; contemporary Kansas artists' paintings; and the Johnson collection of glass, art objects, paintings, and prints. Exhibitions change monthly; many are on loan from other museums, private collections, and the Smithsonian Institution. The permanent collection is displayed during the summer. Permission is needed for the use of cameras. Some lectures, films, and concerts are sponsored by the Fine Arts Department. Occasionally, tours are conducted. The library's circulating and reference art collections are both open to the public. *Africa: Creative Expression in Rural West Africa* was published by the library in 1976. Parking in front of the building. Mon.-Fri. 9-9; Sat. 9-6; Sun. during school 2-6; closed major holidays. Free. (Coming from east or west, exit from I-70 at 10th St.; go west to Washburn. From north or south, leave US 75 at 10th and go west.)

**WICHITA: Edwin A. Ulrich Museum of Art.** Wichita State University, Fairmont & 17th Sts., 67208 ☐ While the McKnight Art Center was under construction on the campus of Wichita State University early in the seventies, Edwin A. Ulrich, a retired businessman from Hyde Park, New York, gave the university a collection of some 300 paintings and a trust to maintain them. (His trove of Waugh paintings remains on display in his Hyde Park, New York, home, Wave Crest.)The museum, which had been included in the original plans for the center, was named in his honor. It opened to the public in 1974, a massive brick structure of varying flat and rotated rectangular shapes intersected by entrance stairs that form a contrasting triangulated perspective. A system of modules or movable panels were designed for the interior, guiding visitors across the black slate and brown-carpeted floors. Remarkable as a university facility, remarkable even as an independent museum in a city with a population of less than 1 million, the Ulrich Museum of Art houses a collection, the core of which is the Ulrich group, of some 725 paintings, 467 drawings and 1,460 prints, 368 sculptures, and 261 pieces of pottery. Although the sum total surveys European, African, pre-Columbian, and American art, the emphasis is on American art of the 20th century. The Ulrich collection includes the most representative group of paintings by Frederick J. Waugh (one of the outstanding marine painters of America) to be found anywhere. Other highlights belonging to the museum are William Hogarth's "Lavina, Duchess of Bolton"; Franz Xaver Winterhalter's "Portrait of a Lady"; Frans Francken's "Nativity"; Albert Cuyp's "Hay Harvest"; and Sir William Beechey's "Portrait of Miss Elizabeth Beresford." The list of

American artists represented here is formidable. In addition to the Waugh paintings and many of Ernest Trova works are works by Childe Hassam, Arthur B. Davies, Robert Henri, Edward Potthast, Jack Levine, George Grosz, Isabel Bishop, Moses Soyer, William Gropper, Henry Varnum Poor, David Burliuk, George L. K. Morris, Hans Hofmann, Willem de Kooning, Frank Stella, John Clem Clarke, Robert Goodnough, Byron Brown, Larry Zox, Max Weber, Jerome Myers, Yasua Kuniyoshi, Fletcher Martin, Peter Hurd, John Kane, Frank Duveneck, Thomas Cole, Jasper Cropsey, and Lawrence Calcagno. The museum's acquisitions of sculptures include the Nevelson "Night Tree" that adorns the entrance and "Moving-Static-Moving Figure," the indoors; and works by Archipenko, Gerhard Marck, Georges Kolbe, Rodin (from his dance series), Calder, and Reg Butler. A small group of watercolors and drawings by Miró, Emil Nolde, Seurat, Modigliani, Milton Avery, William Merritt Chase, and Liu Kuo-sung, and prints by Anthony Van Dyck and Honoré Daumier are here. Far from remaining secluded within its own walls, the museum has spread out over the campus; sculptures have been placed in locations where students can encounter and enjoy art outside a formal academic setting. Chaim Gross's exuberant "Happy Mother" was the first of these large outdoor sculptures to be placed. Others are by Kenneth Armitage, Barbara Hepworth, and Lynn Chadwick, three prominent British sculptors; Ernest Trova; John Kearney; Charles Grafly; and José de Creeft. The schedule of temporary exhibits is impressive: 36 to 40 are mounted each year, all noteworthy. Indeed, some of the nation's most popular exhibits originate here: The 1977–78 Duane Hanson exhibit of lifelike figures attracted record-breaking crowds not only in Kansas but also in Nebraska, Iowa, California, Oregon, Missouri, Colorado, Virginia, and finally the Corcoran Gallery in Washington, D.C., and the Whitney Museum of American Art in New York; an Ernest Trova retrospective of 85 sculptures, paintings, and prints made a similar barnstorming tour of the country. Exhibits that originate in other museums are also installed here. Cameras are permitted.

An adjunct of the university and its art center, the museum concentrates on the display of art; classes are the function of the university department of art. The university art library is open to the public. Lectures, concerts, and some drama presentations are part of the museum program. Publications include catalogs of various exhibits; *Goodnough; Harry Sternberg: A Catalog Raisonné of His Graphic Work; Duane Hanson;* and *Trova.* The museum shop offers these and other books, cards, and prints for sale. Guided tours are available by appointment. Parking nearby. Wed. 9:30–8; Thurs. & Fri. 9:30–5; Sat. & Sun. 1–5. Free. (Leave the Kansas Tpke. at East Kellogg exit and travel west to Oliver; turn right [north] to 17th St., then left [west] to Fairmont.)

**Wichita Art Association Galleries, Inc.** 9112 East Central, 67206 ☐ The Wichita Art Association has made its home since 1965 in a long, low contemporary building set on a 15-acre tract of parklike woodland on the outskirts of the largest city in Kansas. Founded in 1920, when bumper wheat crops and the discovery of oil were restoring prosperity to the former "cow capital," the association has gathered an interesting collection of 19th- and 20th-century paintings from Europe and America, especially the Midwest; prints; Oriental scrolls and decorative art; 20th-century art glass; and pottery. Exhibitions are changed monthly Oct.–Apr.; the permanent collection is displayed for the balance of the year. Permission is required for the use of cameras. The association runs a school of arts and crafts; classes are conducted in painting, drawing, weaving, silversmithing, sculpture, ceramics, dance, and drama. Lecture series and children's theater productions are scheduled during the year. Guided tours are conducted by appointment, and visitors are welcome to the library. A shop offers books and the usual gift items as well as student art and crafts for sale. Parking on the grounds. Tues.–Sun. 1–5. Free. (East Central runs parallel to and 1 mile north of US 54.)

**Wichita Art Museum.** 619 Stackman Dr., 67203 ☐ The Wichita Art Museum, a massive geometric edifice of varying textures and planes overlooking the Little Arkansas River and the skyline of downtown Wichita, is one of the treasures of Kansas, not only for its impeccable collections, but also for the building itself. The original structure, built in 1935, was designed by Clarence Stein in the shape of a cube. The enlargement, executed in 1976 and 1977 by Edward Larabee Barnes, superimposed another cube around the original, this larger one rotated 45 degrees. Curving ramps lead to the main entrance on the upper level (there are three), from which one can look through the building to the sculpture deck in the rear. The display galleries are on this level. The ground and lower levels serve as a community center for lectures, meetings, and other activities, and for maintenance and utility purposes. The Roland P. Murdock collection of American Art was the result of a bequest by Louise Caldwell Murdock, Wichita's first interior designer: a trust was established for the purpose of building an art collection, with preference given to American art, in memory of her husband, owner and publisher of the *Wichita Eagle*. Mrs. Murdock's young assistant in the decorating business, Elizabeth Stubblefield (later Mrs. Rafael Navas) was to select and buy the paintings, and a "suitable place" was to be provided. The first 16 acquisitions by Mrs. Navas were hung in the new museum in 1940. "Kansas Cornfield" by John Steuart Curry, a native of Kansas, was the first purchase; among the others were Luks's "Mike McTeague," Hopper's "5 A.M.," Sloan's "Hudson Sky," Grosz's "The Blue Chair,"

Marsh's "Sandwiches," Burchfield's "December Twilight," Prendergast's "As Ships Go Sailing By," Pène du Bois's "Beach Scene," Glackens's "Luxembourg Gardens," and Eakins's "Portrait of Billy Smith." The group demonstrated the exquisite discernment of Mrs. Navas and signaled the future importance of this fine collection. By 1962, and the acquisition of 167 paintings including 7 major works by members of "the Eight," the trust had been exhausted. The museum's support organization took over the responsibility of increasing the collection still further; additions included works by Benjamin West, Titian Peale, Nevelson, and Motherwell, among others. The museum's other notable collection also focuses on American art. M. C. Naftzger, out of enthusiasm and love of the West, acquired paintings, sculptures, and drawings by Charles M. Russell, which he willed to the Wichita Art Museum. The collection of about 20 objects presents not only a vision of the West as it once was, but also a look at the stylistic development of this prolific artist over a period of 30 years. Enriching further the museum's resources are the L. S. and Ida L. Naftzger collection of master prints and the Gwen Houston Naftzger collection of porcelain birds by Boehm and Doughty. The regular schedule provides for some changing exhibitions that extend over a month to 6 weeks. Cameras without flashes are permitted.

This modern facility provides space for many of the activities typical of an active cultural center—an audiovisual room, educational office, demonstration studio, educational exhibition gallery, theater, conference room, library, and children's room are all included in the floor plan. Art classes for children, lectures and lecture series, a mobile gallery are all part of the program. A 2,000 volume library is open to the public by special permission. The museum's publications include a complete and detailed annotated catalog of the Roland P. Murdock collection and an information brochure on the N. C. Naftzger collection. The education department handles a full schedule of prearranged guided tours. A museum shop offers books, prints, slides, postcards, catalogs, and jewelry; there is also a sales and rental gallery. Luncheon and snacks can be had at the coffee shop. Parking nearby. Tues.–Sat. 10–4:50; Tues. 7–9; Sun. 1–4:50; closed holidays. Free. (Go north off US 54 on Seneca St. to Stackman Dr. Or go east off US 81 bypass [I-235] on Central to Stackman Dr., then go north.)

# KENTUCKY

**BEREA:   Berea College Art Department Collections and Gallery.** 40403 ☐ Berea College increases the population of Berea, Kentucky, in the foothills of the Cumberland Mountains, by about 15 percent; and the teaching collection of art, housed in the Rogers Memorial Building, increases the incidence of master art work by somewhat more. An extension to the 1935 Georgian building was added in 1977 to make more space for the college's Samuel H. Kress collection of Renaissance painting and sculpture; a group of Doris Ulmann photographs; a notable collection of prints; and paintings, sculpture, crafts, and textiles of varying descriptions. Nothing is on exhibit permanently; a changing program rotates the display of holdings such as a Gilbert Stuart "Portrait of George Washington," Dürer's "Life of the Virgin," Blake's "Book of Job," Goya's "Tauromachia," and American painters Moran, Inness, Tanner, and Johnson ("Boy Lincoln"). The Metzger collection of medieval and Renaissance textiles, the Titcomb collection of Chinese and Japanese art, and the Sloniker and Poole collections of prints are other highlights on rotating display. Exhibitions change monthly. Cameras are permitted. The gallery is one of the educational resources of the Berea College art department. The library is open to the public. Parking on campus. Mon.–Fri. 8–5. Free. (Go to Chestnut St.; park off Ellipse St.)

**LEXINGTON:   The Headley Museum, Inc.** 4435 Old Frankfort Pike, 40511 ☐ The Headley Museum developed in the heart of the Bluegrass Region, grew there, and remains one of its artistic resources. It was founded in 1968 by George W. Headley to house his collection of bibelots; it has since been expanded (in 1973 and 1975) to 3 eclectic buildings that incorporate architectural elements ranging from Thai roofs to Greek columns. The 5-acre surrounding farmland was originally part of Headley's La Belle Farm. In a jewel room are displayed the beautiful bibelots and boxes of Headley's own design, crafted by American and European artisans. Another room contains many rare shells. The Heflin collection of Oriental porcelains forms the core of the Oriental display in one wing of the newest building. The Fleischmann collection of paintings, on permanent loan to the museum, contains little-known works by well-known European and American painters of the last 50 years. Special exhibits are mounted on an irregular schedule throughout the year. Cameras are

**117**

permitted. Lectures and slide programs are offered periodically, and guided tours are available to groups on request. The library is open to the public during museum hours. Publications include *The Headley Treasure of Bibelots and Boxes* and *The Unique Collection of the Headley Museum;* a newsletter is issued to members quarterly. A small shop sells cards, books, jewelry, shells, handcrafts, and other gift items. Parking on the grounds. Wed.–Sun. 12–5; large groups admitted other times by appointment. Admission $2 for adults, $1 for students, children free; group rates depend on the size of the group. (From New Circle Road, go 4½ miles west on Old Frankfort Pike.)

**University of Kentucky Art Museum.** 213 Kinkead Hall, University of Kentucky, 40506 ☐ Lexington has many resources to commend it in addition to the brilliantly green and gently rolling horse-farmland that surrounds it. One of these is newborn: a creditable art museum in a spanking new building on the campus of the University of Kentucky. It began as the University Art Gallery, an adjunct to the art department alone; it now serves the university, the larger community of Lexington, and even the state. The collection is varied but focuses mainly on painting and sculpture of the 19th and 20th centuries. However, Oriental art can also be found here; textiles, ceramics, and metalwork from Africa and pre-Columbian America; and a large collection of works of art on paper. Some of the highlights are a Kwakiutl Indian totem pole; a pair of 6-fold 17th-century Japanese screens; an unusually large ancient Peruvian mantle; a small group of ancient ceramics from Colombia; paintings, drawings, cartoons, and prints from WPA projects; and the Robert B. Mayer Loan collection of contemporary art. There are 5 special exhibitions a year as well as a number of smaller exhibits dealing with various aspects of the permanent collection. Permission must be granted for the use of cameras.

The museum sponsors lectures, films, and symposia; a concert series is held in the adjoining concert hall (the museum, in fact, is part of a larger arts complex including a theater, art library, and the concert halls). An educational program is still in the planning stages. Catalogs are published in conjunction with special exhibits; *Art Museum Notes* is published quarterly. The research library is nearby and open to the public. Several restaurants are located nearby; parking on campus. Tues.–Sun. 12–5; closed Thanksgiving, Christmas, Jan. 1. Free. (Hwy. 922 [Newtown Pike] to Main St. and turn left; bear right onto Vine St., right onto Rose St., and go to the corner of Rose & Euclid Aves.)

**LOUISVILLE:    J. B. Speed Art Museum.** 2035 South Third St. Mailing address: P.O. Box 8345, 40208 ☐ Louisville's J. B. Speed Art Museum is not far from Churchill Downs, the oldest and perhaps the most famous racetrack in the United States. The museum commands its own superlatives. Founded in 1925 by Mrs. J. B. Speed as a memorial to her husband, it was opened in 1927, the first and largest art museum in Kentucky and one of the finest examples of classic Renaissance architecture in the South. Two wings were subsequently added, the last in 1973 in an uncompromising contemporary style to house modern art. The museum has a comprehensive collection, covering all periods and styles. The sculpture, both antique and modern, is notable; the Jacobean English room is regarded as one of the finest. The permanent collection also includes Western painting and sculpture from 1200 to the present; Oriental painting and sculpture; art and artifacts from the ancient world—Egypt, Greece, and Rome; French and Flemish tapestries; Western decorative arts from 1400 to the present; Japanese and Chinese decorative arts; American Indian art and artifacts from prehistory to 1900; Kentucky painting, sculpture, and furniture; prints, drawings, and photographs from the 15th century to the present. Works by John James Audubon are included in the Kentuckiana, paintings and portraits unrelated to his masterful reproductions of nature; French painting is represented by Courbet, Monet, and Degas, among others; masters such as Rubens, Goya, and Brancusi are all prides of the museum. Temporary exhibitions every 4 or 5 weeks cover all areas and periods of art, supplementing, whenever possible, the permanent collection. Cameras are permitted.

The museum sponsors lectures and concerts, films, and an extensive photographic program, as well as workshops for both adults and children. Guided tours are offered by appointment; general and specialized tours are announced; a Touch and See Gallery serves the blind. A bulletin, a monthly calendar and news, and exhibition catalogs are published through the year. The library of about 9,000 volumes is open to the public for research. The museum shop sells books, jewelry, prints, cards, and various gift items; there is also a sales and rental gallery. A cafe with service provides full lunches. Parking nearby. Tues., Wed., Fri., Sat. 10–4; Thurs. Oct.–May 10–10, summer 10–4; Sun. 2–6. Free. (Adjacent to the Belknap Campus of the U. of Louisville in the south-central part of the city. Take Eastern Pkwy. exit of I-65 and go directly south from the center of town on 3rd St. Or take the bus on 4th St. It stops 1 block from the museum.)

**MURRAY: Clara M. Eagle Gallery.** Art Department, College of Creative Expression, Murray State University, 42071 □ Visitors who come to Murray before leaving on their hunting or camping trips in the Land Between the Lakes national conservation and recreation area can look in on the Clara M. Eagle Gallery at Murray State University. Housed here is a permanent collection of some 500 works, including the Harry L. Jackson print collection and an Asian Cultural Exchange Foundation collection of Asian arts and artifacts. Cameras are permitted. The gallery sponsors lectures and concerts. Other educational programs are related to the university. Guided tours are offered by prearrangement. Mon.–Fri. 7:30 a.m.–9 p.m.; Sat. 10–4; Sun. 1–4. Free. (Take SR 121 or US 641 to 15th St.)

**OWENSBORO: Owensboro Museum of Fine Art.** 901 Frederica St., 42301 ☐ The high clay banks of the Ohio River turn yellow near Owensboro. Here, pride of place has filled the Owensboro Museum of Fine Art with works by regional and Kentucky artists, living and dead. A gift shop serves up crafted objects and original works by Kentucky and regional artists and craftspeople only. There are audiovisual presentations, classes, guided tours, lectures, and publications. Parking free. Mon.–Fri. 10–4; Sun. 1–4. Free.

# LOUISIANA

**BATON ROUGE: Anglo-American Art Museum.** Memorial Tower, Louisiana State University, 70803 ☐ In this capital city founded by Frenchmen is a museum housed in a northern Italian Renaissance building designed by an American and dedicated to showing the influence of British culture on America through the arts. It was established as Louisiana State University's art museum by an anonymous donation made in 1959. It specializes in British and American art of the 17th through the 20th centuries, with an especially strong collection of decorative arts. Under this roof is also assembled a large collection of paintings, prints, and drawings related to the Baton Rouge area; an excellent collection of the graphic works of 18th-century satirist William Hogarth; a large group of graphics by Caroline W. Durieux, Louisiana's well-known printmaker; many examples of the work of Adrien Persac, recorder of life in the lower Mississippi River valley in the 1850s; and an excellent selection of New Orleans-made silver. The museum mounts 5 or 6 temporary exhibitions annually, some organized by the museum, some borrowed from other large institutions. Cameras are permitted, but not flash attachments. An annual Antiques Forum, lectures, and films are sponsored by the museum. Docents are provided for school and other tour groups; guided tours can be arranged in advance. Catalogs pertaining to the collections are available in the museum office. The library (500 volumes) can be used by special permission. Parking nearby. Mon.–Fri. 8–4:30; Sat. 9–12, 1–4:30; Sun. 1–4:30. Free. (On Highland Rd., southwest section of town. Watch exit markers to the university off I-10.)

**JENNINGS: Zigler Museum.** 411 Clara St., 70546 ☐ George Zigler, and after him his son Fred and his family, lived on a tree-lined street in the town of Jennings. Their home, built not too long after the Southern Pacific Railroad was finished and Jennings was chartered as a town (1888), became the Zigler Museum in 1963, a museum trust established and the property donated by Fred's widow, who all her life had been devoted to the arts. The charming colonial-style house had remained the same for almost three quarters of a century when, in 1972, two years after it was formally opened to the public, it was expanded (two gallery wings were added) and resurfaced in white brick. Housed here in the east wing are 8 dramatic wildlife dioramas that depict the flora and fauna of southwestern Louisiana. In the west wing is a permanent collection of paintings by such eminent European and American artists as John James Audubon, James McNeill Whistler, Johann Overbeck, Louis Jambor, John Constable, Charles Sprague Pearce, Robert Wood, Bruce Crane, Edward Gay, Sir Joshua Reynolds, Jean-Louis Vergne, Gustave Wolff, George Inness, Sir Peter Lely, Albert Bierstadt, and Camille Pissarro. The work of Louisiana artists hangs in the Louisiana gallery. The central gallery is given over to a different artist each month throughout the year. Cameras are not permitted in the permanent collection. The museum sponsors lectures and concerts, and the facilities here are used extensively for group meetings, art-related workshops, and seminars. Guided tours can be arranged in advance. The small library is open to the public. Tues.–Fri. 10–12, 2–5; Sat. & Sun. 2–5; closed major holidays. Free. (Take Jennings-Elton exit off I-10; drive south on Lake Arthur Ave. to Clara St.; turn left and go ½ block.)

**LAFAYETTE: Art Center for Southwestern Louisiana.** Drawer 4-4200, University of Southwestern Louisiana Station, 70504 ☐ The Acadians from Nova Scotia who settled here brought with them a French background and style of life that is still characteristic of this region. Indeed, the Art Center for Southwestern Louisiana, opened in 1968 for the University of Southwestern Louisiana and the community, is one of the finest examples of Louisiana French colonial architecture. Its double brick walls, 24 Doric brick columns (built with wedge-shaped bricks), its pink-tinted plaster exterior, its newel posts and cypress paneling and hand-carved fireplaces all bespeak the elegant traditions of the South. Housed here are 85 paintings by 19th- and 20th-century American (many from

Louisiana) and European artists and some Picasso drawings. Most notable is the collection of 19th-century portraits by American and French artists who worked in New Orleans between 1795 and 1861; included in this group are works by Sully, Rinck, Vaudechamp, Healy, Lion, Amans, and Jarvis. Other museum highlights are Corot's "Venetian Cityscape," "All Hallow's E'en" by Ibbetson, and a portrait by Sir Joshua Reynolds. Special exhibits, which often open with a seminar, change monthly. Cameras are permitted. The center has summer art classes for children and special short-term seminars in painting, art appreciation, and other subjects in addition to its year-round schedule of classes. A variety of programs including slides, films, concerts, lectures, and demonstrations are held on Sunday afternoons. Out-of-state tours to other museums are arranged several times a year. Guided tours are available; lectures in French are given by prearrangement during open hours. Several catalogs have been published and are available at a small sales area together with gift items and books. Parking on the grounds. Mon.–Fri. 10–5; Sun. 2–5. Free. (Exit off Evangeline Thruway to Pinhook Rd.; turn right onto Pinhook, then right onto St. Mary Blvd. and go 3 blocks.)

**NEW ORLEANS: Historic New Orleans Collection.** 533 Royal St., 70130 ☐ The 1792 Merieult House in the Vieux Carré, having been refashioned as a museum, now has 11 galleries that display the extensive historical collection of Brigadier General and Mrs. L. Kemper Williams— paintings, prints, documents, books, and artifacts, all relating to the history of Louisiana. There are prints, oil paintings, watercolors and drawings on the Battle of New Orleans, and old architectural drawings and drawings of forts along the lower Mississippi River (1814). The collection is rotated. Guided tours and gallery talks, a docent program, and a lecture series are offered. The library (5,000 volumes, 15,000 pamphlets) deals exclusively with New Orleans and Louisiana, as does a scholarly series of monographs entitled *Historic New Orleans.* Tues.–Sat. 10–5. Admission $1 for adults, 50¢ for children.

**Louisiana State Museum—The Presbytère.** 751 Chartres St., 70116 ☐ The Louisiana State Museum, established in 1906 to exhibit the history of Louisiana, consists of 8 buildings, each with its own special function. In one, the 1791 Presbytère, are maps, documents, and paintings depicting Louisiana history, but also an extensive collection of portraits of French and Spanish figures prominent in 19th-century Louisiana. Costumes, decorative arts, and old dolls and toys all serve to depict life as it was in the Vieux Carré. Also of particular interest is an original elephant folio of Audubon's *Birds of America.* The museum's resources on Louisiana are enormous and include tens of thousands of documents in the Colonial

Archives (1717–1803); a photographic collection; maps and prints; and a library of 30,000 volumes and periodicals on Louisiana history and general reference. Lectures, guided tours, films, and educational programs are offered to the public on a regular basis. Special exhibition catalogs are also available, as are souvenir medallions, reproductions, books, and prints. Tues.–Sun. 9–5. Admission 50¢ for adults, 25¢ for students, free for children and school tours.

**New Orleans Museum of Art.** City Park. Mailing address: P.O. Box 19123, 70179 ☐ In one of the country's largest municipal parks (1,500 acres), not far from the famous Dueling Oaks, under which many an affair of honor came to its final settlement, is the beautiful Greek Revival New Orleans Museum of Art. It opened in 1912 as the Isaac Delgado Museum, a gift to the city from the wealthy sugar factor whose name it bore. Handsome though it was, it took time and the contributions of private collectors before this museum reached its present proportions. In 1971, the name was changed to the New Orleans Museum of Art and the building was expanded threefold to house the now prominent and diverse collections: Old Master paintings of various schools; a Samuel H. Kress collection of Italian Renaissance and Baroque paintings; the Chapman H. Hyams collection of Barbizon and Salon paintings; pre-Columbian works from Mexico and Central and South America; Latin colonial paintings and sculpture; a group of works by Degas; 20th-century European Art (surrealism and School of Paris are featured); Japanese Edo period paintings; African art; photography and graphics; the Melvin P. Billups glass collection (more than 10,000 objects ranging from antiquity to the 19th century); 19th- and 20th-century American and Louisiana paintings and sculpture; the Latter-Schlesinger collection of European portrait miniatures; the Victor Kiam collection of African, Oceanic, and Northwest coast American Indian art; and 20th-century European paintings and sculpture. The museum takes special pride in the "Portrait of Estelle Mousson Degas" by Degas, whose paintings occupy their own gallery; Degas's short visit to New Orleans in 1873 has been memorialized thus. The museum presents special temporary exhibitions throughout the year covering various phases of the history of art. Cameras are usually allowed; special permission is needed for tripods and flash equipment.

The education department offers regularly scheduled art classes for children and young adults. It also sponsors tours for schoolchildren and adults, teacher workshops, film series, special educational exhibitions, a Speakers Bureau, programming in conjunction with the local PBS television station, and on-site programming with local community groups and agencies. Lectures and concerts are part of the museum's regular programming. Guided tours are offered by prearrangement; French and

Spanish tours are available. The museum publishes exhibition catalogs and brochures, a monthly calendar of events, and an annual report. The Felix J. Dreyfous Library (about 5,000 volumes) is open to the public by appointment. A museum shop sells books and quality gift items. Several fine restaurants are located nearby; a snack bar is in the neighboring building. Parking nearby. Tues.–Sun. 10–5; closed legal holidays. Admission $1 for adults, 50¢ for students; free on Saturdays. (Take the Carrollton Ave. or Esplanade Ave. New Orleans Public Service Bus. Or take I-10 to the City Park/Metairie Rd. exit; or I-610 to the Canal Blvd. exit.)

**SHREVEPORT:   R. W. Norton Art Gallery.** 4747 Creswell Ave., 71106 ☐ The R. W. Norton Art Foundation was established in 1946 by Mrs. R. W. Norton, Sr., and her son, R. W. Norton, Jr. A contemporary building was constructed on its own 40-acre parkland, with wooded areas and azalea gardens, in 1960. About 75 percent of the works are from 19th- and 20th-century America; 25 percent are primarily 19th-century European. The gallery is particularly well known for its excellent collections of art depicting the American Old West—paintings, watercolors, drawings, and sculpture by Frederic Remington and Charles M. Russell; four galleries are given over to their display. Other American artists represented range from the late 17th century through the early 20th: Thomas Cole, Frederick Edwin Church, Jasper F. Cropsey, Arthur F. Tait, Albert Bierstadt, Thomas Sully, and George Inness. Paul Revere is among the group of silversmiths whose work is in the early Colonial silver exhibit. The European section contains six 16th-century Flemish tapestries depicting events of the Second Punic War; animal sculptures and paintings by Antoine-Louis Barye; French, Dutch, and English masters—Corot, Rodin, van Ruisdael, Hobbema, and Sir Joshua Reynolds; bronzes and paintings by Rosa and François Auguste Bonheur representing the Barbizon school; 26 sculptures by Pierre Jules Mêne; and 300 Wedgwood pieces. There are also a large number of American and European miniature portraits. Four to six special exhibitions are held annually. Cameras are not permitted.

The gallery offers slide lectures on the permanent collections and tours for school groups. Guided tours are given by appointment at 10:30 Wed.–Fri. Many catalogs on various aspects of the permanent collection and on special exhibits are available at the sales desk. The library of some 6,000 volumes is open to the public Wed. and Sat. afternoons. Parking facilities on the grounds; both parking lot and building are designed for the handicapped. Tues.–Sun. 1–5; closed major holidays. Free. (Off I-20, take Line Ave. south to Thora Blvd., turn left, and go one block. Off Hwy. 1, turn west at Southfield Rd., which becomes Pierremont; turn right on Creswell, and go 2 blocks.)

# MAINE

**BRUNSWICK:  Bowdoin College Museum of Art.** Walker Art Building, Bowdoin College, 04011 □ On one of the oldest and most beautiful of American college campuses is an impressive building, dignified and serene, not large yet monumental—the Bowdoin College Museum of Art, framed by the towering trees that are typical of this part of Maine. A massive, pleasingly symmetrical rectangle, its broad entrance stairs, bracketed by two strolling lions, lead to a columned portico on either side of which sculptured Romans look out from recesses in the brick facade. The grace of this gem of Renaissance architecture is derivative of two Florentine masterpieces—the Loggia dei Lanzei and Brunelleschi's beautiful Pazzi Chapel—after which it was modeled by Charles Follen McKim, the master builder of McKim, Mead, and White. The collection here lives up to the fine exterior. It began long before the museum was built and, in fact, before the college was founded. In 1811, James Bowdoin III bequeathed to the college 70 paintings collected in Europe, and 2 portfolios of drawings (142 in number) which at the time were valued at $7.50. In 1826, his widow (a Bowdoin herself by birth) added 14 family portraits to the collection. Owing to lack of display facilities, these early gifts were stored away until 1850 when money was given to the college by Theophilus Wheeler Walker to complete the chapel, in which it was decided to include an art gallery dedicated to the memory of his mother. In 1852, 25 more paintings and 7 engravings were presented, and 3 years later, 4 portraits of great value and historical interest. Shortly after, a group of massive Assyrian reliefs from Nineveh came to Bowdoin and were displayed in the chapel. In 1891 the nieces of Theophilus Walker made the gift of the Walker Art Building to honor their uncle. Today, 9 galleries show the treasures owned by Bowdoin. In the entrance rotunda is ancient art and American 19th-century tympana murals, a permanent part of the decorative scheme commissioned to be executed by Kenyon Cox, John La Farge, Elihu Vedder, and Abbot Thayer for the museum. In other display areas are the historical series of excellent Colonial and Federal portraits including works by Smibert, Feke, Copley, and Stuart; Old Master prints and drawings; the Warren collection of classical antiquities; the Winslow Homer collection of wood engravings, watercolors, drawings, and memorabilia; the Molinare collection of medals and plaquettes; and important works by 19th- and 20th-century artists such as Thomas Eakins,

Martin Johnson Heade, George Inness, Robert Henri, John Sloan, and Leonard Baskin. Ten changing exhibitions are scheduled during the year. Cameras without flash equipment are permitted.

The museum sponsors lectures and sometimes series of lectures. Tours of both the Museum of Art and the Peary-MacMillan Arctic Museum (located in Hubbard Hall, with displays of polar artifacts and equipment, personal memorabilia, diaries, photographs, and slides of these two Bowdoin alumni) are offered and can be arranged in advance. Numerous books and catalogs relating to the collections, published by the museum and by outside publishers, are available at a museum shop, which also sells magazines, jewelry, reproductions, cards, slides, pewter, delft, and other gift items. Parking in the rear of the building. Open hours are posted at the door; closed Mon. & holidays. Free. (Take Maine Tpke. [I-95] exit 9, follow signs to Maine St. in Brunswick; go south about ½ mile to the college campus.)

**LEWISTON:   Treat Gallery.** Bates College, 04240 ☐ In the triumvirate of small liberal arts colleges in Maine, Bates is the youngest, despite the fact that it reached its centennial in 1964. On this lovely, tree-shaded campus, in a wing of one of its classroom buildings, is the Treat Gallery, established in 1955. Here a visitor can view a Marsden Hartley Memorial collection (Hartley was a native of Maine); Chinese art objects; and European and American paintings, drawings, prints, and photographs. Exhibits are changed 7 to 8 times a year. Cameras are not permitted. Lectures and concerts are sponsored by the gallery. Catalogs on Donald Lent and Berenice Abbott and *Ninety-nine Drawings* and *Eight Poems and One Essay* by Marsden Hartley have been published. Open school year: Mon.–Fri. 1–4:30, 7–8; Sun. 2–5. Summer: Mon.–Fri. 1–4:30; 7–8 before theater performances. (Watch for Bates College signs from Maine Tpke. [I-95] exits in Lewiston and Auburn. The gallery is 1 block from Rt. 202 at Russell St.)

**OGUNQUIT:   Museum of Art of Ogunquit.** Shore Road, 03907 ☐ The "stern and rock-bound coast" of Maine turns gentle here. The miles of sandy beach stretching northward and the rocky shoreline to the south have made this village by the sea not only popular for summer tourists but for artists as well. There are several galleries here; the Museum of Art is one with a permanent collection. A simple modern building of cinderblock and glass, it opened in 1953, set on landscaped grounds in a rocky cove overlooking the ocean; window walls frame the sea. Assembled here are paintings and sculptures by "Americans of Our Times" (from 1920 on there are Tobey, Graves, Kuniyoshi, and others), including works by many well-known artists of the Ogunquit school of the twenties and thirties,

Marsden Hartley's "Lobster Pots and Buoy" for example, and Marin's "Cape Split, Maine." The museum mounts one exhibition, which remains intact for its 2-month season (July and August). Works are drawn from the permanent collection and loaned from other sources. Cameras are permitted. An illustrated catalog is published annually. Parking on the museum grounds. July–Aug. (through Labor Day): Mon.–Sat. 10–5; Sun. 1:30–5. Free. (Go 1½ miles from Ogunquit Center on US 1.)

**ORONO: University of Maine at Orono Art Collection.** Carnegie Hall, University of Maine, 04473 ☐ Once a library built by Andrew Carnegie in 1904, Carnegie Hall now houses the University of Maine's sizable art collection. In the 30 years since it was started the collection has grown to include more than 2,000 objects, the majority of which represent contemporary American art with particular emphasis on the product of artists who live and/or work in Maine. George Inness's "The Elm" is probably the best known work; others are Winslow Homer's etching "Eight Bells," John Marin's bright blue "A Bit of Cape Split," "Boston—Acorn Street" by Childe Hassam, and "On Bar Island" by Andrew Wyeth. A large group of graphics is international in scope: Rembrandt and Goya, Kollwitz, Manet, Picasso, Sloan, Marsh, Chagall, Dubuffet. Although administered, cataloged, and displayed in Carnegie Hall, the balance of the collection is distributed throughout the Orono and Bangor campuses for students to enjoy while going about their daily routines. Seven exhibits in separate display areas on the Orono campus are scheduled every month; 4 are mounted in Carnegie Hall, one in Hauck Auditorium, one in Memorial Union, and one in Alumni Hall. Cameras are permitted. This collection has sent over 100 traveling exhibitions all over the state. Its publications include a catalog, an annual exhibitions program, and gallery notes accompanying the exhibitions. The educational activities are confined to the university program. The university library is open to the public. Cafeterias and snack bars are located on the campus. Mon.–Fri. 8–4:30. Free. (Exit I-95 at Orono or U.S. 2A.)

**PORTLAND: Portland Museum of Art.** 111 High St., 04101 ☐ Portland's interest in preserving its history is reflected in its Museum of Art—it makes its home in a fine Federal mansion built in 1800 for Major Hugh McLellan, the first 3-story home to rise in the city; and its collection specializes in works related to Maine. The museum was founded in 1882 as part of the Portland Society of Art; in 1908 Mrs. Lorenzo de Medici Sweat bequeathed her home, the McLellan-Sweat House, to the society with funds for a gallery addition to be built in memory of her husband. Today the house stands in a preserved neighborhood among other excellent examples of Federal architecture; the lower 2 floors, furnished with

Federal objects left by the families who lived here, are open to the public. The 1908–1911 gallery addition, an adaptation of the older McLellan House, with sympathetic terra cotta cornices and Colonial Revival detailing, houses 19th-century paintings and sculpture and contemporary prints, as well as a large collection of Portland glass (1863–1873) and a growing group of European works. A major expansion is underway to develop the State of Maine collection and a large selection of paintings by Winslow Homer. Some of the outstanding holdings are "Dead Pearl Diver" by Benjamin Paul Akers (acquired in 1888), "Broad Cove Farm" by Andrew Wyeth, "Moonlight Dance Voulangis," a rare painting by Edward Steichen, "Portrait of Miss Florence Leyland" by James McNeill Whistler, "L'Estaque" by Renoir, and works by Charles Codman and Harrison Bird Brown. Special exhibitions are scheduled regularly throughout the year. Cameras are permitted; special permission is required for flash equipment and tripods.

The museum is affiliated with the Portland School of Art, which offers accredited courses and a 4-year degree-granting program. The museum itself sponsors lectures, concerts, special tours, gallery talks, and a program for students. Guided tours led by docents are available by appointment. Catalogs accompany the special exhibitions; books are published on occasion and are available at the museum shop together with cards, jewelry, glassware, and other gift items. A small library is open to the public upon application. Parking nearby. Tues.–Sat. 10–5; Sun. 2–5; closed holidays. Free; voluntary donations suggested. Admission to the McLellan-Sweat House $1 for adults, 50¢ for children. (Take exit 6A off Maine Tpke. [I-95], entering the city on Danforth St., which comes into High St.; turn left and go up a hill to the corner of High & Spring. Coming from the north on I-295, take the Franklin St. exit; go to Middle, turn right and go to Spring; take Spring to the corner of High.)

**ROCKLAND: Farnsworth Museum.** 19 Elm St., 04841 ☐ Lucy C. Farnsworth died alone—as she had lived—in 1935, the last of a family that had flourished in Rockland for many years. The marshaling of her assets revealed, much to the surprise of her executors, an estate of $1.3 million, the entire amount to be used to establish the William A. Farnsworth Library and Art Museum, and to maintain the Farnsworth homestead. The museum, a handsome Greek Revival structure built to complement the Victorian homestead next door, opened in 1948 after 10 years of planning and purchasing. Today the collection housed in Lucy Farnsworth's museum spans 200 years of American history beginning with folk art from the late 18th century, and including many of the masters of the 19th century (Eakins, Homer, Inness, Fitz Hugh Lane, Stuart, Sully, and Trumbull), and the first half of the 20th century (Bellows, Hopper, Kent,

Luks, Marin, Prendergast, the Wyeths, and William Zorach). The down-stairs exhibition areas, dominated by a striking circular staircase, are given over to changing displays drawn from the permanent collection. Other areas contain materials and artifacts of regional and statewide interest—evidences of Maine's maritime heritage and its Indians. The Upstairs Gallery is hung with the museum's extensive collection of paintings by N. C., Andrew, and Jamie Wyeth—one of the largest in the country for a museum of this size. Cameras are not permitted.

The museum adjoins the Farnsworth Homestead, a fine Victorian home built in 1840 and furnished with the best of that period. It was listed on the National Register of Historic Places in 1973. A school, lectures, concerts, films, and a school program are some of the activites sponsored by the museum. Guided tours are available on request. Catalogs accompany the major exhibitions. The library, with volumes available for use by the public on art history, the decorative arts, and local and maritime history, take up an entire wing. A museum shop offers reproductions and original works of art, crafts, books, and jewelry for sale. Parking facilities behind the museum. June 1–Sept. 30: Mon.–Sat 10–5; Sun. 1–5. Oct. 1–May 31: Tues.–Sat. 10–5; Sun. 1–5; closed holidays. Homestead open June 1–mid-Sept., Mon.–Sat. 10–5; Sun. 1–5. Free. (From US 1 [Main St.] going north, take a left on Museum St. From Union St. going south, take a left on Elm.)

**WATERVILLE: Colby College Art Museum.** Mayflower Hill, 04901 ☐ On the outskirts of Waterville, stretching out over some 900 acres of Maine countryside, is another of the state's old and beautiful small colleges. The neo-Georgian Bixler Art and Music Center in which the Colby College Art Museum began was built in 1959; a contemporary addition was built in 1973 to provide separate space for this museum that serves both students and the population of central Maine. The American art housed here includes works from the early 18th century to the present. American sculpture (12 Nevelsons, Indiana's "ART," works by Calder and Gross among others) dominates the entrance gallery and a sculpture court. Here one can find the American Heritage collection of folk art (78 paintings primarily from New England); the Helen Warren and Willard Howe Cummings collection of American art (portraits by Smibert, Blackburn, and Copley); the Harold T. Pulsifer collection of Winslow Homer (14 paintings); the John Marin collection (25 works by Marin); the Jette American Impressionist collection (Cole, Doughty, Kensett, and Inness represent the Hudson River school); pre-Columbian objects; Far Eastern ceramics; European art; and European and American prints and drawings. An archive of Maine art is devoted to artists past and present. Six loan exhibitions are installed during the course of the year, each lasting 4 to 6 weeks. The permanent collection may be photographed; loan exhibitions may not. Beyond the schedule of exhibitions, the museum's activities include sponsorship of lectures, guided tours for schoolchildren, and study programs for adults. Group tours can be arranged in advance. Among the publications available at the gallery shop are *Maine Forms of American Architecture; Maine and Its Role in American Art; Handbook of the Colby College Art Museum; American Painters of the Impressionist Period Rediscovered;* and sundry catalogs. The library of the art department is open to the public for research. Parking facilities nearby. Mon.–Sat. 10–12, 1–4:30; Sun. 2–4:30; closed major holidays and holiday weekends. Free. (Waterville-Oakland exit off I-95, then on Rt. 11. The museum is off Washington St.)

**Thomas College Art Gallery.** West River Rd., 04901 ☐ The second art assemblage in Waterville is housed in the administration building on the new (1971) campus of Thomas College, in one of the city's lovely suburbs. The college owns only a few works, but the gallery is open 12 months a year showing varied exhibits of paintings and photographs, many relating to Maine. Exhibits change monthly. Cameras are permitted. (Take Waterville-Oakland exit off I-95; go east on Rt. 11. The college is off West River Rd.)

# MARYLAND

**BALTIMORE: Baltimore Museum of Art.** Wyman Park, Art Museum Dr., 21218 ☐ The Baltimore Museum of Art was founded in 1914 and opened soon after in a temporary location at 101 West Monument Street, the home of Miss M. Carey Thomas. Newly received paintings were exhibited there until 1929, when a new building designed by the famous John Russell Pope, who later designed the National Gallery of Art in Washington, D.C., was inaugurated in Wyman Park. This handsome Grecian structure fulfilled the cultural needs of a city that only 25 years earlier had been devasted by the Great Fire of 1904. Today, after years of generous giving by art-conscious Marylanders, the museum is virtually a "collection of collections," each one carrying the distinctive mark of its individual donor. The American Wing had its beginnings before the opening of the Wyman Park building. In 1925 a mid-18th-century room from Eltonhead Manor in Calvert County, Maryland, was presented to the museum. Today the period rooms on display cover 100 years of Maryland history. Two galleries are hung with American paintings, among them Copley's early portrait of Lemuel Cox. The Antioch Court, the core of the building surrounding a small garden, contains the museum's ancient, Byzantine, and Middle Eastern art collections. Outstanding here are the graceful Antioch (ancient Syrian) mosaics, originally floor decorations, and now effectively displayed on the walls. Branching off from the Antioch Court are several wings. In the Cone Wing is displayed one of the largest collections of early works by Matisse in this country, as well as other 19th- and 20th-century artists: Gauguin ("Woman with Mango"), Picasso ("Mother and Child," "The Coiffure"), Cézanne (Mont Ste. Victoire Seen from Bibemus Quarry"). "The Blue Nude—Souvenir of Biskra," the painting that reinforced Matisse's reputation for breaking away from conventional forms and colors, highlights this group of paintings assembled with great taste and foresight by the Cone sisters. Their friendship with Gertrude Stein introduced them to many of the ateliers of Paris, Matisse's among them, and he helped to influence their collection. The Woodward Wing houses a fine collection of "Cherished Portraits of Thoroughbred Horses," presented to the museum in 1956 in memory of the owner and breeder of racehorses at the famous Belair Stables. J. F. Herring, Sr., a British artist who produced some of the best protraits of outstanding horses in the mid-19th century, predominates this group of 18th- and 19th-century paintings. The May Wing, home of the Young People's Art Center, opened in 1950 as a result of Saidie A. May's interest in art education. The gallery, studios, lecture hall, and offices all contribute to the effectiveness of the education program. A study collection of classical, Egyptian, Gothic, and Renaissance objects is installed here, as well as a group of contemporary European works particularly strong in late Cubism and Surrealism, complementing the Cone collection. Temporary exhibits are also held in this wing. The paintings and sculpture in the Old Masters Wing span 400 years of European art, beginning in the 15th century. Rodin's "The Thinker" is here; also Van Dyck's "Rinaldo and Armida," Rembrandt's portrait of his son Titus, Chardin's "Knucklebones," and Monet's "View of the Thames: Charing Cross Bridge." Far Eastern art, art of the Americas, Africa, and the Pacific, prints and drawings, and photography are all represented in excellent displays on the ground floor. Temporary exhibits are also mounted here. A permission slip is needed for camera use.

The museum's facilities include an art school; an auditorium in which lectures, films, concerts, and theatrical performances are held; a sales and rental gallery; a children's library; a noncirculating reference library (16,000 volumes) available to the public; and a downtown gallery, located at Charles and Redwood Streets, that extends the museum's programs to the heart of Baltimore's business district. Guided tours are conducted regularly; self-guiding earphones and multilingual tours are also available. A cafe is open for lunch Tues.–Sat. The museum shop carries gifts, art books, jewelry, postcards, reproductions, and catalogs of the collections. Parking nearby. Tues.–Sat. 11–5; Thurs. 7–10 (except summer); Sun. 1–5. Downtown gallery Mon.–Fri 10–4:30. Closed Jan. 1, Good Friday, July 4, Thanksgiving, Christmas. Free. (Take North Charles St. to 32nd St. & Wyman Park Dr. Proceed through park to Art Museum Dr.)

**Peale Museum.** 225 Holliday St., 21202 ☐ The Peale Museum is the Municipal Museum of Baltimore, housed in what is believed to be the oldest museum building in the United States. Rembrandt Peale, son of famous portraitist Charles Willson Peale and a well-known portrait artist himself, built it in 1814, called it Peale's Baltimore Museum and Gallery of Paintings, and exhibited "Birds, Beasts, Fishes, Snakes, Antiques, Indian Dresses and War Instruments, Shells and Miscellaneous Curiosities" and "The Grecian Beauty, a Statue of Wax, from head to foot, colored like Life—and the picture of the Dream of Love. Both efforts of art to display the beauty, softness, symmetry and grace of the female form . . ." In a skylighted gallery were rows of portraits of American Revolutionary heroes, some copies of his father's paintings and some originals, and his own renderings of Napoleon and other eminent Frenchmen painted during his visit to Paris. After the museum opening Peale was commissioned by the City Council of Baltimore to paint the mayor of Baltimore and leaders in the city's stand against the British in 1814; still later, another city commission added the portrait of Andrew Jackson to the collection. Rembrandt was succeeded as proprietor of the museum by his brother Rubens. After him the collection fell into other hands and the building was used for a succession of purposes until in 1928, neglected and decaying, it was renovated for the purpose of housing objects of interest to the inhabitants of the city of Baltimore. Another renovation took place in 1979. Prints and photographs relating to the city are displayed; the Peale portraits were placed here on permanent loan; other paintings by Baltimore artists past and present and several anonymous works are on permanent exhibit. An architectural file of Baltimore buildings is a major study resource. A replica of Rembrandt's gas-making equipment (the first such equipment to be used for gas illumination) and the remains of the famous "American mastodon" discovered by Charles Willson Peale in New York's Ulster County can also be seen. Temporary exhibits are scheduled regularly. Besides the exhibition program, the museum offers guided tours, lectures, television programs on Baltimore history, historical pamphlets, and a constant research service.

**Walters Art Gallery.** 600 North Charles St., 21201 ☐ Father and son built this collection. William T. Walters (1820–1894) began to collect local contemporary paintings in the 1830s and 40s. An expatriate in Paris during the Civil War, he tapped the resources of the art world there and purchased a prodigious collection of contemporary French works and Chinese ceramics. These acquisitions followed the family back to Baltimore after the war and remained in their home, some on display and some crated, until 1880. An adjoining building was used for storage and display purposes until 1905, when William Delano was commissioned to design a private museum. The resulting neo-Renaissance palazzo, based on the Palazzo Balbi in Genoa, was completed in 1908. Twenty-three years later, Henry Walters (1848–1931), who had added thousands of objects from all the cultures of the world to the collection, deeded the building and its contents to the city, thus enriching it with a massive treasure. By 1974, a sorely needed new wing, designed by Shepley, Bulfinch, Richardson, and Abbott, was added—100,000 square feet of contemporary space built specifically to accommodate the existing collections, which extend from the 8th century B.C. to 1910. The museum is best known for its medieval art (the ivories, enamels, and goldsmith work are among the great collections of this kind in the country); the Byzantine collection, which includes the Hamah Treasure of liturgical silver, a unique assemblage from early Christianity, and a Rubens vase of agate (one of the antiquities in Peter Paul Rubens's collection, acquired by him in 1619 and sold in 1626) dated around A.D. 400; a manuscript collection, often integrated into the exhibitions, which is second in importance only to the one at the Morgan library; Greek and Roman art including the famous 7 carved sarcophagi taken from a burial ground in Rome; Islamic art—one of the fine metalwork collections in the country; Renaissance and Baroque painting including a selection of Italian works by Pontormo, Crivelli, Raphael ("Virgin of the Candelabra"), Vasari, Bellini, Veronese, and Strozzi; an arms and armor collection; and French works by Delacroix ("Sea of Galilee," "Crucifixion"), Manet ("Man at the Bar"), Corot ("Sheepfold"), Gérôme ("Duel After the Masquerade"), Ingres ("Odalisque"), and Monet. Approximately 6 exhibitions are scheduled per year; drawings, manuscripts, and other materials are rotated periodically. Cameras are permitted.

The museum schedules lectures on Mondays at night and Tuesdays at noon, a Christmas concert, and a November concert series with students of the Peabody Institute. The education department handles some 40,000 schoolchildren per year. Tours are provided to the general public on request, or 3 times a day by volunteer guides; tours in French, German, Dutch, and Chinese are also available. The library (65,000 volumes) is open only to members, students, and scholars. A museum shop offers reproductions, cards, jewelry, and the many books and catalogs published by the museum. Parking lot nearby. Mon. 1–5, 7:30–10; Tues.–Sat. 11–5; Sun. 2–5. Summer: Mon.–Sat. 11–4. Free. (Charles St., the major north-south axis of Baltimore, is easily reached from Washington Blvd., I-95, or US 40 by following signs to downtown Baltimore.)

**COLLEGE PARK:** **University of Maryland Art Gallery.** Department of Art, 20742 ☐ Located in a town almost totally devoted to university life, the University of Maryland opened its art gallery in 1964 primarily for the edification of students and faculty. It is now, since 1976, housed in a new building on this huge campus and serves students, faculty, and community. Many of the works on display here were done under various federal patronage projects of the New Deal. American paintings of the 19th century are also on view, as is a growing collection of African art. Temporary exhibits are changed regularly. Cameras are usable by permission only. Although part of the university educational program, the museum sponsors lectures and concerts and offers training fellowships to graduate students. Its most recent publications include *Maurice Prendergast, Art of Impulse and Color* and *French Watercolor Landscapes of the Nineteenth Century: From Delacroix to Cézanne.* Campus eating and parking facilities are available to the public. Mon.–Fri. 9–5; Sat. & Sun. 1–5; closed national holidays and between summer session and fall semester. Free. (Take New Hampshire Ave. exit off the 495 Beltway-Takoma Park exit; make a left on Adelphi Rd. and go to Campus Dr.)

**HAGERSTOWN:** **Washington County Museum of Fine Arts.** City Park, 21740 ☐ The Washington County Museum of Fine Arts is 70 miles west of Washington, D.C., with its formidable array of museums. Here, in the Hagerstown City Park is a Georgian building, appropriate for this setting, as the bold and historic D.C. buildings are for theirs. William H. Singer, Jr., offered this gift to the community in 1929; the museum was built and opened 2 years later. The permanent collection is wide-ranging; the museum began with the gift of Anne Brugh Singer of 19th- and 20th-century French, Dutch, and American works. Today holdings representing America's Hudson River school have increased, and the museum's collections include Italian Renaissance objects, Chinese paintings and jades and other Oriental objects, American pressed glass and other Americana, and Old Master paintings (Flemish, Dutch, Italian). From the American collection are Inness's "Coming Storm, Montclair, N.J."; "In the Rockies" by Bierstadt; "Portrait of Henry Robinson" by Rembrandt Peale; "Portrait of Daniel Webster" by Thomas Sully; "Sunset Hudson River" by Frederick Edwin Church. Special exhibitions—loan collections and traveling exhibits—are changed monthly. There are also annual juried regional photographic salons and annual juried exhibitions of Cumberland Valley artists. Cameras can be used with permission from the director. The museum offers a broad spectrum of facilities and activities: a museum school for adults and children; lectures and concerts from September through June; a film and slide lecture loan library; consultation and restoration services; a Saturday morning youth program; special programs for the handicapped and senior citizens; school outreach programs; a docent training program; and guided tours (by appointment). Catalogs accompany the special exhibits and can be purchased at a shop which also offers museum-quality items for sale. Parking nearby. Tues.–Sat. 10–5; Sun. 1–6; closed Thanksgiving, Christmas, Jan. 1. Free. (Take Virginia Ave. [US 11 south] 4 blocks from downtown Hagerstown.)

**TOWSON: Asian Arts Center.** The Roberts Room, Towson State University, 21204 ☐ Towson State University's Asian Arts Center was established over 100 years after the university itself was founded in this suburb of Baltimore when, in 1971, a local businessman donated his collection of Chinese and Japanese ivory sculpture. The center moved to the Roberts Room in the fine arts building in 1973. Ivories, ceramics, textiles, paintings, prints, and sculpture from India, Tibet, Southeast Asia, China, Korea, and Japan are displayed here. Special exhibits are held only occasionally. Cameras are permitted. An outreach program sends a traveling van, the Asiavan, outfitted with art from the center, to public schools and other institutions in the Baltimore area. Publications include a handlist of the collection, and a catalog of selected objects from the collection. Public parking readily available. Fall and spring semesters 10–12, 2–4; summer 10–12, 1–3. Free. (The fine arts building is at the southeast corner of Osler Dr. & Cross Campus Rd. Reach Osler Dr. from Charles St. via Towsontown Blvd. or from York Rd. via Burke Ave. & Towsontown Blvd.)

# MASSACHUSETTS

**AMHERST: Mead Art Building.** Amherst College, 01002 ☐ Sixty-two years after the town of Amherst was founded in 1759, a college was established to educate "promising but needy youths who wished to enter the ministry." From these resolute beginnings, whence also emerged poets and politicians, one of the most distinguished institutions of learning in the Northeast flowered. It was not, however, for many years that an art museum was to grace this beautiful campus. William Rutherford Mead's generosity to his alma mater resulted in Amherst's first bona fide museum, designed by Mead and his partners, McKim and White. In it, America's art predominates, especially paintings from the 18th and 19th centuries by Copley and Gilbert Stuart, for example, Charles Willson and Rembrandt Peale, and Benjamin West. The museum also has in its possession a collection of ancient art (much of it sent here by Amherst's own graduate missionaries), English and Oriental, and a Kress study collection of Western European art. The decorative arts are covered in a room of early English and American furniture. Exhibitions are changed frequently in all 5 galleries to accommodate the needs of college courses and the public at large. Cameras are not permitted. The museum holds classes for students from all the colleges in the surrounding Connecticut River valley and accepts graduate students from the University of Massachusetts in its graduate program. Lectures and films are also offered periodically. Catalogs are published, usually for major exhibitions. The art library (10,000 volumes) is open for use on the premises. Parking nearby. Sept.–June, Mon.–Fri. 10–4:30; Sat., Sun. 1–5. Summer, Mon.–Fri. 10–12, 1–4; Aug., Mon.–Fri. by appointment. Free. (Take the Northampton exit [Rt. 9] off I-91 and go east for about 5 miles, 1 block from junction of Rts. 9 & 116.)

**University Gallery.** Fine Arts Center, University of Massachusetts, 01003 □ At the University Gallery of the University of Massachusetts, in the Fine Arts Center, which was built in 1970–1974, modern art predominates in the form of drawings, prints, and photographs, and some painting and sculpture. A special collection of modern American photography was given to the university by the class of 1928. Approximately 10 exhibits are mounted during the academic year. Cameras are permitted without flash attachments. The gallery sponsors lectures and concerts, which are held in conjunction with the art and music departments. Tours for groups can be arranged by appointment. Exhibition catalogs and posters are sold. Parking nearby. Free. (Campus is at north end of town. The center is mid-campus, off Massachusetts Ave.)

**ANDOVER:   Addison Gallery of American Art.** Phillips Academy, 01810 □ What is today a leading institution of learning began 200 years ago on a few acres of land in an old carpenter's shop. Phillips Academy was the first boarding school to be incorporated (1780) in the United States. The Addison Gallery of American Art opened in 1931, a gift of alumnus Thomas Cochran in memory of Keturah Addison Cobb. By that time, it was only one of some 160 buildings on a site of over 450 acres. The collection, as stipulated in the deed of gift, is restricted to American works (artists may be born in the United States or naturalized). This specialized collection ranges in time from the 17th century to the present, and includes paintings, sculpture, prints, drawings, photographs, and video. From the Colonial period are works by Allston, Copley, Morse, Stuart, and West. Among many 19th-century paintings are examples by Cole, Doughty, Eakins, Homer, Inness, La Farge, Ryder, Twachtman, and Whistler. Later artists include Calder, Lippold, Moholy-Nagy, Hans Hofmann, O'Keeffe, Pollock, Shahn, and Wyeth. Exhibitions change year round; the museum shows selections from the permanent collection on a rotating basis as well as exhibitions of artists in the Greater Boston and Greater Lawrence area. Exhibitions are also designed to cover a wide range of disciplines such as art history, communications. Request permission to photograph in the museum. The gallery sponsors a series of student-run seminars that cover many facets of the art world and include the showing of films. An Art Therapy Program has been developed through several years of group work with psychiatric patients and other groups with behavioral disorders. Guided tours are offered on a limited basis but not regularly. A variety of catalogs published by the museum are available. Limited parking on campus. Tues–Sat. 10–5; Sun. 2:30–5. Free. (On Rt. 28.)

**BOSTON:  Museum of Fine Arts.** 465 Huntington Ave., 02115 □ Of all the premier museums in the United States, the Boston Museum of Fine Arts is probably the one whose existence, more than others, is traceable to the enthusiasm of the general public—the pride of citizens for their city. It was founded in 1870 in a building on today's Copley Square. It took almost 40 years to finance (without the aid of public funds or large contributors) the huge Greek Revival edifice that opened in 1909. In the beginning, Boston scholars and merchants whose travels took them to the Orient brought objects back to America specifically to fill their museum. The Oriental collection became, and is today, one of the most wide-ranging and comprehensive of its kind in the world. The same process proved profitable to the museum in the field of classical antiquities—the cooperation between Harvard's archaeological department and the museum resulted in the beginnings of large and excellent Egyptian, Roman, and Greek collections, the Egyptian matching the best in the country. Another specialty of this all-around great museum is the American section, with Colonial and Federal furniture, 18th- and 19th-century paintings (including Gilbert Stuart's most famous unfinished George Washington), and a large collection of Paul Revere silver. Paintings from Europe range back to the 12th century, recording the accomplishments of artists up through the present; the Old Masters from Italy and Spain and the Northern school, French Impressionists, contemporary Americans and Europeans—each important school is represented by its masters. Particular beauties are "Bal à Bougival" by Renoir, Hals's "Portrait of a Man," Monet's "La Japonaise," and Cézanne's "Madame Cézanne in a Red Chair." The museum's treasures go further: among a large selection of textiles are French and Flemish tapestries, Coptic and Peruvian weavings, lace and embroideries from Europe and the Near East; a superb collection of prints going back to the 15th century; and musical instruments. The schedule of special exhibitions is continuous.

An art school offers classes for adults and children, graduate and undergraduate students. The department of education has lectures, seminars, and films for adult and school groups. Lecture series, gallery talks, concerts, dance programs are also offered by the museum. Catalogs accompany special exhibitions; the *Museum of Fine Arts Bulletin* is published quarterly, and a calendar of events, monthly. The vast library is available for inter-library loan and is open to the public for noncirculating use. A museum shop sells books, reproductions, cards and paper, and other gift items. In the spring of 1979 the museum opened a branch in the Faneuil Hall Marketplace in downtown Boston. A street-level entrance to the new annex, which occupies 12,000 square feet of the upper story of the South Market Building, makes portions of the museum's wonderful collections easily accessible to the millions of people who come here each year. Tues. 10–9; Wed.–Sun. 10–5. Admission $2.50 for adults, $1.50 for students with ID and senior citizens; free on Fri. for senior citizens and every day for children under 16. Free Tues. 5–9; Sun. 10–1.

**Isabella Stewart Gardner Museum.** 280 The Fenway. Mailing address: 2 Palace Rd., 02115 □ Isabella Stewart Gardner of New York and Boston bought her first Old Master painting, a Madonna by Francisco de Zurbarán, in Seville in 1888, thus beginning the collection that is now housed in the museum that bears her name. And well it should: she bought the land in the Fens in 1898; traveled to Europe to choose the columns, capitals, arches, ironwork, fireplaces, staircases, and fountains to be incorporated into the new building—Fenway Court; made certain that her preference for the Italian Renaissance and her vision of the house as a 15th-century Venetian palace, with galleries opening onto a flowering courtyard, was implemented; and supervised every detail of the construction. The building was finished in 1902, and Mrs. Gardner lived there until her death in 1924, having placed the paintings, arranged the furniture, and positioned the flowers. The museum remains today, according to her stated wishes, in its original superb arrangement, 3 stories of Venetian arches overlooking a lushly planted, inside courtyard. Long before all this took place, Mrs. Gardner, in her efforts at self-improvement, had met a young student named Bernard Berenson in one of Professor Charles Eliot Norton's art history classes. Berenson graduated from Harvard in 1887 and was helped to go abroad by his new friend. It was not long after this that Mrs. Gardner began to rely on Berenson's advice and assistance in acquiring important works of art. The resulting collection consists of about 290 paintings, 280 pieces of sculpture, 60 drawings and 130 prints, 460 pieces of furniture, 250 textiles, 240 objects of ceramic and glass, 350 other objects, and manuscripts and rare books. Of particular importance is the selection of Italian Renaissance paintings and sculpture and the 17th-century Dutch paintings, among them Titian's "The Rape of Europa," 2 paintings by Raphael, 4 by Rembrandt, including a landscape and a self-portrait, drawings by Michelangelo, "The Concert" by Vermeer, 2 Holbeins, and a Rubens. In addition, and from other periods, are "El Jaleo" by John Singer Sargent (hung in a Spanish setting); Sargent's controversial "Portrait of Mrs. Gardner," dominating a Gothic room; and portraits by Degas and Manet. The collection has been called "the finest . . . of its compact size in the world." The museum is never-changing—as stipulated by Mrs. Gardner—except for the flowers in the courtyard, which are freshened seasonally. Cameras are permitted without flashes or tripods.

Concerts are held Tuesday evenings at 8, Thursday and Sunday afternoons at 4. A general tour is offered on Thursdays at 2:30; acoustiguides are also available. Group tours can be arranged for in advance. The museum's list of publications ranges from a large general descriptive catalog to smaller guides and more specific catalogs, all of which are available at the sales desk. Wed.–Sun. 1–5:30; Tues. 1–9:30. Admission voluntary; $1 per person is suggested. (Take Huntington Ave. to The Fenway.)

**Institute of Contemporary Art.** 955 Boylston St., 02115 ☐ The Institute of Contemporary Art, in the center of Boston and a block from the cluster of art galleries on Newbury Street, was founded in 1936 by architect Nathaniel Saltonstall with a group of people interested in bringing traveling contemporary art exhibitions to Boston. With no permanent collection, the institute moved many times until it came to its present Romanesque home. Here, traveling exhibits of 20th-century art—painting, sculpture, video, performance, and crafts—remain in place for 6 to 8 weeks, then move on. Cameras without flashes are permitted. The institute serves the public by its offerings of survey courses, seminars, lectures, and concerts. Tours are conducted every Wednesday afternoon at 2; appointments can be made in advance for tours at other times. The library is open only by special permission. A bimonthly newsletter and exhibition catalogs are published here and are available in the shop, where posters, cards and jewelry are also sold. A restaurant in the building serves Russian cuisine and wine and liquor. Garage is across the street. Tues.–Sat. 10–5; Sun. 12–5; Wed. 10–9. Admission $1, students and children under 12, 50¢. Wed. 2–9, free. (At Massachusetts Ave., opposite Prudential Center.)

**Museum of the National Center of Afro-American Artists.** 300 Walnut Ave., Roxbury, 02119 ☐ The Museum of the National Center of Afro-American Artists was founded in 1969 as a component of its namesake organization and it was developed in cooperation with the Museum of Fine Arts in Boston to collect, present, and criticize art by black Americans, Africans, and West Indians. The collection consists of over 170 African objects, 234 Afro-American paintings, prints, and photographs.

Six to 8 exhibitions are mounted annually, each lasting about 3 weeks. Cameras are not permitted. The museum is associated with the Elma Lewis School of Fine Arts. Concerts, lectures, and films are held on the premises; a Mobile Museum brings the collection to other communities. Guided tours can be arranged. Catalogs, exhibition brochures, a directory, and an occasional journal are among the published materials available from the museum. A slide collection of more than 1,500 reproductions of African, West Indian, and Afro-American works is available for study. Parking nearby. Tues.–Sat. 10–5; Sun. 12–5. Free.

**BROCKTON:     Brockton Art Center—Fuller Memorial.** Oak St., 02401 ☐ In 1969 the Brockton Art Center—Fuller Memorial was opened "in honor of the Fuller family." Geologist and writer Myron F. Fuller was instrumental in achieving this with a $1 million trust left for the purpose. The contemporary structure, 3 miles from downtown Brockton, stands at the outskirts of a 700-acre park. A permanent collection specializes in 19th-century American painting (works by Parrish, Goodwin, Eakins, Tarbell, and the like), and Sandwich glass (a fine collection was recently acquired). Six changing exhibits per year include crafts, photography, Boston painting and sculpture, printmaking, items from the permanent collection, and a 19th-century exhibit. Written permission is needed for the use of cameras. The museum school has 4 sessions during the year with classes in painting, printmaking, photography, weaving, sculpture, and crafts. Lectures and concerts are scheduled regularly. A docent training program, school orientation talks, and programs for "special needs" students are also part of the center's educational activities. Guided tours must be booked in advance. Several catalogs and books published by the center are for sale, together with original works by local craftspeople, at the museum shop. The art reference library is open to members only. Parking on site. Tues.–Sun. 1–5; Thurs. 1–10. Admission $1 for adults, free for children under 16. (From Rt. 24 south, exit at "Mile 33" and take the first right onto Oak St. The center is 1 mile down Oak, on the left.)

**CAMBRIDGE:     Busch-Reisinger Museum.** 29 Kirkland St., 02138 ☐ Harvard University has two fine art museums; the Busch-Reisinger Museum is one, and is unique in the United States. It was founded in 1901 by Dr. Kuno Francke, Professor of German Art and Culture, to house a collection of plaster cast reproductions of German sculpture, architecture, and decorative arts. Thirty years later, under the curatorship of Professor Charles L. Kuhn, the museum began acquiring original works of art. In the beginning the collection was housed in the basement of Rogers Gymnasium. By 1917, Harvard had its Busch-Reisinger Museum, designed by

German architect German Bestelmeyer, with a Baroque exterior and interior spaces that went from Romanesque to Gothic to Renaissance in style. Northern and central European art (German, Swiss, Austrian, Netherlandish) is housed here. The strength of the collection is in German Expressionist art, and art from the Bauhaus (this collection from the school that Walter Gropius founded in Weimar in 1919 is the largest outside Germany). Also included are archives of Gropius and Lyonel Feininger (together with other distinguished artists, he taught at the Bauhaus). Among the works that stand out are "St. Jerome" by Joos van Cleve; "Self-Portrait with Tuxedo" by Max Beckmann; Paul Klee's "Landscape Wagon"; "Jocular Sounds" by Wassily Kandinsky; a triptych, "Convalescence of a Woman," by Erich Heckel; "Light Space Modulator," a sculpture by Moholy-Nagy (he founded a New Bauhaus in Chicago in 1937); and "Pear Trees" by Gustave Klimt. The museum has 4 to 5 special exhibitions a year including traveling exhibitions and borrowed works. Cameras can be used only by special permission.

The museum sponsors gallery talks and special lectures for each exhibit; a Thursday Noon Recital Series features organ music, chamber groups, and choral singers. Tours in English and in German are offered by appointment. Several catalogs published here can be purchased at the sales desk; the museum also publishes a newsletter for members. Parking on the street around the museum. Mon.–Sat. 9–4:45; closed Sat. during July & Aug., national holidays. Free. (From Harvard Square, proceed north to the underpass and Cambridge St.; turn left on Quincy St. The museum is at the intersection of Quincy & Kirkland.)

**Fogg Art Museum.** 32 Quincy St., Harvard University, 02138 ☐ It was over 250 years after its founding that Harvard University got its William Hayes Fogg Art Museum. It began in Hunt Hall in 1895 and moved to its present building in 1927. And while Paul J. Sachs was teaching his Harvard students (many of whom became directors of the country's major museums) to be elitist in the running of their museums (as opposed to the populism of John Cotton Dana at the Newark Museum), the Fogg Museum was growing. Today its holdings span the continents and range from prehistory to modern times. A gift from Harvard graduate Grenville Winthrop in 1943 of more than 3,500 objects expanded the range of the museum significantly. Included in this gift were a magnificent collection of Chinese jades—said to be one of the great such collections in the world—and 18th- and 19th-century English and French drawings. The French drawings, in fact, enriched the already extensive 19th-century collection left to the museum by Sachs. As for the museum's diversity: Antiquities from Egypt can be seen here; sculptures from Persepolis; Greek and Roman sculpture and ancient coins; and from Asia, in addition to the jades, Chinese sculpture, painting, prints, and bronzes, Cambodian sculpture, a Japanese art collection. From Europe, there are Old Master Italian, Flemish, and Spanish paintings, later works from the 17th to 19th centuries (the great Impressionists included). America's paintings and sculpture, silver and Wedgwood, are here as well, and the contemporaries, represented by such as Kline, de Kooning, and Pollock, among others. A distinguished amalgam of the world's creative product, put together in a scholarly way for the benefit of all, but never losing sight, in the tradition of Sachs, of the collection's value as an aid to learning. Special exhibitions are scheduled.

Guided tours, lectures, gallery talks, are sponsored by the museum, which also provides a rigorous educational program for Harvard undergraduates and graduate students. Publications include an annual report, a quarterly newsletter, and exhibition catalogs. The library (140,000 volumes), one of the distingushed fine arts reference resources in the world, can be used by the public on special request only. Catalogs and cards are for sale. Mon.–Sat. 9–5; Sun. 2–5; closed Sat., Sun. July–Labor Day. Free.

**CONCORD:   Concord Art Association.** 15 Lexington Rd., 01742 ☐ By Concord standards, the 1720 house used by the Concord Art Association is relatively young—almost 100 years younger than the town itself. Not surprisingly, in a town so proud of its history, the art association has collected art out of America's and Massachusetts's past and put it on display: early portraits, paintings, sculpture, prints, miniatures, and bronzes. Temporary exhibits include an annual summer display of art relating to the American Revolution; contemporary crafts are also shown periodically. Lectures are open to the public, and competitions are held for artists. An attractive sculpture garden is made more inviting by a waterfall. Tues.–Sat. 11–4:30; Sun. 2–4:30. Admission 50¢.

**DUXBURY:   Art Complex Museum.** 189 Alden St. Mailing address: Box 1411, 02332 ☐ The undulating contours of both Massachusetts Bay and the surrounding countryside of Duxbury—the bay at its door, the hills at its back—are reflected in the curves of the Art Complex Museum, a contemporary structure of glass and wood with a roof line that curls and arches like the waves of the bay and the rolling hills of Massachusetts shore country. It was built in 1971 from a design by Ture Bengtz on 11 acres of John Alden Woods (it was in Duxbury that John and Priscilla are said to have settled). The collection consists of Oriental, European, and American paintings, drawings, prints, ceramics, and glass and a fine group of Shaker furniture and artifacts. Special exhibits are mounted approximately 6 times a year; in an authentic Japanese tea house located on the grounds, tea ceremonies are demonstrated during the summer months. Cameras are permitted by request; no flashes or tripods. The museum sponsors lectures and concerts and provides tours upon request. The library (1,500 volumes), with a particularly good Japanese section, is open to the public. *The Lithographs of Ture Bengtz* was published in 1978. Parking on the grounds. Fri., Sat., Sun. 2–5; other times by special arrangement. Free. (Going north to Boston, make a right turn off Rt. 3 at exit 34 [Rt. 3A]. It runs into Alden St. in Duxbury. Going south from Boston on Rt. 3, take a left at exit 33 [route 14] to Duxbury.)

**FITCHBURG: Fitchburg Art Museum.** Merriam Pkwy., 01420 ☐ The Fitchburg Art Museum, begun in 1925 with a bequest by Eleanor A. Norcross, houses a collection of 19th-century American paintings, drawings and prints, some French provincial furniture, and other decorative art objects such as silver, ceramics, china, and textiles. Changing exhibitions include a regional competition, contemporary fine arts and crafts, and loans. Classes are held from October to June; lectures and demonstrations are also scheduled. An annual report and catalogs are published. The library is open for use on the premises, and there is a gift shop. Sept.–June, Tues.–Sat. 9–5; Sun. 2–5. Free.

**FRAMINGHAM: Danforth Museum.** 123 Union Ave., 01701 ☐ Within the time frame familiar to residents of Framingham (this is an old New England town) the Danforth Museum is but an infant. It was organized by citizens of the South Middlesex area (12 towns west of Boston) in 1973 and opened to the public in 1975 as a regional fine arts museum. Its home is a former school building, built in 1914 in the Chicago Beaux Arts tradition. It began without a permanent collection, but in the few years since its opening it has acquired by purchase and donation an eclectic selection of some 500 works of art. Ever expanding, the present collection includes Old Master and contemporary prints and turn-of-the-century American landscapes, displayed in 6 galleries. There are also changing exhibits that last from 3 to 10 months. Cameras can be used only by special permission. A wide range of fine arts and crafts classes (including a summer session) are offered to both adults and children in large studio-classrooms. School programs, lectures, films, and a docent program are among the special activities of the museum. Facilities include an art library available for use by special permission and a museum shop that sells handcrafted jewelry, ceramics, original prints, cards, books, and museum-published exhibition catalogs. Guided tours (Spanish is available) can be arranged by appointment. Parking possible in front of the museum. Wed.–Sun. 1–4:30. Free. (Rt. 9 goes to Framingham Center. Go to Main St. & Union Ave.)

**GLOUCESTER: Hammond Museum, Inc.** 80 Hesperus Ave., 01930 ☐ The Middle Ages are brought to life in this fishing town by the sea. The Hammond Museum was built in the tradition of a medieval castle by inventor John Hays Hammond, Jr., who lived there looking out over the snug harbor of Gloucester and the threatening tides beyond that wrecked the *Hesperus.* In it he gathered around him the paraphernalia of 12th-, 13th-, and 14th-century Western Europe: furniture, tapestries, sculpture, and stained glass. Tours, lectures, and classes are held here, but most impressive are the concerts given by visiting artists on the huge 8,000-pipe organ. The museum publishes a catalog, a guidebook, and a cookbook. There is a gift shop and a coffee shop for snacks. Late spring, summer, and early fall Mon.–Sat. 10–3:30; late fall, winter, and early spring Mon.–Sat., tours 11–2; Sun. 1:30–4. Admission $2.50 for adults, $1 for children. (5 miles south of Gloucester, 2 miles south of Rt. 127, which leads to Gloucester.)

**HARVARD:   Fruitlands Museums.** Prospect Hill Rd., 01451 ☐ Amos Bronson Alcott, Louisa May's father, attempted to found a utopian colony, based on his lofty Transcendental philosophy, on the land where now stands the Fruitlands Museums. In 1844 Fruitlands was abandoned only months after it had begun, the practical necessities of living having been completely ignored by its idealistic and brilliant leader. What remains in the 1750 farmhouse today recalls Alcott's magnetism—memorabilia of his close relationship with Emerson, Thoreau, and Margaret Fuller. Nearby is a Shaker house (built in 1794) with Shaker arts and crafts, and an American Indian museum with artifacts and dioramas. The Picture Gallery houses a fine collection of Hudson River school landscapes and primitive portraits by itinerant (and anonymous) artists. There is also a library (8,000 volumes, pamphlets, and manuscripts) that focuses on the Transcendental movement, the American Indian, American painting, and Shaker history, open upon request. June–Sept., Tues.–Sun. 1–5. Admission $1 for adults, 25¢ for children. (Harvard is about 10 miles east of Leominster on SR 2.)

**LINCOLN:   De Cordova Museum.** Sandy Pond Rd., 01773 ☐ In one of Boston's suburbs that borders Thoreau's Walden Pond and abuts the historic towns of Concord and Lexington stands the castlelike structure that was once the home of Julian de Cordova, a wealthy merchant and world traveler. At his death in 1945, de Cordova left the castle and its contents, and the surrounding 33 landscaped acres, to the town. His collection was liquidated and the museum's permanent collection is on loan and in storage. It is rarely on view, but included in it are some 600 objects among which are works by major artists such as Kline, Aronson, Levine, and Baskin. Today the Norman château, with gallery space provided by a renovation in 1945 (undertaken by the sixth John Quincy Adams), mounts bimonthly temporary exhibits primarily concerned with contemporary

American art, with special emphasis on works by New England artists. Permission is needed for cameras. The museum offers over 125 classes, 3 times per year. Lectures and film series are held concurrently with exhibits whenever possible. Concert series are programmed during the summer months in the outdoor amphitheater (seats 1,000). A Learning Through Art outreach program sends docents into elementary schools to lecture on art history and appreciation. Tours can be scheduled 2 or 3 weeks in advance. Catalogs are published here for each exhibit; the museum also has published a 2-volume catalog of the permanent collection and *Life and Mind of Julian de Cordova*. All are sold at the museum desk. The art library (1,200 volumes) is open to scholars with special permission. Parking on the grounds. Tues.-Fri. 10-5; Sat. 12-5; Sun. 1:30-5. Admission $1.50 for adults, 50¢ for children. (From Rt. 128, take exit 47W [Trapelo Rd.] toward Lincoln. At the center of Lincoln, Trapelo Rd. becomes Sandy Pond Rd.; the museum is approximately 1 mile from there, on the right side.)

**LOWELL: Lowell Art Assocation.** 243 Worthen St., 01852 ☐ Whistler's mother gave birth to her famous son here, and the Lowell Art Association, like a surrogate mother, strives to preserve his memory. It exhibits works pertaining to his life and art, together with some contemporary paintings. Art classes and lectures are held here; guided tours and/or gallery talks can be arranged by appointment. Concerts, arts festivals and competitions, films, and plays are also presented. A library (300 volumes) can be used on the premises. Tues.-Sun. 2-4:30. Free. (From US 3 north, turn right onto Lowell connector, left onto Gorham St. and follow it to a dead end; go left onto Merrimack St., then left again onto Worthen.)

**MALDEN: Malden Public Library.** 36 Salem St., 02148 ☐ Five miles north of Boston—you can get there by subway—is Malden, where the building used as a public library was also intended, by its donor, to be used as an art gallery. And so it is. Elisha Slade Converse and his wife gave this Romanesque building to the city of Malden in memory of their son Frank Eugene. It was built in 1885; additions in 1896 and 1915 have been used as 2 main exhibition galleries. The collection of paintings here is eclectic, with some well-known artists' work displayed among some less familiar—Copley, Strain, Homer, Macknight, J. M. W. Turner, Pieters, Inness, and Constable. Exhibits are changed, but not on a regular basis, throughout the year. Cameras by special permission only. Afternoon concerts are held during the winter on the first Sunday of every month. Six programs are scheduled in a lecture series during the year. A recording center for the blind employs volunteer readers. A catalog, *Thirty Paintings in the Malden Collection,* can be purchased, as well as slides and notepaper. Municipal parking within walking distance. Mon.–Thurs. 9–9; Fri. & Sat. 9–6; closed holidays & summer Saturdays. (Salem St. is Rt. 60 in Malden. Or by rapid transit, get off MBTA [subway from Boston] at Malden Center.)

**NORTHAMPTON: Smith College Museum of Art.** Elm St. at Bedford Terrace, 01063 ☐ The Smith College Museum of Art is housed in one of the newer buildings in the Connecticut River valley. It looks out on Elm Street, the paradigm of a tranquil, tree-lined residential avenue in a model middle-sized New England town. The modern brick and glass double building, divided by a sculpture courtyard and situated at the edge of the Smith College campus, does not intrude on the quiet early American street setting. Rather it folds its modernity inward to the court, where glass and mirrors reflect and cast light on the sculpture and potted trees that they surround. The first president of Smith, L. Clark Seelye, began the college art collection in 1879 with the purchase from Thomas Eakins of one of his smaller canvases entitled "In Grandmother's Time." The acquisition of a solely American collection his object, Seelye proceeded to visit the studios of contemporary artists—Hassam, Inness, Ryder, Homer—and to buy their paintings. The resulting collection was—and still is—distinguished, but lacked the variety of place and time. By 1914, with the deepening influence of the new (1905) young Professor of History and Interpretation of Art Alfred Vance Churchill, and the stated intention of artist and teacher Dwight Tryon to leave his estate to the college, the decision was made to expand the collection to include European art. A small Rodin bronze was the first acquisition; then came a flood of paintings that described the emergence of modern art after the French Revolution. Today the museum's holdings include art from all periods of history, but its strength and chief claim to excellence are in its works by French masters of the 19th and 20th centuries. Among these, the museum takes particular pride in Courbet's "Toilette de la Mariée" and in "Jephtha's Daughter" by Degas. Added to these two are paintings by Bonnard ("Paysage du Midi"), Monet ("Seine at Bougival"), Corot ("Jumièges"), Cézanne ("La Route tournante à La Roche-Guyon"), and Americans Hassam ("Union Square in Spring"), Ryder ("Perrette"), and Eakins ("Mrs. Edith Mahon"), among a battery of others. Early 20th-century works include Picassos, a Gris, a Tanguy, and "Rolling Power" by Sheeler. Later 20th-century work is represented by Stella ("Damascus Gate, Stretch Variation III"), Kline, Arp, Nevelson, and many more. A print and drawing section extends the time range of the museum back to Rembrandt, and a Chinese jade collection back much further, to the Shang and Chou dynasties. Special exhibits are scheduled throughout the year.

The activities of the museum focus on its teaching responsibilities to the college. Guided tours and occasional gallery talks are available. Catalogs are published with special exhibitions; these and postcards are sold. The library is open for use by scholars. Parking on Elm Street in front of the museum. Tues.–Sat. 11–4:30; Sun. 2–4:30; summer by appointment. Free. (From I-91 take Rt. 9 into Northampton.)

**NORTON: Watson Gallery.** Wheaton College, 02766 ☐ The Watson Gallery at Wheaton College disclaims status as a museum, although it has an interesting and diverse permanent collection. Housed here in the Watson Fine Arts Center are European and American paintings from the 18th to the 20th centuries, with emphasis on the 19th (works by Inness, Gignoux, Melchers, Vedder, A. W. Dow, Stevens, William Merritt Chase, Walter and Winkworth Gay, and Bruce Crane); prints in all mediums ranging from the 16th century to the present with, again, emphasis on the 19th and 20th centuries (works by Rembrandt, Whistler, Le Corbusier, and other European, American, and Japanese masters); drawings, primarily contemporary; Roman and Etruscan bronzes, glass, and alabaster; American 18th- and 19th-century glass; and Greek coins from the Newell bequest. Like most college galleries, only parts of the collection can be shown at one time; exhibitions are changed regularly. Cameras are permitted but not flashbulbs. The gallery functions in conjunction with the college; the fine arts library is in the Watson Fine Arts Center. Lectures that relate to the new exhibitions are often held. Catalogs of the collection are sold. Tours can be arranged in advance. Several visitors' parking lots nearby. Open during academic year Mon., Tues., Thurs.–Sun. 1–5; Wed. 10–12, 2–4; closed college vacation periods. Other times by appointment. Free.

**PITTSFIELD: Berkshire Museum.** 39 South St., 01201 ☐ Zenas Crane, the maker of paper for United States currency, founded the Berkshire Museum in 1903. It is Berkshire County's art, science, and local history museum. Its collection of Old Master paintings is impressive, as is that of early American portraits and of paintings by artists of the Hudson River school. A section is devoted to Far Eastern art and another to a large collection of American and English silver. There is a Berkshire County Historical room and rooms devoted to minerals, biology, animals, birds, and man. Among the Old Masters are works by Juan Pons ("Adoration of the Magi"), de Hooch ("The Music Party"), Van Dyck ("Duke of Richmond"), Raeburn ("Lady Baird"), Rubens ("Vision of St. Ignatius"), Lawrence ("Lady Burdett"), and Reynolds. Other highlights are works by Inness ("Leeds in the Catskills"), Blakelock ("Rocky Mountains"), Edward Moran ("City and Harbor of New York"), Frederick Church ("Valley of the Santa Ysabel"), Bierstadt ("Giant Redwoods of California"),

Charles Willson Peale ("Portrait of General David Forman"), Stuart ("Portrait of Bryant Parrott Tilden"), Calder ("Arc and the Quadrant"), Rodin ("Head of a Youth"), and Epstein ("Meum II"). Three special exhibits and a photo exhibit are scheduled each month. Cameras are permitted for the permanent collection only. The museum holds art classes throughout the year. In recent years, a series of travel lectures has been a great success. School enrichment programs include nature and conservation activities for children. Tours are available on request. A booklet on the museum is available at a shop which also offers books, jewelry, prints, and postcards. A small art and science library (2,000 volumes) is open to the public. Park across the street. Tues.–Sat. 10–5; Sun. 2–5. Also open Mon. during July & Aug. Free; voluntary contributions accepted. (In center of town on South St., which is US 7.)

**PROVINCETOWN: Provincetown Art Association and Museum.** 460 Commercial St., 02657 ☐ At the tip of Cape Cod the world of pleasure—of sun and sand and surf—and the hard, uncompromising world of commercial fishing merge with the world of art. The latter, in the Provincetown of 1914, was concentrated in the summer art classes of Charles W. Hawthorne, E. Ambrose Webster, and William F. Halsall, leaders of the emerging Provincetown Art Association, which grew quickly when artists' retreats in Europe were closed off by the war. By 1921 a new museum was being built which, until 1927, exhibited primarily conservative works by the conservative artists who were prominent at the time. The modernists filtered in at the end of the decade and were finally permitted an exhibition of their own. The Depression of the 1930s and World War II served to slow down the growth of the association, but in 1945, Provincetown again became alive with both pleasure seekers and artists. The Colonial building bulged and was enlaged thrice. Today the collection consists primarily of 20th-century New England artists, particularly works representative of the Hawthorne school (Charles Hawthorne's school of painting opened here in 1899). Some of those whose works appear here are Milton Avery, Marsden Hartley, Edwin Dickinson, William Merritt Chase, Ross Moffett, Karl Knaths, Bud Hopkins, Robert Motherwell, Chaim Gross, and Charles W. Hawthorne. A regular schedule of exhibitions is mounted; emphasis is placed on the summer season when there may be as many as 4 exhibitions running concurrently. Cameras are permitted. The museum's activities include concerts and lectures (many given by musicians and authors who are summer residents here). Educational programs are currently in development stages. Catalogs accompany each exhibit. A library (500 volumes) is open for use by appointment, and a sales desk offers books, prints, and postcards relevant to New England (particularly Provincetown) artists. Parking nearby. Tues.–Sat. 11–2:30, 7–11; Sun. 12–7. Admission 50¢ for adults, children free.

**SALEM: Peabody Museum of Salem.** 161 Essex St., East India Square, 01970 ☐ An overwhelming sense of history in Salem is, naturally, reflected in the Peabody Museum. The seat of government of the Massachusetts Bay Colony was located in this city; here the infamous witchcraft trials took place; and here ships came bearing treasures from all over the world; Nathaniel Hawthorne was born here and took many of his stories and novels from the characters and events he saw every day. The museum was founded in 1799 to exhibit "Natural and Artificial Curiosities" from around the world. Today the 3 areas covered by the museum are American maritime history, ethnology of non-European peoples (Pacific Islands, Japan, and China), and natural history of Essex County. But scattered throughout the maritime and ethnological collections are numerous pieces of artistic merit: Fitz Hugh Lane paintings, for example; a Copley portrait of Sarah Irving; two Sargent portraits; the Roux family marine paintings (about 125); Robert Salmon paintings; the George Chinnery collection of paintings and drawings (about 300); and more. Events and exhibits are scheduled continually throughout the year. Cameras can be used with special permission. The museum holds 5 or 6 evening lectures a year and some daytime courses. Tours are available by reservation. The library (100,000 volumes covering the 3 departments of the museum) is open to the public for a small fee. A museum shop offers reproductions, books, jewelry, postcards, and Oriental objects. Parking nearby. Mon.–Sat. 9–5; Sun. & holidays 1–5; closed Thanksgiving, Christmas, Jan. 1. Admission $1.50 for adults, 75¢ for children. (From Rt. 128 or 1A take Rt. 114 to Salem.)

**SOUTH HADLEY: Mount Holyoke College Art Museum.** 01075 ☐ Mount Holyoke College is yet another gem in the diadem of college campuses that crowns the contoured landscape of the Connecticut River valley. The art collection was begun here in 1876—indeed, it is one of the oldest college collections in the country—and now, a great deal larger, it is housed in a contemporary building (a 2-story teaching facility standing over a one-story museum) dedicated in 1971. Asian art, 19th-century American painting, classical objects, and Italian early Renaissance panel paintings are the high points of this collection. Among the 19th-century Americans are Bierstadt ("Hetch Hetchie Cañon"), Inness ("Conway Meadows"), and Prendergast ("Festival Day, Venice"). There is also a 5th-century B.C. Greek bronze statuette and an excellent group of Chinese paintings. Temporary exhibits occur during the academic year (usually about 5 or 6); occasionally a summer exhibit is mounted as well. Cameras are not permitted.

Classes can be taken only within the framework of the college. However, frequent art department lectures are open to the public. A docent training program is limited to invited persons. An Art Goes to School program provides student lecturers to grade schools and school visits to the museum. Tours must be arranged in advance; multilingual guides can be obtained. Publications include exhibition notices, catalogs (available at a sales desk), and a newsletter. The art building also houses the art library, which is open to the public. Parking nearby. Open academic year Mon.-Fri. 11-5, Sat. & Sun. 1-5; closed during academic holidays. Summer, Mon.-Fri. 1-4. Free. (The college is 5 miles north of Holyoke and 12 miles north of Springfield on Rt. 116. From I-91, exit at Rt. 202 [Holyoke-South Hadley] and proceed east through Holyoke; take the South Hadley Center-Amherst exit to Rt. 116 north.)

**SPRINGFIELD:   George Walter Vincent Smith Art Museum.** 222 State St., 01103 ☐ In the industrial and business complex of Springfield there is a "Quadrangle" of museums facing a grassy common on State Street, which is part of the historic Boston Post Road. George Walter Vincent Smith (1832-1923) was born in New York, retired at the age of 35, and after marrying Belle Townsley, settled in Springfield to spend the rest of his days in the pursuit of art, both as patron and collector. In 1889, he offered his and his wife's collections to the City Library Association. Six years later the present Italian Renaissance building, erected specifically to exhibit the Smith collections, was opened to the public. Its holdings in 19th-century American paintings and Japanese and Chinese decorative arts—Japanese arms and armor, jades, ivories, ceramics, lacquers, illuminated manuscripts, and metalwork—are the pride of this museum. However, there are also fine examples of European painting, furniture, cloisonné, and sculpture, and casts of ancient and Renaissance sculptures. Among the highlights are works by Bierstadt, Cole, Gifford, Inness, and Kensett. "Scene in the Catskills, 1851" by Frederick Church is a star. Of special interest is a rare 16th-century Japanese helmet made by Miochin Nobuiye; several exceptional Japanese pieces are now on loan to the Smithsonian Institution. Approximately 6 temporary exhibits are mounted each year. Annual exhibits include a juried national exhibit of the Springfield Art League, the museum student exhibit, and an exhibit of contemporary Massachusetts artists. Cameras may be used with special permission.

The museum offers studio art classes for adults and children and art history seminars for adults; lectures and concerts; plays and film workshops; educational grants; guided tours for groups of 10 or more (Tues.-Fri. 9-4, Sat. & Sun. 2-4) arranged in advance; internships. Publications relating to the collections are available; the library, also pertaining to the collection, is open by appointment only. Tues.-Sat. 1-5; Sun. 2-5. Free. (From I-91, take exit 91 [Broad St.]; go right at Union St., left at Maple, cross lights at State to Chestnut; Quadrangle is first right. From Mass.

Tpke., take Springfield exit to I-291 from which exit at Chestnut St.; go right at IBM building, left at Dwight St.; at State St. follow sign to Chestnut St. North, then bear left onto Maple, cross lights at State to Chestnut.)

**Museum of Fine Arts.** 49 Chestnut St., 01103 ☐ Another among the group of buildings that form Springfield's Museum Center—the "Quadrangle"— at Chestnut and State, is the Museum of Fine Arts, established in 1933. Eighteen galleries are clustered around a tapestry court, one wall of which is the facade of a 16th-century Spanish palace. Each gallery is devoted to a style, a period, an art form—there is a Gothic gallery and a Renaissance gallery, one for Venetian art, one for Dutch, and one for Flemish. The English, Americans, and French also have their own places. Winslow Homer's "Promenade on the Beach" can be seen here, and in contrast, the fantastic "Historic Monument of the American Republic" by Erastus Salisbury Field; works by Monet, Gauguin, and Pissarro, and a portrait by Delacroix are other choice samplings. The Orient is displayed impressively: Collections from China include ceramics and bronzes that range from the Neolithic age to the 19th century; from Japan there are woodblock prints and from Persia, miniatures, the oldest of which are from the 10th century. The print collection also spans a broad range of time and styles, from Old Masters to moderns. There are always special exhibits. The education department sponsors lectures, films, concerts, and audiovisual programs, a docent program, and an outreach program in the schools. Tours can be oriented to the particular age group involved. The museum publishes a *Museum Handbook,* catalogs, and a bimonthly bulletin. Its library (5,000 volumes on Oriental art) is available for use on the premises. Tues.–Sat. 1–5; Sun. 2–5. Free.

**STOCKBRIDGE: Chesterwood.** Mailing address: Box 248, 01262 ☐ Chesterwood is the summer estate of Daniel Chester French (1850–1931), the sculptor of the "Seated Lincoln" in the Lincoln Memorial and the "Minute Man" at Concord. He called this idyllic setting—120 acres in the Berkshire hills near Stockbridge—"heaven." French's architect friend Henry Bacon (who later designed the Lincoln Memorial) planned the stylized summer studio to the artist's requirements, which included northern light, 22-foot-high double doors, and a flatcar on railroad tracks to move large sculptures in and out of the building. The 2-story Georgian Revival house, also designed by Bacon, was built in 1900–1901. A Barn Sculpture Gallery on the estate is the 150-year-old barn that French found on the property when he bought it. A formal garden and a nature trail designed by French adjoin the studio. In this complex, now a property of the National Trust for Historic Preservation, are assembled French's work, over 500 plaster casts, marble and bronze statues, and plastilene models, including several casts and models of various versions of the "Seated Lincoln" and sketches and working models of some other famous works— "Alma Mater" (Low Library at Columbia University); "Brooklyn" and "Manhattan" (Manhattan Bridge in New York); and the Dupont Memorial Fountain (Washington, D.C.). In addition, works by Ball, Longman, Lukeman, Saint-Gaudens, and Margaret French Cresson (French's daughter) are on view, as well as French's tools, equipment, and drawings. Seasonal exhibitions pertain to sculpture, history of the estate, and historic preservation. Cameras are permitted.

The museum sponsors an antique car show; sculpture demonstrations; a sculptor-in-residence program; a Washington intern program; and an educational program for undergraduates of Elmira College in its Field Experience Program. Specially designed tours for schoolchildren are available as well as the regular tours scheduled every half hour. *Daniel Chester French: An American Sculptor* was published here and can be bought at a museum shop that offers other books, reproductions, clothing, postcards, and posters for sale. The library (5,000 volumes) is available to the public by appointment. Parking nearby. May 1–Oct. 31 daily 10–5. Admission $2 for adults; $1 for children and senior citizens; group rates (10 or more) $1.60; school tours 25¢ per student. (Follow signs from the west end of Main St. in Stockbridge; 2 miles northwest on Rt. 102; turn left on Rt. 183, drive 1 mile to fork in road; turn right, go 75 yards, turn left, continue ½ mile.)

**The Old Corner House: Norman Rockwell Museum.** Main St., 01262 ☐
The Dwights of Stockbridge built their family home in about 1790, less than 60 years after white settlers had established a mission here and bought the surrounding land from the Stockbridge Indians. In 1967 this historic Federal Colonial-style building with hip roof, 2 center chimneys, 5 bays, and a beautiful pilastered doorway was saved from demolition for use as a historical museum. When that use proved impossible, Norman Rockwell's paintings were offered to the directors as an exhibit. And so, in 1967 The Old Corner House opened as the Norman Rockwell Museum. About 150 Rockwell paintings, drawings, and sketches are housed under this historic roof, tracing his work from the early 1900s when he began, to his last large painting, which he did in 1971. Many of his *Saturday Evening Post* cover paintings are on view as well as a number of portraits including "Self-Portrait" and the well-known "Four Freedoms," done to aid the war effort during World War II. Exhibits change seasonally. Cameras are not permitted. Lectures on American painting and folk art are offered occasionally, and the museum sponsors a local group of singers who perform in a series of concerts each winter. Guided tours are available at any time as needed. The museum shop stocks limited edition prints, books, and other

items related to Rockwell. Parking possible on the street. Daily except Tues. 10–5; closed Thanksgiving, Christmas, Jan. 1, and 2 weeks in late Jan. Admission $1 for adults; 25¢ for children to 12; special rates for school groups. (4 miles from exit 2 of the Mass. Tpke. via Rt. 102.)

**TYRINGHAM: Tyringham Galleries.** Tyringham Rd., 01264 ☐ The building that houses the Tyringham Galleries (the Gingerbread House) is nothing if it is not unique—unless it was actually baked in an oven. The roof of this nursery-tale edifice is fashioned in materials that simulate thatching, especially cut and shaped to achieve a rolling effect similar to the Berkshire hills in autumn (the colors are those of autumn as well). Huge natural rock pillars and grottoes front the building; extensive sculpture and wildflower gardens further enhance the exterior. Sir Henry Kitson, sculptor of the "Minute Man" at Lexington and "The Plymouth Maiden" in Plymouth, was the moving force behind the construction of this building in the early 1930s. He designed it as his sculpture studio and named it "Santarella." Today, after much restoration, the galleries display contemporary artists and printmakers, prints by modern Europeans and Americans, and works by Sir Henry. Exhibits of contemporary artists change during July and August. Cameras are permitted. Demonstrations and folk music concerts are included in the special activities. Guided tours can be arranged in advance. Parking available. May–Aug. daily; Sept.– Oct. Sat. & Sun. Admission 25¢ for everyone over 12. (Take Rt. 102 or 20, or the Mass. Tpke. to Tyringham Rd. and go south 4 miles.)

**WALTHAM: Rose Art Museum.** Brandeis University, 02154 ☐ In 1961 the Rose Art Museum, a contemporary glass and concrete building designed by Max Abramovitz of Harrison and Abramovitz, opened on the Brandeis University campus. It was a gift of Mr. and Mrs. Edward Rose of Boston to the rapidly growing university that had begun only 13 years earlier. The museum specializes in 20th-century American and European painting and sculpture; it also has an unusual and comprehensive collection of Tibetan art related to Tantric Buddhism. The entire permanent collection consists of contemporary art (post-World War II); modern art (1800 to World War II), including the Riverside Museum collections and the Teresa Jackson Weill collection; pre-modern art (before 1800); the Helen S. Slosberg collection of Oceanic art; the Mr. and Mrs. Edward Rose collection of early ceramics; Japanese prints; other Oriental art; Tibetan art and American Indian art (both from the Riverside Museum collections); pre-Columbian art; African art. The museum mounts 5 or 6 special exhibitions of approximately one or 2 weeks' duration each. Of these, one or 2 are drawn from the permanent collections; the others are retrospective exhibits of modern and contemporary masters, group exhibitions of younger regional artists, and ethnic and educational exhibitions. Also operated by the museum are 2 exhibition spaces elsewhere on the campus: the Dreitzer Gallery, which houses changing exhibitions of works on paper, theater arts, and student projects; and the Schwartz Hall reception area where the Helen S. Slosberg collection of Oceanic art is permanently installed. Cameras are permitted.

Occasional lectures and films that relate to particular exhibitions are sponsored by the museum. Informal guided tours are scheduled for each exhibit; in addition, group tours can be arranged on weekdays 10–4. Catalogs are published to accompany major shows and can be purchased at the reception desk. Parking nearby. Tues.–Sun. 1–5.; by appointment for groups tours. Free. (From Mass. Tpke. take exit 15 (coming from Boston) or exit 14 (from the west) to Rt. 128 north, and go to Rt. 30 west. Just before the traffic light make a right onto South St. and proceed to the campus.)

**WELLESLEY:   Wellesley College Museum.** Jewett Arts Center, 02181 □ One of 64 buildings on the beautiful campus of Wellesley College, the Jewett Arts Center, which houses the Wellesley College Museum, was dedicated in 1958. The museum, however, was founded in 1889, as a teaching arm of the art history department, to acquire art objects for the purpose of teaching art history from original works. Maintaining that primary function, the museum is also open to the public. Classical, medieval, and Renaissance sculpture, Old Master paintings, prints, and drawings, and contemporary paintings and photographs are gathered here. Some highlights are a Cézanne oil entitled "Portrait Romantique"; a Copley oil, "Portrait of Mrs. Roland Cotton"; a polychrome terra-cotta called "Madonna and Child" by Sansovino; and Rodin's "Walking Man." Exhibitions, including works from the permanent collection and loaned works, are installed throughout the academic year. Cameras are permitted on occasion, with restricted use of flash equipment.

Classes in the Jewett Arts Center can be audited for a small fee. Lectures and concerts are also one of the center's functions. Volunteer docents offer gallery talks on Sundays at 3 during exhibitions and on special request during the week. The museum publishes a catalog of the collection, notecards, postcards, and several other catalogs, all available at a sales desk. The library is open to the public for research. Parking nearby in an area for visitors. Sept.–May, Mon.–Fri. 8:30–5; Sat 8:30–12, 1–5; Sun. 2–5; closed Thanksgiving, Christmas, Jan. 1. Free. (Wellesley is 13 miles west of Boston via either Rt. 9 or the Mass. Tpke. Exit at Rt. 135 or 16. The campus is west of the main shopping area in Wellesley, and the museum is at the intersection of the motor road [off Rt. 135] and the third road on the right.)

**WESTFIELD:    Jasper Rand Art Museum of the Westfield Athenaeum.** 6
Elm St., 01085 ☐ The Jasper Rand Art Museum is housed in Westfield's
neoclassical Athenaeum, built in the late 1920s. Actually an exhibition
gallery with monthly changing exhibits throughout the year, it nevertheless has an extensive permanent collection of works by local and area
artists. Exhibitions present individual or group shows from the greater
Springfield-Westfield area and from New York and Boston. Cameras are
permitted. Classes are held for children and adults; concerts are offered
periodically; tours are available for special groups. Off-the-street parking
across from the museum. Mon., Tues., Thurs., Fri. 9–9; Wed. 9–6; Sat. 9–
5; closed Sat. during summer. Free. (Leave the Mass. Tpke. at exit 3;
proceed south on Rt. 202-10 for about 3 miles.)

**WILLIAMSTOWN:    Sterling and Francine Clark Art Institute.** South St.
Mailing address: Box 8, 01267 ☐ The cultural resources in the Berkshire
Hills vie for attention with the natural beauty to be found there. Robert
Sterling Clark and his French-born wife chose Williamstown for their
museum for this very reason. Today, nestled unobtrusively in the extreme
northwest corner of Massachusetts, this small town yields up no less than 3
museums: The Children's Museum, the Williams College Museum of Art,
and the Sterling and Francine Clark Art Institute. The portion of the
collection housed here that was acquired by Mr. Clark in Paris between
1912 and 1920 consists predominantly of Old Master paintings—Italian,
Dutch, and Flemish. Encouraged by his wife in the twenties and thirties,
he began acquiring the French 19th-century paintings that now dominate
the collection. By 1955, when the museum, a classical building in white
marble, opened, the collection had grown to include prints, drawings,
silver, furniture, china, and more paintings and sculpture. The earliest
works are from the Renaissance: striking portraits by Netherlandish artists
Hans Memling and Jan Gossaert (called Mabuse); paintings by Italian
masters—a Botticelli tondo, a panel painting by Piero della Francesca, and
a "Sepulcrum Christi" by Perugino. French, Flemish, and Dutch artists of
the 17th century are represented by Claude Lorrain, Rubens, van Ruisdael, and Rembrandt. Art from the 18th century includes a powerful
portrait by Fragonard, "Portrait of a Man (The Warrior)" and works by
Gainsborough, G. B. Tiepolo, and Goya plus sculpture, porcelain, and
silver. The selection of 19th-century works, the major strength of the
collection, includes works by Turner and Constable, 7 oils by Winslow
Homer, Sargents, Remingtons, and Innesses. Of the 19th-century works,
however, the French group is outstanding: Géricault, Courbet, Daumier,
Corot, Millet, Daubigny. Impressionists dominate a separate gallery: 7
works by Monet (one from the Rouen Cathedral series), 2 portraits and
several ballet scenes by Degas, and paintings by Sisley, Pissarro, Morisot,

as well as works by Manet, Boudin, and Toulouse-Lautrec. And most impressive of all is the institute's collection of Renoirs—30 canvases (one of them "Sleeping Girl with a Cat") painted over a period of about 30 years—thought to be one of the finest in the country. Sculptures are chiefly from the 19th century: Degas, Rodin, Carpeaux; porcelains, from the 18th and 19th—Höchst, Meissen, Vienna, and Sèvres. Prints and drawings range from 15th to 20th century—Dürer to Picasso, and in between, Rembrandt, Rubens, Watteau, Tiepolo, Delacroix, Daumier, Degas, Toulouse-Lautrec, Gauguin, Bonnard, Whistler, Homer. The silver collection is highlighted by 32 pieces wrought by 18th-century English silversmith Paul de Lamerie. One or more special exhibits are always on display; they change bimonthly. Cameras, but not flashbulbs, are permitted.

The museum's art history program leads to a masters degree and is run in conjunction with Williams College. Lectures, concerts, films, and theatrical performances are all offered. Tours are conducted daily during July and August, by request at other times; acoustiguides are also available. School tours are scheduled Tues.–Fri. at 10; Tues. and Thurs. at 1. Catalogs accompany exhibits; many of them are sold at the museum's shop, which also offers prints, postcards, slides, books, jewelry, games, and sculpture. The library (50,000 volumes) is open to the public. Parking nearby. Tues.–Sun. 10–5. Free. (On South St., ¼ mile south of the intersection of Rts. 2 & 7.)

**Williams College Museum of Art.** 01267 ☐ New England academe, subdued and elegant, nestles in the Berkshire hills like a quiet formal garden along the wooded Mohawk Trail. The Museum of Art at Williams College was founded in 1926 for the benefit of students and community; it was established in Lawrence Hall, constructed in 1848 and enlarged many times thereafter, and remains there today. Spanish Baroque and 20th-century American painting and sculpture predominate in the galleries of this Jeffersonian-style building, but many periods of art are represented: ancient Greek and Roman; Romanesque and Gothic; Italian Renaissance and Baroque; French Impressionist; African, pre-Columbian, Oriental, and works from India; and from all periods, over 1,000 prints and drawings. More than 30 loan exhibits are mounted each year ranging from Oriental to contemporary. Cameras are permitted. Lectures and concerts are offered; tours for schoolchildren and guided tours for other groups are available by appointment. Exhibition catalogs are sold in the museum. Parking nearby, either on the museum driveway or on the street. Mon–Sat. 10–12, 2–4; Sun 2–5; closed legal and college holidays. Free. (On Main St. [Rt. 2] between Spring & Water Sts., at the crest of a rise opposite the Gothic college chapel.)

**WORCESTER: Worcester Art Museum.** 55 Salisbury St., 01608 ☐ A local businessman, Stephen Salisbury III, whose grandfather had come from Boston to set up shop in Worcester some 50 years earlier, began the Worcester Art Museum in 1896. Since then, it has been one of the cultural focal points of central New England. A tract of land and some money for construction of the building was the initial donation that resulted in a neoclassical structure which opened in 1898. Three additions were made subsequently, the latest in 1970, the Higgins Education wing that houses a 3-year professional museum school and studio areas for educational programs for students of all ages. The permanent collection spans 50 centuries of art, with emphasis on painting and sculpture. One can go through the museum and follow the history of art in chronological galleries. Beginning at the entrance on Salisbury Street: The Egyptian and classical galleries exhibit sculpture from ancient Sumeria, Egypt, Italy, and Greece. Four galleries of Persian, Indian, and Far Eastern art are close by. A central Renaissance Court is lined with mosaics from Antioch-on-the-Orontes dating from about A.D. 500 (findings of one of the museum's archaeological digs). A vaulted 12th-century Romanesque Chapter House, used for centuries as a meeting room in a French monastery near Poitiers and transported and reconstructed in Worcester in the 1930s, is one of the stars of the museum. Thirteenth-century frescoes from Spoleto are the earliest European paintings here and are complemented by displays of stained glass, ivories, paintings, and sculpture from the same period. The second floor surveys European painting from the Renaissance onward. Italian paintings of the 14th and 15th centuries include works by Lorenzo di Credi, Raphael, and Piero di Cosimo. Adjacent galleries display northern Renaissance works such as the magnificent Flemish tapestry of "The Last Judgement." A 17th-century Dutch and Flemish collection includes works by Rembrandt, Saenredam, Honthorst, Rubens, and Jan Steen. The Dial collection is on long-term loan; numbering among these works are Matisses, Picassos, Monets, Cézannes, and Braques. The third floor contains the pre-Columbian and early American collections: stone sculptures and gold work represent the pre-Columbian; and among many examples of 17th-century American art is an unknown artist's portrait of "Mrs. Freake and Baby Mary." Several paintings by Sargent and Homer watercolors are also displayed here. A growing contemporary collection contains works by such as Sheeler, Ellsworth Kelly, Franz Kline, and Marsden Hartley. About 3,000 Japanese prints are in the John Chandler Bancroft collection, one of the best of its kind in the world. Four major exhibitions are mounted each year on close to a seasonal schedule. Smaller exhibits—photography, student and faculty exhibits, shows complementing larger exhibitions—are organized continually. Exhibits of the Japanese print collection change every 10 weeks. Cameras, but not tripods, are permitted.

The museum sponsors concert series, organ recital series, and lectures pertaining to the current exhibitions; also an annual film series, docent tours, trips for members, and teaching exhibitions through the College Gallery program. General tours are offered every non-concert Sunday at 3; special tours at 1:30 on second Tuesday of every month. Tours for groups of 12 to 60 or foreign language tours can be arranged. Catalogs are published in conjunction with exhibits; the museum also publishes a bulletin (3 issues per year), an annual report, a 2-volume *Catalogue of European Paintings in the Collection of the Worcester Art Museum,* and a *Handbook of the Worcester Art Museum*—all available in the museum shop. Cards, prints, decorative items, and accessories are also sold. The art reference library (35,000 volumes) is open to the public Tues.–Fri. 10–5; Sun. 2–5 except summer. A cafe serves lunch in the outdoor courtyard during the summer; a year-round restaurant across from the museum is in the planning stage. Parking in front of the building and in lots on Tuckerman Street and on the corner of Wachusett Street and Institute Road. Tues–Fri. 10–5; Sun. 2–5; closed July 4, Thanksgiving, Christmas, Jan. 1. Admission $1 for adults, 50¢ for children and senior citizens. (On Rt. 9, 2 blocks west of Lincoln Square.)

# MICHIGAN

**ALBION:   Brueckner Museum.** Starr Commonwealth for Boys, 26 Mile Rd., 49224 ☐ The Brueckner Museum was founded by Floyd Starr, who also started the Starr Commonwealth for Boys. In a Gothic building finished in 1956, in the suburbs of Albion, is a small collection on permanent display that includes some Wyeth paintings, Montano sculptures, and early American furniture. Cameras are permitted. Mon.–Fri. 9–5. Free. (From I-94, take exit 119 south.)

**ANN ARBOR:   University of Michigan Museum of Art.** Alumni Memorial Hall, 48109 ☐ The University of Michigan's art collection was founded in 1855 by classical scholar Henry S. Freize. By 1910 it had increased to the point where it would occupy its own space in Alumni Memorial Hall, a new, imposing neoclassical building finished that year. In 1945 the Museum of Art was established as a separate administrative unit. The collection housed here includes European and American paintings, graphics, sculpture, and decorative arts from medieval times to the present. It is particularly strong in prints and drawings, especially those of the German Expressionist school and of James McNeill Whistler; and in Chinese and Japanese paintings and ceramics. A listing of some outstanding works indicates the range of time and place in this collection: Joos van Cleve, "St. John on Patmos"; Philippe de Champaigne, "Christ Healing a Deaf Mute"; Guercino, "Esther Before Ahasuerus"; Delacroix, "Lycurgus Consulting the Pythia"; Monet, "Les Glaçons"; Eastman Johnson, "Boyhood of Lincoln"; and Max Beckmann, "Begin the Beguine." Ten or 15 exhibitions, both traveling shows and special exhibits arranged by the museum and the history of art department, are mounted each year. Permission to photograph must be requested. Lectures, symposia, concerts, and theatrical performances are held at the museum frequently. Docents are on hand for tours on Sundays at 2; special tours can be arranged. Publications include an art bulletin, which in 1978 became a joint venture of the Museum of Art and the Kelsey Museum of Archaeology, catalogs on American, European, Near Eastern, and Asian art; all are sold at the shop, which also offers art books, postcards, and posters for sale. Several university parking garages can be used by the public. Mon.–Sat. 9–5; Sun. 1–5; during summer, opening time is 11. Free. (Exit I-94 at State St. and go 2 miles north.)

**BLOOMFIELD HILLS:   Cranbrook Academy of Art Museum.** 500 Lone Pine Rd., 48013 ☐ Cranbrook was founded by George G. Booth, publisher of the Detroit *News.* In 1904 he purchased 300 acres of farmland, named it after his father's birthplace in England, and commenced to transform it into the impressive cultural and scientific complex that it is today. The Academy of Art Museum is but one of several buildings set in magnificently landscaped formal and informal gardens that are strewn with sculptures, fountains, and tree-lined walks. Swedish-born sculptor Carl Milles, who came to Cranbrook in 1931 as professor of sculpture, left 70-some works here, many of which adorn the buildings and lawns. Eight of them, young and lissome figures emerging from a pool and bathed in a misty spray, form the beautiful "Orpheus Fountain" that graces one corner of the museum. The museum itself, built in 1940–41, was designed by Eliel Saarinen in his unique contemporary style. Saarinen, the first president of the academy, left his mark both as the architect of and exhibitor in this museum; his drawings and silver are highlights of the collection. Also housed here are textiles woven under the direction of Loja Saarinen, paintings by Soltan Sepeshy, ceramics by Maija Grotell—all members of the faculty during the period of building the academy (1930–1965). Some of Booth's collection remains in his residence, which is open by appointment. The rest is shown in the museum's frequently changing exhibitions, the preponderance of which are dedicated to contemporary art. During the summer, an exhibition of student work is mounted, including ceramics, painting, printmaking, photography, architecture, fiber, sculpture, design, and metalsmithing. Lectures, concerts, films, and special exhibition previews are sponsored by the museum. A bookstore has an extensive selection of art books, calendars, cards, and fine art posters. Parking in front of and behind the building. Tues.–Sun. 1–5. Admission $2.50 for adults; $1.25 for students and senior citizens; special rates for groups. (Bloomfield Hills is northwest of downtown Detroit via I-75, US 10, or SR 1.)

**DETROIT:    Detroit Institute of Arts.** 5200 Woodward Ave., 48202 ☐ Rodin's "The Thinker" strikes his pensive pose at the entrance of the Renaissance building that is the Detroit Institute of Arts, pondering perhaps on the marvels of the creative accomplishments that "cover the world and cross the centuries" displayed within. Detroit's art museum owes its existence to an art loan exhibition that took place in 1883. Two years after that event took place the museum was incorporated by a group of Detroit citizens who eventually (1919) gave the building (on Jefferson Avenue) and the collection to the city while continuing to administer the endowment, furnish funds, and support educational activities. The present museum, enlarged in recent years, is distinguished by the interior courts formed by the new wings and the marble exterior of the original structure. The feeling of space created in these 3-story inner courts is offset by the intimacy of the small galleries, all 101 of them. Displays here begin in the Great Hall, just beyond the entrance, where armor and tapestries from the Middle Ages are on view. Beyond the Great Hall are collections from Egypt ("Lady from Thebes," made 2,400 years ago) , and from the modern world (Rothko, Warhol), from the Postimpressionists (Van Gogh's self-portrait and Seurat's "View of Le Crotoy"), and the Baroque (Rubens's "St. Ives of Trequier"). There are groups of Flemish and Dutch art (Bruegel's "Wedding Dance," van Ruisdael's "Cemetery," van Eyck's "St. Jerome in His Study," and 4 Rembrandts), English and German paintings and German sculpture, French painting from Louis XIII through Louis XVI (Poussin, Fragonard), Italian and Spanish paintings and Italian sculpture (Caravaggio's "The Conversion of the Magdalene" and Velázquez's "Portrait of a Man"), Oriental and African art, and not the least, the third largest collection of American art in the world. Exhibits of international importance are frequently scheduled here. Photographing is allowed only with signed permission from the museum.

This institution is a hotbed of activity, information about which can be obtained at an information center at both entrances. Gallery aides are stationed throughout the museum to give directions and answer questions. Tours can be arranged 6 weeks in advance. Talks on particular objects in the collection (Masterwork of the Week) and lectures related to the collection of special exhibits are given throughout the year. Classes are offered for all age groups in both the practice and the history and appreciation of art. The museum cosponsors a 2-year master's degree program in museology with Wayne State University. A Teachers' Resource Center provides a variety of teaching aids on loan, free of charge; and teachers' workshops acquaint educators with information about and insight into the various collections and exhibits. The Detroit Youtheatre offers professional musical performances on weekdays in the 1,200-seat auditorium for school groups; programs are designed for grades K–3, 2–5, and 4–8, (special group rates to schools within a 50-mile radius of Detroit); and Saturday performances for families. Chamber concerts, a concert series, and film showings are also offered regularly. The art research library (60,000 volumes) is open to scholars and graduate students and assists the public in identifying works of art. The publications department releases a quarterly bulletin and catalogs of the permanent collections and of special exhibits. One of the 5 regional centers of the Archives of American Art, a branch of the Smithsonian Institution, is located here; these materials, documenting the history of visual arts in the United States, are available for use by the public. The museum shops offer a wide variety of books, cards, slides, prints, posters, reproductions, and jewelry, ceramics, and glass made by Michigan craftspeople. The sales and rental gallery offers both original paintings and reproductions; rentals are available to members only. Outside the museum, the educational program reaches into the classrooms and auditoriums of the area with speakers, packaged teaching materials, lecturers, a Show on the Road exhibition schedule and Youtheatre, and educational advisory services available to both schools and organizations. There is a cafe in the Kresge Court. Parking space in an underground garage at Woodward and Farnsworth Ave. Tues.–Sun. 9:30–5:30. Voluntary admission fee. (Take I-75 to Warren Ave. exit [Cultural Center] or I-94 to the John R exit [also the Cultural Center]. Museum is between Warren Ave. & East Grand Blvd.)

**EAST LANSING: Kresge Art Gallery.** Michigan State University, 48824 ☐ The Kresge Art Gallery is the only museum in the Greater Lansing area. It was founded by Michigan State University in 1959, and funded by the S. S. Kresge Foundation. Housed here for the benefit of both students and public are art works from the neolithic period to the present. Some outstanding works are "Vision of St. Anthony," a 17th-century Spanish painting by Zurbarán; from the 20th century, a Morris Louis painting from the "unfurled" series, and mobiles by Calder and Rickey. Special exhibits change at varying intervals. Cameras without flashes are usually permitted. The gallery is a component of the Kresge Art Center, which also includes the university art department; the gallery, however, is physically separate from the classroom-study area and is also administratively autonomous. Lectures and concerts are held in the center, and a docent training program provides guided tours for school and other groups. The gallery produces some catalogs and a bulletin and newsletter for members. Metered parking nearby; public parking about ¼ mile away. Mon–Fri. 9–5; Tues 7–9; Sat. & Sun. 1–4. Free. (Use the Collingwood entrance to the university from Grand River; go left immediately to Physics Rd. The center is at the end of Physics Rd. next to the auditorium.)

**FLINT:   Flint Institute of Arts.** DeWaters Art Center, 1120 East Kearsley St., 48503 ☐ Once a producer of wagons, the city of Flint came into the automotive age with great ease and is today one of the nation's largest producers of cars. In like manner, but with a shorter history, the Flint Institute of Arts outgrew its several small homes and came into the 1950s with a move to a newly constructed, contemporary DeWaters Art Center, a unit of the Cultural Center that now includes the institute, the Whiting Auditorium, the Dort Music Center (Flint Institute of Music), the Sloan Museum of Transportation, the R. T. Longway Planetarium, the Bower Theater, and the Sarvis Food Center. The institute's collections are diverse: The Bray gallery of Italian Renaissance decorative arts is a treasure trove of tapestries, furniture, sculpture, and ceramics; an Oriental gallery displays Chinese paintings, jades, ivories, ceramics, and bronzes; a fine collection of 19th- and 20th-century French and American art includes works by Renoir, Degas, Chagall, Dufy, Sisley, Utrillo, and Vuillard ("Woman Lighting a Stove in a Studio"), and Sargent ("Study of Vicar's Children"), Cassatt ("Lydia at Tapestry Frame"), Wyeth ("The Sweep"), Heade ("Sunrise on the Marshes"), and Cropsey. Other galleries house the collection of American Victorian furniture, naive paintings, African art, the Bray collection of antique French paperweights, 18th-and 19th-century German drinking vessels, and graphics. Another among the museum's most treasured possessions is "Angel," a painting by Rubens. About 20 special, temporary exhibits are mounted each year. Cameras are permitted.

The institute sponsors a museum school, lectures, concerts, bus trips to other museums in the area, films, and art tours to other countries and other parts of the United States. Docents are available by appointment. Catalogs published by the museum accompany many of the special exhibitions. The library (2,000 volumes) is open to the public by special permission. Books, jewelry, cards, and stationery, gifts, folk art, reproductions, and tapestries are for sale at the museum shop. Parking nearby. Tues.–Sat. 9–5; Tues. (Oct–May) 7–9; Sun. 1–5. Free. (Coming from the south, take I-475 to the downtown exit and follow signs to the Cultural Center. From east or west, take I-69 to the Cultural Center exit. The institute is off Crapo St. between Kearsley & Second.)

**GRAND RAPIDS:   Grand Rapids Art Museum.** 230 East Fulton St., 49503 ☐ The Pike House, in which the Grand Rapids Art Museum is housed, was built by Abraham Pike as his home in 1844, at the end of the period when Greek Revival architecture was all the rage. The building's symmetry, Doric columns, and low pediment at the front portico are typical of this popular style; however, the eavelike extensions on either side are unusual and lend it added grace. Surrounding it in the Heritage Hill Historic District, are some 1,500 houses that illustrate 70 different architectural styles, all built in the 1850s, when Americans were looking to older cultures for inspiration. Twelve paintings formed the nucleus of this collection, but it had no permanent home until the Pike House was provided by a gift in 1924. Today 8 galleries display Renaissance, French 19th-century, American 19th- and 20th-century, and German Expressionist paintings; sculpture; drawings; Staffordshire pottery; and decorative arts. The strength of the collection, however, rests in the prints, with representations by an impressive roster of masters: Goya, Whistler, Cassatt, Picasso, Toulouse-Lautrec, Delacroix, Cézanne, Burchfield, Nevelson, Renoir, Klee, Dürer, Matisse, Chagall, Corot, Gauguin, Degas, and Rouault. Exhibits change monthly and consist of prints from the permanent collection; the work of local artists, and paintings and drawings from the permanent collection on a rotating basis. Cameras are not permitted except under special circumstances.

An extension gallery called the Art Shop, located in downtown Grand Rapids, is run by the museum in conjunction with the bus company. Local artists are shown here; exhibits change monthly. The museum sponsors a weekly film series, lectures by visiting artists, and a rent-a-picture shop. Classes are held in weaving, pottery, and jewelry making. Slide shows are held for many of the special exhibitions. Group tours may be scheduled in advance. Members receive a monthly newsletter and bulletin. The library (12,000 volumes) of general art reference materials is open to the public. A museum shop sells pottery, small sculptures, jewelry, decorative items, cards, books, and gifts. Park in the rear for 25¢ an hour. Mon.–Sat. 9–5; Sun. 2–5; closed Mon. in June, July, Aug. and national holidays. Free. (From Grand Rapids Ford Freeway 196, take College exit south to Fulton St.; turn right, and go 3 blocks.)

**KALAMAZOO:   Kalamazoo Institute of Arts.** 314 South Park St., 49007 ☐ The Kalamazoo Institute of Arts began to acquire works of art in 1961 when it established itself in its newly completed home across from the park. Here, in the heart of the city, a collection of American painting since 1900, photographs, graphics, and sculpture grew. Today it includes a Barlach bronze ("The Singing Man"), Diebenkorn's "Sleeping Woman," a Burchfield watercolor "Street Vista in Winter," Edvard Munch's lithograph "The Death Kiss," and a kinetic sculpture by Rickey called "Four Lines Oblique." Exhibits change monthly. Cameras are permitted. Approximately 1,400 students enroll annually for studio classes here. In addition, the center offers lectures, panel discussions, poetry readings, and tours to major museums. Tour guides are available by prearrangement (2 weeks' notice is needed). A monthly newsletter is published for members as well as occasional exhibition catalogs. The library (4,000 volumes) is open to the public. Cards, books, and jewelry are sold in the gallery shop. Parking nearby. Labor Day–July 3, Tues.–Fri. 11–4:30; July 4–Aug. 1, Tues.–Sat. 10–4. Admission 50¢ for adults, 25¢ for children. (Take Westnedge Ave. & Park St. north off I-94.)

**MUSKEGON:   Hackley Art Museum.** 296 West Webster Ave., 49440 ☐ Charles H. Hackley was a lumber baron to whom Muskegonians owe much—library, manual training school, hospital, parks, monuments, and statuary were all his benefactions. Even after his death in 1905 his gifts continued; the Hackley Art Museum was among them. His will contained a bequest of $150,000 to the Board of Education for the purchase of "pictures of the best kind." The collection thus acquired was housed in the public library until 1912, when it was moved to a new building, classical in design, next to the library in the heart of the city. Today the collection, much of which was derived from Hackley's original bequest, includes objects from ancient times to modern. European painting is represented by such masters as Cranach, Goya, Joos van Cleve, Jan van der Heyden, Sisley, Pissarro, Vlaminck, Vuillard, and Bonnard; American painting by Whistler, Homer, Wyeth, West, Ryder Blacklock, Bellows, Burchfield, and Hopper. The L. C. Walker collection of graphics is noteworthy: in it are works by Dürer, Rembrandt, Cranach, Schongauer, Toulouse-Lautrec, Matisse, Renoir, Chagall, Picasso, and Whistler. The collection of Persian miniatures and manuscripts, Indian Rajput miniature paintings, and Japanese prints gives an interesting sampling of Eastern art. French, Italian, and Spanish illuminated manuscripts from the 14th and 15th centuries are also on view. Sculptures include works by Rodin, Manship, and Lachaise, among others. A regular schedule of changing exhibits from other public and private collections and from contemporary artists complements the museum's own permanent collection. Cameras are permitted. Art classes, lecture series, films, and special events are regularly offered by the museum. Guided group tours can be arranged in advance. Publications include annual reports, exhibit catalogs, and a catalog of the permanent collection, available at the museum shop together with books, jewelry, cards, and reproductions. Parking in nearby lots. Mon.–Sat. 9–5; Sun. 2–5. Free. (From Muskegon Ave. [business road 96], turn toward Webster Ave. The museum is on Webster between 3rd & 2nd.)

**SAGINAW: Saginaw Art Museum.** 1126 North Michigan Ave., 48602 ☐ A thirtieth birthday was celebrated by the Saginaw Art Museum in 1978. Its classical Georgian building was erected in the early 1900s by Clark Lombard Ring to house nothing more auspicious than his own family. The home was given to the museum by his daughters. Hanging here today in 6 galleries is a small collection consisting of Oriental art (from a 1,000-year-old Buddha to a contemporary Chinese painting), English porcelain, American paintings and sculpture (especially by genre sculptor John Rogers), and European paintings (from Old Masters to modern). Traveling exhibitions and an annual photography show are scheduled during the year. Cameras are permitted, but not flashbulbs. Classes are held for both children and adults in jewelry making, ceramics, watercolor, oil, and acrylics. Lectures and concerts are also held. Tours for groups can be arranged. A museum bulletin is mailed to members monthly. The library (1,000 volumes) of books on art history is open to the public. Original paintings, ceramics, woven fabrics, jewelry, prints, books, and cards are for sale in the museum shop. Parking in front and alongside the museum. Tues.–Sat. 10–5; Tues. 7–9; Sun. 1–5. Free. (Go to the intersection of North Michigan & West Remington.)

# MINNESOTA

**DULUTH: Tweed Museum of Art.** 2400 Oakland Ave., University of Minnesota, 55812 ☐ The Tweed Museum, made possible by the financier Duluthean whose name it bears, was established in 1950, and in 1958 the new gallery was ready for occupancy. Then in 1965 the Alice Tweed Tuohy gallery doubled the exhibition area, permitting more of the collection to be on view. George P. Tweed's taste leaned heavily toward 19th-century French and American paintings, so the Barbizon school predominates in his collection of some 500 paintings. Nevertheless, there is a range of other artwork going back to the 16th century. But the French are present in force. Also housed here is an interesting group of contemporary prints. And at the entrance is Jacques Lipchitz's larger-than-life representation of the French explorer who landed here in 1679, Daniel Greysolon, Sieur Duluth, pointing out to the city that took his name. There are approximately 15 major shows each year; additional smaller exhibitions, including an exhibit and sale of student art, fill out a busy schedule. Since the museum serves a wide area around Duluth, its activities are not limited to its function as a university facility. Lectures, films, gallery talks, and guided tours are regular events. The museum also offers an art program for children in cooperation with the public schools. There is an Alice Tweed Tuohy purchase award for student art. Exhibition catalogs are published quarterly. The library (1,500 volumes including catalogs and periodicals) is available for use upon request. Mon.–Fri. 8–4:30; Sat., Sun. 2–5. Free.

**MINNEAPOLIS: Minneapolis Institute of Arts.** 2400 Third Ave. South, 55404 ☐ Ernst Barlach's "The Fighter of the Spirit," the figure of an animal arched under the feet of a brooding angel, greets visitors at the new entrance of an enlarged Minneapolis Institute of Arts. Designed by McKim, Mead, and White in 1911 with the classical elements typical of institutional buildings of the day, the museum was expanded to twice its original size in 1974. The addition of bright, clean-lined rectangular shapes by architect Kenzo Tange and URTEC of Tokyo in association with a Minneapolis firm resulted in a handsome comingling of style and form. Housed here is an outstanding collection of Oriental jades and bronzes, photography, Western paintings, prints, textiles, period rooms, and decorative arts. Approximately 60,000 objects represent all periods and schools of art including European and American paintings and sculpture; ancient, Oriental, African, pre-Columbian, Oceanic, and native North and South American arts. "Lucretia" by Rembrandt, is one of the museum's prides, as are Copley's "Mrs. Nathaniel Allen," Goya's "Self Portrait," Poussin's "The Death of Germanicus," the Pillsbury collection of ancient Chinese bronzes, the Gale collection of Japanese prints, Paul Revere's Templeman tea service, the collection of prints that represent nearly every school and period including a strong group by Rembrandt, ukiyo-e (Japanese paintings and prints of everyday life), 19th-century French works, and the Minnich collection of botanical, fashion, and zoological prints. Four of the museum's 36 annual exhibitions are major. Only objects in the permanent collection may be photographed.

Special classes and workshops are held for all age groups in affiliation with the Minneapolis College of Art and Design. The museum's educational program also includes lectures, concerts, film series, a monthly clinic in which curators attribute art objects, and an Arts Resource and Information Center which provides information about arts-related events in the area. Docents conduct tours; special tours are available for school groups; telesonic audio tours are also offered daily. The library (20,000 volumes) is open to the public. A monthly magazine, *Arts,* is published by the Society of Fine Arts; and the museum publishes an annual bulletin and catalogs for major exhibitions. The museum shop sells art books, postcards, jewelry, posters, silver, and gift items. The Link Restaurant serves lunch and light refreshments Tues.–Sat., and a brunch on Sunday; wine and cocktails are available. Parking ramp on the museum grounds. Tues., Wed., Fri., Sat. 10–5; Thurs. 10–9; Sun. 12–5. General admission $1; children under 12, senior citizens, scheduled school groups free; students and other scheduled groups 50¢; Thurs. 5–9 free, voluntary donation requested. (From I-94, take the 11th St. exit [north] and turn south onto 3rd Ave. From US 12 [east], take Hennepin Ave. exit, turn right onto Lyndale Ave. and left onto 25th St. to the museum.)

**University Gallery,** University of Minnesota, 110 Northrop Auditorium, 84 Church St., S.E., 55455 ☐ Begun as an experiment in 1934, the University Gallery was designed to bring students into close contact with works of art and to serve as an educational resource for the entire university. The collection was and still is housed in Northrop Auditorium, a neoclassical building of brick and stone; the gallery's expansion through the years has made it the primary occupant of Northrop Auditorium today. The strength of this collection is in American paintings, prints, drawings, and sculpture from the first half of this century, most specifically from 1900 to 1930. The gallery's holdings of works by Marsden Hartley and Alfred H. Maurer are exceptional. Limited groups of Old Master prints and drawings, Greek vases, 18th-century European decorative arts (particularly furniture and porcelain) and Far Eastern stone sculpture expand the scope of the collection. The outstanding works, however, are American: "Oriental Poppies," "Oak Leaves," "Pink and Grey," by O'Keeffe; Dove's "The Gale" and "Tree Study"; by Hartley, "Eight Bell's Folly," "Landscape #32," and other works from all periods; "Still Life with Cup" and "Self Portrait" by Maurer; "Star Cage" by David Smith; and works by Marin, Feininger, and Macdonald-Wright. A schedule of temporary exhibitions coincides with the university's academic quarters; the major exhibitions run an entire quarter, the smaller for 3 or 4 weeks. Permission to use cameras must be granted by the director.

Lectures, gallery talks, tours, concerts, and occasional demonstrations are scheduled to complement the small exhibitions; a series of lectures is scheduled to accompany the major exhibitions. Group tours are offered; advance requests are encouraged. The gallery offers internships for master's degree candidates in museology. Access to the university's circulating art library is available to these and other students, staff, and faculty of the university; noncirculating to the public. Catalogs, sold by gallery guards and in the gallery office, accompany most exhibitions. Pay parking lot adjacent to the building. Mon., Wed., Fri. 11–4; Tues., Thurs. 11–8; Sun. 2–5. Free. (Take the U. of Minn. exit off I-94. The Northrop Auditorium is located north of Washington Ave. [US 12] and south of University Ave. [SR 47] just east of the Mississippi River.)

**Walker Art Center.** Vineland Place, 55403 ☐ A gem of a group of Oriental jades in the Walker Art Center is all that remains of lumberman T. B. Walker's multifarious art collection. He had opened it to public viewing in his home in 1879; like Topsy, it grew and grew; he built a separate place for it in 1927; and by 1939, a reorganization transformed his more-or-less traditional museum, affected by the strains of the Depression, into a surefooted and bold-stepping young art center. Today the Walker Art Center, still supported by the T. B. Walker Foundation, occupies a stunning new building, all rectangles and cubes and spirals. It opened its doors next to the Tyrone Guthrie Theater in 1971. There are some 19th-century American paintings here—works for example, by Church, Cole, and Ryder—but the 20th century prevails. The list of artists represented in this collection is a recitation of the masters of this century, from Albers to Warhol. Three sculpture terraces display the likes of David Smith, Calder, and Lipchitz. Several major exhibits are installed each year; many originate at the center.

This is a busy place that tries to be original, beginning with its exhibitions that are becoming familiar nationwide for their inventiveness. Lectures, films, gallery talks, concerts, and dance programs are regular events. A docent program provides tour guides. Classes are held for children and adults, and a training program for professional museum workers. Exhibits are accompanied by catalogs, and very often by films, interpretive lectures, and music. The magazine *Design Quarterly,* well known in its field, is published here, as well as calendars of events and various brochures. The library (5,000 volumes, 30,000 catalogs, vertical files, periodicals, slides, and tapes) is available for use by graduate students on request. A restaurant is located on one of the terraces—the Minneapolis winter is locked outside the indoor section. The museum shop offers books, prints, posters, postcards, and jewelry, among much else, for sale. Summer, Tues.–Sat. 10–8; Sun. 12–6. Winter, Tues., Thurs. 10–8; Wed., Fri., Sat. 10–5, Sun. 12–6. Free. (Vineland place is 1 block south of junction of US 12 & US 169.)

**MOORHEAD:   Plains Art Museum.** Mailing address: Box 37, 56560. **Red River Art Center (Main Gallery).** 521 Main Ave. **Rourke Gallery.** 523 South 4th St. ☐ The Main Gallery of the Plains Art Museum was once the Moorhead Federal Building (1913), a gracefully symmetrical Federal-style structure with Ionic columns stretching across the facade; inside, light filters in through tall arching windows and falls on varicolored marble walls and the barred tellers' windows of the early 1900s. The Rourke Gallery was a former family home, built in 1884, remodeled in the 1920s, yet preserving the period details. Over 3,000 objects housed in this museum include African, Oceanic, pre-Columbian, and North American Indian art, Persian and Oriental art, and Eskimo sculpture. Prints and drawings from the 19th and 20th centuries, 19th-century decorative arts, 20th-century paintings, and photographs are among the major concentrations of the museum. Temporary exhibitions—loan, traveling, and circulating—change frequently. Cameras are permitted; exposed flashbulbs are not. The museum sponsors numerous activities, among them lectures, films, concerts, dance programs, gallery talks, art festivals, studio classes, and art appreciation classes for adults and children. Guided tours are provided through the docent training program. Nine exhibition areas, meeting and classrooms, a research and slide library, a sales and rental service, and museum shop (gift items, cards, jewelry, basketry, and art supplies) are among the facilities. A monthly newsletter, exhibition catalogs, and an annual report are prepared by the staff. Main Gallery: Wed.-Sat. 9-5; Sun. 12-5. Rourke Gallery: Wed-Sun. 9-5 and by appointment; closed Thanksgiving, Christmas, Jan. 1, July 4. Admission by donation. (Main Gallery: Coming from the south, take I-94 to US 75 [8th St.] to Main Ave. and turn left [west]. The museum is at Main & 6th. From the east, take US 10 [Center Ave.] to 6th St. and turn left [south] to Main Ave. From the north, take US 75 to US 10; and from the west [through Fargo], take I-29 to US 10.)

**PARK RAPIDS: North Country Museum of Arts.** Third St. & Court Ave. Mailing address: P.O. Box 328, 56470 ☐ In the forested lakelands at the edge of the prairie (the area is the heartland of Minnesota, where the Mississippi River valley begins), the North Country Museum of Arts came into being. The eclectic Victorian house (built as a county courthouse) that is home for the Hubbard County Historical Society was chosen in 1977 to house a local collector's thirty 17th- and 18th-century European paintings, and to create an art center for the region. A corporation was formed, and a museum was born. Loan exhibitions and locally produced works are shown during the summer months. Cameras are permitted. This young museum sponsors occasional art classes, craft demonstrations, and lectures. Parking one block away. Daily 11-5. Admission $1. (Go 1 block south of SR 34 and 3 blocks west of US 71.)

**ROCHESTER: Rochester Art Center.** 320 East Center St., 55901 ☐ Local artists have their showcase in the Rochester Art Center, founded in 1947 in the city of the Mayo Clinic and IBM, to provide the opportunity to "know, practice, and enjoy the arts." Emphasis is not on collecting but on showing the fine arts and crafts of the upper Midwest. Some 120 works in a permanent collection are primarily by local artists. Thirty exhibits (3 per month) are mounted annually. Cameras are permitted. Classes are offered for both adults and children; occasional workshops are sponsored with special grants from the Minnesota State Arts Council. A 9-month schedule of free community concerts is organized by the music committee. Tours are available by appointment. Catalogs accompany many of the exhibits. A sales gallery offers work in clay, fiber, glass, and metal. Parking nearby. Tues.–Sat. 10–4; Sun. 1–5. Free. (Take US 52 south to 2nd St. S.W. and turn left; go to 3rd Ave. and turn left; go to Center St. and turn right.)

**ST. PAUL:   Minnesota Museum of Art: Permanent Collection Gallery.** 305 St. Peter St., 55102. **Community Gallery.** 30 East 10th St., 55101 ☐ The Minnesota Museum of Art celebrated its 50th anniversary in 1978. Founded as an art school, it was incorporated in 1927, but it was not until the 1940s that the gallery acquired the first works of its permanent collection. Today the museum occupies space in 2 buildings: the Arts and Science Center, built in 1964 with a bond issue; and the Permanent Collection Gallery, purchased in 1971. The Community Gallery, another resource of the museum, is at still another location in Minneapolis and serves as a showcase for educational programs. The museum claims its collection of contemporary drawings to be among the largest in the United States; most well-known American artists are represented here. Other specialties under these roofs are contemporary crafts, sculpture, Asian art, African art, and lace. The museum creates most of its exhibits; only occasionally are loan shows mounted. Exhibits change every 6 weeks and include competitions, local artists, regional, and ethnic shows. Cameras are permitted only in the permanent collection, and only if the flash is protected. Classes, lectures in connection with special exhibitions, and concerts are offered here. An educational program reaches children of grade school, high school, and college level; a program for interns is offered for college credit. Docents trained at the museum lead guided tours. The library (1,500 volumes) is open to the public by special permission. Catalogs are prepared to accompany exhibitions. A restaurant serves luncheon only. Parking at the permanent Collection Gallery is 2–3 blocks away in pay lots; at the Community Gallery, across the street. Permanent Collection Gallery: Tues–Sat. 11–5. Admission 50¢ for adults; 25¢ for children; groups free. Community Gallery: Mon.–Wed. 9–5; Thurs.–Sat. 9–9; Sun. 11–9. Free.

# MISSISSIPPI

**JACKSON:** **Mississippi Art Association, Inc.** 846 North President. Mailling address: P.O. Box 824, 39205 ☐ The Mississippi Art Association was organized in 1911, but a new charter, effective in 1953, launched the organization into education, exhibition, and acquisition. Today the association owns a collection of paintings, prints, sculpture, tapestry, and pottery. Exhibits are held in the **Municipal Art Gallery** (839 North State St., 39201), an old residence that is owned by the city of Jackson. It houses the collection and displays it and other art on a rotating basis. The usual activities of a busy art association are carried on here—lectures, workshops, classes. The association sponsors a travel-lecture program, a speakers' bureau, and many other community related projects. A newsletter is published monthly. Art books, gifts, and artwork are for sale. Tues.–Sat. 9–5; Sun. 2–5. Free.

**LAUREL:** **Lauren Rogers Memorial Library and Museum of Art.** 5th Ave. & 7th St. Mailing address: P.O. Box 1108, 39440 ☐ Laurel, once a lumber camp in the midst of the pine forests of southeastern Mississippi, hardly the place for art and artists to thrive, is nevertheless today the home of a very fine library and museum. Lauren Eastman Rogers, dead in his early twenties, was memorialized by his grandfather Lauren Chase Eastman in 1923 by the opening of this Georgian building to house books and artwork. American art predominates here—works by 19th- and 20th-century Americans such as Blakelock ("Harvest Moon"), Hawthorne ("Girl with Bowl"), Robert Henri ("The Brown Wrap, 1911"), Winslow Homer ("Fisherman's Wife"), George Inness ("Close of a Rainy Day"), Thomas Moran ("Sunset, Long Island Sound"), and John Sloan ("Dolly by the Kitchen Door"). A European room has points of interest: Breton's "The Gleaner," Corot's "Landscape Near Paris," "Strong Man at the Fair" by Daumier, "Old Mill" by Lhermitte, a pastel "First Steps" by Millet, and "The Ferry" by Constant Troyon. Also on view is a collection of Georgian silver, the Gardiner collection of baskets, and some paintings by H. W. Hansen on Indian subjects. The library specializes in genealogy, art, and Mississippiana; especially prized is a page from a 1663 Bible printed in the Algonquin language, a 1780 edition of Alexander Pope's *Essay on Man*, and an 1851 7-volume set of Audubon's *Birds of America*. Temporary exhibits of regional and national artists are changed monthly from September through May. Cameras are permitted. Art Classes, lectures, concerts, programs in art for the public schools are among the museum's services. Docents are available during museum hours. The library (16,000 volumes) is open to the public and for inter-library loan. Parking lot at the intersection of 7th St. & 4th Ave. Tues.–Sat. 10–12, 2–5; Sun. 2–5. Free. (Business Rt. 15 & Rt. 84 lead to the museum.)

**MERIDIAN:   Meridian Museum of Art.** 25th Ave. at 7th St., 39301 ☐ The Meridian Museum of Art, an offshoot of the Meridian Art Association, came into being in 1970. Its collection consists of some 100 objects—paintings, pottery, drawings, lithographs, and silk-screen prints. Exhibitions of works of art from such diverse institutions as the Arkansas Art Center, the High Museum of Art (Atlanta), the Birmingham Museum of Art, the Dallas Museum of Fine Arts, the New Orleans Museum of Art, and the Mobile Art Museum are installed regularly. The museum offers art classes to elementary and high school students and adults. A "Gathering of Artisans" program is operative for artists 17 years and older. Teacher workshops are conducted by the director, and in-school lectures are offered to those who request them. Annual school exhibitions, a juried show, and other special projects are sponsored here. Guided tours are available by appointment. Tues.–Sun. 1–5. Free.

# MISSOURI

**COLUMBIA:   Museum of Art and Archaeology.** 1 Pickard Hall, University of Missouri, 65201 ☐ Pickard Hall is a Victorian structure on Francis Quadrangle, a part of the University of Missouri campus that is on the National Register of Historic Places. It was built in the 1890s to house the university's chemistry department. The interior was renovated in 1976; while the exterior was preserved in its original design to conform to the other buildings on the quadrangle. Here the six Ionic columns of the first administration building (1840), destroyed by fire in 1892, still stand as a memorial to the beginnings of this oldest university west of the Mississippi. Today, Pickard Hall houses the university museum, said to be the third largest art museum, after the two great museums of St. Louis and Kansas City, in the state of Missouri. Ten galleries contain the varied permanent collection, particularly strong in ancient art: a fine collection of Greek, Roman, and Near Eastern pottery and glass; a large selection of archaeological finds from the Mediterranean area; and an interesting assemblage of South Asian Hindu and Buddhist sculpture. The collection also includes Old Master paintings (a group of 14 comprises a Samuel H. Kress study collection) and modern paintings, graphics, and sculpture; Byzantine, early Christian, and Coptic art; objects from South America, Africa, and Oceania; South and Southeastern Asian, Chinese, and Japanese art. Highlights: a rare Egyptian mummy shroud dated around the 2nd century A.D.; a bronze blazon for a Greek shield from the 6th century B.C.; "The Musician," a painting by Thomas Hart Benton; and a rare collection of life-size casts of Greek and Roman sculpture. Each month a different work is selected as the "Exhibit of the Month"; frequent changes are also made in the gallery of prints and drawings. Cameras may be used only by special permission; no flashes are allowed.

The museum, among the other university museums—anthropology, interior design and architecture, arts and crafts, Fine Arts Gallery, the Scruggs-Vandervoort-Barney collection "Missouri, Heart of the Nation," and scientific collections—functions as an educational arm of the university; independently, however, through its support organization, it sponsors lectures and classes for the training of volunteer guides whose activities provide tours upon advance request. The Saul and Gladys Weinberg Traveling Fellowship Fund provides traveling expenses for students in archaeology. The annual report, *Muse,* includes scholarly articles about objects in the collection. The library (5,000 volumes—sales and exhibition catalogs, museum bulletins, and books) can be used on the premises. Books, jewelry, prints, postcards, replicas of ancient Palestinian glass and Greek pottery are sold at the museum shop. Parking is limited; use the visitors' parking lot 2 blocks away, south of the library on Hitt and Conley Aves. Tues.–Sun. 1–5; Mon. 4–10. Free. (From I-70, take Stadium Blvd. exit to College Ave.; turn left to University Ave. and go 2 blocks.)

**KANSAS CITY:   Nelson Gallery of Art and Atkins Museum.** 4525 Oak St., 64111 ☐ North of one of the 50-odd fountains, this one designed by Swedish sculptor Carl Milles, that beautify Kansas City along with 3,700 acres of parks and a renowned system of boulevards, is the Nelson Gallery of Art and Atkins Museum, one of the country's top-rank insitutions of art. This neoclassical building was opened in 1933, having been financed by the family of founder William Rockhill Nelson, also founder of the Kansas City *Star,* and the Mary Atkins estate. It stands on 20 acres of parkland in the center of Kansas City near the Country Club Plaza, the nation's first (1920s) suburban shopping center, magnificently designed in Spanish-style architecture. The museum's collection is a general one representing art from most civilizations from 3000 B.C. (Sumerian) to the present, but its Oriental section is its crowning glory. It is one of the finest in America, and features Chinese painting, sculpture, furniture, and jade, and in the main gallery, a Chinese temple highlighted by a 14th-century fresco and a huge sculpture of the "Bodhisattva Kuan-Yin"; Indian bronze and stone sculpture displayed in an Indian temple room; Persian painting and pottery; and Japanese paintings, paper screens, sculpture, and ceramics. There are 58 galleries and 11 period rooms. In them, collections include classical art, Old Master and modern paintings, sculpture, prints and drawings, decorative arts, medieval and Renaissance sculpture. Among the Occidental paintings are works by Petrus Christus, Caravaggio, El Greco, Goya, Rembrandt, Rubens, Ribera, Titian, Monet, Degas, Cassatt, Gauguin, de Kooning, and Warhol. The Burnap collection of English pottery is outstanding, as is a Samuel H. Kress collection of Italian paintings and sculpture and a Starr collection of portrait miniatures. Special loan exhibits are shown throughout the year. Cameras are permitted.

Creative art classes are offered for children and adults; lectures, concerts, and films are regularly scheduled during the year. Docent guided tours take place Tues.–Sat. 10–11, 12, and 2; Sun. 2, 2:30, 3, 3:30. The library (20,000 volumes) is open to the public. A museum shop offers the catalogs published here (a handbook of the collections in 2 volumes; catalogs of the Burnap and Starr collections) and other books, jewelry, and sculpture reproductions, needlepoint kits, prints, and postcards; the museum also runs a sales and rental gallery. The Coffee Lounge serves snacks and luncheon. Parking on the grounds and nearby. Tues.–Sat. 10–5; Sun. 2–6; closed Jan. 1, Memorial Day, July 4, Thanksgiving, Christmas. Admission free on Sun.; Tues.–Sat. 50¢ for adults, 25¢ for children. (From US 50, take 47th St. to Main St., from which the museum is accessible. The gallery is 2 blocks east of Main, 2 blocks north of 47th, at 45th st.)

**MARYVILLE:   Northwest Missouri State University Art Gallery.** Percival DeLuce Memorial Collection, 64468 ☐ Percival DeLuce became a portrait painter and illustrator of books and periodicals in the 1880s. The Percival DeLuce Memorial Collection, presented to Northwest Missouri State University by his daughter, contains his paintings, drawings, and prints; works by his contemporaries; and family furniture—a 17th-century Boulle writing desk, 2 Napoleonic chairs, and chairs from the workshop of Duncan Phyfe. The collection is shown in rotation, a new display being mounted every 6 weeks. Cameras are permitted. The Olive DeLuce Fine Arts building houses the collection as well as the university art gallery (changing exhibits monthly) and the art department. Parking available. Mon.–Fri. 1–4; other times by special arrangement. (The fine arts building is on College Ave. at 4th St., 7 blocks west of US 71 [Main St.].)

**POINT LOOKOUT:   Ralph Foster Museum.** The School of the Ozarks, 65726 ☐ The Ralph Foster Museum is located on the 940-acre campus of the School of the Ozarks, a college on the banks of the White River in

Taney County, Missouri, that is maintained and run principally by students who work some 20 hours a week in return for room, board, and tuition. The Ozark stone building that houses the museum was built between 1967 and 1977, financed by the Missouri radio pioneer whose name it bears. The preponderance of the 750,000 objects here constitute a Smithsonian-like historical and archaeological collection (the museum is often referred to as the Smithsonian of the Ozarks). Firearms, primitive paintings, coins, Indian objects, and wildlife are some areas of concentration. The fine arts collection consists mainly of 18th-century American and European paintings, most notably works by Rose O'Neill and Albert Bierstadt. There are seasonal exhibits from April through October; September and October are reserved for the annual Forsyth Art Guild exhibition. Cameras are permitted. Tours are conducted by School of the Ozarks students. The Lois Brownell Research Library is open to the public by special permission of the director. Books, jewelry, prints, postcards, pottery, metal crafts, and woven fabrics are sold in the museum shop. Parking nearby. Mon.–Sat. 8–5; Sun. 1–5; closed Mon., Nov. 1–Mar. 31. Free. (Turn onto Hwy. V off US 65, 2 miles south of Branson, Mo.)

**ST. JOSEPH: Albrecht Art Museum.** 2818 Frederick Blvd., 64506 ☐ The eastern starting point of the pony express, the town where Jesse James was killed and the first cross-state railroad reached its western terminus seems hardly the place for Georgian architecture and collections of art. Yet both are present and thriving in St. Joseph's Albrecht Art Museum. A Georgian mansion was built on a 4-acre tract of land by the Albrecht family in the late thirties. Thirty years later the lovely house was given over for use as a gallery by the Albrecht daughter. Handsomely carved woodwork and moldings and decorative marble make a fine backdrop for the collection of 19th- and 20th-century American paintings, drawings, and prints, and European prints from the same period. The landscaped gardens surrounding the house provide attractive space for the display of sculpture. Exhibits change regularly; an art fair is held annually. The museum provides classes for adults and children, lectures, films, concerts, and gallery talks. Guided tours are also available. Publications include a monthly newsletter and several catalogs, one on the architecture of St. Joseph. The library (300 volumes) is open for use on the premises. Jewelry, ceramics, postcards, reproductions, and other gift items are sold. Tues.–Fri. 10–4; Sat., Sun. 1–5. Admission 25¢ for adults, 10¢ for children.

**ST. LOUIS: St. Louis Art Museum.** Forest Park, 63110 ☐ The St. Louis World's Fair of 1904 ran its course and eventually was forgotten, but there were a few especially remarkable features of the fair that were to become part of the American scene: the ice cream cone was one (it was introduced here), the hot dog another (also a first here), and the Palace of Art still another. The Palace was one of the permanent buildings designed by Cass Gilbert as part of a vast Beaux Arts complex of structures, its 90-foot vaulted central hall recalling the Baths of Caracalla. After the fair the building was presented to the city of St. Louis for use as a municipal art museum and, indeed, the St. Louis Art Museum, successor to the oldest art museum west of the Mississippi—the St. Louis Museum of Fine Arts was founded in 1879—set up residence in its home in Forest Park, which had been the fair site. This building, fashioned from the tastes of early 20th-century America, houses objects of art that describe the history of the civilized world. The collections include art from Egypt, the Near East, Greece, and Rome; European art from the Middle Ages through the 20th century, with special emphasis on Northern European works from the Renaissance to Rembrandt, French Impressionists and Postimpressionists, and German Expressionists; American art from Colonial to contemporary; Oriental art including works from China, Japan, and southern Asia; an outstanding assemblage of primitive art including works from Oceania and Africa, and objects of pre-Columbian and American Indian origin; fine examples of 20th-century European sculpture; American and European decorative arts, and Chinese bronzes and porcelains; and a new department of prints, drawings, and photographs. Traveling exhibitions, as well as exhibitions of the permanent collections, are usually on view for a period of 3 months. Cameras (no tripods) and hand-held electronic flashes are permitted.

The education department sponsors art courses periodically for children and adults. Tuesday night lectures, a Friday night film series, concerts, and other special events are part of a regular schedule of activities. A speakers service provides lectures on the museum's collections to interested groups or clubs; a Resource Center for teachers provides slides, slide kits, video cassettes, posters, camera and taping facilities, consultations, and workshops. Guided tours are conducted Wed.–Sun. 11 & 2:30, Tues. at 3. The Richardson Memorial Library (18,000 volumes) is open to the public. A large number of books and catalogs are prepared and published here and sold at the museum shop, which also offers reproductions, postcards, posters, and jewelry for sale. The restaurant serves fine food in a casual atmosphere where original works of art are on display. Parking in the rear and in front of the building. Tues. 2:30–9:30; Wed.–Sun. 10–5; closed Christmas, Jan. 1. Admission to permanent collections free; admission to special exhibitions free on Tues., voluntary Wed.–Sun.

**Washington University Gallery of Art.** Steinberg Hall, 63130 ☐ Originally housed in the St. Louis Art Museum, the Washington University collection came to Steinberg Hall when it opened in 1960. Modern art predominates here: works by Picasso, Ernst, Miró, and more. In addition, other distinguished works are highlighted: paintings by El Greco, Reynolds, Hogarth, and Sir Henry Raeburn; 19th-century Americans such as George Caleb Bingham, Thomas Eakins, and George Inness; selections of 19th-century French works; and important sculptures by Renoir, Rodin, Maillol, and Calder. Special exhibitions mounted periodically focus on a variety of interests. Cameras are permitted. The university's school of fine arts is located in an adjacent building. The museum itself sponsors lectures and concerts periodically. Catalogs of past exhibits are sold. The library (50,000 volumes) is open for use by the public. Parking nearby. Weekdays 9–5; weekends 1–5. Free. (Take US 40 to McCausland Ave. and go north to get to the university, which is located on the edge of St. Louis proper and adjacent to Forest Park.)

**SPRINGFIELD: Springfield Art Museum.** 1111 East Brookside Dr., 65807 ☐ The Ozark highlands stretch to the south of this large residential city in which the art museum is one of the municipal departments. Located in Phelps Grove Park in south-central Springfield, it came to museum status, after several storefront exhibitions, in the forties. In 1958 the museum moved into a new building. Under this unique hyperbolic/parabolic roof is housed an eclectic collection, with emphasis on prints and American painting. Outstanding are prints by Rembrandt and Dürer and paintings by Inness, Shahn, Burchfield, Benton, and Sheeler. Regional and area artists are also included in the collection. The schedule of exhibits varies; in the spring the museum sponsors a competitive exhibit, Watercolor, U.S.A. Cameras without flashes are permitted. Classes are held for both adults and children; lectures, concerts, talks by visiting artists, and film series are also features of the museum's program of activities. Guided tours for groups can be arranged. Catalogs are published for exhibitions initiated here and for Watercolor, U.S.A. The library (3,000 volumes) is open to the public Tues.–Sat. 1–5; Tues. & Thurs. 6:30–9. A sales desk offers craft items, postcards, and reproductions. Parking provided. Tues.–Sat. 9–5; Sun. 1–5; Tues.–Thurs. 6:30–9:30. Free; donations are welcome. (About 6 blocks west of Glenstone Ave. on Bennet St. Bennet becomes Brookside Dr. when it crosses National Ave.)

# MONTANA

**BILLINGS: Yellowstone Art Center.** 401 North 27th St., 59101 ☐ The County Jail (built in 1884) in Billings was converted into the Yellowstone Art Center in 1964. In addition to the classes and workshops common to active art centers across the country, 5 galleries show, in some 20 changing exhibitions, objects from several collections that belong to the center: contemporary graphics, Western Americana (especially Olaf Wieghorst paintings), African sculpture, the Poindexter collection of Abstract Expressionist paintings of the New York school, and photographs. Cameras are permissible according to the exhibition. Films, concerts, and lectures are held here as adjuncts to the educational program. Tours are available by request. The library can be used for browsing, and a sales desk has books, jewelry, prints, postcards, and Montana ceramics. Parking on the street. Tues.–Fri. 11–5 (summer 10–4); Thurs. evening 7–9; Sat. & Sun. 12–5. Free. (From I-90 take 27th St. exit; cross tracks and continue 5 blocks. The center is at the corner of 27th & 4th Ave. North.)

**GREAT FALLS:   C. M. Russell Museum.** Trigg-Russell Foundation, 1201 Fourth Ave. North, 59401 □ Charles M. Russell came to Great Falls in 1880 at the age of 25 and remained there, writing and painting, until his death 46 years later. During those years a Miss Josephine Trigg and members of her family received as gifts around 150 original works by Russell. With the formation, at Miss Trigg's death, of the Trigg-Russell Foundation in 1953, these paintings and sculptures became available to the public in the present museum, to which his studio is attached. Russell predominates here—the museum claims sixth place in the United States in the ranking of C. M. Russell collections—but other Western artists are represented in rotating shows which are changed bimonthly. Cameras are permitted. Films and concerts are scheduled, especially during the tourist season. Guides are available on request. Catalogs published by the museum, original art, pottery, records, and etchings can be purchased at the museum shop. The library (200 volumes) is the repository of books on C. M. Russell and on Montana; it can be used by special permission. Parking facilities are not provided by the museum. May–Sept., Mon.–Sat. 10–5; Sun. 1–5; winter, closed Mon. Admission $2 for families, $1 for individuals, 50¢ for students.

**HELENA:   Montana Historical Society.** Veterans and Pioneers Memorial Building, 225 North Roberts St., 95601 □ Across from the capitol in Helena is Montana's "oldest state institution," the Montana Historical Society, founded in 1865, only 60 years after Lewis and Clark opened up the region, and 24 years before Montana entered the Union. The displays here are primarily, and expectedly, historical—dioramas and display cases depict the history of Montana in visual sequence, and period rooms show 13 different business establishments of a typical 1880s town. However, a central interest in this setting that sets forth the history of the area is a fine collection of paintings and sculptures by Charles M. Russell, depictor nonpareil of America's West. Among some 150 pieces are "When the

Land Belonged to God," "Free Trapper," and "Laugh Kills Lonesome." Other Western art and modern art is exhibited in another gallery where the shows change monthly. Cameras without flashes are permitted.

A docent program focuses on tours to elementary school groups, which can be arranged in advance. Audiophones can be rented for 50¢. During the summer a "tour train" makes a historical tour around Helena. The *Montana Magazine of Western History* is a quarterly published by the society. The State Western History Library, devoted to the history of the Northern Great Plains, Rocky Mountains, and Pacific Northwest, is open to the public for use on the premises. In addition, books on Western history as well as reproductions and gift items are for sale in a display area in the lobby of the building. Parking is limited and difficult in the summer. Memorial Day–Labor Day, daily 8–8; winter months weekdays 8–5, weekends and holidays 12–5. Free. (From I-15, continue on Prospect Ave. to Montana Ave. Follow the signs to the capitol.)

**MISSOULA:   Missoula Museum of the Arts.** 335 North Pattee, 59801 ☐ The Missoula Area Arts Council, at work among the farmers and lumbermen, the paper manufacturers and merchants of Missoula, founded the Missoula Museum of the Arts in 1975 because of "interest shown for such a facility." Its home is an old Carnegie Library building constructed in 1903. There is no permanent collection as yet, but exhibits change every 4 to 6 weeks. No cameras are permitted. Classes, workshops, films are all scheduled activities here, and a docent program prepares people to lead tours as requested. Catalogs and posters relating to the exhibits are sold. Parking on the street only. Tues.–Sat. 12–5. Free.

# NEBRASKA

**LINCOLN:   Sheldon Memorial Art Gallery.** University of Nebraska, 12th & R Sts., 68588 ☐ The Museum of Modern Art Annex and Sculpture Garden in New York and the Sheldon Memorial Art Gallery and Sculpture Garden in Lincoln have a distant kinship through their creator Philip Johnson, architect for both. He designed the Sheldon Memorial Art Gallery in the early 1960s, between working on the Seagram Building (1956) and the New York State Theater at Lincoln Center (1964), both in New York City. In each case, the plans were spectacular; in the case of the Sheldon, the scale was slightly reduced. Sheathed in Italian marble and building-high arched columns, and adjoined on two sides by a sculpture garden, the museum is as stunning as its New York cousins. The art within is mostly 19th- and 20th-century American. The Nebraska Art Association's collections of American art—paintings, sculpture, prints, drawings, ceramics—are housed here together with the university's collections of contemporary paintings, sculpture, prints, drawings, photographs, and ceramics. A group of canvases by Robert Henri shows his development, as do groups of works by Blakelock and Hartley. The 20th century is represented by Rothko, de Kooning, Davis, and Motherwell, among many others. The sculpture garden provides for the 3-dimensional masters of the same time period—Lachaise, Lipchitz, and Nadelman, for example. Exhibits change frequently. The gallery sponsors classes for children, concerts, films, and gallery talks. Guided tours are available. A newsletter and exhibition catalogs are published. The museum shop offers original paintings, sculpture, prints, drawings, ceramics, glass, and jewelry for sale. Tues. 10–10; Wed.–Sat. 10–5; Sun. 2–5. Free.

**Elder Gallery,** Nebraska Wesleyan University, 50th & St. Paul Sts., 68504 □ The Elder Art Gallery in the C. C. White building on campus houses Nebraska Wesleyan University's art treasures: paintings by area artists, and others—Chagall, Rouault, Utrillo, Matisse, Le Brun, Biddle, Baskin, and Arp, for example. Shows change monthly. Cameras are permitted. Concerts are held here throughout the academic year. Parking available. Tues.–Fri. 10–4:30; Sat. & Sun. 1–4:30; closed school holidays. Free.

**OMAHA:    Joslyn Art Museum.** 2200 Dodge St., 68102 □ The Joslyn Art Museum, a pink marble Art Deco building, was finished in 1931 and presented to the public by Mrs. George Joslyn as a memorial to her husband. Although western America is highlighted here in galleries that show life on the prairie, the physical environment of Nebraska, and the history of the Northwest Territory in artifacts, engravings, paintings, and sculpture, the museum's holdings span the centuries from ancient times to the present. Important works of art are displayed with other objects from the same time frame, giving to each a significance in its historical and cultural context. Titian's "Man with Falcon," for example, is shown with a 16th-century Venetian sculpture and Venetian carved furniture. Lorenzo di Credi's "Madonna and Child with Angels" is hung in an early Renaissance gallery where coins, bronzes, and other objects add to the overall picture of the times. The European and American paintings here are numerous and impressive—works by Monet, Rembrandt, Veronese, El Greco, Corot, and Renoir join others by Copley ("Lord Cornwallis"), Inness, Homer, Wood ("Stone City, Iowa"), Benton, Bierstadt, Catlin, and Miller on the walls of this excellent small museum. The history of the area unfolds in on-the-scene representations: The Maximilian-Bodmer collection of paintings and documents elucidates Prince Maximilian's 1833–1834

Upper Missouri River expedition (Bodmer's paintings were done during the expedition); the Stewart-Miller collection depicts the Great Plains in the 1830s (some of these paintings were done by George Catlin); another collection shows the life and look of the Old West, recorded during a Western hunting trip along the Oregon Trail (A. J. Miller was commissioned to make the sketches along the way, and he made 113 of them). Exhibitions change every 6 weeks. Cameras can be used only in the permanent collection. Classes, lectures, concerts, and films are all offered by the museum; guided tours by appointment. The library (8,000 volumes) is open for use by the public and for inter-library loan. A museum shop sells books, jewelry, prints, postcards, pottery, and catalogs. Parking nearby. Tues.–Sat. 10–5; Sun. 1–5. Admission 50¢. (At Dodge St. & 24th St.)

**SEWARD:   Koenig Art Gallery.** Concordia College, 800 North Columbia Ave., 68434 ☐ Concordia College keeps its small art collection in a gallery in the main administration building. Here some contemporary prints, paintings, ceramics, and glass are displayed. There is a Burchfield watercolor, a Rosenquist lithograph ("Continental Divide") and a Rauschenberg pull from the Hoarfrost series. Exhibitions are monthly. Cameras are permitted. Gallery tours are often provided for classes from area schools. Weekdays 8–5; Sun. 2–5; closed a week at Easter, Thanksgiving, and 2 weeks at Christmas. (Take I-80 to the Seward exit [US 34]. From Main St., go north on Columbia Ave. The gallery is in Weller Hall.)

# NEVADA

**LAS VEGAS:   Las Vegas Art Museum.** 3333 West Washington St., 89107 ☐ The adobe brick ranch-style building, built early in the 1900s, that is today the home of the Las Vegas Art Museum has had, like its host city, a checkered career. Early on, the museum grounds were used as a stage stop, later as a ranch, and still later as a dude ranch. In 1945, both land and building were deeded to the city, and five years later, the Las Vegas Art Museum came into being. Contemporary regional artists, many of whom have come through national juried shows, are given exhibition space here; in addition, the collection contains some works by well-known artists. In all, 145 works make up the permanent collection—paintings, prints, photos, sculpture, ceramics, and fiber arts. Exhibits—some one-person shows, some traveling shows—change monthly. Cameras are not permitted. The museum sponsors 2 juried shows per year; demonstrations (fourth week of each month); regularly scheduled 9-week accredited courses; special workshops for advanced students and teachers; summer art camps and neighborhood art for children. Artwork is sent to and displayed in local business places on a rotating basis. Outside festivals are planned in conjunction with other organizations. Funds are available for high school student scholarships to museum classes. A monthly bulletin is sent to members, and an artists' cooperative operates in the building, making a wide range of artwork available for purchase. Parking readily available and convenient for the elderly and handicapped. Daily 10–5; closed Thanksgiving, Christmas, Easter. Free. (1 block west of intersection of Rancho Dr. & Washington St.)

**RENO:  Nevada Art Gallery.** 643 Ralston St., 89503 ☐ Fifty years ago two patrons of the arts founded the Nevada Art Gallery in a Victorian house on Ralston Street, near the center of Reno. A varied collection of 19th- and 20th-century paintings and decorative arts, and Indian baskets and artifacts is on display here. Exhibitions are changed monthly, sometimes 2 or 3 running concurrently. A full program of art and craft classes is repeated in 3 sessions a year. Concerts, lectures, and catalogs accompany exhibits. The docent program sends lecturers into the public schools and offers monthly tours to visiting classes. Other guided tours are available by request. The Shop at the Gallery has one-of-a-kind craft items, prints, photographs, and weavings; the inventory changes with exhibitions and seasons. Parking facilities on the premises. Sept.–July, Tues.–Sun. 1–4; closed Aug. & holidays. Free. (Take North Virginia to 5th St. to Ralston St.)

# NEW HAMPSHIRE

**CORNISH:  Saint-Gaudens National Historic Site.** Mailing address: P.O., Windsor, VT 05089 ☐ In the small rural community of Cornish, at the end of the 19th century, a sophisticated artists' colony flourished around Augustus Homer Saint-Gaudens, one of the great American sculptors of the day. Saint-Gaudens had come here in 1885 to summer under the shadow of Mt. Ascutney, having won the battle against anonymity and become the monument builder of his day. He remodeled what in 1800 had been used as a tavern into a commodious home which he called "Aspet," refashioned a stable into a studio, lavished attention on the grounds by building formal gardens, fountains, and pools, and in 1900 took up permanent residence there. After his death in 1907, his widow and son undertook to preserve the property; they deeded the estate to the state of New Hampshire, and eventually it was designated a National Historic Site by Congress. Here on these 82 acres of the Granite State is exhibited, in the studio, in the gallery, and out-of-doors, the fruit of Saint-Gaudens's labors—sculptures, bas reliefs, portraits, busts, and monumental works. In the garden is a copy of the haunting Adams Memorial (Washington, D.C.) that was commissioned by Henry Adams after the death of his wife. The Shaw Memorial (Boston, Mass.) commissioned by the state in memory of Col. Robert G. Shaw is close by. "The Puritan," the Farragut Monument, and "Standing Lincoln" can all be viewed here, as well as works by the Cornish colony of artists (among them John La Farge, Maxfield Parrish, and Stanford White) and the original furnishings of Aspet. Two to 3 temporary exhibitions of contemporary art or historical works are mounted during the summer months through October. Cameras are permitted.

A series of concerts is held in June, July, and August in cooperation with the trustees of the Saint-Gaudens Memorial. Guided tours are available to educational groups upon prior request. The trustees of the memorial offer a $7,500 scholarship grant to a sculptor or art historian annually, and a sculptor-in-residence program. Demonstrations and interpretations of the processes of 19th-century studio sculpture are held from June through October. Books and pamphlets on the work of Saint-Gaudens are published and sold here together with medals, postcards, and slides. Parking on the estate. Daily May 25–Oct. 31, 8:30–5. Admission 50¢ for adults, children and educational groups free. (Take Saint-Gaudens Rd. off N.H. Rt. 12A; the estate is just north of the Windsor-Cornish covered bridge.)

**HANOVER: Dartmouth College Museum and Galleries.** Dartmouth College, 03755 ☐ One of the beauties of New England is the campus of Dartmouth College, where the brush strokes of early America are still visible despite the more contemporary additions—one of them a huge and handsome building complex (Hopkins Center for the Creative and Performing Arts was built in 1962) that houses facilites for theater, concerts, and the visual arts. Art galleries here and spaces in Carpenter Hall and Wilson Hall display on a rotating basis the permanent collection of Dartmouth College, which consists of some 10,000 objects, including an impressive selection of 19th- and 20th-century art from America and Europe—paintings, sculpture, drawings, and prints. From other places and periods are Assyrian reliefs; early Christian mosaics; classical icons; Chinese art; and a collection from the silversmiths of early Massachusetts. There are contemporaries Rothko and Zox, paintings by Gris and Rattner, Remington and Sloan, and Zurbarán and Goya. Frescoes by Orozco are on the walls of the Baker Library. Exhibitions are continually changing in each of the exhibition galleries; artist-in-residence exhibits occur about 4 times a year. The gallery sponsors gallery talks and annual student shows. Publications include various catalogs including one for each artist-in-residence exhibition. The art library (40,000 volumes) is in Carpenter Hall. Mon.–Sat. 11–4, 7–10; Sun., holidays, intersessions 2–5. Free.

**KEENE:   Thorne-Sagendorph Art Gallery.** Appian Way, Keene State College, 03431 ☐ A large kinetic sculpture by George Rickey adorns the exterior wall of the Thorne-Sagendorph Art Gallery, a wing of the library on the Keene State College campus. The small permanent collection here consists of gifts to the college, many given before the gallery was built (1965), some acquired later. Regional work is shown here, and some work by artists of national prominence. Exhibitions are scheduled throughout the year, generally lasting 4 weeks. Cameras are permitted. The gallery sponsors films, lectures, concerts, workshops, print sales, and other special events. Tours for groups may be arranged in advance. Guest parking across the street from the gallery. Sun.–Fri. 1–4:30, or by prior arrangement. Free. (Take Rts. 12, 9, or 101 into Keene; turn north onto Main St. and proceed to Appian Way.)

**MANCHESTER:   Currier Gallery of Art.** 192 Orange St., 03104 ☐ Manchester boasts one of the leading small museums in New England, in one of the city's loveliest buildings. Copied from an Italian Renaissance palace with a handsome central court, the limestone and marble building rose on the property of Moody Currier, a former governor of New Hampshire, and his wife Hannah, as specified in their will. Funds from their estate also provided the purchasing and operating capability to build and maintain an estimable collection. Today the museum owns European art that ranges across the centuries beginning from the 1400s, including works by Gossaert, Tiepolo, Monet, Rouault, and Picasso; portraits by Copley and Inman; landscapes by Cropsey, Bierstadt, Heade, and Homer; and from the 20th century, paintings by Hopper, Sheeler, Kuhn, O'Keeffe, and Wyeth. A group of American furniture emphasizes New Hampshire craftsmanship, from the country pieces of the Dunlaps to the Federal pieces made in Portsmouth; a selection of new England silver and pewter and choice examples of 19th-century American glass round out a small but high-quality collection. Among the highlights here are Monet's "The Seine at Bougival," Gossaert's "Self Portrait," Tiepolo's "The Triumph of Hercules," "Woman Seated in a Chair" by Picasso, "The Wounded Clown" by Rouault, "The Storm" by Vernet, and a Franco-Flemish Tournai tapestry. Exhibitions change every 6 weeks in 2 of the museum's galleries. Cameras are permitted. The education department offers classes for children and adults, special graded tours (tours in French and German are available on request), classroom programs, slide talks. Lectures and concerts are held regularly. Catalogs accompany exhibitions. The library (3,000 volumes) is open Tues.–Thurs. by appointment only. Art books, cards, museum reproductions, and jewelry are sold in the museum shop. Parking on the street only. Tues.–Sat. 10–4; Sun. 2–5; closed national holidays. Free. (From the Amoskeag Bridge over the Merrimack River, make a right onto Elm St. and a left onto Orange.)

# NEW JERSEY

**CLINTON: Hunterdon Art Center.** 7 Center St., 08809 ☐ The Hunterdon Art Center in Clinton, a picturesque pre-Revolutionary village, prizes one of the outstanding print collections in the state. The gambrel-roofed, stucco-covered stone building that houses the collection was built in 1825 and was used as a gristmill until the 1950s. A group of art-oriented citizens began the art center here in 1952. Special exhibits are mounted monthly, among them a juried exhibit of prints and one of paintings, drawings, and sculpture, a crafts show, an invitational members' exhibit, an antiques show and sale, a folk art bazaar, and a media exhibition. Cameras are permitted. Periodic art classes are held in portraiture, life drawing, and sculpture; a summer children's program offers lessons in pottery and weaving. The center sponsors chamber music concerts every other Sunday throughout the year. Theater productions are staged in the fall and winter. Occasional memorial fellowships are awarded; grant recipients are aided in fulfilling the obligations of their grants. A sales desk offers jewelry, prints, cards, weavings, ceramics, and hand-blown glass for sale. A variety of restaurants are located nearby. Parking on the premises and nearby. Tues.–Fri. 1–4; Sat. & Sun. 1–5. Free; donations are accepted. (At the river, where Main and Center Sts. meet.)

**MONTCLAIR: Montclair Art Museum.** 3 South Mountain Ave. at Bloomfield Ave., 07042 ☐ With a gift of 30 American paintings to the Municipal Art Commission in 1909 from Montclair resident and collector William T. Evans, the Montclair Art Museum was founded. Soon after, Mrs. Henry Lang contributed substantial funds for a building, and in 1914 the new museum, neoclassical in design, opened to the public. American art, primarily paintings, predominates here. There is a particularly fine collection of 18th-century portraits, 19th-century landscapes, and a large group of paintings by George Inness, who lived in Montclair. There is also an interesting permanent display of American Indian art; a collection of North American Indian necklaces; Chinese snuff bottles; silver; European and American prints and drawings and Japanese woodcuts; and American costumes. Except for the permanent American Indian art installation, exhibits change every 4 to 10 weeks. Photographing is allowed by special permission. Art classes are held for adults and children; scholarships are available. A lecture series and 2 concert series are scheduled every year. Sunday afternoon gallery talks, special evening and daytime programs for museum members, and programs for children are all part of the museum's educational activities. Guided tours are offered by prior arrangement; "Discovery Days," luncheon and guided tours for groups and organizations, are also available through the Women's Committee. A bimonthly bulletin, exhibition catalogs, and a catalog of *The American Painting Collection of the Montclair Art Museum,* published by the museum, are sold at the information desk. The library (8,000 volumes) is open to the public for research. The museum shop offers books, cards, handcrafted textiles, ceramics, jewelry, glass, and toys for sale. Parking on the grounds. Tues.–Sat. 10–5; Sun. 2–5:30. Free. (Take Garden State Pkwy. to Bloomfield Ave. exit [#148] and go west. From I-280, take Prospect Ave. exit [8-B] to Bloomfield Ave. and go east. From Rt. 23, go east on Bloomfield Ave.)

**NEWARK:   Newark Museum.** 49 Washington St. Mailing address: P.O. Box 540, 07101 □ The Newark Museum was founded in 1909 by John Cotton Dana, city librarian, as an educational adjunct to the library. It was housed in the Newark Free Public Library until 1925, when it removed to its own home, a new building given to the city of Newark by one of its most successful merchants, Louis Bamberger. Facing it, in the center of the city, is Washington Park, and extending behind, an acre of sculpture garden. The collection of American painting, sculpture, and decorative arts (emphasizing New Jersey) is especially noteworthy, as is the section on Tibetan art and a Schaefer collection of ancient glass, thought to be one of the nation's best. Highlights of the American work are portraits by Stuart, Vanderlyn, and Peale; "N.Y. Interpreted" by Joseph Stella, Hopper's "The Sheridan Theatre," Segal's "Parking Garage," "Greek Slave" by Hiram Powers, and "Untitled" by David Smith. In addition, there is an interesting group of European clocks and a coin collection. The museum also has an extensive science section (natural, physical, and earth), an ethnology section, a Junior Museum and Mini-Zoo, and a planetarium. The 1884 Ballantine House, a Romanesque Renaissance home recently restored, strengthens the museum's holdings in the decorative arts. And behind the museum are Newark's Old Stone Schoolhouse (1784) and the Newark Fire Museum to elaborate on the history of Newark. Frequent changing exhibits feature various facets of the permanent collections. Photographing is permitted except on restricted loans.

A busy schedule of classes and events includes an adult arts workshop; luncheon lecture series and special lectures; monthly concerts, films, children's programs and films; summer jazz in the garden; special art and crafts demonstrations and intensive weekend classes; symposia; summer demonstrations and lectures in the sculpture garden. Docent tours are available by appointment. The many books and catalogs published by the museum are sold in the museum shop, which also offers jewelry, postcards, and objects relating to the museum's collections. The library (18,000 volumes), an art and science resource, is open to the public; New Jersey material is available for inter-library loan. Parking in back of the museum; entrance to lot on University Ave. Daily 12–5; holidays 1–5; closed July 4, Thanksgiving, Christmas, Jan. 1. Free.

**NEW BRUNSWICK:   University Art Gallery.** Fine Arts Collection, Rutgers, The State University of New Jersey, 08903 ☐ The Fine Arts Collection of Rutgers University is housed in the 1904 Renaissance-style building that was once the library. It was renovated in 1966 and today houses close to 5,000 paintings, prints, and sculptures. A long time span is covered by this assemblage of works, but it is especially strong in 19th- and early-20th-century French, English, and American paintings and graphics. The 19th-century French prints and posters are particularly noteworthy. The permanent collection is on display during the summer months; from September to May, the gallery mounts 6 or 7 loan exhibits. Cameras are permitted according to the nature of the exhibit. The gallery offers lectures, concerts, and seminars on the current exhibits from time to time. Saturday morning art appreciation classes are held for children, ages 5–12, night classes for adults. Guided tours are available for groups by appointment. Exhibition catalogs prepared and published by the gallery can be purchased at a sales desk. Only street parking is available. Mon.–Fri. 10–4:30; Sat. & Sun. 12–5. Free. (Take the N.J. Tpke. to exit 9; proceed on Rt. 18 west to Rt. 27 [Albany St., New Brunswick] south; after 2 traffic lights, turn right on George St., left [next light] on Hamilton St. The gallery is on the right, in the middle of the block.)

**PARAMUS:   Bergen Community Museum.** East Ridgewood & Fairview Aves., 07652 ☐ The Bergen Community Museum is housed in a post-Civil War building which was and still is used for county purposes. The space set aside for the museum became available in 1970. Contemporary New Jersey artists have a showcase here, and the museum has a small collection of German bisque dolls. Youngsters and their parents come to see the brace of mastodons, the fossils, and a small nature room with live animals.

The exhibits in 3 galleries are changed monthly. Cameras are permitted. Programs on art and science are scheduled regularly, as are workshops in contemporary crafts. Tours (Tues.-Fri. 9-4) must be arranged in advance. The museum sells books, reproductions of jewelry and antique toys, and postcards. Large parking area adjacent to the building. Wed.-Sat. 1-5; Sun. 2-6. Admission by donation of 50¢ for adults, 25¢ for children; free for senior citizens. (From the Garden State Pkwy. exit at Oradell Ave. and go right at Pascack Valley Rd. From Rt. 4, take Forest Ave. north to East Ridgewood and go left 4 blocks. From Rt. 17, take Midland Ave., River Edge exit, go left at second light and left at the museum sign.)

**PRINCETON:   The Art Museum.** Princeton University, 08540 ☐ Princeton's new (1966) contemporary art museum was built 84 years after the museum was founded (1882) on the same site, and 220 years after the founding of the university. The gracious Georgian look of the campus is not marred by the presence of this new-look structure; with the exception of Picasso's "Head of a Woman," which guards the entrance, the exterior blends into the surroundings by virtue of its simplicity and color. The inner spaces achieve an openness that is markedly 20th century. The museum collections, supporting the curriculum of the Department of Art and Archaeology, are shown in rotation, the exhibits elaborating on subjects being covered in the classrooms. The geographical focus here is Europe, North and Central America, and the Far East; the time frame, from ancient to contemporary. Of particular note is the Greek and Roman art; the Italian, Northern European, American, and Chinese paintings; the prints and drawings; the pre-Columbian art; and the prehistoric Chinese bronzes. There are some loan exhibitions. Hand-held cameras are permitted. Occasional lectures are arranged for the museum's support organization, and lectures sponsored by the Department of Art and Archaeology are open to the public. Guided tours for groups can be arranged in advance. A semiannual bulletin and other books and catalogs published by the museum are for sale here. Municipal parking lots within walking distance. Tues.-Sat. 10-4; Sun. 1-5 (academic year), 2-4 (summer); closed major holidays. Free. (Main entrance to the university is on Nassau St. facing Witherspoon St.)

**TRENTON:   New Jersey State Museum.** 205 West State St., 08625 ☐ The New Jersey State Museum, a complex of 3 buildings—museum, planetarium and auditorium—overlooking the Delaware River, was completed and dedicated in 1965 as part of the state cultural center. Its collections and exhibitions devoted to natural history, archaeology and ethnology, and cultural history are enhanced by a collection of early-20th-century paintings and sculpture. New Jersey artists, or works dealing with New

Jersey subjects, are favored: John Marin, for example, was born in New Jersey, and many of his works are shown here. Other holdings include works by Dove, Hartley, Hopper, Burchfield, Kandinsky, Marsh, and Louis Lozowick. Georgia O'Keeffe's "East River from Shelton" and Max Weber's "Fleeing Mother and Child" are highlights. The museum also prizes a complete collection of graphics by Ben Shahn and 2 large mosaic murals. Sculptures, works by Calder, Hunt, and Rickey among them, are displayed in an outdoor sculpture garden. No gallery is devoted to the exhibition of paintings and sculpture exclusively; rather the museum uses its fine art collection as an adjunct to exhibitions in the other disciplines. Cameras are permitted but not encouraged.

The museum has an extensive educational program, including performing arts programs, gallery talks, and lesson-demonstrations, all of which are free and can be arranged for in advance. Planetarium programs, films, and Sunday concerts are offered regularly, also free of charge. Tours of specific exhibitions are available by advance reservation. The museum publications, including books and pamphlets on natural science, fine arts, archaeology and ethnology, and cultural history are sold at the museum shop, which is primarily for the convenience of visiting school groups. The Artlease Gallery offers a selection of contemporary artwork for rental or purchase. Curatorial libraries in each discipline are open to scholars and students by special arrangement. Parking facilities crowded during the week, plentiful on weekends and holidays. Mon.–Fri. 9–4:45; Sat. & Sun. 1–5; closed Thanksgiving, Christmas, Jan. 1. Free.

# NEW MEXICO

**ALBUQUERQUE:    Museum of Albuquerque.** Mountain Rd. & 19th St. N.W., 87104 ☐ The Museum of Albuquerque came from a 1939 WPA-sponsored building to its new home in 1979. A contemporary building incorporating the most pleasing aesthetic elements of traditional adobe pueblos, it is set in public gardens adjacent to the historic "Old Town" where Albuquerque had its beginnings. The collections here, both fine arts and historical, focus on the southwestern United States. The artwork is predominantly by contemporary local artists and craftsmen, with a good selection of Southwest Indian arts and crafts. The history section covers the eras of Spanish colonization, Mexican territorial rule, U.S. territorial government, and the historical panorama of the Indians of the Southwest. Art exhibits change every 6 to 8 weeks. Cameras can be used with special permission only. In addition to its school, the museum offers lecture series in art, history, and science, and a limited field trip schedule. Suitcase and table-top exhibits accompanied by trained docents are offered to public school classes. Gallery tours are conducted at all times, and can be arranged for in advance. Catalogs accompany most major exhibits. In the museum shop can be found jewelry, books, traditional and contemporary crafts, and museum replicas. On the Old Town plaza are several restaurants serving Mexican-Indian food. Large parking areas on the museum grounds. Tues.–Fri. 10–5; Sat. & Sun. 1–5. Free. (Go north on Rio Grande Blvd. to Mountain Rd.; east on Mountain Rd. to 19th St.)

**American Classical College Museum of Art Gallery.** 6th & McKnight Sts. N.W. Mailing Address: P.O. Box 4526, Station A, 87106 ☐ The artwork of New Mexico's flagellants, a self-castigating religious sect the ancestry of which can be traced to the mid-13th century in Europe, is gathered in the gallery of the American Classical College. In this adobe structure, surrounded by a private garden, are the *santos,* or saints, painted by the flagellants. Also on display are oil paintings attributed to Pintoricchio and Dolci. Cameras are not permitted. Art classes and lectures are held, and in the gallery shop reproductions and books (one a manual of canvas restoration and one on portrait painting) are sold. Parking limited. Daily 10–12. Free. (The pink building with a broad drive-in entrance at the corner of 6th & McKnight Sts. N.W. is the American Classical College Gallery.)

**Lovelace-Bataan Medical Center.** 5400 Gibson Boulevard, S.E., 87108 ☐ If you are in Albuquerque for medical treatment at the Lovelace-Bataan Medical Center, stop to browse through the first-floor lobby gallery in the W. R. Lovelace Building. A permanent exhibit called "The Taos School and the Santa Fe Group of Artists" contains about 30 fine paintings by artists from these Western schools. Open during medical center hours Mon.–Fri. 8–5, Sat. 8–12.

**University Art Museum.** University of New Mexico, Fine Arts Center, Redondo & Cornell N.E., 87131 ☐ The Art Museum at the University of New Mexico was founded and built in 1963 as a part of the College of Fine Arts. The pueblo-style building is the repository for the university's huge and distinguished collection of 19th- and 20th-century prints and photographs; early 20th-century American art, particularly works created in and around Santa Fe and Taos; and Spanish colonial art, particularly silver. Exhibits here, because of limited space, change every 6 to 8 weeks throughout the academic year. Special permission is needed to photograph the collection. The museum sponsors lectures and gallery talks. Catalogs for exhibits organized by the museum and an annual bulletin are available at the museum shop, as well as books and cards. The fine arts library, in the building, is open to the public, as is the print and photograph study room (2 afternoons per week) and the Tamarind Lithography Institute (by appointment). Parking available. Tues.-Fri. 10-5; Sun. 1-5. Admission 50¢ for adults. (About 2 miles east of downtown via Central Ave.)

**Jonson Gallery.** University of New Mexico, 1909 Las Lomas Rd. N.E., 87106 ☐ Also on the University of New Mexico's campus is the Jonson Gallery, built in the style of the Spanish colonies of the Southwest and opened in 1950. Its founder, Raymond Jonson, sought to preserve his own and other artists' works. The Jonson Reserved Retrospective collection consists of over 700 works illustrating all the techniques employed by him. The Other Artists' Work collection contains over 500 items, including representations by Albers, Cook, Diebenkorn, Elaine de Kooning, and Nordfeldt. And a collection of student works from Jonson's classes includes some 375 items. Ten monthly exhibitions, usually one-person shows by New Mexican artists, and a Jonson's Annual Summer exhibition are mounted each year. Cameras are permitted. A small library (400 volumes) is available to researchers upon request. Parking available exclusively for gallery visitors. Tues.-Sun. 12-6. Free. (The gallery is near the center of the campus.)

**ROSWELL:   Roswell Museum and Art Center.** 100 West 11th St., 88201 ☐ The Roswell Museum and Art Center, in this beautiful Pecos Valley city, was founded in 1937, one of the country's many Federal Art Projects. Southwestern art is the primary focus here, along with the early rocket research of Dr. Robert H. Goddard, whose experimental work near Roswell signaled the beginning of modern rocketry. Dr. Goddard's gadgets and replicas of his workshops and rockets are on view for science buffs, as well as natural history exhibits, an aquarium, and a planetarium. And for art fans, in addition to the brilliant collection of works by Peter Hurd and his wife Henriette Wyeth are other works by O'Keeffe ("Ram's Skull with Brown Leaves"), Marin ("Blue Mountain"), Hartley ("Landscape, New Mexico"), and Stuart Davis. Visitors are also served up an excellent collection of Chinese paintings, jades, and bronzes gathered by poet Witter Bynner, who lived in New Mexico, and contemporary Southwest Indian pottery. Exhibitions change every 3 or 4 weeks; the permanent collection is rotated periodically. Cameras are permitted. Art and pottery classes are offered to children and adults. Lectures, films, concerts, and planetarium programs are also on the museum's schedule of activities. Guided tours are available by appointment. Fellowships and grants are offered in painting, lithography, sculpture, and ceramics. Catalogs and a quarterly bulletin are published; a museum shop sells books, jewelry, prints, postcards, and handmade gift items from southwestern craftsmen. Parking on the street and on 2 sides of the museum. Mon.-Sat. 9-5; Sun.

& holidays 1–5; closed Christmas, Jan. 1. Free. (On the corner of Main & 11th Sts.)

**SANTA FE:     Museum of New Mexico, Museum of Fine Arts.** W. Palace Ave., on the Plaza. Mailing address: P.O. Box 2087, 87503 □ The Museum of New Mexico is a complex of institutions—the Palace of Governors (built in 1610), the Museum of Fine Arts, the Museum of International Folk Art, the Laboratory of Anthropology, and the State Monuments—under a central administration. The Museum of Fine Arts was founded in 1907 in the Palace of Governors, mainly for the purpose of preserving this oldest public building, but also to provide space for the artists who were beginning, in the early 1900s, to invade the picturesque Southwest. By 1917 the impact of the art colonies that had grown up in Santa Fe and Taos had created a new museum, fashioned after New Mexico's exhibition building at the Panama-California Exposition of 1913 in San Diego, a structure which drew from the designs of the historic mission churches at Ácoma Pueblo, San Felipe, and Cochiti Pueblo. This "precious child of the Santa Fe sky and the Santa Fe mountains" opened with the paintings of leading artists who lived in or were visiting the state—early New Mexican illustrative works. As a result of the opening, many more artists arrived on the scene. The dual attractions of the gathering of artists and the fine museum engendered still more interest, and nationally known painters such as Sloan and Henri traveled here to work and exhibit. At the same time, artwork of local Indian people was being promoted and encouraged by both museum and artists. Today these early efforts of the Santa Fe and Taos groups and the New Mexican Indians form the core of the museum's large and diverse collection of 20th-century American art, principally from the Southwest, and including a large and fascinating selection of American Indian art. Eastern artists Sloan, Henri, Bellows, Hartley, Marin, and others are also represented here, as well as a scattering of European painters. A regular schedule of exhibitions covers subjects ranging from traditional art of the American West to contemporary lithography and photography. Cameras without tripods or flashes are permitted.

The museum's education division offers classes and occasional lectures and concerts. It also sends traveling shows to communities in the state and "suitcase exhibits" to schools. Multilingual docents are available on request; noontime lectures focus on the current exhibits. In its effort to develop and support the growth of fine arts in New Mexico, the museum sponsors a yearly juried competition, invitationals of regional art, and retrospectives. Catalogs are published with each exhibit; catalogs dating back to 1914 can be perused in the library (6,000 volumes and periodicals), which is open to the public 3 days a week. A museum shop offers books, jewelry, prints, cards, posters, catalogs, and original prints for sale. Municipal parking lots nearby. Daily 9–5. Free.

**TAOS: Harwood Foundation of the University of New Mexico.** 25 Ledoux St. Mailing address: Box 766, 87571 ☐ Elizabeth Case Harwood gave this complex of adobe buildings and their contents to the University of New Mexico in 1936. Here there are old New Mexico santos, works by Taos artists, Persian miniatures, primitive carvings, and tinware. The library (20,000 volumes) has a collection of D. H. Lawrence first editions and books on the art and literature of the Southwest. Mon.–Sat. 10–5. Admission $1.

**Stables Gallery.** Taos Art Association, North Pueblo Rd. Mailing address: Box 198, 87571 ☐ Affiliated with the Taos Art Association, the Stables Gallery provides a showcase for the works of local artists. It is housed in the 1898 Manby House, a Spanish adobe-style hacienda built by Arthur Manby, infamous robber baron of northern New Mexico. Exhibitions are installed every 2 weeks: one-person shows, retrospectives, school shows, Indian student exhibitions, an annual awards show, other special exhibitions, and a continual rotation of the works of the 40-odd artist members of the association. Cameras are permitted. Classes are offered in drama, dance, music, painting, drawing, watercolor, and various crafts. Concert, film, and theater series are programmed regularly. Project Discovery is the children's education program. A newsletter is published monthly. A bookshop is located in an adjacent wing. Municipal parking lot behind the gallery. Free. (On North Pueblo Rd. off US 64 or SR 3.)

# NEW YORK

**ALBANY: Albany Institute of History and Art.** 125 Washington Ave., 12210 ☐ A granddaddy of museums (it was founded in 1791, earlier than all but a few others in the country), the Albany Institute of History and Art is, not unexpectedly, a historical museum which leans heavily on the arts as an expository technique. Albany and its environs, from the period of the Dutch settlers up to the present, is the subject at hand. Early in the 18th century, regional artists (patroon painters) were busily recording the life and the people of the area, and the institute now has many of these paintings on display. Portraits (the subjects identified but not the painters) are in abundance here, as are paintings of biblical subjects; landscapes by Hudson River school painters such as Thomas Cole; sculpture by artists of the Hudson River valley; silver, pewter, furniture, glass, and ceramics all crafted nearby; period rooms dating from the late 17th and 18th centuries; and contemporary paintings and sculpture. There are changing exhibitions in contemporary art and design, an annual regional exhibition of work by artists of the upper Hudson, and a biennial of contemporary American printmakers. The institute sponsors lectures on a broad range of subjects; classes for adults and children; and lectures for children in the public schools on the history of Albany. The library (8,000 volumes, 175,000 manuscripts, photographs, and maps) concentrates on Albany and its history; it is available for use by qualified individuals. A luncheon gallery is in the building. Gifts, books, and prints are for sale. Tues.–Sat. 10–4:45; Sun. 2–5. Free.

**BUFFALO: Albright-Knox Art Gallery.** 1285 Elmwood Ave., 14222 ☐ The Albright-Knox Gallery is one of the treasures of New York State, and one of the first art museums to open in the United States. Its governing body, the Buffalo Fine Arts Academy, was founded in 1862 with a meager collection that was displayed here and there in the buildings of downtown Buffalo. In 1905 what is now referred to as the "old wing"—the Greek Revival Albright Art Gallery—opened by virtue of the generosity of John J. Albright, who single-handedly began the strong artistic and social traditions that attended the growth of this excellent gallery. In 1962 another single benefactor, Seymour H. Knox, made possible the debut of the modern, new wing. Connected to the old wing by a sculpture court, the new wing brought the possibilities of change in both philosophy and size. A Bierstadt painting began the 19th-century collection in 1862; a hundred years later, the museum determined to look into the present and the future to determine the growth of the collection. As a consequence, the collection of contemporary sculpture has become one of the gallery's major assets; in designer Gordon Bunshaft's airy and flexible spaces are sculptures by Baskin, David Smith, Armitage, Nakian, and Butler, to mention a few. Some examples of Renaissance painting and sculpture, Oriental art, Impressionism and Postimpressionism, 18th- and 19th-century English paintings, and 19th-century American paintings are on display, but contemporary painting and sculpture from Europe and the United States predominate. Here hangs the largest collection of paintings by Clyfford Still in the East. Works by the old masters of modern art—de Kooning, Kline, Motherwell, and Pollock—look out over the more contemporary scene from their own quiet setting; works by Lehmbruck, Lipchitz, Maillol, Moore, and Rodin do the same. Van Gogh's "La Maison de la Crau," Gauguin's "Spirit of the Dead Watching" and "The Yellow Christ," Picasso's "La Toilette," Matisse's "La Musique," and Pollock's "Convergence" lend their authority to the young and less well known artists whose works are well represented here. Special exhibits open approximately every 6 weeks. Cameras, with the exception of Polaroids, are permitted; only the permanent collection may be photographed. An education department offers art classes for children and adults. Lectures, concerts, and films are held in the 400-seat auditorium. A community outreach program and an art-to-the-school program fulfill educational needs outside the museum. Tours for groups can be arranged in advance; multilingual guides are available. The museum publishes catalogs in conjunction with the special exhibitions; *Gallery Studies,* an annual collection of essays; an annual report; and a monthly calendar. The library (16,000 volumes) is open to the public. The gallery shop sells books, reproductions, jewelry, cards, and posters. The Garden Restaurant looks out over the sculpture court. Museum parking lot charges 50¢. Tues.–Sat. 10–5; closed Thanksgiving, Christmas, Jan. 1. Admission voluntary; $1 is suggested. (From the N.Y. Thruway, take Rt. 198 [Scajaquada Expwy.]. Large signs indicate the exit that leads to the gallery.)

**Burchfield Center.** 1300 Elmwood Ave., 14222 ☐ The State University of New York, ever more ubiquitous in New York State, shelters under its Buffalo branch the Burchfield Center. Founded in 1966 in honor of one of western New York's best known artists, the center functions as a museum and forum for American art in that area of the state. Its Federal-style home was built around 1932 in a residential area of the city that adjoins Delaware Park, Frederick Law Olmstead's contribution to Buffalo's citizenry. It houses a large collection of the work—paintings, drawings, sketches, wallpapers, journals, and papers—of Charles E. Burchfield, and also the works of artists past and present from western New York. Exhibitions in the main gallery and the 4 adjacent galleries change every 2 months. Cameras are permitted by approval of a written request. Courses in exhibition techniques, independent studies, and docent skills are offered through the State University College at Buffalo. The museum sponsors 3 forum series: artists and critics, poets and writers, and composers and musicians, as well as lectures and special programs. In addition, the educational program reaches out to public schools and homes for the aged and handicapped with traveling exhibitions. A docent training program is offered to community volunteers and college students, and an internship program to secondary school seniors. Guided tours are available by appointment. For many of its exhibits, the museum publishes catalogs that are on sale together with books, periodicals, reproductions, and Burchfield-designed wallpaper at a sales desk. A reference library is open to the public. Dining facilities are on the campus; parking nearby is limited. Mon.–Fri. 10–5; Sun. 1–5. Free. (Entrances to college are on Elmwood Ave. and Grant St.; they lead to a peripheral drive that services all campus buildings. From the east on I-90, take exit 51 [Rt. 33 west] to Rt. 198 west;

exit at Elmwood Ave. S. From the west on I-90, take exit 53 [I-190] to Rt. 198 east; exit at Elmwood Ave. S.)

**CANAJOHARIE: Canajoharie Library and Art Gallery.** Erie Blvd., 13317 □ The village (present population not quite 3,000) of Canajoharie received a gift from Bartlett Arkin in 1927: his collection of 85 traditional American paintings was unveiled at the opening of the Dutch Colonial-style gallery he added to the library to display them. Here, hidden away in the farm country of the Mohawk Valley, are works by the masters of 19th-century American art; there are no less than 20 works by Winslow Homer, and the names of other artists represented form an impressive roster: Gilbert Stuart, Copley, Blakelock, Hassam, Eakins, Inness, Ryder, John Sloan, Prendergast, Benton, Hopper, Burchfield, the Wyeths, O'Keeffe, and others. About 10 exhibits are drawn from this collection a year. Cameras are permitted. A catalog of the permanent collection and post-cards are available for purchase. Mon.–Fri. 10–5; Fri. 7–9; Sat. 10–2; closed holidays. Free. (Corner of Erie Blvd. & Church St.)

**COOPERSTOWN: Fenimore House.** Lake Road, 13326 □ Halls of Fame are not uncommon in Cooperstown; there is the baseball one, and there is Fenimore House. Where the Baseball Hall of Fame pans in on past and present greats of the diamond, Fenimore House sticks to America's past, sports excluded. In fact, it is the headquarters of the New York State Historical Association. There are several interesting sections; folk art (paintings, carvings, and needlework); Hudson River school paintings (by Durand, Cole, and Doughty, for example); early portraits, several by Stuart and one by Benjamin West; life masks of famous Americans; and James Fenimore Cooper memorabilia. American culture is the subject of seminars that are held annually. Tours, lectures, and gallery talks are offered regularly. Classes, workshops, and conferences extend an educational program to nonstudents and children. A program in conjunction with the State University of New York at Oneonta offers graduate degrees. A magazine entitled *New York History* is published quarterly, and a junior magazine called *The Yorker* is published 5 times a year. The Library (50,000 volumes, periodicals, and manuscripts on New York State history) is open to the public upon request. A shop sells books, cards, and prints. Tues.–Sat. 9–5. Admission $2.25 for adults, $1 for children. (1 mile north of Cooperstown on Rt. 80.)

**CORNING: Rockwell-Corning Museum.** Baron Steuben Place, 14830 □ The Corning Glass Foundation and department store owner Robert Rockwell formed an alliance to bring about the Rockwell-Corning Museum in 1976. Rockwell's collection, begun in 1959, was hung in his department store; today it is housed temporarily in the former Baron Steuben Hotel, a 1928 Classical Revival structure in the center of town. Its interior has been revamped to accommodate gallery space and offices, the facade left intact in accordance with the restoration of the business district to its early 1900s appearance. The collection consists of art from the American West (1850–1910), said to be the largest assemblage in the East; Steuben glass (1903–1933), the most extensive selection of glass designed by the famous Carder Steuben; Victorian toys; and Western-related objects such as guns, saddles, Indian artifacts, clothing, and rugs. Paintings by Russell, Remington, Bierstadt, Moran, Catlin, Eastman, and Schreyvogel, among others, and several bronzes by Remington are on view on a rotating basis, one artist featured at a time. Changes are made about 3 times a year. Cameras are encouraged. Special activities of the museum include the presentation of lectures and several audiovisual displays that relate to the collection; a young people's program (in conjunction with other local museums) to acquaint young people with the philosophy and the running of a museum; an orientation program for 4th-grade classes in the district (available to other districts on request); guided tours by special request; a docent-volunteer program. The library, Mr. Rockwell's collection of books on Western artists, is available for use by special permission. *The Painters' West,* a catalog of the collection, is sold at the gift shop, together with cards, prints, books, Indian jewelry. A variety of restaurants are located nearby. The Glass Center, 3 blocks away, provides parking facilities. Memorial Day–Labor Day, Mon.–Sat. 10–6, Sun. 12–5; winter months, Tues.–Sat. 10–5, Sun.1–5. Admission $1 for adults, 50¢ for senior citizens and students, 25¢ for children; special rates for groups with prior reservations. (From Rt. 17, take Pine St., Walnut St. or Cedar St. to Market St. The museum is at the corner of Market & Centerway.)

**ELMIRA: Arnot Art Museum.** 235 Lake St., 14501 ☐ Matthias Arnot was a 19th-century industrialist who filled his neoclassical home in Elmira with paintings representing the artwork of the centuries. Through his bequest in 1910, his home became a museum; 3 years later it was opened to the public. Although today's enlarged collection emphasizes 19th-century academic art and European and American Barbizon paintings— Gérôme, Meissonier, Ludwig Knaus, Jules Breton, Courbet, Daubigny, and Millet—there are other points of interest: "Flemish Fair" by Bruegel, and "Ulysses Discovering Himself to Nausicaa" by Claude Lorrain, for example, are displayed here. Exhibitions change monthly; the entire permanent collection is on view June–Sept. Cameras are permitted. The museum sponsors classes in painting, pottery, printmaking, and photography. Concerts and lectures are also held regularly. Guided tours can be arranged on 48-hour notice. Special exhibition catalogs, a monthly newsletter, and a catalog of the permanent collection are published here. The catalogs are available in the museum shop, which also offers crafts, prints, postcards, reproductions, jewelry, paintings, and pottery for sale. Parking nearby. Tues.–Fri. 10–5; Sat. & Sun. 2–5. Free. (Take Rt. 17 to Church St. exit in Elmira; take Church to Lake St., and turn left.)

**FREDONIA:   Michael C. Rockefeller Arts Center Gallery.** State University College at Fredonia, 14063 ☐ Dedicated to its young namesake, the Michael C. Rockefeller Arts Center Gallery was added to the campus of the State University College at Fredonia in 1968. It was designed by I. M. Pei in concrete and glass; the various wings and courts branch off the entrance lounge, which is gained through an open sculpture court. The simple geometric patterns of the building form the sculptural backdrop for this collection of American prints, drawings, paintings, and sculpture—primarily minor works by contemporary American artists. Four or 5 shows a semester each last about one month. Cameras are permitted. Guest lectures are sponsored in cooperation with the campus art organization Art Forum, generally accompanied by slide presentations and studio demonstrations. Gallery workshop courses given by the director teach the basic problems of museum planning, and hanging and lighting exhibits. Brief explanatory tours can be arranged in advance. Books on the creative and architectural history of Chautauqua County and Fredonia respectively are published and sold here. Eating facilities can be found on the campus; parking near the gallery. Daily; hours change. Free. (Leave N.Y. Thruway at exit 59. Follow signs in Fredonia to the college.)

**GENEVA:   Houghton Art Center.** Hobart and William Smith Colleges, 14456 ☐ The Houghton Art Center is in one of the turn-of-the-century estates that were so common in this Victorian spa located at the foot of Seneca Lake. Formal gardens surround what was once the home of the Houghton (Corning Glass) family. Relandscaping and additions updated the house in the 1930s, and today it is part of the campus of these coordinate colleges. Contemporary paintings and prints—there is an especially fine selection of Japanese prints—are shown here on a monthly schedule of exhibits during the academic year. Cameras are permitted. As college art department, the center offers a range of studio and art history courses. Lectures, concerts, and poetry readings are held during the academic year. Adjacent parking lot has room for 30 cars. Daily 9–5 during academic year. Free. (Use the South Main St. entrance to the colleges on Rt. 14, ⅛ mile south of Jay St.)

**GLENS FALLS:   Hyde Collection.** 161 Warren St., 12801 ☐ The Italian Renaissance comes alive on a street in Glens Falls. The Hyde House, built in 1912, has the look and style of a Florentine villa and is the home of the Hyde Collection. Here, in the house furnished and lived in by the Louis Fiske Hydes, are works of art that range down through the centuries. Ten rooms display a remarkable collection of furniture, tapestries, paintings, and sculpture. A myriad of celebrated names appear on the collection checklist: the 20th century's Bellows, Matisse, Hassam, and Picasso; Turner, Whistler, Ingres, Degas, Homer, Eakins, Courbet, Renoir, Van Gogh, Seurat, Bierstadt, Cézanne, Pissarro from the 19th; Fragonard, Zuccarelli, and Tiepolo from the 18th; from the 17th century, Rembrandt, Van Dyck, Rubens, Hals, and Claude Lorrain; Tintoretto, Veronese, Raphael, and Titian; and della Robbia. Rubens's "Head of a Negro" and Rembrandt's "Christ with Folded Arms" are among the brightest in this galaxy of stars. Special exhibits of works by living artists, works in the permanent collection, sculpture, or decorative arts are mounted periodically. Cameras are permitted without flashes. The collection holds classes for adults in painting and sculpture. Lectures and concerts are offered during the summer. Docents trained here guide tours on a regular basis and for special groups. Publications emanating from the collection relate to the special exhibits and the permanent collection and are available at the museum shop. A small research library (600 volumes) is open to students and scholars. Parking on the grounds and nearby. Tues., Wed., Fri.–Sun. 2–5. Free. (Exit from the Adirondack Northway at #18. In the center of Glens Falls, pass the old post office and the armory on Warren St.)

**GOSHEN: Hall of Fame of the Trotter.** 240 Main St., 10924 ☐ Along with all the trappings and gear of harness racing, the Hall of Fame of the Trotter houses an interesting collection of lithographs by Currier and Ives—all of which feature the harness horse. Two galleries display this collection, as well as paintings and other prints and works depicting trotting races and harness horses in other mediums. Cameras are permitted. Concerts are held 3 or 4 times per year; lectures are provided for groups of schoolchildren. Group tours can be arranged in advance. A library is available for use by advance reservation. The museum shop sells books, prints, jewelry, and postcards. Daily 10–5; Sun. 1:30–5; closed Thanksgiving, Christmas, Jan. 1. Free. (Take N.Y. Thruway to Harriman exit [Rt. 17]; exit from Rt. 17 at 124B to Greenwich Ave.; proceed to Main St. at stop light.)

**HAMILTON: Picker Art Gallery.** Charles A. Dana Arts Center, Colgate University, 13346 ☐ Paul Rudolph designed the Charles A. Dana Art Center on the Colgate University campus. Built in 1966, in Rudolph's "brutalistic" contemporary style, an impressive sculptural form of reinforced concrete and ribbed concrete blocks, it houses the Picker Art Gallery, the Brehman Theater, and the fine arts and music departments of the university. A diverse collection of paintings, sculpture, prints, drawings, photographs, and posters is highlighted by the Luis de Hoyos collection of Guerrero stone sculpture, the most important collection of this pre-Columbian art outside Mexico. An active schedule of exhibitions, some organized here and some on tour, covers a broad spectrum of interest, but particular emphasis is placed on contemporary art, including film and video. Cameras are permitted unless restricted by a special exhibition. Lectures and films are offered. Catalogs and brochures accompany new exhibits. Parking available. Mon.–Fri. 10–5; Sat. & Sun. 1–5; closed during academic recesses and intersessions. Free.

**HUDSON: Olana State Historic Site.** R.D. #2, 12534 ☐ Olana stands high on a hill like a sentinel, looking out over 60 miles of Hudson River valley and the Catskill Mountains to the west. Frederick Edwin Church created this Persian-Moorish villa and 250-acre park in 1870 as his summer retreat, from where he could survey the landscapes that he so often rendered on canvas. The Victorian setting, with furniture and Oriental and Middle Eastern decorative objects intact from Church's day, is apt background for his and other Hudson River school paintings by such as Cole and Heade. Photographing is allowed only by special permission. The museum sponsors many educational activities including lectures, concerts, Hands-on programs, school seminars, tours, and college programs. A series of Catskill mountain hikes takes participants to popular 19th-century sites. Guided tours are conducted every 30 minutes. The library is open to the public by permission only. Books about Church and Olana, a catalog of the museum pieces, and postcards are sold at a museum shop. The grounds of the estate have picnic facilities and grills; guides are available to conduct history and nature tours along the 7½ miles of trails; man-powered boats are permitted on the lake for fishing. Memorial Day–last Sun. in Oct., Wed.–Sun. 9–4:30. Small admission fee. (Take N.Y. Thruway to Catskill [exit 22], Rt. 23 east across Rip Van Winkle bridge; bear right on Rt. 9G for one mile and turn left at the sign to Olana. Or take Taconic Pkwy. to Hudson [exit Rt. 82]; follow Rt. 82 to Rt. 23 west; bear left and go south on route 9G for 1 mile; turn left at the sign to Olana.)

**HYDE PARK: Edwin A. Ulrich Museum.** "Wave Crest"-on-the-Hudson, Albany Post Rd., 12538 ☐ The work of 3 generations of a family of painters, Samuel Bell Waugh (1814–1884), Frederick J. Waugh (1861–1940), and Coulton Waugh (1896–1973)—over 150 years of the creative output of a father, a son, and a grandson—are housed in the Hudson River mansion built by Edwin A. Ulrich. Fashioned from brick and fieldstone in the tradition of an English manor house and overlooking the Hudson, Wave Crest was finished in 1955. Ulrich's interest in the Waughs was unquenchable; he eventually acquired some 350 works by this family: portraits by Samuel (he painted Lincoln and Grant), marine paintings by Frederick, and drawings and palette knife paintings by Coulton. Cameras are not permitted. The museum offers books on the Waughs and prints of Waugh paintings for sale. Biographical material on the Waughs is available for research purposes. Informal talks on the collection are given during visiting hours. May 1–Sept. 30, Fri.–Mon. 11–4; other times by appointment. Admission $1.50; $1 for senior citizens. (1½ miles north of the Hyde Park post office on Rt. 9.)

**ITHACA:  Herbert F. Johnson Museum of Art.** Cornell University, 14853 ☐ Bold and contemporary, itself a massive sculpture of varying juxtaposed rectangular shapes broken by rectangles of sky showing through rectangular arches, the Herbert F. Johnson Museum of Art stands on a knoll overlooking downtown Ithaca, Cayuga Lake, and the surrounding countryside. It was here on this rise, it is said, that Ezra Cornell stood, like Moses on the Mount, and declared his intention to found a university above the waters of Cayuga. The collections shown here, competing with the spectacular views from all sides, were begun in 1953 in the Andrew Dickson White home-turned-museum of art. I. M. Pei was commissioned by Cornell alumnus Herbert F. Johnson, of Johnson's Wax, to design the new museum which he, Johnson, planned to fund and support. Pei's design, incorporating the beauty of the view and fluid inner spaces that flow from lobby to galleries to balconies and wide corridors to still other galleries, was executed in poured-in-place, board-formed concrete, a whole floor poured at a time in order to delineate the levels of the building. Hung against the soft off-white of the concrete is the eclectic collection of art that started as a cultural resource for university students. Although maintaining the broad range originally intended, the collection has developed certain strengths: Asian art, the graphic arts, 19th- and 20th-century American painting, and pre-Columbian art. The Asian collection, with extensive holdings of ceramics from China, Japan, Korea, and Southeast Asia, is enhanced by examples of sculpture, scrolls, bronzes, and prints. Among the American holdings are works by Stuart Davis, Marin, Dove, O'Keeffe, Sheeler, Rattner, Jacob Lawrence, and many others. Some 200 pieces of Tiffany glass comprise an elegant display of American decorative arts. Although the collection of European art is still modest, holdings include 17th-century Dutch, French paintings before Impressionism, and some 20th-century paintings. The print collection, numbering some 7,000, includes works by Mantegna, Dürer, Callot, Hogarth, Canaletto, Piranesi, Goya, and Whistler. Fine examples of 19th-

and 20th-century drawings include works by Whistler, Nolde, Kirchner, Grosz, Léger, Matta, Matisse, and Picasso. A broad range of special exhibits (15 to 20) from all periods of history are mounted each year, some few by students. Cameras are permitted in the permanent collection.

Art Insights: Making Senses is a program of classes for children in art appreciation. Lectures related to exhibits, occasional concerts, and dance programs are offered. Tours guided by specially trained students are available on Saturday and Sunday afternoons or by appointment at other times. Internships (undergraduate) and one assistantship (graduate) are awarded to qualfied students. The museum publishes seasonal calendars and exhibition catalogs which are sold at a sales desk in the lobby, along with cards and posters. The small research library is open to the public by special permission only. Tues., Thurs., Fri., Sat., 10–5; Wed. 10–9; Sun. 11–5. Free. (At end of Central Ave.)

**JAMESTOWN:   James Prendergast Library Association.** 509 Cherry St., 14701 ☐ The city of Jamestown, at the southern end of Chautauqua Lake, was given a gift by Mrs. Alexander T. Prendergast in memory of her son James. A library and funds to purchase works of art for the art gallery, which was included in the building plans, was bequeathed in 1889. Thirty-one oil paintings were purchased, the family portraits and paintings were added, and in 1960, nine more paintings were contributed by another donor. The 19th century predominates in this small collection, with works by Blakelock, Boldini, Cropsey, Hassam, and LeFebvre, among others. Cameras are permitted. Lectures and concerts, occasional art classes, and tours for schoolchildren are among the activities offered. The library's collection of art books is strong and is open to the public. Parking lot next to the library building. Mon.–Fri. 9–9; Sat. 9–6; Sun. 1–4. Free.

**LONG ISLAND:   Guild Hall of East Hampton, Inc.** 158 Main St., East Hampton 11937 ☐ The village of East Hampton is the paradigm of a small, early Colonial village, and Guild Hall, added to the scene as late as 1931, is part of this serene and beautiful setting. The museum section of this cultural center, which celebrates both the performing and visual arts, consists of several galleries and a sculpture garden; the collection tends to favor the work of artists who have lived or worked in the surrounding area: among them are James Brooks, Jackson Pollock, Thomas Moran, Childe Hassam, Ibram Lassaw, Ilya Bolotowsky, Bernard Rosenthal, Robert Gwathmey, and Adolph Gottlieb. About 20 exhibits are launched every year, each lasting about a month. Permission is needed for photographing. In the tradition of cultural centers, Guild Hall offers art and craft classes, series of lectures and concerts, dance recitals, plays, films, and a film festival. It circulates approximately 20 exhibitions to some 30 schools in eastern Long Island and trains interns in the museum section and apprentices in the theater section. It provides guided tours (earphones for some exhibits) that can be arranged in advance. A monthly newsletter is sent to members; a cookbook and catalogs of exhibitions are available at the hall's shop as well as books, posters, cards, handcrafted items, and prints. Park on the street. May–Sept., Mon.–Sat. 10–5; Sun. 2–5; Oct.–Apr., Tues.–Sat. 10–5. Free. (From N.Y.C. take the L.I. Expwy. east to exit 70 [Manorville Rd.]. Proceed to Rt. 27 [Sunrise Hwy.] and go east to East Hampton. Guild Hall is on the corner of Main St. [Rt. 27] & Dunemere Lane, just after the town pond.)

**C. W. Post Art Gallery.** Long Island University, Greenvale 11548 ☐ Hillwood Commons, in which C. W. Post Center of L.I.U. shelters its works of art, is a contemporary structure of gray stone built in 1973 on land sold to the university by the daughter of breakfast cereal magnate C. W. Post. The gallery, one of the many facilities in this student complex, seeks to expose the surrounding community to a variety of visual experiences. Permanently residing here are lithographs (Dali, Rauschenberg, Grooms), paintings, sculptures, and photographs. The schedule of exhibits is varied. Cameras are permitted. A course on gallery and museum management is offered to students and the general public. Exhibitions are often accompanied by lectures and catalogs (sold at the reception desk). Tours are available by appointment. Top of the Commons is a restaurant and bar open daily for lunch and dinner. Parking behind the building. Mon.–Fri. 10–5; Sat. & Sun. 1–5. Free. (Take the L.I. Expwy. to exit 39N; go right, continue to Rt. 25A and make a right turn. Proceed to C. W. Post signs on right and make a right turn at the first entrance. Hillwood Commons is on the left after the road curves. The gallery is on the second floor.)

**Emily Lowe Gallery.** Hofstra University, Hempstead Turnpike, Hempstead 11550 ☐ The beneficence of Joe and Emily Lowe reached Hofstra University in 1963, only 10 years after they had presented Syracuse University with funds for its art center. The collection here is eclectic: European and American paintings coexist with sculpture from Japan, Oceania, Africa, South America, Puerto Rico, and India; prints come from 17th-century Japan and 20th-century America, and photographs from 20th-century Europe and America. "Retreat from the Storm" by Millet, "Portrait of a Woman" by Gauguin, "Otarie Rouse et Juane" by Calder, are among the highlights of this collection. Cameras are permitted by request. Lectures relating to current exhibits are sponsored periodically, as are children's art workshops. Tours can be arranged. Exhibition catalogs are available on request. Parking nearby. Mon.–Thurs. 10–5; Tues., Wed. 10–9; Sun. 1–5. Free. (From Manhattan, take the L.I. Expwy. to Northern

State Pkwy. to Meadowbrook Pkwy. [south]; exit at M5, Hempstead Tpke. west.)

**Heckscher Museum.** Prime Ave. & 25A, Huntington 11743 ☐ The Heckscher Museum is located in Heckscher Park; park, museum, and collection were presented to the people of Huntington in 1920 by August Heckscher, a German immigrant whose mining fortune provided the funds for all three. The original Heckscher bequest consists of works from the 16th through the 20th centuries; the American holdings, particularly those from the 19th century, are outstanding. The earliest painting is by Lucas Cranach, dated 1534. Other outstanding European artists include Bastien-Lepage, Courbet, Jacque, and Diaz de La Peña. Names such as Thomas Moran, George Inness, and Arthur Dove suggest the strength of the American selection. In 1967 the museum acquired a major George Grosz and since then has added works by Thomas Eakins, George Luks, Marsden Hartley, Stuart Davis, and other leading contemporary artists. Six major exhibits and 3 or 4 small, one-artist, one-gallery exhibits are scheduled through the year. Cameras are permitted only in the permanent exhibit galleries. Children's art classes are scheduled during the summer. Lectures and lecture series are coordinated with major exhibitions. Guided tours can be scheduled by appointment. Catalogs are published for major exhibitions and are sold at a sales desk, which also offers postcards and slides. Picnic tables in the park are available for alfresco dining. Park on the street nearby. Tues.–Fri. 10–5; Sat., Sun. 1–6; closed Election Day, Thanksgiving, Christmas, Jan. 1. Free. (From the L. I. Expwy. go to Northern State Pkwy., then to Jericho Tpke. east to Rt. 110. Go north on 110 to 25A [Main St., Huntington]; right on 25A to the first traffic light; left on Prince Ave. to the park entrance.)

**Parrish Art Museum.** 25 Jobs Lane, Southampton 11968 ☐ In 1897 Samuel Longstreth Parrish founded this museum to display his collection of Renaissance panel paintings and classical statuary. Looking like a Venetian villa in the shape of a Greek cross, the building is surrounded by a sculpture garden with several busts of the Caesars and an arboretum of rare and exotic trees. Within, Mr. Parrish's Renaissance collection now shares space with a fine selection of 19th- and early-20th-century American paintings, including an extensive collection of works by William Merritt Chase. Lorenzo Lotto's "Man with a Book," Hassam's "Church at Old Lyme," and Chase's "Prospect Park" (among about 50 other Chase paintings) can be seen here, bridging the chasm of centuries and styles. Here also are Chinese ceramics and Japanese prints and stencils. About 20 exhibits are mounted yearly in 3 galleries. Permission is required for the use of cameras. Classes are held for children and adults, as well as concerts, lectures, and films. Programs for schools, including classroom extension programs, docent tours (group tours by appointment), and internships for college and high-school students are also among the educational activities. Exhibition catalogs are available on request. The Aline B. Saarinen Art Library (2,000 volumes) is open to the public 10–12 and 2–4 on Tues., Thurs., and Fri., and by appointment. A museum shop offers cards, glassware, books, and decorative items for sale. A village parking lot adjoins the museum grounds. Tues.–Sat. 10–5; Sun. 2–5; closed major holidays. Free. (Take the L. I. Expwy. or Rt. 27 to Southampton; the museum is at the main intersection of town.)

**Museums at Stony Brook.** Route 25A, Stony Brook 11790 ☐ Among the Museums at Stony Brook, a complex of 19 buildings on 13 acres of land in this quiet residential village, is a Carriage Museum (1951), a new History Museum, an Art Museum (1974), and 6 period buildings (a blacksmith shop, an 1877 school, a barn, a carriage shed, and two 18th-century structures that are located in the town of Stony Brook). This elaborate project was begun simply in 1935, in one building known as the Suffolk Museum at Stony Brook, by a group of local residents interested in the natural history of the area. Buildings were acquired through the years, and in 1974 the Art Museum was built in the Federal style of architecture that predominates here. Housed in the museum are more than two thirds of the output of genre painter William Sidney Mount, who lived and worked in the area. The collection of some 300 horse-drawn vehicles is widely admired, as is the sizable collection (275) of decoys. Also notable is the collection of 19th- and 20th-century costumes and 15 miniature rooms. Exhibitions change in the Art Museum approximately 4 times per year. Cameras of nonprofessionals are permitted without flash equipment.

A full educational program for schoolchildren and a 4-semester professional craft school are sponsored here. Lectures, guide training, and museum workshops are further features of the museum's special programs. Guided tours are offered upon request. The museum publishes a quarterly newsletter, *Long Island Folklife*, exhibition checklists, brochures, and an annual report. The library (2,000 volumes) is open by appointment. Books, prints, postcards, antiques, early American toys, and home furnishings are sold at the museum shop. Parking available. Wed.–Sun. & most Mon. holidays 10–5. Admission $2 for adults, $1.50 for students and senior citizens, $1 for children over 6, free for under 6. (Take the L.I. Expwy. to Nichols Rd.; go west on 25A, left at the traffic light; the entrance is the next right.)

**MOUNTAINVILLE: Storm King Art Center.** Old Pleasant Hill Rd., 10953 ☐ About 7 miles from Newburgh, where General George Washington announced the end of the Revolution and disbanded his troops, there has grown up another army—peaceful, fixed in place, mute. Scattered over 200 acres of landscaped gardens and rolling fields that surround the 1935 French Normandy-style mansion of Mr. Vermont Hatch, some 90 sculptures, half the total number housed here, stand silent watch. The Storm King Art Center was designated an art museum by the State of New York in 1960. Since then, the collection, devoted to the acquisition of modern artworks (1950 to the present), has expanded to include many oversize sculptures that can be shown to advantage only in open spaces. (For example, 13 large sculptures by David Smith were acquired in 1967.) In addition to these, paintings, graphics, and smaller sculptures are exhibited in the museum galleries, and outstanding works are borrowed from other museums, artists, and private collections to be displayed with the permanent collection. Two or 3 exhibits are installed in the 6 months (May through October) that the museum is open. Photographing is permitted only with hand-held cameras. Guided tours for groups of 15 to 50 (adults only; $35 fee daily except Tues., 2–5:30) can be arranged in advance. Art teachers may conduct their own tours but must have reservations. Picnicking is not permitted. A brochure of the art center costs $1. Parking on the estate. Daily except Tues. 2–5:30. Suggested donation, $2. (From N.Y.C., take the N.Y. Thruway to exit 16 [Harriman]; go north 11 miles on Rt. 32 to the bridge over Moodna Creek; cross the bridge and take an immediate left onto Orr's Mill Rd.; follow the signs to the art center. From Newburgh and points north, take Rt. 32 south 6 miles to the Moodna Creek bridge; go right [do not cross the bridge] on Orr's Mill Rd. to Old Pleasant Hill Rd.)

**NEW YORK CITY: Asia House Gallery.** Asia Society, Inc., 112 East 64th St., 10021 ☐ The Asia Society was founded in 1957 to promote understanding between East and West. The Asia House Gallery was opened in 1960 to familiarize Americans with the art of Asia. To accomplish this aim, 3 large exhibits, the objects for which are borrowed from both foreign and U.S. collections (there is no permanent collection here), are installed during the year. The range of the exhibitions is broad, including Japanese, Indian, Chinese, and Tibetan art. Recorded lectures are available to visitors. The society holds film, dance, and musical programs. Catalogs are published for every exhibit, and an *Archives of Asian Art* annually; they are for sale. Mon.–Fri. 10–5; Sat. 11–5; Sun. 1–5. Closed June 1–Oct. 1; Dec. 15–Jan. 15; Mar. 15–Apr. 15. Free.

**China House Gallery.** 125 East 65th St., 10021 ☐ China House, founded in 1966 to exhibit Chinese classical art, has one gallery in which exhibitions change twice a year. Scholars arrange shows and choose areas of classical Chinese art not commonly dealt with in the West. Films and lectures on

Chinese culture and art are held for groups of schoolchildren or adults. There are 6 visiting lecturers each year; 50 gallery talks are scheduled; concerts and classes are all part of an active educational program. Catalogs are published with every exhibit. Open during exhibitions Mon.–Fri. 10–5; Sat. 11–5; Sun. 2–5.

**The Cloisters.** Fort Tryon Park, 10040 ☐ A medieval turret rises over the trees of Fort Tryon Park and casts its somber shadow over the cliffs that descend to the Hudson River. Here at the Cloisters, a branch of the Metropolitan Museum of Art, the Middle Ages come alive; the quiet chapels and cloisters, the Chapter House from Pontaut, the Gothic and Romanesque Halls seem to echo the receding footsteps of the former robed and hooded occupants. Yet it was created by a modern man (John D. Rockefeller, Jr.) in modern times (1938). The medieval-style building houses authentic 12th- and 13th-century rooms and galleries brought here, stone by stone, from France and Spain, and set out in a chronology that moves from Romanesque to Gothic, from the 11th century to the 15th. On the main floor a Romanesque Hall and apse, a Benedictine cloister from an abbey in southern France, a chapel with the interior choir stonework from a 12th-century church in southern France, a Chapter House (monk's meeting room) from Gascony, a tapestry room containing a set of 14th-century French tapestries depicting the medieval Nine Heroes, and an early Gothic Hall flow around the 12th-century pink and white marble Cuxa Cloister from the monastery of St. Michel-de-Cuxa in the eastern Pyrenees. The chronology proceeds to the ground floor—a Gothic chapel with 13th- and 14th-century tomb monuments, 2 cloisters, a glass gallery with examples from the 15th and 16th centuries, and 3 rooms (the Treasury) devoted to the museum's brilliant collection of small objects such as goldsmith work, enamels, illuminated manuscripts, ivories. Again on the main floor is the Boppard Room with late Gothic stained glass and a 15th-century Spanish altarpiece; the Hall of the Unicorn Tapestries, the famous set of Franco-Flemish 15th- and 16th-century hangings that depict the hunt and capture of the unicorn, and another room with more 15th-century tapestries; the Spanish room, dominated by Robert Campin's altarpiece "Annunciation" and filled with objects that resemble those in the painting; the Late Gothic Hall, reserved for changing exhibits; and the Froville Arcade from a Benedictine priory in eastern France. Hand cameras without flash attachments are permitted; permits are needed for tripods.

The educational services pertain to all ages, and are available by appointment; programs are free to public school groups from New York City. A guided tour of the collection is offered on Wednesdays at 3. Groups of 10 or more must arrange for their visits in advance; chartered or school buses must have permits (obtainable by application to the Cloisters) to enter Fort Tryon Park. Music is an integral feature of the museum; programs of medieval music are played daily, and weekly special concerts are announced in advance. A sales desk offers a variety of reproductions, cards, and books, many of which are prepared and published by the museum. Limited parking on the museum grounds. Tues.–Sat. 10–4:45; Sun. & holidays 1–4:45; Sun., May–Sept. 12–4:45. Admission voluntary; free for children under 12 & senior citizens, weekdays only. (By car, take Henry Hudson Pkwy. north; leave parkway at first exit after George Washington Bridge. Or by the 8th Avenue subway, take the "A" train to 190th Street-Overlook Terrace; reach the street by elevator and take #4 bus or walk through the park. Simplest of all: take the Madison Ave. bus #4 ["Fort Tryon Park-The Cloisters"] directly to the door of the museum.)

**Cooper-Hewitt Museum.** The Smithsonian Institution's National Museum of Design, 2 East 91st St., 10028 □ Andrew Carnegie's baronial mansion, which he built opposite Central Park on Fifth Avenue, a mile north of Henry Clay Frick's baronial mansion opposite Central Park on Fifth Avenue, was presented to the Smithsonian Institution as a new home for the Cooper-Hewitt Museum in 1972. Before that, the museum was an integral part of the Cooper Union, the remarkable educational institution—a free school, a library, and a lecture forum—established by Peter Cooper in 1859. Some time in the late 1800s, Cooper's granddaughters Sarah, Eleanor, and Amy Hewitt established the museum planned, but not accomplished, by their grandfather, and in 1897 the Cooper Union Museum for the Arts of Decoration was opened in the original building on Astor Place. Several important private collections made this opening possible: J. Pierpont Morgan's 3 collections of European textiles; the Italian architectural and decorative drawings belonging to the curator of the Borghese collection; and, acquired several years later, Sèvres architect and interior designer Léon Décloux's samples of 18th-century French decoration in drawings, woodwork, hardware, prints, and books. Having operated many free facilities for many years, the trustees of Cooper Union, in 1963, found it necessary to close the doors of the museum. Not long after, it was taken over by the Smithsonian. In 1968 the museum became the Cooper-Hewitt Museum of Decorative Arts and Design, Smithsonian Institution. Today the museum's holdings make up one of the foremost collections of decorative arts and design in the world. Objects come from all parts of the globe, from every historical period, and cover every category of design. The drawings and prints housed here are primarily related to architecture, design, and ornament; it is the largest collection in the United States (some 30,000 works). The 18th- and 19th-century Italian

University Art Museum, University of California, Berkeley, California

COLIN MC RAE

Los Angeles County Museum of Art, Los Angeles, California

Norton Simon Museum of Art, Pasadena, California

Rosicrucian Egyptian Museum, San Jose, California

Denver Art Museum, Denver, Colorado

Hill-Stead Museum, Farmington, Connecticut

Wadsworth Atheneum, Hartford, Connecticut

Yale Center for British Art, New Haven, Connecticut

THOMAS BROWN

Aldrich Museum of Contemporary Art, Ridgefield, Connecticut

Hirshhorn Museum and Sculpture Garden, Smithsonian Institution, Washington, D.C.

National Gallery of Art's East Building, Washington, D.C.

Norton Gallery, West Palm Beach, Florida

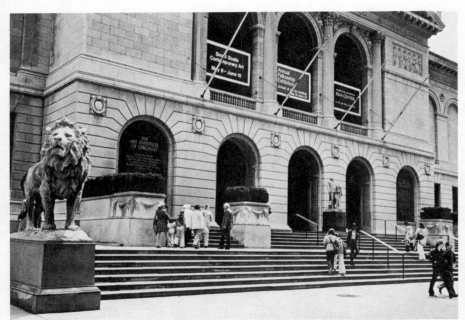

The Art Institute of Chicago, Chicago, Illinois

Indianapolis Museum of Art, Indianapolis, Indiana

I. M. Pei Wing, Des Moines Art Center, Des Moines, Iowa

Helen Foresman Spencer Museum of Art, Lawrence, Kansas

Wichita Art Museum, Wichita, Kansas

J. B. Speed Art Museum, Louisville, Kentucky

New Orleans Museum of Art, New Orleans, Louisiana

R. W. Norton Art Gallery, Shreveport, Louisiana

WILFRED RANDALL

The Art Complex, Inc., Duxbury, Massachusetts

Smith College Museum of Art, Northampton, Massachusetts

Chesterwood, Stockbridge, Massachusetts

Cranbrook, Bloomfield Hills, Michigan

Detroit Institute of Arts, Detroit, Michigan

Minneapolis Institute of Arts, Minneapolis, Minnesota

William Rockhill Nelson Gallery of Art, Atkins Museum of Fine Arts,
Kansas City, Missouri

St. Louis Art Museum, St. Louis, Missouri

ROBERT PETTUS

Herbert F. Johnson Museum of Art, Cornell University, Ithaca, New York

Solomon R. Guggenheim Museum, New York, New York

Metropolitan Museum of Art, New York, New York

Brooklyn Museum, Brooklyn, New York

Everson Museum of Art, Syracuse New York

Munson-Williams-Proctor Institute, Utica, New York

Taft Museum, Cincinnati, Ohio

Cleveland Museum of Art, Cleveland, Ohio

Scaife Sculpture Court, Museum of Art, Carnegie Institute, Pittsburgh,
Pennsylvania

Frick Art Museum, Pittsburgh, Pennsylvania

Brookgreen Gardens, Murrells Inlet, South Carolina

Hunter Museum of Art, Chattanooga, Tennessee

Amon Carter Museum of Western Art, Fort Worth, Texas

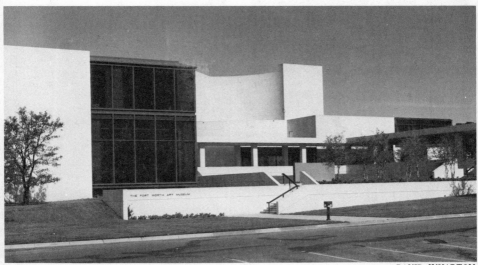

Fort Worth Art Museum, Fort Worth, Texas

Museum of Fine Arts, Houston, Texas

Bundy Art Gallery, Waitsfield, Vermont

Seattle Art Museum, Seattle, Washington

Elvehjem Museum of Art, University of Wisconsin, Madison, Wisconsin

Milwaukee Art Center, Milwaukee, Wisconsin

Royal Ontario Museum, Toronto, Ontario

Winnipeg Art Gallery, Winnipeg, Manitoba

ERNEST MAYER

architectural and ornamentation drawings are incomparable anywhere; the collection of several thousand French designs for textiles and decoration and French ornament prints is unrivaled; the group of American wood engravings is surpassed only by the one in the Library of Congress; numerous North European woodcuts and engravings by Schongauer, Dürer, van Leyden, and Rembrandt enrich the print collection, as do a group of over 200 prints by the Tiepolo family; and a remarkable section of drawings—over 400 by Winslow Homer, some 2,000 sketches by Frederick Edwin Church, and works by Daniel Huntington, Elihu Vedder, and Thomas Moran—brings 19th-century American art into focus. Beyond the drawings and prints, the decorative arts collections include wallpapers, textiles, ceramics, glass, furniture, woodwork, metalwork, and jewelry, and encompass every discipline from architecture and urban and industrial design to advertising, fashion, interiors, and home furnishings. The temporary exhibitions are changed periodically and usually include objects from the permanent collection. Hand-held cameras without flash attachments are permitted.

The museum sponsors an extended program of classes, seminars, tours, lectures, concerts, and poetry readings for adults and young people. Guided tours are offered by appointment. The library, "developed as a complimentary expansion of the museum's collections," is still another of the museum's assets: it provides a comprehensive reference collection on design, decorative arts, and textiles second to none; rare books; and an encyclopedic picture collection. The myriad publications, both catalogs and books, prepared here are sold at a sales desk, which also offers slide sets of objects in the permanent collection, cards, and reproductions. The renovation that took place after 1972 to prepare the house for its new occupant included the restoration of Andrew Carnegie's large and luscious garden (it was for this that he built his home on the upper reaches of Fifth Avenue), which is open for the public to wander through and enjoy. Parking is extremely difficult; take public transportation. Tues. 10–9; Wed.–Sat. 10–5; Sun. 12–5. Admission $1; children and senior citizens free. (Southwest corner of 5th Ave. & 91st St.)

**The Frick Collection.** 1 East 70th St., 10021 ☐ The former residence of Henry Clay Frick, Pittsburgh coke and steel industrialist, houses this exquisite collection. Designed by American architect Thomas Hastings in the tradition of 18th-century European domestic architecture and built in 1913–14, the building reflects the quiet Old World elegance of a country estate. The sculptures and paintings—Renoirs, Vermeers, Fragonards, El Grecos, Goyas, Gainsboroughs, Romneys, Titians—are displayed in the grandly furnished rooms of the Frick household. Frick bequeathed both his collection and his home to a board of trustees empowered to make both available to the public; the Frick Collection was incorporated in 1920 and opened in 1935, with the express purpose of maintaining the residential setting as it was during Frick's lifetime. Emphasizing this home atmosphere are fresh flowers, ticking clocks, an absence of display cases, and a minimum of restraining barriers. The Collection does not attempt a didactic or encyclopedic approach to art history; rather it is an "anthology of selected works of art of exceptional interest," set in the sumptuous surroundings of wealth and good taste.

Illustrated lectures are given Wednesday, Thursday, and Saturday afternoons from October through May. Introductory lectures are scheduled at 11 a.m. Tuesdays through Fridays. A videotaped Introduction to the Collection is offered several times every day. Chamber music concerts are held, without charge, on occasional Sundays at 4 p.m. The Frick Collection publications can be purchased at a sales desk at the Collection, as well as catalogs, photographs, postcards, greeting cards, color prints, and slides. Catalogs can be ordered by mail. Sept.–May, Tues.–Sat. 10–6; Sun., Feb. 12, Election Day 1–6. Summer hours: June–Aug., Wed.–Sat. 10–6, Sun. 1–6. Closed Jan. 1, July 4, Thanksgiving, Dec. 24, 25. Admission $1; children under 10 not admitted; under 16 must be accompanied by adult. Group visits by appointment only. (5th Ave. & 71st St.)

**Solomon R. Guggenheim Museum.** 1071 Fifth Ave., 10028 ☐ One of New York City's landmark structures, and one of its most controversial, the Solomon R. Guggenheim Museum, completed in 1959, was designed by Frank Lloyd Wright. Guggenheim commissioned Wright in 1943 and approved the plans before his death in 1949; construction began in 1957. Looking like a giant sculpture poised across the avenue from Central Park, its concrete casting forms a spiral ramp (a "giant snail") that rises from ground to dome some 95 feet above. The ¼-mile interior ramp, although unbroken in its circular descent, is honeycombed with 74 bay areas used for display purposes. Paintings can be viewed from the usual close range, and also from across the broad expanse of the empty central core, giving exhibitions the added dimensions of space and distance.

Solomon R. Guggenheim began his collection early in the 20th century. The fourth of seven brothers, he expanded the mining fortune of his Swiss immigrant father into a great mining empire, supporting with it, in the tradition of the times, organizations, philanthropies, and his own unformed and undirected tastes in art. His first purchases consisted of an eclectic assortment ranging from some Old Masters to American landscapes. It was not until the middle twenties that his collecting took on definite focus, influenced by the future director of his expanding collection, the Baroness Hilla Rebay von Ehrenweisen. An avant-garde artist herself, she introduced him to the world of nonobjective art, and his new enthusiasm resulted in many purchases of this genre. Soon the collection, too large for his apartment at the Plaza Hotel in New York City, had to be moved to separate office space in Carnegie Hall; Miss Rebay looked after the paintings. After several important loan exhibitions had been mounted, and the collection was converted into a foundation in 1937, the Solomon R. Guggenheim Collection of Non-Objective Paintings opened in rented quarters at 24 East 54th Street in 1939. There the works of modern masters such as Kandinsky, Bauer, and Delaunay, framed heavily in gold and silver, were displayed in a modern setting. Less than 10 years later, land for the Wright project having been secured on Fifth Avenue between 88th and 89th Streets, the collection moved to a mansion on the site of the present building. At this time, over 700 items were added by the purchase of a prominent New Yorker's estate; among them were Kokoschka's "Knight Errant," 18 Kandinskys, 110 Klees, 6 Chagalls, 24 Feiningers, and 54 Kirchner watercolors and prints.

After the death of Guggenheim in 1949, the foundation having acquired the balance of his private collection, and the retirement of Miss Rebay 3 years later, the name of the museum was changed to the Solomon R. Guggenheim Museum, signaling a new broader policy which was to include into the museum the whole range of contemporary art. Display techniques were changed, draperies and heavy frames removed, walls painted white, and with the encouragement of the board, paintings were cataloged and conserved. Sculptures, lacking before, were acquired, among them works by Brancusi, Archipenko, Calder, Duchamp-Villon, Arp, Miró, Maillot, Moore, Max Ernst, and Giacometti. Paintings by Cézanne, Braque, Miró, Picasso, Kline, Pollock, de Kooning, and Stuart Davis were also purchased. Another large estate added Brancusi's oak "Little French Girl," an Archipenko bronze of 1919, a 1935 Calder string mobile, Duchamp-Villon's "Cat"; a Mondrian "Composition" of 1929, and a 1916 Gris "Still Life." Acquisitions of still another administration continued with the same objectives: to fill historical gaps and to continue to enlarge the contemporary representations with such masterpieces of the 1960s as "Nunc Stans" and "Bidon l'Esbroufe" by Dubuffet, Bacon's triptych "Crucifixion," David Smith's "Cubi XXVII," and Morris Louis's "Saraband." The Justin K. Thannhauser Foundation collection enriched the historical content by bringing to the Guggenheim a group of Impressionist and Postimpressionist masterpieces. Among these 75 paintings and sculptures, designated as a bequest to the museum after Thannhauser's death but already on permanent display, are Daumier's "The Chess Players," Pissarro's "Les Coteaux de l'Hermitage, Pontoise," and major works by Manet and Renoir. Postimpressionists include 4 Cézannes, several Van Goghs, and pastels by Toulouse-Lautrec and Degas. Thirty-four Picassos include "Moulin de la Galette," "Woman Ironing," and the later "Woman

With Yellow Hair." Also notable in the Thannhauser collection are 2 Modiglianis, a double Vuillard cityscape, a Fauve Braque, Soutine's "The Venetian," Rouault's "Christ and the Fisherman," bronzes by Degas and Matisse, and drawings by Matisse and Van Gogh. In 1971, from the Hilla Rebay estate, the museum acquired numerous Kandinskys, the total number in the collection reaching over 130. Subsequently, the lesser of these were sold at auction.

Seen as a whole, the museum continues the original intentions of its founder, whose sizable collection formed the nucleus of this institution that now houses some 3,000 paintings, sculptures, and works on paper from the 19th and 20th centuries. An active exhibition program includes 8 to 12 shows per year, loan exhibitions as well as exhibitions drawn from the permanent collection. Group and one-person shows feature established modern masters as well as experimental artists. There are also programs of special events and art education, films, lectures by museum staff members or visiting authorities, performing arts events, and poetry readings scheduled throughout the year. Taped tours are available for rent, and guided tours are available for adult groups by appointment 3 weeks in advance. A bookstore offers a wide range of exhibition catalogues, art books, lithographs and prints, posters, slides, postcards, notepaper and greeting cards. Lunch and refreshments are available in a cafe that opens its outdoor terrace during the summer months. The museum reference library of about 10,000 volumes is open by appointment only; it has reference books as well as vertical file materials. Wed.–Sun. & holidays, 11–5; Tues. 11–8. Adults $1; over 62 50¢; students with ID 50¢; children under 7 free. Tues. eves. free. Student groups accompanied by teacher, by appointment (Tues.–Fri.) 25¢ each. $10 annual pass provides for unlimited visits. (5th Ave. & 89th St.)

**Hispanic Society of America.** 613 West 155th St., 10032 □ Archer Milton Huntington's collections of books and works of art are housed by the Hispanic Society of America, which he founded in 1904. At the entrance, 2 limestone lions by Anna Hyatt Huntington guard the paintings, sculpture, and decorative arts within, all works of art representing the culture of the Iberian peninsula from prehistory to the present. Paintings by Goya, El Greco, Velázquez, Morales line the walls of a Spanish Renaissance main court; in another room, objects from the 15th to the 17th centuries, including a 1490 *retablo* signed by Pere Espalargues, are arranged in a chapel-like setting; a series of paintings by Joaquín Sorolla y Bastida show regional Spain in the Sorolla room. More treasures: a 15th-century illuminated Hebrew Bible; a Hispano-Moresque bowl dated around 1400; a sample of Mudejar silk from the 1400s. And a terrace connecting the 2 buildings owned by the society contains more of Anna Hyatt Huntington's sculptures. Cameras are not permitted.

The society's library contains one of the fine collections of books, manuscripts, maps, and graphics on Spanish and Portuguese art, history, and literature; it is open for scholarly research. The reading room is open to the public Tues.-Fri. 1-4:30; Sat. 10-4:30. Tape tours are available at the sales desk, which also offers the many books published by the museum relating to the collection, cards, color prints, and slides. Special events scheduled here include lectures, films, concerts, plays. An educational program is tailored for both adults and children; groups of children must be accompanied by one adult for every 10 children. Parking on the street is difficult. Tues.-Sat. 10-4:30; Sun. 2-5; closed Jan. 1, Feb. 12, Easter Sun., May 30, July 4, Thanksgiving, Christmas (Dec. 24, 25, 31). Free. (Take #4 or 5 bus to West 155th St. & Broadway. Or take the 8th Ave. subway [Washington Heights local] to West 155th; or the 7th Ave. IRT local to 157th St. & Broadway.)

**Japan House Gallery.** 333 East 47th St., 10017 ☐ Visitors to New York (or New Yorkers themselves) who warm to Oriental art have the privilege of stopping in at the triannual exhibitions held at the Japan House Gallery. These major exhibits, on loan from sources in Japan or the United States, are installed in the delicately and serenely Oriental surroundings of the Japan Society's headquarters; bamboo trees, reflecting pools, and pebble gardens are all here to enchant, and a small study collection is permanently available for perusal. Lectures are open to all; gallery talks and classes, films, concerts, and dance programs are all available. Catalogs accompany each exhibit. The library (4,500 volumes) is open for use on the premises. Open only during exhibitions daily 11-5; Fri. 11-7:30. Contributions are accepted.

**Jewish Museum.** 1109 Fifth Ave., 10028 ☐ The elegant Gothic home of Felix M. Warburg, designed by Cass Gilbert in 1904 on the upper reaches of mansion-studded Fifth Avenue, was given to the Jewish Theological Seminary by Mrs. Warburg in 1947 for use as the Jewish Museum. The collection brought here from its former home at the seminary contained thousands of ceremonial objects, paintings, and graphics, antique and contemporary, that had to do with Jewish culture. In 1963, the old Warburg mansion was given a contemporary addition: The Albert A. List wing, funded by the man whose name it bore, added space and a new look to the museum. Today it houses the largest collection of Judaica in the United States—plaques and medals, Eastern European art, coins from the Holy Land, a mosaic wall believed to have been part of a 16th-century Persian synagogue, Palestinian pottery from the Iron and Bronze Ages, the most comprehensive collection of Judaic textiles in the Western Hemisphere, treasures from the lost Jewish community of Danzig, Tissot watercolors illustrating the Old Testament, and a sizable assemblage of contemporary art. Approximately 8 to 10 special exhibits are installed each year from the permanent collections and on loan. Cameras (no flashes) are permitted.

An extensive education program for children involves both elementary school and high school students. The Tobe Pascher Workshop is an artist-in-residence program dedicated to training adults to create Jewish ceremonial objects in metal, glass, and ceramics. Needlecraft classes are held periodically. The museum sponsors lectures and concerts regularly. Guided tours with trained docents are available for individual visitors on Sunday afternoons without reservations, or for groups by advance appointment. The museum publishes a quarterly calendar of exhibitions and events, catalogs for particular exhibitions, posters, and an original graphic each year, which are sold in the museum shop along with books, cards, needlecraft, reproductions from the permanent collection, soft sculpture and jewelry, ceremonial objects, and other objects relating to Jewish culture. Parking is difficult but there are garages nearby. Mon.–Thurs. 12–5; Sun. 11–6; closed Fri., Sat., & Jewish holidays. Admission $1.75 for adults, $1 for children and students, voluntary for senior citizens. (At 92nd St.)

**Metropolitan Museum of Art.** Fifth Avenue at 82nd St., 10028 ☐ The Metropolitan Museum of Art, quite simply, is one of the great art museums in the world. It began with fewer than 200 paintings in 1870, hung in a former dancing academy on Fifth Avenue, remained for a time in the Douglas mansion on 14th Street, and in 1880, moved to its present location in Central Park. Calvert Vaux, one of the architects of the park, designed the Gothic Revival building that was to be enlarged many times in many different styles to create what is today a massive and impressive complex of buildings and wings. (The original Vaux building is now Wing A, or Medieval Hall; the North and South Wings were added in 1884 and 1889, designed by Theodore Weston in the style of a 16th-century Italian villa; The Great Hall, with neoclassical elements designed by Richard Morris Hunt, was opened in 1902; additions to the Fifth Avenue facade, designed by McKim, Mead, and White in the mode of the Italian Renaissance, were begun in 1900 and completed in 1926; the American Wing, designed by Grosvenor Atterbury, was added in 1924; and the master plan, executed by Kevin Roche and John Dinkeloo in 1969, took some 10 years to complete.) About 3 million objects span the course of human history from the ancient Near East up to the present; collections of arms and armor, American painting, American decorative arts, costumes, drawings, Egyptian art, European paintings, Far Eastern art, Greek and Roman, Islamic, and medieval art, musical instruments, primitive art, prints and photographs, European decorative arts—all are prominent. In the American wing, 3 floors filled with the creative product of America's past and present, are 35 period rooms, galleries devoted to general displays of styles, and galleries devoted to paintings alone. All, or nearly all, the American masters of all schools are represented here. The collection of the Costume Institute, an entity in itself, encompasses the history of dress here and abroad, and mounts frequent major exhibits with interesting and popular themes. The collections of drawings and prints are unique in the country; French and Italian works predominate. The Temple of Dendur, saved from the flooding Nile behind Aswan and given to this country by the Egyptian government, is but another of the fabulous installations in the Egyptian section. European paintings cover every school and every country—Giotto, Raphael, Vermeer, Rembrandt (among some 30 is "Aristotle Contemplating the Bust of Homer"), Titian, Tintoretto, Tiepolo, El Greco ("View of Toledo"), Velázquez ("Portrait of Juan de Pareja"), Poussin, Fragonard—the list is long and all-encompassing. Far Eastern art is highlighted by a Chinese sculpture collection said to be the most significant in the West; the Islamic section is unequaled in the world outside Istanbul. Among the Greek holdings is the priceless Calyx Krater, painted by Euphronius. The medieval collection is divided between the museum and the Cloisters (q.v.). The primitive art collection was given a boost in 1969 with Nelson Rockefeller's gift in memory of his son Michael, who died while on a research expedition in the South Pacific; African, Oceanic, and pre-Columbian art stand out here as well as objects from the New Hebrides and New Caledonia. The 20th century, succeeding the great Armory Show of 1913, is displayed in its own setting; masters such as Hartley, Sheeler, Hopper, Wyeth, and O'Keeffe are shown together with the newer breed of Abstract Expressionists and pop artists. The Lehman Pavilion, donated to the museum in 1969 by Robert Lehman with the stipulation that the collection from his residence be displayed intact in a homelike setting, not only enlarged the museum's collection of 14th- and 15th-century Italian paintings, Old Masters, Impressionists, and Fauves, but also extended the drawing collection and indeed, the decorative arts collection with Renaissance bronzes, Limoges enamels, and Gothic tapestries. Exhibits in this national treasure of a museum are continually changing, new ones overlapping with the old. Hand-held cameras without flashes are permitted; more elaborate equipment is allowed only with special permission.

The rich resources of the museum are utilized in a variegated array of special events and activities. Courses, concerts, films, gallery programs for young people, studio workshops, demonstrations, lectures, community programs, school programs, a junior museum, tours, and gallery talks are all daily occurrences in this beehive of activity. The library (185,000 volumes) is available for use by graduate students, researchers, and visiting scholars. The Photograph and Slide Library (290,000 slides; 250,000 black and white photographs; 6,000 color prints) covers the history of art and is open for use by the public; slides may be rented for lecturing. Introductory tours and gallery talks are offered free of charge, as well as films and lectures in the auditorium and special Sunday programs. School groups must make appointments in advance. Subscription courses are offered in a Learning from the Original series, and recorded tours for certain collections may be rented. In 1977, 21 fellowships and scholarships were offered to qualified graduate students and scholars to study various aspects of the museum's collections in depth; professional travel stipends were offered to 14 members of the museum's staff for study abroad. The myriad of catalogs and books prepared and published by the museum are sold in an extensive book store; the museum shop offers exquisite reproductions of jewelry and sculpture, silver, pewter, porcelain, furniture, and glass for sale. The Fountain Restaurant, an elegant cafeteria (wine and beer; liquor at a bar) with tables clustered around a restful lagoon and fountains, is open Tues.–Fri. 11–3, 3–4:30; Tues. 5–8:15; Sat. 11:30–3:45; Sun. 12–4:15. An underground parking lot has space for 472 cars. Tues. 10–8:45; Wed.–Sat. 10–4:45; Sun. & holidays 11–4:45. Pay what you wish; suggested admission $2; senior citizens free.

**Pierpont Morgan Library.** 29 East 36th St., 10016 ☐ Madison Avenue at 36th Street retains a hint of the elegance that was old New York. Here, the pink marble Renaissance-style building that McKim, Mead, and White built for J. Pierpont Morgan in 1906 still stands among the high-rise office buildings. Under this roof is probably the most extraordinary library in the world; illuminated medieval and Renaissance manuscripts and printed books from the 15th century are commonplace here. Rare possessions are exhibited in a gallery in what was once Morgan's home. The West Room, once Morgan's study and still looking very much as it did in his day, is where some of his art collection is displayed—as it was, in fact, when he used the room. Works by Old Masters line the ruby damask walls. Another room, to the east, contains the library and a stunning collection of drawings that span the 6 centuries from the 14th to the 19th, including works by such diverse masters as Fra Filippo Lippi, Tintoretto, Van Gogh, and many more. Rembrandt also has a place here—in a collection of his etchings. Special exhibitions are installed regularly. Accredited scholars, after approval of their applications, are given cards for the Reading Room. But the library sponsors lectures and concerts, and of course opens the doors of its permanent and temporary exhibitions to the public. Library publications (books, pamphlets, catalogs, and cards) and slides are for sale. Sept. 7–July 31, Tues.–Sat. 10:30–5; Sun. 1–5. Free.

**El Museo del Barrio.** 1230 Fifth Ave., 10029 ☐ El Museo del Barrio is unabashedly ethnic. Here in the heart of El Barrio, New York City's primarily Puerto Rican community, paintings and graphics by Puerto Rican artists are displayed together with handcrafted objects from Puerto Rico. Temporary and traveling exhibitions share this space with the permanent collection. Activities include lectures, films, classes in all the media for both adults and children, and guided tours. The museum also sponsors workshops and classes in music and dance. A mobile unit and a school loan service are the means by which the museum reaches into the community. A library (500 volumes) on the culture and history of Puerto Rico and bilingual educational materials are available for use on the premises. The museum shop offers handcrafted items, books, and calendars for sale, as well as the publications prepared here. Mon.–Sat. 9–4. Free. (Between 104th & 105th Sts.)

**Museum of American Folk Art.** 49 West 53rd St., 10019 ☐ Not what is commonly called the fine arts, but a fine display of man's craving for beauty and his raw instinct for design.

**Museum of the American Indian.** Heye Foundation, Broadway at 155th St., 10032 ☐ North, Central, and South American and Caribbean Indian artwork and artifacts are displayed here. It has the most extensive North American Indian collection in the world.

**Museum of the City of New York.** Fifth Avenue at 103rd St., 10029 ☐ All facets of the city's history are documented here: its politics, economy, its social and cultural fabric, and its expansion.

**Museum of Modern Art.** 11 West 53rd St., 10019 ☐ Art of the 20th century has its temple here. The Museum of Modern Art was begun in 1929 in an office building on Fifth Avenue and 56th Street with the aim of building a collection of modern art, enhanced by samplings from the art of the 1880s that led the way to the modern movement. The museum opened the doors of its present building in 1939 with a ceremony presided over by no less than President Roosevelt. Twenty-five years later a new wing was added to the east of the original building and two years after that, the museum overflowed into the neighboring building to the west, what had formerly been the Whitney Museum. The area in the rear of the building became one of the very few sculpture gardens in the city, an enchanting place for footsore visitors to relax and peruse the wonderful shapes of Moore ("Family Group"), Maillol ("Nude"), and Rodin ("Balzac"). Like the 20th century itself, the art inside MOMA is enormously diverse. The optimistic gaiety and soft, shimmering colors of the Impressionists give way to the brutality of Picasso's "Guernica" and the sharp edges of the Abstract Expressionists. A walk through the upstairs galleries is a visual journey through all the great movements of modern art. Picasso is here in his own gallery, as are Matisse and Brancusi. Of the thousands of objects owned by the museum, only some are always on view, but like beacons of light on a shifting sea, they are steady, friendly, and familiar. Prints, more than 10,000 of them, are available for study. Photographs (the museum owns 14,000) are installed in a new gallery. The museum has some 3,000 drawings, 800 illustrated books, 3,000 posters and graphics, 400 architectural drawings, 4,500 films, and 3,000,000 film stills. Major special exhibitions are installed on the ground floor in the east wing. Smaller changing exhibits can be seen on the ground floor level on the west side of the building.

The many activities of this vital institution are interesting and well attended. Film series drawn from its own collection are extremely popular, as are lectures, symposia, and summer concerts in the sculpture garden. Recorded tours are available; gallery talks are offered frequently. Educational programs for children, graduate students, and professional museum workers are offered. The library (30,000 volumes) can be used by researchers and graduate students by appointment. The museum publishes books and catalogs continually; most of them are available in the bookstore, the museum's newest addition next door. Also sold here are reproductions, gifts, jewelry, posters, and postcards. A cafeteria has a view into the sculpture garden. Mon., Tues., Fri., Sat., Sun. 11–6; Thurs. 11–9. Admission $2.50 for adults, 75¢ for senior citizens and children under 16; $1.50 for students with ID; donations accepted on Tues.; student group rates by appointment.

**New York Historical Society.** 170 Central Park West, 10024 ☐ The New York Historical Society, its own past a thread woven through the fabric of New York City's history, is (and was, beginning in 1804) the repository of "material pertaining to the history of the United States, and of New York State in particular." It is the second oldest historical society in the country. Having moved from government building to government building, from the Remsen Building at Broadway and Chambers Street to the Stuyvesant Institute at 659 Broadway, to New York University on Washington Square, it finally, in 1857, acquired its own building on 2nd Avenue and 11th Street, where it stayed for half a century. In 1908 the present building was completed and the society moved to 76th Street overlooking Central Park. Here one can see America as it has been: the 17th- and 18th-century silver; the John Rogers statuette household gods popular in the late 1880s; an exhibit of 3 centuries of transportation in New York; 19th-century toys, especially travel toys—a display of early transportation in miniature; 18th- and 19th-century decorative arts in the home—pottery, pewter, paintings, furniture, paperweights, and glass. Embellishing these historical displays are paintings and prints. In the Audubon Gallery are hung a selection of the original watercolors that John James Audubon made for *Birds of*

*America* (the society owns 433 of the total 435). American genre painting and folk art—needlework, household utensils, shop signs, weathervanes, lighting devices, glass bottles and flasks, and New York stone glaze pottery—occupy another gallery. The museum has an outstanding collection of Hudson River school landscapes, 18th-century portraits of New Yorkers by itinerant artists, and portraits by John Trumbull, Gilbert Stuart, and Rembrandt Peale, among others; and a display of old New York in early photographs and a collection of 19th-century carriages, stagecoaches, sleighs, and fire trucks restored and installed in a large basement area. Special exhibitions are held regularly. Cameras are permitted.

The education department is an active one, scheduling programs for children and adults, concert series, films, story hours. Guided tours can be arranged by appointment only. The noncirculating library (500,000 volumes) is a major asset, one of the foremost reference libraries of American history in the country, and is available for use at a fee of $1 per day (open Tues.–Sat. 10–5). A museum shop sells the many books and catalogs published here. Parking is difficult. Tues.–Fri. 11–5; Sat. 10–5; Sun. 1–5; closed Jan. 1, Memorial Day, July 4, Labor Day, Thanksgiving, Christmas. Free. (Between 76th & 77th Sts.)

**Nicholas Roerich Museum.** 319 West 107th St., 10025 ☐ Nikolai Konstantinovitch Roerich emigrated to the United States from Russia in 1920, after which he led an expedition, as a proponent of Theosophism, to central Asia. He then lived and worked in northern India. In Europe he was one of Diaghilev's designers, and in America he was a contributor to *World of Art* magazine. The Nicholas Roerich Museum was formed in 1955 to exhibit his paintings—from Russia, from America, and from Asia. In addition to the permanent Roerich collection, gathered from a number of private collections, exhibits of contemporary artists are mounted every month in a smaller gallery. Cameras are not permitted. Lectures and concerts are held; tours may be arranged in advance. The museum publishes a biography of Roerich and *The Invincible,* written by Roerich. These are available, as well as reproductions and postcards of Roerich paintings, at a sales desk. Metered parking on the street. Mon.–Sun. 2–5. Free. (Between Riverside Drive & Broadway.)

**Whitney Museum of American Art.** 945 Madison Ave., 10021 ☐ An austere yet serene modern building amid the sophisticated and fashionable shops of Madison Avenue, the present Whitney Museum of American Art, designed by Marcel Breuer and Hamilton Smith with Michael H. Irving as consultant architect, opened its doors to the public in 1966. Its founder, Gertrude Vanderbilt Whitney, daughter of railroad magnate Cornelius Vanderbilt, was herself a sculptor whose interest in young contemporary artists led her to support their work through the Whitney Studio, started in 1914; the Friends of Young Artists, 1915–1918; and the Whitney Studio Club and its successor, the Whitney Studio Galleries, 1918–1930. In 1930 the founding of the Whitney Museum of American Art was announced. The next year it opened to the public in a group of converted brownstone buildings at 10 West 8th Street.

From the beginning, Mrs. Whitney's aim was to provide young artists with a place to exhibit their work. In 1931, as it does today, the museum adhered to that central purpose, but it broadened its perspective by establishing a permanent collection encompassing the whole span of American art. Mrs. Whitney's original gift of 500 paintings, drawings, and sculptures, as well as 100 additional works purchased by her before the museum's opening, formed the nucleus of this collection. In 1949, unable to compete with other institutions in historical representations of American art, the museum directorate decided to divest itself of all works executed before 1900, so that with the funds thus acquired, it would be able to purchase more contemporary art. By 1966, however, this policy was modified, a curator of 18th- and 19th-century art was appointed, and the museum began once again to cover early American art as well, maintaining its emphasis on 20th-century works.

The museum grew rapidly, and larger quarters became a necessity; construction on a new building began in 1949, on land at 22 West 54th Street, offered to it by the Museum of Modern Art. It opened at this location in 1954, remaining there for the 12 years until its spectacular move to the present location. Here, expansion encompassed not only its acquisitions, but also its programs: More loan exhibitions than ever before were mounted in architecture, photography, and folk art; a film program (films are shown every day except Monday) brought the Whitney recognition as a showcase for noncommercial filmmakers; an education program which was extensive in nature and concept, operated, to a large extent, outside the confines of the building (a warehouse on the lower east side, the basement of a former bank, and a downtown branch in the financial district—55 Water Street). In fact, the intimate exhibition facility begun by Mrs. Whitney grew into a large and complex public institution, national in scope, supported by members, visitors, and both the state and federal governments.

In the building on Madison Avenue, a sales desk offers a selection of art books, catalogs, reproductions, posters, cards, and gift items. The restaurant is downstairs. Wed.–Sat. 11–6; Tues. 11–10; Sun. & holidays 12–6. Admission $1.50; Tues. eves. free; children under 12 accompanied by adult, students with ID, and senior citizens free. (At 75th St.)

---

**Bronx Museum of the Arts.** 851 Grand Concourse, Bronx 10451 ☐ The Bronx Museum of Art makes up for its lack of a permanent collection by serving as a "conduit for other museums . . . to bring their works to the community and for local artists to have their work viewed. . . ." It was founded in the Bronx Courthouse, a block away from Yankee Stadium, in 1972 by the Bronx Council on the Arts. Most frequently, the museum shows contemporary abstract and surrealistic artwork; continually changing exhibits feature all forms of artistic expression—painting, sculpture, photography, crafts, papier-mâché, antiques. Cameras are permitted. Seven satellite galleries are located throughout the borough serving people who would not travel to an exhibition outside their own neighborhood. Workshops are conducted for children and senior citizens; lectures are given periodically and concerts on Sunday afternoons. An Artist-Adopt-a-School program brings professional artists, for periods of from 4 to 6 weeks into the public schools where there is no art program. Guided tours can be arranged in advance. A gift shop offers books, original artwork, prints, jewelry, postcards, and craftwork. Parking in the vicinity; the Yankee Stadium parking area is close by. Mon.–Fri. 9–5; Sun. 1–3:30. Free. (At 161st St. & Grand Concourse.)

**Brooklyn Museum.** 188 Eastern Parkway, Brooklyn 11238 ☐ In 1825 the Marquis de Lafayette, taking a 6-year-old child named Walt Whitman in his arms, dedicated the cornerstone of the Apprentices' Library. Some 20 years later, the library became known as the Brooklyn Institute, and in 1846 a permanent art gallery was established there. The present Roman Revival building, imposing among the low-rise residential apartment buildings that face it, was built between 1892 and 1925, designed by the famous architectural firm of McKim, Mead, and White. The fabulous Brooklyn Botanical Garden is its neighbor on the west; Frederick Law Olmstead's favorite Prospect Park is close by. This museum claims to be the seventh largest in the United States. The collections here are, without doubt, among the country's treasures. Best known are the ancient Egyptian holdings, the American paintings, American decorative arts and period rooms (26 rooms from 1675 to 1930), pre-Columbian and African art, costumes and textiles, and prints and drawings. Greek and Roman art can also be seen here as well as Middle Eastern art, Oriental, American Indian, and European paintings and sculpture from medieval times to the 20th century. About 40 special exhibitions are mounted every year. Cameras are permitted in the permanent collection, but not in special exhibitions that are on loan.

A major cultural center in this most heavily populated borough, the museum sponsors educational activities that encompass a wide assortment of lectures, concerts, poetry readings, and film series; a museum school; an after-school children's program; and video and artist-in-residence programs. Group tours may be arranged by appointment. Publications with the museum imprint include catalogs and books pertaining to the collections. Two libraries are open to the public; the art reference library Wed.–Fri. 1–5; the Wilbour Library of Egyptology, by appointment. A gallery shop sells crafts from around the world, reproductions, and antiques; a book shop, books, postcards, and posters. A cafeteria provides light fare. Parking behind the museum. Wed.–Sat. 10–5; Sun. 12–5; holidays 1–5. Free. (Take the 7th Avenue IRT to the Brooklyn Museum-Eastern Parkway stop. Or by car from Manhattan, cross the Manhattan Bridge and go straight [Flatbush Ave.] to Grand Army Plaza; make a ¾ circle around the plaza to Eastern Parkway. Or cross the Brooklyn Bridge and go straight to Atlantic Ave.; left to Washington Ave; right to Eastern Parkway.)

**Queens College Art Collection.** Paul Klapper Library, Queens College of the City University of New York, Flushing 11367 ☐ In 1957, the Paul Klapper Library at Queens College opened a small display area for the purpose of exhibiting art objects pertinent to the current curriculum. The collection from which it drew consisted of about 300 WPA prints, some 250 ancient artifacts and antique glass objects, and a few Oriental, medieval, and Renaissance pieces. A drawing by Gorky, one by Calder, and another by Pereira are among the more important pieces. Displays are chosen according to the needs of the curriculum. Cameras are permitted. Catalogs and monographs that pertain to the collection are published here. A separate art library (20,000 volumes) is open for reference use by the public. Mon., Wed. 9–8; Tues., Thurs. 9–6; Fri. 9–5. Free. (By car take the L.I. Expwy. and Kissena Blvd. Or, take the Flushing line #7 [IRT] to Main Street, Flushing [the last stop]. Then take #25/34 bus on Main Street to the main gate of the college on Kissena Blvd.)

**Jacques Marchais Center of Tibetan Arts.** 338 Lighthouse Ave., Staten Island 10306 ☐ New York's most rural borough with the smallest population supports several historical houses and museums, a college, a zoo, and a conservation center—resources common to all the boroughs of Manhattan. The Jacques Marchais Center of Tibetan Art, however, is unique in the city. A Tibetan temple and gardens, it was established in 1946 to house a library and museum of Buddhist (primarily Tibetan) philosophy, art, and religion. The art collection maintained here comes from Tibet. Several lectures are offered during the course of the year. Tours are available by prearrangement. Some prints and reproductions are sold. The library (1,100 volumes) is available for use on the premises. Garden for picnic lunch. Apr.–Nov., Sat. & Sun. 2–5 or by appointment. Admission $1 adults, 50¢ children. (By car, from Verrazano Narrows Bridge take I-278 to Richmond Rd.-Clove Rd. exit; follow exit ramp alongside highway to second traffic light; make left onto Richmond Rd., follow it to Lighthouse Ave., and make right up Lighthouse Ave. to top of hill. From ferry, take bus #113 to foot of Lighthouse Ave.; it is a short walk up the hill.)

**Staten Island Museum.** 75 Stuyvesant Place, Staten Island 10301 ☐ The Staten Island Museum, governed by the Staten Island Institute of Arts and Sciences, began in 1881 as a society of natural scientists. Moving from place to place until the present neo-Georgian building was opened in 1918, the museum gradually developed collections that gave it a broader base. Today it is a general museum of science and art; the fine arts focus on American art with emphasis on Staten Island and New York regional artists. Approximately 3 special exhibits are held each year. Cameras are not permitted. Natural science lectures and chamber music concerts are held regularly. The education activities include a program for public school children. A library is open by special permission only. The museum shop offers books, antiques, and small gift items for sale. Tues.–Sat. 10–5; Sun. 1–5. Free. (Take the Staten Island Ferry at the southern tip of Manhattan. The museum is located in St. George, 2 blocks up the hill from the ferry terminal.)

**NIAGARA FALLS: Native American Center for the Living Arts, Inc.** 25 Falls Street Mall, 14301 ☐ The turtle, Iroquois symbol for the earth, is celebrated in the design of this Native American Center: a central dome with 4 extensions forming the legs. Recently completed, the center began as a storefront gallery in 1974 to promote the culture, art, and traditions of Native Americans. Today it exhibits all manner of past and contemporary Native American art representing over 100 nations, but emphasizing the Iroquois, Southwest, and Plains cultural areas. Paintings, sculpture, pottery, rugs, beadwork, stonework, clothing, and prehistoric artifacts are shown here. Exhibits are changed several times a year and last from 2 to 4 months. The use of cameras is limited to certain areas in the center. Craft workshops, a winter lecture series, an Indian education program, and an artist-in-residence program are sponsored. Tours can be arranged during the week. A shop offers books, records, crafts, art, jewelry, and souvenirs for sale. A restaurant features Native American foods (wine is available) and a cafeteria, quick service. City parking facilities nearby. Mon.–Fri. 10–5; Sat., Sun. 12–5. Admission $2 for adults, 50¢ for children. (Take the Robert Moses Pkwy. or Buffalo Ave. to Rainbow Blvd.)

**OGDENSBURG: Remington Art Museum.** 303 Washington St., 13669 ☐ Although he never lived there, Frederic Remington is memorialized in the Parish mansion in Ogdensburg. His studio collection of paintings, sketches, and bronzes; his library and letters; his furniture and portraits of the Remingtons; and a re-creation of his last studio are housed here. The house was built as a residence for the Parish family in 1810 and was occupied by them and a Madame Ameriga de Vespucci until 1859. Eventually, after her husband's death in 1909, Mrs. Remington lived in the house with her sister, and remained there until her death in 1918 when her late husband's work and effects were turned over, by her bequest, to the Ogdensburg Public Library. In 1923 the Parish mansion was turned into the Remington Art Memorial. Here the Old West comes to life in Remington's well-known naturalistic depictions of cowboys, Indians, and pioneers—the largest single collection of Remington's works extant. The Vespucci room displays rosewood parlor furniture by John Henry Belter and a portrait of Madame Vespucci; 2 other galleries contain an excellent collection of Victorian decorative arts. Special exhibits are mounted throughout the year. Photographing is not permitted. The museum offers guided school tours on request. The shop offers art prints, postcards, books, paper items, tiles and gift items, and slides for sale. Parking in lots within a 2-block area. June 1–Oct. 1, Mon.–Sat. 10–5; Sun. 1–5. Admission $1 for adults, 50¢ for students, under 12 free.

**POUGHKEEPSIE:** **Vassar College Art Gallery.** Taylor Hall, Raymond Ave., Vassar College, 12601 ☐ Matthew Vassar founded the Vassar College Art Gallery in the same year that he founded the college on the rocky cliffs overlooking the Hudson River. The original collection, consisting mostly of Hudson River school paintings, was bought by him from Elias Magoon and was housed in the main building of the new college. In 1917, a neo-Gothic-style building, Taylor Hall, was built and became the repository of Magoon's, now Vassar's collection. Today this group of paintings still remains one of the highlights of the gallery, along with the large selection of Rembrandt and Dürer prints. Among the Hudson River school works are paintings by Church, Cole, Durand, Gifford, Inness, Moore, and Whittredge. French masters Cézanne, Corot, Delacroix, and Daubigny are represented here, as well as Italians Bacchiacca, Chimenti, Giordano, Rosa, Sacchi, and Serodine. The 20th century is represented by Baziotes, Beckmann, de Kooning, Dove, Hartley, Henri, Léger, Masson, Matisse, Nicholson, O'Keeffe, Perlstein, Rothko, Diebenkorn, Hartigan, and Sage. Two large special exhibits and other smaller ones are mounted each semester. Cameras without flashes are permitted. Lectures are occasionally given at the gallery by guests of the college. Catalogs published here are sold in the museum shop together with postcards and prints. A cafeteria and snack bar are located on the campus not far away. Parking along Raymond Avenue in front of the museum. Open only when school is in session: Mon.–Sat. 9–5; Sun. 1–5.

Free. (From the N.Y. Thruway, get off at Newburgh exit; take I-84 east to Rt. 9 exit and go north to Vassar Rd.; take Vassar Rd. to Raymond Ave. and go right. Or from the Taconic State Pkwy., get off at Rt. 55 exit; follow Rt. 55 into town where it becomes Main St.; turn left on Raymond.)

**PURCHASE: Neuberger Museum.** State University of New York, College at Purchase, 10577 ☐ The Roy R. Neuberger collection of 19th- and 20th-century American art is installed in yet another of Philip Johnson's spectacles. His building's severe exterior shelters America's somewhat less severe 19th-century artists and more strictly modern 20th-century lights such as Avery, Davis, Levine, and Pollock. George Rickey's collection of constructivist art (objects made using industrial materials and engineering techniques, following the philosophy of an early 20th-century Russian group) is here; Rickey's work is included. Another collection of American and European artists includes the work of the collector, Hans Richter. African art was brought here by other collectors. "Threnody," a sequence of 14 large paintings, is artist Cleve Gray's solution to the challenge of an entire empty gallery. Other artists' attempts will follow. Changing exhibitions are hung regularly. Guided tours, films, lectures, and symposia, and the well-known annual series of Yaseen lectures are held here. Tues.–Sat. 11–5; Sun. 1–5. Free. (On Anderson Hill Rd., 4 miles north of Cross Westchester Expwy.)

**ROCHESTER: Memorial Art Gallery of the University of Rochester.** 490 University Ave., 14607 ☐ The Memorial Art Gallery opened in its Italian Renaissance-style home in 1913 on the original campus of the University of Rochester with a few paintings and sculptures. Today it is the largest small museum in New York State, with collections that come from all places and all periods of time, from Assyria and ancient Egypt to present-day Europe and America. Mrs. James S. Watson, who contributed funds to the university for the museum, gave still more money to enlarge it in 1926. And in 1968 the original space was doubled yet again, making room for what had grown by then into the extensive holdings of a fine general museum, especially rich in medieval art. In the impressive collection is a 13th-century capital taken from a French church—the figures of 3 of Christ's apostles looking on as Christ displays his wound to Doubting Thomas—only one small gem from the Middle Ages housed here. Some of the paintings on display are by El Greco, Strozzi, Tintoretto, Rembrandt, Hals, Rubens, Constable, Ingres, many of the Impressionists, Matisse, Picasso, and American masters of the 19th and 20th centuries— Warhol and Tobey among the most contemporary. Sculptures are from Assyria and Egypt, from the Orient and the American continent (pre-

Columbian), from Africa, and from Romanesque, Gothic, and Renaissance Europe. A work by Moore dominates the sculpture garden near the entrance; other modern sculptors, Lachaise and Noguchi among them, can be seen here. Exhibitions change regularly; there is an annual juried Rochester-Finger Lakes exhibition open to competitors from west-central New York State; in addition, the museum holds an annual Clothesline Art Show and Sale.

Lectures, gallery talks, concerts, films, and demonstrations are sponsored by the gallery, as well as classes for adults and children, workshops, studio classes, and a summer school. The gallery also sponsors an inner city art school, and art classes for the handicapped. Guided tours are available. A gallery shop sells art books, catalogs (many published here), reproductions, prints, original artwork, and posters. The library (7,500 volumes) can be used on the premises. Tues. 10–9; Wed.–Sat. 10–5; Sun. 1–5. Admission 50¢ for adults, 25¢ for students, senior citizens, and unaccompanied children; free Tues. 5–9.

**ST. BONAVENTURE:   St. Bonaventure Art Collection.** Friedsam Memorial Library, St. Bonaventure University, 14778 ☐ The Friedsam Memorial Library on St. Bonaventure's campus houses the collections of Col. Michael Friedsam, successor to B. Altman as president of the B. Altman Company in New York, and of Dr. T. Edward Hanley, art connoisseur from Bradford, Pennsylvania. Friedsam's 25 paintings and 100 Chinese porcelains, and Hanley's 150 art objects range up through the 19th and 20th centuries; together the 2 collections include works by Rembrandt, Bellini, Rubens, Velázquez, Romney, Inness, Hawthorne, and some 60 other American artists who worked prior to 1914. Friedsam's collection of Chinese porcelains dating from the Ming dynasty is on permanent display; the paintings are rotated periodically. Cameras are permitted. The library (200,000 volumes) is the repository of rare books, manuscripts, archives of St. Bonaventure, stamp and coin collections, and rare reference materials. All are open for use by faculty, students, and area residents. Eating facilities are in Reilly University Center nearby. Parking also nearby. Open when the library is open. Free. (The university is located 3 miles west of Olean, on the south side of Rt. 417, in the town of Allegany.)

**SARATOGA SPRINGS:   Hathorn Gallery.** Skidmore College, North Broadway, 12866 ☐ What was once a carriage house in the salad days of Saratoga Springs, when 19th-century elegance and gaiety attracted the rich and famous (President Grant partied here and died here) to its hotels and inns, became the original home of Skidmore's art gallery. A contemporary building, recently completed, has taken over the function of housing part of the college art collection (the balance is either in storage or dispersed throughout the school) and its art department. Prints, including works by Goya, Rembrandt, Whistler (49 of them), Manet, Kirchner, and Hopper, and works pertaining to Saratoga can be seen here, in 10 special exhibits during the academic year (traveling exhibits, invitationals, faculty and student exhibits included). Cameras are permitted. Informal talks by exhibiting artists, art historians, or gallery-connected speakers, and films are offered periodically, as well. Catalogs of past shows are available. Parking near the gallery. Open during academic sessions, Mon.–Fri. 9–5:30; Sat. & Sun. 12–5:30. Free. (From the Northway [I-87] take exit 15 toward Saratoga Springs and turn right onto East Ave., then right onto North Broadway and left at the Skidmore College sign. Follow signs to the art building. Or coming north on US 9, which turns into Broadway, continue onto North Broadway.)

**SYRACUSE: Everson Museum of Art.** 401 Harrison St., Community Plaza, 13202 ☐ Flanked by business and apartment buildings on the Community Plaza in downtown Syracuse, the Everson Museum of Art resembles a scattering of great concrete blocks aglow with the pink Croghan granite embedded in them. It was designed in 1966 by I. M. Pei and opened in 1968 to house the collections of the Syracuse Museum of Fine Arts. Although it had been founded in 1896 by one of the founders of the Metropolitan Museum of Art and first dean of the College of Fine Arts at Syracuse, George Fisk Comfort, it had never had a building of its own. Helen S. Everson willed $1 million to correct this deficiency. The huge inner space of a 2-story-high sculpture court is broken by 4 cantilevered galleries connected by bridges. Scattered through 3 exhibitions levels is American art, including what is said to be the largest contemporary ceramics collection in the country; fine displays of decorative arts; English pottery and porcelain; Oriental art; and African art. Works by Arthur B. Davies, Childe Hassam, Robert Henri, and John Sloan can be seen here; in the sculpture court are Moore, Hepworth, Jason Seley, and Ernest Trova. Ten Greek vases, small treasures from ancient Syracuse, counterpoint the extensive display of modern ceramics. Photographing is allowed by special permission only.

Special activities abound in this active museum. A museum school offers painting, drawing, ceramics, and multimedia classes to children and adults. Series of lectures, concerts, and films fill out a rich education schedule which includes an outreach program, training for professional museum workers, classes for psychiatric patients and the handicapped, TV programs, internships in the curatorial department, and the well-known

National Ceramic Bi-Annual that, since 1932, has brought together the leading craftspeople in the country. Multilingual guides are available to lead tours (Sept.–June, 2-week notice requested); mini-tours are conducted weekdays 12–2. Books published here relate to the collections and are available at the sales gallery (open Tues.–Fri. 12–4:30), which also carries a wide selection of original graphics, paintings, and craft items, as well as the usual museum shop fare. The Luncheon Gallery is open Tues.–Fri. 12–2, Sat. & Sun. 12–4, serving sandwiches and luncheon entrees. Underground parking adjacent to the museum. Tues.–Fri. 12–5; Sat. 10–5; Sun. 12–5; closed July 4, Thanksgiving, Christmas, Jan. 1. Free. (On the corner of State & Harrison.)

**Joe and Emily Lowe Art Gallery.** Sims Hall, Syracuse University, 13210 ☐ On a rise overlooking downtown Syracuse is Syracuse University. Here, for many years, an impressive art collection was housed in the Joe and Emily Lowe Art Center, which had opened in 1952. By 1975, having outgrown the facilities in the art center, the collection was relocated in Sims Hall, which provided expanded exhibition and staging areas. The gallery is fronted by a sculpture court adjacent to the university's main quadrangle. Twentieth-century American works predominate in this museum; special attention has been paid to the Depression and War years. George Arents, benefactor of the Arents Research Library, donated a superb collection of 19th-century European Salon paintings. Some 12,000 prints survey the history of printmaking, many of them from American studios. Korean, Japanese, and American ceramics, pre-Columbian and contemporary Peruvian ceramics, and Scandinavian metal, wood, and clay designs are included in the decorative arts section. A collection of Asian-Indian folk art and one of West African tribal art present surveys of these 2 areas. In all, the gallery houses approximately 19,000 objects of original art. The schedule of exhibits, which change monthly, includes shows from the permanent collection and traveling shows. Cameras are permitted. The gallery is part of the Syracuse University College of Visual and Performing Arts, a professional art school offering bachelor's and master's degrees in 16 areas of art. A museum training program is open only to graduate students. The museum offers teaching assistantships and fellowships for museology and art students. Catalogs are produced to accompany exhibits. Small tours can be arranged by request. Parking on the university campus only during the weekend. Tues.–Thurs., Sat., Sun. 12–6; Fri. 12–9. (Sims Hall is on College Place. The gallery may be entered from the street or from the College Place driveway entrance.)

**UTICA: Munson-Williams-Proctor Institute.** 310 Genesee St., 13502 ☐ The three families responsible for this institution came to the Mohawk

Valley before Utica was a city; indeed, they were leaders in its emergence, the Munsons as bankers, the Williamses as politicians, and the Proctors as hotel owners and manufacturers. The endowment that created the Munson-Williams-Proctor Institute was established in 1919, and the institute became active under its charter in 1935. Today it consists of a school of art established in 1941; a museum of art designed by Philip Johnson and opened in 1960; Fountain Elms, the Proctor family home, which was restored in 1960 as a house-museum; and a Meetinghouse, which opened in 1963. Johnson's building, a masterpiece of classical simplicity in a modern architectural statement, is a flattened cube that, supported by bronze piers and crossbeams, seems to float over recessed glass walls; the main entrance, gained by crossing a platform bridge over the moatlike sunken terrace on 3 sides of the building, leads to the sculpture court and large uncluttered galleries. The museum houses a collection of more than 5,000 items, primarily American—paintings, drawings, prints, sculpture, and decorative arts. The contributions of Edward W. Root, during his lifetime and at his death, were major: Old Master prints; 20th-century American prints; Japanese woodcuts; over 225 20th-century American paintings and drawings; and a library of 700 volumes. Other collections include more 20th-century art; small groups of pre-Columbian, Persian, Greek, and Etruscan art; and Fountain Elms, the 1850 restored Italianate house, the rooms of which are furnished to display the museum's decorative arts collection. Highlights are Thomas Cole's 4-painting series "Voyage of Life"; "The Tree" by Mondrian; 2 still lifes by Raphaelle Peale; a still life by Harnett; works by Burchfield, Tobey, Pollock, Picasso, Kandinsky, Klee, and Léger. Calder and Moore are among the sculptors represented. Exhibitions change monthly. Cameras are permitted.

The museum's activities include a full-fledged school of art; a Great Artist series; a Utica Arts Festival—open-air performing arts and a sidewalk exhibition of paintings and sculpture—staged for a 10-day period in July. Lectures, films, trips to other museums, guided group tours (not on a fixed schedule) are also features of the educational program. A lending library of 1,000 items is available to members; a reference library and a music library are both open to the public. Many catalogs and publications emanate from this museum and are available for purchase at the museum shop, which also sells jewelry, prints, postcards, ceramics, paintings, and sculpture. Parking facilities nearby. Tues.-Sat. 10-5; Sun. 1-5; closed holidays. Free.

**WEST POINT:   West Point Museum.** United States Military Academy, 10996 □ Among the military artifacts here—West Point has one of the largest collections of these in this part of the world—is a collection of Sully portraits, Rindisbacher watercolors, and military paintings and prints. Visitors can attend lectures or take guided tours around the museum. Make an appointment to use the library (1,600 volumes) on arms, armor, and things military. West Point souvenirs are sold. Daily 10:30–4:15. Free. (Take the Old Storm King Hwy. [Rt. 218]; it is one of the beauties in the East. Or take US 9W.)

**YONKERS: Hudson River Museum at Yonkers, Inc.** 511 Warburton Ave., 10701 ☐ The Victorian mansion, enlarged by a modern wing, that overlooks the Hudson River from Trevor Park in Yonkers was the fashionable home of John Bond Trevor. Its interior, designed by John Locke Eastlake, displays the style and decorative arts popular in the late 19th century. The permanent collection of paintings for the most part underlines the look of 19th-century America—many of these works are the ones that could have hung here in the 1800s; those of the Hudson River school, for example, reproduce the scene that one can see from the windows of the house. There are also some 20th-century paintings. Exhibitions in art, history, and technology change regularly. Established in 1924 as the Yonkers Museum of Science and Art, it has a planetarium and a geophysical section. Concerts, lectures, films, and gallery talks take place regularly. Study clubs and classes are offered, as well as training programs for professional museum workers. Extension programs to schools and community groups, mobile vans, and a school loan service send the museum's resources into the community. The library (3,000 volumes) is available for use on request. A catalog and booklets published here, crafted objects, educational materials, and books are for sale. Mon.–Fri. 10–5; Wed. 7–10; Sun., holidays 1–5. Free.

# NORTH CAROLINA

**ASHEVILLE: Asheville Art Museum.** Civic Center, 28801 ☐ Here, in the middle of Thomas Wolfe's "Altamont," is a museum dedicated to works by living regional artists. A few European and Asian works are the exception. Some of the artists represented here are Piranesi, Favre, Baskin, Rasmussen, Mevi, Dorn, Bireline, and Dangerfield. Exhibitions change monthly. Photographing is permitted if the photographer signs a release. The museum sponsors lectures, films, and concerts in addition to the classes offered in the museum school. Trained docents lead groups on prescheduled visits. A museum shop offers jewelry, prints, postcards, and crafted items for sale. Parking nearby. Tues.–Fri. 10–5; Sat. & Sun. 1–5. Free. (Take the Montford Ave. exit off US 70. The Civic Center is on Haywood St., the main artery through Asheville. Haywood may also be reached from US 19, 23–Merrimon Ave.; and from US 25, 70, & 74 from Biltmore Ave. and Hendersonville Rd.)

**Biltmore House and Gardens.** 28803 ☐ The house that George W. Vanderbilt built took 5 years and about 1,000 workmen to complete, and can easily be mistaken for a French Renaissance castle. It is set amid 35 acres of formal gardens which themselves are only a small part of the entire tract, a sizable domain. Beyond the landscaped acres are forests, thousands of acres of them, which were managed and watched over during Vanderbilt's residency, and which are now part of Pisgah National Forest. The inside of the castle dazzles—the Persian rugs, the tapestries, the mantels, the sculpture and decorative objects combine to resemble the great halls of the Renaissance. Daily 9–5. Admission $6 for adults, $4 for children 6–16. (Take US 25 south off I-40 and go 2 miles.)

**CHAPEL HILL: William Hayes Ackland Memorial Art Center.** Columbia & Franklin Sts., University of North Carolina, 27514 ☐ Tennesseean William Hayes Ackland, in his desire to advance the cause of art in the South, willed a substantial sum of money to be used to establish an art museum in a major Southern university. After years of litigation over the site, the courts awarded the bequest to the University of North Carolina at Chapel Hill. The building, financed by the Ackland Trust, was begun in 1951 and completed in 1958. Ackland's remains, in true Renaissance style, are entombed within in a sarcophagus overlaid with his carved reclining figure. Except for a print collection owned previously by the library and art department, all the objects housed here today were acquired since the opening in 1958. They include works that span the centuries from Egyptian and classical antiquity to the present day. French 19th-century painting and sculpture are particular strengths among a total of some 250 paintings, 170 sculptures, and 3,000 prints and drawings. There is also a room of period furniture and a collection of silver and decorative arts. Among the stars of the museum are a Greek 2nd-century B.C. bronze female head; "Cleopatra and the Servant" by Delacroix; and "View of the Ile St.-Louis" by Rousseau. Temporary exhibits change every 4 to 6 weeks during the academic year; during the summer months an exhibition is drawn from the permanent collection. Indeed, the museum varies its schedule of exhibits, using the resources of other institutions (loan shows), faculty and students, and its own collection. Cameras can be used upon request.

Art studio and art history courses are offered to graduates and undergraduates affiliated with the university. Gallery talks on the temporary exhibits are open to the public, as well as lectures and films. Docent tours can be arranged in advance. The museum publishes numerous catalogs and books related to the collection, all of which can be purchased from the museum guards. A 34,000-volume library is available for interlibrary loan and by special card. University parking lot adjacent to the museum for weekend use; municipal lot 2 blocks away for weekdays. Tues.–Sat. 10–5; Sun. 2–6; closed one week in Aug. Free. (On the southeast corner of Franklin, the main street of Chapel Hill, and Columbia Sts.)

**CHARLOTTE: Mint Museum.** 501 Hempstead Pl., 28207 ☐ Before the California Gold Rush (1849), Charlotte was in the center of the nation's largest gold-producing region. A branch U.S. Mint was established here in 1836 in a Federal-style building that had been designed for the purpose by the renowned William Strickland of Philadelphia. In this building, reconstructed on its present site in 1936, exactly 100 years after its opening, is one of the prides of Charlotte, the Mint Museum. Over 5,000 objects— paintings, sculpture, ceramics, and decorative arts—are housed here; the building, itself an object of historical interest. The collection emphasizes the Renaissance, Baroque, 18th-century English, and 19th- and 20th-century European and American painting; and a pre-Columbian collection is on permanent display. But the museum is particularly well known for its comprehensive collection of pottery and porcelain—English, Continental, and Oriental—ranging from the Han Dynasty to the late 18th century. This collection and a library dedicated to the subject of ceramics constitute an institution for the research and study of ceramics. Some highlights among the paintings are works by Stuart, Henri, Sloan, Sully, Prendergast, Anuszkiewicz, and Bearden, and among the sculpture, works by Chicago artist John Henry. There is also an interesting group of artwork by Southeastern artists and craftsmen as a result of the museum's 2 biennial competitive exhibitions for artists living in the Southeastern states—the Piedmont Painting and Sculpture Exhibition and the Exhibition of Piedmont Crafts. Exhibits change approximately every 6 weeks. Cameras are permitted, preferably without flashes.

Elsewhere in the city, on Shamrock Drive, is the Mint Museum of History, serving as a center for the study and preservation of local history. In addition, the museum maintains a special exhibition room in downtown Charlotte (Spirit Square) for changing monthly exhibits. Classes on antiques and antique furniture are held twice a year, drama classes, during the summer. Either art lectures or concerts are offered every Sunday. A "Museum in the Schools" program sends slide lectures on art appreciation and history into the city's classrooms. The docent training program provides guides for tours that take place almost daily; groups must make arrangements 3 weeks in advance. Catalogs accompany all major exhibitions. The library (2,800 volumes) is open to the public by special permission. The museum shop offers books, cards, and museum replicas for sale. Parking on the grounds. Tues.-Fri. 10–5; Sat. & Sun. 2–5. Free. (SR #16 passes within a few blocks of the museum. Street signs and arrows on Hempstead Pl., Eastover Rd., or Colville Rd. guide visitors to 501 Hempstead Pl.)

**DAVIDSON: Davidson College Art Gallery.** Mailing address: Box 2495, 28036 ☐ On this small college campus near Charlotte, where there are no less than 4 pre-Civil War buildings, 2 of them still in use with some of the original furnishings, is gathered a stunning collection of graphics. Begun in 1950 as a teaching aid and an addition to the cultural resources of the community, the gallery soon became host to the Davidson National Print and Drawing competition, one of the largest of its kind in the country, bringing to the campus each spring the product of the nation's finest printmakers. Thus the strength of the collection is in 20th-century graphics, despite its broad range in time over the preceding 5 centuries. Recent acquisitions have included works by Isabel Bishop, Calder, Levine, Soyer, and Tobey. Also to be seen are prints and drawings by Corinth, Corot, Goya, Hogarth, Toulouse-Lautrec, and Miró, among others. Four to 6 special exhibits, each focusing on the work of a noted contemporary artist, are installed annually. Cameras are permitted. Frequently artists visiting the campus give gallery talks. The college library (500,000 volumes) is open to the public only by special permission. Parking on the campus. Weekdays 10–5; Sat. & Sun. 2–5. (Take the Davidson College exit off I-77.)

**DURHAM: Duke University Museum of Art.** 27708 ☐ On the East Campus of this 2-campus university, a 1920s neo-Georgian structure which was once the science building is now (since 1969) the Duke University Museum of Art. The clever reorganization of this building has effected simple, quietly elegant galleries and spaces, well lighted, temperature-controlled, secure from fire and theft. The prime collection here, the Ernest Brummer collection of medieval and Renaissance sculpture and decorative arts, consists of over 250 objects, most of them superior in quality. Other collections are perhaps smaller but equally fine: 16th- to 18th-century bronzes; Chinese jades and porcelains; pre-Columbian objects and African art; a full set of the wood engravings of Winslow Homer, done during his 20 years as illustrator for *Harper's Weekly;*

classical art emphasizing pottery; and graphics, paintings, meerschaum pipes, Greco-Roman coins, Navajo rugs, and shells, all of which add to the diversity of this interesting museum. In addition to the varying display of the permanent collection, the museum mounts 4 or 5 loan exhibits during the academic year. Photographing is permitted for noncommercial use only. The museum is available to all university departments for various functions including lectures, concerts, and classes. The docent program trains volunteers to give tours of the permanent collections; these can be arranged for groups by appointment made 2 weeks in advance. The many catalogs and pamphlets published here relate to the collections. Visitors are welcome to the campus cafeteria located only 2 buildings away from the museum. Visitor parking behind the museum. Mon.–Fri. 9–5; Sat. 10–1; Sun. 2–5. Free. (From I-85, take the Gregson St. exit to Trinity Ave. and turn right onto Trinity to the entrance to the East Campus. This road leads to the parking lot behind the museum.)

**Museum of Art, North Carolina Central University.** 27707 ☐ North Carolina Central University's museum opened in 1976, a modern facility to celebrate the nation's bicentennial. It was established in smaller quarters in 1971 as a repository for the works of Afro-Americans and other minority groups, and so it still serves. There is a small group of African art, and a small Oceanic collection. Black Americans predominate: this collection includes paintings by William H. Johnson and Alvin D. Loving, Jr., and a sculpture by Richard Hunt. A program of monthly changing exhibits is designed to serve the university community. Cameras are permitted. Tues., Wed., Thurs. 12:30–3:30; Sun. 2–4; or by appointment. Free. (Fayetteville St. leads to the main entrance gate of the campus. Look for the Fine Arts complex next to the administration building.)

**FAYETTEVILLE: Fayetteville Museum of Art.** Stamper Rd. Mailing address: P.O. Box 35134, 28303 ☐ For the first 6 years of its existence, the Fayetteville Museum of Art was housed in the Market House, a 1780 building listed as a National Historic Landmark that once served as the state capitol. Today the museum has a modern home that opened in 1978. The permanent collection consists primarily of works by contemporary regional artists: Claude Howell, Robert Nelson, Richard Kinnaird, Ralph Steeds, Richard Coleman. A full schedule of exhibitions is planned during the year, each show running 4 to 6 weeks; they include one-person shows by North Carolina artists, faculty shows from North Carolina colleges and universities, loan exhibitions from the North Carolina Museum of Art, exhibitions of work by local schoolchildren, and works selected from the museum's annual competition for North Carolina artists. Cameras without flashes are permitted. The museum holds classes and, with the Fayetteville

Parks and Recreation Department, cosponsors a series of lectures, workshops, and films for adults. For children, the museum and the department cosponsor a Children's Art Fair, an Art Day Camp, and a series of workshops. With the city schools it holds art history and art appreciation programs in classrooms. Tours of the museum are available. A museum shop is planned. Parking lots behind the adjacent shopping center and in front of the museum. Tues.–Fri. 10–4; Sun. 2–5. Free. (Find the Eutaw Shopping Center on Bragg Blvd. The museum is behind it.)

**GREENSBORO: Weatherspoon Art Gallery.** University of North Carolina at Greensboro, 27412 ☐ In 1942, when what is now the University of North Carolina at Greensboro was still the Women's College of the University of North Carolina, the Weatherspoon Art Gallery was founded as an adjunct of the department of art. In 1960 the McIver Building opened and the gallery moved into the wing set aside for the art department. With small collections of Oriental and ethnographic art, the gallery concentrates mainly on the 20th century—paintings, sculpture, and graphics—and more specifically on American contemporary art. De Kooning's "Woman" is among the best known works in this category, together with works by Calder, Nadelman, and Henri. The Cone collection of graphics and bronzes by Matisse and other 20th-century artists and the Dillard collection of American works on paper purchased from the gallery's annual Art on Paper exhibitions enrich the sum total of the holdings here. A sculpture garden (to be developed further) contains works by Nadelman, Baizerman, and Rickey. Exhibitions are scheduled throughout the academic year. Hand-held cameras without flash attachments are permitted. Occasional lectures are held to which students are invited. An informal docent program provides tours for student and adult groups upon request. The gallery is staffed by graduate and undergraduate students by means of assistantships and student-aid/work-study programs. The annual catalogs for Art on Paper exhibitions and an annual bulletin are published here and are available for purchase. Reference files on the artists in the permanent collection are available for use by students and researchers. Parking on nearby city streets. Open during academic session Tues.–Fri. 10–5; Sat. & Sun. 2–6. Free. (On Walker Ave. between Tate & McIver Sts.)

**HICKORY: Hickory Museum of Art, Inc.** Third St. & First Ave., N.W. Mailing address: Box 2572, 28601 ☐ In the heart of downtown Hickory, a small industrial city in the foothills of North Carolina and near the Blue Ridge Mountains, is the pride of the city's 40,000 people—the Hickory Museum of Art. It was founded in 1944 by Paul W. Whitener to collect and foster American art, and it has done so ever since. The collection focuses strongly on late-19th- and early-20th-century painters, including Thomas Cole, A. B. Durand, Kensett, and F. Worthington Whittredge. Some American Impressionists represented are Homer D. Martin, Bruestle, Potthast, and George Smillie; later American Impressionists exhibited are Robert Reid and George Elmer Brown. The museum also owns a small collection of European art including works by Tintoretto, Turner, Sir Thomas Lawrence, Pierre Miguard, Rousseau, and others. There are monthly exhibitions, including local and regional shows and periodic national shows. Cameras are permitted on special request. The museum offers art classes for adults and children, lectures, and other events on an irregular basis. Guided tours for schoolchildren and special groups are available. Mon.–Fri. 10–5; Sun. 3–5. Free.

**RALEIGH:  North Carolina Museum of Art.** 107 East Morgan St., 27611 ☐ There is one painting by Stephan Lochner, the 15th-century German master ("St. Jerome in His Study"), in the United States, and it hangs in the North Carolina Museum of Art. There is one Cellini bronze in existence, and it is housed at the North Carolina Museum of Art. Add a large Kress collection; European and American paintings, sculpture, and decorative arts; pre-Columbian, African, Oceanic, and Indian art; the Phifer collection of paintings; and about 60 galleries in which to hang them—and you have the ingredients of a very fine museum. It was established by the North Carolina Art Society with Robert F. Phifer's paintings long before it opened in 1956. Today, still aided by Phifer funds, the galleries overflow with the work of painters such as Rubens, de Vos (from Rubens's workshop), Van Dyck, Rembrandt, and Raphael; and among the Americans, Copley and Gilbert Stuart, Bellows and O'Keeffe. Some ancient pieces, a North Carolina collection, and a gallery for the blind enhance still further the resources of this institution. There are approximately 10 temporary exhibits per year, including annual North Carolina artists' competitions and traveling exhibits. The educational program is strong, reaching out into many communities with a statewide extension program. Lectures, films, concerts, workshops, and guided tours are offered; catalogs, a quarterly bulletin, brochures, and a calendar of events are published. There is a reference library (12,000 volumes) and a museum shop. Tues.–Sat. 10–5; Sun. 2–6. Free.

**WILMINGTON:  St. John's Art Gallery.** 114 Orange St., 28401 ☐ The holdings of the St. John's Gallery consist of a small number of paintings and watercolors by Elizabeth Chant, teacher of Wilmington artists and founder of the Wilmington Art Association; "Portrait of a Gentleman" by

Jacob Marling, early 19th-century North Carolina portrait painter; a collection of Jugtown pottery; and a collection of 19th-century scent bottles. The Georgian building, a Wilmington landmark, was erected in 1804 to house the first Masonic lodge in North Carolina. Eleven exhibitions are scheduled per year; these include loan exhibits from the North Carolina Museum of Art and shows of the work currently produced by North Carolina artists. Cameras are permitted. Art classes are conducted by an artist-in-residence; lectures, concerts, workshops, films, and slide presentations are also offered. A sales gallery sells original art, postcards, and notepaper. Parking on the street only. Tues.–Sat. 10–5. Free. (From US 17, cross Memorial Bridge and go north on Front or 3rd St.)

**WINSTON-SALEM: Museum of Early Southern Decorative Arts.** 924 South Main St. Mailing address: Salem Station, 27108 ☐ The decorative arts flourish in Winston-Salem in both this museum and in Reynolda House, not far away. Founded in 1965, the Museum of Early Southern Decorative Arts is devoted exclusively to the study of Southern decorative arts from 1680 to 1820. Collections of furniture, paintings, silver, and textiles, and complete room interiors illustrate the Colonial way of life in Maryland, Virginia, Georgia, Kentucky, Tennessee, and the Carolinas. There is no regular schedule of special exhibitions. Cameras are not permitted. Series of lectures bring leading authorities to Winston-Salem to speak. A summer institute offers graduate credit in 2 courses. Trained guides lead groups of 4 to 6 people every 15 minutes. Publications include a general catalog and a semiannual *Journal of Southern Decorative Arts.* The library is available for use by special permission. A bookstore offers titles related to the subjects covered by the museum. Restaurants are located nearby; parking adjacent to the museum. Mon.–Sat. 10:30–5; Sun. 1:30–4:30; closed Christmas. Admission $2, students $1. (At Old Salem restoration.)

**Reynolda House.** Reynolda Rd. Mailing address: Box 11765, 27106 ☐ Richard Joshua Reynolds came to Winston, North Carolina, from his home in Patrick County, Virginia, in 1874, to establish the R. J. Reynolds Tobacco Company with a little over $7,000 in cash. In 1905 he married, and in 1917 he built a house—Reynolda House—for his growing family. The house was designed by a fashionable Philadelphia architect, Charles Barton Keen, on a 1,000-acre tract of land that was to be a model self-sustaining community, including a dairy, stables, a smokehouse, a blacksmith shop, a greenhouse, a post office, a school, and a church, a central heating plant, and residences for nearly 100 souls. Reynolds died 8 months after moving into the house, but his family remained and continued to develop the dream of the builder. By 1965 the house was no longer in use by the family and was opened to the public as a museum, dedicated to the advancement of education and the arts. The Reynolda House American Art collection, which opened to the public in 1967, spans the whole range of American art from 1755 to the present and can be viewed in the comfortable surroundings of a beautiful home. The work on display includes such widely diverse paintings as Leonard Baskin's "Old Artist" (one of the more recent), and John Singleton Copley's "Portrait of John Spooner" (one of the oldest). Also on exhibit here are works by Avery, Benton, Bierstadt, Cassatt, Eakins, Harnett, Peale, and Andrew Wyeth, to name only a few. The group of prints is somewhat smaller and more contemporary, with works by Dine, Johns, Rosenquist, and Mark Tobey among them. Another pride of the museum is the singular collection of porcelain birds designed by Dorothy Doughty and first made in 1935 by the Royal Worcester Porcelain Company; it is said to be the only complete collection of Doughty birds on public display. Family costumes from 1910 to 1940 are also a source of information and enjoyment to visitors here. Cameras are permitted.

The activities of Reynolda House include chamber music concerts, drama, lectures, and festivals, as well as several art classes, which can be taken for graduate or undergraduate credit by arrangement with local universities. The museum also offers fellowships to graduate students in the American Foundations summer seminar, fellowships to January interns, and artist-in-residence positions to poets, musicians, and painters. The library (1,000 volumes) is open to the public; its focus is that of the collections of art, ceramics, and costumes. Guided tours are available only for large groups that have made arrangements in advance. Postcards and brochures on the collection can be purchased at a sales desk. The gardens, designed by Philadelphia landscape architect Thomas Sears, and the greenhouses are spectacular in season; they are open the same hours as the museum. Parking on the grounds. Tues.–Sat. 9:30–4:30; Sun. 1:30–4:30; closed Christmas, Jan. 2–Feb. 1. Admission $1 for adults, 50¢ for children and students. (About 2 miles northwest of downtown on Rt. 67.)

**Southeastern Center for Contemporary Art.** 750 Marguerite Dr., 27108 □ Although the Southeastern Center for Contemporary Art maintains no permanent collection other than the period furnishings in its restored building in Old Salem, nevertheless the continually changing exhibitions represent the contemporary creative work going on in 11 surrounding southeastern states. Exhibitions—either one-person or group shows in all media—change in 9 gallery areas every 4 to 8 weeks. Occasionally the center holds juried competitions and installs traveling or exchange exhibitions. Cameras are not permitted. The center functions as an active cultural fount of the community, sponsoring educational programs and classes, seminars, workshops, panel discussions, hands-on exhibits, trips, lectures, concerts, and more. A fellowship is offered to an artist residing in the 11-state southeastern area. Docents conduct tours on request. In the center shop, visitors can purchase fine crafts, books, art gifts, paper products, jewelry, and children's items. Parking on the museum grounds. Tues.–Sat. 10–5; Sun. 2–5. Free. (Off Reynolda Rd.)

# NORTH DAKOTA

**MINOT: Minot Art Gallery.** Samuelson House, North Dakota State Fairgrounds. Mailing address: P.O. Box 325, 58701 ☐ The Minot Art Gallery, located on the North Dakota State Fairgrounds, was established in 1970. With only a small permanent collection of works by Robert A. Nelson, Warrington Colescott, C. Robert Schwieger, and Bud Sharkin, the gallery holds monthly exhibits of living artists, both local and national. There are also art fairs and competitions. Cameras are permitted. The gallery offers lectures, art classes, and guided tours for special groups. A gift shop sells paintings, frames, and crafts by North Dakota artists. Tues.–Sun. 1–5. Admission 50¢ for adults, 10¢ for children.

**VALLEY CITY: 2nd Crossing Gallery.** Room 210 McFarland Hall, Valley City State College. Mailing address: Box 1319, 58072 ☐ In October 1973 Valley City State College was enlarged by one art gallery, opened in the administration building to provide art shows to the students and to the population at large. The small collection (16 pieces) is displayed in a 28-by-40-foot space with modern lighting and movable standards. Approximately 11 shows, generally on loan, are installed annually; there is also a biennial national juried art show. Photographing by permission only. Small scholarships are awarded. Catalogs are prepared to accompany exhibitions. Parking available. Mon.–Fri. 1–4; Mon., Wed. 7–9; Sun. 2–4. Free.

# OHIO

**AKRON: Akron Art Institute.** 69 East Market St., 44308 ☐ Although Dr. Benjamin Franklin Goodrich opened his first rubber plant in Akron in 1870, the city (which is now the world's leading producer of rubber products) began to thrive in the 20th century with the "horseless carriage."

Thus, it is appropriate that Akron's museum features 20th century art. The institute celebrated its 50th anniversary in 1972, after many years of moving and uncertainty, in its Beaux-Arts home that was once the Carnegie Library. Today the collection includes works by Stella, Magritte, Picasso, Warhol, and Robert Indiana, and earlier works by Burchfield, Chase, and Henri among others. Paintings from 15th- to 18th-century Europe can also be viewed here. Twenty-odd exhibitions are mounted yearly, some of which feature local artists. Cameras are permitted. The activities of this lively museum are myriad. Classes for adults are offered year round; for children, on Saturdays, Sept.–May. Lectures, demonstrations, and concerts are held regularly. Schoolchildren are given tours and demonstrations, and other groups are offered guided tours by trained docents. An artmobile visits city parks and county schools. Federally funded programs for inner-city young people include such activities as painting urban walls and planning playground equipment. Catalogs are published to accompany special exhibits and are available at the shop, together with other art books, jewelry, prints, and more. The library (4,000 volumes) is open to the public. Parking nearby. Tues.–Fri. 12–5; Sat. 10–5; Sun. 1–5. Free.

**ASHTABULA: Ashtabula Arts Center.** 2928 West 13th St., 44004 ☐ Ashtabula's Art Center was founded in 1953 in the home of its inspiration and patron, Katharine E. Hill. It came to its own home in 1972; on 5 acres of wooded land in suburban Ashtabula, the building was awarded a state architectural award in 1973. The small collection here consists of the work of contemporary regional artists. National, regional, and local exhibits are rotated monthly. Cameras are permitted. This active art center offers classes in all branches of the arts, 4 terms per year; a limited number of scholarships are awarded to students who meet qualification standards. Sunday lectures and music and drama programs are offered regularly. The educational activities extend to 10 schools in Ashtabula County and the Warren public schools. A schedule of classes, a monthly calendar, an annual report, and other miscellaneous publications emanate continually from the center. A shop offers books and jewelry for sale. Parking on the grounds. Mon.–Thurs. 8:30 a.m.–9:30 p.m.; Fri. & Sat. 8:30–5; Sun. 1–4. (Take US 20 to Lake Ave.; turn off Lake at 13th St.)

**CANTON: Canton Art Institute.** 1001 Market Ave. N., 44702 ☐ The Canton Art Institute was established in 1935, almost 40 years away from the "Front Porch" provincialism of William McKinley, who started the practice of law here. Italian, Spanish, and American paintings; 18th- and 19th-century English and American portraits; contemporary regional art, sculpture, graphics, and decorative arts—all reside very comfortably in Canton, Ohio. Exhibits change regularly and frequently. The Institute offers guided tours, lectures, films, gallery talks, and classes for adults and children. Catalogs are published with exhibits. The library (4,000 volumes) is open for use by the public. A shop offers toys, reproductions, jewelry, books, postcards for sale. Tues.–Thurs. 9–5, 7–9; Fri., Sat. 9–5; Sun. 2–5. Free.

**CINCINNATI: Cincinnati Art Museum.** Art Museum Dr., Eden Park, 45202 ☐ The Cincinnati Art Museum was founded in 1881. The original, and still central building was completed in 1886 in a style known as "Richardson Romanesque." Wings were added in 1906, 1910, 1927–30, 1937, and 1962–65. This general art museum reviews the major civilizations over a span of 5,000 years through paintings, sculpture, prints, drawings, photographs, decorative arts, tribal arts, costumes, and textiles. Both its Near Eastern and American collections are notable, as are the ancient musical instruments (Eastern and Western) and the Herbert Greer French collection of prints from the 15th to the 20th century. The collection of American Indian art is outstanding in the country. Many well-known paintings can be seen here, among them Mantegna's "Esther and Mordecai," "Portrait of Philip II" by Titian, "Crucifixion with View of Toledo" by El Greco, and 12th-century Spanish frescoes from San Baudelio de Berlanga. There are works by Frank Duveneck and Henry Farny; Grant Wood's "Daughters of the Revolution," a Cézanne still life painted in 1865 and a watercolor of 1904; Chagall's "Red Rooster"; Van Gogh's "Figures in Undergrowth"; important ancient and medieval sculptures; and unique 1st- and 2nd-century Nabataean sculptures from Jordan. Eight to 10 temporary exhibitions are planned each season, some from the permanent storage holdings, some from other institutions. Cameras are permitted.

The Cincinnati Museum Association parents both the museum and the Art Academy of Cincinnati, which is an adjoining professional art school. The museum itself sponsors creative arts classes for children, lectures, and films. Lectures and tours are available for individual groups by appointment; public tours led by museum-trained docents are offered Wed. and Sun. at 2, Sat. at 10:30 and 2. Background music enhances the musical instrument collection on weekdays (10:30, 1:30, 3) and Sun. (1:30, 3). Publications emanating from the museum include a quarterly bulletin and the museum *News,* books, catalogs, and checklists relating to specific holdings; all are sold at the museum shop, which also offers reproductions, postcards, jewelry, and other objects relating to the museum's collections. The library (29,500 volumes) is open to the public Tues.–Fri. 10–4:45. A cafeteria is open Tues.–Fri. 10–3:30, Sat. 10–2. Parking on the museum grounds. Tues.–Sat. 10–5; Sun. 1–5; closed major holidays. Free on Sat.; weekdays $1 for adults, 50¢ for ages 12–18, free for children under 12 and scheduled tour groups through grade 12. (From downtown Cincinnati, go east on 7th St. to Gilbert Ave. to Eden Park entrance.)

**Contemporary Arts Center.** 115 East 5th St., 45202 ☐ The Contemporary Arts Center, operating on what it terms the *kunsthalle* model, maintains no permanent collection, yet its aim—and that of its founders in 1939—is to fill the need for the representation of modern art in Cincinnati. It has defined itself as a museum of ideas, not of objects. Only a sculpture ("Hecuba") by Ruben Nakian and a mobile by Alexander Calder are always on display to complement the architectural features of the space. Exhibits in all the visual arts change every 2 months. Cameras without flashes are permitted. The center sponsors lectures and workshops, dance company residencies, chamber music concerts, and recitals. Tours can be arranged in advance. Posters and exhibition catalogs published here are sold at the information desk. Tues.–Sat. 10–5; Sun. 12–5. Admission 50¢ for adults, 25¢ for students; free for children under 12. (In the Formica Building, between Main & Walnut Sts.)

**Taft Museum.** 316 Pike St., 45202 ☐ The elegant Federal-style mansion facing Lytle Park in Cincinnati was inhabited by a mayor of Cincinnati; by Nicholas Longworth, member of the House of Representatives and Alice Lee Roosevelt's husband; and by Charles Phelps Taft, proprietor and editor of the Cincinnati *Times Star,* and half brother of the twenty-seventh President of the United States. Indeed, it was in this entrance portico in 1908 that William Howard Taft accepted the Republican presidential nomination. Anna Sinton and Charles Phelps Taft amassed a stunning collection of paintings and objets d'art while they lived here. When it became a museum in 1932, 112 years after it was built, the building was restored to its original state and decorated in the style of the period, with Duncan Phyfe furniture and Regency and Empire fabrics and hangings. The Tafts' collection of portraits by Rembrandt ("Man Leaning on a Sill," "Portrait of a Young Man"), Hals, Van Dyck, Goya ("Toreador," "Portrait of Queen Maria Luisa"), and Whistler, and landscapes by Ruisdael, Gainsborough, and Corot remained on the walls. And the superb collections of over 200 Chinese 17th- and 18th-century porcelains and French Renaissance enamel portraits were further enhanced by the grace and beauty of their 19th-century surroundings. What was once the ballroom of the house became and still is the setting for Sunday afternoon concerts. Adjacent to the gardens at the rear of the house is the Garden Gallery, where exhibitions of historical and community interest and contemporary art are presented. Guided tours are offered by advance appointment to groups during the week. Informal tours are given by volunteer guides on weekdays 10–4. Weekdays 10–5; Sun. 2–5; closed Thanksgiving & Christmas. Free.

**CLEVELAND: Cleveland Museum of Art.** 11150 East Blvd., 44106 ☐ Four men are responsible for the birth of the Cleveland Museum of Art. Three of them, independently of one another, made bequests in their wills that designated money for the building of a museum; they were John P. Huntington, Horace Kelley, and Hinman B. Hurlbut. Land (given in 1892), art objects, and funds for further purchases were donated by J. H. Wade II, who later became the museum's second president. The museum was incorporated in 1913, and the white marble neoclassic building opened to the public in 1916. It was built on an elevation overlooking a pond; today that pond and elevation, beautifully landscaped and graded, help to make the Cleveland one of the most beautiful museums in the world, its elegant facade reflected in a lake and overlooking the terraced gardens that are known as Wade Park. Within this templelike edifice has grown one of America's major museums. Its constantly growing collection (more than 43,000 objects), reviewing the art of all cultures down through the ages, is installed in chronological order. The Oriental collection is considered to be one of the finest in the western world; it contains Chinese and Japanese paintings and ceramics, Chinese bronzes, Japanese screens, and Indian sculpture. The medieval collection, also famous, contains gold, silver, ivory, and enameled reliquaries, crosses and decorative objects, illuminated books and manuscripts, wood and stone religious sculpture, altarpieces, and other paintings on panels. The single most illustrious item in this collection is the Guelph Treasure, 9 sacred objects dating from the early 11th century, from the Cathedral of St. Blasius in Brunswick, Germany. Its acquisition in 1931 raised the Cleveland Museum to rank with the leading museums of Germany, France, and England in the field of medieval art. The assemblage of European and American paintings represents almost every school and period from the Middle Ages to the present. Particularly fine is the collection of 14th- and 15th-century European paintings; most important are "The Holy Family with the Infant St. John and St. Margaret" by Filippino Lippi, and 2 panel paintings of "St. Anthony Abbot" and "St. Michael" also by Filippino Lippi. Renaissance paintings include Titian's "Adoration of the Magi" and Tintoretto's "Baptism of Christ." The Baroque painting collection is strong and growing; a recently acquired masterwork by Caravaggio, "The Martyrdom of St. Andrew," hangs with works by his followers, Terbrugghen, Gentileschi, van Honthorst, and de la Tour. Other masterworks of Baroque art are Reni's "Adoration of the Magi" and Rubens's "Diana and Her Nymphs Departing for the Chase." The museum is also rich in

Spanish paintings; El Greco's "Christ on the Cross with Landscape" and "Holy Family" are well known, as is Zurbarán's "The Holy House of Nazareth." There are 3 exceptional portraits by Goya and works by Murillo and Ribera. Dutch painting of the 17th century includes portraits by Rembrandt, notably "Old Man Praying," and a number of fine landscapes, particularly those of van Ruisdael. The small group of 18th-century French and English paintings contains portraits by Rigaud, Reynolds, Lawrence, and Gainsborough. English landscape paintings include a view of Hampstead Heath by Constable and one of the museum's most celebrated works, Turner's "The Burning of the Houses of Parliament." Three important works in the large collection of 19th-century French paintings are "Cupid and Psyche" by David, "Grand Panorama of the Alps" by Courbet, and "Summer" by Puvis de Chavannes. A gallery devoted to the Barbizon school contains outstanding paintings by Corot and Daubigny. The large American painting collection is distinguished by John Singleton Copley's portrait of Nathaniel Hurd and portraits by Stuart and Sully. Nineteenth-century American landscape is particularly strong, with important pictures by Cole, Church, Gifford, and Heade, and fine examples by Inness and Homer. Later 19th-century American romantics and realists are exemplified by Ryder's "Death on a Pale Horse," Chase's "Portrait of Miss Dora Wheeler," Eakins's "Biglin Brothers Turning the Stake," and Bellows's "Stag at Sharkey's." The museum is distinguished for its collection of Impressionist and Post-impressionist paintings: Degas's "Frieze of Dancers," Monet's "Water Lilies," Van Gogh's "The Road Menders at Arles," Gauguin's "L'Appel," Toulouse-Lautrec's "Monsieur Boileau at the Café," and Cézanne's "The Pigeon Tower at Montbriand." Recent acquisitions of works by Picasso and Braque have strengthened the museum's collection of cubist paintings. Picasso's work is particularly well represented, with examples of almost every phase of his production, including "La Vie," the masterpiece of his Blue Period, and "Harlequin with Violin," an exceptional example of synthetic cubism. Since 1960 the museum has built a representative collection of contemporary paintings, including important works by Hofmann, Kline, Rothko, and Louis. French furniture and decorative arts of the 18th century, with exquisitely crafted tables, cabinets, and clocks, and a Louis XVI boudoir from a house in Rouen are some of the other treasures here. There is also one of the 3 or 4 best textile collections in the United States, including the largest and most complete collection of medieval Persian textiles in the world and a very good selection of early Egyptian textiles. The collection of Greek vases and classical bronzes is small but very select. Quality has been the principal consideration in the selection of works for the extensive prints and drawings collection. There is a choice group of 18th- to 20th-century American drawings. The print collection has many fine 15th-century Italian, German, and Netherlandish prints, and is also strong in works by 16th-century German and Dutch, 18th-century Italian, and 19th-century English and French printmakers. Sculpture in the museum (exclusive of Oriental) ranges from a stone figure of Gudea, governor of the Sumerian city of Lagash, dating from 2200 B.C., to American contemporary artist Louise Nevelson's 1958 wood sculpture "Sky Cathedral-Moon Garden Wall." Sculpture is displayed with paintings and decorative arts of the same period; next to late Gothic paintings are wood sculptures by the German artist Riemenschneider; in the galleries for early-19th-century French painting is Canova's neoclassic marble sculpture of "Terpsichore"; and in the galleries for late-19th-century French painting, Rodin's "Age of Bronze." A small collection of African and Oceanic art is adjacent to the 20th-century galleries; and on the museum's ground level is American Indian art and a fine collection of pre-Columbian art. About 12 special exhibits, organized by the museum or circulated by other institutions, are presented through the year; they include The Year in Review, an annual exhibition of works acquired during the previous year, and the May Show, an annual juried exhibition of works by artists and craftspeople of Ohio's Western Reserve region. Photographing of museum-owned works is permitted without the use of flashes or tripods.

The Department of Art History and Education offers studio and art history classes for young people and adults. Many lectures by visiting scholars and museum curators, and concerts are scheduled throughout the year. The museum also offers advance placement courses to Cleveland area high school students and in conjunction with Case Western Reserve University, undergraduate and graduate courses in art history for which 2 fellowships are available. An extensions division designs and installs exhibits drawn from its own collection in schools and libraries (changed every 6 weeks) throughout greater Cleveland, and in a gallery (Karamu House) in the inner city and one in a Cleveland suburb. Gallery talks are provided by education department instructors on Sun. and Wed. at 1:30. Guided tours for groups of 15 or more must be arranged in advance. The museum publishes many books and catalogs, available at the sales desk along with slides and reproductions, and a scholarly bulletin ten times a year, available by subscription. The library (86,000 volumes, 180,000 slides, 223,000 photographs) is open to visiting scholars, curators, and graduate students. The cafeteria is open for lunch and afternoon tea, Tues.-Sat. Parking on the grounds and nearby. Tues., Thurs., Fri. 10-6; Wed. 10-10; Sat. 9-5; closed July 4, Thanksgiving, Christmas, Jan. 1. Free. (In University Circle, a 500-acre educational and cultural center 10 minutes from downtown Cleveland. From Public Square [downtown Cleveland], take Euclid Ave. to East Blvd. and go north; or take Memorial

Shoreway Dr. [I-90] to Liberty Blvd. and go south through Rockefeller Park.)

**Salvador Dali Museum.** 24050 Commerce Park Rd., 44122 ☐ The private collection of Mr. A. Reynolds Morse, consisting of about 50 oil paintings, 60 to 75 drawings and watercolors, and over 100 graphics, all by Salvador Dali, are housed in a wing of the Morse office building (I.M.S. Company) in Commerce Park. Works from Dali's childhood, from his student days, several surrealist efforts leading to his classic period are all on view here. Three large canvases—"The Discovery of America by Christopher Columbus," "The Ecumenical Council," and "The Hallucinogenic Toreador"— highlight this more or less permanent retrospective. The graphics are rotated every 3 to 6 months. Signed permission is required to photograph the exhibit. Short explanatory lectures are offered to large groups upon request. The museum's shop offers Dali-related items: books on Dali, reproductions, lithographic posters, graphics, plates and medallions, slides, postcards, and other miscellanea. Tues.–Sat. 10–12, 1–4 by appointment only. Free. (The I.M.S. Company building is on the east side of Cleveland in the suburb of Beachwood. Exit from I-271 at Chagrin Blvd.; go west 3 blocks to Commerce Park Rd. on the left.)

**COLUMBUS:    Columbus Gallery of Fine Arts.** 480 East Broad St., 43215 ☐ On the star-studded roster of artists whose work is on display at the Columbus Gallery of Fine Arts, George Bellows's name has a special prominence. He was, after all, born in Columbus, and his works here constitute the largest publicly shown collection known—20 paintings, 4 drawings, and over 60 lithographs. The handsome Italian Renaissance-style building which houses them was opened in 1931. A new wing was added in 1974 to accommodate the wide-ranging collections gathered here, works from 2000 B.C. to the present. The Ferdinand Howald collection is one of the most interesting. This Columbus businessman amassed one of the country's great collections of American art—works by Marin (28 watercolors), Demuth, Prendergast, Sheeler, Dickinson, Ernest Lawson, Blume, Weber, and Kuniyoshi. He gave them all—Americans, some Picassos and Matisses, a large group of Pascins, a selection of Majolica and Isnik plates, and medieval paintings—to Columbus. The Frederick W. Schumacher collection is another gem. Its focus is on paintings and sculpture by Dutch, Flemish, English, French, and Italian masters, but it also includes medieval tapestries and furniture. The Derby Fund collection is a potpourri of great masters, one of the most spectacular being "Christ Triumphant Over Sin and Death," an altarpiece done by Rubens in 1618. Van Dyck, Constable, Eakins, Lawrence, Reynolds, Rembrandt, and Le Brun are others represented in the Derby group. "Sky Catherdral: Night

Wall" by Nevelson and "Canna Lily" by O'Keeffe are among the more recent acquisitions. The new wing, opening out from the soaring central court, is used for large contemporary paintings and sculpture and temporary exhibits which are scheduled monthly. Cameras are permitted in the permanent collection only; no flashes are allowed.

Art classes and seminars for children and adults are offered through the education office. The gallery also sponsors regular "Box Lunch Chats" (reservations required), lectures, concerts, poetry readings, and film series; all are open to the public. Docent-guided tours are available by appointment. Many catalogs and books are published here and are for sale. A print study room can be used by appointment. The Designer-Craftsman Shop sells original crafts by Ohio artists, including jewelry, pottery, and ceramics, and prints and postcards. The Collector's Gallery offers works by local and national artists for rent or sale. Parking on the museum grounds. Tues., Thurs., Fri., Sun. 11–5; Wed. 11–8:30; Sat. 10–5. Admission $1.50 for adults, 50¢ for children 6–17, senior citizens, and students. (Off Washington Ave.)

**Ohio State University Gallery of Fine Art.** Hopkins Gallery and Sullivant Gallery. Office: 128 North Oval Mall, 43210 ☐ The Ohio State University Gallery of Fine Art is incorporated into 2 university buildings, Hopkins and Sullivant. Begun in 1975, the permanent collection here celebrates the seventies in art. Works by Lichtenstein, Stella, de Kooning, Rauschenberg, and Kelley are on view on a rotating basis in the Collection Gallery, located in Sullivant Hall. A Main Gallery, 2 lobbies, and a corridor in Hopkins Hall and the Main Gallery in Sullivant are utilized for changing temporary exhibits of work from other institutions, by visiting artists, or by students and faculty. Cameras are permitted. The gallery sponsors rug concerts on Thursday (12 noon) while school is in session, lectures in conjunction with exhibitions (often by exhibiting artists), and workshops. Several individual catalogs and one reviewing the entire year's exhibits are published here. Parking nearby. Hopkins Gallery open Mon.–Fri. 9–5; Sullivant Gallery open Tues.–Thurs. 9:30–5:50, Fri. 9:30–5, Sat. 10–4, Sun. 2–5. Free. (I-71 to 17th Ave. exit; follow signs to the university. Sullivant Gallery is at 15th Ave. & High St.; park in Union or Mershon garages on either side. Hopkins Gallery is between North Oval Mall & 17th Ave., 2 blocks west of High; park in Mershon garage.)

**Schumacher Gallery.** Capital University, 2199 E. Main St., 43209 ☐ The Schumacher Gallery is Capital University's teaching gallery for the academic community; it also serves the community at large. Eight gallery areas on the top floor of the library building house the holdings of the university: American watercolors, contemporary prints, 19th-century paintings, sculpture, Oceanic tribal arts, and works by Ohio painters.

Woodcuts by Dürer, a 16th-century Pietà by Willem Key, a landscape by Bellows, and watercolors by Reginald Marsh, William Zorach, and others are among the gallery's most notable works. Exhibits change monthly. Cameras are permitted. Lectures are regularly scheduled and guided tours are available by reservation. The gallery has produced a film strip and tape called "Major Ohio Painters" which may be used by outside groups. Parking nearby. Mon.–Fri. 1–5; Sun. 2–4. Free. (From downtown Columbus, take I-70 to Capital University exit, then take east Main St. 2 blocks to the library building.)

**DAYTON: Dayton Art Institute.** Forest & Riverview Ave. Mailing address: P.O. Box 941, 45401 ☐ High on a hill overlooking the Miami River and Dayton is the Dayton Art Institute, looking very much like a 16th-century Italian palazzo. This ornate sandstone recollection of the Renaissance, with the arcaded inner courts of its predecessors—the Villa d'Este and the Villa Farnese at Caprarola, after which it was modeled—was given to Dayton by Mrs. Harriet G. Carnell. The museum is known for its American collection, which is housed in a new American wing; for the Oriental collection that began with Mrs. Carnell and has grown to notable proportions, to be housed in its own wing; and for the European section, which contains fine works from Italy, France, Belgium, and Holland. Works from ancient cultures, from pre-Columbian America, and from primitive cultures (American Indian, African, and Oceanic, for example) are also here. A series of national exhibits are brought to Dayton each year; several smaller shows run concurrently with these. Photographing is allowed only by special permission.

The education department offers classes for children and adults, school tours, and Action Packs for schools in the area. Every month lectures and gallery talks are given by the curatorial staff. Films and concerts are also part of the regular schedule of events. A docent training program supplies guides for all types of tours, including special tours for the handicapped. Scholarships are available through the youth program. The museum publishes a monthly calendar of events, books, and catalogs of the permanent collection as well as temporary exhibits. The library (20,000 volumes) is open to the public Mon.–Fri. 9–5. A sales shop (open Tues.–Sun. 1–4) offers antique and modern jewelry, books, handmade baskets, boxes, fabrics, toys, and collectors' items. Parking in a lot behind the museum. Tues.–Fri. & Sun. 12–5; Sat. 9–5. Free. (Take I-75 to Main St. exit; go north over the bridge to Riverview Ave. The museum is at the intersection of Riverview & Forest.)

**Fine Arts Gallery at Wright State University, Inc.** Wright State University, 45435 ☐ The Fine Arts Gallery at Wright State University began in 1974 as an art department gallery in the then sparkling new contemporary Creative Arts Center. The collection of painting and sculpture is limited, but there is a growing number of works on paper, primarily prints done by contemporary artists. The specialty here is the exhibition of works designed for the specific spaces provided by this particular gallery. These temporary exhibits change about every 3 weeks. A signed release is needed for camera users. The activities of an active university arts center take place here. Tours are offered by appointment. A sales and information desk offers books and publications from previous exhibits (the gallery's own) for sale. Parking nearby. Mon.–Sat. 10–4; Wed. & Thurs. 5–7. Free. (From downtown Dayton, take Rt. 4 to Rt. 444 to Kauffman; or take 3rd St. to Colonel Glenn.)

**MASSILLON: Massillon Museum.** 212 Lincoln Way E., 44646 ☐ James Duncan founded the town of Massillon and built what was to become its museum. In fact, the original Federal-style building was his home. It was bequeathed to the town by its owners to be used as a library or a museum or both. In 1933 the museum was opened, and 3 years later a wing was added to accommodate the growing library. The museum's paintings, prints, photographs, china, glass, ceramics, and costumes concentrate on the fine arts and crafts of Ohio and the history of the region. There is a sculpture by William Zorach, paintings by William T. Mathews, a portrait by G. P. A. Healy, a landscape by Albert Blakelock, and some early portraits dating from 1826 to 1845. Exhibits in 2 areas are changed monthly; a period room and an early kitchen are changed once a year. Cameras are permitted. Classes in the arts, pottery, photography, and drama are offered to adults and children. Lectures, demonstrations, and occasional musical programs are also offered, as well as displays for classrooms and workshops in Merit Badge requirements. Catalogs accompany exhibits. Guided tours can be scheduled any time. The museum shop offers paper items, jewelry, pottery, and toys for sale. Park on the street or in lots on weekends. Tues.–Sat. 9:30–5; Sun. 2–5. Free.

**OBERLIN: Allen Memorial Art Museum.** Oberlin College, 44074 ☐ Oberlin's Allen Memorial Art Museum, the first college museum west of the Alleghenies, was designed by architect Cass Gilbert soon after his resounding success with the Woolworth Building in New York City. The handsome Italian Renaissance-style building, a gift of Mrs. F. F. Prentiss of Cleveland in memory of her first husband Dr. Dudley Peter Allen, opened in 1917 with some artifacts and a few paintings that belonged to the college. Today the collection is one of the finest of any on an American college campus. All periods are covered, from ancient Egypt to the pres-

ent, but the museum's particular strength is in Northern European painting, Old Master prints, Japanese woodblock prints, and modern art. Stars
are Terbrugghen's "St. Sebastian," Hobbema's "Landscape," Monet's
"Gardens of the Princess, Louvre," and Gorky's "Plough and the Song." A
canvas by Rubens, prints by Dürer and Rembrandt, and works by Kokoschka, Modigliani, Picasso, Braque, Matisse, Dine, Poons, and Stella
take the collection up through the centuries. Likewise, the sculpture begins
with the Sumerians and finishes with Arp and Oldenburg. American
pressed glass goblets (1,400 of them), Oriental rugs, and a fine costume
collection add to the range of interests. Six to 8 temporary exhibits are
mounted during the school year; some are loan shows and some are from
the permanent collection. Cameras without flashes are permitted; tripods
require special permission.

A lecture series is administered by the art department, which is housed
in the same building complex (a 1937 addition to the original building is
used for classrooms and studios and a 1976 addition for the art library,
restoration laboratory, and gallery of contemporary art). Gallery talks are
offered to school or other groups on request. Occasionally catalogs accompany exhibits, but the *Allen Art Museum Bulletin* appears biannually; both
are for sale at a sales desk that also offers postcards and museum reproductions. The art library (30,000 volumes) is available to the public by
permission and for inter-library loan. Parking in front of the museum on
Main Street. Open during the school year: Tues. 11–8, Wed.–Fri. 11–5,
Sat. & Sun. 2–5; during school vacations, Jan. term, and summer, Wed.–
Sun. 2–5. Free. (At the intersection of Rts. 10 & 58.)

**OXFORD: Miami University Museum.** Miami University, 45056 ☐
Ground for the Miami University Museum was broken in 1976, more than
10 years after the university art collection was assembled in the temporary
Art Center in Rowan Hall. The collection that was moved to the new
museum consists of 18th-, 19th-, and 20th-century paintings and prints,
ancient (Gandharan) sculpture, decorative arts (Roman glass and ceramics, Persian manuscript pages, European and American 18th- and
19th-century glass and ceramics, European 18th–20th-century furniture),
and an ethnographic collection of pre-Columbian ceramics; African masks
and sculpture; European, Central American, and Mideastern folk arts—
costumes, textiles, and embroideries. An exhibition schedule keeps 5 galleries on constant rotation with special traveling exhibits and a rotating
permanent collection. Cameras may be used with special permission only.
The new museum sponsors lectures and other educational programs. Arrangements can be made for gallery talks and tours. A small research
library is open for use by special permission. Parking on the grounds.
Mon.–Sat. 9–5; Sun. 1–5; closed legal holidays and some portion of uni-

versity holidays. Free. (The new museum is on Hwy. 27, in the south-western corner of the western campus.)

**SPRINGFIELD:   Springfield Art Center.** 107 Cliff Park Rd., 45501 ☐ The Springfield Art Association built its art center in 1967 to accommodate all the activities of a busy cultural center. The small permanent collection displayed here belongs predominantly to this century and the last. Exhibits are changed monthly. Cameras are permitted. Art classes and lectures are held here; tours are led by docents; scholarships are available to children and young people. The center occasionally publishes catalogs in conjunction with an exhibit. The library is open to the public. Original art and crafts of area artists are sold. Parking nearby. Tues.–Fri. 9–5; Sat. 9–3; Sun. 2–4. Free.

**TOLEDO:   Toledo Museum of Art.** 2445 Monroe St. Mailing address: P.O. Box 1013, 43601 ☐ Here in the glass-producing capital of the world is the world's most comprehensive glass collection. Edward Drummond Libbey, having brought the glass industry to Toledo in 1888, was instrumental, because of his love of art, in the founding of the Toledo Museum of Art in 1901. He supplied some of the first paintings. By 1912 the museum had its own Greek Revival building. Enlarged twice over a period of 30-odd years, the museum is now the repository of a wide-ranging collection that includes works of art from ancient Egypt to the present. Old Master and 20th-century paintings, a medieval cloister, and classical and Oriental art objects are housed here as well as Egyptian objects, Near Eastern ceramics and statuary, 17th- to 20th-century French paintings (Matisse, Bonnard, Modigliani, for example), 19th-century English works, an American section that includes works from all the major periods, Spanish works by Velázquez, El Greco, Zurbarán, and Goya, and sculpture (Rodin's "Eve" and Moore's "Reclining Figure" among them). The museum has a yearly schedule of changing exhibits either drawn from the permanent collection or on loan from other collections or institutions. Cameras are permitted except in the temporary loan exhibits.

The museum's School of Design is well known in the field. Lectures are held regularly, and concerts take place in the peristyle, an auditorium that resembles a Greek amphitheater. Free Saturday classes in art and music are offered to children, and classes in studio art and art history to University of Toledo students. The museum also offers a complete master's degree program; fellowships are available in art education and museum training. Art Museum docents conduct tours on art and music by prearrangement. Many publications emanate from this fine institution, among them the *Quarterly Museum News,* a *Guide to Collections,* a catalog of European paintings, *Art in Glass,* and *Corpus Vasorum Antiquorum;* all are available at the museum shop. The library (30,000 volumes, 40,000 slides) is open to the public, as are a print study room, a glass study room, and a glass crafts building. Visitors may dine in the museum's cafeteria; park in the museum's lots. Tues.–Sat. 9–5; Sun. & Mon. 1–5. Free. (Take Collingwood Ave. exit from I-475 to Monroe St.)

**WOOSTER: College of Wooster Art Center Museum.** E. University St., 44691 ☐ The College of Wooster Art Center Museum was established as an educational adjunct to the college. Its John Taylor Arms collection of some 5,000 prints, from Dürer to Dali, is outstanding. Also housed here are Chinese artifacts and African sculpture. A regular schedule of exhibits encompasses a wide range of interests; each year at least one exhibit features a painter, a printmaker, sculpture, faculty or student work, ethnic groups, or crafts. Cameras are permitted. The Community Art Center that uses the same plant offers classes on a regular quarterly schedule. Lectures are given in conjunction with exhibitions; catalogs also accompany exhibitions. The museum has published *Wooster in 1876,* which is available for purchase. Field trips to museums in the area are scheduled occasionally. Refreshments are available on campus at the student snack bar in the Union or at the Wooster Inn. Park on the street or behind the student union. (From the north, take Rt. 83 to Wooster and exit at the blinker; go south on Burbank Rd., which becomes Bever St.; turn left at the corner of Bever and University and go 1 block. From the south, take US 30 to College of Wooster exit [Bever St.] and go north; go 1 block past the 6th stoplight and turn right on University.)

**YOUNGSTOWN: Butler Institute of American Art.** 524 Wick Ave., 44502 ☐ A white marble Italian Renaissance palace rose in Youngstown, Ohio, in 1919 to become the Butler Institute of American Art. Joseph G. Butler, Jr., having suffered the loss of much of his art collection in a fire 2 years before, hired the famous McKim, Mead, and White architectural firm to build a new structure that would last. The building was to house new acquisitions of American art, bringing a balancing cultural resource into the coal and steel country of the Mahoning River valley. Today, the collection ranges the country's history from Colonial times to the present. Oil paintings, watercolors, drawings, and prints, some 3,500 of them, are housed here, bought by 3 generations of Butlers. A Winslow Homer ("Snap the Whip") began the succession of purchases that built this impressive collection; an Audubon followed, a Morse, and an Inness. Works by Copley, Stuart, Peale, Sully, West, Eakins ("The Coral Necklace"), Ryder ("Roadside Meeting"), Whistler ("The Thames from Battersea Bridge"), Cassatt, and others came later. Hopper, Shahn, and Marin are among those who represent the 20th century. Other Americana includes a unique collection of miniatures of all the United States presidents; a group of paintings and drawings of American Indians; oil paintings and scale models of clipper ships; and more than a hundred antique glass bells. The institute has several annual exhibits and one-person shows, as well as its exhibit of American Indian oils and photographs. Cameras are permitted. Art classes are held for elementary and high school students throughout the year. Lectures and films are also part of the institute's regular schedule. An Art Holiday program is offered for inner city schools. Tour guides are available Tues.–Fri. 11–3. The institute's catalogs and color reproductions are on sale, with jewelry, ceramics, and cards, at its shop. Permission is needed to use the library. Parking facilities on the north side of the building. Daily 11–4; Sun. 12–4. Free. (From the south and east, take exit 16 off Ohio Tpke. and go north on Rt. 7. From the north and west, take I-80 to I-680 to Wick Ave.)

**Youngstown State University Kilcawley Center Art Gallery.** 410 Wick Ave., 44555 ☐ The Kilcawley Center Art Gallery is Youngstown State University's answer to the needs of its students. Both center and gallery were opened in 1973, the gallery with a collection of pop art—works by Warhol, Lichtenstein, Oldenburg, and Rosenquist, for example. A total of 10 exhibits, each running about 3 weeks, are mounted every academic year. Cameras are permitted. Eating facilities on premises; parking available. Mon.–Thurs. 10–8; Fri. 10–3. Free.

**ZANESVILLE: Zanesville Art Center.** 1145 Maple Ave., 43701 ☐ Fine pottery is made in Zanesville, and the art center displays it with great pride. In addition, there are permanent collections of European and American paintings, sculpture, drawings, and prints; Oriental art objects; and Mexican and African art. Exhibits change regularly. Lectures, tours, classes, concerts, and other entertainments—all the activities of a busy art center—take place here. The library (4,100 volumes) is open to the public. Mon.–Thurs., Sat. 9:30–5; Sun. 2–5. Free.

# OKLAHOMA

**BARTLESVILLE: Woolaroc Museum.** Route 3, 74003 ☐ Buffalo, deer, elk, Texas longhorns, brahmans, Scotch Highland cattle, and water buffalo wander across the 3,500 acres of timberland refuge that surround the Woolaroc Museum. In 1929 Frank Phillips of the Phillips Petroleum Company (located in Bartlesville) built a home for the airplane "Woolaroc," winner of the 1927 Dole flight, a race from Oakland, California, to Honolulu. A collection of western and southwestern art and Indian art and artifacts was assembled, rooms were added, and a museum was born; the Woolaroc Museum opened to the public in 1948. Displayed among the baskets and blankets of the Pueblos, Apaches, and Navajos, with the pioneer stagecoach and the archaeological materials, are paintings by Remington ("The Last Stand"), Russell ("The Bolter"), Leigh ("Visions of Yesterday"), and other western artists. Cameras without flashes are permitted. The museum hosts thousands of schoolchildren each year. Occasional lectures are scheduled; short orientation talks are given to groups upon prior request. The museum publishes *The Woolaroc Story,* booklets describing the collection, and a children's book, all of which are sold at the museum shop; also available are prints, postcards, Indian turquoise jewelry, slides, and miscellaneous Woolaroc items. A snack bar in another building serves barbecued buffalo and squawbread. The Lodge, Frank Phillips's nearby summer home, is open for viewing daily 10–4:30. And an Indian Guide Center presents a multimedia·production, "Arrows Skyward," that focuses on the Indian heritage. Nature trails crisscross the refuge. Parking on the grounds. Daily 10–5; closed Thanksgiving, Christmas. Free. (From Bartlesville, take SR 123 southwest. From Tulsa, take SR 11 to Barnsdall, then 123 to Woolaroc.)

**NORMAN: Museum of Art, University of Oklahoma.** 401 West Boyd St., 73069 ☐ Like many museums in western and midwestern towns and universities, the University of Oklahoma's museum was established in the 1930s, when art projects had government aid and support through the WPA. Contemporary American and European paintings and graphics can be seen here as well as Oriental painting and sculpture. There are examples of American Indian artwork and some paintings by Flemish and Dutch artists. Exhibitions are changed regularly—some are circulating shows, some are from the permanent collection. Gallery talks and guided tours aid visitors to the exhibits. Lectures, films, and concerts are held periodically. A docent program is also offered. Cards and catalogs (some published here) are for sale. The library (1,500 volumes) is available for use on special request. Tues.–Fri. 10–4; Sat. 10–1; Sun. 1–4. Free.

**OKLAHOMA CITY: National Cowboy Hall of Fame and Western Heritage Center.** 1700 Northeast 63rd St., 73111 ☐ Persimmon Hill, the 37-acre site of the National Cowboy Hall of Fame, overlooks a segment of the old Chisholm Trail, the gateway to the West. In 1964 a building suggesting a pioneer's tent, or a circle of wagons surrounding a campfire, was completed on this site; a year later the Cowboy Hall of Fame opened, with the stated purpose of preserving the heritage of the West and honoring those who contributed to it. Seventeen western states sponsor this memorial, the idea of which came from the dreams of Chester A. Reynolds, a Kansas City businessman. Among other attractions at the hall is an impressive collection of art: works by Russell ("Smoke Talk," "Red Man's Wireless"), Remington ("In From the Night Herd" and "Hunters' Camp in the Bighorns"), Schreyvogel (his studio collection), Farny, Miller, Fechin (studio collection), Sharp, Rungius, Henri, N. C. Wyeth, Moran, Link, Leigh, Bierstadt, Hill, and others. One of Russell's sketchbooks containing 87 sketches, is here, and some letters that he illustrated. A selection of bronzes includes "Coming Through the Rye," "Bronco Buster," and "The Outlaw" by Remington; "The Last Drop" by Schreyvogel; "Meat for Wild Men," "The Buffalo Runner," "Counting Coup," and "The Bronc Twister" by Russell (the hall has over 50 bronzes by Russell). The Taos collection, artifacts and paintings representing the Taos school, consists of works by Ufer, Sharp, Berninghaus, and others. Two imposing statues are memorable: "Buffalo Bill," which stands 30 feet high and is surrounded by fountains, pool, and a stone plaza, and "End of the Trail," a defeated Indian warrior sitting dejected on his exhausted horse, by James Earle Fraser, designer of the buffalo-Indian head nickel. Changing exhibits are presented in the contemporary Western art gallery year round. Cameras are permitted.

Thousands of schoolchildren visit the hall each year. Tours for children or adult groups of ten or more are led by trained docents and can be scheduled Mon.-Fri. 9-4:30 (2-week advance notice is necessary). Films produced by the hall about the museum are available. The National Academy of Western Art, created in 1973, selects artists to exhibit at an annual competitive exhibit. A Western Heritage Awards program was established in 1960 to encourage excellence in films, literature, and music dealing with the West. The Rodeo Hall of Fame honors outstanding cowboy and cowgirl competitors with displays of trophies, saddles, and bronzes relating to rodeos. A great electrified map of America (45 feet by 60 feet) shows the development of settlements, trails, and railroads across the West. The West of Yesterday gallery unfolds the history of the West in life-size exhibits complete with sound tracks. Gardens with streams and stone walks and many varieties of trees and shrubs enhance the exterior and are open for leisurely wandering. A noncirculating library (6,000 volumes) is open to the public. The museum publishes a quarterly magazine and sponsors the publication of books under its own imprint. A gift shop carries books, reproductions, slides, postcards, and a variety of Western items. A parking area on the grounds has space for 350 cars. Daily 9:30-5:30; summer 8:30-6; closed Thanksgiving, Christmas, Jan. 1. Admission $2 for adults, $1 for children; special rates for groups of 10 or more.

**Oklahoma Museum of Art.** 7316 Nichols Rd., 73120 ☐ The Oklahoma Museum of Art, an offshoot of the older Oklahoma Art Center, was founded in 1960 as a repository for the conservative and realistic values in art. Having gone through a series of moves into increasingly larger rented spaces, the museum, in 1975, became the occupant of its present building, a 1937 English Regency-style private residence built by an early Oklahoma oil millionaire. Before that, the museum's collection was minimal: about 125 drawings and prints by National Academy artists, and a few 20th-century paintings by academic artists. Since 1975 works by 19th- and 20th-century artists such as Sir Thomas Lawrence, Eugène Boudin, Gustave Courbet, Delacroix, Solimena (Italian, 18th century), Blakelock, and J. F. Murphy have been acquired. A number of high-quality prints and drawings and a few examples of ornamental 20th-century American porcelains have been added. Six- to 8-week exhibits are scheduled throughout the year, augmenting the small permanent collection. Cameras are allowed only with special permission and only in the permanent collection galleries.

The museum offers classes for children and adults in studio and art history and painting workshops. Lectures, occasional concerts, and films are also scheduled. Each weekend, a lecture on the special exhibits and the permanent collection is given by docents, who also guide group tours, which can be booked in advance. The museum also arranges occasional tours to major art shows in other cities. Scholarships are offered to talented children for special 2-week studies in the summer. The museum publishes a monthly calendar, exhibition catalogs, and books. A small library (100 volumes) is open for use on the premises. Gift items, reproductions, jewelry, postcards, and prints are for sale. Parking lot on the museum grounds. Tues.–Sat. 10–5; Sun. 1–5; closed major holidays. Admission $1 for adults; under 18 free. (From the north on I-35, take the exit to Britton Rd., go 5 miles west to Nichols Rd., then south 8 blocks. From I-40, take the Pennsylvania Ave. exit and go north 7½ miles to Wilshire; go east 1 block to Nichols Rd., north 3½ blocks. From downtown, go north on Western Ave. to Wilshire, west ¾ miles to Nichols, then north 3½ blocks.)

**Oklahoma Art Center.** 3113 Pershing Blvd., 73107 □ Another Oklahoma art facility, established in 1936 and incorporated in 1946, the Oklahoma Art Center has a permanent collection of American masters' and contemporary paintings and sculpture and contemporary graphics and drawings. Exhibitions include an Annual National Print and Drawing Exhibition and an Eight State Exhibition of Painting and Sculpture. Guided gallery tours, lectures, gallery talks, films, and classes all take place in this active center. Catalogs are printed annually. The library (2,000 volumes) is open for use on the premises. Art books, small sculpture, cards, posters are for sale. Tues.–Sat. 10–5; Sun. 1–5. Free. (At State Fairgrounds, near junction of I-40 & I-240.)

**TULSA: Gilcrease Institute of American History and Art.** 2500 West Newton St., 74127 □ Thomas Gilcrease was an Oklahoma oil man whose Creek Indian origins sparked an interest in Americana—from art to artifacts, manuscripts, and imprints. The museum that he started and, in fact, designed with an eastern Woodland Indian longhouse in mind, opened under his private ownership in 1949. Since 1954 the museum has been owned and operated by the city; it was enlarged in 1963 and 1977. America is on display here—artifacts from 10,000 B.C.; Indian documents from 1512 to 1900; art from Colonial days through Catlin, Miller, Moran, Remington, and Russell to the 20th century. The collection, ranking second only to the Smithsonian's, consists of 6,000 works of art, 80,000 books and documents, 250,000 artifacts. Here are Jarvis's paintings "Black Hawk" and "Whirling Thunder," Bierstadt's "Sierra Nevada Morning," Sully's "Charles Carroll of Carrollton," Sir Joshua Reynolds's "Syalust Ukah," 21 oils and 18 bronzes by Remington, among them his "Stampeded by Lightning," Russell's "Jerked Down" (total by Russell: 29 oils, 25 watercolors, 28 bronzes), Audubon's "Wild Turkey," A. J. Miller's "Fort Laramie," Vanderlyn's "Washington and Lafayette at the Battle of Brandywine," 74 oil paintings and 137 watercolors by Catlin, and an entire gallery of romantic landscapes by Thomas Moran. Portraits by Feke, Earl, Smibert, Benjamin West, and Charles Willson Peale show the great Americans who helped bring civilization to the wild and beautiful country that is detailed on these walls. Usually the exhibits in one large gallery and several smaller areas are rotated every month. The seasons are celebrated by the hanging of different landscape paintings every 3 or 4 months; fall becomes winter, spring, and summer indoors as well as out. Permits are necessary for cameras.

Slide talks or lectures are available to public schools or other groups. Gallery tours are offered if requested; guides are available on Sunday afternoons and weekdays. Newsletters appear monthly—*The Curator* and *The Gazette* alternate—and *The American Scene* magazine is published quarterly. The library is open by appointment. Books, Indian jewelry, prints, and postcards are sold. Parking on the museum property (there are 126 acres); 22 of the landscaped acres are open until dark. Mon.-Sat. 9-5; Sun. & holidays 1-5; closed Christmas. Free. (From downtown Tulsa, take North Denver to Edison St. to 25th Ave. West. From highway approaches to Tulsa, take Keystone [US 64, SR 51] and exit at 25th Ave. West.)

**Philbrook Art Center.** 2727 S. Rockford Rd. Mailing address: Box 52510, 74152 □ Oil brought Waite Phillips to Tulsa in 1918. In less than 10 years, having bought leases, struck rich pools, and then extended his holdings into Arkansas, Kansas, and Texas, he began the construction of a new home, which proved to be one of the most ornate and elegant mansions in

Oklahoma. Villa Philbrook was fashioned after the styles of the Italian Renaissance, complete with great hall, Corinthian columns, painted ceilings, and formal gardens. Phillips donated it to the Southwestern Art Association in 1936 to be used as a museum, and after alterations and renovations, the Philbrook Art Center opened in 1939. Since then, gifts and purchases have made it an outstanding cultural resource in the Southwest, especially as a preserver of American Indian culture and art. The Clark Field collection of Indian pottery and basketry is superb, as is the collection of contemporary American paintings and the paintings acquired over 30-odd years of a juried American Indian Artists exhibition. The other collections are also outstanding: a Kress collection of Italian Renaissance paintings and sculpture leads the list; also gathered here are primitive African sculpture, Chinese art, southeast Asian tradeware, Japanese screens and scrolls, 19th- and 20th-century European and American art, the Starr collection of miniatures, and the Standard Oil collection of paintings of the oil industry. Temporary traveling or loan exhibitions are mounted seasonally. During the summer special exhibitions feature works from the permanent collection; and a contemporary Oklahoma artists' gallery features regional shows that rotate every 6 weeks. Photographing is permitted, using available light only.

A year-round museum school offers art and craft classes for all ages. Monthly lectures by prominent scholars, a summer lawn concert series, a film series, and occasional theater productions are among the many activities of this institution. A junior gallery program provides an introduction to the museum for grade-schoolers. Docent guided tours are available for groups; 2-week advance notice is necessary. A bimonthly bulletin and calendar and exhibition catalogs are published here. The library (3,500 volumes with a particularly important collection of American Indian art and history books) is available to the public by appointment only. The museum shop sells books, prints, jewelry, postcards, and imported gift items. Parking on the grounds. Tues.–Sat. 10–5; Sun. 1–5. Admission $1.50 for adults, 75¢ for senior citizens and college students; high school students free. (From I-44 exit at Peoria Ave.; follow it north to 27th Pl. and go east directly into the museum grounds. From Rt. 64/51, exit at 21st St.; go west on 21st to Peoria Ave., then south to 27th Pl.; go east on 27th Pl. into the museum grounds.)

# OREGON

**COOS BAY:  Coos Art Museum.** 515 Market Ave., 97420 ☐ An old
Carnegie Library, built in 1917, was taken over by the Coos Art Museum
and became one of the fine galleries in the state of Oregon. Here, where
the Pacific provides both livelihood (Coos Bay is the largest shipping port
for forest products) and pleasures (it is a paradise for deep-sea fishermen),
a museum affords another sort of diversion. Contemporary American
artists' prints are collected and exhibited in Coos Bay. There is a changing
exhibition every month; the permanent collection is shown once every 2
years. Cameras are permitted. Classes in painting, drawing, and crafts, and
lectures, concerts and films are scheduled regularly. A gift shop offers a
large variety of crafted items. Tues.–Sun. 1–4. Free. (3 blocks from Hwy.
101.)

**EUGENE:  Museum of Art.** University of Oregon, 97403 ☐ The Murray
Warner collection of Oriental art formed the nucleus of the Museum of
Art at the University of Oregon when it was built in the early 1930s. The
Gothic-style building that rose in the center of the campus housed, by the
completion of the Warner bequest in 1940, art from China and Japan
principally, but also from Cambodia, Korea, Mongolia, Tibet, and Russia,
and American and British works executed in traditional Oriental style.
This collection grows constantly, recent purchases adding sculpture from
Gandhara (region in Pakistan and Afghanistan) and India; Chinese jade,
ceramics, and textiles; Persian miniatures and ceramics; Syrian glass; and
contemporary Japanese arts and crafts. American glass, artifacts from New
Guinea and Mexico, and a new group of African arts and crafts primarily
from Ghana and Nigeria have added diversity to the museum's holdings.
The contemporary Pacific Northwest collection, originated by a gift from
the Haseltine family, contains over 1,400 works, most notable of which are
18 major paintings by Oregon-born Morris Graves, and a Graves archival
collection of almost 500 items including his drawings, sketches, prints, and
other objects. A group of architectural photographs by Pietro Belluschi, a
northwestern architect, and other prints by outstanding American photographers are also part of the contemporary American collection. An
extensive program of changing local, national, and international exhibits is
scheduled. Cameras are permitted.
  The museum is an affiliate of the university, and as such serves as a

resource for students and faculty. A museology course is offered annually by the director of the museum. An outreach program known as Visual Art Resources sends packaged art exhibitions from the museum's permanent collection or by Oregon artists to communities throughout Oregon and beyond, to other western states. In addition, this program offers artist workshops to Oregon communities. A docent council provides guided group tours in English or French by appointment. Grants to students and artists are obtainable through the university. The museum has some catalogs of the permanent collections, and some on temporary exhibitions; they can be purchased at the museum shop, which also offers books, jewelry, cards, antiques, and handcrafted toys for sale. Parking nearby. Tues.–Sun. 12–5; closed university holidays and Aug. 14–Sept. 24. Free. (In the center of the university campus, north of 13th St., south of 18th St., east of Kincaid St., and west of University St.)

**PORTLAND:    Portland Art Museum.** 1219 S.W. Park Ave., 97205 ☐ The Portland Art Museum was founded in this beautiful city in 1892, exactly 50 years after the first inhabitants settled here. It moved into its present building, a modern classical-style structure designed by the well-known northwestern architect Pietro Belluschi, in 1932. Located on the "park blocks," a mile-long corridor of park running through downtown Portland, it has a collection that reflects the pride in the culture and heritage of the area typical of many northwestern institutions. Northwest coast Indian and Eskimo arts are a feature here, and there is a superb collection of arts from Cameroon, said to be the only one on view in the United States. But there is much more: classical antiquities; ancient Chinese sculptures, bronzes, ceramics, and furniture; Japanese prints; Oriental painted screens and lacquers; Persian and Hindu miniatures; pre-Columbian art; a small Samuel H. Kress collection of Renaissance paintings and sculpture; a large and important collection of English silver; French paintings and sculpture from the 16th through the 20th centuries; Ethiopian crosses; Oriental rugs; contemporary paintings, sculpture, drawings, and prints; English watercolors; and European and American painting and sculpture of all periods. Thirteen or 14 changing exhibitions, each lasting from 4 to 6 weeks, are scheduled each year. A pass is required for cameras.

The museum runs a professional degree-granting Museum Art School with an accredited studio and humanities program (some scholarships are awarded). Evening and Saturday classes and a 6-week summer program are held for adults and children. A wide variety of lectures, concerts, plays, and other events are part of the regular schedule. Tours are offered Fri. evenings and Tues., Thurs., and Sun. afternoons at 2. Publications include a monthly calendar, exhibition catalogs, an annual report, and scholarly notes on the collection (also annual). The library is open to students of the art school only. A gift shop offers books, jewelry, prints, cards, and re-productions. Public parking lots nearby. Tues.–Sun. 12–5; Fri. 12–10; closed major holidays. Admission $1 voluntary contribution for adults, 50¢ for students; children and senior citizens free; Fri. 4–10 free.

**SALEM:   Bush House Museum and Bush Barn Art Center.** 600 Mission St. S.E., 97301 ☐ Asahel Bush, pioneer newspaper editor, politician, and banker, built his Victorian house amid a stand of oaks in the winter of 1877–78. It remained a private residence until 1953, when the city of Salem purchased both house and surrounding 80 acres for a historic museum and park. The art center is next door. This antique house con-tains furniture, paintings, and prints, decorative arts and costumes from the period of 1877 to 1900; the original wallpapers, imported from Europe a century ago, remain intact throughout. The Bush Barn Art Gallery features contemporary Oregon art in both its permanent collection and the exhibitions that are scheduled monthly. Cameras without flashes are per-mitted. An art school offers classes for adults and children year round. Lectures and other cultural events are also scheduled through the year. Docents lead tours around the house, tours at the gallery upon request. A Collectors' Corner in the center is an outlet for Oregon arts and crafts, as well as books, prints, jewelry, and postcards. Parking lot between the house and the barn. House open in summer: Tues.–Sat. 12–5, Sun. 2–5; winter: Tues.–Sun. 2–5. Barn open Tues.–Fri. 9:30–5; Sat. & Sun. 1–5.

# PENNSYLVANIA

**ALLENTOWN:   Allentown Art Museum.** Fifth & Court Sts. Mailing address: Box 117, 18105 ☐ In the grid of streets that is downtown Allen-town an abandoned church was remodeled in 1959 to house an important Samuel H. Kress collection of European paintings. The neoclassical-style church had been built in 1905 and was enlarged with a contemporary addition in 1975. The Allentown Art Museum, founded in the 1930s, began its real life with the 1959 acquisition and remodeling. Its Kress collection includes works from Italy and the Netherlands from 1350 to 1750, paintings, for example by Bugiardini, Dossi, Hals, Massys, Rem-brandt, Ruisdael, and Steen. Another collection consists of American paintings executed in the 19th and 20th centuries: works by Hicks, Getz, Gross, Inness, Rauschenberg, Rudd, Shanks, Stevens, and Zorach. Yet another concentrates on prints. In addition, a period room (c. 1912) dis-plays the genius of architect-designer Frank Lloyd Wright. Six or 8 major exhibits, each lasting 6 or 8 weeks, and 12 smaller ones are mounted each year. Cameras are permitted, but not flashes or tripods. The Baum School of Art is operated and financed separately, but is housed in the museum building. The museum itself sponsors lectures, concerts, films, seminars, and art demonstrations. Group tours are conducted on request. Many catalogs are published here, most related to exhibitions organized by the museum. They can be purchased at the shop, which also offers gift items and paperbacks. The library (5,000 volumes) is open for use by the public. Parking nearby. Tues.–Sat. 10–5; Sun. 1–5. Free. (From I-78 take Rt. 145 south to 7th & Hamilton; go left to 5th and left again to Court.)

**BETHLEHEM:   Lehigh University, Exhibitions and Collection.** Mailing address: Chandler-Ullmann Hall, Building #17, 18015 ☐ Lehigh University's impressive permanent holdings are displayed in constantly changing exhibitions that are mounted in 2 galleries, one in the **Ralph L. Wilson Gallery** in the Alumni Memorial Building, and one in the **DuBois Gallery** in Maginnes Hall. Several periods and styles are represented: The Grace collection of paintings includes English artists such as Raeburn, Romney, Reynolds, Gainsborough ("Crossing the Stream") and a painting by Goya, one by Hobbema, a Corot, and a Daubigny. The Wilson collection contains paintings by "the Eight," including a Henri, 29 paintings by Arthur B. Davies, a Sloan, a Bellows, and others. There is a group of French paintings—"Scène de Jardin" and "Study of Miss Nathanson" by Bonnard, and paintings by Sisley, Vuillard, Courbet, and Picasso; one of watercolors by such as Burchfield and Marin; of prints by Rembrandt, Whistler, Marsh, Warhol, Oldenburg, and Motherwell; another group of prints including works by French, Dutch, German, and Italian artists; and another by early American printmakers. (The university's Baker collection of Chinese porcelain [110 pieces] is on display at the Allentown Art Museum.) Various campus sites serve as excellent settings for sculpture. Special exhibits changing every month are installed in both galleries from September to June. Cameras are permitted. The working study collection is available to students and community by appointment. Gallery talks and visiting artists' lectures are scheduled throughout the year. Guided tours are available. A spring and fall calendar are published as well as catalogs, brochures, and posters. The Office of Exhibitions and Collection has a library that is open to the public. Ralph L. Wilson Gallery: Mon.–Fri. 8–5; Sat. 9–12; Sun. 2–5. DuBois Gallery: Mon.–Fri. 9–10, Sat. 9–12. Free. (Campus is at Brodhead & Packer Aves., on south side of city.)

**CHADDS FORD:   Brandywine River Museum.** Mailing address: P.O. Box 141, 19317 ☐ Thirty miles southeast of Philadelphia and 15 miles north of Wilmington, Delaware, the Brandywine River Museum looks out over a beautiful, lazy landscape. It was built as a grist mill in 1864, in the sturdy stone and wood of the countryside. Today the picturesque structure, standing on a rise near the river, surrounded by wild-plant gardens and nature trails, houses a fine and up-to-date museum that came into existence with major interior renovations in 1971. The art history of the Brandywine River valley is displayed here: works by artists such as Bass Otis, T. B. Reed, Jefferson Chalfont, F. V. C. Darley, George Cope, and other 19th-century landscape painters. A major focus is the work tradition in art and illustration engendered by Howard Pyle in the late 19th century. Paintings and illustrations by his students, among America's most famous illustrators, and the work of the Wyeth family (N. C., Andrew, James), Peter Hurd, and others form the major portion of the collection. Especially treasured are the famous nudes by Andrew Wyeth and 6 paintings by Siri Erickson. Special exhibits change seasonally; many are devoted to single artists (Clifford Ashley, N. C. Wyeth, Maxfield Parrish, Horace Pippin, Hurd, and Cope) as well as thematic subjects. Cameras are not permitted. The museum sponsors occasional concerts and conducts education programs for students and adults. Special tours are available to groups by previous arrangement. A studies program in art, history, and natural sciences is offered to school classes. A quarterly bulletin is sent to members; catalogs are published with special exhibits. They are for sale at a shop, which also offers books, reproductions, and postcards. Cafeteria on premises; parking on grounds. Daily 9:30–4:30; closed Christmas. Admission $1.75 for adults, $1 for senior citizens; 75¢ for students and children. (On US 1, near intersection with SR 100.)

**GREENSBURG: Westmoreland County Museum of Art.** 221 North Main St. 15601 ☐ The Westmoreland County Museum of Art was given to Greensburg by one of its native daughters, Mrs. Cyrus E. Woods. By her instructions, the site of her family home was used for a new Georgian building that was completed in 1958. In it was to be exhibited, in Victorian period rooms, the furniture and objets d'art that she brought back from Europe and the Orient. The collection grew, and in 1968 a new modern wing was added. On view are 18th-, 19th-, and 20th-century American paintings, prints, drawings, sculpture, and decorative arts; 18th- and 19th-century Pennsylvania folk art; a suite of 4 mid-Victorian period rooms; 2 18th-century English pine-paneled rooms; 18th- and 19th-century English and Continental paintings and drawings; modern and contemporary European prints; and a collection of American and European toys from the 19th century to 1940. A regional invitational exhibition is held in Oct., a Christmas exhibition in Nov. and Dec., one-person shows Jan.–Mar., and larger exhibits from the permanent collection June–Sept. Cameras are permitted. The museum sponsors films, concerts, and lectures regularly.

Docents conduct tours of both the permanent collection and special exhibitions. The library (4,000 volumes) is open for research. *250 Years of Art in Pennsylvania* and catalogs published by the museum are sold at the museum shop together with postcards and small gifts. Visitors' parking area. Tues. 1–9; Wed.–Sat. 10–5; Sun. 2–6. Free. (Rt. 119N leads onto Main St.; at top of hill turn right. From Rt. 22, take Rt. 66S, which also leads onto Main St.; turn left at top of hill.)

**LANCASTER: Rock Ford Foundation.** Rock Ford Rd., Lancaster County Park, 17604 ☐ Rock Ford was the home of General Edward Hand, an adjutant general in the Continental Army. Washington was a guest in this large 1792 Georgian house, which remains as it was when he visited. The barn was built around the same time and was moved to this site for its opening as a museum in 1976. The furnishings and structural details of the house illustrate Colonial times in this region; in contrast, the barn museum exhibits today's art and, infrequently, antiques. Exhibits are planned monthly. Cameras are permitted. Lectures and concerts are given on the premises; programs on the house and family are sent out to schools requesting them. The house can be viewed by means of guided tours only; visitors are conducted around whenever they arrive; groups can make prior arrangements. Four candlelight tours are given between April 1 and Nov. 30. A library is open by special permission. Books, postcards, prints, toys, and handcrafted items are sold in a craft shop. Parking on the grounds. Mon.–Sat. 10–4; Sun. 12–4. Admission $2 for adults, $1 for children 6–18. Candlelight tours $2.50 for adults, $1.25 for children. Groups $1.50 for adults, 75¢ for children. (Go south on Duke St. to Chesapeake; right on Chesapeake to the bottom of the hill; turn left into Lancaster County Park and follow signs to Rock Ford.)

**LORETTO: Southern Alleghenies Museum of Art.** Saint Francis College Mall. Mailing address: P.O. Box 8, 15940 ☐ Woods and mountains surround the Southern Alleghenies Museum of Art, which was cleverly transformed into its present state from an unused gymnasium belonging to St. Francis College. In the context of *New Uses for Old Buildings* (published in London), this unusual building is exemplary. When it opened in 1976, after a year of renovations, it became the only repository for fine arts in a 6-county area. The collection is primarily American and includes works by Baskin, Baziotes, Benton, Bierstadt, Burchfield, Cassatt, De Creeft, Kuhn, Levine, Sargent, Shinn, and Sloan. From December through February, when the entire permanent collection is on display, there are no temporary exhibits; other times, the museum has changing exhibitions every 6 weeks. Cameras are permitted; no flashes or tripods. The art department of St. Francis College and the continuing education department of the museum conduct art classes in the basement of the building. Lectures, films, demonstrations, modern and classical dance recitals, choral music, theater productions, dramatic readings, and chamber music concerts are all scheduled by the museum. Tours, some with luncheons, can be arranged in advance. Parking available. Wed.–Fri. 10–5; Sat. & Sun. 1:30–5:30. Free. (It is easier to find the museum than it is to find Loretto. Take US 22 from the east or west to Ebensburg and proceed to Loretto on the Ebensburg-Loretto road.)

**NEW BRIGHTON: Merrick Art Gallery.** 5th Ave. & 11th St. Mailing address: Box 312, 15066 ☐ Beginning in 1884, Edward Dempster Merrick planned a series of additions to New Brighton's abandoned train station, which had been built about 30 years before. He wanted to use it to display the paintings that he had collected. He added a second floor to the existing structure in 1884, an extension on the south side some time later, and the largest gallery in 1901. Both European and American 19th-century works predominate here: paintings by Prud'hon, Winterhalter, Hans Makart, Courbet, and Americans Richards, Sully, Thomas and Edward Moran, Kensett, and Blakelock. The museum hosts several one-person shows throughout the year. Cameras are not permitted. Classes in drawing, painting, sculpture, calligraphy, and drama are offered, usually in the fall and spring. Concerts and lectures are also scheduled periodically. The gallery sponsors an arts and crafts fair during the month of June. Tours are given by request. A catalog, *History Through Industry,* was printed for the nation's bicentennial, and a newsletter comes out 6 times a year. The catalog and prints are for sale. The library (Mr. Merrick's books) is open to the public by appointment only. Parking on the street. Tues.–Sat. 10–5; Sun. 1–5; summer months Wed.–Sat. 10–3:30 & every other Sun. (From Pittsburgh, take Rt. 65, which becomes 3rd Ave. [the main street] in town. The gallery is at the southwest corner of 5th Ave. & 11th St.)

**PHILADELPHIA: Athenaeum of Philadelphia.** 219 S. 6th St., 19106 ☐ The Athenaeum of Philadelphia is located in the heart of Society Hill, one of the famous Colonial restoration areas in America, and on the edge of Independence National Historic Park. It faces Washington Square (one of the original public squares laid out in the 17th century by William Penn) and has its own 2,500-square-foot Victorian city garden. From the time of its founding in 1814 by members of the American Philosophical Society to collect books and other objects relating to the history of America, to 1847 when the present Italianate Revival-style building was completed, the Athenaeum was located in Philosophical Hall on Independence Square. Restored and expanded in 1976, the building is now a National Historic Landmark. Under this distinguished roof are the only research library in

America specializing in 19th-century social and cultural history, and interesting collections of fine arts and decorative arts, especially from 1825 to 1850. Furniture by Michel Bouvier and Anthony Quervelle and decorative objects from the collections of Joseph Bonaparte are particularly notable. Exhibits change seasonally; all relate to the Victorian period in America. Cameras are permitted. The Athenaeum sponsors a regular series of lectures and chamber music concerts. Guided tours are offered daily at 10:30 and 2, other times by appointment; tours concluding with a sherry reception are available to groups by advance reservation. Books written in the 19th century are republished with new introductions or commentary and sold here. The library (100,000 volumes and 400,000 items relating to architecture) is open to the public upon application Mon.–Fri. 9–5. Two underground parking lots are a half block away on 6th St. Mon.–Fri. 9–5; closed bank holidays. Free.

**Barnes Foundation.** North Latch's Lane & Lapsley Rd., Merion Station. Mailing address: Box 128, Merion Station 19066 ☐ The Barnes Foundation was chartered in 1922 as a privately endowed educational institution. Its creator and benefactor was Dr. Albert C. Barnes, the inventor of Argyrol, whose stance on admitting a limited number of visitors to his collection is legend. Having begun to feel the economic benefits of his popular medicines, he proceeded to collect artwork, with the help of his friend William Glackens. By the early 1920s he was able to show at the Philadelphia Academy of Art a notable group of Impressionist paintings that Glackens had brought back from Europe. The shocked reaction of conservative Philadelphians to his Cézannes and Matisses was enough to cause the retreat of Barnes and his paintings behind the closed doors of his own gallery, which he had built on a 12-acre site in Merion—a retreat that persists today. The building, designed by Paul Philippe Cret in the architectural style of southern France, with room for the collection and for classrooms, was dedicated in 1925 as a school. It has continued as a school ever since and wishes to be known as such rather than as a museum in the traditional sense. But in fact, many museums have less discerning selections and fewer paintings than this "non-museum." Although the lighting is less than perfect, the paintings themselves—piled 2 and 3 tiers high, hung over windows, and lining stairwells—illuminate the small galleries. The initial impact is breathtaking—a score of Renoirs, several Cézannes and Matisses, including his languorous "Joie de Vivre" and a large mural of dancing nudes, are displayed in the first gallery, 2 stories high. There are hundreds more Renoirs, roughly 60 Matisses, 100 Cézannes, and 25 Picassos scattered along the crowded walls of the baker's dozen galleries in the 30-room mansion. This amazing collection includes works by a myriad of others—van Gogh, Soutine, Courbet, Corot, Modigliani, Seurat, Rousseau, Pascin, Manet, Degas, de Chirico, Utrillo, Monet, Gauguin, Klee, Miró, da Silva. Some Americans represented include Demuth, Glackens, Charles and Maurice Prendergast, Lawson, and Pippin. Among the Old Masters sharing the hanging space are Titian, Tintoretto, El Greco, and Veronese, together with early Dutch, Italian, French, Spanish, German, and Flemish primitives. Works are hung without attention to grouping according to traditional styles or periods of art. Following his own notions of color and composition, which are taught at his school, Barnes mixed Old Master paintings with primitives, antique tools (of which he amassed a sizable collection) with Impressionist paintings, African sculpture with American and European drawings. The result is eminently successful visually. But the lack of labels on the objects and furniture, titles or dates on the paintings (they are labeled with the artist's name only), and even a catalog of the collection, makes a visit to the Barnes Foundation a somewhat bemusing experience. One stands in awe of the prodigious number of masterworks squeezed together on these walls, at the same time wanting to know more about each work. Cameras are forbidden.

The foundation offers a tuition-free 2-year course in the philosophy and appreciation of art. The course of study includes lectures and discussions with observation and verification in the works in the collection. It is only since 1951 that the public has been admitted to view this collection, and reservations must be made by mail or phone (215-667-0290). One hundred reservations per day are taken on weekdays, and on Fridays and Saturdays 100 people are admitted without reservations. On Sunday, 50 people with reservations and 50 without are admitted. No children under 12. Sept.–June, Mon.–Sat. 9:30–4:30; Sun. 1–4:30; closed July & Aug. and on legal holidays. Admission $1. (From center city, take Schuylkill Expwy. [I-76] west to City Ave., then go southwest on City Ave. to Old Lancaster Rd., turn right and go to Latch's Lane, then make a left and proceed a few blocks.)

**Drexel Museum Collection.** Drexel University, 32nd & Chestnut Sts., 19104 ☐ The educational institution that Anthony Drexel planned and founded in 1891 was intended to include a museum collection to support the 3 foci of the institute: art, science, and industry. The intent was achieved in art by the pooling of 2 collections: Drexel's and his brother-in-law John D. Lankenau's (he built the Lankenau Hospital). Both favored the work being done in their own time. Thus the works that form the nucleus of this small museum afford a survey look at the trends in European and American art in the 19th century. Works from France by Corot ("Dawn"), Daubigny ("On the Seine River"), Dupré ("Solitude"), and from Spain, Italy, Norway, and Germany are on display together with European textiles, ceramics, and china. The Rittenhouse clock, made in

1773 by David Rittenhouse, astronomer, mathematician, first director of the United States Mint, and member of the Pennsylvania Constitutional Convention of 1776, tells the time of day, plays 10 melodies, and indicates the day and date, phases of the moon, orbit of the moon around the earth and the earth around the sun, signs of the zodiac, equation of time and the planets. It is the pride of the museum, together with a chess table used by Napoleon during his exile on St. Helena, and the "Water Boy," a figure by Frédéric Auguste Bartholdi, sculptor of the Statue of Liberty. One or 2 special exhibits are mounted each year. Cameras are permitted. The museum was founded as an adjunct to Drexel University and still fulfills that function. Tours can be arranged by appointment. Catalogs and small brochures on objects of interest are available. Parking nearby. Mon.–Fri. 9–5. Free. (Cross the Schuylkill River on Chestnut St. to get to "University City.")

**Gallery for the La Salle College Study Collection of Art.** La Salle College, 20th St. & Olney Ave., 19141 ☐ Ten years ago the La Salle College study collection of art was installed in galleries converted from cellar storage space. Here, a few paintings from each century, beginning with the 16th, are displayed, each century in its own room. Special exhibits are held occasionally. Lectures are given in the galleries. Guides are available on request. A growing research library is open for use by the public. Parking during school hours is difficult. Weekdays 10:30–3:30, or by special arrangement. (The La Salle campus is in North Philadelphia near Roosevelt Blvd. From center city, go north on Broad St. to Olney Ave., then turn left on Olney to 20th St.)

**Violet Oakley Memorial Foundation.** 627 Saint George's Rd., 19119 ☐ The Violet Oakley Memorial Foundation provides the means by which her studio, a massive, columned, 1815 barn, remains open to visitors. Her paintings, drawings, furniture, and objets d'art are on view here in the place where she worked. Her murals decorate the walls of the State Capitol, the Supreme Court of Pennsylvania, the County Courthouse in Cleveland, Ohio, and other public buildings. Cameras are permitted by special arrangement. Parking in a small courtyard or on the street. Open by appointment (telephone 215-247-0633). Admission $1.50. (In Mt. Airy. Take Schuylkill Expwy. to Wissahickon Dr. to McCallum, then left 1 block north past Allen's Lane to St. George's Rd.)

**Pennsylvania Academy of the Fine Arts.** Broad & Cherry Sts., 19102 ☐ Charles Willson Peale, Rembrandt Peale, and William Rush, together with 68 civic and business leaders in Philadelphia, founded the Pennsylvania Academy of the Fine Arts, the first museum and art school in America, in 1805. Its purpose was then and still is to cultivate the fine arts in America, to display the best of them, and to train future generations in them. The academy's building, designed by Philadelphia architect Frank Furness, was a celebration of high Victorian architecture when it opened in 1876, with elements drawn from Gothic, Byzantine, Renaissance, and classic architecture; the pink granite, brownstone, and brick facade is further bedecked with elaborate floral patterns that are echoed in the interior. American art, expectedly, predominates here. The academy's holdings are widely considered to be among the 3 premier collections of American art in the United States. It is particularly rich in late-19th-century painters, with a large number of works by the Peale family, Thomas Sully, Gilbert Stuart, and John Neagle. Among the outstanding works are "The Fox Hunt" by Winslow Homer, the familiar portrait of George Washington by Stuart, "William Penn's Treaty with the Indians" by Benjamin West, "Walt Whitman" and "The Cello Player" by Thomas Eakins, "Man Cub" by Alexander Stirling Calder (1870–1945), father of the Alexander Calder of "mobile" fame, "Young Washington at Princeton" and "The Artist in His Museum" by Charles Willson Peale, and many others. Four major special exhibits are shown each year in addition to an annual student exhibition and 6 shows of works by individual contemporary artists. Peale House, at 1819 Chestnut Street, is an adjunct building that contains studios, classrooms, a few offices, and gallery space, part of which is used for student exhibitions. Cameras are permitted.

The Academy School is the oldest art school in the United States, with an enrollment of about 400 full-time day students. Lectures and concerts are sponsored by the women's committee; the academy also organizes exhibition-related lectures by outside authorities, panel discussions, and slide presentations. The education department offers tours Tues.–Fri. at 11 and 2, and weekends at 2, and a school program called "Triad," which consists of an in-class slide presentation, a tour of the museum, and a follow-up exercise. Special tours can be arranged by calling the museum; tours in French, Italian, Dutch, German, Spanish, and Yiddish are available. The museum publishes an annual school catalog, a newsletter and annual report, a layman's guide called *Faces of the Pennsylvania Academy*, and exhibition catalogs that can be purchased in the shop along with other books on art and architecture, reproductions, postcards, and gift items. Several good restaurants as well as parking facilities are nearby. Tues–Sat. 10–5; Sun. 1–5. Admission $1 for adults, 50¢ for children under 12, students, and senior citizens.

**Philadelphia Museum of Art.** 26th St. & Benjamin Franklin Pkwy., 19130
☐ The Philadelphia Museum of Art, the Greco-Roman building that dominates Fairmount Park, and in fact Philadelphia, its Minnesota dolomite exterior and glazed blue roof tiles gleaming over the city, celebrated

its 100th birthday in 1976 (it had been created for the Centennial Exposition of 1876). At that time it was housed in Memorial Hall, the only exposition building that still stands, in West Fairmount Park. The present imposing Parthenon look-alike was erected in 1928 on the site of what once had been a reservoir, at the entrance to the largest inner-city park in the world. The museum's treasures, over 500,000 of them from all parts of the globe, are displayed in 200 galleries and period rooms, and range in time from the 1st century A.D. to the 20th. (The Far Eastern and Indian sections are strong.) The John G. Johnson collection was given to the museum by this avid collector (he acquired about 1,200 paintings dating from the 14th century to the early 20th in 30-odd years) at his death in 1917. In 1933 the entire magnificent collection was moved from his house to the museum; it included a group of Flemish paintings by van Eyck ("Saint Francis Receiving the Stigmata" is one), Bouts, and Campin; Italian Renaissance works by Fra Angelico, Lorenzetti ("Virgin and Child Enthroned"), Botticelli, and Veronese; 15th-century Northern European artists such as Gerard David, Bosch, and van der Weyden ("The Virgin and Saint John" and "Christ on the Cross"); and 19th-century works by Courbet, Manet ("The Alabama and Kearsarge"), and Pissarro. The museum's section on 20th-century art is large, with an early Picasso ("Three Musicians") and a Léger among the Cubists; Joan Miró's "Dog Barking at the Moon" and other surrealists Dali and Ernst; Rauschenberg, Lichtenstein, and Wesselmann ("Bedroom Painting No. 7") from the pop art world; and abstractions by Stuart Davis ("Something on the 8 Ball"), Avery, and Gorky. The Arensberg collection of over 200 more modern masterpieces, a great many of which were acquired during and after World War I with the advice of Marcel Duchamp, includes the largest group of Brancusi's sculpture in the country ("Bird in Space" and "The Kiss"); cubists Picasso, Braque, and Gris ("Man in the Cafe"); surrealists Dali, Ernst, and Tanguy; and many works by Duchamp himself, most particularly his famous "Nude Descending a Staircase" that caused a furor at the New York Armory Show of 1913. Calder's 24-foot mobile "Ghost" hangs from the ceiling of the Great Stair Hall, a set of Rubens-designed tapestries adorns the walls, and 15th- and 16th-century German, Italian, and English arms and armor fill the Armory. Medieval European art has its own space on the second floor, as do the museum's impressive collections of Near Eastern and South Asian art, Far Eastern art, English art from 1700 to 1850, and European art from 1400 to 1700, from 1700 to 1870, and after 1870. Some of the famous paintings of the world are hung on these walls: Cézanne's "Large Bathers," van Gogh's "The Staircase Group," Andrew Wyeth's "Ground-Hog Day," portraits by Gainsborough, and landscapes by Monet. The museum is full of the treasures of many cultures, frequently displayed in period settings that reflect the times in which they were created. It also administers the Rodin Museum (q.v.); the Fairmount Park houses, three 18th-century American homes; the Eakins House (1729 Mount Vernon St.), a community center with the beginnings of a memorabilia collection on Thomas Eakins's studio; and the Samuel S. Fleisher Art Memorial (719 Catharine St.), where free art classes are offered, special exhibitions are hung, and a Romanesque chapel is on view. Major exhibitions are scheduled at the Philadelphia Museum throughout the year.

Occasional classes are held here, but the schedule of lectures, concerts, and films is extremely heavy. Gallery talks, special programs for school groups, and ethnic programs are also offered by the museum. Guided tours are available every hour 10–3; tours in 9 foreign languages can be arranged in advance. The museum publishes a large number of exhibition catalogs, a quarterly *Bulletin,* a monthly newsletter, handbooks, and calendars. Many are sold in the shop, which also handles cards, reproductions, jewelry, and gift items. The library (90,000 volumes) is open only to scholars with library cards. Cafeteria in the building. Parking for 300 cars. Daily 9–5; closed legal holidays. Admission $1.50 for adults, 75¢ for children, senior citizens, and students with ID; free on Sun. 9–1.

**Norman Rockwell Museum.** 601 Walnut St., 19106 ☐ Childhood collections are often nostalgic, but notable only to the collector. The brothers Stoltz, however, in 1976, turned their early enthusiasms into a book, and then into a museum—the Norman Rockwell Museum—where all of Norman Rockwell's original *Saturday Evening Post* covers are gathered and displayed. In fact, there are some 700 pieces here—the covers (324 in all), a series Rockwell did for the Boy Scouts of America, and one he did for the Massachusetts Mutual Life Insurance Company, 3 original works, and 2 preliminary sketches. The originals can be found in a replica of his studio. An explanatory slide and sound presentation is offered in the museum's Four Freedoms Theater, and the same program is sent out, with a lecturer, to groups and schools on request. The large gift shop sells Rockwelliana of all shapes and descriptions, at all prices. A catalog is available as well. Daily 10–4. Admission $1.50 adults, 12 and under free, special group rates.

**Rodin Museum.** Benjamin Franklin Pkwy. at 22nd St., 19101 ☐ American filmmaker Jules E. Mastbaum commissioned the house, fashioned after Rodin's home in France, that shelters his (Mastbaum's) collection of Rodin's work—80 bronze casts, marble and plaster sculptures, drawings, and watercolors. A repository of the single largest collection of Rodin work outside the Musée Rodin in Paris, the house was completed and given to the city of Philadelphia in 1929. One must pass by "The Thinker" to enter and see other well-known works such as "Age of Bronze," "St. John the Baptist Preaching," "The Burghers of Calais," and "The Gates of

Hell." The museum is administered by the Philadelphia Museum of Art. Daily 9–5; closed legal holidays. Admission by donation.

**Philip H. and A. S. W. Rosenbach Foundation Museum.** 2010 DeLancey Pl., 19103 ☐ The Rosenbach brothers were well-known American bibliophiles and collectors whose choices of porcelain, silver, miniatures, paintings, original drawings for book illustrations (by such as Daumier, Fragonard, and William Blake) and 18th-century furniture (Chippendale, Hepplewhite, and Louis XV) adorn the rooms of their 19th-century Philadelphia town house. However, the main attraction of the Rosenbach Museum is a collection of 100,000 manuscripts (including James Joyce's *Ulysses* and works by Conrad, Dickens, Robert Burns, and Dylan Thomas), a collection of 25,000 rare American and English books from the days of the Spanish explorers in the New World to World War II, and from Chaucer to the 20th century, and the archives (manuscripts, correspondence, library, and personal effects) of American poet Marianne Moore. The permanent displays here enhance the changing exhibitions drawn from the museum's collections. Guided tours are available to groups by reservation on weekdays from 9 to 5. Gallery talks are given; no advance notice is needed. The museum's publications are sold, together with postcards and catalogs. The library is open for scholars by appointment Mon.–Fri. 9–5. Admission $1.50 for adults, $1 for groups of 8 or more, 50¢ for students under 18. (East of 21st St., 1 block south of Spruce St., near Rittenhouse Sq.)

**Woodmere Art Gallery.** 9201 Germantown Ave., 19118 ☐ Charles Knox Smith left his roomy 1867 Victorian home, his property on Chestnut Hill, and his art collection to the people of Philadelphia in 1916. An eclectic collector, he had gathered together, in the circular, skylighted gallery he added to the house for the purpose of displaying them, not only paintings and sculpture, but also furniture, Oriental rugs, porcelains, ivories, Oriental embroideries and prints. Since 1940, when the Woodmere Art Gallery was incorporated, works (predominantly traditional) by area artists have been added. Among the rugs are examples of Kashan, Mosul, Sarouls, Anatolian silk, and Bokhara. Examples of Meissen, French Vienna, Sèvres, and Capo Di Monte are notable among the porcelains. Works by American artists West, Powers, Cropsey, Anshutz, Read, May, Moran, Bailey, Rogers, and Daniel Garber, and by Europeans Sir Thomas Lawrence, Carpentier, Dupré, de Quiriers, and Franceschini are on display here. Six 4-week exhibitions (Sept.–June) include a members' and a juried show. Cameras are permitted. Classes for adults and children are held Sept.–June; weaving is taught by instructors from the Philadelphia Guild of Handweavers. The gallery also sponsors an annual concert and 5 educational programs relating to current exhibits for fifth-graders in area schools. Guided tours are available on request. A shop offers jewelry, prints, cards, pottery, weaving, small sculpture, miniature furniture, dolls, small paintings and drawings. Parking on the gallery property. Mon.–Fri. 10–5; Sun. 2–5. Free. (From downtown Philadelphia, take East River Dr. and Lincoln Dr. to Germantown Ave. From the Pa. Tpke., take the Plymouth Meeting exit and go south on Germantown Pike.)

**PITTSBURGH: Fisher Collection.** Fisher Scientific Company, 711 Forbes Ave., 15219 ☐ The Fisher Scientific Company in downtown Pittsburgh seems an unlikely place for Old Master paintings. Yet here they are, displayed in their own special gallery that shuts out the business world. This is not a museum, but the collection, which specializes in alchemical art and traces the history of science from crude alchemy to the emergence of true chemistry in the 18th century, is held to be unique in the world. Many of the paintings are 17th-century Dutch and Flemish, among them "The Alchemist" by David Teniers the Younger; "The Chemist" by Pietersz Bega; Rembrandt's etchings "The Magic Disk" and "The Deliverance of Dr. Faustus"; van Hellemont's "The Medical Alchemist"; Webb's "The Search"; Heerschopp's "An Explosion in the Alchemist's Laboratory"; and "Rich Poverty" by Adrian van der Venne. Cameras are permitted. Guided tours are available by appointment during working hours. There is a company cafeteria in the building. Public parking nearby. Weekdays 9–4. Free.

**Frick Art Museum.** 7227 Reynolds St., 15208 ☐ The discovery of coal in the hills around the Golden Triangle, and the building of a blast furnace there in 1792, signaled the beginning of Pittsburgh as the "Iron City." The Golden Triangle, named for its location at the confluence of the Allegheny, Monongahela, and Ohio Rivers, spawned the great fortunes of the Fricks, the Carnegies, and the Mellons, and all three families left their mark in parks, buildings, and cultural institutions. The Frick Art Museum, for example, is located close to the Frick estate and faces Frick Park. Helen Clay Frick, daughter of Henry Clay Frick, had this Italian Renaissance-style structure built in 1970 to serve as a museum for the enjoyment of the citizens of Pittsburgh; it would house some of her private collection, and other objects as they were acquired. The concentration here is on Italian, Flemish, and French paintings from the early Renaissance through the 18th century. There is a French 18th-century period room; Renaissance decorative arts; Chinese porcelains; Italian Renaissance bronzes; French and Flemish tapestries; and rare Russian silver from the 17th and 18th centuries. Outstanding pieces are a Savonnerie rug, 2 portrait busts and a classical figure of a Vestal Virgin by Jean Antoine Houdon, a Florentine 15th-century glazed terra cotta plaque of the Madonna and

Child from the atelier of Andrea della Robbia, a small Italian panel by Duccio, 2 small panels and a "Madonna and Child with Angels" by Sassetta, an oil on copper by Antoine Le Nain, a portrait of a woman by Fragonard, "The Music Lesson" by Jan Steen, a portrait of Princesse de Conde by Rubens, a harpsichord, and a set of musical glasses or grand harmonicon. Cameras are not permitted.

The museum schedules a series of free concerts and lectures each year, usually from October to May. Lectures about the collection are offered to groups on request, as are guided tours. Among the publications available are *Treasures of the Frick Art Museum, The Arts in Changing Societies,* and *Frick Art Museum Pittsburgh* by Walter Read Hovey, *Henry Clay Frick, The Man* by George Harvey, and *Madame Jean Antoine Houdon* by Miss Helen Clay Frick. The sales desk offers these, art postcards, and notepaper. Free parking lot adjacent to the building. Wed.–Sat. 10–5:30; Sun. 12–6. Free. (Forbes, Dallas, and Penn Aves. all lead to the Point Breeze residential area in the east end of the city where the museum is located.)

**Museum of Art, Carnegie Institute.** 4400 Forbes Ave., 15213 ☐ Following the belief, which he expounded in an article ("Wealth") in the *North American Review* in 1889, that the fortunes of the rich should be used to benefit everyone, Andrew Carnegie sold his gargantuan steel business in 1901 and devoted his full energies to philanthropy. But even before the sale, he was practicing what he preached. He founded the Carnegie Institute in 1895–96, a triple-purpose (two museums and a music hall) gift to Pittsburgh, where his fortunes began. He envisioned the institute's Museum of Art, as opposed to its Museum of Natural History, as the repository of a permanent collection growing out of an International Exhibition of Contemporary Art. The vision began to materialize when the first of these internationals was held in 1896. Immediately, the museum was unique by virtue of its concentration on contemporary works rather than the Old Masters. The Carnegie Internationals became an annual event until 1950, after which they were held every 3 years, bringing together the works of hundreds of contemporary artists from all over the world. As a result of them, the collection that grew in this French Renaissance building reflects the late 19th and early 20th centuries. French Impressionists and Postimpressionists are especially well represented; and the 19th-century American collection is major. In 1974 all the holdings of the Carnegie Institute Art Museum were moved to a new wing, designated the Sarah Scaife Galleries, which was designed by Edward Larrabee Barnes. Here, in huge spaces, between towering glass walls that allow a view of a landscaped sculpture courtyard, Andrew Carnegie's dream of benefiting his fellow man is at work. Monet's "Nympheas" is here; Renoir's "The

Garden in the Rue Cortot, Montmartre"; van Gogh's "The Plain of Auvers"; Cézanne's "Landscape near Aix, the Plain of the Arc River"; "The Thousand and One Nights" by Matisse; "The Old King" by Rouault; Whistler's "Arrangement in Black: Pablo de Sarasate"; "Picnic" by Prendergast; "Venetian Interior" by Sargent; 8 oils by John Kane and 25 works by David G. Blythe, both Pittsburgh artists. There is also a fine display of decorative arts in the Ailsa Mellon Bruce galleries, a small group of Old Masters in its own quiet setting, and a strong presentation of Pittsburgh talent. Exhibitions are changing constantly in the new Heinz galleries, used for this purpose only; several new exhibits can be seen in one visit since they overlap in time. Hand-held cameras may be used to photograph the permanent collection only.

The institute is a vital and active cultural center, with its huge library (40,000 volumes), music hall, and 2 museums. The Museum of Art itself sponsors Saturday art classes for children, an art lecture series with guest speakers, docent guided tours 3 times daily, and the Selmas Burke Art Center in East Liberty. Publications include a myriad of catalogs and the excellent *Carnegie Magazine* (10 issues per year). The museum shop offers them for sale, as well as postcards, jewelry, ethnic clothing, pottery, and glassware. A cafe overlooking the sculpture court serves snacks, lunch, and tea; a more informal cafeteria is also available. Parking nearby. Tues.–Sat. 9–5; Sun. 1–6. Admission by suggested donation of $1 for adults, 50¢ for students. (At the corner of Forbes & Craig in the Oakland area east of downtown Pittsburgh.)

**READING: Reading Public Museum and Art Gallery.** 500 Museum Rd., 19611 ☐ A 25-acre park surrounds the Reading Public Museum and Art Gallery. In 1925 ground was broken for this neoclassical building, which would house 19th- and 20th-century American paintings; a Pennsylvania-German collection; Renaissance, Baroque, and 18th-century paintings; an ornithological (10,000 specimens) and an entomological (500,000 specimens) collection. Among the 16th-, 17th-, and 18th-century paintings are works by Rubens, Bruegel, Kneller, Lely, and Reynolds. The 19th century is represented by such as Bierstadt, Blakelock, Raphaelle Peale ("Lemons and Sugar"), Church ("Cotopaxi"), Eakins, Homer, Inness, Harnett, Hassam, Luks, Parrish, Ryder, Sargent, Stuart, and Sully. Avery, Baziotes, Bellows, Davies, Shinn, Soyer, and Wyeth are included in the 20th-century group. The museum has an Easter and a Christmas show and other temporary exhibits during the year. Cameras can be used only by permission of the director. School classes are held here daily. Lectures and concerts are also regularly scheduled, and tours are available. The library (12,000 volumes on natural history) is open to the public with special permission. A sales desk supplies postcards, jewelry, prints, museum publications, posters, and rock specimens. On the grounds are a planetarium, an arboretum, and a botanical garden. Parking available. Mon.–Fri. 9–5; Sat. 9–12; Sun. 2–5; closed Sat. during the summer. Free. (From US 422, take Penn Ave. to West Reading. The museum is directly behind the Reading Hospital.)

**SCRANTON:   Everhart Museum of Natural History, Science and Art.** Nay Aug Park, 18510 ☐ Scranton became the largest city in northeastern Pennsylvania because of coal—in 1840 the Scranton brothers built 5 newfangled iron furnaces that revolutionized the manufacture of iron and steel. But eventually, in 1902, the mills moved away, and the town turned its attentions elsewhere. In 1908 Dr. Isaiah F. Everhart, a civil war surgeon and naturalist, gave the building in Nay Aug Park to the Scranton community. Today visitors are treated to the naturalist collections of the founder and more—a folk art collection, a glass collection, and what is said to be the largest group anywhere of paintings by John Willard Raught. Temporary loan exhibitions in the fields of history, science, and art are scheduled frequently. Cameras can be used with permission from the staff. Art classes covering several media are taught by local artists. Film and lecture series and trips to other museums are organized by the museum association. Tours guided by museum staff can be arranged, and a museum catalog is available. The library is open to the public. A shop offers arts and crafts, postcards, plants, and decorative pieces for sale. Parking available. Tues.–Sat. 10–5; Sun. 2–5. Free. (Take I-81 to Central Scranton Expwy. exit; follow signs to downtown Scranton and Jefferson Ave. Make a right turn onto Jefferson, go 2 blocks and make a right onto Mulberry St., which leads to Nay Aug Park.)

**STATE COLLEGE:   Museum of Art, Pennsylvania State University.** Mailing address: University Park, 16802 ☐ The museum at Pennsylvania State University opened in 1972 to serve the needs of students and the citizens of central Pennsylvania. The attempt is to build a study collection emphasizing American art in general and Pennsylvania art in particular, with some European and Oriental art. A list of 12 holdings includes a Grausman, a Diebenkorn, a Prendergast, a Shinn, and an Eichholtz, a Vuillard, a de Wint, a Pierfrancesco Mola, a Chinese artifact from the 1st century, a Khmer (Cambodian) jar from the 12th or 13th century, a 17th-century Chinese depiction of a "Lotus" (ink on paper), and a bronze decoration from a 3rd-century Roman table. Three floors feature changing and special exhibitions. Cameras can be used with special permission. The museum sponsors lectures once a month and guided tours at 1:30 on Sundays, or on request. A shop is open to visitors. Parking nearby. Tues.–Sun. 12–5. Free. (On US 322.)

**YORK: Currier and Ives Prints and Antiques Gallery.** 43 West King St., 17401 ☐ If you fancy Currier and Ives, stop at the Currier and Ives Prints and Antiques Gallery in a renovated 1870 Victorian home that is the place of business of the Kling brothers, who own the collection. Over 300 prints are assembled here, probably the largest private collection of Currier and Ives extant. Antiques of the period are also on view. Cameras are permitted. Tours are conducted twice daily at 10 and 3 during the week. Antiques can be purchased at the gallery shop. Street parking is available, and a public parking lot is nearby. Mon.–Fri. Admission $1.50.

# RHODE ISLAND

**BRISTOL: Bristol Art Museum.** Wardwell St., 02809 ☐ The works of art created in Bristol, Rhode Island, for about 40 years (1893–1934) were not the sort that are displayed on walls—they were the sailing vessels, built in Bristol's Herreshoff Boatyard, that successfully defended the America's Cup during that period. In 1963, however, Bristol's museum opened, and the fine arts—paintings and sculpture—took their place in the life of the town. Temporary and traveling exhibits are scheduled. Sat.–Thurs. 1–5; Fri. 1–5, 7–9; closed alternate Tuesdays & Wednesdays. Free.

**NEWPORT: Redwood Library and Athenaeum.** 50 Bellevue Ave., 02840 ☐ Abraham Redwood was a wealthy Quaker merchant, a group of whose friends gave land and funds for this rusticated wood Roman temple as a memorial to him. Peter Harrison designed the original section, which was completed in 1750, three years after it was chartered by the Colony of Rhode Island. Works by Gilbert Stuart (6 portraits), Sir Thomas Lawrence, Robert Feke, Charles Willson Peale and Rembrandt Peale, and 40 portraits by Charles Bird King can be seen here. Exhibitions change bimonthly. Cameras are permitted. *Redwood Papers* is a bicentennial book published by the library and sold there. Guided tours are available on request. Parking across the street. Mon.–Sat. 10–6; Aug. 10–5. Free. (Between Redwood St. & Old Beach Rd.)

**PROVIDENCE: Bell Gallery.** 64 College St., List Art Building, Brown University, 02912 ☐ Brown University's Albert and Vera List Art Building was designed in 1971 by Philip Johnson in Philip Johnson modern—a reinforced concrete exterior emphasizes the cantilevered sunscreens and an uneven roofline of skylights. Bell Gallery occupies a section of this extraordinary building, with an excellent collection of contemporary paintings and prints. Approximately 8 special exhibits are mounted during the school year; they range from one-person shows of living artists to a scholarly art history show produced annually by graduate students. Cameras can be used with permission from the staff. Lectures are sponsored by the art department and are sometimes held in conjunction with exhibitions. The Bell Gallery exhibitions are also utilized in university instruction. Guided tours can be arranged in advance. Mon.–Fri. 11–4; Sat., Sun., & holidays 1–4 during exhibitions. Free. (From downtown Providence follow the river until you can turn right to cross it. Go straight to a dead end, then left on South Main St. and right on College St.)

**Annmary Brown Memorial.** 21 Brown St. Mailing address: Box 1905, Brown University, 02912 ☐ The Annmary Brown Memorial has been affiliated with the Brown University Library since 1947, 40 years after it was founded by General Rush C. Hawkins in memory of his wife Annmary and given to the city of Providence. It is a mausoleum that houses a collection of books printed before 1501, 17th- to 19th-century American manuscripts, about 100 paintings, and sundry Brown family memorabilia. Cameras are not permitted. Parking on the street only. (On Brown U. campus.)

**Museum of Art, Rhode Island School of Design.** 224 Benefit St., 02903 ☐ Reverberations from the Philadelphia Centennial Exposition were felt in the art world of Providence. The following year (1877) the Rhode Island School of Design and its museum were founded by the Ladies' Rhode Island Centennial Commission with a surplus of $1,675 from their exposition funds. They established their institution with three basic purposes in mind: the instruction of artisans as related to trade and manufacture; the training of students in the practice of art; and the general advancement of art education. In 1878, three rooms in the Hoppin Homestead, where the school began operations, were set aside for an industrial museum. The school moved, the museum moved; in 1904 an 18th-century Georgian-style house (Pendleton House) was given to the museum; and in 1926 the museum came to its present home. Pendleton House remains the "American wing," housing a fine collection of American Georgian-style furniture and decorative arts. The galleries of the main building are arranged around 3 sides of a sculpture courtyard, which is bounded on the fourth side by Pendleton House. They display strong collections of ancient art (jewelry, sculpture, bronzes, Greek vases), 19th-century French paintings, 20th-century graphics, and a John D. Rockefeller collection of Japanese bird and flower prints. The classical collection is superb, one of the 3 best in the country, especially the Roman frescoes and portrait busts. Other facets of the permanent collection are numismatics; medieval art; 15th–20th-century painting, sculpture, and decorative arts; 20th-century American art; modern Latin American art; costumes; Oriental textiles and art;

18th-century European porcelain; an Abby Aldrich Rockefeller collection of Japanese prints; and ethnographic art. Some important works are: a 10th-century Japanese Buddha; the "Providence Painter" Greek vase; Monet's "Bassin d'Argenteuil"; Rodin's "Balzac"; a late 1700s bombé chest of drawers; Manet's "Le Repos"; a Babylonian lion; and "On a Lee Shore" by Winslow Homer. This first-rate collection, varied in time and place, is shown at great advantage by limiting the number of objects on display. The museum sets its treasures out sparingly, and handsomely. Between 12 and 20 special exhibitions are mounted annually, including in-house and traveling shows. Hand-held cameras are permitted; photographing of works on loan is not permitted.

The Rhode Island School of Design is a degree-granting institution with courses of study in the fine arts, architecture, and design disciplines. The museum itself offers children's classes throughout the school year and also sponsors a variety of lectures, tours, lecture series, and concerts, beginning and advanced docent programs, and a school loan service of slides and reproductions. Much attention is given to school and children's art exposure and tour programs. The museum publishes an annual catalog known as *Museum Notes, Rhode Island School of Design,* catalogs of special exhibitions and of the permanent collection, pamphlets, and a calendar of events, all of which can be purchased at the museum shop; the shop also offers jewelry, crafts, postcards, posters, and prints for sale. The museum library (44,000 volumes) and the school library are one; it is open to the public for use on the premises; books are available for inter-library loan. Eating facilities are located nearby as are parking lots. Winter: Tues., Wed., Fri., Sat. 11–5; Sun. & holidays 2–5; Thurs. 1–7. Summer: Tues.– Sat. 11–4:30; Sun. & holidays 2–4:30. Closed Thanksgiving, Christmas, Jan. 1, July 4, and Aug. Admission $1 for adults, 25¢ for children 5–18. (From I-95, take 195 exit onto Wickendon St.; follow signs to Benefit St. Traveling west on I-195 take South Main St. exit, turn right on College St. and left on Benefit St.)

# SOUTH CAROLINA

**CHARLESTON: Gibbes Art Gallery.** 135 Meeting St., 29401 ☐ The list of firsts that describes Charleston's history is long and diverse. The first permanent colonial settlement in the Carolinas, it had the first playhouse designed solely for dramatic productions, the first museum, the first public school, the first municipal college in America, and the first fire insurance company on the continent; the first shots of the Civil War were fired here against Fort Sumter. Cleaving to this tradition of early starts, the Carolina Art Association was founded early—in 1858—and out of it grew the Gibbes Art Gallery, which was built for the association in 1905. The neoclassical building with cupolas and pillars to spare, and an awesome rotunda domed with Tiffany glass 30 feet up, provides the space for a fine American collection. Colonial and Federal portraits by Stuart, Morse, Sully ("Mrs. Gilmor"), Washington Allston, Theus, Charles Willson and Rembrandt Peale ("John C. Calhoun"), Vanderlyn, and Wollaston ("Judith Smith") are a source of pride, but are not always all on view. Early Charleston residents are memorialized in a stunning group of some 300 miniatures, executed by such outstanding artists as Edward Greene Malbone (America's foremost in the miniature field), Trumbull, Fraser, and Rainage. The selection of Japanese woodblock prints, thought to be among the finest in the country, includes works by Harunobu, Hokusai, Sharaku, and Hiroshige; they are rotated (35 to 55 are shown at one time) every 2 months. Another first belonging to Charleston is Henrietta Johnston, said to be America's first artist, or certainly America's first woman artist. Five of her works can be seen here. The gallery's holdings of modern art are increasing as the result of a Living Artist Fund, which serves as an encouragement to South Carolina artists particularly. Among the contemporaries are works by Pearlstein, Lawrence, Hendricks, Hirsch, Perlmutter, and Bechtele. Six galleries are utilized for leased or borrowed exhibitions that change every 60 days. Cameras are not permitted.

The Gallery Art School, with an annual enrollment of more than 1,000, offers courses in all manner of fine arts and crafts for both adults and children; the Dudley Vail Memorial Bindery offers instruction in bookbinding. Lectures and concerts are held 3 times per year. There is a special audiovisual art history room in the gallery; outside, the gallery reaches into the schools with slide talk shows and instruction. Docents conduct tours frequently. The library (92,500 volumes) is available for inter-library loan and is open to scholars by appointment. Books, ceramics, prints, objets d'art, reproductions, and postcards are sold in the gallery shop. County parking garage nearby. Tues.-Sat. 10–5; Sun. 2–5. Free. (Between Horlbeck & Queen Sts., a block away from City Hall.)

**City Hall Art Collection.** City Hall, 80 Broad St., 29401 ☐ Charleston's City Hall was built in 1801, relatively late in the history of this old city (founded in 1670), yet it is the oldest council chambers in active use in the country. Gathered here are the portraits of the council's famous visitors through the years, a distinguished collection of men represented by a distinguished roster of painters: "George Washington" by John Trumbull, "Andrew Jackson" by John Vanderlyn, "James Monroe" by Samuel F. B. Morse, "Lafayette" by Charles Fraser, to name only a few. Special permission is required to photograph the collection. Guides are on hand Mon.–Fri. 9–5. Parking nearby. Mon.–Fri. 9–5. Free. (Broad St. at Meeting St.)

**CLEMSON: Rudolph Lee Gallery.** College of Architecture, Lee Hall, Clemson University, 29631 ☐ Not only did Thomas Green Clemson leave his money to the state of South Carolina to found a state college, but he also left a collection of 17th- and 18th-century Flemish and Dutch paintings which today form the nucleus of the Rudolph Lee Gallery at Clemson University. Located in the College of Architecture building, the gallery also shows contemporary American paintings and graphics, and architectural designs and models. Student and faculty exhibits are interspersed with traveling and other special shows. The gallery comprises a resource for the entire Southeast; extension services provide material and traveling exhibits to museums and colleges, and a lending service. Lectures by visiting speakers are open to the public, and gallery talks and tours are scheduled. Catalogs and an annual exhibition bulletin are published here. Mon.–Fri. 9–4:30; closed holidays. Free.

**COLUMBIA: Columbia Museum of Art and Science.** 1112 Bull St., 29201 ☐ The heart of South Carolina beats in its capital city, Columbia (less than 3 miles off the state's geographic center), and in the heart of Columbia are its Museums of Art and Science. The 24-room 1908 house that has served as its headquarters since 1949 is located on a 4-acre block. In the original spacious mansion, maintained in the eclectic architectural style of the early 1900s, and in the 1954 and 1962 additions, are housed a superb Samuel H. Kress collection of Italian Renaissance art (the pride of the museum), a collection of contemporary graphics, European and American paintings and decorative arts, costumed dolls, a group of South Carolinian dispensary bottles, and a Spanish Colonial collection. The Kress collection is assembled in 3 galleries that separate the works into the early Christian era, the High Renaissance, and the Baroque. Paintings by Tintoretto ("A Gentleman of the Emo Family"), di Giovanni ("Madonna and Child with St. Catherine of Siena and St. Sebastian"), and Botticelli can be seen here together with appropriately placed furniture on display. Van Dyck and Rubens are in other galleries, as well as American painters Allston, Theus, and John Wesley Jarvis ("Portrait of James McCord"). Approximately 18 special exhibits—seasonal, regional, national, juried, and foreign—are scheduled every year. Cameras are permitted; flashes can be used only with special permission. Classes are held in painting, drawing, sculpture, ceramics, and jewelry making. Three or 4 lectures are given each season; concerts and films are held in series. Trained docents lead school tours that can be arranged by advance reservation. The library

(4,000 volumes), said to be one of the most comprehensive in South Carolina, is open to the public. The science museum and planetarium, which was built in 1960, is a strong attraction. Catalogs of the art collection are available at the sales desk, with postcards, books, and prints. Parking is limited. Tues.–Sat. 10–5; Sun. 2–6. Free.

**FLORENCE:   Florence Museum.** 558 Spruce St., 29501 ☐ The Florence Museum came out of the basement of the County Library with the advent of its prime mover, Dr. William Burns, who came to Florence from the San Diego Museum of Natural History. The museum's present home, a 26-room mansion built in 1939 in international modern, was the residence of Sanborn Chase. Its collections are devoted to art, science, and the history of South Carolina; it takes particular pride in its groups of Egyptian, Oriental, and African objects, many of which were sent back to Florence, unsolicited, from around the world, by friends of the museum. The Oriental collection acquired thus includes ceramics, jade, and a Chinese moon gate at the gallery entrance. The southwestern Indian pottery started the museum; several hundred works by local and regional artists expanded it. Special exhibits are installed regularly, averaging 2 per month. Cameras are permitted. Art classes are held year round for adults and children; elementary and secondary school curricula are supplemented in the museum's formal teaching program. Lectures are held on special occasions; also films, slide presentations, and demonstrations. The library, the Jane Evans Research Center located next door, is open to the public. Parking available. Tues.–Sat. 10–5; Sun. 2–5; closed legal holidays and the last 2 weeks in Aug. Donations are appreciated. (On the edge of Timrod Park & the City Rose Garden.)

**GREENVILLE:   Greenville County Museum of Art.** 420 College St., 29601 ☐ This relatively small (population 65,000), blue-collar, manufacturing community, the "textile center of the world," has succeeded, by dint of enthusiasm, hard work, and innovative community planning, in building a new 56,000-square-foot museum, the first to be raised in South Carolina in a half-century. The museum was begun in the 1950s by the Greenville Art Association in an old mansion. Lacking funds, it became moribund in the early 1960s and was reborn when the Greenville County legislative delegation decided to support private efforts to stimulate the cultural resources of the county. The new museum is a stunner: It is trapezoidal in shape; 2 angled, 4-level wings meet at a point where the levels open up to a ground-to-ceiling skylight. The visual arts of the North American continent are featured here, from the pre-Columbian period to the present—a range of over 2,000 years. Approximately 1,000 objects include works by Benjamin West ("Figure with Shield," pen and ink),

Charles Fraser ("Unknown Portrait"), Washington Allston ("View Near Harvard College"), Sloan ("Stein Visits"), Henri ("View in Volendam"), Burchfield ("Raven in the Summer Rain"), Beal ("Central Park"), Lowell Nesbit ("Poppy"), and de Kooning (untitled ink on paper). The museum makes a special effort to acquire artwork and crafts produced in the Southeast and puts particular emphasis on contemporary works. Cameras without flashbulbs are permitted.

The museum school of art offers courses in aesthetics, art history, and film, as well as practical courses in fine arts and crafts. Audiovisual techniques are explored in a program of multimedia productions known as Electragraphics, used for instruction and exposure. This experimental technique, which combines the visual with music and narrative, is only one of the educational opportunities offered here; in fact, the educational program forms a "continuum of informative experiences from pre-school through post-graduate level with appropriate programs at each level." Lectures, films, demonstrations, workshops, seminars, and an Independent Filmmakers Series fill out an active schedule. Scholarships to the art school are available. The museum publishes catalogs regularly. The museum shop sells original works by artists and craftspeople from the southeastern states and other unique items. Parking lot nearby. Mon.–Sat. 10–5; Sun. 1–5; closed July 4, Labor Day, Thanksgiving, Christmas, Jan. 1. Free. (At Heritage Green, the cultural center in downtown Greenville.)

**Bob Jones University Art Museum.** Wade Hampton Blvd., 29614 ☐ The "World's Most Unusual University" guards the foothills of the Great Smokies and the Blue Ridge Mountains on a 200-acre tract of South Carolina soil. Bob Jones University was founded by evangelist Dr. Bob Jones, Sr., in 1927, to "train outstanding Christian leaders for all walks of life," to stand "without apology for the old-time religion and absolute authority of the Bible." The museum houses, in a building remodeled for the purpose in 1965, one of America's outstanding collections of sacred art. More than 400 paintings, including European works from the 13th through the 19th centuries, are displayed in 30 galleries. Rembrandt can be seen here, with Tintoretto, Titian, Veronese (altarpiece), Sebastiano del Piombo, Cranach the Elder ("Salome With the Head of John the Baptist"), Gerard David, Ribera, Rubens, Van Dyck, and Honthorst ("The Holy Family in the Carpenter Shop"). Wood-paneled Gothic and Renaissance rooms supply the backdrop for some of the paintings and some of the fine Renaissance furniture. The War Memorial Chapel nearby is the home of a series of religious works by Benjamin West with the theme "Revealed Religion," which he was commissioned by George III to paint for a chapel the king planned at Windsor Castle. The chapel plans never materialized, the paintings were returned to West, and then they were sold after West's death to a Member of Parliament, in whose country house they remained until 1962, when they were offered for sale. Six were acquired for Bob Jones University, and then a seventh, all to find their final home here in South Carolina. Cameras are not permitted. Since the museum is an arm of the university and its extensive School of Fine Arts, its activities have only to do with the display of art. Guided tours are available (Sept.–May) upon advance request. Catalogs of the collection, postcards, and reproductions of the paintings are sold in a sales room. Parking adjacent to the museum. Tues.–Sun. 2–5; closed Dec. 20–25, Jan. 1, July 4. Free. (Go 3 miles north of downtown on Wade Hampton Blvd. [US 29] to main entrance of campus.)

**MURRELLS INLET:  Brookgreen Gardens.** 29576 ☐ Scattered across this fertile land along the Atlantic, where indigo and rice were once harvested, are the sculptures of Brookgreen Gardens. What was a planta-tion yesterday is today a showcase of southern horticulture and botany—and American sculpture. Moss-laden oaks and boxwood, and indigenous southern plants and trees growing in ordered profusion are lovely com-panions to works by Weinman, Manship, Remington, Saint-Gaudens, French, Anna Hyatt Huntington, Edward McCartan, Solon Borglum, and many others. Over 380 19th- and 20th-century American sculptures are beautifully displayed here, and have been since Archer M. Huntington thought of the idea in 1931. Cameras are permitted. The gardens are enhanced by a wildlife park, nature trails, and the presence of the state of South Carolina as overseer of a portion of the property called Huntington Beach State Park, where visitors can camp out, picnic, and swim. Guided tours of the gardens and the wildlife park are conducted during the summer months. Catalogs of the sculpture and other pamphlets, postcards, photographs, and color slides are available at a shop in the new Visitors' Pavilion. Parking on the museum grounds. Daily 9:30–4:45; closed Christ-mas. Admission $1.50 for adults, 50¢ for children 6–12. (Entrance on the west side of US 17, 18 miles south of Myrtle Beach and 18 miles north of Georgetown; 3 miles south of Murrells Inlet.)

# SOUTH DAKOTA

**BROOKINGS:  South Dakota Memorial Art Center.** Medary Ave. at Harvey Dunn St., 57007 ☐ The South Dakota Memorial Art Center is on the west campus of the state university, South Dakota's largest institution of higher learning. In 1969 a windowless, cubical structure was built to house the art of South Dakota and the Northwest. Sixty-odd paintings and drawings by South Dakota native Harvey Dunn, who gained fame as an illustrator, World War I combat artist, and painter of pioneer life on the Dakota prairies, are on display here. "Something for Supper" and "Bringing Home the Bride" are fine examples of the prairie scenes, "Street Fight" and "The Doughboy," of World War I. Nine works by Yanktonai Sioux painter Oscar Howe are on view, along with works by over 80 other South Dakota artists. The center's collection of embroidered linens by Vera May Marghab (another native South Dakotan) is particularly popular—it is perhaps the only such collection. Sioux artist Andrew Standing Soldier, Rockwell Kent, Reginald Marsh, and Thomas Hart Benton are also represented here. Special exhibits are scheduled at the rate of about 10 or 12 per year. Cameras are not permitted. Regular art and theater classes offered by South Dakota State University are presented in the center; and the center offers 2 art scholarships at the university each year. In addition, the center staff trains volunteer docents who are available to lead tours; 2 earphone units are also available. The center sponsors 4 to 6 lectures a year, and publishes a newsletter every month, a bulletin quarterly, reports annually, catalogs of exhibitions when they occur, and an *Index of South Dakota Artists* and *Art of South Dakota*. The library (2,000 volumes) is open to the public. A museum shop sells reproductions, Indian jewelry, crafts, linens, postcards, and books. Parking available. Mon.–Fri. 8–5; Sat. 10–5; Sun. 1–5. Free. (From I-29 take exit onto Business Spur [6th St.]. Proceed west to Medary Ave., turn onto Medary, then right onto Harvey Dunn St.)

**VERMILLION: W. H. Over Museum.** University of South Dakota, 57069 ☐ The Carnegie Library building, which houses the W. H. Over Museum of the University of South Dakota, marks the site of the first institution of higher learning in the Dakota Territory. There are anthropological, natural history, ethnological, and ecological displays here, and among them is the gallery and studio of contemporary Sioux artist Oscar Howe, whose paintings reflect Sioux traditions and culture. Traveling and loan exhibits are mounted. The museum sponsors research in all aspects of the region. Craft classes are offered in addition to lectures and films, courses in museum techniques, and school loan exhibits. *The South Dakota Museum,* a magazine, is prepared here, and there is a gift shop. Mon.–Fri. 8–4:30; Sat. 10–4:30; Sun. 2–4:30. Free.

**Shrine to Music Museum.** Clark & Yale Sts. Mailing address: USD Box 194, 57069 ☐ The fine arts, strictly defined, do not include musical instruments, yet many of them are works of art. The Shrine to Music Museum, operated by the University of South Dakota, has one of the most comprehensive collections of the world's musical instruments. The Arne B. Larson collection forms the nucleus of this museum's holdings, which include more than 2,500 items representing all the world's cultures and historical periods. During the academic year the museum sponsors concerts that utilize the instruments in the collection. It cooperates with the College of Fine Arts of the University of South Dakota in its master of music program. Lectures, lecture-demonstrations, and an annual American Musical Festival fill out the yearly schedule. Guided tours are available by appointment. Assistantships are available for graduate students interested in the history of musical instruments. The museum offers 2 recordings, *The Golden Age of Bands,* Vols. I and II, and postcards for sale. The library is open for research by permission of the director. Restaurants are within walking distance, as are parking facilities. Mon.–Fri. 9–4:30; Sat. 10–4:30; Sun. 2–4:30. Free.

# TENNESSEE

**CHATTANOOGA: Hunter Museum of Art.** 10 Bluff View, 37403 ☐ The Hunter Museum of Art is situated on a bluff overlooking the Tennessee River, surrounded, as is all of Chattanooga, by the names—Lookout Mountain, Chickamauga, Missionary Ridge—and memorabilia of the Civil War. It was started in 1924 as the Chattanooga Art Association, which sponsored art exhibitions in sundry available spaces until 1951, when the Hunter Mansion, a 1904 Classic Revival-style structure, was bequeathed to the association. By 1975 the citizens of Chattanooga had raised enough money to build a new addition and to renovate the mansion. The new museum opened that year with the added acquisition of a sizable gift of American paintings. As a result, American art, particularly from the century between 1850 and 1950, predominates here. A highlight of this fine survey collection is a group of 5 paintings by Charles Burchfield. There are also works by Benton, Marsh, Marin, Guy Pène du Bois, Blakelock, Homer, Andrew and Jamie Wyeth, and members of "the Eight," and a notable collection of prints by contemporary Americans. A sculpture garden that is part of the new complex is surrounded by hand-wrought iron fencing made especially for the museum. About 35 special exhibits are mounted each year on a rotating basis in 3 galleries. A regional gallery displays work by local artists in one- and 2-person shows that change every 3 weeks. Cameras without flashes are permitted.

The museum school offers classes for all age groups day and evening in 4 term sessions; its facilities include a printmaking studio for intaglio and lithography and a ceramics workshop. Chamber music concerts are held one Sunday per month from September to May. Lectures, films, demonstrations, workshops, and programs for children are scheduled regularly. Guided tours are available to groups on 2-week advance notice; an audio-cassette treasure hunt leads children through the museum to several highlights of the collection. The library (700 volumes), concentrating on American art, is open to the public by request. A museum shop offers cards, jewelry, crafts, toys, books, notecards, and small sculpture for sale; works in the regional gallery are also for sale. Parking lot adjacent to the building. Tues.–Sat. 10–4:30; Sun. 1–4:30. Free; contributions are accepted. (From I-24, take I-124 north to 4th St. exit; turn right on 4th, go up the hill, and turn left at High St. The museum parking lot is at the end of High.)

**KNOXVILLE: Dulin Gallery of Art.** 3100 Kingston Pike, 37919 ☐ John Russell Pope, long before he became famous as the architect of the National Gallery, the Jefferson Memorial, and other monumental structures in Washington, D.C., designed the neoclassical residence in Knoxville of Hanson Lee Dulin, Esq. The structure was completed in 1917 and was home for the Dulin family until 1961, when Mrs. Dulin died and the house passed to her daughter. She in turn founded the Dulin Gallery of Art in memory of her parents. Aside from the beauty of the building itself (it is listed on the National Register of Historic Places), there is much to be seen here. The collection consists of about 250 contemporary American prints, drawings, and paintings, and a beautiful group of Thorne miniature rooms. Approximately 9 exhibits, from international sources and the Smithsonian, are held every year. A National Print and Drawing Competition is also held annually. The permanent collection is displayed during the summer. Workshops and multimedia programs are conducted for all age groups. Lectures, an Arts-to-the-Schools program, slide lectures, gallery tours for school groups, and a Young Artists' Gallery featuring students' artwork are more features of the educational program. Guided tours for sixth-graders are conducted Tues.–Fri. 9:30 and 10:30 throughout the academic year. The gallery has produced booklets on the Dulin residence and the Thorne miniature rooms and a book on the architecture of Barber and McMurry. The library (700 volumes) is open to the public. Parking on the grounds. Tues.–Sun. 1–5. Admission $1 for adults, free for children and students. (Go .7 mile west of Alcoa Hwy. interchange.)

**MEMPHIS: Brooks Memorial Art Gallery.** Overton Park, 38112 ☐ The Brooks Memorial Art Gallery was founded in 1915 by Bessie Vance Brooks in memory of her husband Samuel Hamilton Brooks. Overton Park greenery softens the marble exterior, which was modeled after the Morgan Library in New York City. In 1958, when the Kress Foundation gave a collection of some 30 works to the gallery (Kress's first "5, 10, and

25 Cent Store" opened in Memphis in 1896), a wing was added. Another addition was made in 1973. In addition to the Kress collection (Italian, Spanish, and Flemish paintings and sculpture) the gallery prides itself on its Northern European paintings and sculpture (16th through 18th centuries); English portraiture and landscapes (18th and 19th centuries); French paintings and etchings (16th–20th); American paintings (18th and 19th); a 20th-century international collection of paintings and sculpture; an extensive print collection; and a fine group of porcelain and glass. Rubens's "Portrait of a Lady" is here, as well as Renoir's "L'Ingénue"; "La Sente de la Justice à Pontoise" by Pissarro; Ralph E. W. Earl's "Portrait of General Andrew Jackson"; and "Sacrifice III," a bronze sculpture by Jacques Lipchitz. Contemporary American art is featured in the works of Okada, Stamos, Andrew Wyeth, and others. Exhibits change monthly. The museum sponsors lectures and concerts throughout the year. Regular tours are conducted daily at 1, and by appointment for particular groups; tours for the handicapped are also available. Fellowships are offered through the Southwestern College, the Memphis Academy of Arts, and Christian Brothers College work-study program. The museum shop sells the exhibition and permanent collection catalogs published by the museum as well as books, jewelry, prints, and postcards. The library (10,000 volumes) is open to the public. Parking nearby. Tues.–Sat. 10–5; Sun. 1–5. Free. (Just north of Poplar Ave.)

**Dixon Gallery and Gardens.** 4339 Park Ave., 38117 ☐ The Ionic columns at the entrance of this Georgian home signal the elegance within, reflecting the life-style of its former owner Hugo Dixon. Outside, 17 acres of formal and informal woodland gardens supply the setting. The house was built as late as 1940, used by Dixon until his death in 1974, and, by his testamentary request, opened to the public in 1976 after 7 new galleries were added. Dixon left his art collection here intact; it includes work from the major movements of the 18th, 19th, and 20th centuries, among them French and American Impressionists and related schools, Postimpressionists, and British portraits and landscapes. Degas, Cassatt, Gauguin, and Matisse are represented here, and there are portraits by Reynolds, Raeburn, and Romney and landscapes by Constable and Turner. The home is furnished with English antique furniture; the decorative arts are exemplified by Sheffield silver pieces, Waterford crystal, stoneware by Mason, Chinese porcelain vases, and Chelsea and Sèvres porcelain. Exhibits change every 6 weeks. Photographing is permitted using existing light only. Lectures, films, and concerts are sponsored throughout the year. Representatives from the gallery present programs on the collection in schoolrooms or at group meetings. Docent tours for groups are available upon request; regular tours are conducted during open hours. Interns in both gardens and gallery are accepted from universities across the country. Catalogs on the permanent collection are sold at the reception desk. The library (3,000 volumes) is open to the public upon request. Parking on the museum grounds. Tues.–Sat. 11–5; Sun. 1–5. Admission $1 for adults, 50¢ for children 5–12; special rates for senior citizens and groups. (From the east on I-240 take Poplar Ave. exit; go west to White Station Rd., turn left, go one block to Park Ave. and turn right. From the south, go east on I-240, exit at Getwell Rd. and continue north to Park.)

**NASHVILLE:    The Parthenon.** Centennial Park, 37203 ☐ As if to prove the aptness of Nashville's designation as "Athens of the South," the Parthenon, in perfect repair (as it is not in Greece) and symmetry (as it most certainly is in the original), occupies a place in Centennial Park. Surrounded by the modern world—banks, insurance companies, industries, stores, and country music—this exact-size replica of Athena's temple (like its counterpart, the columns are not uniformly sized or spaced, no lines are perfectly straight, no steps are the same height) was built in wood and plaster in 1897 to celebrate the Tennessee Centennial. Thirty-four years later it was cast in more permanent reinforced materials, still accurate to the 39 pediment figures on the east and west facades and the griffins at the four corners of the roof. Visitors come to see the temple alone, but are rewarded with the bonus of an art collection inside. In addition to reproductions of the famous Elgin marbles which were once part of the original Parthenon and are now at the British Museum, there is a notable collection of 19th-century American paintings including works by Homer, Moran, Ennis, Church, and Benjamin West. Exhibitions of contemporary art rotate every month. An exhibit of art from 13 central Southern states takes place in May, and a Tennessee state exhibit is shown in November. Cameras are permitted. Classes in the arts and crafts, lectures, and tours (on request) are provided by the Metropolitan Board of Parks and Recreation, which is the governing authority. A shop offers slides, books, jewelry, cards, and other gift items. Parking nearby. Mon.–Sat. 9–4:45; Sun. 1–4:45; closed legal holidays. Free. (Centennial Park is located between West End Ave. & 25th Ave. N.)

**Tennessee Botanical Gardens and Fine Arts Center, Inc.** Cheekwood, Cheek Rd., 37205 ☐ Among elegant residences, rolling hills, and forests, only 8 miles from the heart of Nashville, is Cheekwood, the former home of Leslie Cheek, whose company helps to supply the populations of the world with their morning, midmorning, afternoon, and evening bracers—Maxwell House coffee. With architect Bryant Fleming, Cheek traveled through the British Isles and returned to Nashville with structural elements and treasures from many of the great English mansions, all to be incorporated into a new Georgian-style country home. Cheek died in 1932, soon after finishing the house, and left it to his daughter, who lived in it and then, in 1944 gave it to a private, nonprofit corporation created to maintain it as a cultural center. The Tennessee Botanical Gardens and Fine Arts Center opened in 1960, after which the holdings of the Nashville Museum of Art were transferred to it, and in 1970 the Nashville Museum collection became the permanent property of the center. A Botanic Hall was added, also in 1970. Contemporary and older American art, Georgian decorative arts, the work of Tennessee painters and sculptors, both today's and yesterday's, an outstanding collection of snuff bottles (17th–19th centuries), a selection of old Sheffield silver, and pre-Columbian and Oceanic artifacts can all be seen here. There are many works by Red Grooms in this collection, among them "Mr. and Mrs. Rembrandt." Andy Warhol's "Portrait of Jamie Wyeth" and Jamie Wyeth's "Portrait of Andy Warhol" are both on view, as well as number one of Larry Rivers's "Dutch Masters Series" and Frank Duveneck's "Whistling Boy." Exhibits change monthly. During the summer months a larger-scale exhibition is installed for a 3-month period. Cameras without flash attachments are permitted.

Saturday and evening classes are offered, as well as concerts and lectures. Exhibits are available for loan to public places. Guides, available daily, lead tours that concentrate on various facets of the museum: the art gallery, the gardens (the boxwood garden is said to be the finest in the South), decorative arts, and the building itself. The museum has published a long list of books, which are sold in its extensive gift shop. A restaurant serves 90 people; groups are advised to make advance reservations. Picnic tables are provided on the grounds. Ample parking near the mansion. Tues.–Sat. 10–5; Sun. 1–5; grounds open sunrise to sunset. Admission $2 for adults, $1 for students 7–17. (Go out Harding Rd. to the intersection of Hwys. 70 & 100; turn left onto Hwy. 100 and go ¼ mile to Cheek Rd.)

**Vanderbilt University, Department of Fine Arts.** West End Ave. at 23rd Ave., 37235 ☐ The Vanderbilt Art Collection was established in 1956 by the Department of Fine Arts to make original works of art available to the university and Nashville communities. The gallery is part of a Victorian building, originally built as a gymnasium in 1880 and renovated to house the department of fine arts in 1961. The building, on the National Register of Historic Places, is itself something to see. The collection is a general one, with the purpose of providing representative works from as many cultures as possible. There is an outstanding collection of Old Master prints and an excellent selection of Oriental art. Seven to 9 exhibits are scheduled during the course of a year. Cameras are permitted. The Vanderbilt Art Association sponsors an annual series of lectures each winter titled "Sites and Insights into Art." Parking nearby. Mon.–Fri. 1–4; Sat. & Sun. 1–5. Free.

**Carl Van Vechten Gallery of Fine Arts.** Fisk University, 18th Ave. & Jackson St. North, 37203 ☐ Jubilee Hall, where Fisk University's Carl Van Vechten Gallery of Fine Arts is located, is a landmark in itself. It is on the site of a Civil War fort, its neo-Romanesque design conceived and executed in 1888. The collection here has much to do with photographers and photography: Van Vechten's photographs are here, and Alfred Stieglitz's collection of 101 works of modern art. In addition, there are works by Milton Avery and Hans Moller; a collection of sculpture, prints, and paintings by black Americans; and a group of contemporary and traditional objects from West Africa. Temporary exhibits are held, and the gallery offers lectures, films, concerts, and gallery talks. Guided tours are available, as is a training program for professional museum workers. Catalogs and *Fisk Art Magazine* are published here. The library (4,500 volumes) can be used on the premises by the public. Mon.–Fri. 8:30–12; 2–5; Sun. 4–6. Free.

# TEXAS

**ABILENE: Abilene Fine Arts Museum.** South 7th & Mockingbird Sts. Mailing address: Box 1858, 79604 ☐ The Abilene Fine Arts Museum serves an area that fans out 75 miles in all directions in the heart of Texas. It was chartered in 1954 as an educational institution; its present plant was built in 1964. The very small permanent collection here is rarely shown. Changing exhibits are the order, one every month. Cameras are permitted. Classes and workshops are held in painting, drawing, writing, jewelry, pottery, and photography. Occasional lectures, an all-Texas art competition, a public-school children's art show, and a tri-college art show are scheduled. Docents conduct 10,000 to 14,000 schoolchildren through the museum every year. A scholarship fund is available for worthy art students. The gift shop offers jewelry, wall hangings, pottery, books, and prints for sale. Parking nearby. Tues.–Fri. 10–5; Sat. & Sun. 1–5. Free.

**AUSTIN: Laguna Gloria Art Museum.** 3809 West 35th St. Mailing address: P.O. Box 5568, 78763 ☐ The Laguna Gloria Art Museum is housed in a Mediterranean-style villa built in 1916 by Clara Driscoll Sevier and her husband as their winter home. In 1943 Mrs. Sevier deeded it to the Texas Fine Arts Association for use as a museum; Laguna Gloria assumed operation of the museum in the 1960s. Here, on 24 acres of landscaped grounds bordering Lake Austin, 20th-century American art, from varied national and regional sources, is on display. The small permanent collection is rarely exhibited. Special permission is needed for cameras. A museum school of art holds sessions 3 times yearly. Concerts, films, and lectures are held periodically. Art After School offers classes in the schools and is taught by working artists. An active docent program provides guides for tours, available upon request; docents are on duty every Sunday 2–4. A branch gallery at the First Federal Bank in downtown Austin has monthly changing exhibits and programs during lunchtime hours. An appointments calendar featuring photographs by Austin artists is available for purchase at the shop; also for sale are gifts, books, prints, and postcards. Parking on the grounds. Tues.–Sat. 10–5; Thurs. 10–9; Sun. 1–5. Free. (At the end of West 35th St. The MoPac Freeway is adjacent to it, and the West 35th St. cutoff leads to the museum's front gate.)

**Elisabet Ney Museum.** 304 East 44th St., 78751 ☐ At the age of 59, in 1892, some 20 years after she had terminated a successful career in Europe to concentrate on living a quiet life in America, sculptor Elisabet Ney came to Texas and built a studio in Austin. This studio, a limestone "castle" with crenellated towers (added in 1902) and classical porches, has been preserved as a memorial since shortly after her death in 1907, and to this day presents a vivid picture of how and under what conditions a sculptor worked in the 19th century. It is full of her works: full-size figures in plaster of Stephen Austin, Sam Houston, and "Lady Macbeth," the marbles of which are in Washington, D.C.; many busts done from life of such figures as Jacob Grimm, Schopenhauer, Garibaldi, Bismarck, William Jennings Bryan, and Ludwig II of Bavaria; and a large medallion of "St. Cecilia" by Donatello, which she owned. Cameras are permitted. The museum sponsors classes in sculpture and life drawing for adults and classes for children; lectures and concerts are also held. Tours are conducted at all times. *Sursum,* an annotated book of the letters of Elisabet Ney, is published and sold here. The library is open to the public. Parking on the grounds. Tues.–Fri. 11–4:30; Sat. & Sun. 2–4:30. Free. (From I-35, go west on 38th St. to Ave. H, then north to 44th.)

**University Art Museum, University of Texas.** 23rd St. & San Jacinto Blvd., 78705 ☐ Three hundred 20th-century American canvases given to the University of Texas by James A. Michener, Latin American paintings and drawings, and at least a thousand graphics, both old and new, adorn the walls of the museum here. Changing exhibits emphasizing art in the Americas bring onto the campus artwork from other museums and collections. Lectures, films, and gallery talks are offered, and catalogs are published with exhibits. Mon.–Sat. 9–6; Sun. 1–5; closed school holidays. Free.

**BEAUMONT: Beaumont Art Museum.** 1111 Ninth St., 77702 ☐ In Beaumont, near the nation's largest concentration of petroleum refineries (it was here, in 1901, that the first great Texas oil well blew), is the small Southern-Regency-style mansion that is the home of the Beaumont Art Museum. The museum moved its holdings there in 1970, having previously been located for 20 years at the Southeast Texas Fairgrounds. The focus of the collection is 19th- and 20th-century American art and contemporary Texas painters and sculptors. Temporary exhibits change monthly. Cameras are usually not permitted. The museum's schedule of events includes lectures, films, concerts, gallery talks, tours to other cities, guided tours for children and adults, and an annual arts and crafts festival. An extensive educational program is offered in the schools. Trained docents conduct tours on request. Exhibition catalogs are published. A Gift Gallery offers jewelry, baskets, books, pottery, glasswork, and crafted items for sale. Parking on the beautifully landscaped and wooded grounds. Tues.-Fri. 10–5; Sat. & Sun. 2–5. Free. (Coming from the east on I-10, take the 11th St. exit, stay on the access road, go under the freeway, and turn right on 9th St. The museum is 5 blocks south. Coming from the west, take the 7th St. exit, and turn right on 9th.)

**BROWNSVILLE: Brownsville Art League.** 230 Neale Dr. Mailing address: P.O. Box 3404, 78520 ☐ The Brownsville Art League has a new modern building (dedicated in 1977) right next to the antique (1834) building that it still uses for classes. The league's collection of some 150 works is housed in the new building; paintings in all media are here, pen and ink drawings, woodblock prints, and lithographs. A particular pride is "The Locating Engineer" by N. C. Wyeth; there are also paintings by Dale Nichols, Harry De Young, and Roy Keister. Exhibits change seasonally. Cameras are permitted. Classes are held 5 days a week. Lectures and demonstrations are given by visiting artists. A bimonthly publication, *Brush Strokes,* is sent to members and interested visitors. Parking nearby. Weekdays 9:30–3; Tues. 1–4. Free.

**CORPUS CHRISTI: Art Museum of South Texas.** 1902 North Shoreline Blvd., 78401 ☐ The Art Museum of South Texas came into being in 1944 as the result of the interest in an exhibition and sale of art gathered together from a national competition by the Corpus Christi *Caller-Times.* The newspaper, the Corpus Christi Art Guild, and the South Texas Art League subsequently banded together to form the Centennial Art Museum, which took its name from the small building in South Bluff Park in which it was installed: it had been built in 1936 to commemorate the Texas Centennial. In 1961 the museum was chartered by the state. Rapid growth necessitated larger quarters, and in 1972, a new building designed by Philip Johnson was completed. It houses paintings, sculpture, graphics, photographs, and a group of 27 works on paper by contemporary American artists. Approximately 20 exhibitions are mounted each year.

Cameras are permitted, but tripods are not. The museum sponsors an experimental program for 4–10-year-old children who are encouraged to try their hands at several mediums in an informal atmosphere. Guest lecturers are invited periodically. Docent tours are available on request. Catalogs are published in conjunction with many exhibits. The library (1,000 volumes) is open to the public Tues.–Fri. 10–5. A museum shop offers ceramics, handcrafts, games, toys, and items of clothing for sale. Parking in front of the museum or on the public barge dock at the basement level. Tues.–Sat. 10–5; Sun. 1–5. Admission is a voluntary 50¢ for adults, 25¢ for children. (From I-37 go to Water St.; turn left to Hirsch St., then turn right.)

**DALLAS: Dallas Museum of Fine Arts.** Fair Park, 2nd & Parry Aves., 75226 ☐ Of the many buildings constructed for the 1936 Texas Centennial in Dallas's Fair Park, 15 are still in use. One of them, an art deco shell-stone building, houses the Dallas Museum of Fine Arts. The concept of a fine arts museum in this city was initiated by the Dallas Art Association in 1902. Sporadic exhibitions in libraries and theaters and minor collecting activities with title transferred to the city of Dallas resulted in a Foundation for the Arts collection which, combined in 1963 with the collection from the Dallas Museum for Contemporary Art, added up to a noteworthy amalgam of art. The two major areas of concentration are pre-Columbian art of Central and South America and African sculpture. Researchers and scholars come from afar to study the extraordinary Peruvian work— textiles, the large gold collection, the most complete silver collection outside Peru, and the impressive pottery and figurative sculpture in the Nora and John Wise collection of ancient South American art. The Stillman collection of Congolese sculpture and the Schindler collection of African art constitute the bulk of the African collection, said by many to be one of the nation's most important. A few works stand out: a Peruvian mantle dated c. 300–100 B.C.; the African mask collection; Jackson Pollock's "Portrait of a Dream"; works by Monet ("La Seine à Lavacourt") and Gauguin ("I Roro te Oviri"); Osias Beert's "Basket of Flowers" (1615); Andrew Wyeth's "The Gentleman"; "The Tale of the Bamboo Cutter" by Shibata Zestin; a 4th-century Greek "Figure of a Young Man from a Funerary Relief"; and Thomas Hart Benton's "The Prodigal." About 12 or 14 temporary exhibits are mounted every year; of these, 4 or 6 are produced by the museum, while the others are traveling or on loan. Cameras are not permitted.

Classes are held in series of 3 to 5 sessions to discuss current exhibitions. Drama, music, and art projects are also part of the educational activities. Lectures are given every Wednesday at 11; tours, Tues., Thurs., Fri. at 11, Wed. at 1, Sun. at 2. A concert series alternates on Sundays with a film series. National authorities lecture through Museum League seminars. The museum also carries out a strong outreach program. Four internships are awarded each year, 2 for educational projects and 2 for children's programs. A Texas Artists' Resource File keeps up-to-date information and slides on state artists. A bimonthly newsletter, an annual report, and catalogs of special exhibits are published here. The library is open to researchers Tues.–Sat. 10–5; Sun. 1–5. A shop offers books, gifts, handcrafted items, jewelry, prints, postcards, T-shirts, textiles, and posters for sale. Gallery Buffet serves a one-price luncheon Tues.–Fri. 11:30–1:30. Parking free on grounds adjacent to the museum. Tues.–Sat. 10–5; Sun. 1–5. Free. (Take I-30 east to Fair Park 2nd Ave. exit and turn left after the signal light into the parking lot.)

**Meadows Museum.**    Southern Methodist University, 75275 ☐ The Meadows Museum is in the Owens Art Center on the campus of Southern Methodist University, a 5-minute drive north of downtown Dallas. It specializes in Spanish art—paintings, prints, and drawings—from the late 15th century to modern times. There is also a modern sculpture garden. Paintings by Velázquez ("Portrait of King Philip IV"), Murillo ("Jacob Laying the Peeled Rods Before the Flocks of Laban"), Goya ("The Madhouse of Saragossa" and "Los Caprichos, Disasters of War") and Picasso ("Still Life in a Landscape") are particularly noteworthy. No camera flashes are permitted. The museum is used as a teaching aid for art, art history, and Spanish classes. Group tours are conducted only by prearrangement. A catalog of the collection, published by the museum, is available for purchase at the entrance. The fine arts library, which has a section on Spanish art, is open to researchers. Parking nearby. Daily 10–5; Sun. 1–5. Free. (Exit from Central Expwy. west on Mockingbird. Go north on Bishop Blvd. onto the SMU campus; the Owens Art Center is on Bishop Blvd., 2 blocks north of Mockingbird.)

**EL PASO: El Paso Museum of Art.** 1211 Montana Ave., 79902 ☐ An imposing classic structure encircled by 2-story Corinthian columns was built in 1910 as the home of State Senator and Mrs. W. W. Turney. The home was to be sold after Mr. Turney's death in 1939, and the directors of what had been chartered in 1930 as the International Museum Association sought to buy it. They did so with the combined moneys from a public appeal, donations, and a gift from Mrs. Turney, and settled in the upper floors of the house while the first floor was being utilized for "Bundles for Britain" and soon, "Bundles for America." In 1947 the International Museum opened. Ten years later, with the offer of a Samuel H. Kress collection, a 2-wing addition was planned, built, and launched in 1960 as the newly chartered El Paso Museum of Art, a municipal institution supported by tax dollars. The Kress collection of 57 works is on permanent display in 3 galleries of the west wing corresponding generally to 3 periods of art history: Early Renaissance, High Renaissance, and Baroque-Rococo. This is a beautiful group of paintings that includes a Bellini ("Saint Luke and a Carmelite Saint"), a Botticelli ("Madonna and Child"), a Crespi ("Cupids Frolicking"), 2 Tiepolos ("Allegory of Winter" and "Young Woman with a Parrot"), a Ribera ("Saint Bartholomew"), a Zurbarán ("The Immaculate Conception"), and a Van Dyck ("Portrait of a Lady"). In another corner of the museum is a collection of American paintings, among them Remington's "Sign of Friendship" and Inness's "Landscape," pre-Columbian pottery and artifacts, and Mexican colonial paintings and sculpture. The decorative arts of the 18th, 19th, and early 20th centuries are displayed in the Heritage Gallery. Exhibits on loan, traveling, or from the permanent collection change monthly. Cameras without flash attachments are permitted.

The museum's art school offers 12-week classes the year round for adults and children. Lectures and concerts are also held on a regular schedule, as well as workshops, master classes, and studio visits. Annual scholarships are awarded to El Paso high school students for the art school or for college art courses. Guided tours are available upon request; multilingual, especially Spanish docents can be requested. Catalogs are published now and then. The library (500 volumes) is open with special permission by appointment. A museum shop sells books, jewelry, prints, postcards, and pottery. Parking on the museum grounds. Tues.–Sat. 10–5; Sun. 1–5. Free. (Take I-10 to North Mesa; North Mesa to Montana Ave.)

**FORT WORTH: Amon Carter Museum of Western Art.** 3501 Camp Bowie Blvd. Mailing address: P.O. Box 2365, 76101 ☐ Amon G. Carter, born and raised in a frontier community, expressed his interest in and love of the West in many ways. He founded and published the Fort Worth *Star-Telegram,* he helped in the development of west Texas and Fort Worth, and he collected the creative output of artists inspired by the character and traditions of western America. Ultimately, he provided in his will that his wonderful collection be brought together under one roof—the Amon Carter Museum of Western Art. It opened in 1961; designed by Philip Johnson, the new building provided the open spaces and wide vistas of Texas in a modern idiom that recalls the classical. A front portico of tapered columns shades the bronze-framed glass facade, which looks out over Fort Worth in the distance, and a lowered terrace close by, where Henry Moore's totemlike "Upright Motives" looks back. Inside the glass front, a 2-story-high gallery stretches the length of the building. One of the best collections of Remingtons ("Bronco Buster" and "Coming Through the Rye") and Russells are housed here, as well as an extensive group of

19th-century landscapes. Modern art is represented by O'Keeffe, Davis, Marin, Shahn, and more. The museum also has an extensive print collection that numbers over 150,000 items. In addition, this museum was one of the first to collect art from the far northern portion of the country; several Eskimo objects are included in this category. Recent notable acquisitions were Martin Johnson Heade's "Thunderstorm Over Narragansett Bay," Homer's "Crossing the Pasture," Nadelman's "Tango," Fitz Hugh Lane's "Boston Harbor," and 6 rare platinum prints by photographer Laura Gilpin. These were added to a collection that includes works by such American masters as Bingham, Bierstadt, Kensett, Moran, Catlin, Harnett, Dove, Audubon, Zorach, Calder, Cropsey, Kuhn, Peto, and many others. The museum changes exhibits approximately every 6 weeks. Selections from the permanent collection are displayed on a rotating basis. Works of art are not to be photographed.

The museum theater sponsors a full range of activities including lectures, film series, audiovisual programs, symposia, meetings, and musical festivals. It hosts the city's fifth-grade students annually for a tour and a lesson in American art. Docents provide conducted tours daily at 2. Over 30 books have been published at the continuing rate of about 2 a year; they are available in the museum shop together with posters, slides, prints, and belt buckles. The library (13,500 volumes) is available for inter-library loan but is open to the public by appointment only. Parking lot near the Camp Bowie entrance. Tues.–Sat. 10–5; Sun. 1–5:30. Free. (From I-20 exit at Montgomery and continue north until Montgomery intersects Lancaster Ave. & Camp Bowie Blvd.)

**Fort Worth Art Museum.** 1309 Montgomery St., 76109 ☐ The Fort Worth Art Museum is one of the three art museums on Carter Square (the other two are the Amon Carter and the Kimbell), where the population of Fort Worth comes for its cultural diversions. Working together not to duplicate collections but to complement one another, each has become noteworthy in its own field. The Fort Worth Art Museum began in 1901 as a gallery in the public library, run by the Art League and devoted to contemporary art. After several reorganizations of the support group and a successful bond drive dedicated to building an independent facility, the collection, bursting out of its quarters at the library, moved to its own contemporary building adjoining the William Edrington Scott Theater in 1954. This building, enlarged in 1974 to about twice the original size, houses a collection devoted primarily to modern art. Picasso's "Femme Couchée Lisante" is here, as well as Eakins's "The Swimming Hole" (in fact, the museum's expansion started with the purchase of this painting in 1925 by the support group from which the present Art Organization is descended), Picasso's "Vollard Suite," and Rauschenberg's "Whistle Stop." Among other 20th-century masters to be seen here are Kandinsky

("Above and Left"), Shahn ("Allegory"), Rothko ("Light Cloud-Dark Cloud"), Sheeler, O'Keeffe, Oldenburg, and Stella. Changing exhibitions are mounted throughout the year on an irregular schedule. Camera users must sign a release; tripods and flashes are not permitted.

Art workshops are offered for children and adults. Lecturers are invited to discuss the exhibits; concerts and dance and drama performances fill out a program of special activities. The Fort Worth Art Association supplies docents to all the museums on the square; their office is located in the FWAM building. Exhibitions are accompanied by extensively illustrated catalogs which are sold in the museum store together with other books and prints. The library is open to the public by appointment. Parking in a museum lot or on the surrounding streets. Tues.–Sat. 10–5; Sun. 1–5. Most exhibitions are free; occasionally there is an admission charge. (From I-20 take Montgomery exit, turn right, go to Lancaster, and turn right. The museum is at the corner of Montgomery & Lancaster.)

**Kimbell Art Museum.** Will Rogers Rd. West, 76107 ☐ The late Kay Kimbell, Fort Worth industrialist, left his entire fortune to the Kimbell Art Foundation, which he had established in 1936. His dream was to create a first-rate art museum for the city where enterprises in milling, food, oil, grain, insurance, and real estate made him a wealthy man. His own collection and that of his wife, whose interest sparked his, began in the mid-1930s. For the next three decades, the Kimbells, particularly enthralled with 18th-century British portraiture and late Renaissance works, acquired a fine collection that finally became too extensive to keep at home. Through the foundation, paintings were placed on long-term loans in colleges and universities, churches, and libraries. In 1966 the foundation, which had been further enriched by the joining of Mrs. Kimbell's share of the community property, began to implement the dream of the founder. The city provided space for a building near the Amon Carter Museum of Western Art and the Fort Worth Art Museum. The new museum, concentrating as it would on European art from classical times through the 19th century and arts of the Far East, Africa, and pre-Columbian America, would perfectly complement the already existing ones close by. Acquisitions in this cooperative spirit began immediately and covered an entire spectrum of styles and schools excluding what had already been covered: the 1250 Barnabas Altarpiece (English painting on panel); Goya's portrait of his friend, matador Pedro Romero; landscapes from the early Flemish Joos de Momper to Fauvist André Derain, from Canaletto to Monet, and including many 17th- and 18th-century Dutch works; Renaissance and Baroque paintings by di Paolo, Mantegna, Tintoretto, Tiepolo, Rubens ("Duke of Buckingham"), Hals, Van Dyck, El Greco, Ribera, Murillo, Rosa, and Bellini ("Christ Blessing" and "Madonna and

Child"); Olmec, Aztec, and Mayan art; Indian, Chinese, and Japanese works. This much-enlarged Kimbell collection (American art and art by living artists is excluded) came under public scrutiny for the first time in its extraordinary new home in 1972; the building, consisting of a series of cycloidal vaults, was designed by the aging Louis I. Kahn and completed only two years before his death. The spectacular exterior, admired by architects and engineers alike, creates a gigantic interior shell, with uninterrupted spaces (there are no supporting walls or columns) that permit tremendous variety of installation, as the paintings demand. Special exhibitions are on view at various times throughout the year but are not regularly scheduled. Cameras are permitted; no flashes or tripods.

Lectures, films, and concerts are scheduled the year round. A docent training program prepares docents, in a 5-month art history course, for all the museums in Fort Worth. Tours are available at the Kimbell Museum by appointment. A catalog of the collection and a book entitled *Light Is the Theme* have been published by the museum; they are for sale at the bookstore with other books relating to the collection. A noncirculating library (17,000 volumes) is open to scholars by appointment only. Snack bar on premises; parking off Arch Adams St. Daily 10–5; Sun 1–5. Free. (From I-20 take University Dr. exit and travel north; turn west on Lancaster, go 1 block, then right on Arch Adams. The museum is on the left. The Kimbell is easily accessible from downtown Fort Worth via W. 7th St., which becomes Camp Bowie Blvd.; from Camp Bowie, turn south on Arch Adams; the Kimbell is on the right.)

**HOUSTON: Museum of Fine Arts.** 1001 Bissonnet at Main, 77005 ☐ In 1900 the Art League of Houston founded the Museum of Fine Arts to house its small collection and to make art available to Houston schoolchildren. A neoclassical building was formally opened in 1924; 2 spectacular additions, in 1958 and 1974, designed by Mies van der Rohe, extended the museum's capability both to exhibit and teach. Today the collection spans the 5,000 years from antiquity to modern times. This general art museum is especially strong in 17th- and 18th-century European art; Impressionism and Postimpressionism; western Americana; modern American art; and photography. Cullinan Hall, the first of Mies's additions, houses the contemporary works of the permanent collection: Frankenthaler, Poons, Christiansen, and Brooks are among the artists here. In the Pavilion are the pre-Columbian, American Indian, and African and Oceanic collections, a special gallery housing what is said to be one of the largest private collections of Frederic Remingtons, and a gallery of prints and drawings. The Robert Lee Blaffer Memorial group contains Cézanne's "Portrait of Madame Cézanne" and Renoir's "Still Life with Bouquet"; a

Kress collection includes works by Tintoretto and Bellotto ("Market Place in Pirna"); a Strauss collection has more Italian Renaissance paintings and sculpture—paintings by Memling and Fra Angelico ("Temptation of St. Anthony, Abbot"), sculpture by Cellini and Verrocchio. Several galleries trace French art from classicism to Postimpressionism. The antiquities are highlighted by the great 7½-foot figure of Ephebus. The museum has 6 temporary exhibition galleries, with exhibits changing about once every 2 months in 4 of them and a semipermanent exhibit in the others. Photographing is allowed with a special permit from the museum.

Lectures, concerts, symposia, films, and guided tours are some of the activities sponsored by this increasingly important institution. The schedule of guided tours is copious. Sun. at 1, 2, & 3; Tues. at 12:15; Wed., Thurs., Fri. at 1; Sat. at 11 & 2. The library (13,000 volumes) is open to the public for research. Exhibition catalogs published by the museum are sold in the shop, which also handles posters, prints, reproductions, jewelry, art replicas, sculpture, books, and slides. Cafeteria on premises (beer and wine served). Free parking across the street. Tues.–Sat. 10–5; Sun 12–6. Free. (At the intersection of 3 major Houston Streets: Bissonet, Montrose, & Main.)

**The Bayou Bend Collection of the Museum of Fine Arts.** 1 Westcott St. Mailing Address: Box 13157, 77019 ☐ The American decorative arts collection of the Museum of Fine Arts of Houston, the largest in the Southwest, is housed in a "Latin colonial" mansion built as a private residence for Miss Ima Hogg, daughter of Texas Governor James Stephen Hogg, in 1927. Miss Ima, as she is known in Houston, began her collection with the specific ultimate purpose of giving it to the state. The house was built on the bayou with the gift in mind; it served as her home until 1958, when it was turned over to the Museum of Fine Arts. By 1966 furniture, paintings, and objets d'art were appropriately sorted out and arranged, and the Bayou Bend collection was opened to the public. Twenty-four period rooms show the progression of American design and decorative arts from 1650 to 1850 and American paintings from the 18th and early 19th centuries. Smibert, Feke ("Portrait of Ann McCall"), Copley ("Mrs. Paul Richards"), Stuart, Peale, and Cole are among the artists whose work hangs in this expansive house-museum set in 14 acres of beautiful bayou woodland 3 miles from the center of the city. The Bayou Bend is a branch of the Houston Museum of Fine Arts; it can be visited by reservation only. Two-hour guided tours through the house are available Tues.–Fri. and Sat. morning. A tour of no more than 4 people leaves every 15 minutes, morning and afternoon; a maximum of 48 people are conducted through the house each day. Larger groups can make special arrangements for tours. A lecture series is held each year, and slide programs are offered to fifth-graders and elderly citizens in nursing homes. A catalog of the collection is available for purchase at a small sales desk. The library (2,000 volumes) can be used on special request. Parking nearby. Free. A deposit of $1 is required with your reservation; it is refunded later. (Just off Memorial Dr.; go west from downtown and turn south onto Westcott.)

**Rothko Chapel.** 3900 Yupon St., 77006 ☐ Not a museum, the Rothko Chapel nevertheless proclaims the power of modern art beyond pure aesthetics. The ecumenical spirit of the place is reinforced by its octagonal shape and by Rothko's 14 panels of modern religious art, the antecedents of which reach back to the Renaissance and before. In front, a 26-foot-high steel obelisk, "Broken Obelisk" by Barnett Newman, memorializes Dr. Martin Luther King, Jr. Daily 10–6. Free.

**Sarah Campbell Blaffer Gallery.** University of Houston, 77004 ☐ The Sarah Campbell Blaffer Gallery was built as part of the University of Houston arts complex in 1973 to serve the university population and the surrounding community. The paintings here range from the 15th to the 20th century. A pre-Columbian collection, a rapidly growing contemporary print study collection, and a group of Mexican graphics are also on view. Some highlights are works by Ribera, Mantegna, Greuze, Pintoricchio, Murillo, Corot, Casentino, Cranach, and Bonnard. The schedule of exhibits (approximately 8 to 10 per year) coincides with the academic year. Cameras, but not flashes, are permitted. Lectures are held in conjunction with exhibitions. Guides are available, but not regularly. Publications pertinent to the exhibits are available for purchase. Parking nearby. Tues., Wed., Fri., Sat. 10–6; Thurs. 10–8; Sun. 1–6. Free. (Use entrance 5 off Cullen Blvd.)

**SAN ANTONIO: McNay Art Institute.** 6000 North New Braunfels. Mailing address: P.O. Box 6069, 78209 ☐ A portrait bust of Marion Koogler McNay is surrounded by some of her most treasured paintings—El Greco's "Head of Christ" and Diego Rivera's "Delfina Flores"—in the entrance hall of the museum that she began. Her collection formed the nucleus of the McNay Art Institute that opened in 1954 in her 1927 Spanish-Mediterranean-style home. The tropical inner patio and 25 landscaped acres provide a most congenial setting for the various collections that are exhibited here. The main emphasis is on 19th- and 20th-century art, a great many in the Expressionist tradition: Gauguin (including a self-portrait), Van Gogh, Modigliani, Rouault, Soutine, Cézanne, Dufy, Matisse, Kirchner ("Portrait of Hans Frisch"), and Picasso ("Portrait of Sylvette") are among the masters whose works were acquired by Mrs. McNay. In a separate gallery are the items of furniture, textiles, pottery, jewelry, and votive images from greater New Mexico that she loved. Gothic and medieval art fills another gallery, a permanent installation assembled and presented to the museum by Dr. and Mrs. Frederic G. Oppenheimer. A graphic arts collection with master prints by Delacroix, Redon, Toulouse-Lautrec, and Gauguin, is rotated in its own gallery. The Sylvan and Mary Lang galleries house a collection rich in modern sculpture and American paintings by Homer, Marin, O'Keeffe, and Dove. The Jack and Adele Frost galleries are also filled with American art. Special exhibits are hung every 6 weeks. Cameras are permitted.

A varying number of lectures and concerts is scheduled at the institute. A docent program provides tours for school and other groups. Some exhibits are accompanied by catalogs, which are on sale at the sales desk; also available are postcards, reproductions, and books published by the museum. The library (5,000 volumes) is open to the public. Parking on the museum grounds. Tues.–Sat. 9–5; Sun. 2–5; closed Jan. 1, July 4, Thanksgiving, Christmas. Free; contributions are welcome. (At the junction of US 81 [Austin Hwy.] & N. New Braunfels Ave. It is possible to take the Broadway-Terrel Heights bus from Houston & North St. Mary's Sts. or Broadway & Houston St.)

**San Antonio Museum of Art.** 200 W. Jones Ave., 78215 ☐ Three museums function under the aegis of the San Antonio Museum Association: the Witte, the Museum of Transportation, and the San Antonio Museum of Art. The Witte Memorial Museum, oldest of the three, was founded in 1926 by Ellen Schulz Quillan as a museum of natural history and science. Like Topsy, it grew and grew, and from it, the association formed the Museum of Transportation in 1969. But still the Witte grew; to the natural history and science collections had been added art of the Americas—Texas furniture and decorative arts, American contemporary paintings and sculpture, contemporary photography, and an American Indian collection. The art and archaeological collections were then moved (1980) to the association's most recent creation—the San Antonio Museum of Art, fashioned out of what were formerly the buildings of the Lone Star Brewery (worthy of the National Register of Historic Places) on the San Antonio River. A sculpture garden and a park abut the museum, which is accessible along the riverfront. Among the works are paintings by Hicks ("A Peaceable Kingdom with Quakers Carrying Banners"), Hartley ("New England Still Life"), Pearlstein ("Female Model in Robe Seated on Platform Rocker"), Segal ("Her Arm Crossing His"), Frankenthaler ("Eden Revisited"), and Lawson ("Harlem River High Bridge"). There is also space for large traveling exhibits.

The museum maintains a full program of lectures, films, and slide presentations in conjunction with touring exhibits. Trained docents conduct tours. The SAMAVAN, part of the education department outreach program, provides a mobile media extension of the museum with audiovisual programs, study guides, replicas, and art materials. The curatorial staff authors books and catalogs pertaining to exhibitions. The museum shop features gifts from around the world, not found elsewhere in the city; also for sale are locally produced crafts, locally found artifacts, and publications. Parking facilities are located nearby. Weekdays 9–5; weekends 10–6; closed Christmas, Jan. 1, Fiesta Friday. Admission by voluntary donation. (West of Broadway and east of St. Mary's St., just north of downtown.)

**SNYDER: Diamond M Foundation Museum.** Diamond M Building, 911 25th St., 79549 ☐ Oilman C. T. McLaughlin's "hankering to own some nice pictures" resulted in a fine collection of art objects from all over the world, all personally selected. McLaughlin came to Texas in 1920 and worked in the oil fields around Wichita Falls. In 1934 he bought the Diamond M Ranch near Snyder, only to find that his newly acquired land rested over the heart of the Canyon Reef oil pool, one of the largest in the world. Sixteen years, and many purchases of "nice pictures" later, he created the Diamond M Foundation, and 14 years after that, on the second floor of the Diamond M Industries building, the Diamond M Foundation Museum. McLaughlin's true love, art of the American West, predominates among more than 300 paintings, 80 bronzes, and 150 jade, ivory, and china objects. There are several paintings by N. C. Wyeth, 3 small paintings and a few bronzes by Remington, works by Andrew Wyeth, Frank Schoonover, Cornwall, Storey, Johnson, Leigh, and so on. He bought more than 100 paintings and a number of bronzes by young artists whose work he wanted to encourage. He also bought the work of English artists F. W. Hulme and George Cole and animal bronzes by French artist P. J. Mene. Cameras are permitted. Guided tours can be arranged for in advance. Parking nearby. Mon.–Fri. 9–12 and by appointment. Free.

**VICTORIA: The Nave Museum and McNamara House.** Victoria Regional Museum Association, 306 West Commercial St., 77901 ☐ The Nave Museum opened on November 20, 1976, in a Greek Revival building erected in 1933 and given to Victoria by Royston Nave's family to be used as a fine arts museum for the region. Royston Nave painted in and around Victoria in the 1920s, and his paintings are hung here. The museum has started an expanding permanent collection. Exhibits change every 8 weeks. Cameras are permitted. Lectures and seminars, tours for schools and study groups are offered. Parking close by. Wed.–Sun. 1:30–5:30;

Wed–Fri. 10–12, and by appointment. (At the corner of Moody & Commercial.)

**WACO:   The Art Center.** 1300 College Dr., 76708 ☐ A renovated 1924 Mediterranean-style building looking out over the Brazos and Bosque River valleys and surrounded by cedars is the home of Waco's Art Center, which houses a small collection of contemporary regional art. Primary emphasis, however, is on an exhibition program that brings a wide variety of fine art to the Waco area. Fifteen exhibits are scheduled each year. Cameras without flashes are permitted. Classes in ceramics, painting, drawing, sculpture, and art history are offered both children and adults in four 8-week sessions per year. Lectures, occasional films, workshops, and local school tours are scheduled throughout the year. Docents and staff members are available to lead tours. Scholarships are awarded to local students. Catalogs accompany exhibitions. A small library is open for use by the public. The center shop handles books, handcrafted items, and jewelry. Parking nearby. Tues.–Sat. 10–5; Sun. 1–5. Free. (Between North 19th & Lake Shore Dr.)

**Baylor Art Museum.** Baylor University, 76703 ☐ The Baylor Art Museum is the only museum within a 100-mile radius of Waco. It serves both the university, with teaching functions, and the community at large. The artwork gathered here represents New Guinea (figurines), Africa (sculpture), and the region around Waco (paintings). Cameras are permitted. Parking available. Daily 8–5. Free. (The building is at the intersection of I-35 & S. 5th St., Baylor exit.)

**WICHITA FALLS:   Wichita Falls Museum and Art Center.** 2 Eureka Circle, 76308 ☐ Wichita Falls, located on the gently rolling plains of the Red River valley, acquired its museum and art center in 1964. It was founded by a coalition of civic leaders. By 1967 the museum was established in a contemporary boxlike structure which was to house what had already been acquired and what was to be purchased by a matching grant from the National Endowment for the Arts. The resulting collection centers on American printmakers from 1880 to the present. About 150 prints include a Currier and Ives "American Game," Oldenburgs's "Letter Q as Beach House with Sailboat," "Drouet Sculpteur" by Whistler, and fine works by Homer, Benton, Albers, Warhol, Ray, Diebenkorn, Johns, Dine, Stella, Grooms, and Pearlstein. History exhibits change yearly; science exhibits change twice a year; art exhibits change monthly. Photographing is allowed with special permission. Art, cooking, and science classes are offered by the center; lectures, occasionally. Planetarium shows are on a regular schedule; group tours are conducted on request. A catalog of the collection is available to visitors. The sales desk handles books, jewelry, cards and games, posters, and candles. Parking nearby. Mon.–Fri. 9–5; Sat. 9–4:30; Sun. 1–5. Free. (Exit from US 281 at Midwestern Pkwy.; go west to Eureka Circle and turn left. The museum is last building on circle.)

# UTAH

**BRIGHAM CITY:    Brigham City Museum-Gallery.** 24 North 3rd West, 84302 ☐ The Brigham City Museum-Gallery stands at the edge of Brigham Young Park, which marks the place where Young delivered his last public address in 1877. The museum was built in 1970 to function as a three-in-one facility: it houses a historical museum, a natural history collection, and an art gallery. A small but expanding permanent collection of regional and local art and traveling exhibits are shown here on a monthly schedule. Cameras are not permitted. Lectures and concerts are sponsored periodically. Events such as the Peach Days Art Festival, a local competition, and the Community Art Week, a week of school participation in demonstrations and lectures, add to the educational functions of the museum. The library (on Mormon and western history) is open to the public. A sales area offers books, jewelry, prints, postcards, and handcrafted items. Parking nearby. Mon.–Sat. 11–7. Free. (3 blocks west of the city's main intersection, Main & Forrest.)

**CEDAR CITY:    Braithwaite Fine Arts Gallery.** Southern Utah State College, 84720 ☐ The Braithwaite Fine Arts Gallery at Southern Utah State College, which is central to no less than 4 national parks, was completed in 1976. It brought together the collection developed by the college over a period of 80 years. In its colonial-style home the gallery displays a selection of 19th- and 20th-century American art, with a scattering of some English 18th- and 19th-century canvases. The gallery administers a year-round exhibition program, including traveling exhibits and an annual national juried competition. Permission must be granted for the use of cameras. Lectures, art demonstrations, film programs, string concerts, poetry readings, and recitals are regularly scheduled. Guided tours are provided by gallery personnel. Parking nearby. Weekdays 10–5; Sat. 1–6. Free. (Take I-15 to Cedar City and exit at the second of 3 exits, regardless of north or south direction. The campus is at 300 South St., between Center & 200 South Sts.)

**PROVO:  Brigham Young University Art Gallery.** Harris Fine Arts Center, 84602 ☐ The Harris Fine Arts Center opened on the Brigham Young University campus in 1965; the center's art gallery opened at the same time with the collection that had been acquired by the university up until then. The priority of interests are first, Mormon art—works by Mormon artists or dealing with Mormon history or subject matter; second, American art—primarily Utah artists, then Western and other schools; and third, pre-Columbian and Indian art. The gallery prides itself on a large collection of works by Western artist Maynard Dixon, among them "Free Speech"; an equally extensive selection by Julian Alden Weir ("In the Sun" and "Autumn Stroll"); paintings, sculpture, and prints by Mahonri Young; murals by C. C. A. Christensen; and not least, "Massasoit," the 12-foot bronze Indian by Cyrus Dallin. Approximately 40 shows in all take place in the 5 exhibition areas of the building; 2 competitive exhibits are held annually, one for Mormon artists, one for students. Cameras are permitted. The gallery's activities coincide with the needs of students. Occasional lectures are given on particular exhibitions. Tours can be arranged by appointment. Several books published by the museum relating to its collections can be purchased at the college bookstore. Eating and parking facilities are on campus. Mon.–Fri. 8–5 (Secured Art Gallery and Foyer); Mon.–Sat. 8–10 (B. F. Larsen Gallery, 4th & 5th Level Exhibition areas).

**SALT LAKE CITY:  Salt Lake Art Center.** 20 South West Temple, 84101 ☐ Salt Lake Art Center was founded as a community art school and exhibition space in 1931 and has since collected the work of Utah artists and craftsmen. The new modern facility opened in May 1979. Exhibitions change often; selections from the permanent collection are shown twice a year. Cameras are generally permitted. An active art school provides professional teaching. Some small scholarships are offered. Chamber music concerts, films, lectures are held about twice a month. Docents conduct guided tours by prearrangement. A rental-sales gallery offers the work of Utah artists, and a shop features work of area craftspeople, books, postcards, and gift items. Parking available. Tues.–Sun. 10–6; Wed. 10–9. Free.

**Utah Museum of Fine Arts.**  104 Art & Architecture Center, University of Utah, 84112 ☐ The Utah Museum of Fine Arts was founded in 1951, a century and a year after the University of Utah itself was established. The museum is in the Art and Architecture Center, near the library on the university's 1,500 acres. Of interest here are the 19th-century landscapes (American and French); a Rubens; 18th-century French tapestries; some Italian Renaissance paintings; antiquities from Egypt; and a group of objects from various Buddhist cultures. There are continuous changing exhibitions—some organized by the museum, some on loan, and occasional faculty shows. The museum offers guided tours, concerts, films, and lectures. Tours for schoolchildren can be arranged in advance. The library (500 volumes) can be used for research. Catalogs are prepared for many of the exhibits. Mon.–Fri. 10–5; Sat. & Sun. 2–5. Free. (East end of 2nd South St.)

**SPRINGVILLE: Springville Museum of Art.** 126 East 400 South, 84663 ☐ The museum that bears the name of this quiet residential town at the foot of the Wasatch Mountains was begun in 1903 by native sons John Hafen (painter) and Cyrus Dallin (sculptor). Each donated a work of art to the high school students of the city. Thenceforward, for more than 60 years, students continued to acquire artwork, after which the collection was taken over by the city. The Spanish-style structure that became the museum's home in 1935 was a WPA project, funded with federal, city, and school district money; red tile roofs and a stucco exterior suggest the handmade tile floors and fine red oak woodwork of the interior. The collection here represents 20th-century American art interspersed with some earlier European works such as Turner's "Ship Burning at Sea" and a landscape by Gainsborough. A group of Dallin bronzes leads off the American collection; Rockwell Kent, Childe Hassam, and Anna Hyatt Huntington ("Lady Godiva") are among the notables. There has been a national competition and invitational show in April of every year since 1921; a regional quilt show in June; and a High Schools of Utah show in February. Cameras are permitted for noncommercial use only. Oil painting instruction is offered year round. Concerts are held in series and band concerts in the summer. Tours are available on request. A catalog of the permanent collection and a book entitled *Cyrus E. Dallin, Let Justice be Done* have been published by the museum. They can be purchased at the museum shop, which also offers jewelry, reproductions, calendars, photographs, and prints for sale. Parking in front of the building. Tues. 10–9; Wed.–Sat. 10–5; Sun. 2–5. Free.

# VERMONT

**BENNINGTON: Bennington Museum.** West Main St., 05201 ☐ Like so many public places in Vermont, where old buildings are preserved with the passion of pride, the Bennington Museum is housed in what was once built for another purpose. Erected in 1855, it was the first Roman Catholic church in southern Vermont. It opened as a museum in 1928, with 2 owned objects and a few items on loan. Today the museum surveys the history and creative heritage of the region in a thrice-enlarged building. The famous Bennington flag (the oldest) can be seen here; early Bennington pottery; rare American blown and pressed glass; furniture, documents, costumes and uniforms, firearms and swords, toys and dolls, and household items are all packed into this museum. And as if to confirm the authenticity of it all, there are the paintings by Anna Mary Robertson Moses—Grandma Moses—displayed by themselves and reviewing 100 years of a life-style familiar in this portion of the country. (In fact, Anna Mary Robertson Moses was born in, spent most of her life in, and died in New York State.) The Grandma Moses Schoolhouse Museum enhances the portrait of the artist with its displays of family paintings and memorabilia. One special gallery changes exhibits 5 times during the 9-month season. Cameras are permitted except in the Grandma Moses Gallery. The museum sponsors a winter lecture series, and an annual European tour for members. Close cooperation with area schools results in guided tours, classroom lectures, and "colonial kits" for history classes. Groups can request guided tours. Several books published by the museum are availale at the gift shop; reproductions and souvenirs are also sold. Parking on museum grounds. Mar. 1–Nov. 30: winter 9:30–4:30; summer (Memorial Day–Oct. 15) 9–6. Admission $2 for adults; $1 for 12–17; 25¢ for unaccompanied children under 12; free for children under 12 with an adult; special group rates. (About 2 miles west of intersection of US 7 & SR 9.)

**BURLINGTON:   Robert Hull Fleming Museum.** University of Vermont, Colchester Ave., 05401 ☐ McKim, Mead, and White designed the neoclassical building that was named for Robert Hull Fleming (University of Vermont, 1862) in 1931. Into it were moved the university's collections of Vermontiana and Vermont archaeology, geology, and zoology; Sioux Indian artifacts; Zulu beadwork and African artifacts; and objects from Central America. The fine arts collections were developed during and after the 1950s. Soon archaeological, zoological, and geological specimens were moved to their respective departments, and the museum was left with the fine, decorative, and ethnographic arts. It has an ancient and medieval gallery, an Asian gallery, and particularly strong collections in American, African, pre-Columbian, and American Indian art. Exhibits are planned to coincide with the university schedule; 3 galleries change regularly, showing the works of art teachers, acquisitions, and Vermont and other artists. Special permission is required to use a camera. Students use the museum for their studies; the art history department is on the lowest floor. Some classes for children are offered. A lecture series and gallery talks by artists are scheduled to coincide with the university semesters. Children's tours, conducted by an education coordinator, can be arranged in advance. Internships and work-study programs are available to students of the university. Catalogs accompany special exhibits. The library (1,300 volumes) is open to the public on weekday afternoons. A sales desk offers books and cards; a craft shop is open at Christmastime. Parking is difficult, but buses come from downtown Burlington every half hour (Winooski or Essex Junction bus). Mon.–Fri. 9–5. Sat. & Sun. 1–5. Free. (Take exit 14W off I-89. From Williston Rd. turn left onto East Ave., go to the end, and make another left turn onto Colchester Ave. The museum is about ⅛ mile from the East Ave. turn.)

**MANCHESTER: Southern Vermont Art Center.** 05254 ☐ A Colonial-style mansion built in 1910 on 375 acres off West Road in Manchester has housed the Southern Vermont Art Center since 1950. Paintings, sculpture, and graphics from the early 20th century are on view here during the summer months. Concerts, dance programs, and light opera are presented in a music pavilion not far from the main house. Art classes, films, and special exhibits are also offered here, as well as botany and nature walks through the center's own stretch of Vermont countryside, a portion of which is given over to a sculpture garden. During the winter, activities and small exhibits are held at the Winter Gallery on Seminary Avenue in Manchester Village. (Dec.–May, Mon.–Fri. 10–4; free.) June–mid-Oct., Tues.–Sat. 10–5; Sun. 12–5. Admission $1 for adults; 50¢ for students; children under 12 free; Tues. free.

**MIDDLEBURY: Johnson Gallery.** Department of Art, Middlebury College, 05753 ☐ The Johnson Gallery shares the Christian A. Johnson Memorial Building (1968) with the departments of art and music at Middlebury College. The college's eclectic teaching collection includes a painting by Hans von Aachen ("Judith and Holofernes"), a Calder mobile, a mobile sculpture by George Rickey, and early Renaissance and modern prints. Exhibitions are changed every month. Cameras are permitted. All art classes at the college use this gallery. Three or 4 outside lecturers are invited by the department of art each year. Parking nearby. Mon.–Fri. & Sun. 12–5; Sat. 9–12, 1–5; closed during college vacations. Free. (US 7 goes through Middlebury. From either direction, go west on Rt. 125, turn right at the bottom of the hill below the marble Romanesque Roman Catholic church, then take the second left turn up the hill to student parking lot B.)

**MONTPELIER: Thomas Waterman Wood Art Gallery.** Kellogg-Hubbard Library, 135 Main St., 05602 ☐ Thomas Waterman Wood began a gallery in his native city to house and exhibit his own paintings and those of some of his 19th-century contemporaries—Asher Brown Durand, Alexander Wyant, M. F. H. de Haas. From the old Colonial house where it was originally located the collection was moved to the Kellogg-Hubbard Library. There, occupying the second floor, are over a hundred of Wood's paintings and works by Joseph Stella, Reginald Marsh, Durand, Wyant, and others. Wood's works, on exhibit at all times, are rotated monthly; local and regional work is also shown monthly. Cameras are permitted. Art classes are offered in 6- to 10-week sessions in the fall and spring. Concerts are given at Christmas and in spring; the gallery also sponsors occasional films and lectures. A monograph on Wood and works by Vermont printmakers are available for purchase. Parking at meters in front of or in a small area behind the library. Tues.–Sat. 12–4; summer, Tues.–Fri. 12–4, Sat. 9–1. Free. (From I-89 follow signs to State House on State St. Go past the capitol and continue until the first traffic light; make a left on Main St. and go 2 blocks to the library.)

**ST. JOHNSBURY:  St. Johnsbury Athenaeum.** 30 Main St., 05819 □ The provenance of the St. Johnsbury Athenaeum can be traced to the invention of the platform scale. The scale was built in 1830 by Thaddeus Fairbanks in St. Johnsbury. The Athenaeum was built as a public library with Fairbanks money and support in 1871; in 1873 an art gallery was added by the same means. It is said to be the oldest gallery in its original form in the United States. Under this Victorian mansard roof are gathered approximately 100 paintings and sculptures. The Hudson River school predominates; in many cases, works were painted to order or purchased directly from the artist. The huge "Domes of the Yosemite" canvas by Albert Bierstadt is a highlight; there are also works by Gifford, Colman, Whittredge, Asher B. Durand, and Jasper Cropsey. Cameras are permitted. A catalog of the collection and postcards of "Domes of the Yosemite" are sold at the library's front desk. Metered parking in front of the building. Mon. & Fri. 10–8; Tues., Wed., Thurs., 10–5; Sat. 10–2. Free. (At junction of US 2 & US 5 on the corner of Eastern Ave. & Main St.)

**SHELBURNE:  Shelburne Museum, Inc.** 05482 □ Thirty-five 18th- and 19th-century buildings on 45 acres of beautifully landscaped lawns and gardens make up the Shelburne Museum. It was founded in 1947 by Electra Havemeyer Webb and her native Vermont husband J. Watson Webb. Raised by pioneer collectors in New York, Electra began her own collecting early, and with her husband, who was enthralled with all manner of Americana, amassed some 125,000 objects before they bought land in Shelburne and restored an early 19th-century house to serve as a museum. Thus began the collecting of buildings from other parts of Vermont and New England as well as additional historical objects and works of art. One by one the buildings were brought here; there are homes, barns, a railroad station and a train shed, a blacksmith shop, a meeting house, a jail, a smokehouse, a school, an inn, a covered bridge, and a general store. The fine arts are displayed in several new buildings. In the Beach Gallery (built in 1962) are paintings of North American big game by Carl Rungius and works by Remington, Sydney Laurence, A. F. Tait, and Rosa Bonheur. The Webb Gallery (built in 1960) contains 18th- and 19th-century American primitive and academic paintings—works by Copley, Morse, and Homer are included here—and some rooms devoted to Vermont scenes. Georgian paneled rooms, furnishings of the Webbs' New York apartment, and their collection, inherited from the Havemeyers, of European paintings (Rembrandt, Goya, Corot, Manet, among others) and Degas bronzes can be viewed in the Electra Havemeyer Webb Memorial Building (built 1967). And in the Colchester Reef Lighthouse Gallery (built in 1871 and brought here from Colchester Reef, Lake Champlain) are maritime prints and paintings and ship figureheads. The resources of this complex of buildings are enormous, most particularly in the field of American art ranging from folk art and crafts through architecture and the finer decorative arts, and including quilts, textiles, tools, decoys, dolls, pewter, glass, ceramics, carriages and sleighs, railroadiana (a private railroad car) and the sidewheeler S.S. *Ticonderoga,* the last ship of its kind in America. All displays are permanent. Photography permits ($1) are required; you must specify the objects to be photographed and you are restricted to a maximum of 6 shots.

Summer courses are offered for graduate or undergraduate credit at the University of Vermont. A summer lecture series lasts for 7 weeks every year. Guides serve as interpreters of the exhibits in all buildings; some are bilingual (French-English). The museum publishes many books and catalogs for sale in a shop that also offers postcards, jewelry, and decorative household items. A cafeteria-snack bar has indoor seating and outdoor picnic tables. Parking on the grounds. May 15–Oct. 15, daily 9–5. Admission $5 for adults, $2.50 for the 2nd day; $2.50 for children 6–16. (Shelburne is on US 7 south of Burlington. Car ferries operate across Lake Champlain via I-87 from Port Kent, NY, to Burlington and from Essex, NY, to Charlotte, VT. Museum is 1 mile south of Shelburne on US 7.)

**SPRINGFIELD: Springfield Art and Historical Society.** 9 Elm Hill, 05156 ☐ The Springfield Art and Historical Society makes its headquarters in a beautiful 1825 Victorian home that was given to the town in 1956 to be used for the arts. In addition to the historical and decorative objects on display—the Bennington pottery, Richard Lee pewter, Springfield dolls and toys—there are primitive portraits and paintings by Joe Henry, Horace Brown, Herbert Meyer, Stuart Eldredge, Russell Porter, Thomas Clark,

and Marion Eldredge. Monthly exhibits of paintings, sculpture, and crafts
are held. Cameras are permitted. Art classes and concerts are given during
the summer. Guided tours are available upon request. Small scholarships
are awarded to local high school students who want further training in art
or music. The library (200 volumes) is open to the public. Books, notepaper, and prints are for sale. A large driveway provides ample parking
space. Mon.–Fri. 12–4:30. Free.

**WAITSFIELD: Bundy Art Gallery.** Mailing address: Box 19, 05673 ☐
At the center of 80 acres of untouched Vermont countryside, about 4½
miles south of Waitsfield, is a 12-acre plateau of meadowland where the
Bundy Art Gallery stands. Its strong rectangular shapes, in sharp contrast
to Vermont's softer profile, are fashioned from Norman brick, copper, and
glass rising 5 levels from the ground. An L-shaped lagoon girding the
building on 2 sides is itself buttressed by man-made rolling mounds beyond which the natural environment takes over—an orchard gives way to a
stand of spruce, a maple grove edges a deep ravine that drops to a stream
below. The gallery was founded and designed by Harlow Carpenter and
named in memory of his mother Helen Bundy Carpenter; its purpose, to
bring contemporary arts into rural Vermont—a contemporary country museum. On the grounds, in hollows and on knolls, along wooded paths and
in clearings, and scattered across the lawn and through the woods are
sculptures of the past 25 years. Nevelson ("Distant Land"), Robert Rohm
("Number One Sport"), Minguzzi ("Studio per Pas de Quatre" and "Gli
Amanti"), and Subirachs ("The Law Table") become a part of the landscape. Inside are paintings by Marca-Relli ("The Passage"), Afro ("Three
Under Lock and Key"), Mathieu ("Bodhi"), Soulages ("July–August
1956"), and Tapies ("Untitled"); the largest canvases are displayed in the
22-foot-high main gallery. Displays change 5 or 6 times during the year.
Cameras are permitted. A museum school offers art classes to schoolchildren and members as well as occasional lectures, outdoor concerts in
the summer, and indoor concerts in the main gallery during the winter.
The library (450 volumes), arranged to be enjoyed with paintings as
background, is open for use by the public and for inter-library loan. Some
catalogs of exhibits are available. Parking on the museum property. Daily
10–5; Sun. 1–5; closed holidays & Nov. Free. (4½ miles south of Waitsfield
on SR 100.)

# VIRGINIA

**CHARLOTTESVILLE: University of Virginia Art Museum.** Bayly Memorial Bldg., Rugby Road, 22903 ☐ Thomas Jefferson founded and planned the University of Virginia, one of the most beautiful campuses in the country, but it was not until 1935 that the Palladian-style art museum came into existence. The collection here includes American art, European art in the age of Jefferson, Asian art, contemporary painting and sculpture, prints and drawings, and African and American Indian art. Special exhibits are mounted occasionally. Cameras are permitted. A lecture series is held during the academic year in conjunction with the university department of art. A docent program provides guided tours by appointment. Some exhibition catalogs are published and are available in a shop with other books, postcards, jewelry, ceramics, textiles, and crafts. Parking across Rugby Road. Tues.–Sun. 1–5; closed Christmas–Jan. 1. Free. (US 29 to University Ave. [US 250] to Rugby Rd.)

**FREDERICKSBURG: Belmont—The Gari Melchers Memorial Gallery.** 224 Washington St., 22401 ☐ American artist Gari Melchers (1860–1932) lived and worked at Belmont, a 27-acre tract of land on the Rappahannock River. His home, a Georgian manor house that was built in 1761 and added to in 1843, and a studio that he built in 1920, were deeded to the state of Virginia as a memorial museum and an art center. The main house, now a National Historic Landmark, is furnished with the period and contemporary pieces collected by the Melcherses in Holland and Germany. The galleries in the large fieldstone studio building show over 75 works by Gari Melchers and a small variety of additional paintings and drawings—one by Frans Snyders, a small sketch by Jan Bruegel, etchings by Childe Hassam, a drawing by Rodin. The museum has special exhibits, but not on a regular schedule. Cameras are permitted. Lectures and films are offered periodically, as well as educational tours for local school groups. Tours for visitors are conducted regularly. Reference materials are available to scholars on request. The museum shop sells postcards and a booklet on Belmont. Parking on the grounds. Daily 1–4 except Tues. & Thurs. Admission $1 for adults, 40¢ for students, 75¢ for senior citizens. (From I-95, take US 17 east 1¼ miles toward Falmouth and turn right halfway down a long hill. From US 1, go west ¼ miles on US 17 to the first left turn.)

**HAMPTON:  College Museum.** Hampton Institute, 23668 ☐ The College Museum of the Hampton Institute is devoted to ethnic art—traditional art objects and artifacts of sub-Saharan Africa, Asia, Oceania, and the American Indian, and contemporary Afro-American and African art. The African collection of over 1,000 objects from all over the continent began in 1911 with a purchase of some 400 objects that had been collected in the Congo between 1890 and 1910 by Dr. William H. Sheppard, a Hampton alumnus. In the American Indian collection, consisting of objects from nearly all the cultural areas of North America, the Plains Indian predominates. This unusually fine collection derives from a federal policy in the late 19th and early 20th centuries of sending groups of young American Indians from western reservations to Hampton Institute. Oceania is represented notably by sculptures from the Philippines, Australia, Melanesia, Micronesia, and Polynesia. The contemporary ethnic art collection includes works in a variety of media by 20th-century Afro-American and African artists. The museum offers guided tours and lectures and an educational program for public schools in surrouding communities. The library (1,000 volumes) is open to the public. Changing exhibitions from its own collection, loans, and traveling exhibits, faculty and student art shows, and shows of works by regional artists are mounted regularly. Weekdays 8–5. Free. (Take exit 5 off I-64. Institute is at east end of Queen St.)

**LYNCHBURG:  Randolph-Macon Woman's College Art Gallery.** 2500 Rivermont Ave., 24504 ☐ The first accredited woman's college in Virginia began its fine collection of American paintings and graphics long before 1952, when the gallery was built. Today the gallery displays part of the permanent collection and special changing exhibits. A catalog of the collection is available. Daily 2–5 or by appointment. Free.

**NEWPORT NEWS:  Mariners Museum.** Museum Dr., 23606 ☐ The Mariners Museum is just that—with every conceivable accoutrement of seafaring on display: miniature ships, small craft, ship equipment and armament, sailors' crafted objects, figureheads, and on and on. There is also a collection of some 17,000 prints, paintings, and drawings of watery subjects. The material rotates annually in the museum's 9 galleries. Tours, lectures, gallery talks, and demonstrations figure in the activities of this seafarer's paradise. The library (53,000 books, maps, charts, logs, periodicals, manuscripts) deals with marine topics. A photograph archive and a film library are available for research and loan respectively. Books, prints, and ship models are on sale. Mon.–Sat. 9–5; Sun. 12–5. Admission $1.50 for adults, 75¢ for children; half price for groups of 15 or more. (At junction of US 60 & J. Clyde Morris Blvd.)

**NORFOLK:** **Chrysler Museum at Norfolk.** Olney Rd. at Mowbray Arch, 23510 ☐ A Florentine Renaissance-style building that was begun in the 1920s was finished with the help of WPA funds in 1933 and became the Norfolk Museum of Arts and Sciences. Into it was moved a collection of paintings and tapestries that had been donated in 1905 to the Irene Leache Memorial Association to honor this popular Norfolk teacher. After the founding in 1917 of the Norfolk Society of the Arts, an alliance between these two art-oriented associations was formed for the purpose of building the museum that finally opened its doors in the thirties. Almost 40 years later, in 1971, Walter P. Chrysler, Jr., brought his collections from the Chrysler Museum of Provincetown to Norfolk; the museum thus became the Chrysler Museum at Norfolk, and in five years was enlarged to accommodate the now augmented collection. Chrysler brought examples of the art of virtually every major civilization, including Egyptian, Greek, Roman, European, and Oriental. The museum has outstanding galleries of Dutch, Flemish, Italian Baroque, French, English, and modern art. Over 7,000 glass objects include a major group of Tiffany and Sandwich glass. An Art Deco collection, thought to be among the finest, and a group of decorative arts broaden the scope of the museum, but the Italian Renaissance and Baroque paintings and sculpture are the most significant. "Virgin and Child with Saints" is one of the few works by Veronese in this country that has been fully documented. Here also are Guido Reni's "Abigail and David," Guercino's "Samson Bringing Honey to his Parents," and "Bust of the Savior," Bernini's last work. Other important acquisitions are La Tour's "St. Philippe," Vouet's "Vierge au Rameau," Boucher's "Vegetable Vendor"; Flemish and Dutch 17th-century works by Terbrugghen, Teniers, Everdingen, and Rubens ("Portrait of a Man" and "Portrait of the Archduchess Isabella"); Impressionists Renoir ("Daughters of Durand-Ruel"), Degas ("Danseuse aux Bouquets"); Academic and Salon painters Bouguereau, Gérôme, and Gleyre; American art from the 18th and 19th centuries—Bierstadt, Durand, Remington, Homer, Sargent, and Cassatt. Temporary exhibits are changed monthly. The Irene Leache juried exhibition is held annually. Cameras without flashes are permitted.

A docent training program provides guides for the more than 25,000 schoolchildren from nearby cities who come to tour the museum. College students and docents are offered gallery talks by artists. A film series, lectures, and concerts are available, as well as guided tours for any groups of 10 or more (tours are offered in 4 languages). The museum catalogs of exhibitions it has sponsored are sold at a shop together with reproductions, books, and a large assortment of gift items. The library (200,000 volumes), an amalgam of Chrysler's personal art reference library (40,000 volumes) and the M. Knoedler and Co. Ltd. art reference library, although partially in storage, is open to scholars by appointment. A landscaped courtyard and sculpture garden offer visitors a fine escape from city bustle. Parking on the museum property. Tues.–Sat. 10–4; Sun. 1–5. Visitors are asked to donate $1 voluntarily. (The Waterfront Dr. exit of I-64 becomes Duke St., which runs in front of the museum.)

**Hermitage Foundation Museum.** 7637 North Shore Rd., 23505 ☐ Overlooking the Lafayette River in Norfolk is the gracious Tudor-style mansion in which the collection of William and Florence K. Sloane is housed. Here, in 13 informal galleries, is a potpourri of Oriental, Near Eastern, European, and Amercan art. Of special interest are Oriental jades, ivories, and bronzes, and rugs, Russian icons, and lace from Italy and France. Tour guides elucidate on the collection regularly; lectures are scheduled about 10 times a year. The library (600 volumes) is available for use by appointment. Daily 10–5. Admission $1 for adults, 25¢ for children, students free.

**RICHMOND:   Virginia Museum of Fine Arts.** Boulevard & Grove Ave., 23221 ☐ The Virginia Museum was founded by an act of the General Assembly of Virginia in 1934 and opened to the public in 1936, becoming the first museum of art in the country to have state sponsorship. The original Georgian building, completed for the opening, and 3 additional wings house the objects that, through a statewide program, are seen over the length and breadth of Virginia. Collections spanning 5,000 years of world history are permanently housed here. Most notable, in some of the 14 main exhibition galleries, are Russian Imperial jeweled objects made for the Romanov family by Peter Carl Fabergé; one of the country's leading collections of art from India, Nepal, and Tibet; American decorative arts; Byzantine art; and Art Nouveau. In addition, the classical, the Oriental, and the medieval are represented here; other works come from all over Europe, reaching back in time and forward into the 20th century. Individual high points are diverse and plentiful: Guardi's "Piazza San Marco," Constable's "Pond at Hampstead Heath," Goya's portrait of General Nicholas Guye, a huge statue of the Roman emperor Caligula, Monet's "Iris by the Pond," 6 Gobelins Don Quixote tapestries, paintings by Courbet, Renoir, and Picasso, Hopper and Shahn. The sculpture court holds more treasures: Maillol's "The River," Moore's "Reclining Nude," and works by Lipchitz among them. A dozen major exhibits and 20 to 30 smaller shows are mounted during the year. Hand-held cameras are permitted; tripods and flashes must be approved in advance.

Unique in this museum are the orientation theaters attached to many of the collections: Visitors learn background information on what they are about to see from short films shown in a room adjacent to the gallery. Indeed, teaching is one of the strong points of the Virginia Museum.

Studio art and lecture classes are held throughout the year; lectures are given in connection with all major exhibitions; there are special residency programs for students; lecture-demonstrations and artmobiles tour the state; guided tours are available to those who request them 2 weeks in advance; fellowships are awarded to undergraduates, graduates, and professionals in all areas of the arts; the museum's theater offers productions by a professional resident theater company. Publications include catalogs and a scholarly journal, published three times a year. The library (40,000 volumes) is open to the public for research Mon.-Fri. 9-5. A shop offers reproductions, books, and a full range of gifts for sale (open Tues.-Sat. 10:30-4:30, Sun. 2-4:30). A cafeteria is open Tues.-Fri. 11:30-2, Sat. 12-3, Sun. 1-3. Ample parking nearby. Tues.-Sat. 11-5; Sun. 1-5. Admission 50¢, under 16 and senior citizens free. (Entering the city on I-95, use exit 14. Trailblazer signs will direct you to the museum.)

**Anderson Gallery.** Virginia Commonwealth University, 907½ West Franklin St., 23220 ☐ The stable that has been, since 1970, the Anderson Art Gallery has gone through several phases since its original bequest in 1920 for use as an art gallery. After years of service as classroom space and then as a library, it was taken over and utilized once again as a gallery. Today the 4-story structure, considerably altered since its days as a stable, exhibits contemporary works in all mediums and a small cache of prints by Van Gogh ("Portrait of Dr. Gachet"), Bonnard ("Les Boulevards"), Homer ("Eight Bells"), Marsh ("Two Girls in Subway"), Calder ("Bouboules"), Matisse ("La Petite Liseuse"), and Dürer ("Christ Before Caiaphas"). One to 5 exhibits are mounted per month in the 6 display areas. Photographing with permission only. Lectures are often presented by exhibitors on topics related to the exhibits. Tours are conducted by request. Brochures accompany many exhibits. Parking on neighboring streets. Mon.-Fri. 10-4. Free.

**WILLIAMSBURG:  Colonial Williamsburg.** 23186 ☐ Colonial Williamsburg need not be described here. It is simply one of the most remarkable and extensive restoration projects in the country, encompassing about 170 acres with nearly 500 (more than 100 restored and open) structures of various kinds—homes, taverns, shops, public buildings. The thrust is historical; the purpose, to show life as it was lived in the capital of the Virginia colony before the Revolution. Of course, in the restored parlors and bedrooms and public rooms are the paintings and sculptures that would have been part of the 18th-century decor. Visitors should check at the Information Center for activities that include slide lectures and forums, films, guided tours, concerts and theater productions typical of the 18th century, and temporary exhibits. Many books and brochures on

Williamsburg are sold at the Information Center and several shops. The library (25,000 volumes), focusing on 18th-century Virginia and Colonial and United States history, is open for research by special arrangement. Restaurants are part of the complex. Reproductions, gifts, and souvenirs are sold. Exhibition buildings and shops are open daily 9–5; extended hours during summer. Various combination tickets available; prices vary depending on number of exhibits and activities.

**Abby Aldrich Rockefeller Folk Art Collection.** South England St., 23185 ☐ The Abby Aldrich Rockefeller Folk Art Collection is one of the preeminent collections of its kind in the country. Over 2,000 objects—paintings, sculpture, needlework, decorative implements, decoys, painted furniture—from the 18th and 19th centuries are collected under one roof. Exhibitions change about 6 times a year; there is an annual Christmas show. The collection offers guided tours, lectures, and gallery talks; traveling exhibitions and lecturers; and films on folk art. A guide to the collection and temporary exhibit catalogs are available. The library (1,200 volumes) is open by appointment. Winter: daily 12–6; summer: Mon.–Sat. 10–9, Sun. 12–9. Free.

# WASHINGTON

**BELLEVUE:   Bellevue Art Museum.** 10310 N.E. 4th, 98004 ☐ In 1975 the Bellevue Art Museum was formed by the Pacific Northwest Arts and Crafts Association. Here, in its Mission Revival-style building, the museum specializes in small educational exhibitions emphasizing 20th-century European and American art, most particularly Pacific Northwest artists and craftsmen. Exhibits change every 6 weeks to 2 months; there is a crafts invitational exhibit every Christmas and a juried competition at Easter. Cameras are permitted. The Bellevue Art Museum School offers a full range of courses approved by Western Washington University for academic credit. Scholarships are available to full-time students in need. Lectures that relate to the current exhibition are scheduled, and catalogs are published. Concerts are held in summer, poetry readings during the winter. A film series features the work of independent filmmakers. Docents conduct tours daily at 2 or by appointment. The library (500 volumes) is open to the public on Tues. & Thurs. 10–2. A sales desk offers books and reproductions. Parking adjacent to the museum. Tues.–Sun. 12–5; closed Thanksgiving, Christmas, Jan. 1, Easter, Aug. Free. (Heading east from Seattle on the Evergreen Point Bridge, take the Bellevue/Renton [south] exit onto I-405; proceed south to N.E. 8th exit, and go west to 104th. Turn left, go to 4th, and turn right.)

**BELLINGHAM: Whatcom Museum of History and Art.** 121 Prospect St., 98225 ☐ The Whatcom Museum of History and Art was founded in 1940 and 8 years later became the Bellingham Public Museum. It is housed in a restored 1892 city hall building that is now on the National Register of Historic Places—a fine example of late Victorian civic architecture. The museum concentrates in 3 areas: the ethnography of the Pacific Northwest coastal Indians; the history of Whatcom County from 1850 to the present; and artwork by contemporary West Coast and northwestern artists. About half the gallery space is utilized for exhibits that change every month or so. Cameras can be used with special permission only. A museology program is conducted in conjunction with Western Washington University, and the museum also offers art studio classes. Concerts, lectures, and special events are scheduled through the year. Guided tours are available by appointment. Grants for linguistic and anthropological studies are given by the Melville and Elizabeth Jacobs Foundation, which the museum administers. Several catalogs are published here and are available at the museum's shop along with crafts, jewelry, prints, and imported items. The small library is open for use by appointment. Small parking lot and on-street parking. Entrance ramp for wheelchair visitors. Tues.–Sun. 12–5. Free. (Take the State Street-City Center exit from I-5 and follow the signs from Iowa to State to Champion to Prospect.)

**GOLDENDALE: Maryhill Museum of Fine Arts.** Mailing address: Star Route 677, Box 23, 98620 ☐ The elegance and grace of Versailles are present on a windswept hill looking south over the Columbia River into Oregon. It was here in 1914 that Samuel Hill began the construction of his home, a château modeled after the Petit Trianon. Hill died in 1931, convinced by his friend Loie Fuller, an American dancer who became famous in France, that his home should be made a museum. The museum opened in 1940. Twenty-two galleries house a distinguished collection of Rodin sculptures and drawings; icons and ecclesiastic embroideries; furniture and memorabilia of Queen Marie of Romania; Indian artifacts and baskets; and a large variety of chessmen. Special exhibits are mounted seasonally. Cameras are permitted, but not flashes. The museum sponsors lectures and concerts and offers guided tours by appointment. A souvenir booklet is available from the museum shop, which also stocks postcards, books, and petroglyph rubbings. Parking on the grounds. Mar. 15–Nov. 15 daily 9–5. Admission $1.50 for adults, $1 for senior citizens, 50¢ for students. (In Maryhill. From Goldendale, take US 97 south 11 miles, then go west 2½ miles on SR 14.)

**PULLMAN: Washington State University Museum of Art.** Fine Arts Bldg., 99163 ☐ The Museum of Art at Washington State University was founded around a core of American paintings collected by a former president of the university. The collection was removed from the university library in 1974 to the Fine Arts Building and has grown there since that time. About 150 paintings represent the years between the late 19th century and the present, with an emphasis on the Ashcan school and Northwest regional art. The list of painters, however, crosses schools of art and regions of the country: Bellows, Blakelock, Duveneck, Glackens, Henri, Inness, Shinn, Sloan, and Twachtman are all here. And representing the past and other countries are etchings by Goya and lithographs by Daumier. About 10 or 11 exhibits are mounted each year. Cameras are usually permitted, depending on the exhibit. Lectures and concerts are sponsored by the museum. A class is taught by museum personnel under the auspices of the fine arts department. The museum's Washington State Art Services program provides traveling exhibitions, regional art symposia, museum tours, exhibition modules, and museum management workshops. An annual art symposium brings distinguished speakers to the university for several days of discussion often related to a major current exhibition. Staff-guided tours are available on advance request. Two or 3 catalogs are published each year, and a bookstore is open weekdays 12-4. The library (300 volumes) is accessible to the public. University cafeteria across the street; parking in the building. Weekdays 10-4; Mon. & Fri. evenings 7-10; Sat. & Sun. 1-5. Free. (Take Wilson Rd. off Stadium Way.)

**SEATTLE: Charles and Emma Frye Art Museum.** 704 Terry Ave. Mailing address: P.O. Box 3005, 98114 ☐ Charles and Emma Frye left their collection of paintings and the bulk of their estate to be used to maintain a museum in perpetuity. In 1952 the museum, small and contemporary in style, the inner spaces determined by the explicit wishes of Charles Frye, opened in Seattle. The Frye collection became one of the proud cultural resources of the city. The 19th-century predominates here—paintings by 99 artists from 14 countries representing the Munich school of art, German Secessionists, French Academicians, and pre-Impressionists. In addition, works by the Wyeths, Grant Wood, Everett Shinn, Childe Hassam, and Mary Cassatt can be seen on these crowded walls. Exhibits change every 3 weeks; there are shows by local and nationally known artists, loan exhibits, and once a year, a competitive exhibit for artists from the Puget Sound area. Cameras are not permitted. Guided tours are provided upon request; a docent is always available. A small sales desk offers postcards, a Frye Museum catalog, and a gallery guide. Parking lot at the rear of the building and one across the street for museum patrons. Mon.-Sat. 10-5; Sun. & holidays 12-6; closed Thanksgiving and Christmas. Free. (The museum is on the northwest corner of Terry and Cherry. Coming from the south on I-5, take the James St. exit, turn right on James to Terry Ave., turn left and go 1 block north to Cherry. Coming from the north on the same road, take the James St. exit and go to Cherry; at the first traffic light turn left to Terry.)

**Seattle Art Museum.** Volunteer Park, 14th Ave. E. & E. Prospect St., 98112
☐ In the depths of the Depression, Dr. Richard E. Fuller and his mother, Mrs. Eugene Fuller, financed construction of the first art museum in the Northwest, to be built in Volunteer Park on Capitol Hill, overlooking Puget Sound and beyond to the Olympic Mountains along the coast. At its dedication in 1933 the Seattle Art Museum, an "arte moderne" structure filled with Fuller's limited collection, was given to the city, and a program of acquisitions was set into motion. Today the museum's collections are ample and diverse. Approximately half of the 10,000 objects housed here are Asian in origin—they come from Japan, China, Korea, Nepal, India, Southeast Asia, and the Islamic world—and constitute one of the great assemblages of Eastern art in this part of the world. The Japanese holdings in particular are considered to be the most exceptional collection outside Japan. Oriental sculpture, paintings, screens, and jade represent 6,000 years of art; marble animals that once led to the tombs of Chinese royalty now adorn the museum entrance and grounds. Other major areas of concentration are pre-Columbian ceramics and textiles, 18th- and 19th-century European porcelains, and African tribal Kongolese miniatures. The Western art includes an Isaacson porcelain collection, and Renaissance, Baroque, primitive, and American paintings, many from a Samuel H. Kress collection. A ceiling by Tiepolo (there are only two in this country) and a Rubens sketch of "The Last Supper" are among the Kress treasures. The **Modern Art Pavilion** (2nd Ave. N. & Thomas St.), an annex of the museum located in Seattle Center (take the monorail from downtown) houses the 20th-century and Northwest art collection. Works by Duchamp, Léger, Klee, Frankenthaler, Stamos, and most particularly the "Northwest Mystics" Morris Graves and Mark Tobey are on display here. Rotating exhibitions lasting about 45 days take up half the gallery space; they come from other museums or from the permanent collection. Photographing of the permanent collection only is permitted.

Art history classes are held primarily to train docents, but are open to the public. Lectures and lecture series deal with special exhibits. Sunday afternoon chamber music concerts are presented fall, winter, and spring. "Senior Days"—one day every month of lectures, concerts, and other art-related programs—are designed for senior citizens. The children's program includes docent school tours and a "Treasure Box" outreach—boxed objects from other cultures are transported by trained volunteers to area schools. Docent-guided tours are offered Tues.–Sun. at 2 at the Seattle Art

Museum in Volunteer Park; Thurs., Sat. & Sun. at 2 at the Modern Art Pavilion; tours conducted in Spanish, Japanese, Cantonese, and a number of European languages are available by prearrangement. The museum publishes a variety of materials from Christmas cards to nationally recognized reference materials: *Asiatic Art in the Seattle Art Museum, Lewis and Clark's America,* and *Skagit Valley Artists,* for example. The library (9,000 volumes) is open to the public Tues.–Sat. 10–12, 1–5 for research. Books, jewelry, prints, postcards, gift items, and reproductions are sold at the sales desk, and ceramics, fabric designs, and Northwestern crafts, at the Guild shop. Parking is limited. Seattle Art Museum, Volunteer Park: Tues.–Sat. 10–5; Sun. & holidays 12–5; Thurs. evening 7–10. Modern Art Pavilion, Seattle Center: Tues.–Sat. 11–6; Thurs. evening 6–8. Admission $1 for adults, 50¢ for students and senior citizens; free on Thurs. (For main museum in Volunteer Park: From I-5, take exit 168A [Harvard Ave.- Roanoke exit], turn left on Roanoke [over the freeway] and get into the right-hand lane. Turn right on 10th, which goes into Broadway, and follow it to Prospect; turn left and proceed to Volunteer Park. Or take exit 166 [Stewart-Denny exit], get into the left-hand lane, turn left on Denny, and follow it to 14th Ave. Turn left on 14th and proceed to the park entrance.)

**Henry Art Gallery.** University of Washington, 98195 ☐ The Henry Art Gallery was built on the University of Washington campus in 1927, the building and its contents a gift from Horace C. Henry. Born on the other side of the continent, Henry made his fortune, like many displaced eastern entrepreneurs in the late 1800s, in railroading and timber. His home on Capitol Hill filled up with the paintings he acquired from 1893 on, and he soon built a small gallery to accommodate them and to make them available to public viewing. In time, having resolved to give his art collection to the people of Seattle, he chose the university as the repository of his gift: $100,000 for the construction of the building and 151 paintings from the Barbizon school, academic works from the Paris Salon, Hudson River school landscapes—predominantly 19th-century works. The museum's holdings have grown to number about 2,000 items: Works by artists of the Pacific Northwest include 91 drawings and paintings by Morris Graves and 35 drawings and paintings by Mark Tobey; other drawings and prints represent the work of Rouault (58 prints from the "Miserere" suite), Motherwell ("The Madrid Suite"), Rauschenberg ("Booster" and 7 studies for it), Indiana (10 in his "Numbers Suite"), Hogarth, and Piranesi; contemporary Japanese folk pottery comprises an important group of holdings. Exhibitions change about every 4 weeks; the use of cameras without flashes or tripods is permitted during some of them.

The gallery sponsors a variety of lectures, performances, and workshops usually associated with exhibition programs. *The Index of Art in the Pacific Northwest* and *Quarto* are published for the gallery by the university; the *Index* is a series of publications devoted to northwestern art and artists and to works of art in Northwestern public and private collections; *Quarto* is a series of treatises on subjects related to exhibitions. The gallery also publishes exhibition catalogs. A registry of Northwestern artists housed here accounts for all the visual arts in the Pacific Northwest; it serves governmental groups which select art for public places. Underground parking adjacent to the gallery; 50¢ to $1.25 depending on how long your car is there. Mon.–Fri. 10–5; Thurs. evening 7–9; Sat. & Sun. 1–5. Free. (Take the 45th St. exit from I-5, travel east to 15th N.E., turn south to N.E. 41st.)

**TACOMA:    Tacoma Art Museum.** 12th St. & Pacific Ave., 98402 ☐ The Tacoma Art League was established in 1891; almost 75 years later the Tacoma Art Museum was incorporated. Here, at the edge of Puget Sound, there are collections of 20th-century American and European art and a group of Japanese woodblock prints. Far from home, Andrew Wyeth's "Braddock's Coat" hangs here, and there are also works by Graves, Tobey, Motherwell, Glackens, Dubuffet, Stella, and Rauschenberg (one of the "Moon Shot Series"). Changing exhibitions are scheduled regularly. The museum provides all the services of a busy cultural center: lectures, concerts, classes, seminars. Docents give gallery talks. A fine children's gallery has the latest audiovisual equipment. Television and radio programs are prepared here. The library (1,000 volumes) can be used by the public. Catalogs are prepared with most exhibits. Mon.–Sat. 10–4; Sun., holidays 12–5. Free.

**WALLA WALLA:    Olin Gallery.** Whitman College, 345 Boyer Ave., 99362 ☐ The first chartered institution in the state of Washington, Whitman College, is centrally located in downtown Walla Walla. The Olin gallery was established in one of the newer (1969) buildings on this historic campus. It is student oriented with a small permanent collection. Rotating exhibits are linked with school schedules. Cameras are permitted by request. The gallery offers school group tours and provides tape recorders to individual visitors if desired. The student union nearby is open to the public for beverages and light snacks. Parking on campus. Hours are variable. Free.

# WEST VIRGINIA

**CHARLESTON:** **Sunrise Foundation, Inc.** 755 Myrtle Rd., 25314 ☐ The Sunrise Foundation, Inc. is custodian of an art gallery, a children's museum, a planetarium, and a garden center; its headquarters are on 16 acres of gardens and woodlands in one of Charleston's residential neighborhoods. The gallery, housed in a Georgian-style mansion built in 1928 by West Virginia's ninth governor for his son, was founded in 1963. Its holdings survey American art, with particular emphasis on the 19th and 20th centuries. A variety of changing exhibits on the arts of the Americas are scheduled throughout the year; 10 major exhibits are mounted. Permission is needed to photograph the artworks. Classes are offered to young people and adults, and lectures, films, concerts, and other special events are often held here. The foundation's outreach program utilizes the resources of the entire complex. An artist-in-residence program is another of the gallery's educational efforts. Docent-led tours may be scheduled for groups and individuals. The gallery publishes a monthly newsletter and exhibition catalogs. The library is open by special permission. A museum shop offers pottery, jewelry, books, and folk art for sale. Parking on the grounds. Tues.–Sat. 10–5; Sun. 2–5. Free. (Take Dickinson St. to the South Side Bridge over the Kanawha River. Stay on Bridge Rd., which runs into Myrtle Rd. and the entrance of the estate.)

**HUNTINGTON:** **Huntington Galleries.** 2033 McCoy Rd., Park Hills, 25701 ☐ Collis P. Huntington of the Chesapeake & Ohio Railroad started this city in 1871. Its museum, founded in 1947 and opened in 1952, stands on 50 acres of woodland through which serpentines a 2½-mile nature trail. In 1970 the museum doubled in size with an addition, designed by Walter Gropius, that created a complex of library, auditorium, galleries, 2 sculpture courts, and 6 studio workshops (3 in a separate structure). In 1976 a third building was added. Emphasis here is on American art and decorative arts. The Daywood collection, a major part of the galleries' permanent holdings, comprises paintings, prints, and bronzes, and among others, works by Winslow Homer, Andrew Wyeth, Childe Hassam, Burchfield, Hopper, and "the Eight." The Fitzpatrick collection, with which the galleries opened, consists of Georgian silver, Oriental prayer rugs, French and American paintings, prints, and bronzes. The Bagby collection adds English portraits by Reynolds, Romney, Raeburn, and Gainsborough and selected 18th- and early-19th-century pieces of furniture. The Dean collection of arms has over 400 rifles, pistols, powder horns, swords, crossbows, and accessories. Works by Calder, Motherwell, and Rickey are among the large contemporary group. Special exhibits are scheduled regularly. Photographs may be taken of objects in the permanent collection only. Classes and workshops in the fall, spring, and summer offer subjects such as painting, drawing, photography, ceramics, and weaving. Lectures, theatrical performances, and chamber music concerts are regular events. Long- and short-term artist-in-residence programs have been in effect, but not invariably. Guided tours may be arranged 2 weeks in advance. Catalogs are published and sold here, and in the museum shop (Collectors' Corner), consigned goods from regional artists and craftsmen and articles purchased from dealers approved by the Museum Store Association are sold. The library (3,000 volumes) is open to the public. Parking on the grounds. Tues.–Sat. 10–4; Sun. 1–5. Free. (Take 8th St. out of Huntington or the 5th St. exit off I-64 & Miller Rd.)

# WISCONSIN

**BELOIT:    Theodore Lyman Wright Art Center, Beloit College.** 53511 ☐
The Theodore Lyman Wright Art Center was dedicated in 1930 on the campus of what started out as Beloit Seminary—a school with New England biases founded by displaced New Englanders. In the center are housed strong collections of Oriental and contemporary art. There are also prints by Rembrandt, Dürer, Whistler, and others. Exhibitions are changed monthly. Lectures, demonstrations, classes, concerts, and gallery talks are offered. Catalogs accompany exhibits. Mon.–Fri. 9–5, 7–9; Sat. 11–5; Sun. 1–5. Free. (On US 51.)

**GREEN BAY:    Neville Public Museum.** 129 South Jefferson St., 54301 ☐
The Neville Public Museum grew out of an antique exhibit that took place in 1915. Housed in an old Gothic library building, its present collections are those of a general museum covering history, earth sciences, and art. Among the paintings, drawings, prints, and sculpture are works by contemporary and older artists; acquisitions, however, are now generally limited to living Wisconsin artists. Traveling exhibits, local artworks, and the permanent collection are shown in monthly rotation. Photographing by permission only. Workshops designed for children, lectures, gallery talks, demonstrations, hands-on programs, films, and classes fill a busy activities schedule. Guided tours are offered by appointment. Articles relating to the exhibits are for sale. Parking on surrounding streets. Mon.–Sat. 9–5; Sun. 2–5. Free. (On the northeast corner of Jefferson & Doty Sts.)

**MADISON:   Elvehjem Museum of Art.** 800 University Ave., University of Wisconsin, 53706 ☐ The Elvehjem Museum's modern exterior cloaks an interior that is derived directly from Florentine Renaissance concepts: an inner open courtyard at the core surrounded by balconies that open onto it. The museum was built during the incumbency of President Conrad E. Elvehjem, whose studies of campus deficiencies resulted in the gathering together of the scattered University of Wisconsin art collection under one roof. It would also house an art school, auditorium, and art library. A teaching museum as well as a community resource, the general collection here illustrates all periods of art ranging from classical Greece to contemporary America. Included are Greek and Roman coins; Roman marble statues; Syrian mosaics; Dutch and Renaissance paintings ("Adoration of the Shepherds" by Vasari); 17th- and 18th-century French and English paintings (Gainsborough) and furniture; 19th-century French painting and furniture; American painting, sculpture, and furniture from the 18th through the 20th centuries; Soviet Socialist Realist paintings (presented to his alma mater by former Ambassador to Russia Joseph E. Davies); a large print and drawing collection with examples by all major printmakers from Dürer to Whistler and including a complete set of Goya's "Caprichos"; English and Chinese export porcelain; ancient glass; Indian miniatures; and African and pre-Columbian artifacts and sculpture. Twelve to 14 temporary exhibitions are held each year in 2 galleries; they change alternately every 2 to 3 weeks and are designed to bring types of objects that are not in the permanent collection to Madison. The use of cameras must be authorized by the museum staff.

The museum sponsors occasional lectures, seasonal concerts, and weekly performances by student and faculty groups. The education department produces gallery guides, offers conducted tours, and holds art classes for children. General tours are conducted on Sundays at 3; visiting groups can arrange in advance for tours at other times; Spanish-, French-, and German-speaking guides are available. The museum publishes several catalogs each year, a quarterly calendar of events, an annual bulletin, and general brochures. The Kohler Art Library (70,000 volumes), the largest public university art library in North America, is open to the public and for inter-library loan 7 days a week. A museum shop offers gift items, jewelry, art books, catalogs, and postcards for sales. Public parking (Lake Street Ramp) is located one block from the museum. Mon.–Sat. 9–4:45; Sun. 11–4:45. Free.

**Madison Art Center.** 720 East Gorham St., 53703 ☐ In 1968 the Madison Art Association received a bequest of some 1,200 works of art from Professor Rudolph E. Langer (University of Wisconsin). A year later the Madison Art Center, an incorporation of the association and the fundraising Madison Art Foundation, became the occupant of a former elementary-school building on the shore of Lake Mendota (the largest of Madison's four). Where before 1968 had been a small collection of works by local artists acquired from juried shows, graphic arts now predominate: European masters from Dürer to Matisse, over 300 woodblock prints, 200 Mexican prints, and an excellent selection of 20th-century American works. The Langer collection's stars are Hiroshige, Kollwitz, Piranesi, and Rouault. Among the paintings and sculpture are works by Alma-Tadema, Benton, Curry, Dewing, Epstein, Hartley, Inness, Lhote, Troyon, and Vedder. At present, acquisitions focus almost exclusively on contemporary art, the new and innovative works of the midcentury. The center's 7 galleries are rehung about 6 times per year, so that more than 40 events are on the exhibition calendar. One gallery draws its exhibits from the print collection, one is traditionally devoted to photography, and a hallway area displays the major paintings owned by the center. Photographs may be taken of works in the permanent collection; special permission is needed to photograph works on loan.

The center offers classes (2 winter terms and one summer term) for adults and children in painting, drawing, ceramics, textiles, photography, and filmmaking. The educational program also includes small lecture series, print loans to public schools, an Art Cart to visit city playgrounds, an Art Fair on the Square that attracts craftspeople from all over the nation, and bus tours to museums in other cities. Docents conduct groups on gallery tours by appointment. A monthly newsletter and 3 or 4 catalogs are published each year. A sales and rental gallery provides paintings and graphics by area artists, crafted items, imported gifts, cards, and toys for sale. Large parking lot behind the building. Wed., Fri., Sat. 9–5; Tues., Thurs. 9–9; Sun. 1–5. Free. (From the north or east, take East Washington Ave. to Blount St.; turn right and drive 4 blocks to E. Gorham St.; cross Gorham toward the lake, then turn right to the center parking area. From the south or west, take Park St. to Johnson; turn right onto Johnson to Blount, and proceed same as above.)

**MANITOWOC: Rahr-West Museum.** North 8th St. at Park St., 54220 ☐ The influence of Sir Christopher Wren on architecture during the reign of Queen Anne reached all the way to Manitowoc, Wisconsin, in 1891—a place and a time Wren could not have dreamed of. The brick and shingle residence that was donated to Manitowoc by the Rahr family in 1941 for use as a museum was built in 1891 in a style reminiscent of the homes Wren designed. The collections include dolls, Chinese ivory carvings, native American and Wisconsin artifacts, period furniture from the late 19th and early 20th centuries, and mid-20th-century paintings and prints.

Among the paintings are Bouguereau's "The Pouter" and "Downtown Street" by Stuart Davis. Art exhibits change monthly. Cameras are permitted. Some art classes, lectures, and musical programs are sponsored. Guided tours are offered when requested. The library (2,000 volumes) is open to the public. Off-the-street parking for about 30 cars. Tues.–Thurs. 9–4:30; Sat. & Sun. 2–5. Free. (Take US 141 directly into the city onto Washington; continue on Washington, turn left at 8th, and go north until 8th intersects Park.)

**MILWAUKEE:   Charles Allis Art Library.** 1630 East Royall Pl., 53202 ☐ The Charles Allis Art Library is an extension of the Milwaukee Public Library. This 1908 Tudor-style house and its contents were given to Milwaukee by the Allis family in 1945; included were Mr. Allis's library; Oriental pottery and porcelain; Chinese jade; Italian bronzes; Oriental rugs; the fine antique furniture and appointments of an art connoisseur's home; a collection of paintings by 19th-century American (particularly landscapes) and Western European (many of them Barbizon paintings) masters; and etchings and engravings by Rembrandt, Dürer, Whistler, and others. Temporary exhibits are mounted. Guided tours, lectures, concerts, and films are included in the schedule of activities. The library (500 volumes) is available for inter-library loan and for use on the premises. Tues., Thurs.–Sun. 1–5; Wed. 1–5, 7–9:30. Free.

**Marquette University Gallery.** Memorial Library, 53233 ☐ Marquette University established a gallery in 1953 to house its growing collection, in which religious art predominates. Flemish and Italian paintings of the Renaissance and French tapestries (17th to 19th centuries) are highlights, together with an estimable selection of Dürer prints. A Reynolds, a Matisse, and a Dali also hang here. There are special exhibits from time to time. Lectures, concerts, and dramatic programs are held at the gallery, which maintains a library and a photograph collection. Open daily. (Campus is on W. Wisconsin Ave. from 11th to 16th Sts.)

**Milwaukee Art Center.** 750 North Lincoln Memorial Dr., 53202 ☐ Eero Saarinen designed the War Memorial that also houses Milwaukee's Art Center. Completed in 1957, it dominates one of America's most beautiful lakefront drives. The museum had been an entity since 1888, but the added building and the gift of a rambling collection of American and European art moved Milwaukee into a new phase in the development of this facility. The Layton collection (the original collection) consists of late-19th- and early-20th-century American and European paintings. The Bradley collection (the 1950s gift) comprises 800 paintings and pieces of sculpture, contemporary American and European for the most part. Rothko, Stella, and Segal are here, and Kandinsky, O'Keeffe, Picasso,

Hanson's "The Janitor," a Dubuffet, and a Wesselmann—indeed, the whole galaxy of 20th-century painters and sculptors. There are two biennials—Wisconsin Painters and Sculptors, and Wisconsin Designer-Craftsmen—and many special exhibitions.

Classes, tours, concerts, films, lectures are all regular art center occurrences. There is a docent program, a Children's Art Lending Library, and an active support group program. The library (15,000 volumes) is available for inter-library loan and for use on the premises. Reproductions, books, cards, folk art, and antiques are for sale. Catalogs are prepared to accompany special exhibits. Tues.–Sun. 10–5. Admission $1 for adults, 50¢ for students and senior citizens; free for children under 12. Free the first open hour of each day.

**University of Wisconsin-Milwaukee, Fine Arts Galleries.** School of Fine Arts, 3200 Downer Ave., 53201 ☐ The School of Fine Arts at the University of Wisconsin in Milwaukee established a gallery in 1967. In it are housed a large graphics collection, 20th-century drawings, Oriental woodcuts, photographs, and current art. Special exhibitions are scheduled regularly. Lectures sponsored by the gallery are opened to the public, as are gallery talks. Student works are for sale. Mon.–Fri. 10:30–4; Wed. 5:30–9:30; Sat. 10–3. Free.

**OSHKOSH: Paine Art Center and Arboretum.** 1410 Algoma Blvd., 54902 ☐ Nathan Paine started to build a home for himself in the 1920s, but it was destined not to be finished in his lifetime. Work stopped during the Depression, and in 1947, after her husband's death, Jessica Paine directed the completion of the building. The stately Tudor manor house that resulted was opened in 1948 as Paine Art Center. Period rooms show furnishings from Nathan Paine's home; other period rooms show models of life in Gothic, Tudor, Elizabethan, Jacobean, and Victorian times. The permanent collection of fine art can be seen in a Main Gallery, where paintings by Blakelock, Corot, Daubigny, Diaz, Homer, Inness, Millet, Rousseau, Stuart, Wright, and many others are on display. Persian rugs, icons, and Chinese decorative arts enrich the sum of the museum's holdings. Highlights among the paintings are "The Watering Place" by Corot; "Morning on the Oise" by Daubigny; "Off the Coast of Cornwall" by Inness; a Millet ("Le Delaissée"); a Rousseau ("The Cow Pond"); and one of Stuart's 3 portraits of George Washington. An arboretum and flower gardens cover 15 acres of land that display native and exotic trees, shrubs, herbaceous plants, and an 18th-century English garden. About 7 loan exhibitions, each lasting 4 to 6 weeks, supplement the permanent collection. Non-flash, hand-held cameras are permitted. Art and gardening classes are held throughout the year. The center also sponsors lectures and educational and music programs. Docents are trained to lead tours through both art center and arboretum; special tours are conducted for students and young children (arrangements for these must be made in advance). For individual visitors, guides are stationed in each room. A handbook describing the contents of the museum and arboretum is available for purchase, as are other books, postcards, and gifts. The library (1,300 volumes) is open to the public with permission from the director. Parking on the streets around the center. Tues., Thurs., Sat. & Sun. 1–4:30 in winter; Tues.–Sun. 1–4:30 in summer. Admission $1, children free. (Turn east off US 41 onto SR 21 and proceed 1 mile to junction with SR 110.)

**RACINE:    Charles A. Wustum Museum of Fine Arts.** 2519 Northwestern Ave., 53404 ☐ Charles A. Wustum was descended from early settlers of this heavily Danish city that intrudes itself into Lake Michigan. He left his 12-acre estate and buildings to Racine, his wife Jennie financed it with an endowment to the city, and in 1941 the Charles A. Wustum Museum of Fine Arts became a reality. The collection includes a large number of WPA artworks, but the museum shows particular interest in the watercolors of contemporary Wisconsin artists. The changing exhibits often feature regional artists, as does an annual juried exhibition, Watercolor Wisconsin, which also tours the state. Cameras are permitted. Classes are available for adults and children. Lectures, concerts, closed circuit television programs, films, workshops, and demonstrations are all programmed at irregular intervals during the year. A short audiovisual orientation program has been prepared for visiting groups. The museum's shop offers art, jewelry, cards, and handcrafted items for sale. Parking for about 100 cars on the grounds. Mon.–Thurs. 11–9; Fri.–Sun. 1–5. Free.

**WEST BEND:    West Bend Gallery of Fine Arts.** 300 South 6th Ave. Mailing address: P.O. Box 426, 53095 ☐ The West Bend Gallery of Fine Arts was founded by the family of local industrialist A. J. Pick in 1961. A large number of paintings by Carl von Marr, Mrs. Pick's uncle, adorned the walls of the Pick home and the homes of other of Marr's many relatives in West Bend. Brought together, they formed an interesting retrospective collection of his work—60 paintings and 30 drawings done between 1870 and 1936. Temporary exhibits change each month. Cameras are permitted. Classes in pottery and painting are held for adults in the winter months; children's classes are offered in the summer. Travelogues are held once a month. The library is open by special permission only. Parking on the grounds. Wed.–Sun. 1–4:30. Free. (2 blocks west of Main St. & US 45.)

# WYOMING

**BIG HORN:   Bradford Brinton Memorial Ranch.** Mailing address: Box 23, 82833 ☐ An Illinois industrialist, Bradford Brinton, built his summer home in the foothills of the Big Horn Mountains between the towns of Sheridan and Big Horn in the late 19th century. His life here was typical of a wealthy rancher's in that era. In 1966, 30 years after his death, a gallery was added to the ranch to house some 600 oils, watercolors, and sketches, most of which represent the creative product of the West at the end of the 19th and beginning of the 20th centuries. Works by Russell, Remington, Borein, Gollings, Kleiber, Benson, Audubon, De Yong, Reiss, Tenney, Johnson, and James hang here. The gallery's exhibits, taken from the collection, change seasonally. Cameras are not permitted. Lectures are offered during the summer and tours whenever requested. The gallery produces monographs of some of the artists whose work it owns, guide books, postcards, reproductions, and slides, all of which are available at its shop. Parking on the grounds. May 15–Labor Day, daily 9–5. Free. (On I-90, watch for Brinton Memorial signs at Sheridan Interchange [coming from the north] and Meade Creek Interchange [coming from the south]. Exit onto US 87, proceed to SR 335, and go southwest through and past Big Horn to the ranch.)

**CASPER:   Nicolaysen Art Museum.** 104 Rancho Rd., 82601 ☐ The Central Wyoming Museum of Art changed its name to Nicolaysen Art Museum in 1979. Loan exhibitions are shown here while the museum is starting a permanent collection. Daily. 11:30–4:30. Free.

**CHEYENNE:   Wyoming State Museum.** Barrett Building, Central Ave. & 23rd St., 82002 ☐ The Wyoming State Museum is primarily a historical museum. A small art gallery features Wyoming artists and artists whose paintings depict Western subjects. Mon.–Sat. 9–5. Free.

**CODY:   Buffalo Bill Historical Center.** Sheridan Ave. & 8th St. Mailing address: P.O. Box 1020, 82414 ☐ The Buffalo Bill Historical Center consists of the Buffalo Bill Museum (dedicated in 1927) which displays a vast collection of personal and historical memorabilia of Col. William F. (Buffalo Bill) Cody; the Whitney Gallery of Western Art (begun in 1959), with paintings and sculptures that document the colorful history and stark beauty of the Old West; the Plains Indian Museum (opened in 1969), reflecting the traditions and life patterns of the Plains tribes; and the Winchester Museum (1976), containing a comprehensive collection of over 5,000 projectile arms outlining the development of firearms in America. Looking out to the majestic mountain vista that appears in the paintings it houses, the Whitney Gallery of Western Art is perhaps singular in the country. Here are gathered the reminders of a faded legend, the Old West as seen through the eyes and imaginations of American artists whose sense of adventure and beauty drove them west and held them in thrall. The collection was begun by Buffalo Bill Cody himself and was displayed in his Irma Hotel until his death. In 1942 the 31 paintings that were Cody's (among them was Rosa Bonheur's equestrian portrait of Cody), were given to the Buffalo Bill Museum. The Whitney Gallery opened with many more paintings and sculptures representing a diverse group of artists—some trained in the academies of Europe, some self-taught; some fine artists, some illustrators. Among them are the artist-explorers: George Catlin ("Attack of the Grizzly"), a Pennsylvania lawyer who turned artist and painted nearly 40 Indian tribes; Karl Bodmer, a Swiss artist who traveled the upper Missouri with scientist-explorer Prince Maximilian in 1833 and painted the Indians they encountered on their 13-month expedition; Alfred Jacob Miller ("Louis—Mountain Trapper," "The Lost Greenhorn"), who painted mountain men, traders, and Indians on the Green River south of Jackson Hole in 1837 on an expedition with Scottish laird Captain William Drummond Stewart; and John Mix Stanley ("Last of their Race"), an itinerant portrait painter whose Victorian romanticism portrayed the Indian as "noble savage." The landscape painters used the mountains and the plains as their studio: Albert Bierstadt's canvases depict electrifying, romanticized landscapes ("Yellowstone Falls," "Wind River, Wyoming," "Indian Encampment in the Rocky Mountains," "Sunset on Peak"); Thomas Moran's show a Turner-influenced vision of the Western scene ("Gateway to Yellowstone"). Indian conflicts absorbed Charles Schreyvogel ("How Kola") and Edgar S. Paxson ("Custer's Last Stand"), while the move West was immortalized by Harvey Dunn ("The Scout"). Frederic Remington and Charles Russell—the paradigms of Western artists—are here in numbers. It is their vision of the West that is etched in the minds of succeeding generations of Americans, even more perhaps than the picture evoked by the real artifacts that are displayed in the buildings nearby. Here lovers of Western art can see Russell's "Roundup on the Musselshell," "The Bronc Twister," "Bringing Home the Spoils," "Attack on the Wagon Train," and "Single Handed," and Remington's "The Mountain Man," "Prospecting for Cattle Range," and "The Night Herder." Also on display are the early-20th-century painters who, even after the frontier had reached the coast and the old traditions had surrendered to modern ways, were still caught by the romance and excitement of the West: Edward Boren, W. Herbert Dunton, Frank Tenney Johnson, W. H. D. Koerner, N. C. Wyeth, Carl Rungius, and Maynard Dixon are some of them. Cameras are permitted.

Classes, seminars, and lectures are all offered by the center in fulfillment of its educational goals. Recorded tours are available, as are docents, on 24-hour notice. Many books (published by the center), slides, reproductions, and prints are sold in Keeley's Museum Shop. The library (2,000 volumes) is open to the public. Parking near the center. Daily 7 a.m.–10 p.m. (June, July, Aug.); daily 8–5 (May, Sept.); Tues., Thurs., Sat., Sun. 1–5 (Oct., Nov., Mar., Apr.). Admission $2 for adults, $1 for children 6–15.

**LARAMIE:  University of Wyoming Art Museum.** Fine Arts Center, 82071 ☐ Laramie could have been the setting of a Hollywood western, complete with the spur-and-saddle variety of machismo, the railroad men and the hunters, the saloons and brawls, and vigilante law. But the desperado town progressed into the 20th century with great aplomb. The Union Pacific pushed farther west; yesterday's saloons were replaced by today's businesses and schools; drunks and brawls were supplanted by the quiet resolve of a residential community enlarged by the presence of a state university. A collection of paintings would have seemed out of place here in the early days, but not today. The Fine Arts Center that houses the University of Wyoming Art Museum was opened in 1972. The museum focuses on 19th- and 20th-century American and European paintings and prints. Outstanding among them are Benton's "Lewis and Clark at Eagle Creek," Moran's "Grand Canal, Venice," Jules Dupré's "Summer Landscape," Ernest Lawson's "Autumn on the River," Kuniyoshi's "Woman with Hat," "Victorian House in Winter" by Burchfield, "Mother and Child" and "Whiskey Bill-John Noble" by George Luks, Avery's "Girl with Hat," Loiseau's "Rue à Pont-Aven," and Alfred Stevens's "Femme aux Fleurs." Exhibits are changed approximately every 2 weeks. Cameras are permitted only in the permanent collection area. The museum sponsors lectures in conjunction with some exhibits. Many other activities derive from the close cooperation between the museum and the departments of the university. Guided tours can be arranged. The museum has published several books, among them *One Hundred Years of Artist Activity in Wyoming, 1837-1937,* which are available at a sales desk. Visitor parking directly in front of the center or at other campus locations. Daily except Sat. 2–5. Free. (Take the Grand Ave. exit off I-80; it leads to the university complex on 15th St. Turn north on 15th and follow a U-shaped loop [Fraternity-Sorority Row] at the end of which is the Fine Arts Center. The museum is on the lower level.)

**ROCK SPRINGS:    Sweetwater Community Fine Arts Center.** 400 C St., 82901 ☐ In an old Mormon church remodeled for the purpose, in the coal mining area of Rock Springs, is an art collection acquired by the generations of students of Rock Springs High School, beginning in 1939. The collection—255 works including a Grandma Moses, a Norman Rockwell, a Raphael Soyer, a Rufino Tamayo, a Peter Hurd, and an Alexander Calder—is perhaps one of the grandest of high-school collections. A regular monthly schedule of exhibits includes a National Art Show and Competition and photography shows. Cameras are permitted. Art classes and workshops are held in the host fine arts center, as are lectures and concerts. Parking on the museum grounds. Mon.-Fri. 1–5, 6:30–8:30; Sat. 2–5 (winter), 10–12, 2–5 (summer). (Take the Rock Springs Elk St. exit off I-80 and proceed to the center of town.)

# CANADA

# ALBERTA

**CALGARY:   Alberta College of Art Gallery.** Southern Alberta Institute of Technology, 1301 16th Ave. N.W., T2M 0L4 ☐ Southern Alberta Institute of Technology is on the North Slope of the Bow River looking out over downtown Calgary and the Rocky Mountains. Its art gallery dates back to 1959, when it was opened as a resource for Alberta College of Art students. Since 1973 the gallery's "Class A" facilities have been open to the public in a new building. The permanent collection is composed of works by graduates of the college and by teachers and is displayed in the various departments of the institute. The gallery's forte is its temporary exhibition program, which presents bimonthly showings of contemporary art, graphic design, and crafts. Many of these changing exhibits are arranged by the curatorial office; some are on loan. Photographing is allowed with permission from the curator's office. The college of art offers noncredit evening courses, and the gallery itself presents artists and lectures to the public. Group visits from schools or communities are encouraged. Free catalogs are available for about half of the temporary exhibits. The library (4,000 volumes) is open to the public for research. The college cafeteria is open during gallery hours. Parking adjacent to the building. Tues.–Fri. 12–8; Sat. & Sun. 2–5. Free. (From downtown Calgary, proceed west along 6th Ave. S.W. to the 14th St. ramp [approximately 10 blocks]. Follow 14th St. N.W. another 10 blocks to the institute.)

**Glenbow Museum.** 9th Ave. & 1st St. S.E., T2G 0P3 ☐ The Glenbow Museum, located in the Glenbow-Alberta Institute complex, began in 1954 when Eric L. Harvie, Q.C., formed the Glenbow Foundation to collect and display the art and artifacts of western Canada. The Glenbow-Alberta Institute was incorporated in 1966, the legislature of Alberta becoming a partner of the Glenbow Foundation to maintain the now international collection. Historical exhibits in this sedately modern structure tell the history of western Canada from the "Indian Before the White Man" to the "20th Century to the Discovery of Oil"; there are also exhibits of Oriental arms and armor, antique guns, and rare minerals. On the second floor, devoted to art, is a permanent collection of paintings, sculpture, prints, and drawings that includes works from all over the world as well as those of Canadian and regional artists, both past and present. Art exhibitions change frequently. School programs, special tours, lectures, films, and special events demonstrate the museum's strong educational resolve. Tours for groups can be arranged in advance. The library (25,000 volumes) on western Canadiana is available for inter-library loan and to the public for research on the premises. A museum shop offers books, gifts, catalogs, Glenbow publications, and other materials for sale. Daily 11–9. Admission $1 for adults, 50¢ for students, senior citizens; free for children under 12; $2.50 for a family.

**EDMONTON:  Edmonton Art Gallery.** 2 Sir Winston Churchill Square, T5J 2C1 ☐ The Edmonton Art Gallery's holdings—Canadian paintings, sculpture, and graphics, and contemporary art—are rotated in some 40 exhibitions a year. Guided tours, lectures, films, gallery talks, concerts, and dance programs, and art classes for adults and children are all supported by the gallery. A library (1,500 volumes) is open for research, and books are available for inter-library loan. Books, handcrafts, ceramics, prints, and reproductions are on sale. Catalogs accompany the changing exhibitions; the Edmonton Art Gallery *Bulletin* is published monthly. Mon., Tues., Fri., Sat. 10–5; Wed., Thurs. 10–10; Sun. 1–5. Free.

# BRITISH COLUMBIA

**BURNABY:  Burnaby Art Gallery.** 6344 Gilpin St., V5G 2J3 ☐ In Burnaby, one of Vancouver's suburbs, the Art Society founded in 1958 became, within 10 years, the Burnaby Art Gallery Association and proud owner of a 1909 "West Coast Tudor" building in which to open up shop. It was renovated by the city as part of the 1967 centennial project in what became known as Century Park, which the city also endowed with rhododendron gardens, a lake, and several arts-related buildings. The gallery houses primarily contemporary Canadian prints. Exhibitions of contemporary British Columbian art, historical and international paintings, prints, drawings, sculpture, and crafts change continually; generally they last 5 weeks. Cameras are permitted. The gallery sponsors lectures, tours, and workshops in the various mediums; they are conducted in the gallery itself on Sunday afternoons, in outlying schools, or at community gatherings. In fact, the extension department services communities throughout the province. Educational kits on a variety of local subjects (Salish weaving, for example) are circulated in the lower mainland elementary schools. A gallery shop offers local crafts, pottery, glass, weaving, bookbinding, prints, reproductions, and cards for sale. Parking nearby. Mon.–Fri. 10–5;

Wed. 10–9; weekends & holidays 12–5. (Take Hwy. 1 or Canada Way to Sperling Ave. S.; turn onto Gilpin at the Municipal Hall complex.)

**VANCOUVER:   Vancouver Art Gallery.** 1145 W. Georgia St., V6E 3H2 ☐ The Vancouver Art Gallery was established in 1931 on a site provided by the city. After 20 years it was enlarged to its present size. With annual grants from the city and other sources of income, the gallery has grown to include European paintings (particularly English) spanning the centuries from the 17th to the 20th; a fine collection of Canadian painting, sculpture, and graphics; an Emily Carr collection; and a group of contemporary American paintings and graphics. There are several special exhibitions during the year. The gallery has popular noon hour programs of music, poetry, or drama, evening lectures, and daily tours and films. A broad extension program sponsors activities in Vancouver and in the rest of the province. The library (6,500 books, periodicals, slides, catalogs, and reproductions) is available for reference use. Catalogs and a monthly newsletter, *Vanguard,* are published here. Mon., Tues., Thurs., Sat., holidays 10–5; Wed., Fri. 10–10; Sun. 2–5. Free.

**VICTORIA:   Art Gallery of Greater Victoria.** 1040 Moss St., V8V 4P1 ☐ Since 1945 the Art Gallery of Greater Victoria, housed in a mansion built in 1895 with later, modern wings, has been impressive. In addition to its historic home, interesting in its own right, its holdings are diverse and unusual in British Columbia: Oriental, European, Canadian, American, and primitive art can all be found here. The contemporary section contains art by primarily American, Canadian, and European artists; the 16th to the 19th centuries are covered in European and decorative arts; and the Oriental section encompasses art from Japan (ancient and modern), China, Tibet, India, and Persia. Exhibits change every 2 or 3 weeks. Special activities include lectures, films, concerts, dance and drama programs, and guided tours. Classes and a docent program are among the educational offerings. The library (3,000 volumes) is open by special request. A gallery shop sells crafts, books, and reproductions. Tues., Wed., Fri., Sat. 10–5; Thurs. 10–5, 7:30–9:30; Sun. 2–5. Admission 50¢ for adults, free for students and children.

**Maltwood Art Museum and Gallery.** University of Victoria. University Centre. Mailing address: P.O. Box 1700, V8W 2Y2 ☐ The Maltwood Art Museum and Gallery is located in University Centre, the University of Victoria's main performing arts and public service facility. Four major exhibition facilities—a formal exhibition gallery, a permanent collections gallery, an interior temporary sculpture court, and an exterior permanent sculpture court—contain the Maltwood collection (left in 1964 by English sculptress Katherine Emma Maltwood) and the University of Victoria art collection (begun in 1953 for the practical purpose of adorning the buildings and exteriors of the campus). Oriental ceramics, costumes, rugs, 17th-century English furniture, and Canadian paintings are included in the Maltwood collection. And in the university collection are over 350 paintings and sculptures by contemporary western Canadian artists. There are approximately 15 formal exhibitions per year—a mix of national and international traveling exhibits, exhibits of student and faculty art, and exhibits generated from the university's own holdings. The museum trains advanced students in exhibition design and preparation. Traveling exhibits are organized here and circulated; the museum makes its collections available on loan for research or exhibition. Catalogs are published with most exhibitions, and elaborative faculty lectures are scheduled in conjunction with exhibitions. Gallery talks, tours, and dramatic programs are also held. A library (500 volumes) is available for researchers, and there is a book shop. Several books are published here. Mon.–Fri. 10–4. Free. (University Centre is located just inside the Ring Road adjacent to the Sports and Aquatic Centre, the Campus Retail Services Bldg., and the Student Union Bldg. and Library.)

# MANITOBA

**WINNIPEG:   Gallery III, University of Manitoba.** School of Art, R3T 2N2 ☐ Gallery III was established in 1965 as a facility of the University of Manitoba's School of Art, and it doubles as a facility for the public at large. The collection focuses on contemporary Canadian and American painting, sculpture, and prints. Exhibits are brought here from many of the larger institutions in Canada and the United States; there are also annual exhibits of works by students of the School of Art. Workshops, discussions, gallery talks, and lectures are offered regularly. Catalogs accompany exhibits. May 1–Sept. 1: Mon.–Fri. 8:30–4:30. Sept. 16–Apr. 30: Mon., Thurs., Fri. 9–5; Tues., Wed. 9–5, 6–9; Sat. 9–12. Free. (Campus is in South Winnipeg, off Pembina Hwy.)

**Winnipeg Art Gallery.** 300 Memorial Blvd., R3C 1V1 ☐ The oldest civic art gallery in Canada, the Winnipeg Art Gallery was founded in 1912 by the Western Art Association of Winnipeg. It was moved from here to there until the 1950s, when it was lodged in the Civic Auditorium where a systematic policy of acquisitions was developed and carried out for 20 years. In 1971 a geometric, clean-lined 4-story triangular building faced in

Manitoba limestone opened in the heart of the city. The Winnipeg Art Gallery, having reached the age of 59, was moving into its own permanent home to grow old and distinguished. Here, in 9 major galleries and a roof sculpture garden, is housed Canadian art; Inuit (Eskimo) art consisting of over 5,000 objects and said to be one of the largest collections of its kind in the world; a collection, left to the gallery by Lord and Lady Gort, of Gothic and Renaissance German panel painting; 16th-century Brussels tapestries; 15th-20th-century prints and drawings; and modern European art. Among the important works are Cranach the Elder's "Portrait of a Lady," Canadian Lawren S. Harris's "Clouds, Lake Superior," a sculpture by Canadian Douglas Bentham, and "Reclining Figure No. 2" in bronze by Henry Moore. The permanent collection is rotated in exhibitions, some of which are long-term and some not; exhibits drawn from other public and private collections and traveling exhibits complete a full schedule. Cameras are not permitted.

Classes, lectures, concerts, and theater programs fulfill the gallery's aim of developing a well-rounded artistic environment in Winnipeg. Courses for college credit are offered in conjunction with the University of Winnipeg. The gallery has a senior citizens' program (lectures, recitals, tours, films), and a children's program brings art classes into the city parks in the summertime. Guided tours are available for specific exhibitions; group tours of the building can be booked in advance. The gallery offers curatorial, education, and administration internships. The number of catalogs published annually varies; a calendar of events is published monthly. The library (13,500 volumes) is open to the public. The gallery shop, run by volunteers, offers books, jewelry, prints, postcards, ceramics, glassware, and original Eskimo sculpture. Gallery Restaurant (liquor served) and cafeteria (wine and beer) on premises; paid public parking across the street. Tues.–Sat. 11–5; Sun. 12–5. Free; donations are welcome. (Trans-Canada Hwy. 1 to Rt. 62; go south ½ block to Memorial Blvd. & Portage Ave.)

# NEW BRUNSWICK

**FREDERICTON: Beaverbrook Art Gallery.** 703 Queen St. Mailing address: P.O. Box 605, E3B 5A6 ☐ An endowment fund and the Beaverbrook Canadian Foundation support the Beaverbrook Art Gallery, which was established in 1959 across from the Legislative Assembly building on Queen Street. English and Canadian paintings, English porcelain, graphics, and sculpture are on display here. Some highlights: works by Sir

Joshua Reynolds, Gainsborough, Graham Sutherland, Cornelius Krieghoff, watercolors by Sir Winston Churchill, and Dali's "Santiago el
Grande." The gallery schedules gallery-sponsored and traveling exhibits
regularly. An art education program includes lectures, tours, films, gallery
talks, and a school loan service. An extension program encompasses the
entire province. Catalogs are produced with special exhibitions and are for
sale at the gallery shop, which also sells reproductions and cards. Summer:
Sun., Mon. 2–9; Tues.–Sat. 10–9. Winter: Sun., Mon. 12–5; Tues.–Sat. 10–
5. Admission 25¢ for adults, free for children, students, tour groups.

**MONCTON: Galerie d'Art, Université de Moncton.** Edifice Champlain,
E1A 3E9 □ In 1965 the Université de Moncton Galerie d'Art opened with
a collection of Canadian paintings, prints, and drawings. There is a permanent exhibit as well as temporary (traveling) installations. The gallery
arranges guided tours, lectures, films, and gallery talks. Sept.–June: Mon.–
Wed. 1:30–4:30, 7–9; Sat., Sun. 2–4. July & Aug.: Mon.–Fri. 2–4. Free.

**SAINT JOHN: New Brunswick Museum.** 277 Douglas Ave., E2K 1E5
□ The New Brunswick Museum can trace its beginnings back to 1842—it
is the oldest public museum in Canada. It was not until 1934, however,
that the doors to the present Greek Revival building overlooking the St.
John River were opened. Originally planned as a natural science and
history museum focusing on the province of New Brunswick and sec-
ondarily on Canada in general, the museum's devotion to the fine arts was
almost an afterthought, initiated to encourage and exhibit local talent in
the arts and crafts and to display examples of the applied arts. The
painting collection here consists of work by provincial artists. There is also
a fine furniture collection. Traveling exhibits pass through the New
Brunswick Museum. Educational programs are offered to school classes;
there are also art classes and a university-level course to students of the
University of New Brunswick. Guided tours are available to school groups
that book in advance. A large variety of publications are produced by
museum staff and sold in the museum shop. A library (28,600 volumes) is
open to the public. Parking nearby. Sept.–May 2–5; summer 10–9. Admission $1 for adults, free for children under 6, students with ID, senior
citizens. (Exit from highways at Reversing Falls and turn onto Douglas
Ave. Or follow Main St. to Douglas Ave. and turn left.)

# NEWFOUNDLAND

**ST. JOHN'S:** **Art Gallery, Memorial University of Newfoundland.** Arts and Culture Centre, Prince Philip Dr., A1C 5S7 □ Several superlatives speak for St. John's: it is one of the oldest cities in North America; it is the closest city on the North American continent to Europe; it is home for the oldest organized sport event in North America—its famous annual regatta; it is the largest port in the province which it governs. And it is host to the only public art gallery in the province. The gallery was founded in 1962—more than 400 years after the city's birth in the 1500s—as one of the elements of the Memorial University of Newfoundland. By 1967 it had moved into one section of the newly constructed, multilevel Provincial Arts and Culture Centre, which had space for two theaters, a children's and an adults' library, and a provincial crafts school. The collection concentrates on the artwork (particularly on paper) of Canada from 1960 on. Approximately 850 items include the compete graphics of Christopher Pratt and some of his paintings. Exhibits change monthly in 3 galleries; some are organized by the gallery itself, others are on loan from other galleries. Much of the permanent collection is dispersed through the university buildings. Cameras are not permitted. There is an annex gallery in the downtown area of St. John's where small shows, new artists, and experimental work are exhibited. In addition, the gallery supplies exhibits to centers across the province, some schools, and occasionally museums. Through the extension section of the center, the gallery provides art courses and workshops to outlying communities. A lecture series on art history, talks by artists, concerts, films, poetry readings, all figure in the active schedule of events. Guided tours can be booked in advance. Small catalogs are produced for gallery-originated shows. A small library of catalogs, magazines, and some books is open by permission. Prints and postcards are sold. There is a snack bar and restaurant in the center. Parking nearby. Tues.–Sun. 12–10. Free. (The Arts and Culture Centre is at the corner of Prince Philip Dr. & Allandale Ave. in the east end of the city.)

# NOVA SCOTIA

**HALIFAX: Centennial Art Gallery.** Halifax Citadel National Historic Park. Mailing address: P.O. Box 2262, B3J 3C8 ☐ A star-shaped stone citadel guards the harbor from Citadel Hill in the first city in Canada settled by the British (Halifax was founded by Edward Cornwallis in 1749 as a British depot). Construction of the citadel was begun in 1828 on the site of three former forts and was completed 30 years later. Today it houses a military museum, part of the Nova Scotia Museum collection, and the Centennial Art Gallery (in the powder magazine). There are paintings, prints, and sculptures here, almost 200 objects in all. Exhibitions change approximately every month. Lectures, gallery talks, art classes for adults and children, and tours are among the activities sponsored by the gallery. A monthly catalog is published. Winter: Mon.–Sat. 10–5; Sun. 12–5; summer: Mon.–Sat. 9–7:30; Sun. 12–7:30. Free.

# ONTARIO

**HAMILTON: Art Gallery of Hamilton.** 123 King St. West, L8P 4S8 ☐ In 1912 the family of artist Blair Bruce donated a collection of 30 paintings to be housed in a new temporary gallery on the second and third floors of the library in this sleepy industrial city. Sixty-five years later the city had tripled in size, local industry had contributed to an active economy, and the 30-piece art collection had moved from the library to its own building, where it had grown to substantial proportions. In 1977 it was moved once again into the modern brick and concrete buttressed building that will be its permanent home, one of the elements of the Civil Centre urban renewal development in Hamilton. The collection today is one of the most important in Canada. Among approximately 4,000 objects, the group of Canadian paintings is outstanding throughout the dominion; the collection of British paintings, prints, and sculpture covering the first 60 years of this century is one of three that are preeminent in the country; the collection of American paintings and prints from the same period is unique in Canada. The Group of Seven are represented here, as are the Ashcan school and French Impressionists. Monet and Sisley, Thomson and

**375**

Krieghoff and A. Y. Jackson—these names and many more are on the roster of distinguished artists. Approximately 30 exhibitions are mounted each year; about half are initiated and produced by the gallery itself, while others are organized and sent here by other galleries and museums. Only authorized cameras are permitted.

In the heart of Hamilton, the center's new building is a beehive of activity. Art classes and workshops are held regularly, as are lectures, concerts, films, and tours. A docent training program supplies guides for tours, which must be prearranged; cassette tapes are available for some exhibits. Slide packages to accompany school curricula and extension exhibits are prepared and sent into outlying communities. Catalogs, brochures, and bulletins are published. The library is open to the public. A gallery shop offers books, jewelry, prints, postcards, pottery, stained glass, and reproductions for sale. An art rental gallery also offers Canadian paintings and drawings for sale. The gallery has a lounge and a bar; food and drink facilities are restricted to Wed., Sat., Sun.; the bar operates only during openings. Tues.–Sat. 10–5; Thurs. 7–9; Sun. 1–5. Free. (Take Hwy. 403 to Main St. East, then to McNab St.)

**KINGSTON:    Agnes Etherington Art Centre.** Queen's University, K7L 3N6 ☐ Kingston looks out over Lake Ontario, near the place where the waters of the lake meet the St. Lawrence River and combining, splash up against the shores of the Thousand Islands. Agnes Etherington gave her house near the lake to Queen's University in 1957 to be used as an art gallery for both the university and the city. Today it is the only public art museum in Kingston. Two additions, one in 1962 and another in 1975, and some structural alterations in 1978, have changed not only the look of this Georgian-style house but also the capabilities and efficiency of it. The collection emphasizes Canadian painting and sculpture from the 19th and 20th centuries; there is a large number of graphics from earlier European schools and a growing collection of European paintings, particularly 17th-century Dutch. Some highlights include works by the Group of Seven (Lismer, J. E. H. Macdonald, Tom Thomson, for example); many Canadian Abstract Expressionists; and a large group by 19th-century watercolorist Daniel Fowler. From Europe are works by Flinck, Lievens, and Allegrain, among many others. There is also a small collection of 18th-century British domestic silver. About 24 exhibitions are scheduled each year, some historical, some contemporary, some Canadian, and some international; many are prepared by the staff. Permission is required for photographing; flashes are not permitted.

Art classes are held for adults and children, and lectures relating to exhibition themes and special public lectures on general art topics are offered. Recitals are scheduled about twice a year. Special 2- or 3-day seminars are held on various subjects of interest to the public. Docent guided tours are available for school groups and for adult groups on request. Grants emanating from the Ontario Arts Council are administered by the center; selection is made by a committee of local artists. The center publishes many books and catalogs, all of which are sold here. The library (4,000 volumes) is open to the public on request. Underground parking garage across the road; weekends and evenings, the main university parking lot adjacent to the art center is open and free. Tues.–Fri. 10–5; Sat., Sun. 1–5; Tues., Thurs. 7–9. Free. (At the corner of University Ave. & Queen's Crescent. It can be reached from King St. [west from City Hall], Barrie St., or Stewart St. [by the hospital]; the entrance to the parking garage is near the corner of Stewart St. & University Ave. Or from Union St., go south on University.)

**KITCHENER:  Kitchener-Waterloo Art Gallery.** 43 Benton St., N2G 3H1 ☐ The Kitchener-Waterloo Art Gallery was established in 1956 with a small collection of predominantly contemporary Canadian artworks. Exhibitions change monthly. Although the gallery is in Kitchener, it serves Waterloo as well by means of an extension program: Traveling exhibits are circulated and individual artworks are loaned. Lectures, concerts, and classes for adults and children take place in Kitchener. A *Gallery Bulletin* and occasional catalogs are published. Tues.–Fri. 10–5, 7–9; Sat. 10–5; Sun. 1–5. Free.

**KLEINBURG:  McMichael Canadian Collection.** L0J 1C0 ☐ Twenty minutes northwest of Toronto is the village of Kleinburg, where, among the old homes and parklike surroundings, the McMichael Canadian Collection is situated in what was once the private home of Robert and Signe McMichael. The McMichael home was built in 1954 (additions have been made since 1965 when they gave it to the province of Ontario) of huge ancient logs and fieldstone. Picture windows throughout the 32 rooms bring the panorama of the Humber River valley into competition with the canvases that show artists' versions of the Canadian scene. The collection, begun by the McMichaels and continued by private donations, focuses on Canadian painting between 1890 and 1935; it is particularly noted for the fine selection of works by the Group of Seven and Tom Thomson. In addition, it has the first permanent collection in Canada of the art of the Woodland Indians. There is also an excellent group of Inuit prints and sculpture, and art of the northwest coast Indians. Among the Group of Seven works are "Summer Shore," "Georgian Bay," and "Woodland Waterfall" by Tom Thomson; A. Y. Jackson's "First Snow Algoma" and a sketch of "Red Maple"; Lawren Harris's "Pic Island"; and L. L. Fitzgerald's "The Little Plant." Also to be seen are Norval Morrisseau's "Artist's Wife and Daughter," Charles Edenshaw's carvings, and magnificent Indian masks, carvings, and prints. One gallery is devoted to 3-month special exhibitions of contemporary paintings and sculpture. Cameras are permitted.

The education department provides study sessions for students from kindergarten through university in the areas of Canadian art and studies. Concerts are held on Sunday afternoons. Staff members deliver lectures to outside groups on request. An extension program provides exhibits to communities and schools. Guided tours are available in several languages; they must be booked in advance. *The McMichael Canadian Collection* and *Group of 7 and Tom Thomson* are books published by the museum on sale at the shop, which also offers many Canadian crafted items. The library is open to the public by special permission. A restaurant and a snack bar are in the house; the restaurant is available for convention groups by appointment. Parking on the museum grounds. Tues.–Sun. 12–5:30. Free. School tours are conducted, by appointment, Sept.–June, 9–5. (Take Hwy. 401 [on the northern boundaries of Toronto] to Hwy. 400; go north on 400 to Major McKenzie and drive west to Islington Ave.; go north on Islington 1 mile to Kleinburg.)

**LONDON:   McIntosh Art Gallery.** University of Western Ontario, N6A 3K7 ☐ The University of Western Ontario's McIntosh Art Gallery was founded early in the forties. The Canadian collection here consists of paintings, drawings, and prints from the 19th and 20th centuries, but is predominantly contemporary. The gallery also shows works from 18th- and 19th-century Europe, most particularly from England. There are approximately 14 to 16 changing exhibits per year, most taking place between September and April, some from May to August. Lectures, films, demonstrations, and concerts are sponsored by the gallery. Grants from the Ontario Arts Council are distributed by the gallery to artists in the area. A few books, periodicals, and catalogs are sold. Space for visitors' cars in university parking areas. Sept.–Apr.: Mon.–Fri. 12–5; Wed., Thurs. 7–9; Sat., Sun. 2–5. May–Aug.: Mon.–Fri. 12–4; Sun. 2–5. Free. (From Hwy. 401, take Wellington Rd. north to the end [Pall Mall St.] and turn left [west]. Go 1 block to Richmond St., turn right [north] and proceed to university gates.)

**OSHAWA:   Robert McLaughlin Gallery.** Civic Centre, L1H 3Z3 ☐ A group of Canadian artists called Painters Eleven, who adhere to the principles of Abstract Expressionism, are featured at the Robert McLaughlin Gallery. Among the 300 works are also paintings by other Canadian artists, Fenwick Landsdowne bird charts, and Japanese woodblock prints. Exhibits change every 3 weeks; some are on loan, some originate in the gallery. As a rule, cameras are not permitted. The extension division here serves the entire district. Lectures, concerts, and classes are held in the center throughout the year. A Canadian Art Lecture series features prominent speakers from across Canada who expand on the current exhibit. Docents conduct tours for students and other groups. And if the students do not come to the gallery, it goes to them in the form of circulating exhibits. The library (4,000 volumes) is open for research. A shop offers the gallery's several publications and catalogs for sale as well as crafts and gift items. Parking at the rear of the building. Mon.–Fri. 10–6; Tues. 7–9; Sat. 12–5; Sun. 2–5. Free. (East of Toronto on Hwy. 401, exit at Simcoe St., Oshawa; go north to Bagot St., west on Bagot to the gallery.)

**OTTAWA: National Gallery of Canada.** Elgin St., K1A 0M8 □ The National Gallery of Canada was founded in the capital of Canada by the Governor-General in 1880; it was incorporated in 1913 to develop and maintain the national collections; and in 1968 it became part of the National Museums of Canada Corporation. Since 1960 it has been housed in a building which was named after the Marquess of Lorne. Not surprisingly, Canadian art—painting, sculpture, and decorative arts from the 17th century to the present—is a preoccupation of the museum, and its major field of research. In fact, at its incorporation, it was charged not only with the development and care of the country's collections, but also with the task of promoting art in Canada. Europe is not neglected, however, nor is the United States; Canada takes pride in its European paintings and sculpture that range from the present all the way back to the 14th century, and its American contemporary art. Prints and drawings make up a large section of the gallery's holdings; this group includes works by such diverse masters as Picasso, Rouault, Rauschenberg, Warhol, Gainsborough, and Cézanne. Many exhibitions are scheduled throughout the year, many are sent abroad, and many are loaned to museums and institutions all over Canada.

The gallery offers lectures, films, gallery talks, and tours. Films on art are available for loan. The library (47,000 volumes) is open for interlibrary loan and for use on the premises. Publications prepared here on the history and development of Canadian art, catalogs, and monographs are for sale, as well as reproductions and postcards. The gallery also publishes annual reviews, a semiannual *Bulletin,* and *National Programme Journals.* Mon., Wed., Fri., Sat. 10–6; Tues., Thurs. 10–10; holidays 2–5; closed Mon. Sept.–Apr. Free. (Between Albert & Slater Sts.)

**OWEN SOUND: Tom Thomson Memorial Gallery and Museum of Fine Art.** 840 1st Ave. W. Mailing address: Box 312, N4K 5P5 □ The leader of Canada's "national movement" of art, depicting the scenes of his native land with intensity and drama, is memorialized here. Tom Thompson paintings, drawings, and memorabilia, other Canadian and Indian artists, and graphics are on display here on the banks of Georgian Bay. Tours, films, lectures, and concerts are available to adults, art and crafts classes, to children. A library (400 volumes) relating to the collection can be used by the public. The museum's publications (pamphlets on Owen Sound and Tom Thomson) are for sale. Sept.–June: daily 12–5, Wed. & Fri. 7–9. July–Aug.: daily 12–5, Wed.–Fri. 7–9. Admission 25¢ for adults, free for children.

**ST. CATHARINES:   Rodman Hall Arts Centre.** 109 St. Paul Crescent, L2S 1M3 ☐ In a Tudor Revival manor house, in what is known as the Garden City, is the Rodman Hall Arts Centre, founded in 1960 by the St. Catharines and District Arts Council. In this historic house, built in 1853, is shown contemporary Canadian art—332 examples of it. In 4 galleries, 3 exhibitions per month (Sept.–June) are installed, and the permanent collection is on view during the summer. Exhibits are either on loan from Canadian, American, or other institutions, are initiated by the center itself, or come from the center's permanent collection. Cameras are permitted, but not invariably. The center's activities are those of a well-utilized cultural center: Lectures, concerts, films, dance and arts festivals, classes, and special children's events are everyday occurrences here. Docents conduct tours by appointment. A monthly poster describing current center events, and occasional catalogs are published. The library (250 volumes) is open for public use on the premises. A shop offers books, jewelry, prints, cards, ceramics, and woven items for sale. A tea room serves snacks. Parking lot in front of the building. Tues., Thurs., Fri. 9–5; Wed. 9–10; Sat., Sun. 1–5. Free. (Take Queen Elizabeth St. to Ontario St.; Ontario to St. Paul St. Turn right on St. Paul West, left on Bellevue Terrace, then left to Rodman Hall.)

**STRATFORD:   The Gallery/Stratford.** 54 Romeo St. N., N5A 4S9 ☐ The City of Stratford Pumping Station, built in 1883, is the historic home of The Gallery/Stratford. The collection that is growing here is composed primarily of contemporary prints and drawings, both Canadian and American, with some sculptures and theater designs. Exhibits change monthly; a large traveling exhibit is installed during the summer months. There are art classes here, and many activities relating to schoolchildren, including an art-in-schools program. Recitals, concerts, lectures, guided tours, films are all part of a busy schedule of events. Traveling exhibitions are organized, and exhibition catalogs are published triannually. Summer: Mon.–Sat. 10–8; Sun. 12–6. Admission 75¢ for adults. Sept.–May: 1–5; Sat. 10–5. Free.

**SUDBURY:  Laurentian University Museum and Arts Centre.** John St. Mailing address: Department of Cultural Affairs, Laurentian University, P3E 2C6 ☐ William Joseph Bell, a lumber magnate in the Sudbury district, built his home in 1906 on a rocky knoll overlooking Lake Ramsey. Hundreds of tons of local stone were cut and blocked for the exterior; the interior was lined with oak; 50 teams of horses took 6 weeks to haul the soil that was needed to landscape the site. In 1966 the Sudbury Chamber of Commerce commenced the conversion of this beautiful and elegant estate into a museum and arts center; it opened the next year, and in 1968 was turned over to Laurentian University. The permanent collection consists of more than 400 works, primarily Canadian, dating from the late 1800s and early 1900s to the present: the Group of Seven, Eskimo sculptures and prints, contemporary Canadian prints, and earlier Canadian works (by Verner, Martin, Watson, for example) are included. Exhibits are changed every 3 weeks. Cameras are not permitted. There are summer art classes, and lectures, concerts, recitals, and films are presented throughout the year. Artists are often present to give lectures or talks in connection with their exhibits; these "Meet the Artist" programs are extended to school groups and the general public. Groups can arrange tours by appointment. The center recommends possible recipients for Ontario Arts Council grants. Catalogs, postcards, art books, and original prints are offered at a sales desk. Parking on the grounds. Tues., Fri. 12–9; other days 12–5. Free. (From the south: Hwy. 69; Paris St.; John St. From the east: Hwy. 17; Paris St.; John St.)

**TORONTO:  Art Gallery of Ontario.** 317 Dundas St. W., Grange Park, M5T 1G4 ☐ The Grange, a Georgian manor house built in 1817, was the first repository of the collections now in the Art Gallery of Ontario. Today the gallery is next door, while the historic building, face-lifted and refurbished in the style of the 1830s, holds visitors to Grange Park in thrall. The Gallery of Ontario, however, is tough competition: Its holdings are copious and impressive, ranging the centuries and across continents. European art here includes works by Italian (15th–18th centuries), Dutch (17th), French (17th–20th), and British (18th–20th) masters; from North America there is Canadian and American 19th- and 20th-century work. And, as though this were not enough, there is the Henry Moore Sculpture Centre containing what is said to be the largest collection of Moore sculpture extant, and an interesting collection of illustrated books from 19th-century England. Special exhibits are frequent and varied. This gallery circulates exhibitions throughout the province of Ontario; about 90 exhibition centers receive some 50 shows that originate here. Art classes are held for both adults and children, lectures, films, concerts on Sundays, guided tours, dance and drama programs for adults. There is a large loan collection of slides and a study collection of prints. The library has 20,000 volumes on art. The museum's publications, reproductions, and catalogs are sold at its shop. A dining room and a cafeteria are on the premises. May–Oct.: Mon., Tues., Fri., Sat. 10–5; Wed., Thurs. 10–10; Sun. & holidays 12–5. Voluntary donations accepted as admission.

**Royal Ontario Museum.** 100 Queen's Park, M5S 2C6 ☐ The Royal Ontario Museum opened its doors in downtown Toronto in 1914 as 5 separate museums of archaeology, geology, mineralogy, paleontology, and zoology. All shared the west wing of the present building. The east wing and the rotunda opened in 1933. The **Canadiana Building** (14 Queen's Park Crescent West) opened in 1951 and the McLaughlin Planetarium in 1968. Of its 20 curatorial departments of art, archaeology, and the natural sciences, the museum is most famous for its Chinese collection, which spans some 4,000 years—the most comprehensive in the world. Also in the field of fine and decorative arts are the collections from Islam, India, Greece, and Rome, Egypt and western Asia, Europe (medieval; Italian and Spanish Renaissance; 16th-, 17th-, and 18th-century continental Europe; Central European Baroque; Continental porcelain and glass; medieval to 1660 England; 17th-, 18th-, and 19th-century England), the Northwest Pacific coast, American Subarctic and Woodlands, Africa, Mexico, Inuit, Peru, American Southwest, and Canada (the entire Canadiana collection—furniture, crafts, paintings, prints, silver, ceramics, and glass—in its own building). There are always a number of temporary or special exhibits in progress that cover a wide range of subjects, last 3 weeks to 3 months or longer, and are installed in regular galleries or the major exhibition hall. Cameras (no tripods or light stands) are permitted.

The Education Services Department offers classes in the museum's galleries that are closely integrated with school curricula. Lectures, films, and concerts are also offered here. Clubs and programs are organized for special groups such as senior citizens and young people. Tours (a different one every day) are available on weekdays; a general tour is available in French and German. The museum publishes a myriad of books and catalogs, all of which are for sale in one of its 3 shops: the gift shop also sells jewelry, prints, cards, crafts, pottery, and objets d'art; the Mini Shop, designed for children, sells books, cards, models, toys, and T-shirts; the planetarium shop sells items related to astronomy. Cafeteria and snack bar on premises; several municipal parking lots within a 5-to-10-minute walk of the building. Sept.–June: daily 10–6, Tues. 10–9, Sun. 1–9; July & Aug.: daily 10–9, Sun. 1–9. Admission $1.50 for adults, 75¢ for students with ID and children, 50¢ for senior citizens, $3 for families. Canadiana Building open daily 10–5; Sun. 1–5. Free. (From the north, take Hwy. 401 to the Avenue Rd. exit and drive south on Avenue Rd. to the museum. From the south, take the Gardiner Expwy. to the University Ave. exit and drive north on University to the museum. Or, by public transit, take the Avenue Rd. bus or the Yonge-Spadina subway to the museum station.)

**Art Gallery of York University.** Ross Building N. 145, 4700 Keele St., Downsview M3J 1P3 ☐ Downsview, a satellite suburban town northwest of Toronto, is located in the borough of North York, one of Toronto's five; it is the home of York University, which itself is surrounded by large residential areas and a recently developed industrial estate. The university's art holdings are administered from the art gallery, which was established in 1970 to provide for the needs of the academic community and for the general public. The collection has been built following a policy of acquiring paintings, sculpture, drawings, and prints by contemporary Canadian artists; certain older objects, however, have been acquired by donation. Modern and earlier Inuit carvings and artifacts are also part of the collection, some of which is on display in various buildings on the campus and some of which is in storage. Museum facilities are planned as part of a Center for Performing and Visual Arts to be built in the future. An exhibition program (Sept.–May) includes events initiated by the gallery and exhibits circulated by other institutions; exhibits change frequently. Cameras are permissible only in special cases and for eligible purposes. As an arm of the university, the gallery's activities are limited to acquiring, exhibiting, and publishing. However, the gallery itself sponsors occasional lectures relating to the material on exhibit. The curator of art is available to conduct groups through exhibits by prearrangement. Handsome catalogs are prepared with the exhibits; past and present gallery publications can be purchased here. Art reference materials make up a substantial section of the university library, which is open to the public by special permission. Cafeteria in the same building; parking nearby. Mon.–Fri. 10–4:30. Free.

**WATERLOO: Art Gallery, University of Waterloo.** N2L 3G1 ☐ The University of Waterloo began its art gallery in 1961 to provide for a permanent collection and traveling exhibits. Many foreign embassies have donated artworks, thus broadening the range of the collection, primarily of contemporary Canadian works. Exhibits change monthly, and a brochure is published for each. The gallery holds lectures, films, and seminars in conjunction with the exhibits and also schedules concerts. Sept.–July, Mon.–Fri. 9–5; Sun. 2–5. Free.

**WINDSOR: Art Gallery of Windsor.** 445 Riverside Dr. W., N9A 6T8 ☐ The Art Gallery of Windsor was established in 1943 in a Tudor mansion built in 1904. Of the more than 1,000 objects here, works of art from

Canada predominate: paintings, sculpture, graphics, and Eskimo artwork from the 18th century to the present. Artists from southwestern Ontario are given an annual exhibition here; another annual exhibit brings together works from all across Canada. Lectures, demonstrations, and concerts are regularly scheduled events. Trained docents guide schoolchildren by the thousands through the collection. The gallery's support organization holds an outdoor art festival at nearby Willistead Park and supports and operates a sales and rental gallery. A shop offers pottery, Eskimo artwork, and jewelry for sale. Mon.–Wed. 10–5, 7–9; Thurs.–Sat. 10–5; Sun. 2–5. Free.

# PRINCE EDWARD ISLAND

**CHARLOTTETOWN:    Confederation Centre Art Gallery and Museum.** Confederation Plaza, Queen & Grafton Sts. Mailing address: P.O. Box 848, C1A 7L9 ☐ One hundred years after the Confederation Conference that was held on Prince Edward Island in 1864, Queen Elizabeth II opened the Confederation Centre of the Arts, Canada's national memorial to the fathers of the dominion, with a library, a theater, public archives, a convention area, and a gallery, all dedicated to the preservation and exhibition of Canadian arts. Four large areas display the permanent holdings and circulating exhibits from other institutions. Among the Canadian painting, sculpture, graphics, and decorative arts, and a small collection of historical artifacts and porcelain is a major collection, said to be the largest in existence, of works by Robert Harris, the Canadian who painted the famous "The Fathers of the Confederation." There is also a specialized collection of contemporary crafts from all 10 provinces and territories. Exhibits change monthly; July and August are devoted to major exhibitions to coincide with the Charlottetown summer festival. Photographing by special permission only. The gallery's educational schedule provides art classes, lectures, concerts, film programs. Its extension program reaches all island communities; traveling exhibitions are circulated, materials and individual art objects loaned. Docent or staff-guided tours are available on request. The gallery publishes catalogs for certain exhibitions and *Ars-Atlantic,* a quarterly journal of the arts. The library (1,500 volumes) is open for inter-library loan, and to teachers and students by appointment. A sales desk specializes in Canadian objects. The restaurant serves wine. Parking nearby. Thurs.–Sat. 10–5; Sun. 2–5; daily 10–9 during July & Aug. Free; donations accepted.

# QUEBEC

**JOLIETTE:  Musée d'Art de Joliette.** 145 Wilfrid Corbeil St. Mailing address: P.O. Box 132, J6E 3Z3 ☐ In 1943 a retrospective collection of Canadian paintings was begun at the Séminaire de Joliette by one of its former students, a Dr. Roméo Boucher. During the next 20 years, it was enlarged and enriched by acquisitions of both European and Canadian works, made possible by other former students of the séminaire; the burgeoning collection was housed in the residence of the Clercs Saint-Viateur. By 1968 it was obvious that it was too extensive and too important not to have its own home—a proper museum building. The new, modern Musée d'Art de Joliette opened in 1976. Canadian painting and sculpture are only one facet of this gem; the others shine as bright: sculpture from the Middle Ages and the Renaissance; 15th- to 18th-century paintings; Russian and Byzantine art; sacred art of Quebec; and decorative arts. Exhibits change monthly; there are about 18 per year. Cameras can be used only with authorization. The museum's educational activities include classes, concerts, lectures, and films. Tours are conducted by guides who speak French and English (Tues.–Sat. 9–5; reservations required). A large and comprehensive catalog of the collection, a brochure, a calendar of events, and postcards are published and are available at the sales desk. The library (1,000 volumes) is open for research. Parking behind the building. Tues., Thurs. 9–5, 7–9:30; Sat., Sun. 2–5. Admission $1 for adults, 25¢ for students.

**MONTREAL:  McCord Museum.** 690 Sherbrooke St. W., H3A 1E9 ☐ David Ross McCord, Q.C., donated his extensive historical collection to McGill University in 1919. Three years later his holdings were on exhibit in the Jesse Joseph house at the corner of McTavish and Sherbrooke Streets. At the end of 1936 the collection was closed to the public and available only to students of the university. It continued to grow, however, and reopened in 1957 in what was once the McGill Student Union building, remodeled for use as a museum. The focus of the McCord Museum is the social history of Canada: The ethnological collection, the prints and photographs, the costumes (the only collection of its kind in Quebec and one of the few in Canada), the decorative arts, all serve to expound on Canada's development. The paintings and drawings serve the same purpose. Displayed for their documentary content are works by Beaucourt, Berczy, Duncan, Hamel, Krieghoff, and Leduc, among others. Two galleries are used for temporary exhibits. Cameras are not permitted. The museum's extension program circulates exhibits throughout Canada. Municipal parking lot nearby (charges by the hour). Wed.–Sat. 11–5. Free. (Go ½ block west of University St. on Sherbrooke.)

**Montreal Museum of Fine Arts.** 3400 Avenue du Musée, H3G 1K3 ☐ The Montreal Museum of Fine Arts was founded in 1860. It houses a general collection of paintings, sculpture, and decorative arts—works from Spain, the Netherlands, England, and Canada; a Norton collection of ancient glass; and Chinese, Near Eastern, Peruvian, and primitive art. Special exhibits are scheduled. The museum's School of Art and Design offers a full 3-year diploma curriculum in visual arts, animation design, and interior design. There are also continuing education evening courses and Saturday afternoon children's art classes. The museum provides guided tours, lectures, gallery talks, films, and other programs. The library (50,000 volumes) on fine and applied arts, decorative arts, and costumes is open for reference only; vertical files deal with Canadian art and artists. The museum publishes a quarterly bulletin called *M,* a handbook of the collection, a catalog of paintings, and a guide, as well as catalogs for special exhibitions. They are available at the shop where visitors can also buy original Eskimo and Indian art, graphics, reproductions, books, cards, and jewelry. A restaurant is in the building. Tues., Thurs.–Sat. 10–4:45; Wed. 10–9:45; Sun. 1–4:45. Free.

**Musée d'Art Contemporain.** Cité du Havre, H3C 3R4 ☐ The echoes of thousands of footsteps had hardly faded in the shut-down International Gallery of Montreal's Expo '67 when its doors were opened for another purpose. The modern cuboid structure had been turned over, almost immediately, to the Museum of Contemporary Art. Housed in the Château Dufresne since its founding in 1964, the museum had been created to promote and exhibit contemporary art in Quebec, and indeed, in Canada. And so it does. The permanent collection includes more than 1,800 works of art created during the period between 1940 and the present by Quebecois and Canadian artists from the other provinces (half the collection is Canadian), and by important international artists. Paintings, engravings, sculpture, drawings, photographs, tapestries, stained glass, and enamels from the world of contemporary art are on display here; an important collection of the Automatist (Surrealist) movement includes more than 100 Paul-Emile Borduas works; Post-Automatists and Abstract Expressionists are also numerous. There are selections of works by Molinari, Pellan, Riopelle, Tousignan, Dallaire, Alleyn, Lyman, Gagnon, and more, all from Quebec. Work from elsewhere in the dominion is represented by Carr, Bush, Saxe, and Ronald, and others. The European section includes works by Picasso ("L'homme au Chien"), Klee, Vasarely, Matisse ("Portrait au Visage Rose et Bleu"), Rouault, and Soulages ("5 Février 1964"). American works by Poons ("Street Singer"), Hans Hofmann ("Classic Fragments"), Albers, and Rauschenberg are also part of this impressive young collection. There are 2 or 3 temporary exhibits a month.

The educational services of the museum include presentations that address themselves specifically to schoolchildren. Films on art or video productions often accompany exhibitions, conferences, or lecture series. Three concerts a year present avant-garde music. Guided tours for groups are available in French or English on weekdays. The museum publishes a bimonthly paper, *Ateliers,* containing general information on contemporary art. The library (4,000 volumes) is well endowed with periodicals, catalogs, and audiovisual material. A sales desk offers books, postcards, magazines, catalogs, and posters for sale. Space for parking in front of the museum. Tues.–Sun. 10–6; Thurs. 10–10. Free. (In the Cité du Havre, not far from downtown Montreal. Take bus number 12 [Nun's Island], which connects with the McGill subway station. Or, by car, go south on University St., continue on the Bonaventure Hwy., and exit at Cité du Havre [first exit on the right]. Or, from the south bank, cross to the island on Champlain Bridge and proceed to Bonaventure Hwy.)

**Sir George Williams Art Galleries.** Concordia University, 1455 W. De Maisonneuve Blvd., H3G 1M8 ☐ The Sir George Williams Art Galleries, affiliated with Concordia University since 1966, are dedicated to the showing of Canadian art, from the past and the present. Three exhibition halls make it possible to have a different exhibit of paintings, sculpture, graphics, mixed media, and decorative arts every 2 to 3 weeks. There are thematic exhibits, retrospectives, and student and staff shows. The galleries invite visiting lecturers to speak on art-related topics; the facilities are also used for concerts, theater programs, and gallery talks. Artworks are circulated throughout the area around Montreal. The gallery has published catalogs of special exhibits and of the permanent collection every 2 years. Mon.–Fri. 11–9; Sat. 11–5. Free.

**QUEBEC CITY: Musée de Québec.** Parc des Champs de Bataille, G1S 1C8 ☐ The Musée de Québec was established in the first quarter of the century under the auspices of the government of the province of Quebec. The archives of the province occupy the ground floor. Elsewhere are paintings, sculpture, and decorative arts; a highlight is the collection of furniture made by Quebec artists from the 1600s to the present. Special exhibits are scheduled. The museum provides guided tours of the collection. Lectures, films, and concerts are offered as well. The library (1,200 volumes) is open to the public. Daily 9–5. Free.

**SHAWINIGAN:   Centre Culturel de Shawinigan.** 2100 Dessaules, G9N 6V3 ☐ Shawinigan's cultural center (formed in 1967) has an art gallery that displays a permanent collection of paintings, watercolors, works on paper, and sculpture plus traveling exhibits. In all, about 20 shows are mounted each year. The center sponsors concerts, dance and drama programs, and classes and workshops in the arts. Original art objects, photographs, and slides are available for loan. Mon.–Fri. 9–5; Sat., Sun. 2–5, 7–9. Free.

**SHERBROOKE:   Centre Culturel de l'Université de Sherbrooke.** Cité Universitaire, J7K 2R7 ☐ The cultural center at the University of Sherbrooke was established in 1964 to provide for both the campus and the community. The permanent collection of the gallery focuses on Canadian art. Exhibitions are changed every month. Gallery talks and tours are offered here, and the center also provides theater, music, lectures, and films. The university library (200,000 volumes) is open for use by the public and for inter-library loan. Mon.–Thurs. 12–9:30; Sun. & holidays 1–5. Free.

# SASKATCHEWAN

**REGINA:   Norman Mackenzie Art Gallery.** College Ave., S4S 0A2 ☐ Regina was the home of the Northwest Territorial government for almost 25 years before Saskatchewan became a province in 1905. It then became provincial capital, and now, although located in the grain belt of Canada and preoccupied with light industry, potash mining, and agriculture, it supports many cultural resources. The Norman Mackenzie Art Gallery, for example, is attached to and administered by the University of Regina. The lawyer and collector whose name it bears gave his collection to Regina College (now the university) in 1936. It was put in storage until 1953, when the first gallery of the yet to be completed (1956) building opened in Wascana Center near Wascana Lake. Enlarged by gifts and acquisitions, the collection is predominantly Canadian, but there is a solid teaching collection of 19th- and early-20th-century European drawings, prints, and watercolors that is constantly being expanded. There are also European prints and drawings from the 15th, 16th, and 17th centuries, and some contemporary American works by Hofmann, Stella, Wiley, and

Olitski, for example. Exhibitions, some originated by the gallery and some touring, change approximately every 6 weeks from Sept. to June. During the summer months the permanent collection is on display. Special permission is required to use a camera. The gallery's educational program is carried on in conjunction with the public school system; trained volunteers operate a Traveling Arts program that introduces art into classrooms. A Wednesday evening series of films, lectures, and demonstrations attempts to enlarge on current exhibitions; and a bring-your-own "Lunch and Art" series includes films and more interpretive talks on art. A docent program provides guides for regularly scheduled tours. Many catalogs are published here. An excellent book on the building of the collection tells an interesting and human tale of Mackenzie's efforts to acquire art, and enumerates and describes many of the museum's holdings and the artists who created them. A Resource Centre (library) is open to the public. Postcards, books, and catalogs are available at the sales desk. Parking nearby. Mon.–Fri. 12–5; Sat., Sun. 1–5; Wed., Thurs. 7–9. Free. (Museum is just east of Albert St.)

**SASKATOON: Mendel Art Gallery and Civic Conservatory.** Saskatoon Gallery and Conservatory Corporation, 950 Spadina Crescent East. Mailing address: P.O. Box 569, S7K 3L6 □ The Mendel Art Gallery and Civic Conservatory is located on the west bank of the South Saskatchewan River across from the University of Saskatchewan and near the city's business district. Fred S. Mendel, art connoisseur and industrialist, brought ·it into existence, with funds for the building and a group of Canadian paintings to form the nucleus of a permanent collection. In 1964 the center opened with his 20th-century Canadian group. Today the gallery also owns a selection of Eskimo art and graphics. Exhibits change monthly. Cameras are permitted. The gallery sponsors art classes for children, workshops, lectures, concerts, and films. Guides are available for tours. A monthly newsletter, "Folio," and catalogs are published here. The library (3,000 volumes) is open to the public for research. Books, jewelry, prints, postcards, pottery, and handcrafted items are sold. Parking on the grounds. Daily 10–10; closed Dec. 25, Good Friday. Free; donations are welcome. (Spadina Crescent East is north of University bridge.)

# WHERE TO FIND SPECIAL COLLECTIONS

### African
College Museum, Hampton Institute (VA)
College of Wooster Art Center Museum (OH)
Dallas Museum of Art (TX)
Flint Institute of the Arts (MI)
Jacksonville Art Museum (FL)
Kimbell Art Museum (TX)
Museum of African Art (DC)
Museum of the National Center of Afro-American Artists (MA)
New Orleans Museum of Art (LA)
Philbrook Art Center (OK)
Seattle Art Museum (WA)
University Gallery, U. of Florida (FL)
U. of Maryland Art Gallery (MD)

### Afro-American
Museum of Art, North Central U. (NC)
Museum of the National Center of Afro-American Artists (MA)

### American, general
Addison Gallery of American Art (MA)
Amon Carter Museum (TX)
Anglo-American Art Museum (LA)

Bryant Art Museum (AR)
Butler Institute of American Art (OH)
Canajoharie Library and Art Gallery (NY)
Cincinnati Art Museum (OH)
Cleveland Museum of Art (OH)
Corcoran Gallery of Art (DC)
Cummer Gallery of Art (NH)
Dayton Art Institute (OH)
Denver Art Museum (CO)
El Paso Museum of Art (TX)
Gilcrease Institute of American History and Art (OK)
Greenville County Museum of Art (SC)
Hackley Art Museum (MI)
Hickory Museum of Art (NC)
Huntington Galleries (WV)
Lang Art Gallery, Scripps College (CA)
Los Angeles County Museum of Art (CA)
Malden Public Library (MA)
Munson-Williams-Proctor Institute (NY)
Museum of Art, Pennsylvania State U. (PA)
National Collection of Fine Arts (DC)
National Portrait Gallery (DC)
Newark Museum (NJ)
New Britain Museum of American Art (CT)

New York Historical Society (NY)
Randolph Macon Woman's College Art Gallery (VA)
Saginaw Art Museum (MI)
San Antonio Museum of Art (TX)
Schumacher Gallery (OH)
Southern Alleghenies Museum of Art (PA)
Springfield Art Museum (MO)
Sweetwater Community Fine Arts Center (WY)
Telfair Academy of Arts and Sciences (GA)
Tennessee Botanical Gardens and Art Center (TN)
Timken Art Gallery (CA)
Edwin A. Ulrich Museum of Art (KS)
University Art Collections, Arizona State University (AZ)
U. of Virginia Art Museum (VA)
Westmoreland County Museum of Art (PA)
Wichita Art Museum (KS)
Yale U. Art Gallery (CT)
Zigler Museum (LA)

### American, 17th and 18th centuries
Albany Institute of History and Art (NY)
Bennington Museum (VT)
Berkshire Museum (MA)
Colby College Museum of Art (ME)
Colonial Williamsburg (VA)
Concord Art Association (MA)
Denver Art Museum (CO)
Diplomatic Reception Rooms (DC)
Everson Museum of Art (NY)
Fenimore House (NY)

Florida Gulf Coast Art Center (FL)
Ralph Foster Museum (MO)
Gibbes Art Gallery (SC)
High Museum of Art (GA)
Montclair Art Museum (NJ)
New Bedford Whaling Museum (MA)
Smith College Museum of Art (MA)
Edwin A. Ulrich Museum (NY)
Vassar College Art Gallery (NY)

### American, 19th century
Albany Institute of History and Art (NY)
Allentown Art Museum (PA)
Charles Allis Art Library (WI)
Art Center for Southwestern Louisiana (LA)
Art Gallery of Ontario (CAN)
Athenaeum of Philadelphia (PA)
Ball State U. Art Gallery (IN)
Beaumont Art Museum (TX)
Berkshire Museum (MA)
Belmont—Gari Melchers Memorial Gallery (VA)
Bennington Museum (VT)
Birmingham Museum of Art (AL)
Braithwaite Fine Arts Gallery (UT)
Brandywine River Museum (PA)
Brockton Art Center (MA)
Bryant Art Museum (AR)
Burpee Art Museum (IL)
Bush House Museum and Bush Barn Art Center (OR)
Amon Carter Museum of Western Art (TX)
Chesterwood (MA)

City Hall (Charleston) Art
Collection (SC)
Colby College Museum of Art
(ME)
Colonial Williamsburg (VA)
Colorado Springs Fine Arts
Center (CO)
Cornell Fine Arts Center,
Rollins College (FL)
E. B. Crocker Art Gallery (CA)
Currier and Ives Antiques
Gallery (PA)
Dartmouth College Museum
and Galleries (NH)
Delaware Art Museum (DE)
Denver Art Museum (CO)
Des Moines Art Center (IA)
Dimock Gallery (DC)
Diplomatic Reception Rooms
(DC)
Everson Museum of Art (NY)
Fine Arts Gallery of San Diego
(CA)
William A. Farnsworth Museum
(ME)
Fitchburg Art Museum (MA)
Freer Gallery of Art (DC)
Georgia Museum of Art (GA)
High Museum of Art (GA)
Housatonic Museum of Art
(CT)
Hudson River Museum (NY)
Hunter Museum of Art (TN)
Herbert F. Johnson Museum of
Art, Cornell U. (NY)
Lowell Art Association (MA)
Mead Art Building, Amherst
College (MA)
Merrick Art Gallery (PA)
Milwaukee Art Center (WI)
Mint Museum (NC)
Montclair Art Museum (NJ)

Montgomery Museum of Fine
Arts (AL)
Morse Gallery of Art (FL)
Mount Holyoke College Art
Museum (MA)
Museum of Art, Carnegie
Institute (PA)
Nashville Parthenon (TN)
Neuberger Museum (NY)
New Orleans Museum of Art
(LA)
R. W. Norton Art Gallery (LA)
Violet Oakley Memorial
Foundation (PA)
Olana State Historic Site (NY)
Parish Art Museum (NY)
Pennsylvania Academy of the
Fine Arts (PA)
Philbrook Art Center (OK)
Phillips Collection (DC)
Pioneer Museum and Haggin
Galleries (CA)
Portland Museum of Art (ME)
Redwood Library and
Athenaeum (RI)
Remington Art Museum (NY)
Reynolda House (NC)
Lauren Rogers Memorial
Library and Museum of Art
(MS)
St. Johnsbury Athenaeum (VT)
Saint-Gaudens National Historic
Site (NH)
Shelburne Museum (VT)
George Walter Vincent Smith
Art Museum (MA)
Smith College Museum of Art
(MA)
Society of the Four Arts (FL)
Springfield Art Center (OH)
T. C. Steele State Memorial (IN)
Sunrise Foundation (WV)

Edwin A. Ulrich Museum (NY)
U. of Maryland Art Gallery
 (MO)
U. of Nebraska Art Galleries
 (NE)
U. of Wyoming Art Museum
 (WY)
Wadsworth Atheneum (CT)
Washington State U. Museum
 of Art (WA)
Watson Gallery, Wheaton
 College (MA)
West Bend Gallery of Fine Arts
 (WI)
Wood Art Gallery (VT)

**American, 20th century**
Allentown Art Museum (PA)
Art Center for Southwestern
 Louisiana (LA)
Art Gallery of Hamilton (ON,
 CAN)
Art Gallery of Ontario (ON,
 CAN)
Ball State U. Art Gallery (IN)
Beaumont Art Museum (TX)
Bellevue Art Museum (WA)
William Benton Museum of Art
 (CT)
Blanden Art Gallery (IA)
Braithwaite Fine Arts Gallery
 (UT)
Brandeis U., Rose Art Museum
 (MA)
Brandywine River Museum
 (PA)
Burchfield Center (NY)
Burpee Art Museum (IL)
Amon Carter Museum of
 Western Art (TX)
Colby College Museum of Art
 (ME)

Colorado Springs Fine Arts
 Center (CO)
Cornell Fine Arts Center,
 Rollins College (FL)
Salvador Dali Museum (OH)
Dartmouth College Museum
 and Galleries (NH)
De Cordova Museum (MA)
Delaware Art Museum (DE)
Des Moines Art Center (IA)
Dimock Gallery (DC)
Everson Museum of Art (NY)
Fine Arts Gallery of San Diego
 (CA)
Georgia Museum of Art (GA)
Hartnell College Gallery (CA)
Henry Gallery (WA)
Housatonic Museum of Art
 (CT)
Hunter Museum of Art (TN)
Herbert F. Johnson Museum of
 Art, Cornell U. (NY)
Johnson Gallery, University of
 New Mexico (NM)
Kalamazoo Institute of Art (MI)
Joe and Emily Lowe Art
 Gallery, Syracuse U. (NY)
Loch Haven Art Center (FL)
Lyme Historical Society,
 Florence Griswold House
 (CT)
McNay Art Institute (TX)
Charles H. MacNider Museum
 (IA)
Milwaukee Art Center (WI)
Mint Museum (NC)
Montgomery Museum of Fine
 Arts (AL)
Museum of Art, Houston (TX)
Museum of Art of Ogunquit
 (ME)
Neuberger Museum (NY)

New Orleans Museum of Art (LA)

R. W. Norton Art Gallery (LA)

Norton Gallery and School of Art (FL)

Old Corner House: Norman Rockwell Museum (MA)

Parish Art Museum (NY)

Pennsylvania Academy of the Fine Arts (PA)

Philbrook Art Center (OK)

Phillips Collection (DC)

Queens College Art Collection (NY)

Reynolda House (NC)

Lauren Rogers Memorial Library and Museum of Art (MS)

de Saisset Art Gallery and Museum (CA)

Smith College Museum of Art (MA)

Society of the Four Arts (FL)

Southeast Arkansas Arts and Science Center (AR)

Springfield Art Center (OH)

Springville Museum of Art (UT)

Sunrise Foundation (WV)

Tomoka State Museum (FL)

Treat Gallery (ME)

University Art Museum, Berkeley (CA)

University Art Museum, U. of Texas at Austin (TX)

U. of Maryland Art Gallery (MD)

U. of Minneapolis, University Gallery (MN)

U. of Nebraska Art Galleries (NE)

U. of Northern Iowa Gallery of Art (IA)

U. of Wyoming Art Museum (WY)

Washington State U. Museum of Art (WA)

Whitney Museum of American Art (NY)

Williams College Museum of Art (MA)

**American, contemporary**

California State U., Northridge Fine Arts Gallery (CA)

Coos Art Museum (OR)

Des Moines Art Center (IA)

Dulin Art Gallery (TN)

Evansville Museum of Arts and Science (IN)

Fresno Art Center (CA)

Greenville County Museum of Art (SC)

Jacksonville Art Museum (FL)

National Gallery of Canada (ON, CAN)

Newport Harbor Art Museum (CA)

Michael C. Rockefeller Arts Center Gallery (NY)

Vancouver Art Gallery (BC, CAN)

Weatherspoon Art GAllery (NC)

**American, Hudson River school**

Fruitlands Museums (MA)

St. Johnsbury Athenaeum (VT)

Washington County Museum of Fine Arts (MD)

**American Indian**

Brigham Young University Art Gallery (UT)

Cincinnati Art Museum (OH)

Museum of Art, North Carolina Central U. (NC)
Museum of New Mexico (NM)
Native American Center for the Living Arts (NY)
New Orleans Museum of Art (LA)
W. H. Over Museum (SD)
University Gallery, U. of Florida (FL)

**American, Midwest**
Alford House, Anderson Fine Arts Center (IN)
Indianapolis Museum of Art (IN)
Massillon Museum (OH)
Neville Public Museum (WI)
Rochester Art Center (MN)

**American, New England**
Bennington Museum (VT)
De Cordova Museum (MA)
Mattatuck Museum (CT)
New Bedford Whaling Museum (MA)
Provincetown Art Association and Museum (MA)
Springfield Art and Historical Society (VT)

**American, New York**
N.Y. Historical Society (NY)
Staten Island Museum (NY)

**American, Northeast**
Albany Institute of History and Art (NY)
Guild Hall of East Hampton (NY)
Museums at Stony Brook (NY)
Portland Museum of Art (ME)
U. of Maine Art Collection (ME)

**American, Northwest**
Bellevue Art Museum (WA)
Bush House Museum and Bush Barn Art Center (OR)
Henry Gallery (WA)
Museum of Art, U. of Oregon (OR)
Olin Gallery, Whitman College (WA)
Seattle Art Museum (WA)
South Dakota Memorial Art Center (SD)
Washington State U. Museum of Art (WA)
Whatcom Museum of History and Art (WA)

**American, South**
Anglo-American Art Museum (LA)
Asheville Art Museum (NC)
Fayetteville Museum of Art (NC)
Historic New Orleans Collection (LA)
Louisiana State Museum (LA)
Montgomery Museum of Fine Arts (AL)
New Orleans Museum of Art (LA)
Lauren Rogers Memorial Library and Museum of Art (MS)
St. John's Art Gallery (NC)
Tennessee Botanical Gardens and Art Center (TN)

**American, Southwest**
Art Museum, U. of New Mexico (NM)
Colorado Springs Fine Arts Center (CO)
Heard Museum (AZ)

Johnson Gallery, U. of New
  Mexico (NM)
McNay Art Institute (TX)
Museum of Albuquerque (NM)
Museum of New Mexico (NM)
Roswell Museum and Art
  Center (NM)
Tucson Museum of Art (AZ)
Woolaroc Museum (OK)

**American, West**
Beaumont Art Museum (TX)
Bradford Brinton Memorial
  Ranch (WY)
Brigham City Museum-Gallery
  (UT)
Brigham Young U. Art Gallery
  (UT)
Buffalo Bill Historical Center
  (WY)
Amon Carter Museum of
  Western Art (TX)
E. B. Crocker Art Gallery (TX)
Diamond M Foundation
  Museum (TX)
Downey Museum of Art (CA)
William S. Hart County Park
  (CA)
Laguna Beach Museum of Art
  (CA)
Las Vegas Art Museum (NV)
Montana Historical Society
  (MT)
Monterey Peninsula Museum of
  Art (CA)
Museum of Fine Arts, Houston
  (TX)
National Cowboy Hall of Fame
  and Western Heritage Center
  (OK)
R. W. Norton Art Gallery (LA)
Oakland Museum (CA)
Phoenix Art Museum (AZ)
Rockwell-Corning Museum
  (NY)

Rogers House Museum Gallery
  (KS)
Will Rogers State Historic Park
  (CA)
C. M. Russell Museum (MT)
San Jose Museum of Art (CA)
Sioux City Art Center (IA)
Sweetwater Community Fine
  Arts Center (WY)
Triton Museum of Art (CA)
Whatcom Museum of History
  and Art (WA)
Woolaroc Museum (OK)
Yuma Art Center (AZ)

**Archaeology**
Museum of Art and
  Archaeology (MO)
U. of Chicago, Oriental Institute
  Museum (IL)

**Architectural drawings**
U. of California Art Museum,
  Santa Barbara (CA)

**Asian**
Asia House Gallery (NY)
Asian Art Museum of San
  Francisco (CA)
Asian Arts Center (MD)
Birmingham Museum of Art
  (AL)
Fine Arts Gallery of San Diego
  (CA)
Honolulu Academy of Arts (HI)
Herbert F. Johnson Museum of
  Art, Cornell U. (NY)
Los Angeles County Museum of
  Art (CA)
Mount Holyoke College Art
  Museum (MA)
Seattle Art Museum (WA)
U. of Virginia Art Museum
  (VA)

**Barbizon School** *(See also* French, 19th century)
Arnot Art Museum (NY)
Paine Art Center and Arboretum (WI)

**Baroque**
El Paso Museum of Art (TX)
Mint Museum (NC)
New Orleans Museum of Art (LA)
Ringling Museum of Art (FL)
Wadsworth Atheneum (CT)

**Baroque, Dutch and Flemish**
Birmingham Museum of Art (AL)

**Baroque, Spanish**
Fine Arts Gallery of San Diego (CA)
Williams College Museum of Art (MA)

**Bauhaus**
Busch-Reisinger Museum (MA)

**Buddhist**
Florida Gulf Coast Art Center (FL)

**Byzantine**
Dumbarton Oaks Research Library and Collection (DC)
Musée d'Art de Joliette (PQ, CAN.)

**Canadian**
Art Gallery of Greater Victoria (BC, CAN)
Art Gallery of Hamilton (ON, CAN)
Art Gallery, Memorial U. of Newfoundland (NF, CAN)
Art Gallery of Ontario (ON, CAN)

Art Gallery of Windsor (ON, CAN)
Art Gallery, U. of Waterloo (ON, CAN)
Art Gallery of York U. (ON, CAN)
Beaverbrook Art Gallery (BC, CAN)
Burnaby Art Gallery (BC, CAN)
Centre Culturel de l'Université de Sherbrooke (PQ, CAN)
Confederation Centre Art Gallery and Museum (PE, CAN)
Edmonton Art Gallery (AB, CAN)
Agnes Etherington Art Center (ON, CAN) .
The Gallery/Stratford (ON, CAN)
Gallery III, U. of Manitoba (MB, CAN)
Glenbow Museum (AB, CAN)
Laurentian U. Museum and Arts Center (ON, CAN)
McCord Museum (PQ, CAN)
McIntosh Art Gallery, U. of Western Ontario (ON, CAN)
Norman Mackenzie Art Gallery (SK, CAN)
Robert McLaughlin Gallery (ON, CAN)
McMichael Canadian Collection (ON, CAN)
Maltwood Art Museum and Gallery (BC, CAN)
Memorial U. of Newfoundland Art Gallery (NF, CAN)
Montreal Museum of Fine Arts (PQ, CAN)
Musée d'Art Contemporain (PQ, CAN)

Musée d'Art de Joliette (PQ, CAN)
Musée de Québec (PQ, CAN)
National Gallery of Canada (ON, CAN)
New Brunswick Museum (NB, CAN)
Rodman Hall Arts Center (ON, CAN)
Royal Ontario Museum (ON, CAN)
Saskatoon Gallery and Conservatory Corporation (SK, CAN)
Tom Thomson Memorial Gallery and Museum of Fine Art (ON, CAN)
Vancouver Art Gallery (BC, CAN)
Sir George Williams Art Galleries (PQ, CAN)
Winnipeg Art Gallery (MB, CAN)

**Caribbean**
Museum of the National Center of Afro-American Artists (MA)

**Ceramics**
Fisher Community Center (IA)
Everson Museum of Art (NY)

**Chinese** *(See also* Far East; Near East; Oriental)
China House Gallery (NY)
Norton Gallery and School of Art (FL)
Royal Ontario Museum (ON, CAN)
Washington County Museum of Fine Arts (MD)

**Contemporary** *(See also* American, 20th century; American, contemporary; Modern; 20th century)

Akron Art Institute (OH)
Albright-Knox Art Gallery (NY)
Aldrich Museum of Contemporary Art (CT)
Anderson Gallery, Virginia Commonwealth U. (VA)
Bell Gallery, Brown U. (RI)
Bundy Art Gallery (VT)
Fine Arts Gallery at Wright State U. (OH)
Florida Gulf Coast Art Center (FL)
Headley Museum (KY)
Houghton Art Center, Hobart and William Smith Colleges (NY)
Housatonic Museum of Art (CT)
La Jolla Museum of Contemporary Art (CA)
Madison Art Center (WI)
Minnesota Museum of Art (MN)
Musée d'Art Contemporain (PQ, CAN)
Museum of Contemporary Art (IL)
Smith-Mason Gallery-Museum (DC)
Tyringham Galleries (MA)
U. of Arizona Museum of Art (AZ)
University Galleries, U. of South Florida (FL)
U. of Virginia Art Museum (VA)
Visual Arts Gallery, Pensacola Junior College (FL)
Wellesley College Museum (MA)

**Cuban**
Museum of Arts and Sciences (FL)

**Decorative Arts** *(See also* Furniture; Glass; Porcelain)
  Anglo-American Art Museum (LA)
  Birmingham Museum of Art, (AL)
  Currier Gallery of Art (NH)
  Cooper-Hewitt Museum (NY)
  Diplomatic Reception Rooms (DC)
  William A. Farnsworth Museum (ME)
  Henry Morrison Flagler Museum (FL)
  J. Paul Getty Museum (CA)
  Headley Museum (KY)
  Huntington Galleries (WV)
  Joe and Emily Lowe Art Gallery, Syracuse U. (NY)
  Museum of Fine Arts (FL)
  Museum of Fine Arts, Houston (TX)
  Philadelphia Museum of Art (PA)
  Portland Museum of Art (ME)
  Slater Memorial Museum and Converse Art Gallery (CT)
  Telfair Academy of Arts and Sciences (GA)
  Tennessee Botanical Gardens and Art Center (TN)
  Vizcaya (FL)
  Winterthur Museum (DE)

**Drawings** *(See also* Graphics)
  E. B. Crocker Art Gallery (CA)
  Pierpont Morgan Library (NY)
  Watson Gallery, Wheaton College (MA)

**Dutch, 17th century**
  Allen Memorial Art Museum (OH)
  Allentown Art Museum (PA)

  Agnes Etherington Art Center (ON, CAN)
  Fisher Collection (PA)
  Isabella Stewart Gardner Museum (MA)
  Indianapolis Museum of Art (IN)
  University Galleries, U. of Southern California (CA)

**Egyptian**
  Brooklyn Museum (NY)
  Metropolitan Museum of Art (NY)
  Museum of Fine Arts, Boston (MA)
  Rosicrucian Egyptian Museum (CA)

**English, general**
  Anglo-American Art Museum (LA)
  Beaverbrook Art Gallery (NB, CAN)
  Dixon Gallery and Gardens (TN)
  Huntington Library, Art Gallery and Botanical Gardens (CA)
  Yale Center for British Art (CT)

**English, 18th century**
  Evansville Museum of Arts and Science (IN)
  Indianapolis Museum of Art (IN)
  Mint Museum (NC)

**English, 19th century**
  Evansville Museum of Arts and Science (IN)
  Indianapolis Museum of Art (IN)
  Philbrook Art Center (OK)

**English, 20th century**
  Art Gallery of Hamilton (ON, CAN)

**Eskimo**
Anchorage Historical and Fine
Arts Museum (AK)
Art Gallery of Windsor (ON,
CAN)
Saskatoon Gallery and
Conservatory Corporation
(SK, CAN)
Winnipeg Art Gallery (MB,
CAN)

**European, general**
Allentown Art Museum (PA)
Art Gallery of Ontario (ON,
CAN)
Cleveland Museum of Art (OH)
Currier Gallery of Art (NH)
Dayton Art Institute (OH)
Denver Art Museum (CO)
Bob Jones U. Art Museum (SC)
Kimbell Art Museum (TX)
Malden Public Library (MA)
National Gallery of Canada
(ON, CAN)
U. of Virginia Art Museum
(VA)
Vancouver Art Gallery (BC,
CAN)
Zigler Museum (LA)

**European, 17th century**
Museum of Fine Arts, Houston
(TX)

**European, 18th century**
Museum of Fine Arts, Houston
(TX)
Saginaw Art Museum (MI)

**European, 19th century**
Des Moines Art Center (IA)
Fine Arts Gallery of San Diego
(CA)
Housatonic Museum of Art
(CT)

Joe and Emily Lowe Art
Gallery, Syracuse U. (NY)
Merrick Art Gallery (PA)
Milwaukee Art Center (WI)
Mint Museum (NC)
Phillips Collection (DC)
Saginaw Art Museum (MI)
Society of the Four Arts (FL)
Southeast Arkansas Arts and
Science Center (AR)
U. of Wyoming Art Museum
(WY)

**European, 20th century**
Blanden Art Gallery (IA)
Des Moines Art Center (IA)
Fine Arts Gallery of San Diego
(CA)
Housatonic Museum of Art
(CT)
Metropolitan Museum and Art
Centers, Inc. (FL)
Milwaukee Art Center (WI)
Mint Museum (NC)
New Orleans Museum of Art
(LA)
Phillips Collection (DC)
Rose Art Museum, Brandeis U.
(MA)
Society of the Four Arts (FL)
University Art Museum,
Berkeley (CA)
U. of Wyoming Art Museum
(WY)

**European, Western**
Martin D'Arcy Gallery of Art
(IL)
J. Paul Getty Museum (CA)
Honolulu Academy of Arts (HI)
Norton Simon Museum of Art
at Pasadena (CA)

**Far Eastern** *(See also* Chinese; Japanese; Oriental)

Freer Gallery of Art (DC)
Yale U. Art Gallery (CT)

**Flemish, 17th century**
Fisher Collection (PA)
Indianapolis Museum of Art
(IN)
University Galleries, U. of
Southern California (CA)

**Folk art**
Abby Aldrich Rockefeller Folk
Art Collection (VA)

**French, general**
California Palace of the Legion
of Honor (CA)

**French, 18th century**
Smith College Museum of Art
(MA)

**French, 19th century** *(See also* Bar-
bizon school)
William Hayes Ackland
Memorial Art Center (NC)
Charles Allis Art Library (WI)
Evansville Museum of Arts and
Science (IN)
Indianapolis Museum of Art
(IN)
Museum of Art, Rhode Island
School of Design (RI)
Norton Gallery and School of
Art (FL)
Pioneer Museum and Haggin
Galleries (CA)
Smith College Museum of Art
(MA)
Tweed Museum of Art (MN)
University Art Gallery, Rutgers
(NJ)
Wadsworth Atheneum (CT)

**French, 20th century**
Norton Gallery and School of
Art (FL)

Smith College Museum of Art
(MA)

**French Impressionist**
Sterling and Francine Clark Art
Institute (MA)
Dixon Gallery and Gardens
(TN)
Hill-Stead Museum (CT)
Museum of Art, Carnegie
Institute (PA)

**Furniture** *(See also* Decorative arts)
Diplomatic Reception Rooms
(DC)
Henry Morrison Flagler
Museum (FL)
Hyde Collection (NY)
Museum of Art, Rhode Island
School of Design (RI)
Vizcaya (FL)
Winterthur Museum (DE)

**General**
William Hayes Ackland
Memorial Art Center (NC)
Allen Memorial Art Museum
(OH)
Lyman Allyn Museum (CT)
Arkansas Art Center (AR)
Art Complex Museum (MA)
Art Gallery of Greater Victoria
(BC, CAN)
Art Gallery, Springfield Art
Association (IL)
Art Gallery, U. of Notre Dame
(IN)
Art Institute of Chicago (IL)
Art Museum, Princeton U. (NJ)
Baltimore Museum of Art (MD)
Barnes Foundation (PA)
Bass Museum of Art (FL)
William Benton Museum of Art
(CT)
Martha Berry Museum and Art
Gallery (GA)

Sarah Campbell Blaffer Gallery (TX)
Bowdoin College Museum of Art (ME)
Brooklyn Museum (NY)
Brooks Memorial Art Gallery (TN)
Brownsville Art League (TX)
Brueckner Museum (MI)
Bryant Art Museum (AR)
Chrysler Museum at Norfolk (VA)
Cincinnati Art Museum (OH)
Cleveland Museum of Art (OH)
Columbus Gallery of Fine Arts (OH)
Cooper-Hewitt Museum (NY)
Danforth Museum (MA)
Denver Art Museum (CO)
Detroit Institute of Arts (MI)
Duke U. Museum of Art (NC)
Elvehjem Art Center, U. of Wisconsin (WI)
Evansville Museum of Arts and Science (IN)
Exhibitions and Collections, Lehigh U. (PA)
Fine Arts Museum of the South (AL)
Robert Hull Fleming Museum, U. of Vermont (VT)
Fogg Art Museum (MA)
Fort Wayne Museum of Art (IN)
Frick Art Museum (PA)
Frick Collection (NY)
Heckscher Museum (NY)
Highland Area Arts Council (IL)
Indianapolis Museum of Art (IN)
Johnson Gallery (VT)
Joslyn Art Museum (NE)
Kimbell Art Museum (TX)

Krannert Art Museum, U. of Illinois (IL)
Kresge Art Gallery, Michigan State U. (MI)
La Salle College Gallery (PA)
Los Angeles County Museum of Art (CA)
Emily Lowe Gallery (NY)
Memorial Art Gallery, U. of Rochester (NY)
Metropolitan Museum of Art (NY)
Miami U. Art Center (OH)
Minneapolis Institute of Arts (MN)
Montreal Museum of Fine Arts (PQ, CAN)
Museum of Art, Springfield (MA)
Museum of Fine Arts, Boston (MA)
Museum of Fine Arts, Houston (TX)
Museum of Fine Arts of St. Petersburg (FL)
National Gallery of Art (DC)
Nave Museum (TX)
Nelson Gallery, Atkins Museum (MO)
Peabody Museum of Salem (MA)
Philadelphia Museum of Art (PA)
Philbrook Art Center (OK)
Phoenix Art Museum (AZ)
Picker Art Gallery, Colgate (NY)
Plains Art Museum (MN)
Portland Art Museum (OR)
Reading Public Museum and Art Gallery (PA)
Royal Ontario Museum (ON, CAN)
Saginaw Art Museum (MI)

St. Bonaventure Art Collection (NY)
St. Louis Art Museum (MO)
Schumacher Gallery (OH)
Stanford U. Museum of Art (CA)
Taft Museum (OH)
Toledo Museum of Art (OH)
University Art Gallery, Rutgers (NJ)
U. of Michigan Museum of Art (MI)
Vanderbilt U., Dept. of Fine Arts (TN)
Virginia Museum (VA)
Wadsworth Atheneum (CT)
Walters Art Gallery (MD)
Woodmere Art Gallery (PA)
Worcester Art Museum (MA)
M. H. de Young Memorial Museum (CA)

**German, 19th century**
E. B. Crocker Art Gallery (CA)

**German Expressionist**
Busch-Reisinger Museum (MA)
Norton Simon Museum (CA)

**Glass** *(See also* Decorative Arts)
Newark Museum (NJ)
Toledo Museum of Art (OH)

**Graphics** *(See also* Prints, Drawings)
Art Institute of Chicago (IL)
William Benton Museum of Art (CT)
Berea College Art Dept. (KY)
Blanden Art Gallery (IA)
California Palace of the Legion of Honor (CA)
Cincinnati Art Museum (OH)
College of Wooster Art Museum (OH)

Currier and Ives and Antiques Gallery (PA)
Davidson College Art Gallery (NC)
Davison Art Center, Wesleyan U. (CT)
The Gallery/Stratford (ON, CAN)
Henry Gallery (WA)
Huntsville Museum of Art (AL)
Herbert F. Johnson Museum of Art, Cornell U. (NY)
Loch Haven Art Center (FL)
Madison Art Center (WI)
Museum of Art, Rhode Island School of Design (RI)
U. of Michigan Museum of Art (MI)
Frederick S. Wight Art Galleries, UCLA, Grunwald Center for the Graphic Arts (CA)

**Greek and Roman**
J. Paul Getty Museum (CA)
Los Angeles County Museum of Art (CA)
Mt. Holyoke College Art Museum (MA)
Princeton U. Art Museum (NJ)
Santa Barbara Museum of Art (CA)
Slater Memorial Museum and Converse Art Gallery (CT)

**Hawaiian**
Contemporary Arts Center of Hawaii (HI)
Tennent Art Foundation (HI)

**Impressionist**
Art Institute of Chicago (IL)
Fisher Community Center (IA)
Hackley Art Museum (MI)

Museum of Fine Arts, Houston
(TX)
Phillips Collection (DC)

**India**
Los Angeles County Museum of
Art (CA)
Museum of Fine Arts (FL)

**Italian, early** *(See also* Renaissance,
Italian)
Yale U. Art Gallery (CT)

**Japanese** *(See also* Far East; Oriental)
Allen Memorial Art Museum
(OH)
Gibbes Art Gallery (SC)
Henry Gallery (WA)
Japan House Gallery (NY)
Museum of Art, Rhode Island
School of Design (RI)
New Orleans Museum of Art
(LA)
Seattle Art Museum (WA)

**Jewish**
Jewish Museum (NY)

**Latin American**
Denver Art Museum (CO)
Metropolitan Museum and Art
Centers (FL)
University Art Museum, U. of
Texas at Austin (TX)
University Gallery, U. of
Florida (FL)

**Marine**
Mariners Museum (VA)

**Medieval**
Cleveland Museum of Art (OH)
Cloisters (NY)
Hammond Museum (MA)
McNay Art Institute (TX)

Musée d'Art de Joliette (PQ,
CAN)
Yale U. Art Gallery (CT)

**Mexican**
El Paso Museum of Art (TX)
Phoenix Art Museum (AZ)
Tucson Museum of Art (AZ)

**Modern** *(See also* American, contemporary; American, 20th century; Contemporary; 20th century)
Allen Memorial Art Museum
(OH)
Solomon R. Guggenheim
Museum (NY)
Hirshhorn Museum and
Sculpture Garden (DC)
Los Angeles County Museum of
Art (CA)
Phillips Collection (DC)
Norton Simon Museum (CA)
Ulrich Museum of Art (KS)
University Gallery, U. of
Massachusetts (MA)
Washington U. Gallery of Art
(MO)

**Mormon**
Brigham Young U. Art Gallery
(UT)

**Near East** *(See also* Oriental)
Cincinnati Art Museum (OH)
Freer Gallery of Art (DC)
U. of Chicago, Oriental Institute
Museum (IL)
Yale U. Art Gallery (CT)

**Nepalese**
Los Angeles County Museum of
Art (CA)

**19th Century**
Arnot Art Museum (NY)
Drexel Museum Collection (PA)

Fort Lauderdale Museum of the
  Arts (FL)
Charles and Emma Frye Free
  Public Art Museum (WA)
McNay Art Institute (TX)
Maryhill Museum of Fine Arts
  (WA)
Nevada Art Gallery (NV)
Northwest Missouri State U. Art
  Gallery (MO)
Oklahoma Museum of Art (OK)
James Prendergast Library
  Association (NY)
Society of the Four Arts (FL)
Sheldon Swope Art Gallery (IN)
U. of Iowa Museum of Art (IA)
Utah Museum of Fine Arts
  (UT)

**Old Masters**
Lyman Allyn Museum (CT)
Berkshire Museum (MA)
Evansville Museum of Arts and
  Science (IN)
Frick Collection (NY)
Hackley Art Museum (MI)
Hispanic Society of America
  (NY)
Bob Jones U. Art Museum (SC)
New Orleans Museum of Art
  (LA)
Pierpont Morgan Library (NY)
Timken Art Gallery (CA)
U. of California Art Museum,
  Santa Barbara (CA)
Washington County Museum of
  Fine Arts (MD)
Wellesley College Museum
  (MA)

**Oriental** *(See also* Chinese; Far
East; Japanese; Near East)
Art Institute of Chicago (IL)

Blanden Art Gallery (IA)
Cleveland Museum of Art (OH)
College of Wooster Art Center
  Museum (OH)
Denver Art Museum (CO)
Flint Institute of Arts (MI)
Indianapolis Museum of Art
  (IN)
Kimbell Art Museum (TX)
Museum of Art, U. of Oregon
  (OR)
Museum of Fine Arts, Boston
  (MA)
Nelson Gallery-Atkins Museum
  (MO)
Paine Art Center and
  Arboretum (WI)
Santa Barbara Museum of Art
  (CA)
Slater Memorial Museum and
  Converse Art Gallery (CT)
George Walter Vincent Smith
  Art Museum (MA)
Philbrook Art Center (OK)

**Photography**
Berea College Art Dept. (KY)
Chicago Center for
  Contemporary Photography
  (IL)

**Pop art**
Youngstown State U. Kilcawley
  Center Art Gallery (OH)

**Porcelain** *(See also* Decorative arts)
Cummer Gallery of Art (FL)
Indianapolis Museum of Art
  (IN)
Jacksonville Art Museum (FL)
St. Bonaventure Art Collection
  (NY)
Seattle Art Museum (WA)

**Portraits**
National Portrait Gallery (DC)
West Point Museum (NY)

**Postimpressionist**
Art Institute of Chicago (IL)
Dixon Gallery and Gardens
(TN)
Museum of Art, Carnegie
Institute (PA)
Museum of Fine Arts, Houston
(TX)
Phillips Collection (DC)

**Pre-Columbian**
Brigham Young U. Art Gallery
(UT)
Dallas Museum of Fine Arts
(TX)
Dumbarton Oaks Research
Library and Collection (DC)
Fort Lauderdale Museum of the
Arts, Inc. (FL)
Jacksonville Art Museum (FL)
Loch Haven Art Center (FL)
Herbert F. Johnson Museum of
Art, Cornell U. (NY)
Kimbell Art Museum (TX)
Mint Museum (NC)
New Orleans Museum of Art
(LA)
Picker Art Gallery, Colgate U.
(NY)
Seattle Art Museum (WA)
Tucson Museum of Art (AZ)
Yale U. Art Gallery (CT)

**Pre-Raphaelite**
Delaware Art Museum (DE)

**Prints** *(See also* Graphics)
Art Museum, U. of New Mexico
(NM)
Boston Public Library (MA)
Coos Art Museum (OR)

Georgia Museum of Art (GA)
Hall of Fame of the Trotter
(NY)
Joe and Emily Lowe Art
Gallery, Syracuse U. (NY)
Mills College Art Gallery (CA)
Portland Museum of Art (ME)
C. W. Post Art Gallery (NY)
Queens College Art Collection
(NY)
Springfield Art Museum (MO)
University Art Collections,
Arizona State U. (AZ)
U. of California Art Museum,
Santa Barbara (CA)
Vassar College Art Gallery (NY)
Watson Gallery, Wheaton
College (MA)
Wichita Falls Museum and Art
Center (TX)

**Puerto Rican**
El Museo del Barrio (NY)

**Religious**
Bob Jones U. Art Museum (SC)
Rothko Chapel (TX)

**Renaissance**
Berea College Art Dept. (KY)
Biltmore House and Gardens
(NC)
Denver Art Museum (CO)
Frick Art Museum (PA)
El Paso Museum of Art (TX)
Hyde Collection (NY)
Mint Museum (NC)
Musée d'Art de Joliette (PQ,
CAN)
U. of California, Santa Barbara
Art Museum (CA)

**Renaissance, Italian**
Allentown Art Museum (PA)
Ball State U. Art Gallery (IN)

Columbia Museums of Art and Science (SC)

Fine Arts Gallery of San Diego (CA)

Flint Institute of Art (MI)

Isabella Stewart Gardner Museum (MA)

High Museum of Art (GA)

Mount Holyoke College Art Museum (MA)

New Orleans Museum of Art (LA)

Philbrook Art Center (OK)

Ringling Museum of Art (FL)

Yale U. Art Gallery (CT)

**Renaissance, Northern European**
Birmingham Museum of Art (AL)

Ringling Museum of Art (FL)

**Russian**
Musée d'Art de Joliette (PQ, CAN)

Nicholas Roerich Museum (NY)

**Santos**
American Classical College Museum of Art Gallery (NM)

Harwood Foundation of the U. of New Mexico (NM)

**Sculpture**
Albright-Knox Art Gallery (NY)

Art Gallery of Ontario (ON, CAN)

Brookgreen Gardens (SC)

California Palace of the Legion of Honor (CA)

Los Angeles County Museum of Art (CA)

Maryhill Museum of Fine Arts (WA)

Meadows Museum, Southern Methodist U. (TX)

Metropolitan Museum and Art Centers (FL)

Elisabet Ney Museum (TX)

Storm King Art Center (NY)

Lorado Taft Midway Studios (IL)

Wellesley College Museum (MA)

Frederick S. Wight Art Galleries, UCLA (CA)

**Spanish**
Hispanic Society of America (NY)

Meadows Museum, Southern Methodist U. (TX)

**Spanish Colonial**
Art Museum, U. of New Mexico (NM)

Denver Art Museum (CO)

Tucson Museum of Art (AZ)

**Stained glass**
Morse Gallery of Art (FL)

**Swedish, 20th century**
Granbrook Academy of Art Museum (MI)

**Tibetan**
Los Angeles County Museum of Art (CA)

Jacques Marchais Center of Tibetan Arts (NY)

Newark Museum (NJ)

Rose Art Museum, Brandeis U. (MA)

**20th Century** *(See also* American, 20th century; American contemporary; Contemporary; Modern)
Arkansas State U. Art Gallery (AR)

Fort Lauderdale Museum of the Arts (FL)

Fort Worth Art Museum (TX)
Institute of Contemporary Art
  (MA)
Le Moyne Art Foundation (FL)
McNay Art Institute (TX)
Maryhill Museum of Fine Arts
  (WA)
Museum of Modern Art (NY)
Nevada Art Gallery (NV)
Northwest Missouri State U. Art
  Gallery (MO)
Oklahoma Museum of Fine Arts
  (WA)
Rahr-West Museum (WI)

San Francisco Museum of
  Modern Art (CA)
Norton Simon Museum of Art
  at Pasadena (CA)
Society of the Four Arts (FL)
Sheldon Swope Art Gallery (IN)
U. of Iowa Museum of Art (IA)
Wadsworth Atheneum (CT)
Walker Art Center (MN)
Weatherspoon Art Gallery (NC)
Yale U. Art Gallery (CT)

**Video art**
Long Beach Museum of Art
  (CA)

# INDEX